# *GRIEVANCE GUIDE*

## *ELEVENTH EDITION*

# GRIEVANCE GUIDE

## ELEVENTH EDITION

*by the*
**BNA EDITORIAL STAFF**

**The Bureau of National Affairs, Inc., Washington, D.C.**

**Library of Congress Cataloging-in-Publication Data**

Grievance Guide / by the BNA editorial staff.--11th ed.
    p. cm.
    ISBN 1-57018-393-7
    1. Grievance procedures--United States. 1. Bureau of National Affairs (Washington,
    D.C.)
    HD6972.5 .G74 2003
    658.3´155–dc21

2003048180

Published by BNA Books
1231 25th St., NW, Washington, DC 20037-1165
*http://www.bnabooks.com*

International Standard Book Number 1-57018-393-7
*Printed in Canada*

# PREFACE

When the first edition of the *Grievance Guide* was published by the Bureau of National Affairs, Inc., it provided a picture of how arbitration works in the real world. In subsequent editions, BNA has continued that tradition of providing descriptions of actual cases as a way to give pratical guidance to both employers and employee representatives.

Although the intervention of neutral third parties to settle disputes has a long and varied history, arbitration of labor disputes had its formal beginnings in the 1940s, when unions and employers needed a way to quickly resolve labor-management disagreements and thus avoid hindering the country's war effort. From those experiences emerged the publication *War Labor Reports*, which was introduced by BNA in 1942. Seventeen years later, BNA began issuing *Grievance Guide*, which has provided discussions of arbitrators' decisions in a broad range of situations and workplaces.

In the past, arbitrators generally interpreted the letter and spririt of a particular collective bargaining agreement, but in recent years, they also have dealth with the interplay between labor contracts and new statutes. Since the early 1990s, arbitrators have had to resolve cases in light of the Americans with Disabilities Act, the Family and Medical Leave Act, and various state laws that echo the mandates and prohibitions of those federal statutes. In addition, the principles of federal and state disability and leave laws also have been explicitly incorporated into many collective bargaining agreements.

The *Grievance Guide* appears in both *Union Labor* and *Labor Relations*, two reference services for union officials and labor relations staff, respectively, as well as in the *Human Resources Library*, BNA's Web product for human resource professionals.

The *Grievance Guide* presents synopses of current arbitration cases, complete with citations to the full text of arbitration awards that BNA publishes in its *Labor Arbitration and Dispute Settlements*, which contains coverage of major decisions and reports on arbitrators, fact-finding bodies, and other agencies that are involved in settling labor disputes. (A citation such as 110 LA 214 translates as Vol. 110 of *Labor Arbitration and Dispsute Settlements*, page 214.)

The 11th edition of *Grievance Guide* was prepared by AnnTherese Carlozzo, an editor with the BNA *Human Resources Library*.

Leslie A. Goldman
Managing Editor
*Human Resources Libary*

---

# INTRODUCTION

Once a union has been certified or recognized as the representative of a bargaining unit and has negotiated its first collective bargaining agreement, the bargaining agreement, not the National Labor Relations Act, determines the rights and obligations of each party in most cases.

This addresses the problems that employers and employees encounter in the day-to-day business of living under a collective bargaining agreement. The arbitration cases discussed were chosen to illustrate general arbitration principles in a variety of collective bargaining situations. Readers should keep in mind the following principles while using this book:

- An arbitrator's function is to give the most appropriate judgment in interpreting collective bargaining agreements. Although arbitrators are not bound by precedent, there are nonetheless precedents that have implications for their decisions, and those decisions are not made without reference to other legal settings.

- No two collective bargaining agreements are identical in every detail, and nuances in contract language may make all the difference in the outcome of a given dispute. In recent years, in addition to provisions of specific contracts, arbitrators also have taken into account certain federal laws, such as the Americans with Disabilities Act and the Family and Medical Leave Act, as well as comparable state laws.

- The meaning of a contract clause may be determined in large part by the past practice of the parties—i.e., how the bargaining agreement had actually been interpreted or applied in the particular workplace setting.

- The fact that certain kinds of employer conduct are permitted under a bargaining agreement does not necessarily make those actions lawful or proper, and the inverse is also true.

# CONTENTS

**Part 1**

# Discharge and Discipline:
# In General

# Just Cause for Discipline

―――――――――――――――――――――――― **OVERVIEW** ――――――――――――――――――――――――

A basic principle underlying most disciplinary procedures is that management must have "just cause" for imposing the discipline. This standard often is written into union contracts or read into them by arbitrators. Even in the absence of a contract, "just cause" sums up the test used by employees in judging whether management acted fairly in enforcing company rules.

Although the definition of "just cause" necessarily varies from case to case, one arbitrator listed seven tests for determining whether an employer had just cause for disciplining an employee.

► Was the employee adequately warned of the consequences of his or her conduct? This need to warn an employee may be waived in cases of certain kinds of conduct—e.g., insubordination, coming to work drunk, drinking on the job, or stealing employer property—that are so serious that the employee is expected to know it will be punishable.

► Was the employer's rule or order reasonably related to efficient and safe operation of its business?

► Did management investigate before administering the discipline? The investigation normally should be conducted before the decision to discipline is made. Where immediate action is required, however, the best course is to suspend the employee pending investigation with the understanding that he or she will be restored to the job and paid for time lost if found "not guilty."

► Was the investigation fair and objective?

► Did the investigation produce substantial evidence or proof of guilt? There need not be a preponderance of evidence, nor must it be conclusive or "beyond reasonable doubt," except where the alleged misconduct is of such a criminal or reprehensible nature as to stigmatize the employee and seriously impair any chance for future employment.

► Were the rules, orders, and penalties applied evenhandedly and without discrimination? If enforcement has been lax in the past, management cannot suddenly reverse its course and begin to crack down without first warning employees of its intent.

► Was the penalty reasonably related to the seriousness of the offense and the person's employment record? If one employee's record is significantly better than that of another employee, the employer properly may give the former a lighter punishment for the same offense.

## SUMMARY OF CASES

### Just Cause for Discipline

In addition to the checklist outlined above, arbitrators have suggested that employers should:

▶ enjoy reasonable discretionary powers to prescribe rules of conduct;

▶ publicize these rules either by direct publication or by consistent enforcement;

▶ apply disciplinary policies "seriously and without discrimination";

▶ regard industrial discipline as corrective rather than punitive;

▶ avoid arbitrary or hasty action when confronted with a situation;

▶ evaluate each situation in the light of the employee's disciplinary record; and

▶ tailor the punishment to fit the crime .

To protect employees, the following criteria should be applied when in evaluating just cause for disciplinary action.

*Equal Treatment*—All employees must be judged by the same standards, and the rules must apply equally to all. This does not mean, however, that the same penalty always must be given for the same offense (see above).

*Rule of Reason*—Even in the absence of a specific provision, a contract protects employees against unjust discipline and permits a challenge to any employer procedure that threatens to deprive employees of their rights.

*Internal Consistency*—The pattern of enforcement must be consistent, whether an employer disciplines on a case-by-case basis or uses a set of rules.

### Just Cause for Discipline Upheld

Initially, if management has acted in good faith after a fair investigation and fixes a penalty that is consistent with similar cases or what would be considered fair, an arbitrator should not attempt to second guess management, an arbitrator ruled. If the causes for discharge appear to be fair, the grievant must suffer the consequences of the misconduct, the arbitrator emphasized (*Smith & Wesson-Fiocchi Inc.*, 60 LA 366).

In this regard, just cause for discipline has been upheld where:

● a sales clerk failed to follow proper store procedures and displayed unbecoming conduct toward fellow employees and customers (*Goldman's Department Store*, 65 LA 592);

● An employer had just cause to discharge an employee for falsifying a job application. When filling out a job application the employee stated he was never convicted of any crime, which was not true. The arbitrator rejected the employee's argument that his criminal convictions were irrelevant because he had paid his debt to society by spending time in jail. The employee's contention did not excuse his obligation to answer job application questions "fully and truthfully" (*Pacific Telesis Group*, 116 LA 526).

● a drill press operator negligently misdrilled an aircraft part and then attempted to cover up the mistake by throwing the part into a trash bin (*Rohr Industries Inc.*, 65 LA 982);

● an employee made excessive use of the employer's telephone to transact personal business in violation of employer policy (*Canned Foods Inc.*, 65 LA 409);

● an employee made telephone threats that a bomb was going to blow up the employer's plant (*Vulcan Materials Co.*, 64 LA 773);

● an employee, while on vacation, refused to accept the employer's telephone calls and a telegram advising the worker of his shift on his return to work (*Anaconda Co.*, 61 LA 1221);

● an employer fired an employee who was seen sitting in a bar with a glass of beer in front of him, a violation of his reinstatement agreement from a previous discharge for alcoholism. Under that pact, he had agreed to refrain from consuming alcohol "anywhere, at any time" (*Sterling Drug Inc., Local 342*, 67 LA 1296);

● an employer discharged a driver/salesman for falsifying and tampering with cash tickets, even though the contract did not contain an express provision that discharge shall be only for "cause" or "just cause," because the agreement as a whole expressed the parties' adoption of the "just cause" concept (*Dayton Pepsi Cola Bottling Co.*, 75 LA 154);

• an employer discharged a shift electrician for failing to pass a test that the electrical superintendent administered to determine his competence in correcting malfunctions of paper machines for which he was responsible, given that the union did not provide impartial experts to challenge the fairness of the test and there was no evidence that the superintendent devised questions that were so deliberately difficult that the worker could not be expected to answer them (*St. Regis Paper Co.*, 74 LA 896);

• an employer fired an employee after she refused to raise her pants leg to reveal the nature of bulges that a plant guard had noticed, because it is not customary for people to have odd bulges under their pants leg and it would have been a clear dereliction of duty for the guard to see that and do nothing (*Aldens Inc.*, 73 LA 396);

• an employer imposed a 10-day suspension on an employee for drinking beer during a four-hour off-duty interval of her split shift under a plant rule prohibiting employees from consuming alcoholic beverages of any kind during a tour of duty, given that management had adequately communicated the rule to employees and applied it in an evenhanded fashion (*General Telephone Co. of California*, 77 LA 1052);

• an employee audio-recorded, and made no effort to stop recording, a counseling session held to end her unauthorized use of audio and video equipment in the workplace (*Prescription Health Services*, 98 LA 16);

• a telephone employer operator was suspended for three days when she rudely addressed a customer and failed to give her name when asked (*American Telephone & Telegraph*, 98 LA 102); and

• a home-delivery meal driver was discharged for failing to deliver hot meals to certain senior citizens, since he tried to falsify records and the misconduct was so egregious that it threatened the senior citizens' health (*Bay County Division on Aging*, 98 LA 188).

## Just Cause for Discipline Not Upheld

Arbitrators are unwilling to uphold an employer's disciplinary action where management has failed to meet certain requirements. Discipline was *not* justified in the following cases where:

• a city employee who received gifts from a city supplier was discharged, while other city officials, who were guilty of the same offense, were only suspended (*City of Binghampton*, 65 LA 663);

• an employer discharged a locomotive brakeman who accidentally shot himself while trying to shoot a crow near the employer's railroad track, because the worker's action was not related to his railroading duties (*Erie Mining Co.*, 65 LA 880);

• an employee was discharged for obtaining payroll information on fellow employees from the employer's desk drawer, which was made the basis of a union grievance, given that there was no employer rule declaring the drawer and its contents off limits (*Meat Fair Meat Market*, 65 LA 1112);

• an employer fired a bench inspector for harassing the employer by filing 16 grievances and writing notes of protest to management in a four-year period, in light of the fact that most of the worker's grievances had merit (*Caterpillar Tractor Co.*, 62 LA 645);

• an employee was fired for urinating on the floor of his delivery vehicle by choice and not by necessity. Even if the worker's conduct was offensive, there was nothing in the parties' contract subjecting an employee to immediate discharge merely because his personal behavior is offensive and vile (*Pepsi Cola Bottling Co.*, 76 LA 54); and

• an assistant bookkeeper was discharged over an incident in which she allegedly spent the night with a married store manager at the home of a fellow employee following a party, but an employee's off-duty conduct away from employer premises was not subject to discipline or discharge, under the contract,

unless it adversely affected the operation
of the employer's business (*Ralph's Grocery Co.*, 77 LA 867).

---

# Disciplinary Procedures

## OVERVIEW

In ruling on the fairness of discipline for such offenses as insubordination, misconduct, absenteeism, and poor work, arbitrators do not concern themselves merely with whether the workers involved are guilty. They also examine the procedures followed by the employer in punishing the workers and the nature of the punishment itself.

Many agreements specify procedural requirements for discharge or discipline. Arbitrators have refused to uphold management's action in discharging or disciplining an employee where management failed to fulfill some procedural requirement specified by the agreement, such as a required statement of charges against the employee, or a notice or investigation requirement, or a requirement for a hearing or joint discussion before assessing a punishment.

In numerous other cases, however, compliance with the spirit of such procedural requirements has been held to suffice even when the employee has not been adversely affected by the failure of management to accomplish total compliance with the requirements.

Every employer is forced at some time or other to administer discipline, but there are good ways and bad ways of doing so. A study of many successfully administered policies reveals that the following guidelines can foster more successful results.

• Employer rules should be carefully explained to employees. This is especially true for new employees, although any changes in rules should be dealt with as if all employees were new hires. Indoctrination courses, employee handbooks, bulletin board notices, and many other methods can be used.

• Accusations against employees should be carefully considered to see if they are supported by facts. Witnesses must be interviewed, their statements recorded, and a careful investigation made to see that the many sides of the story are elicited and fairly presented. Circumstantial evidence should be kept to a minimum in judging the facts, and personality issues, as well as unfounded assumptions, should be eliminated.

• A regular "warning" procedure must be worked out and applied; some employers have found that it is wise to put all warnings in writing. An alternative procedure is to deliver the initial warning orally (while a written copy of it is filed), and put subsequent warnings in writing. Warnings should be given for all except the most serious offenses—those that management has made clear will prompt for immediate discharge.

• Some employers bring the union into the discipline case early in the procedure. In those cases, copies of warning notices should go to the union, giving it advance notice of other disciplinary actions that management intends to take. Sometimes the action is held up until the union has time to make its own investigation.

- Before disciplinary action is taken, the employee's motives and reasons for violating the rules should be investigated. Then the penalty can be adjusted to fit the facts—whether the employee's action was in good faith, partially justified, or totally unjustified.

- Before disciplinary action is taken, the employee's past record must be taken into consideration. A good work record and long seniority should be viewed as mitigating factors, particularly where a minor infraction or first offense is involved. Previous offenses should not be used against the employee unless he or she was reprimanded at the time they occurred or warned that they would be used in any future disciplinary action.

- Employers should ensure that all management agents, and particularly first-line supervisors, know the employer's disciplinary policies and procedures and carefully observe them. This is particularly important in the case of verbal warnings or informal reprimands.

- Discipline short of discharge should be used wherever possible.

- Generally, an employer must issue discipline in a timely manner—i.e., within a reasonable period following the occurrence of the alleged misconduct. Such a requirement may be expressly stated in a contract.

## SUMMARY OF CASES

### Right to Adopt Rules

It is generally agreed that management is authorized to make and to post reasonable rules of conduct as long as they are consistent with the collective bargaining agreement (97 LA 542, 93 LA 1082, 90 LA 625, 90 LA 341, 88 LA 1164).

Once promulgated, the rules may be subject to challenge through the grievance procedure if they are found to be contrary to the contract or arbitrary, unfair, or discriminatory (65 LA 1077, 63 LA 267).

Although an employer's right to make reasonable rules is recognized, particular rules may be voided if they are found to be unreasonable, vague, ineffective, or arbitrary (97 LA 675, 96 LA 122).

The test of reasonableness of a rule is whether or not the rule is reasonably related to a legitimate objective of management (55 LA 283). Rules must be reasonable, not only in content but also in application.

- An employer's rule—that male employees on the day shift had to wear neckties while male employees on the second shift did not have to wear them, and female employees could dress as they pleased—was discriminatory, an arbitrator ruled. Pointing out that this discriminatory enforcement of the rule violated the contract, the arbitrator concluded that the rule was not predicated on a reasonable standard, because it appeared that the necktie requirement was based on the personal taste of the department head (*Union Tribune Publishing Co.*, 70 LA 266).

Even reasonable rules have been held unenforceable if they have not been brought to the attention of employees (18 LA 866), infringe unduly on an employee's private life (18 LA 400), or are applied discriminatorily (26 LA 934).

- An employer could not enforce a rule prohibiting employees from wearing beach clothes when walking to and from plant gates, in amplification of its general safety rule barring wearing of loose clothing or jewelry when employees are moving around machinery, an arbitrator ruled. The rule went substantially beyond the scope of the general rule, and constituted unreasonable interference with the personal freedom of employees to come and go from their workplace, the arbitrator concluded (*Babcock & Wilcox*, 73 LA 443).

## Posting of Plant Rules

The decision as to whether to post plant rules is management's and the posting of rules ordinarily is not a condition precedent to management's right to discipline employees for violations.

Except where the nature of the prohibited activity is such that employees should know it is unacceptable, plant rules should be communicated to employees in some consistent manner. Thus, in the absence of posted rules, management's freedom of action may actually be more restricted than it would be if rules were posted.

• In rejecting a union's contention that an employer could not discipline employees in the absence of properly promulgated and communicated plant rules, an arbitrator observed that many plants operate without formal rules, relying instead on employees' having a modicum of common sense (*Davey Company*, 60 LA 917).

Other arbitrators have held that plant rules need not be put in writing (*Ohio Power Co.*, 50 LA 501); that an employer's reliance on the "grapevine" to announce a disciplinary policy was acceptable (*Pacific Northwest Bell Telephone Co.*, 48 LA 498); and that there is no one way of either setting or publicizing a rule, which can become effective through experience and practice (*Eastern Airlines Inc.*, 44 LA 459).

## Consistent Enforcement

Where management has winked at violations of a rule, it should announce its intention to require observance of the rule before it hands out heavy penalties. This is especially true where the rule applies to conduct that, unlike stealing or assaults on supervisors or co-workers, is not inherently objectionable or clearly wrong. Lax enforcement of rules may lead employees to a reasonable belief that management actually approves of the conduct in question (94 LA 297, 93 LA 302, 66 LA 953).

Although arbitrators have no jurisdiction to pass on management's treatment of its supervisors, they may set aside penalties imposed on rank-and-file workers if supervisors who were guilty of the same offense are given lesser penalties. Thus, when both a supervisor and a worker were cleared of an offense, the arbitrator found management guilty of double standards when it reinstated only the supervisor (39 LA 823).

## Pay for Time Spent in Disciplinary Interview

Is a worker who is being questioned or interviewed to determine possible disciplinary action entitled to pay for the time spent in this way? Typically, arbitrators (and the courts as well) view that time as useful for both management and worker.

[**Note:** A number of states have passed laws that specifically make such time compensable, even in light of the fact that those same states usually have laws forbidding management to contribute financially to a union that represents its workers.]

• At least one arbitrator has ruled that workers could not be docked for the time spent in disciplinary interviews held on employer time. Both management and the worker stand to profit from such interviews, he pointed out, and there is no reason why the employee should have to suffer a monetary loss (*Bethlehem Steel Co.*, 19 LA 261).

• Similarly, a union steward's pay was improperly docked one-half hour because the worker left his job early to discuss his own disciplinary grievance with union attorneys, an arbitrator ruled, noting that the steward left the plant with the permission of the employer (*County Sanitation District*, 64 LA 521).

• Furthermore, another arbitrator ruled that workers should be paid for time spent in a disciplinary conference held on their off time. In this instance, the workers were called in on a Saturday, so the arbitrator awarded them four hours' pay for the time spent in conference under the "call-in-pay" provision of the contract (*Bethlehem Steel Co.*, 21 LA 579).

• On the other hand, an employee was not entitled to pay for time spent in a grievance meeting where a fight between the worker and a co-employee was discussed, an arbitrator decided, because the contract expressly stated that the "company will not pay for time spent at meetings" (*Brockway Glass Co. Inc.*, 74 LA 601).

## Pay for Training Time

A sheriff's office was not required to pay for training employees needed to obtain certification, one arbitrator ruled. Before 1992, a county sheriff's office had paid newly hired correctional officers for the costs of their continuing training, but after 1992, the employer refused to pay the corrections officers for training time and required them to train on their own time as a prerequisite for hiring. At the time of the change and for several years afterward, the union made no comment or complaint.

The parties also agreed, the arbitrator observed, that "the establishment of pre-hiring conditions" by the employer was not subject to collective bargaining. Finding the employer's actions consistent with the contract and past practice, the arbitrator rejected several employees' reimbursement request (*Pickaway County Sheriff*, 112 LA 742).

## Staggered Penalty

Where management penalizes a group of workers by suspending them, can it stagger the suspensions so that the workers are not all off at the same time? Arbitrators typically rule that management has that right.

● In one case where workers struck in violation of the contract, the arbitrator reasoned that if management suspended everyone at once, the result would be a work stoppage, the very thing the disciplinary action was intended to penalize (*United States Steel Corp.*, 40 LA 598).

● Another arbitrator came to a similar conclusion, adding that although management was not free to schedule the discipline "at its convenience" any time after the stoppage, it was entitled to reasonable latitude in deferring the suspensions (*Bethlehem Steel Co.*, 39 LA 686).

## Challenging New Rule

A union lost any right to challenge the discharge of a worker for violation of a new plant rule forbidding drinking during lunch breaks when it did not protest at the time the rule was posted, an arbitrator ruled. A worker was caught drinking on his lunch break and was fired. The arbitrator denied the union's grievance, holding that management was justified in enforcing a new rule that it considered had full union support (*International Pipe & Ceramics Corp.*, 44 LA 267).

## Union's Right to Disciplinary Forms and Reports

The personnel forms management develops are its own business and ordinarily need not be given to the union, one arbitrator has ruled. The same arbitrator, however, suggested that this rule may not hold where a form is used in imposing discipline.

● When an employer developed three new personnel forms to replace a single reprimand form, the union demanded that it be given a copy whenever one of the forms was used. Management was willing to supply one that was to be used solely for reprimands, but it refused to hand over one used to record attendance and changes of address or one entitled "Employee Performance & Conduct Memo."

The arbitrator said the employer had the right to develop its own forms without any discussion or negotiation with the union. In addition, if a form was to become merely part of management's records, the union had no more right of access to it than management would have had to union records. He noted that the employer had established the sound practice of supplying reprimand forms, so he concluded that the new reprimand form had to be given to the union whenever it was used, the Performance & Conduct Memo had to be supplied only if used as a reprimand, and the attendance and change of address form could be withheld altogether (*Harshaw Chemical Co.*, 32 LA 86).

## Notice to Union

Where a contract calls for notice of disciplinary action to be given to the union, arbitrators are likely to require strict compliance with such a provision. They operate on the theory that a worker's rights are seriously abridged if the union is not given a chance to get in on the ground floor.

• Even if the disciplined employee clearly was guilty of misconduct, the penalty may be mitigated if the union was not given proper notice. Thus one arbitrator ordered a discharged employee reinstated without back pay where the employer failed to adhere to the contractual requirement of consultation with the union over discharges (*Hayes Mfg. Corp.*, 17 LA 412; see also 94 LA 7, 86 LA 503, 65 LA 690, 64 LA 425, 64 LA 67).

• Another arbitrator ruled that an employer that had failed to comply with notice requirements had to give an employee pay for time lost between the date of his discharge and the date of the first grievance meeting, even though his discharge was for just cause (*National Lead Co.*, 13 LA 28).

## Union Representation

An employer's failure to follow contractual procedures regarding union presence at disciplinary meetings may invalidate an employee's discharge.

[**Note:** In recent years, federal appeals courts have ruled that not only must unions be given notice so that an employee may have a union representative present at any meeting that could lead to discipline, but also that this so-called "Weingarten" right applies to workers in nonunion workplaces. The U.S. Supreme Court let stand an appeals court decision to that effect, the only difference being that nonunion workers had the right to request that a co-worker—rather than a union representative—accompany them to investigatory interviews that might result in discipline. The ruling emphasizes the need for representation during any get-together that is potentially a disciplinary meeting, whether or not the contract specifically requires it (*Epilepsy Foundation of Northeast Ohio v. NLRB*, 88 LRRM 2689).]

• A collective bargaining agreement mandated that a union steward be allowed to attend any meeting "where possible disciplinary measures may be taken" and gave the union the right to notice "prior to any discharge" and "to be present when formal charges are made." An employee was given a disciplinary notice for neglecting to perform scheduled maintenance of a forklift. A union steward was present then but not later at a meeting when the employee was suspended or when the worker was later discharged. The union contended the discharge should be invalidated because the employer failed to follow contractual procedures on union notification and representation.

The employer countered that its prompt written notice to the union after the discharge followed the "spirit of the contract," and that procedural violations should not invalidate a discharge unless the employee shows that the violations adversely affected him or her.

Conceding that the employer had just cause to discharge the employee for negligence, the arbitrator noted that the express provisions of the contract involved a more extensive right to union representation than is the norm, and concluded that the employer failed to meet its obligation to ensure the presence of the steward when it suspended and discharged the employee (*S and J Ranch and United Farm Workers*, 103 LA 350).

• If a bargaining agreement gives employees the right to union representation when disciplinary action is taken against them, do they also have the right to have a union official on hand when the employer is conducting preliminary investigations held prior to disciplinary action? Arbitrators are divided on this question. Some feel that employees have the right to union representation during preliminary investigations on the theory that this is the beginning stage of a grievance (66 LA 581, 60 LA 1066, 60 LA 832, 60 LA 9).

• Others, however, take the position that union representation is not required unless the employee actually requests it (73 LA 1092), is charged with an offense, or until the beginning of the investigation.

## Union Representation Waived

Under a contract giving a disciplined employee the right to representation, what happens if the employee is not in the plant when he or she is discharged or other discipline is imposed? Arbitrators generally hold that representation requirements are waived if the employee is absent when disciplinary action is taken or if the penalty is imposed via mail or telegram.

• An employer did not violate a contract's provision requiring the presence of union representation at the discharge of an employee when the employer sent a telegram to the employee at his home notifying him of his discharge, an arbitrator ruled. The arbitrator reasoned that the contract required the presence of a union representative "if practical" and the presence of a union representative at the home of the grievant when the telegram was delivered was not practical. The contract provision contemplated that discharges would occur on employer premises during regular working hours (*Rexall Drug Co.*, 65 LA 1101).

# Types of Penalties

―――――――――――――――――― **OVERVIEW** ――――――――――――――――――

The type of penalty assessed for wrongdoing usually is either a temporary suspension or discharge. A temporary suspension, or "disciplinary layoff," results in loss of pay (and sometimes loss of seniority) for the period of suspension and mars the employee's record. When an arbitrator reinstates a discharged employee without back pay, the end result is not unlike suspension.

Warnings are a lesser type of discipline. Failure to warn an employee of the consequences of violating a rule is one of the most frequent reasons given by arbitrators for setting aside disciplinary layoffs or discharges.

An employer may be on shaky ground if it attempts to use types of penalties other than warnings, suspensions, and discharge. Increasingly, however, common forms of conditional reinstatement are appearing in the form of so-called "last-chance" agreements and disciplinary probation.

[**Note:** Such agreements have become more common, as employers seek to reconcile the sometimes disparate requirements of the Americans with Disabilities Act and particular union contracts.]

Factors relevant to an arbitrator's review or evaluation of an employer's penalties include:

- the nature of the offense;
- due process and procedural requirements;
- pre-discharge conduct of the employee;
- the possibility of double jeopardy;
- the employee's work record;
- the employee's length of service with the employer;
- the employer's previous lax enforcement of company rules; and
- discriminatory or disparate treatment of the employee, either in the specific case at hand or earlier in the employment relationship.

―――――――――――――――――― **SUMMARY OF CASES** ――――――――――――――――――

**Discipline Other Than Discharge**

The fact that a contract gives an employer the right to discharge for cause or mentions certain offenses that are grounds for discharge usually does not preclude management's imposing lesser forms of discipline. Under the principle that the greater includes the lesser, arbitrators have upheld management's right to impose various degrees of penalties.

If, however, a contract mandates progressive discipline, including warnings, suspension, and discharge, arbitrators may not uphold management's right to apply other types of penalties, particularly if such measures contravene other provisions of the contract. Thus, arbitrators have held that employers had no right to apply the penalties of denial of a promotion.

- When an employee went for his paycheck, the payroll clerk was carrying on a personal telephone conversation. The employee waited 10 minutes, then broke the connection to get the clerk's attention. She complained about his conduct, and he was told to apologize. When he refused, he was fired.

The employee was unnecessarily rude to the clerk, the arbitrator figured, because he could have attracted her attention in some other way. A short layoff would, however, have been adequate discipline, given that the offense was minor and the clerk's conduct irritating. The employer's attitude, the arbitrator found, put the employee on the spot; he was required to say he was wrong when he felt he was not. The employer's action, the arbitrator held, was out of line (*Magnavox Co.*, 28 LA 449).

● Although an employer had just cause to fire an employee because of repeated absences and tardiness, an arbitrator decided that he deserved a last chance to change his ways. During a 16-month tenure with a company, the employee was reprimanded for numerous absences, early departures, and failures to call in when absent. He was given many warnings and eventually was fired, at which point he revealed that he had been taking care of his ailing grandmother. The employer gave him another chance, but on the day he was to report for work, he failed to show up and did not call. After five days passed, he was fired. Although the company had just cause for discharge, the arbitrator said, the employee should have one last chance (*Penske Truck Leasing*, 115 LA 1386).

### Warnings

Arbitrators in general seem to feel that some form of warning should precede a discharge (75 LA 819, 75 LA 1254, 64 LA 778, 64 LA 563), except where the employee is guilty of serious misconduct such as stealing or intoxication on the job (64 LA 880).

● A written warning is particularly important where a worker has been let off lightly for past offenses and management intends to crack down on future offenses (77 LA 940, 65 LA 894). A discharge for a "last straw" offense might be set aside unless the worker was warned previously that he would be dealt with more severely (74 LA 814, 65 LA 829, 64 LA 981).

### Progressive Discipline

For most offenses, management is expected to use a system of progressive discipline under which the employee is warned or given disciplinary suspensions before being hit with the ultimate penalty of discharge. A common pattern is: oral warning, written warning, disciplinary layoff, and discharge.

Extreme situations—e.g., violent behavior, bringing weapons to work—usually can legitimately prompt employers to dispense with progressive discipline, and in cases where the employee repeatedly fails to meet the most minimal standards, arbitrators agree that that can obviate the need for incremental action by an employer.

● Management is not, however, bound by a progressive-discipline formula in cases of serious offenses. Some offenses, such as stealing or drunkenness on the job are regarded as so serious that no specific warning or prior disciplinary action need precede discharge. Employees are presumed to know that such serious offenses will lead to discharge (66 LA 286, 27 LA 768).

● If progressive discipline were to apply to every case, one arbitrator noted, an employee who brutally assaulted his foreman or a fellow employee would get off with a simple warning slip if it were only his first offense. Thus, he held, the schedule of penalties spelled out in the contract was intended to apply to the offenses referred to and other violations of specific contract provisions and was not intended to apply to other offenses, including serious infractions of plant rules (*Alliance Machine Co.*, 48 LA 457).

● In one case, an employer had just cause to discharge an employee who accumulated a horrible attendance record that deteriorated into a no-show, no-call problem, according to the arbitrator. Shortly after passing her 90-day probationary period, an employee began accumulating unexcused absences. So blatant was her disregard of attendance requirements that at one point her union had a "heart-to-heart" discussion in an attempt to convince her of the need to at least show up. She declared that she "just forgot" to report to the plant and refused employer requests to at least call when she was not going to work. The union, however, argued that the company did not properly apply progressive discipline when it imposed a second written reprimand leading to discharge. The "important point to be made regarding this argument" was, however, that there was "no negotiated 'progressive disciplinary' system" in the particular collective bargaining agreement, the arbitrator said, upholding the discharge (*Tembec Paper Group*, 117 LA 250).

• As one arbitrator explained, "the policy of progressive discipline does not mean that for any given employee each penalty must necessarily be more severe than the immediate preceding one, regardless of the offense involved. What progressive discipline does mean is that progressively more severe penalties may be imposed on each given employee each time any given offense is repeated." The arbitrator also noted that "progressive discipline also means that after a specified number of offenses, regardless of whether the offenses are identical or not, the employer may have the right to discharge the given employees." Finally, the arbitrator said "both of these interpretations of progressive discipline avoid the inequitable meting out of discipline, and at the same time serve the dual purpose of progressive discipline, namely, the discouragement of repeated offense by employees, and the protection of the right of the employer to sever completely its relationship with any employee who by his total behavior shows himself to be irresponsible" (*Bell Aircraft Corp.*, 17 LA 230).

• An employer had just cause to fire a warehouse loader who failed to refrigerate honey mustard packets, said one arbitrator. The loader forgot to properly store some 140 boxes of the item, a mistake that the distributing company said could pose a health risk for its customers. At the time, the loader had on his record a verbal warning, a written warning, and a suspension for poor work performance. Under the firm's progressive discipline policy, a fourth infraction within a rolling six-month period was grounds for automatic termination, and the company followed through and fired the man. The

union argued against such "mechanical application of progressive discipline," but the employer was not required to be lenient, given that the rules were explicit and known to all, the arbitrator concluded (*Golden State Foods*, 117 LA 632).

## Double Jeopardy & Delays

It is a well recognized principle that discipline should be reasonably prompt and that a penalty, once announced, should not be increased absent evidence that the offense was more serious than it initially appeared to be. In addition, arbitrators have been held that an employee is entitled to expect full discipline within a reasonable time and to assume that the penalty received is the complete one.

The principle of double jeopardy has been applied by arbitrators to prohibit the imposition of two successive penalties for the same offense, such as a recorded warning and a suspension (76 LA 758, 12 LA 129, 59 LA 414, 90 LA 435, 96 LA 657, 97 LA 8, 97 LA 60, 97 LA 121, 97 LA 393, 97 LA 774, 98 LA 102).

• One arbitrator pointed out that the legal "double jeopardy" rule assumes that a full hearing has been held and that disclosures at that hearing are the basis for the penalty imposed. Nonetheless, "normal industrial plant disciplinary procedures" do not contemplate the kind of hearing that is the basis of the legal rule, he pointed out, upholding the discharge of employees who already had been laid off for participating in a wildcat strike where evidence obtained after the layoff showed that they actually instigated the job action (*International Harvester Co.*, 13 LA 611; see also 74 LA 1012, 81 LA 564, 83 LA 833, 85 LA 302, 91 LA 544).

*Court and Employer Penalties*—The fact that an employee has paid a fine or served a jail sentence for acts committed in connection with his or her job does not preclude management from imposing discipline for the same acts. An arbitrator, however, may consider the legal punishment in determining the severity of the penalty imposed by management (*Westinghouse Electric Corp.*, 26 LA 836).

• An arbitrator ruled that a branch of the U.S. military was justified in imposing a three-day suspension on an employee after the worker pleaded guilty and was convicted of making fraudulent claims against the government because the double jeopardy defense does not apply where the misconduct of the employee also amounts to a violation of the law (*Air Force, Dept. of and Government Employees, AFGE, Local 1857*, 74 LA 949).

*Delays*—Management may delay in imposing a penalty for a reasonable time, but arbitrators sometimes find that excessive delay is almost the same as double jeopardy because an employee then has the threat of the penalty hanging over him or her for months (*Ashland Oil & Refining Co.*, 28 LA 874).

## Demotion as Discipline

Many arbitrators disapprove of demotion as an ordinary tool of discipline. It permits unequal penalties for similar offenses, they reason, and may have side effects more drastic than the intended punishment, as where a demoted employee subsequently loses his job because of the change in his seniority status (*Lukens Steel Co.*, 42 LA 252).

● Other arbitrators, however, have allowed demotions for such matters as carelessness and negligence, poor work attitudes, and incompetence (74 LA 1131, 74 LA 991, 66 LA 588, 60 LA 197, 59 LA 988).

● In such cases, the arbitrator's approval of the employer's action frequently is grounded in the theory that the demotion is not really a form of discipline but an adjustment required by the employee's inability to do his job (17 LA 328, 18 LA 457).

● An employee who had worked for a supermarket chain for about 14 years had served two long stretches as head of a meat department. Each time he had been demoted to cutter, first class, for unsatisfactory performance. Nevertheless, he talked the employer into giving him another chance at running a department. He was told at that time, however, that he would have to maintain a satisfactory profit margin.

Although the employer could not point to specific defects in the employee's subsequent handling of the department, his profit margin consistently was below the all-store average, was below his predecessor's average, and was, in fact, the worst of any of the employer's 40 stores. After 14 weeks of this, the employee was warned in writing; a week later, when the picture had not improved, he was demoted.

An arbitrator upheld the demotion, but he clearly did not view it as discipline. Instead, he treated the employee's 15 weeks as a department head as a trial period during which he had failed to demonstrate his ability to handle the job (*Hart's Food Stores Inc.*, 43 LA 934).

## Discharge or Resignation?

Where the facts and circumstances are such as to lead management to reasonably conclude that an intent to resign exists, the matter may be treated as a resignation (or "voluntary quit") even though the individual never actually stated his or her intentions (97 LA 297, 96 LA 585, 93 LA 1047, 92 LA 930, 92 LA 259, 90 LA 1194, 90 LA 149, 86 LA 1160, 86 LA 888).

● Because of an increase in workload, an employer cancelled vacations scheduled to begin in August and informed the two employees who were affected that later dates would be assigned. One of them, disregarding the employer's notice, did not call in for his work assignment on August 21, and when contacted by an employer representative, reported that he was going on vacation. The employee was told that, if he did so, his act would be construed as a voluntary quit. Upholding management's viewpoint, the arbitrator stressed that the scheduling and taking of vacation time is a "mutual responsibility," under which the employee may select his leave dates provided they are agreeable to the employer. It is clear that the grievant's chosen vacation time was not agreeable, the arbitrator observed, pointing out that the other employee whose leave was cancelled was able to reach agreement with the employer for a later vacation date (*B.B.D. Transportation Co. Inc.*, 66 LA 64).

● An employee voluntarily quit and was not discharged, an arbitrator held, when the worker angrily left the plant without either clocking out or reporting to his foreman following confirmation that the job he had bid on was awarded to someone else. Rejecting the union's contention that the employee at the time of his walkout was suffering from acute stomach pains that precluded his clocking out, the arbitrator ruled that although it is possible that the employee's anger over not getting the job had caused him to become ill, the evidence did not establish that the worker was so incapacitated as to justify his leaving the plant without either punching out or notifying his foreman (*Owens Manufacturing Inc.*, 63 LA 585).

● The fact that an employee leaves work without permission because of dissatisfaction or upset over something that has occurred does not necessarily mean that management may be justified in treating the worker as a voluntary quit (97 LA 297, 88 LA 1265, 88 LA 597, 86 LA 144, 82 LA 569).

● Arbitrators have held that the test in these cases is whether the employee intended to permanently sever the connection with his or her employer. As one arbitrator stated, "the overwhelming weight of authority holds that there is no voluntary quit by reason of an employee's refusal to perform work to which he is assigned. Unless some affirmation of an intent to quit the job is manifested by the employee, the employer's subsequent refusal to let the employee continue his status constitutes a discharge rather than a resignation" (*Oklahoma Furniture Mfg. Co.*, 24 LA 522; see also 41 LA 913).

● An employer that reinstated a worker who had resigned and permitted him to maintain his original seniority did not violate its labor agreement, one arbitrator held. A machinist gave two weeks' notice and resigned. When the employee asked for his old job back after only six days at the new company, he was reinstated with no loss of seniority. The union filed a grievance, arguing that the employer should have treated the employee's purported resignation as a voluntary quit. The arbitrator found for the employer, saying that it had in essence given the employee a chance to pursue a new job with the understanding that he could return. The company unintentionally processed his resignation, and the reinstatement with full seniority did not violate the contract, the arbitrator ruled (*Lufkin Industries Inc.*, 115 LA 1631).

***Circumstances beyond employee's control***— Employees have been held not to have voluntary quit their jobs when they are forced by other commitments or circumstances to miss or stay away from a job. If the intent to resign is not adequately evidenced, or if a statement of intent to resign is involuntary or coerced, an alleged resignation will be treated as a discharge and subject to the usual test of "just cause."

● An employee whose military training extended beyond a return-to-work date—specified in a memo granting a leave of absence—did not voluntarily quit his job, despite the fact that the memo stated that failure to report would be considered a resignation, since the employee failed to demonstrate a clear and unequivocal intent to sever the employment relationship (*Rustco Products Co.*, 92 LA 981; see also 96 LA 216).

● Even when an employee is warned that persisting in a certain action or behavior will be construed as quitting, the employee's persistence might not be viewed as a voluntary quit (67 LA 1061, 66 LA 19).

● A foreman who offered to resign from his job was constructively discharged, an arbitrator ruled, where the foreman made the offer following the employer's indication of its dissatisfaction with the worker's performance as supervisor. The employer also had stated that the employee would not receive any salary increases.

Concluding that it was reasonable for the foreman to assume that the employer was really telling him that he might as well look for another job, the arbitrator pointed out that the employer's plant superintendent admitted that he would have terminated the foreman had the worker not resigned (*Rodman Industries Inc.*, 59 LA 101).

### Mental State at Time of Quit

When an employee who is suffering from a mental illness or disturbance announces an intent to resign, an arbitrator may have to decide whether the worker was capable of making a rational decision at the time. Even if the employee is merely upset when he or she precipitously exits the workplace, many arbitrators will look askance at the employer that insists the person voluntarily quit.

● An employee who told his supervisor he did not feel like working and then left work for the day did not voluntarily quit his job, an arbitrator ruled. A produce worker called to say he would arrive late one day, but when he showed up, he had an unpleasant conversation with his manager. After that, the employee left and did not return. There are three ways an employee can resign voluntarily: through written statement, oral statement, or by actions, the arbitrator said. The employee did not exhibit any of those actions, the arbitrator concluded, ordering the employee reinstated without back pay (*Royal Farms Supermarket*, 115 LA 1495).

● An employee suffered from a nervous condition and was unable to sleep or eat for several days. During this period, the worker approached his supervisor and for no apparent reason said: "I quit. I saw you smiling at me." The supervisor immediately called two union stewards to his office, and asked the employee to repeat the statement. The employee, however, did not reply, but instead retrieved his tools and left the plant. Subsequently, the employee was admitted to a mental institution for observation. Following a two-week stay there, he returned to the plant, attacked a union steward, and damaged the steward's car. At the time, the employee still was under psychiatric care and was receiving medication. A few months later, the psychiatrist told management that the employee was able to return to work; however, the employer, contending that the employee had voluntarily quit, refused to allow him to return to the job.

Agreeing that the employee had suffered a nervous breakdown when he allegedly quit and was not responsible for his statements that day, the arbitrator held that the employee did not have the necessary mental capacity to make a meaningful decision to quit work. The employee should be reinstated, the arbitrator decided, but only if two psychiatrists affirmed that he was mentally fit to return (*Herr-Voss Corp.*, 70 LA 497).

● For several years, an employee suffered from a mental condition that frequently caused irrational reactions. After the employee experienced a new nervous disorder, a physician stated that the condition was "not totally disabling," and recommended that the worker be allowed to return to work on a limited basis. After being back at work for only a short period of time, however, the employee decided that it would be in his own best interest to quit.

After management reluctantly accepted his resignation, the employee's doctor contended that the worker was in no condition to make prudent decisions.

Finding that the employee was in a rational frame of mind when he reached the "deliberate decision" that the tensions associated with his work were more than he could handle, an arbitrator ruled that he voluntarily quit his position. Despite efforts by management and union officials to dissuade the employee from quitting, he was determined to abide by his decision, the arbitrator pointed out (*Kellogg Co.*, 71 LA 494; see also 74 LA 980).

## Rescinded Resignations

Generally, an employee who voluntarily quits loses his or her status as an employee. Therefore, if the person subsequently tries to rescind the resignation, the decision as to whether to accept the retraction is seen as being be solely within management's discretion (40 LA 469, 29 LA 700).

● Where an employee's resignation and subsequent request to withdraw it were an admitted attempt to defraud the employer by gaining time off with pay, an arbitrator ruled that the employer's refusal to honor the withdrawal was reasonable, even though contrary to its past practice (*A.R.A. Manufacturing Co.*, 67 LA 1195; see also 53 LA 1103).

● Some arbitrators have held that extenuating or mitigating circumstances may justify a departure from "rigid" application of the general rule. An employee who resigned after being charged with being off employer premises and using marijuana was entitled to rescind his resignation after getting an opportunity to evaluate the facts, an arbitrator ruled, where the recision caused no detriment to the employer (*Renaissance Center Partnership*, 76 LA 379).

## Restitution for Negligence

An arbitrator held that an employee may be compelled to reimburse an employer for financial loss that resulted from the employee's negligence, in a case where the parties' collective bargaining agreement allowed the employer to choose between discipline and reimbursement in cases of lost and damaged parcels.

According to the arbitrator, an employee was justly made to reimburse his employer for negligent loss of a parcel containing a $12,000 diamond ring that he had picked up from a customer. The employee, a delivery person for a package delivery service, had left the parcel containing the piece of jewelry unattended, and it was stolen. The arbitrator held the loss was solely attributable to the employee's failure to follow proper safekeeping procedures for high-value parcels. The arbitrator dismissed the union's contention that the employee's actions were due to insufficient training and not negligence (*United Parcel Service Inc.*, 106 LA 637).

# Proving Misconduct

## OVERVIEW

In most disciplinary cases, particularly those involving discharge, management generally has the burden of proving guilt or wrongdoing, particularly where a collective bargaining agreement requires "just cause" for discharge (117 LA 1149, 55 LA 435).

The amount or degree of proof required to prove misconduct, however, is not a cut-and-dried matter. It may vary with the severity of the alleged offense, the type of evidence at hand, and the individual arbitrator's analysis of particular facts in a given case.

Strict observance of legal rules of evidence usually is not necessary, unless expressly requested by the parties.

## SUMMARY OF CASES

### Determining Degree of Proof

In disciplinary or discharge hearings, arbitrators frequently tend to stress burden of proof considerations. In such cases, the arbitrator is concerned with two areas of proof. The first involves proof of wrongdoing, and the second—assuming that the employee's guilt has been established—concerns the issue of the appropriate penalty.

• The degree of proof required by arbitrators for proving misconduct may vary, depending on the type of offense the employee allegedly has committed. Arbitrators generally agree that a "preponderance" of the evidence, "clear and convincing" evidence, or evidence "sufficient to convince a reasonable mind of guilt" is necessary to uphold management's disciplinary action in cases involving ordinary misconduct (77 LA 978, 77 LA 569, 77 LA 483, 77 LA 210, 75 LA 574, 74 LA 877, 74 LA 737).

• A higher degree of proof, however, may be required where the alleged misconduct is punishable under criminal law or regarded as morally reprehensible. In such cases, the common law standard of "proof beyond a reasonable doubt" may be required (64 LA 1099, 66 LA 619).

• An arbitrator ruled that the penalty of discharge was too severe for an employee who allegedly participated in an attempt to steal company-owned property, since the employer failed to establish the worker's guilt beyond a reasonable doubt. The "drastic nature of the sanction of discharge" requires a higher standard of proof, the arbitrator pointed out, emphasizing that not only is a discharged employee out of a job, but also (especially where the worker is discharged for dishonesty) the opportunities for reemployment are greatly reduced (*Daystrom Furniture Co. Inc.*, 65 LA 1157).

• Four employees who repeatedly used improper computer keying were discharged with just cause, said one arbitrator. In this case, management discovered that the four manipulated company software while operating forklifts equipped with computer screens and keyboards used to assign and track in-house goods. The employer accused the four of using a keying sequence that artificially inflated their productivity figures, which were used to determine both bonus payments and discipline. The union argued that the men thought the keying produced "a more accurate performance record," was not willful manipulation, and should have been subject to progressive discipline. The arbitrator found, however, that the four employees "did not engage in run-of-the-mill, minor misconduct, for which progressive corrective discipline is normally applied," but rather, engaged in "dishonest misconduct warranting summary dismissal" (*Ralphs Grocery Co.*, 117 LA 833).

• An employer failed to establish beyond a reasonable doubt that an aluminum ladder and other items found in an employee's garage were company property that the worker had removed from the workplace, an arbitrator decided. The charge of theft, the arbitrator noted, was based on a statement by the employee's estranged wife that her ex-husband had brought the property home from work. Although the employee may have removed the property from company premises, it was equally as possible that it was not removed by him and that his disgruntled ex-wife set up the situation, the arbitrator pointed out, concluding that there was no proof that the worker stole the materials (*Standard Oil Of Ohio*, 75 LA 588; see also 74 LA 1163, 73 LA 1066).

### Evidence Gathering

When management discharges or disciplines an employee, it should have enough facts in hand at the time of the action to establish "just cause." Efforts to build up a good case by extensive research after a grievance is filed generally will be a waste of time, since arbitrators usually hold that management's case must stand or fall on the basis of facts it had at the time it acted (12 LA 108, 10 LA 117, 1 LA 153).

• The most important evidence in a discharge or discipline proceeding usually comes in the form of testimony from witnesses—the facts that led to the employer's disciplinary action being of great importance (77 LA 721, 75 LA 1147, 73 LA 771, 73 LA 610, 71 LA 1109, 71 LA 949).

In weighing the credibility of evidence offered by management and the union, an arbitrator might consider the following.

• any conflict or contradiction in the evidence;

• any inconsistency in the testimony of the accused employee and other witnesses (60 LA 703, 64 LA 107); and

• the source of the witnesses' testimony—whether it is firsthand knowledge or merely hearsay and gossip.

### Witnesses

One arbitrator devised the following criteria to be used to determine the credibility of witnesses' testimony; including, but not limited to:

• the relative strength of their recollections;

• the consistency in testimony given on the same subject at different times during hearings and in different settings;

• the showing of obvious bias or prejudice;

• the showing of emotional stress or other feelings that would impair ability to respond to questions carefully and accurately;

• evasiveness;

• the quality and reasonableness of testimony; and

• the existence of corroborating testimony (*Safeway Stores Inc.*, 96 LA 304).

• Arbitrators sometimes bring in outside experts for impartial study of the disputed matter (6 LA 218, 18 LA 447, 21 LA 573).

Arbitrators have accepted testimony of handwriting experts and have based their awards principally on such testimony.

• In a case involving the discharge of an employee for allegedly writing and posting three obscene notices slandering female employees, the arbitrator ignored the employee's refusal to take a lie detector test, holding that he was within his rights in so refusing. The arbitrator did, however, rely on the testimony of a handwriting expert in upholding the discharge. He noted that the examiner's qualifications as an expert were substantial and that his identification of the employee as the author was both positive and firm (*Seaview Industries Inc.*, 39 LA 125).

### Polygraph Tests

Arbitrators generally have been reluctant to uphold discipline based on the results of polygraph tests. Some arbitrators have held that test results should be given no weight whatsoever in determining guilt.

- Granting that such tests are used extensively in government and industry, one arbitrator said, the fact remains that most courts have ruled them inadmissible as evidence in criminal and civil cases. The same rule should apply to arbitration proceedings, the arbitrator concluded (*Continental Air Transport Co.*, 38 LA 778; see also 75 LA 574, 75 LA 313, 71 LA 1202, 70 LA 909, 70 LA 100, 68 LA 581).

- Another arbitrator discounted the use of polygraph-test results in a proceeding involving a discharge for theft, where state law forbade the reference to, or use of, polygraph tests in court proceedings (*Deer Lakes School District*, 94 LA 334).

- Traditional arbitral skepticism about the reliability of polygraphs may be changing, according to one arbitrator, who observed that arbitrators have begun to adopt a "more favorable attitude" toward such testing in recent years. He cautioned, however, that "polygraph tests are more useful in verifying the truthfulness of testimony than in detecting its unreliability" (*Daystrom Furniture Co. Inc.*, 65 LA 1157).

- Similarly, another arbitrator maintained that "the pace of acceptance of polygraph results has accelerated somewhat in recent years" and that the tests "can provide helpful supplemental evidence" in industrial discipline cases (*Bowman Transportation Inc.*, 64 LA 453; see also 88 LA 1019, 77 LA 1259).

- Other arbitrators have held that test results may be considered as a "factor of evidence" but may not serve as the sole basis of proof (39 LA 470, 39 LA 893, 43 LA 450).

- Still others have said that an employee's refusal to submit to a test cannot be used against him, especially where the company is fishing for a guilty party among a group of employees and has not yet accused any particular person (73 LA 304, 32 LA 44, 39 LA 470).

- One arbitrator set forth these guidelines on the use of lie detector tests in cases involving dishonesty. He said the employer could offer these tests to employees on a voluntary basis when there was a reason to suspect them of dishonesty and could consider the failure to take a test as an additional possible factor in determining whether to proceed with discharge action. In cases where the employer had nothing else to go on but an employee's unwillingness to take a test, it could not use this factor as a basis for discipline (*Lag Drug Co.*, 39 LA 1121).

- One arbitrator upheld an employee's discharge for refusal to cooperate in the investigation of a theft where the missing articles were found in the employee's car, and he refused to offer a satisfactory explanation or submit to a polygraph test (*Allen Industries Inc.*, 26 LA 363).

[**Note:** A number of states have passed laws that limit the use of polygraph tests in employment situations.]

## Use of Surveillance/Listening Devices

The suspension of a telephone operator for poor work performance was upheld by an arbitrator, where supervisors used multiple listening devices to monitor her performance. Discipline need not be limited to eyewitness observation by supervisors, the arbitrator held (*Michigan Bell Telephone Co.*, 45 LA 689).

- Use of a television surveillance system was knocked down by another arbitrator, but only on the ground that installation of the cameras was a substantial enough change in working conditions to require negotiation with the union. The arbitrator did not completely close the door to the use of closed circuit cameras as a supervisory tool. For one thing, he rejected the union's claim that this constituted an unlawful invasion of privacy or spying.

In ruling that the camera system had to go, the arbitrator relied heavily on the fact that the company failed to show any particular need for or benefit from the system (*EICO Inc.*, 44 LA 563).

## Unnamed Accusers

Some arbitrators have refused to sustain discipline based on charges by persons whom the employer refused either to identify or produce at the arbitration hearing.

• On the other hand, in cases where a discharge was based on the report of a professional "spotter" employed to detect irregularities, an arbitrator held the company did not have to produce the spotter at the hearing, because this would have destroyed his effectiveness, which was the result, in part, of his anonymity (*Shenango Valley Transportation Co.*, 23 LA 362).

## Biased Accuser

The arbitrator also might examine the relationship between the employee and his accuser. Arbitrators generally recognize that the accused employee has "a strong incentive for denying guilt," in that the worker stands immediately to gain or lose in the case (48 LA 812), and that normally there is no reason to presume that a supervisor would unjustifiably select and accuse the employee of misconduct. Nevertheless, the testimony of the accuser would be subject to doubt and might be carefully scrutinized if there is evidence of ulterior motives or ill will against the accused employee (60 LA 206, 60 LA 688, 63 LA 244, 64 LA 304).

• An employee was discharged for being a "goof-off." Two of his fellow workers said they'd rather clock out and go home than be assigned to work with this employee because of his habit of wandering off and leaving them to shoulder the whole load. It so happened that one of these employees was a brother-in-law of the discharged employee's foreman and the other was a neighbor of the foreman. The discharged employee on an earlier occasion had turned in the foreman for being intoxicated on the job.

The arbitrator did not put any stock in the testimony of the foreman's allies but relied instead on the testimony of other employees who said they had never had any trouble working with the discharged employee (*Scientific Data Systems Inc.*, 53 LA 487).

**Part 2**

# Discharge and Discipline: Categories

# *Absenteeism/Tardiness*

## Absenteeism/Tardiness

────────────────────────── **OVERVIEW** ──────────────────────────

Generally, arbitrators agree that chronic or excessive absenteeism is just cause for discharge, but the real problem has been to determine when absenteeism is excessive. No general rules are laid down, so arbitrators must consider a variety of factors in deciding such cases.

In determining whether an employer acted reasonably in disciplining an employee for absenteeism or tardiness, most arbitrators use a case-by-case approach, focusing on the particular details of the immediate situation. Several factors are examined by arbitrators, including:

• the duration or the frequency (i.e., length of time between incidents) of the employee's absenteeism or tardiness (*Albertson's Inc.*, 105 LA 913; see also 64 LA 12, 74 LA 623, 94 LA 409, 95 LA 1169);

• the reasons for the worker's absences (64 LA 672, 74 LA 1185, 98 LA 57);

• the nature of the employee's job;

• the attendance records of other employees (64 LA 483);

• whether the employer has a clear disciplinary policy relating to absenteeism, on that is known to all employees and is applied fairly and consistently (63 LA 1315, 65 LA 919, 77 LA 249); and

• whether the employee was adequately warned that disciplinary action could result if the person's attendance failed to improve (63 LA 148, 71 LA 129, 71 LA 744, 72 LA 347, 98 LA 105, 98 LA 203).

────────────────────────── **SUMMARY OF CASES** ──────────────────────────

### Reasons for Absenteeism

Balancing the employee's right to job security against the employer's right to expect a reasonable degree of job attendance is the primary task of arbitrators dealing with a problem of excessive absenteeism. In achieving this balance, the arbitrator's decision often turns on whether the employee has provided a reasonable or justifiable excuse for being absent from work.

Some of the problems in striking this balance are discussed below.

### Chronic Illness

Illness is typically the most common excuse given by employees who are absent from work. Although it is reasonable for employees to be excused for occasional absences due to illness, manage-

ment does have the right to guard against false claims of sickness.

In evaluating whether excessive absenteeism due to illness justifies the disciplinary penalty, arbitrators often consider whether or not the employee's attendance record has fallen below an acceptable range for an unreasonable period of time. In determining this, management may consider the employee's previous attendance habits, his length of service, his apparent desire to be a faithful employee, his efforts to improve, the nature of the absences, the extent to which they exceed the norm, the effect upon efficiency and morale, and the prospects for the future.

Management's case for justifying a discharge will be strengthened if it has sought through counseling, warnings, and health care to rehabilitate the employee. Nonetheless, the fact that a final absence would not by itself support discharge is immaterial, as long as the employer has given adequate warning.

• An employer had just cause to discharge an employee for excessive absenteeism, even though the employee suffered from migraine headaches, an arbitrator determined. The employee, who had a dismal attendance record, attributed his frequent absences to chronic migraine. On one occasion, the employee suffered a migraine at work and left to go to the hospital. When he returned to work two days later, a supervisor told him to report for duty the following Monday. He failed to do that and was fired for excessive absenteeism. The union claimed that the employer should have told the employee that his absences could have been covered under the Family and Medical Leave Act. Rejecting that assertion, the arbitrator said the employee was in fact properly terminated for violating the attendance policy in the collective bargaining agreement. Regardless of his disabling migraines, the employer had a right to expect regular attendance, the arbitrator noted (*GAF Building Materials Corp.*, 114 LA 1528).

• One arbitrator ruled that illness, injury, and other incapacitation caused by forces beyond the employee's control are mitigating circumstances, excuse reasonable periods of absence, and are important factors in determining excessive absences. He added, however, that if an employee cannot maintain an "acceptable attendance record" due to chronic bad health or injury proneness, an employer may discharge the employee after having sought to improve the attendance through counseling and warnings (*Louisville Water Co.*, 77 LA 1049; see also *Drummond Company Inc.*, 106 LA 250 (psychological/medical problems); 77 LA 1049, 78 LA 673, 79 LA 128, 79 LA 916, 80 LA 7).

• Similarly, an employer properly discharged an employee who had been absent because of illness 14 or 15 weeks out of a six-month period. In upholding the discharge, an arbitrator said "no

plant can operate profitably unless it can depend on fairly regular attendance of employees." The arbitrator added that any situation that "results in or tends toward unprofitable operations is against the best interests not only of the company, but of the employees themselves" (*Celanese Corp. of America*, 9 LA 143; see also 74 LA 205, 74 LA 362, 74 LA 531, 74 LA 623, 74 LA 681, 74 LA 858, 94 LA 41, 94 LA 409, 95 LA 1169, 97 LA 653).

• It is generally felt that employees should be put on notice and given an opportunity to improve before the discharge penalty is invoked (*Ambac Industries Inc.*, 72 LA 347; see also 64 LA 1283).

• It may be relatively easy for a company to justify a discharge for excessive absenteeism where the employee has had frequently recurring illnesses for short periods taking place over a long period of time while showing symptoms of psychosomatic origin or chronic bad health. On the other hand, it may be more difficult for the employer to justify the termination of an employee who has several genuine illnesses, each lasting a long time (36 LA 1042; see also 75 LA 430).

• An arbitrator reinstated an employee where an employer's attendance-control policy in a collective bargaining agreement recognized the mitigating nature of an employee's illness—in this case, a chronic kidney ailment—in determining proper discipline. The arbitrator said that valid "no-fault" absentee plans must distinguish between "malingering and honest misfortune" (*Owens-Brockway Packaging Inc.*, 96 LA 950; see also 98 LA 112).

• Also, discharge was premature and possibly without just cause for an employee whose off-duty back injury had caused sporadic absences, despite claims that the employer had a responsibility to protect the worker and itself from the risk of further injury and even though there was no indication that absenteeism would improve, in light of the fact that a doctor's statements did not limit employee's work activities after his recovery (92 LA 837).

• In addition, just cause did not exist to discharge a 28-year employee suffering from anxiety and depression, even though she had accumulated seven absenteeism-related discipline slips in 23 days and did not seek treatment until more than two weeks after discharge. A letter from a treating psychologist confirmed that she was unable to care for herself or to act rationally during period in question (96 LA 1174).

## Family Member's Illness

An employee who stayed home from work to care for her retarded son was unjustly terminated, an arbitrator ruled. A 27-year employee of a packaging plant took a day off from work to care for her son when his regular caregiver could not do so. The employer had warned the employee about her chronic absenteeism and maintained that the federal Family and Medical Leave Act referred specifically to medical treatment, not day care, and required employees to give employers advance notice of time needed to take off. Her union asserted that the employer's absenteeism policy was arbitrary; a state family leave law did not require employees to give advance notice for emergencies; and the employee was required to furnish a reason for her absence only if the employer asked for it, which it did not. The company's six-day work week, coupled with the employee's 10-hour work days and frequent Saturday shifts, were an obvious burden on her, the arbitrator determined. Although the employer's absenteeism policy was acceptable, the FMLA was created to deal with such emergencies and the employee followed protocol under the law, the arbitrator concluded, ordering her reinstated with back pay (*Tenneco Packaging Burlington Container Plant*, 112 LA 761).

## Alcoholism

Generally alcoholism is viewed as an illness, and many companies have developed programs aimed at spotting and rehabilitating alcoholics, especially in the wake of the Americans with Disabilities Act. Employers are not obligated to retain indefinitely an employee whose alcoholism keeps him or her from working on a regular basis.

● An employee had been warned on numerous occasions about his absences, eventually prompting a seven-day disciplinary suspension. This was followed by more counseling concerning the seriousness of his absenteeism and his drinking problem, and finally by a 30-day suspension (pending discharge) with the understanding that he would be given one more chance if he committed himself to the state alcoholic hospital and successfully underwent treatment. After temporarily getting "on the wagon," the employee subsequently began drinking again, losing a week of work and ending up in the state hospital again. The company finally decided to discharge him.

Refusing to set the discharge aside, an arbitrator noted that when a "last-chance" agreement has been reached, another chance must rest entirely within the company's discretion. If he were to rule otherwise, it might jeopardize the chance of other employees to obtain reinstatement on the same condition, the arbitrator noted (*Mohawk Rubber Co.*, 47 LA 1029).

● Similarly, an employer properly discharged an alcoholic who had received his fourth warning for excessive absences instead of allowing the worker to take retroactive credit against his paid vacation for his unexplained absences, an arbitrator ruled. Pointing out that it is not unfair for an employer to place more stringent reporting requirements on an employee who has had warning notices about poor attendance, the arbitrator concluded that management did not act precipitously (*General Electric Co.*, 72 LA 355).

[**Note:** For more arbitral standards and decisions concerning employee alcoholism, see another section under this tab, "Intoxication and Alcoholism."]

## Imprisonment

Arbitrators are by no means unanimous in their attitude toward absence caused by an employee's confinement in jail. Some hold that it is just cause for discharge, while others say that it is a legitimate excuse for absence. In between are those who hold that it is not necessarily one or the other and that disposition depends on the circumstances of each particular case.

• In determining the propriety of discipline for an absence caused by a jail sentence, a number of factors may be taken into consideration. These include the duration of the absence, the nature of the act causing the confinement, and the effect the employee's reinstatement would have on plant morale, the ease or difficulty of having the absent employee's duties performed by others, the employer's past practices with respect to absenteeism generally and to arrest-caused absences specifically, the employee's length of service, the person's disciplinary record, and his or her record of dependability (87 LA 500, 87 LA 691, 87 LA 1273, 89 LA 1150, 94 LA 1206, 96 LA 216).

• An employee who had 37 years of service was arrested in a local movie house on a morals charge. He was held in a jail a couple of days before being released and later was tried, convicted, and sentenced to a year and a day in prison. Upon his release, he began receiving treatment from doctors and psychiatrists in an effort to eliminate the "sociopathic personality disturbance, sexual deviation" that had landed him in jail. The company later decided to terminate him permanently.

Although the arbitrator conceded that the employee was mentally ill and that his illness had manifested itself in a way that was repugnant and unlawful, he directed his reinstatement. The illness did not impair his ability to do his job, the arbitrator noted, and the company had not shown that the illness-precipitated bad behavior could not be eliminated or substantially improved by medical treatment. Nor was it shown that the employee's absence had affected the efficiency of his department or had significantly increased the company's insurance charges. Aside from sheer speculation, there was no basis for finding that his return would result in bad feelings or tensions in his department. All of this, plus his previously spotless 37-year record, convinced the arbitrator there was not just cause for discharge (*U.S. Steel Corp.*, 41 LA 460).

• An arbitrator ruled that an employee's incarceration did not trigger his discharge under a last-chance agreement. After compiling an unsatisfactory record of absences, the employee had signed the last-chance agreement, under which any absence or tardiness for the subsequent six months would result in his termination. When the employee was absent from work two months later, he was discharged; the termination was later rescinded, contingent on the employee's entering an alcohol rehabilitation program—and the employee incurred no further absences over the next three months. After he was later arrested for allegedly selling drugs, however, the company fired the employee for being absent. The criminal case against the employee was later dropped. His union grieved the discharge, claiming that the employee had no control over his absence, he was innocent of the charge, and he had fully intended to report for work until he was arrested.

Ordering the employee reinstated, the arbitrator held that the employer was not justified in assuming that the employee was guilty of the criminal charges simply because he was arrested. Because the charges were dropped, the employee must be presumed innocent, the arbitrator noted. Under the company's absenteeism policy, the employer is required to discern absences beyond employees' control, as in this case, the arbitrator says, and the last-chance agreement cannot override the requirement of "good and sufficient cause" for discharge (*Orpack-Stone Corp.*, 102 LA 545).

• An arbitrator upheld the grievance of an employee jailed on drunk driving charges who was discharged after reporting his absence as sick leave. Ordering the employee reinstated, the arbitrator reasoned that although the employee's claim of illness was an "incomplete" explanation, the employee, because he *was* legitimately too sick to come to work, did not intend to deceive the employer (*Indianapolis Water Co.*, 102 LA 316).

• On the other hand, after juggling his schedule in order to appear in court on a workday, an employee was convicted of a felony and incarcerated. The worker's wife reported his whereabouts to the company the following day, and after he had missed a week of scheduled workdays, the employee was suspended for an unjustified absence. Later, after considering the worker's record of absenteeism and discipline, management decided to change the penalty to a discharge. The union, on behalf of the prisoner, requested that the company grant the worker either his vacation leave or a leave of absence until the employee was given a work release, which occurred four weeks later. Management contended it had no obligation to do so and stuck by the discharge.

Saying there was no reason the company should consider the employee's imprisonment to be in error or forced upon him for reasons beyond his control, the arbitrator asserted that management "is not required to sit idly by, and in effect, carry an employee who is serving a jail sentence for acts committed against society." Finding that the employer had no contractual obligation to place the worker on annual leave, the arbitrator concluded that the worker's confinement, in light of his prior discipline and "significant absenteeism problem" warranted discharge (*United States Steel Corp.*, 69 LA 225; see also 72 LA 613, 73 LA 196, 86 LA 1237, 88 LA 167, 88 LA 1092, 89 LA 804, 91 LA 1225).

## Religious Beliefs

Management's right to discipline an employee for absences caused by his religious beliefs is complicated by the ban on religious discrimination in Title VII of the federal Civil Rights Act and by similar bans in many state fair employment practice laws.

Guidelines issued by the Equal Employment Opportunity Commission call for employers to "reasonably accommodate" the religious needs of their employees when this can be done without undue hardship to the business.

## Weather Conditions

On occasion, bad weather, civil disturbances, or other outside conditions make it difficult for employees to report to work. Even, however, when an "Act of God" is considered a reasonable excuse for absence, there still may be difficulties in determining how long the condition provides an acceptable excuse.

• Under an absentee control program that assigned "points" to employees for certain types of tardiness and absences, but imposed no penalties for "Acts of God," an employer wrongly assigned points to employees who were absent from work one day after a severe winter storm that was considered an Act of God, an arbitrator ruled. Despite management's contention that strict enforcement of the absence program was necessary and that conditions did not have a "sufficient impact" on the total workforce since 80 percent of the employees were able to report, the arbitrator maintained that the company could have extended the Act-of-God allowance to the 20 percent who were still hindered by snow and ice the following day, without retarding or impairing the overall effectiveness of the absence program (*Environmental Elements Corp.*, 70 LA 912; see also 95 LA 906).

• Although an employer had the right to establish a "snow day" policy excusing absence of employees due to weather conditions only when more than 50 percent of employees were absent, an arbitrator decided that the application of the policy on the day a snowfall caused absence or tardiness of 36 percent of employees was improper because the employees were not notified of the policy (*Marley Cooling Tower Co.*, 71 LA 306).

• An employer that closed its business during a flu epidemic must reimburse at a premium rate those employees who were called in to work, an arbitrator held. The employer, a mental health facility, closed to enrollees and staff members for two days during an outbreak of influenza. The employees' union asked that the employer compensate employees who were called in to work during that period at two and one-half times their regular rate of pay because the flu outbreak constituted a "calamity day" under the parties' collective bargaining agreement. The employer refused, arguing the epidemic did not constitute an "Act of God" as defined by the agreement. On the contrary, the arbitrator ruled, an outbreak where "almost everyone was hit with some type of flu" does qualify as an "Act of God" and is precisely the type of event that was intended to be covered by the contract language (*Erie County Board of Mental Retardation and Developmental Disabilities*, 111 LA 1121).

### 'Personal Business'

Employees at times are reluctant to disclose their reasons—good or bad—for wanting to take time off from work. To avoid unpleasant situations, employers frequently are willing to accept personal business as a valid excuse for absences in some situations, but there is by no means consensus on this issue among arbitrators.

● When a company decided to crack down on absenteeism because of suspected abuses, an arbitrator held that it could require employees to come up with something more than "personal business" as an excuse for absences. It is appropriate in such cases, the arbitrator said, for the company to inquire into the *general* nature of the business without invading the privacy of the employee's personal affairs. Because it would be next to impossible to prescribe a set formula covering every situation, the arbitrator advised, each personal absence should be dealt with based on the facts at hand (*Fairbanks Morse Inc.*, 47 LA 224).

This case-by-case approach generally is followed by arbitrators.

● An employee who had a record of extensive absenteeism and failing to call in or give explanation for his absences, gave as an excuse for a one week's absence that he had been out on "personal business." Because this explanation was considered inadequate, he was asked on several occasions to come up with a more substantive explanation. When he failed to do so, he was terminated. Only then did he explain that the reason for his absence was a highly personal situation involving domestic difficulties that he found embarrassing to make public. If the employee had not had the poor past record of unex-

plained absences, the company might have been in the position to have given him the benefit of the doubt, an arbitrator said, but in view of his record, a request for an explanation was justified (*Mead Corp.*, 51 LA 1121).

### Notification of Absence

Company rules usually require both notice to the employer when the employee is going to be absent and a justifiable excuse for such an absence. Notice alone, without a good excuse, does not fulfill the employee's obligation. On the other hand, a good excuse for the absence does not necessarily justify an absence without notice.

### Lack of Notice

If employees are expected to give notice of their absences, a failure to attempt to meet this requirement may justify discipline, regardless of how good the reason for the absence (60 LA 680, 63 LA 1262, 81 LA 657, 98 LA 23).

● An employer that imposed "last-chance" re-employment on an employee who had a drinking problem was justified in discharging the employee after he was absent from work for more than one week without complying with a condition requiring him to give notice of an intended absence and the circumstances involved to either of two general supervisors (*United States Steel Corp.*, 63 LA 274; see also 74 LA 507).

● An employer's discipline of an employee was not unreasonable after he failed to report to work, did not call in, and had no good excuse, an arbitrator ruled. Company rules on absenteeism provided that unreported absences were punishable by a one-day suspension. When the employee returned to work the next workday, he was informed of his violation and suspended for a day without pay. His union managed to get the suspension reduced to a written warning, but the employee had already served his suspension and when the company refused to reimburse him for his lost pay, the union refused to withdraw the grievance. Because "the obligation to report an absence, barring a legitimate excuse, is unchallengeable," the only issue to decide is whether the penalty is legitimate, the arbitrator said, noting that he was obligated to defer to the employer's judgment (*Smith & Loveless Inc.*, 116 LA 235).

## Failure To Notify Not Voluntary Quit

An employee's failure to notify an employer of his or her whereabouts or reasons for an absence can be considered a "voluntary quit." Occasionally, however, if the employee's reasons are good enough, a discharge may be reduced to a suspension (96 LA 216, an employee's imprisonment; and 95 LA 881, an employee's drug relapse).

## Defective Notice

If an employee makes a good-faith effort to comply with the notice requirement but is unable to do so, he is more likely to be treated leniently *if* a sincere effort at compliance has been made.

• An employee was taken ill shortly before the time he was to leave for work. Having no telephone, he asked a fellow employee to transmit the message to management, but the message never arrived. An arbitrator credited the employee with an honest effort to meet the notice requirement. The employee's obligation is met, the arbitrator said when "he employs a means of reporting that is, under all circumstances, reasonable and calculated, in all probability, to result in actual receipt of the notice" (*Goodyear Clearwater Mills*, 11 LA 419; see also 72 LA 312, 73 LA 133).

• An employee who wanted to extend his vacation mailed a letter to this effect to the employer at the end of his originally scheduled time off. The employer's rule specified that absence without notice "for three consecutive working days" meant termination. The employee's letter was mailed within the three-day period, but the employer did not receive it until later.

The employee did not meet the notice requirement, an arbitrator held, because the employer must actually receive notice within the three-day period (*Lear Sieglar Inc.*, 48 LA 276).

## Other Absenteeism Problems

Special absenteeism problems, apart from the issues of excuse and notice, are discussed below.

## Overstaying Leave/Vacation

Vacations, layoffs, and leaves of absence often give rise to absenteeism problems when employees report back late. Arbitrators tend to judge these situations as they would any other absenteeism case, with particular attention to the reason for the absence and the consistency of the company's enforcement of rules against leave-stretching.

• An employee did not return to work until one week after the end of her scheduled two-week vacation. She claimed that she could not get transportation back from the distant place where she spent her vacation unless she waited for her husband to finish his three-week vacation. Discharge of the employee for violating the company's rules was upheld by an arbitrator who said the employee probably had deliberately chosen not to return to work on time. In any event, she had demonstrated an irresponsible attitude toward her job (*Packaging Corp. of America*, 42 LA 606).

• In another case where an employee overstayed her vacation by a week, an arbitrator found that her excuse was good enough to warrant reducing her discharge to a suspension without pay. The reason for her absence was that she was attempting to save her marriage, which the arbitrator felt outweighed the employer's need for her presence (*Vellumoid Co.*, 41 LA 1129; see also 74 LA 847).

## Effect of Unionization

Five employees should not have been disciplined for violating an employer's policy on absenteeism, an arbitrator found. For many years, a job corps facility's instructors were unrepresented, but a first collective bargaining agreement became effective in 1998. Seven months later, the employer disciplined five instructors for exceeding the number of absences permitted by the employer's absentee and tardiness policy. Protesting the discipline, the union argued that the employees' charged absences included paid leaves that were approved by the company. The company's policy, however, counted them as "chargeable incidents," the union added, which violated the contract. The employer responded that the policy on absenteeism had been in effect well before the new labor agreement and the contract did not modify or cancel this policy, which should be recognized as a past practice. The arbitrator disagreed and said that a past practice can only exist if it has been "mutually acknowledged and practiced by both the employer and the union" over an extended period of time (*Career Systems Development Corp.*, 113 LA 920 ).

## Past Leniency

The fact that management has been lenient with an employee in the past does not necessarily bar it from resorting to discharge if the employee persists in his misconduct. A decision to give an employee a break in hopes that he will straighten out will not later be held against management by an arbitrator. But where management, over an extended period of time, gives only lip service to a rule of conduct, arbitrators will insist that discharge be preceded by effective notice that the rule will be enforced.

● In an effort to get a delinquent employee to mend his ways, management sent him a total of five "final" warnings over a three-year period. It ultimately fired him. Overruling the discharge, an arbitrator noted that the "final" warnings all read exactly alike. Thus it was not surprising that the employee did not think anyone actually was concerned about his absences. If somewhere along the line management had let the employee know that it meant business, either by specific warning or disciplinary suspension, then discharge for subsequent absences probably would have been upheld. Instead, management had completely nullified the effectiveness of its warnings by repeatedly threatening discharge and then taking no disciplinary

action, the arbitrator concluded (*Limestone Greer Co.*, 40 LA 343).

## Absence on Usual Day Off

When management schedules work on a Saturday, holiday, or other day that normally is not a working day, it usually faces a greater degree of absenteeism than usual. Arbitrators are agreed, however, that as a general principle, the right to schedule work belongs to management, except to the extent that this right has been specifically limited by contract.

● Even where a contract gives employees the right to decline to work on a Saturday or holiday, arbitrators usually have held that once an employee accepts an assignment to work on such an overtime day, his duty to the company is the same as it would be on a regular work day (11 LA 947, 12 LA 770, 29 LA 672).

## Insubordination

The offense of absenteeism often is compounded by insubordination where employees after being denied permission to take time off, take the time anyway. Arbitrators usually find just cause for discipline in such cases (43 LA 1070, 24 LA 593).

● A municipal employer could not fire an employee for insubordination for taking unauthorized time off, an arbitrator held. The employee worked for approximately 12 years as a laborer for a city government. Assigned to street maintenance, he was disciplined several times for numerous instances of tardiness and excessive absences. Finally, the worker was cited for insubordination for being "absent without leave" and for excessive tardiness under the state personnel rules. The employer said the worker was told one day that he could not leave work before the end of his shift, but he still left more than an hour early. The union filed a grievance, arguing that the collective bargaining agreement governed discipline for absences, not state personnel rules. The arbitrator agreed, adding that "tardiness is not insubordination" and ordering the employee reinstated with back pay (*City of Eastpointe*, 116 LA 577).

## Failure To Report

An employer properly discharged an employee for refusing to report to a job offered under a reinstatement award, where union officials urged him to accept position pending arbitral clarification of award, and resolution was "equivalent" to the former job, and the worker had been reinstated on probation and without back pay because of previous improper resort to self-help (97 LA 489; see also 96 LA 740).

• In another case, however, just cause did not exist to discharge an employee for "unauthorized absences" following an automobile accident, even though he did not report to work on the first date specified in a medical release, where the date of his actual return was one week after the return-to-light-duty date specified by a chiropractor. In addition, the date of the worker's actual return was one week prior to the earliest date he would be released for regular duties, and the employer had told the worker on similar occasions that there was no light-duty work, and the worker was entitled to a period of readjustment (97 LA 572; see also 95 LA 784, 95 LA 881, 95 LA 1135, 96 LA 38, 98 LA 194).

## Pattern of Absenteeism Justifying Proof of Illness

Related to management-rights provisions in collective bargaining agreements, an employer may be justified in requiring medical certification of an employee's illness where there appears to be a reasonable basis for such action based on the unique circumstances of the case.

• An arbitrator held that an employee's pattern of absenteeism justified his employer's insistence on a proof of illness. A municipal employee was notified that a review of his sick-leave record showed excessive use without any apparent reason. If he failed to provide a reason for these earlier absences, the notice said, he had to, in the future, bring in written verification from a physician each time he used sick leave. The union grieved. The city argued that the management-rights clause of its contract authorized it to re-

quire proof of illness when this appears reasonable on the basis of individual circumstances.

The arbitrator concluded that the contract did not invalidate the disputed policy. The contract provided that sick leave is to be used only for illness, and under the management-rights clause, the city had the right to manage in the interest of efficient operations unless this right were limited by specific provisions of the agreement. Finding that the contract's sick-leave provisions did not limit the employer's right to insist on a physician's certificate when the city reasonably suspected an abuse of sick leave in individual cases, the arbitrator denied the grievance (*City of Ann Arbor*, 102 LA 801).

• Another arbitrator held that an employer acted unreasonably when it established a new rule requiring employees to provide a physician's statement verifying that their absences due to illness were "excused." The arbitrator stated that, although the new rule followed standard industry practices and the employer had a legitimate concern for preventing the abuse of sick-leave claims, it encompassed employees with good as well as bad absenteeism records and thus went beyond the realm of reasonableness (*Altec Corp.*, 71 LA 1064).

## Tardiness

Although tardiness is not as serious an offense as an absence without excuse or notice, it is a proper subject for discipline. Given that the reported cases commonly involve discipline of employees for a combination of absenteeism and tardiness, it would appear that the employee who is guilty of one is likely to be guilty of the other (77 LA 947, 76 LA 1066, 76 LA 324, 74 LA 290, 74 LA 205, 72 LA 347, 71 LA 129).

• As with absenteeism, a program of progressive discipline (e.g., counseling, warning, suspension) generally is viewed as the proper way to encourage a delinquent employee to mend his ways (89 LA 1237, 90 LA 131, 91 LA 231, 91 LA 339, 93 LA 441, 95 LA 983, 97 LA 708). As with absenteeism, however, excessive and consistent tardiness can reach the point of rendering a worker no longer suitable for employment.

## When Does Tardiness Begin

Can employees be counted tardy if they are not at their workstations at the time the contract says the workday starts, even though they clocked in on time?

• Under a contract that failed to specify whether the workday began at the time clock or at the workstation, an arbitrator held, management had no right to fire a worker for tardiness because he did not clock in before the beginning of his shift. According to the contract, the "standard day shift" ran from 7:30 a.m. to 4:00 p.m. The employer construed this to mean that workers had to be at their workstations by 7:30, and it issued a notice stating that they would be considered late if they failed to clock in before then. A worker who persisted in clocking in exactly at 7:30 was given a written warning. He appealed the matter to a labor-management committee but was turned down. Eventually he was discharged on three counts, one of which was tardiness. The arbitrator, noting that the employer bore the burden of proof, decided that the charge of tardiness would not stand up. Nothing in the contract, he pointed out, established whether the parties intended the workday to begin at the time clock or at the workstation; therefore there was no basis for the company rule. For either the grievance committee or the arbitrator to "interpret" the contract on this issue would actually be an amendment to the contract, and therefore improper, the arbitrator concluded (*Pacific Air-Motive Corp.*, 28 LA 761; see also 85 LA 207, 92 LA 658, 95 LA 248).

• An arbitrator decided that an employer properly suspended an employee who either had another worker punch in for him so that he could go to the convenience store, where the plant manager saw him 10 minutes after the start of the shift; or punched in himself and then temporarily left the plant (*Peerless Mfg. Co.*, 73 LA 915; see also 84 LA 613, 85 LA 411).

• An employer did not have just cause to discharge a grocery store checker for chronic tardiness, an arbitrator found, citing several mitigating factors. The employee, who had worked at the store for 30 years, was discharged under the employer's absenteeism policy after she was late to work 10 times in one year. The final incident of tardiness involved her being three minutes late. The union protested, contending that the last tardiness event was beyond her control and therefore exempted from consideration under company rules. The arbitrator disagreed with that contention but said the employer failed to abide by its past practice of excusing late arrivals to work of five minutes or less. This especially would apply in the employee's case, he said, because more than half of her disciplines for tardiness had been for being less than five minutes late for work. This factor plus her nearly 30 years of seniority prompted him to order the employee reinstated with full seniority but without back pay (*Albertson's*, 115 LA 46).

• Refusing to "instantaneously" report for call-in work and uttering profanities later when confronted were insufficient reasons to dismiss an employee, one arbitrator ruled. The employee, whose job made him subject to required call-in duties, was asked to report to work immediately. The employee was undergoing hair treatment at the time, but the employer claimed the employee hung up on his supervisor and refused to report to work. The employee asserted that he told his supervisor that he would report to work after his treatment was completed, and in fact did so within an hour. When confronted by management later to discuss a disciplinary suspension, an argument ensued and the employee allegedly shouted profanities. The employee was subsequently terminated for insubordination, and his union argued that under the circumstances, the employee's outbursts should be excused. The employer argued that the employee had unreasonably delayed his arrival and later uttered profanities in violation of work rules. The testimony did not support the severity attributed to the incidents by the employer, the arbitrator found, expressing concern that "covert racial attitudes" had influenced the employer's actions. He ordered the termination rescinded and the employee fully reinstated with back pay and restoration of benefits, but with a written warning for his use of profane language (*Bunge Corp.*, 111 LA 1201).

## Tightening Rules on Tardiness

If it becomes necessary for a company to adopt stricter rules on tardiness, are there any limitations on the penalties it can impose?

• One arbitrator has taken the position that a new set of rules on tardiness must be judged not only on their merits but also by how they compare with past practice. Applying this reasoning, he refused to approve a rule that departed radically from past practice. After trying a number of approaches to the problem of tardiness, a company finally laid down a rule stating that an employee would be discharged if he was tardy 12 times in a 12-month period.

The arbitrator held that this rule was arbitrary and unreasonable. Looking at past practice, he found that none of the rules promulgated by the company in the past eight years had provided for discharge without prior warning. Moreover, the penalty of discharge had never been invoked on the basis of as few as 12 instances of tardiness in a 12-month period. It sometimes may be all right to define "chronic tardiness" in terms of a fixed number of instances of tardiness, the arbitrator said, but in his view it was unreasonable to do so where the number of instances of tardiness was reduced from

the number allowed in the past, where notices were not issued to the employees, and the rules made no provision for a graduated system of penalties (*The Maccabees*, 27 LA 99).

• Another arbitrator ruled that a company had no right, after signing its first contract, to start docking workers for tardiness. Nobody had ever been docked for tardiness before the contract was signed. In addition, the company had agreed that no clause in the contract would be interpreted to "imply a lowering of the working conditions heretofore existing."

The arbitrator found the contract language of special significance, because it was a first contract, and said it granted the workers all rights, privileges, and benefits they previously enjoyed plus the new ones in the agreement. He concluded that to start docking for tardiness after the contract became effective was a lowering of previously existing conditions (*Hellenic Lines Ltd.*, 39 LA 31; see also 97 LA 988).

• An employer violated a contract provision obligating parties to keep shop rules and penalties in effect without change for the duration of the bargaining agreement, an arbitrator ruled, when it promulgated a rule setting new discipline for tardiness. The employer's action was an improper modification of offenses and penalties under the contract the arbitrator reasoned, concluding that the evidence established a past practice by which employees regularly had been disciplined under existing rules for tardiness and absence (*Wolverine Aluminum Corp.*, 74 LA 252).

# *Insubordination*

# Refusal to Obey Directives

## OVERVIEW

Most cases of insubordination involve a worker's refusal or failure to follow the directive of a duly designated member of management or comply with an established procedure. On reviewing the propriety of discipline in such cases, arbitrators generally consider not only the magnitude of the offense and earlier occurrences of such behavior, but also whether:

- the order or procedure in question was clearly expressed;
- the employee was made aware of the possible consequences of the action; and
- the discipline was applied in a nondiscriminatory and progressive manner.

## SUMMARY OF CASES

### Rules, Orders, & Procedures

Violations of clearly expressed orders typically constitute insubordination and provide grounds for discipline.

- An employee was properly suspended for refusing to obey an order to move her car. After the employee refused to comply with a request to move her automobile, which was parked in a restricted area on the company's parking lot, the safety manager issued her a ticket. It warned the employee that she was parked illegally in an area reserved for motorcycles. When the employee refused to accept the ticket, her supervisor ordered her to accompany him to the associate manager's office where she would be given a memo directing her to move the car.

Despite these actions, the employee again refused to comply and subsequently was suspended for insubordination. The employer argued that the employee was "flagrantly" insubordinate in failing to move her car and report to the manager's office. The union, on the other hand, insisted that the worker should not have been required to report to the manager's office unless a union representative was allowed to accompany her.

It has long been established that an employee first must follow an order and then turn to the grievance procedure for

further relief, the arbitrator declared, upholding the disciplinary action. Pointing out that an "air of insubordination" surrounded the employee's conduct, he concluded that the worker's "open defiance" of management's directives constituted just cause for discipline (*Federal Correctional Institution*, 75 LA 295; see also 93 LA 203, 96 LA 212, 96 LA 633).

- In another case, however, an employee who was charged with five separate acts of insubordination during a 20-minute period was improperly dismissed because he was not warned about his behavior, another arbitrator ruled. The employee first was told to adjust the brakes on a piece of machinery. Refusing to comply, the employee used obscene language toward his supervisor, who then ordered the worker to report to a manager. When the employee refused to obey that command, the supervisor told him to clock out and leave the premises.

The employee insisted on staying and worked at his machine until management summoned the police to remove him from the premises. Subsequently, management discharged the worker, maintaining that he had committed five separate acts of insubordination by refusing to comply with orders to repair a machine, talk to the manager, stop working, clock out, and leave the premises. Protesting the discharge, the employee claimed that because all the incidents took place within 20 minutes, they constituted a single infraction.

Rejecting the employee's argument that the insubordinate acts constituted a single incident, the arbitrator pointed out that the employee was "instructed to perform or not to perform several distinctly different tasks or acts." Although holding that the worker was "guilty of committing several acts of insubordination," the arbitrator decided to overturn the discharge because of a "procedural error" made by the worker's supervisor. Noting that the supervisor had "failed to forewarn" the worker of the grave consequences of his disobedient behavior," the arbitrator stressed that such a warning "might have shocked" the worker "back to his senses" (*St. Regis Paper Co.*, 75 LA 819; see also 93 LA 773, 95 LA 302, 97 LA 592, 98 LA 131).

A refusal to take a polygraph examination, many arbitrators agree, warrants special consideration and does not automatically constitute insubordination.

• One arbitrator declared that an employer's demand that a worker take a polygraph test was an invasion of the right of privacy and the constitutional protection against self-incrimination, even though the worker had signed pre-employment forms agreeing to take such tests. The employment form had not been approved by the union, the arbitrator found, and could not stand up as an individual contract (*Lag Drug Co.*, 39 LA 1121; see also 39 LA 332, 38 LA 778).

• In a similar fashion, another arbitrator stressed that polygraph test results are "generally held to be inadmissible evidence" in arbitration proceedings. Furthermore, the arbitrator continued, refusing to take such tests is "analogous to refusing to work under hazardous conditions" because it "exposes the employee to another sort of danger, that of self-incrimination." An employee who submits to a polygraph test may be forced to reveal information that "may be placed in the hands of the employer to his future detriment, whether accurate or not, and whether or not material to the investigation at hand," the arbitrator

pointed out. Even though management had required the test only after a series of in-house thefts, the arbitrator concluded, it improperly discharged a worker for failing to take the exam (*Temtex Products Inc.*, 75 LA 233).

• Another arbitrator decided that management was within its rights to discharge a worker for a similar refusal, especially because the employee had signed a pre-hire agreement to submit to lie detector tests at the employer's request. "Employees may be required by their employer to undergo polygraph tests as a part of an investigation, and may be disciplined or discharged for refusal to submit to such a test," the arbitrator asserted, especially "when the employees sign a statement at the time they are hired agreeing to submit to a polygraph test during their employment at any time the employer may request." In this case, the arbitrator observed, the employee failed to comply with the agreement he made at the time he was hired. The company was within its rights in requiring the employee to take the test and discharging him when he refused to do so, the arbitrator concluded (*Grocers Supply*, 75 LA 27).

Failure to comply with procedures typically leaves the worker open to discipline. The grievance process, arbitrators agree, is the proper mechanism for protesting directives once the worker has complied with the order.

• An employee who refused to report to his supervisor at the beginning and end of his shifts was properly discharged. The worker was clearly informed of the procedure and warned of the consequences of noncompliance but repeatedly refused to follow the check-in procedures on the grounds that the rule was unreasonable and discriminatory because it applied only to a two-employee unit.

"The mere fact that an order is directed at two people does not per se render it discriminatory," the arbitrator asserted. Noting that management often had difficulty locating workers in the unit because of their inability to answer pages when performing certain tasks, the arbitrator decided that the employer's "rule of check-in and check-out" was "reasonable." Despite his supervisor's warnings, the employee "continued to flout the rule," the arbitrator stressed, upholding the worker's discharge (*Washington Hospital Center*, 75 LA 32).

• An employee who refused to sign a form making him responsible for company-issued tools was properly discharged for insubordination, an arbitrator decided. An employee was assigned to a job that required the use of special tools. He also was told that he would have to sign a voucher that said that a sum equivalent to the value of the tools would be deducted from the worker's paycheck in the event that the equipment was not returned. The employee refused to sign the voucher, even though his supervisor told him to do so. Subsequently, management discharged the worker for "deliberate refusals to comply with work instructions and unreasonable insubordination." Protesting the discharge, the employee argued that he had refused to sign because he believed that the form amounted to a "blank check" for the company to make unauthorized deductions from his wages. Stressing that he had "never" signed for a tool before and "was not starting now," the employee claimed that in the past supervisors commonly took responsibility for the workers' tools.

The arbitrator said that "it is clear" from the worker's "own admission that he was insubordinate." The employee's attitude "amounted to a deliberate defiance of the legitimate exercise of managerial authority in terms of the requirement that employees sign for the tools and materials they are issued." Rejecting the worker's argument that signing the voucher was equivalent to signing a "blank check," the arbitrator stressed that there was "no evidence that the employer had ever made improper or unauthorized deductions from employee paychecks in the past as a result of their having signed the voucher" (*Budd Co.*, 75 LA 281; see also 43 LA 46, 40 LA 562).

• A teacher who required his students to complete an examination during a bomb threat was properly suspended for failing to comply with established procedures. The teacher protested the discipline, arguing that false alarms were common at the school and that it was within his "judgment to allow the students to complete" the important exam. The arbitrator, however, agreed with management that the teacher had endangered the pupils by requiring them to stay in the building and "deliberately and willfully" disobeying "clear and reasonable policy and legal guidelines." Because the teacher's actions were "most serious" and his judgment in the situation "clearly faulty," the arbitrator declared, the one-day suspension was for just cause (*Whitehall-Coplay School District*, 76 LA 325).

Meanwhile, given the importance of established work procedures, some arbitrators have held that an employee may not be disciplined for insisting on complying with such practices even in the face of orders to the contrary.

• An employee was improperly suspended for refusing to sign a time card his supervisor had altered, an arbitrator decided. The worker, a union steward, attended a grievance meeting that started a half hour before the end of his shift. At the end of the two-hour meeting, the employee clocked out. His supervisor subsequently changed the worker's time card to reflect the time he had stopped working rather than the time he had left work. The employee refused to sign the time card, claiming that the card had been "tampered with." Following the worker's repeated refusals to initial the card, management suspended him for insubordination. The worker protested, claiming that he did not sign the card because he disagreed with its contents.

The supervisor's insistence that the worker sign the card "in the face of his fear of signing away his claim" for pay "served no legitimate business purpose and did not constitute a valid work order," the arbitrator declared, especially in light of the fact that the employer was "free" to calculate the worker's pay in any way it thought proper, whether or not the worker signed the time card. Because the employee had not refused a valid work order, the arbitrator continued, he could not be guilty of insubordination. Stressing that an "essentially trivial" incident "ought not result in serious consequences," the arbitrator decided that the employer did not have "proper cause" to suspend the worker (*Kilsby Tubesupply Inc.*, 76 LA 921).

• A worker who had followed one set of procedures for 11 years was improperly discharged for refusing to follow new operating procedures, an arbitrator ruled. A messenger for an armored car service, who was entrusted with delivering and picking up bags of currency, previously had been required to pack and seal damaged bags in a separate container. Suspecting that currency was being "extracted" from holes or tears in the bags, management established a new policy requiring messengers to break the seal on a bag and count the currency whenever a hole was discovered. Confronted with this situation, the employee, however, refused to obey the directive even though a supervisor ordered him to do so. When the worker continued to insist that "tampering" with the seal would be illegal, he was discharged for insubordination.

Although the arbitrator agreed that the employee did defy a clear order that did not involve an illegal or contractually forbidden act, he ruled that the penalty of discharge was too severe. For 11 years, the employee had been taught by "direction, custom, and practice" never to break the "sacrosanct seal," he stressed, concluding that the employer could not expect to "turn back the clock" on such experience and training simply by issuing a new directive (*Brinks Inc.*, 76 LA 1120).

*Flight Attendants*—Arbitrators have held that flight attendants and members of flight crews are required to have special schedules because of the unique nature of their work and requirements of their employers. Thus, one arbitrator found that an airline had just cause to issue a seven-day suspension to an airline flight attendant who refused to work an assignment of an extra flight to replace an ill attendant, where none of her several excuses constituted an emergency or justified the refusal (*Piedmont Airlines Inc.*, 103 LA 751).

## Safety & Working Conditions

The leading exception to the "obey now, grieve later" standard arises when an employee has reasonable cause to believe that the work ordered performed is unusually hazardous, substantially injurious to the health, or abnormally dangerous. When an employee raises the issue of safety as a reason for refusing to obey orders, some arbitrators have taken the position that the worker has the burden of proving the existence of unsafe conditions (103 LA 824, 61 LA 607, 62 LA 605, 63 LA 653, 64 LA 369).

• On the other hand, most arbitrators have held that an employee is protected in refusing to perform work, even if in actuality conditions are safe, as long as he or she honestly believes that the situation is hazardous. As one arbitrator put it, the employee should not be disciplined if he is "sincere in his belief of danger and so long as he makes a 'reasonable' appraisal of the potential hazards" (*A.M. Castle & Co.*, 41 LA 666; see also 30 LA 833, 67 LA 486).

• Furthermore, both the National Labor Relations Act and the Occupational Safety and Health Act prohibit certain disciplinary measures against workers who refuse to perform under hazardous conditions. Noting that under the NLRA, quitting work in good faith because of abnormally dangerous conditions does not constitute a strike, the U.S. Supreme Court has held that employees refusing to work on the basis of this provision cannot be disciplined so long as there is objective evidence that the work is dangerous to that degree (*Gateway Coal Co. v. Mine Workers*, U.S., 1974, 85 LRRM 2049).

• The Supreme Court also upheld similar rights provided workers by OSHA. In one case, for example, the court ruled in favor of two employees who had refused to work on a suspended screen from which a co-worker previously had fallen to his death. Arguing that the workers were engaging in unlawful acts of "self-help," management suspended the two for the rest of the day and issued written reprimands for insubordination.

Dismissing the employer's allegations, the court found that the workers were protected by OSHA regulations that served to further the OSH Act's fundamental objective of preventing occupational deaths and serious injuries. It would be a deviation from the purpose of the law to construe it as prohibiting an employee, with no other reasonable alternative, the freedom to withdraw without fear of reprisal from a work environment that he or she reasonably believes is highly dangerous, the court concluded (*Whirlpool Corp. v. Marshall*, U.S., 1980, 8 OSHC 1001).

● A worker was improperly suspended for insubordination after refusing to operate a vehicle he believed was in unsafe condition, an arbitrator ruled. After experiencing problems over a prolonged period of time with a vehicle's brake system, the worker told his supervisor that he had no "desire" to continue operating the machine. Finally, after again being assigned to the vehicle, the employee said he would "rather not" operate it. He was then suspended for a "clear act" of disobedience. Finding, however, that the worker's desire not to operate the vehicle was based on a legitimate concern for his personal safety, the arbitrator decided that the suspension was unjust (*Georgia Pacific Corp.*, 76 LA 808; see also 98 LA 72).

● An arbitrator reduced a discharge to a suspension for a truck driver who refused a work assignment on the ground that a tractor was unsafe to drive. The arbitrator held the employee failed to show the employer evidence of "snow-plowing" on a gravel surface allegedly caused by faulty steering and further failed to suggest that someone else drive the vehicle after a mechanic pronounced it safe (*CF Motor Transport*, 103 LA 303).

● Another arbitrator ruled that a refusal to obey an order may be justified by a good-faith fear for personal safety, whether or not the danger actually exists. In that case, an outside electrician refused to throw two high voltage outside switches unless another outside electrician were present, not the inside electrician the company promised. Discharging the employee for insubordination, management insisted that a worker who relies on safety factors to justify a refusal to obey an order must demonstrate that a danger actually exists. Dismissing this argument, the arbitrator stressed that the employee's fear was "real" enough, and warranted his reinstatement (*Hercules Inc.*, 48 LA 788).

● In another case, an arbitrator held that a group of employees erred in refusing to work under abnormal conditions despite the protective equipment furnished by management. The employees refused to work in the presence of an acid mist, which they considered abnormally dangerous to their health, although the company offered to provide respirators to filter out 95 percent of the mist. The employees, however, refused to wear them, contending that use of the respirators would not reduce the danger of the acid. The arbitrator found the company's arguments the more convincing of the two and pointed out that the employees showed only that there were "abnormal conditions " in the work area, not that such conditions were "abnormally dangerous." In upholding the suspensions for the refusal to work, the arbitrator added that the employees could not assume that the respirators would have been ineffective (*Bunker Hill Co.*, 65 LA 182).

● Arbitrators have held that, even if employees are not in danger themselves, they may be justified in refusing to perform a work assignment out of consideration for the safety of others. Thus, an arbitrator found a company in error when it disciplined a worker for refusing to work with another worker who performed his job in such a way as to endanger the safety of others (*Midland Structural Steel Corp.*, 30 LA 38).

*'Hazardous' versus 'Uncomfortable'*—Whether working conditions are "hazardous" or merely "uncomfortable" sometimes is the boundary line for what constitutes a proper as opposed to improper refusal to obey a work order or assignment. In deciding whether an employee's claims of dangerous working conditions are valid, arbitrators may have

to distinguish between mere discomfort on the employee's part and a real threat to occupational health or safety.

• An arbitrator found that an employer's use of portable toilets at a shipyard was not a serious threat to the safety and health of the employees because there was no evidence that the toilets themselves were unsanitary. The employees had objected to the toilets, claiming that it was unpleasant to use such facilities without the benefit of hot and cold running water. The arbitrator concluded that the employees had not proved that any disease or ailment had been contracted by the use of the facilities and that, therefore, there was no basis for their complaint (*National Steel and Shipbuilding Co.*, 64 LA 466).

Where working conditions are uncomfortable, as distinguished from hazardous, it is generally agreed that the proper method of securing relief is to file a grievance or request permission to leave. An employee who walks out to protest the heat or the lack thereof normally is subject to discipline, although arbitrators may reduce discharge penalties if they find mitigating circumstances.

• Seven employees who were working on overtime told their foreman they were going home on a day when the temperature in the plant approached 100 degrees. Their foreman told them they were making a mistake, but they left nevertheless.

An arbitrator reduced the discharges imposed by management to two-week disciplinary layoffs. He agreed with the company that the employees had violated the well recognized standard of conduct in industry that an employee does not leave during a shift—either regular or overtime—without permission. Mitigating circumstances were found here, however, particularly in the foreman's vague response, which was at best only a half warning. He probably could have forestalled the walkout if he had told the employees that they had a duty to remain and that they would be disciplined if they left without permission, the arbitrator observed (*Phelps Dodge Aluminum Products Corp.*, 52 LA 375).

• A woman who claimed extreme nervousness moved her work area farther away from the noisy area of the plant despite her foreman's order to remain until she substantiated her complaint with a doctor's slip. Upholding her discharge, the arbitrator found that the woman repeatedly disobeyed orders to stay at her regular workstation, ignored a warning of discharge, and "acted with full knowledge of the consequences" (*Scripto Inc.*, 48 LA 980).

• A distinction may be made between working conditions that are merely uncomfortable and conditions that are so bad as to make it unreasonable for management to require employees to continue working. The latter type of situation was found by an arbitrator in a steel fabricating plant where the heat was turned off for renovation during the winter and the thermometer dipped to 20 degrees. Disciplinary suspensions of workers who walked out were set aside by the arbitrator (*Berger Steel Co.*, 46 LA 1131).

• Safety rules may be established and enforced by management in order to protect the health and safety of the workforce. Absent specific contract provisions to the contrary, most arbitrators agree, management has the right, as well as the obligation, to promulgate and enforce reasonable safety rules and regulations (61 LA 824, 63 LA 574, 64 LA 894, 65 LA 360, 65 LA 751).

• Observing that such rules must bear a reasonable relationship to the promotion of safety and health on the job, as well as "being reasonable in application," an arbitrator ruled that management was justified in enforcing a requirement that employees wear safety shoes. Failure to wear the shoes, the arbitrator noted, was a potential health hazard to workers handling heavy objects (*Ingalls Iron Works Co.*, 61 LA 1154).

Arbitrators also have held that the punishment must fit the crime, i.e., that extenuating circumstances must be considered in weighing the propriety of a disciplinary penalty.

• A senior miner objected to a new rule requiring the wearing of safety glasses, complaining that the glasses, in his view, were more hazardous than helpful. After being given several warnings, he was told to wear the glasses or else, and he chose the latter.

An arbitrator conceded that management had authority to discharge, after suitable warning, for refusal to comply with the safety-glasses regulation. The employee's record was a good one, and his fears apparently were genuine, so the arbitrator was moved to permit him to return, but without back pay and provided he pledged to cooperate in the future (*Bunker Hill Co.*, 43 LA 1253).

### Reasonable Belief of Inability to Perform Work Not Insubordination—

An arbitrator held that an employee who had tendonitis was not insubordinate when she refused a work assignment with the reasonable belief that she physically could not perform the work because of her documented medical condition (*Stockham Valve and Fittings Inc.*, 102 LA 73).

## Overtime Assignments

In the absence of contract language specifically permitting or forbidding management to compel overtime work, arbitrators generally hold that overtime work may be required. Before discipline is imposed for a refusal to work overtime, however, certain conditions usually must be met:
• the overtime must be reasonable in amount;
• a notice must be given except in emergencies;
• overtime must be distributed equitably on a departmental basis;
• it must be assigned first to qualified workers who are willing to work extra hours; and
• only if there are not enough willing workers may unwilling employees be required to work overtime (*Sunbeam Electric (P.R.) Co.*, 41 LA 834).

The general "rule of reason" often applied to required overtime—it must be of reasonable duration; commensurate with employee health, safety, and endurance; and ordered under reasonable circumstances (*Texas Co.*, 14 LA 146)—"has generally been construed to mean that an employee's refusal may be justified, and that reasonable excuses for not working overtime must be accepted" (*American Body & Equipment Co.*, 49 LA 1172). Common types of excuses are reviewed below.

### Physical ailments as an excuse—

Claims of physical inability, when substantiated, may protect a worker from reprisals for refusing to work overtime. As one arbitrator asserted, "that genuine illness is a proper excuse for nonperformance of a work assignment—overtime or regular—goes beyond reasonable question" (*United States Steel Corp.*, 63 LA 608).

• An employee who had a "recent history of disability and severe back pain was justified in refusing to obey a supervisor's order to work overtime because of the "serious hazard" posed by such work, one arbitrator decided (*Pet Dealers Supply Co.*, 60 LA 814).

• In another case, an arbitrator found that management properly disciplined an employee for refusing overtime because he was "sick" from the "heat." The worker's "excuse of sickness," the arbitrator decided, was "for the sole purpose of avoiding overtime work and did not represent a true account of his physical condition at the time such excuse was made" (*Becton, Dickinson & Co.*, 60 LA 913).

• Despite an employee's claim that he had medical problems, his employer had just cause to fire him for insubordination when he refused to work nine-hour shifts, one arbitrator ruled. A coal mining contractor had to extend its work shifts to nine hours to fill a large order on time and told the employee he was needed for that task. The employee said he could only work eight-hour shifts because he was on medication for a health problem. Subsequently, on four workdays, the employee worked his regular shift and went home. Management warned that he must provide a doctor's note, but the employee never complied. According to the arbitrator, the employee refused to follow management's instructions on at least nine occasions, including "four when he refused to work overtime, four times when he refused to provide a medical slip, and once when he refused to grant a release of medical information." He added that the employee never produced a doctor's note to verify his alleged illness, noting that the employer had just cause for discharge by "a wide margin" (*Key Rock Energy*, 115 LA 462).

Employees' religious beliefs and practices may lead to scheduling difficulties. Although employers are required to make reasonable accommodations for sincerely held beliefs, an employee's religious involvement may not automatically be considered a valid reason for refusing to work overtime.

● One arbitrator held that employees' refusal to work on Christmas and New Year's Eves was not punishable as insubordination in view of the "peculiar and sacred" place those holidays occupy in the culture and in view of the irretrievable loss that would result if the employees followed the "obey now, grieve later" rule (*Kaiser Steel Corp.*, 31 LA 567).

● In upholding the discharge of an employee who refused overtime because he had "certain duties to perform as a minister," another arbitrator ruled that "this very high calling does not entitle an employee to exceptional consideration" (*Food Haven Inc.*, 62 LA 1246).

● In another case involving religious reasons, an arbitrator insisted that "chaos" would follow if an employee were permitted to "determine for himself, for reasons sufficient to him, whether he will regularly not work on a workday" that "management has the right to schedule" (*Combustion Engineering Inc.*, 49 LA 204).

Personal inconvenience or hardship resulting from extra work requirements also is cited as an excuse for refusing overtime. Depending on the severity of the hardship, arbitrators may accept the excuse as a valid reason for the refusal.

● "There are circumstances of emergencies, disasters, and perils, unforeseeable and foreseeable, where all but the very most vital needs of a good faith employee must give way to working the overtime," an arbitrator observed. He continued, however, that in most cases

there must be some give and take between employer and employee, to reach a "common sense" adjustment of overtime problems. With that reasoning, the arbitrator found an employer unjustified in forcing an employee to work on the day her house was being moved to a new location (*Southwestern Bell*, 61 LA 202).

● An employer did not violate its labor agreement by giving a two-day suspension to an employee who refused to work emergency weekend overtime, ruled one arbitrator. When a refinery employee was informed that he was needed to work the weekend, he refused, claiming unspecified "personal business" prevented him from doing so. Despite being warned by supervisors that the failure to respond to the company's emergency would be grounds for discipline, the employee did not report. As a result, he was suspended for two days and given a final warning, prompting the union to charge that there had been a woeful lack of progressive discipline for the 20-year employee, and disparate treatment. The final warning violated the contract, the arbitrator said, but the employee's refusal to work without providing a plausible explanation had left the company no alternative (*Phillips Petroleum Co.*, 116 LA 1251).

● An employer had the right to reject an employee's attempt to use his car pool as a permanent exemption from overtime duty, an arbitrator ruled, even though the employer had encouraged employees to form car pools and was required by contract to excuse employees from overtime, where overtime would cause hardship or serious inconvenience (*American Can Co.*, 65 LA 12).

*Moonlighting*—Generally, moonlighting is not recognized as a valid excuse for refusing overtime. Employees owe their first loyalty to their primary employer, and cannot use a second job as a reason for avoiding required extra work (*Shamrock Oil Co.*, 41 LA 1250).

● Where management has followed a policy of trying to accommodate overtime assignments to employee wishes, discharge was too severe a penalty for a moonlighting employee who refused the extra work. Reducing the termination to a disciplinary suspension, the arbitrator stressed that substitute workers were available to handle the overtime and that other employees with the same work assignment had been excused (*Budd Co.*, 52 LA 1290).

## Mitigating Circumstances

Unique conditions surrounding an alleged incidence of insubordination have led arbitrators to reduce or completely set aside discipline for the infraction.

• An arbitrator reversed the discharge of a union trial-board member for insubordination after he left work without permission to attend a union convention, despite the general application of the "obey now, grieve later" rule to insubordination cases. Because the international union ordered a trial board to reconvene at a convention, the employer was required to grant a leave of absence to any employee "designated by the union" to attend a convention "or other official union business." In addition, internecine union politics made swift resolution of the member's predicament unlikely before the convention, the arbitrator concluded (*Dole Refrigerating Co.*, 96 LA 787).

• An arbitrator reduced from a discharge to a suspension the penalty imposed on a 60-year-old employee who violated a plant rule prohibiting workers from sitting during their tour of duty. Although acknowledging "management rights to impose plant rules unilaterally," the arbitrator stressed that "to sustain actions taken thereunder, such rules must be within the bounds of reason, considering all the circumstances surrounding their application." The arbitrator added that the "no-sit-down rule in a cement plant where operations are at least semiautomatic and therefore to an extent monotonous, temperatures at least at some spots above normal, and floors hard," the arbitrator declared, "would seem to go beyond the bounds of reason" (*Ideal Cement Co.*, 13 LA 943).

• Another arbitrator overturned the discharge for insubordination of a professional employee who failed to follow new policy and procedures after being told to use her own discretion about how to run a detached facility. The employee, as the sole laboratory technician at a clinic located five miles from her supervisor, had to exercise more independent judgment than might otherwise have been required, the arbitrator noted, adding that the physical separation undoubtedly made effective communications difficult and contributed to a number of misunderstandings. Furthermore, the arbitrator pointed out, the employee, upon challenging the policy changes, had been assured by her supervisor that she could continue to use her discretion in regards to the facility's operating procedures (*Permanente Medical Group*, 52 LA 217; see also 98 LA 194).

• An arbitrator held that an employer did not have just cause to discharge an employee who refused to comply with an order to stop publishing an offensive, albeit 10-year-old, internal newsletter and to stop downloading race results on the employer's computer system during work hours where the employer failed to adequately warn the employee that his conduct could lead to discharge. Specifically, the arbitrator said, the employer failed to define what constituted "serious misconduct" under the contract, which would have fairly warned the employee that he could be terminated immediately (*Alliedsignal Engines*, 106 LA 614).

• Another arbitrator ruled that a supervisor must be the judge of when, and of what, tasks are to be performed. In that case, the employee, a service worker, claimed that he was too busy to comply with his supervisors' instructions. Although the pressure of dealing with the public may increase the potential for friction, the arbitrator emphasized, it does not warrant abandoning the standard of "obey now, grieve later." It would be destructive of proper labor-management relations, the arbitrator concluded, to allow employees to be the final judge of what instructions they would follow or honor (*National Lawyers Club Inc.*, 52 LA 547).

## Failure to Obey Order to Ignore Valid Legal Right

An arbitrator has held that an employee's failure to obey a supervisor's order to ignore a valid legal right is not the same as failing to obey a supervisor's order regarding work duties. An arbitrator ruled an employee's refusal to attend nondisciplinary instructional training because she erroneously felt she was entitled to union representation during the session did not constitute gross insubordination, and although a serious offense, was not the sort of behavior that should be subject to discharge (*Health Care and Retirement Corp.*, 105 LA 449).

## Walking Off Job as 'Voluntary Quit'

Employees who walk off a job based on a misunderstanding of material fact should not be assumed to have quit voluntarily, arbitrators have held.

● An employer treated an employee as having voluntarily quit after he walked off his job on his first day back after a three-month medical leave. The employee expected to be returned as mill operator's job he had been performing as a trainee for a few months prior to his leave of absence but was told he was being reassigned to a laborer's position. The arbitrator held the mere fact the employee had refused to perform the laborer's job did not automatically translate into a voluntary resignation, and the employer should not have concluded that was his intention. Generally, an employee does not voluntarily quit when he or she walks off a job to control anger, the arbitrator said, and here the employer knew the employee did not intend to quit and he contacted the union less than 24 hours after the incident. The employee simply was confused over his right to the mill operator's job and was not aware of the employer's absolute authority to assign him to the laborer's position, the arbitrator concluded (*Buckeye Steel Castings*, 104 LA 825).

● Another arbitrator ruled an employer's refusal to accept the retraction of a resignation may be considered a violation of the employee's good-cause rights, particularly if the employee has a good work record (*Atlantic Southeast Airlines*, 102 LA 656) and was upset at the time of resignation (*Moss Supermarket*, 99 LA 408).

● Another arbitrator cautioned that even individuals who were somewhat impaired should be assumed to have sufficient mental capacity to understand what they are doing unless there is clear evidence to the contrary. A showing of some inability to think clearly is insufficient, the arbitrator said, noting that reinstatement usually is awarded when a health professional who was treating the employee can confirm the employee was unable to make a sound decision (*Cowlitz County Public Utility*, 99 LA 80).

## Failure to Understand Directive

Arbitrators may refuse to uphold an employer's discipline of an employee where the employee failed to understand the employer's directive/order due to a nonfluency or nonproficiency in a particular language.

● An arbitrator held an employer did not have just cause to suspend a Spanish-speaking employee who refused to sign a document confirming that supervisors had given him safety instructions, where the employee in good faith did not understand why he had to sign the document (*Bud Antle Inc.*, 106 LA 101).

# Abusive Behavior

## OVERVIEW

Abusive behavior toward employer representatives constitutes insubordination, and therefore, grounds for discipline. Within this general category, are several types of offenses of varying degrees of severity, ranging from displaying a disrespectful attitude to verbally abusing or even physically assaulting management representatives. Each class, of course, and the circumstances surrounding the specific insubordinate behavior will determine the appropriateness of a disciplinary penalty.

Nevertheless, arbitrators typically uphold the ultimate penalty of discharge in cases where an employee has directed threats, abusive language, or physical violence toward a management representative (51 LA 633, 51 LA 688, 63 LA 765, 63 LA 1130, 65 LA 631, 65 LA 1119, 66 LA 206, 67 LA 426, 92 LA 3, 94 LA 1277, 95 LA 895, 97 LA 121). "Where this type of grievous on-the-job misconduct occurs," one arbitrator stressed, an employer "is obligated in the protection of its employees to mete out stern disciplinary action promptly and consistently" (51 LA 462).

Following are arbitral reviews of discipline for abusive behavior.

## SUMMARY OF CASES

### Physical Assault

An assault on a supervisor is considered a very serious offense, particularly where it would have the effect of undermining employees' respect for an employer's authority if it went unpunished. Most arbitrators agree that an employer's right to control operations in an efficient manner rests on the assumption that employees will exhibit respect for their supervisors. Assault and battery on a supervisor, for example, was described by one arbitrator as "the antithesis of civilized conduct and the behavior code of employment" (51 LA 462). Similarly, another arbitrator maintained that threats by an employee to inflict bodily harm on a supervisor were "a potent form of intimidation no less serious than actual physical attack" (50 LA 232).

To be considered insubordination, the assault need not occur on company property or during working hours if it is work related and has its roots in the employer-employee relationship. On the other hand, it would not be considered insubordination if the assault occurs off company property and outside of working hours and results from a purely personal matter. A distinction is drawn between the civil law that governs the normal relations between people and the "private" law of industrial relations that governs job-related relationships.

In cases where an employee is accused of physically abusing a supervisor, arbitrators generally consider the type of assault committed, the degree of violence involved, whether the worker was the aggressor in the altercation, or whether the employee merely was defending him- or herself.

● An employer was held justified in discharging an employee who was the aggressor in a fight with his supervisor on company premises, even though the supervisor might have struck the first blow. Remarking that the employee exceeded his right to self-defense by chasing the supervisor with a piece of iron after the fight had ended, the arbitrator ruled that the use of a dangerous weapon constituted an aggravated infraction of the plant rules (*Southern Iron & Equipment Co.*, 65 LA 694).

• An arbitrator upheld the discharge of a delivery truck driver who assaulted his supervisor during an argument that occurred when the supervisor tried to improve the driver's efficiency. While the employee's frustration and anger at repeatedly being told that his work was not up to par might have been understandable, his frustration was no excuse for the method he used to manifest his emotions, the arbitrator decided, asserting that a contrary conclusion would invite "industrial anarchy" (*United Parcel Service Inc.*, 67 LA 861).

An employee was properly discharged for assaulting his supervisor after an argument in which the foreman collapsed and died of a heart attack. Although the worker argued that he was not guilty of an "assault" because he had not physically attacked the foreman, the arbitrator decided that the discipline was just. The argument, coupled with the worker's shaking a rod in front of the supervisor's face as a "weapon to threaten or intimidate the foreman," put "great stress" on the deceased. "Making verbal threats and poking the rod at the supervisor's face" were sufficient grounds for discharge "just as pulling a knife would be enough," the arbitrator reasoned, pointing out that in the latter case there would be "no question that a supervisor would not have to be stabbed before a discharge was proper" (*Quality Electric Steel Castings Inc.*, 74 LA 558).

• An arbitrator ruled that two employees were properly disciplined for "supporting" an off-duty assault on a supervisor by blocking the exit and refusing to intervene in the scuffle. Even though the employees did not "physically participate" in the assault, the arbitrator noted, they did "aid and abet" the attackers. Because they prevented others from coming to the supervisor's assistance, stood by "passively," and failed to "attempt to restrain" the attackers, they were "accomplices to the assault," the arbitrator

ruled, and deserved the suspensions. A failure to uphold an employer's right to punish workers for such conduct, the arbitrator concluded, "unquestionably would have an intimidating effect on a foreman's willingness to exercise discipline in his department" (*Murray Machinery Inc.*, 75 LA 284).

• Another arbitrator decided that a worker was improperly discharged for kicking a supervisor, who had bent over to pick up something he had dropped, on the grounds that the kick was a "spontaneous kind of horseplay without malice or evil intent or any feeling of animosity or anger." Although the employer argued that the kicking incident jeopardized the "respect, consideration, and loyalty" that the supervisor needed to function on the job, the arbitrator found the contrary to be true. There was much "playing around" in the "relaxed" atmosphere of the worksite, the arbitrator pointed out, declaring that a "playful kick can be a compliment among friends" (*Tyrone Hydraulics Inc.*, 75 LA 672).

• So-called "road rage" is another problem that is likely to get an employee fired, as it did in the case of a 22-year city employee, who, while driving a pickup truck from the city's wastewater plant to its offices, was cut off by another motorist. When the employee honked his horn at the motorist and was greeted with an obscene gesture, he followed the motorist home, got out of his truck, and grabbed the person. Only then did he return to his duties, driving to headquarters, where the motorist also went and demanded an apology. The employee failed to give a sincere apology, and the motorist filed a criminal complaint, which prompted management to fire the employee. The sum total of the employee's actions clearly fit within the contractual prohibition of "serious abusive behavior toward a member of the general public," the arbitrator found. Despite considering a long list of potentially mitigating circumstances put forward by the union, she concluded that the employee's egregious behavior justified the termination "without the benefit of progressive discipline" (*City of Petoskey*, 116 LA 1176).

***Off-Duty Assaults***—Such assaults, as noted above, typically are viewed by arbitrators in the same light as on-premises misconduct. Although the arbitrator acknowledged that public authority is available to deal with those who willfully commit assault and battery, he declared that an employer still retains the right to maintain discipline and protect supervisors from retaliatory action by disgruntled employees, whether inside the plant or away from its premises (*U.S. Steel Corp.*, 35 LA 227).

● In another case, an employee who followed a supervisor to his residence and punched him was properly terminated, an arbitrator decided. After an argument on the job, the employee and his supervisor agreed to meet at a nearby parking lot to "box it out." The supervisor went to the parking lot but left before the employee arrived. When the employee was unable to find the supervisor at the lot, he went to the manager's residence and threw a punch at him. The employer subsequently discharged the worker for "seriously offensive conduct." To condone "violence, intimidation, and threatened attacks on supervisory personnel, for whatever reason and wherever committed," the employer argued, would "lessen efficient production and undermine authority." Protesting the discharge, the worker contended that his conduct was "only incidentally related" to the workplace and "was not so reprehensible as to justify his discharge."

The employee's "aggressive" behavior was the "culmination of a brooding resentment" toward his supervisor, the arbitrator found. Stressing that the worker had "plenty of time to reflect and back off," the arbitrator decided that the employee's pursuing the supervisor to his residence warranted the discipline imposed by the company (*Texstar Automotive*, 74 LA 210).

## Threats of Violence

In determining the propriety of an employer's disciplinary action in situations where an employee allegedly has threatened to assault a supervisor, arbitrators might consider the following:

▶ Was the employee's language directed toward the supervisor in an insulting manner and in front of other employees?

▶ Did the employee intend to, or could the employee, carry out the threat of bodily harm?

▶ Was the employee provoked?

▶ Was the employee's threat ambiguous or not?

● An employer had just cause to fire a bakery employee for threatening another worker. The employee in question was a 316-pound dough divider operator on one of the company's mass production bread lines. One day a co-worker hid the employee's tools in a nearby stockroom as payback, he said, for similar behavior by the employee. Returning from break, the employee found out what had happened and began yelling obscenities at the other man and chasing him over slick, slippery, and greasy floors, all the while threatening to hurt the 140-pound co-worker. He ignored a supervisor's order to stop, and subsequent testimony by bystanders suggested most of them believed that if he could have caught the co-worker, the man would have been seriously hurt. An employer cannot be expected to tolerate an employee who physically intimidates and threatens other employees, the arbitrator said, finding that the company had "not abused its discretion in determining that termination is the proper discipline" (*Interstate Brands Corp.*, 116 LA 1414).

● An arbitrator decided an employer was justified in discharging an employee who had reacted to an assigned task of picking up dog manure by dumping the manure on the supervisor's desk, breaking the supervisor's office window with a steel pipe, and threatening to "bust" the supervisor's head. Even assuming that the supervisor, by words or gestures, had provoked the employee's conduct, there was no justification for the employee's threat of physical violence, the arbitrator reasoned. Noting that the employee's assignment did not represent a threat to his health or safety, the arbitrator stressed that "the worker had committed three serious offenses in succession, each of which standing alone merited dismissal" (*Marley Cooling Tower Co.*, 66 LA 325).

● In another case, an arbitrator ruled that an employee who had threatened to have his foreman killed by a hired assassin was properly discharged. Emphasizing that the employee's threat against the foreman's life, which was made in front of co-workers, had "a chilling effect on the entire workforce," the arbitrator pointed out that, if the employer condoned the employee's conduct, then other workers might be tempted to engage in similar misbehavior, without fear of reprisal (*Protective Treatments Inc.*, 61 LA 1292).

● A worker was terminated for just cause after he followed his supervisor's car one morning, swerved in front of the other vehicle, and then threatened to kill the foreman. Dismissing the worker's denials of the incident, the arbitrator found that the supervisor's "positive testimony" carried more weight. Furthermore, the arbitrator noted, the employee had a history of run-ins with various supervisors, as well as having recently been suspended for absenteeism (*Central Soya Co. Inc.*, 74 LA 1084).

● An employer properly discharged a worker for raising his fist against a supervisor and telling the foreman to "lay off me, boy, or I'm going to beat your ass." Protesting the discipline, the worker maintained he had been responding to racial remarks, and that he had not threatened the supervisor but only told him to "beat the hell out of my face before things happen that we don't want to happen." Rejecting the employee's claims, the arbitrator pointed out that even if he had made the latter remarks, these words "certainly promised physical harm if the supervisor did not modify his behavior to comply" with the employee's wishes. In addition, while the supervisor might have made some derogatory racial utterances, the arbitrator observed, the employee's "proper response" would have been something other than "mayhem" (*United Parcel Service Inc.*, 76 LA 1086; see also 92 LA 3, 94 LA 1277, 95 LA 895, 97 LA 121).

● An arbitrator held that an employer had just cause to discharge a nurse who told co-workers at a government medical center that she would like to hit her immediate supervisor and that she was capable of buying and firing a gun at the supervisor. The arbitrator said the employee, among other things, had made three indirect threats against the supervisor, committed "disrespectful conduct," and violated government standards by engaging in other conduct prejudicial to government (*VA Medical Center*, 106 LA 907).

● In another case, an arbitrator decided that discharge was too severe for a 12-year employee who had an otherwise spotless record but who had threatened to run over a supervisor with a Mack truck. The arbitrator agreed with the employer that the worker's threats were a "direct subversion of the company's right to maintain order and to direct the workforce" and underscored the worker's attempt to "exercise self-help" over the matter leading up to the altercation. Nonetheless, while the conduct "justified punishment," the arbitrator ruled, termination was too severe in light of the "principles of progressive discipline." Instead, he concluded, a "substantial layoff" would be "in order" (*Brockway Glass Co. Inc.*, 74 LA 601; see also 95 LA 302, 95 LA 519, 95 LA 543, 97 LA 473, 97 LA 750).

● An arbitrator held an employer lacked just cause to discharge an employee who had told his supervisor he could get someone to injure him because the employee had a 14-year record of unblemished service and good work performance; his threat was ambiguous and he did not have the propensity to carry it out; the threat was borne out of nothing more than the worker's frustration with the particular day's events; and the threat was not accompanied by an overt physical act, other than putting his arm around the supervisor and drawing him close (*Pepsi-Cola Co.*, 104 LA 1141).

## Abusive Language

Generally arbitrators do not require companies to tolerate employees' verbally abusing their foremen. Use of profane and obscene language by an employee does not necessarily subject him to drastic discipline, but if such language is used to embarrass, ridicule, or degrade a supervisor, it would be considered an insubordinate act, especially if other employees were present to hear it.

• When profane, obscene, or abusive language is coupled with a refusal to obey an order or other insubordinate act of the employee, arbitrators typically uphold a discharge or other severe penalty (*Hastings Mfg. Co.*, 26 LA 713).

**Profanity Toward Management**—Such profanity generally is upheld as grounds for discipline. Except where employees have consistently used such abusive language even in the face of repeated warnings to cease, arbitrators generally will not sustain discharge for profanity alone. On a few occasions, arbitrators also have accepted employee claims that profanity—"shop talk"—is a normal practice in the workplace.

• An employee who used obscene language and made a vulgar gesture toward a foreman should have been suspended, not terminated, an arbitrator ruled. The arbitrator noted that the incident occurred during a series of mechanical breakdowns that left the shop in "turmoil." Finding that the "profane words and gestures" had a "relevant significance" to the "frustration, excitement, and confusion that prevailed," the arbitrator ordered that the discharge be reduced to a three-day suspension (*Mead Packaging Co.*, 74 LA 881).

• Another arbitrator ruled that discharge was too severe a punishment for a long-term employee who went into a rage at a grievance meeting held to discuss her alleged use of foul language toward her supervisor. Insisting that it could not condone or tolerate this type of behavior, the employer discharged the worker for "gross insubordination." Reducing the penalty, the arbitrator pointed out that the worker was a well-trained, long-term employee who had held several positions within the company. Under the circumstances, the arbitrator concluded, she deserved a "last chance" to correct her unacceptable behavior (*TRW Inc.*, 76 LA 782; see also 94 LA 610, 94 LA 767, 94 LA 1075).

• An arbitrator upheld the discharge of a union activist, where, in the presence of other employees, the activist walked off the job almost eight hours early, and shouted obscenities immediately after attending a meeting called by the employer to discuss the need to have employees work a full day (*Transco Railway Products*, 106 LA 103).

• Another arbitrator upheld the discharge of an employee who used profanity and in very obscene terms suggested that his foreman perform an act of indignity upon himself. The foreman told him he would be given a warning for such language and started to walk away. The employee called after him and repeated the remark with emphasis. Between 10 and 20 employees were in the vicinity at the time.

In upholding the employee's discharge, an arbitrator conceded that the term used was in common usage in the plant, but the way in which it was used is the important consideration. Use of the term in ordinary banter may be tolerated, but it is vastly different when such an expression is used in anger and with the intent to degrade and insult the recipient. The company must maintain the respect of both employees and supervisors; it cannot condone repeated insubordination, such as this, without losing this respect. To permit one employee to be disrespectfully insubordinate, the arbitrator concluded, could undermine the morale of the entire workforce (*Paragon Bridge & Steel Co.*, 43 LA 864).

**Name-calling**—According to one arbitrator, name-calling may be just cause for discipline where the employee, instead of executing an order, argues about it and calls the supervisor a name; the employee calls the supervisor a name in front of other employees; the employee calls the supervisor a name privately but afterward brags to other employees about telling off the boss; or the employee calls the supervisor a name privately, is warned by the supervisor, but continues to indulge in the name-calling (*Arkansas Louisiana Chemical Corp.*, 35 LA 887).

• In some name-calling cases, arbitrators have reduced discharge penalties in view of mitigating factors, such as the employee's good work record, common use of profanity in the shop, or reciprocal use of profanity by the supervisor (25 LA 439, 27 LA 611, 39 LA 58, 39 LA 661, 39 LA 849, 64 LA 751, 64 LA 1065, 65 LA 25, 94 LA 1087).

• Calling a supervisor a "liar" usually is regarded as a major offense that may warrant the discharge penalty. A discharge for this offense was upheld even where the employee had an "erroneous impression" that led him to think the supervisor had told an untruth (*Pacific Mills*, 3 LA 141).

• Another arbitrator noted that "most people would consider the accusation 'liar' to be more abusive and contemptuous than some casual vulgarism." In that case, the employee not only called his supervisor a liar in front of union and employer officials, but also refused to follow work assignments and even sprayed his foreman with a high-pressure hose. Finding that the worker's conduct was "no simple act of incivility," but rather "an egregious expression of contempt for supervisory authority," the arbitrator ruled that the employer was within its rights to terminate the employee (*ITT Continental Baking Co.*, 75 LA 764).

• In another case, an employee managed to hold onto his job after calling his foreman a "damn liar" only because he had a good work record and because there were no other employees within hearing at the time. Furthermore, there was some evidence that the foreman had initiated the use of abusive language (*Higgins Industries Inc.*, 25 LA 439).

### Disrespectful Attitude

Few things are likely to annoy a supervisor more than the employee who always replies with a flip or sour remark when told to do something; however, it often is difficult to draw a line between defiance or disrespect that would undermine discipline and harmless, minor griping. And it is not at all rare for a supervisor to put up with questionable remarks and then finally get angry and take action.

*Back Talk and Grumbling*—Such behavior may be tolerated over a period of time without precluding an employer's deciding that an employee finally has

gone too far. It may be necessary, however, to warn the employee that an employer's patience has run out before serious disciplinary action is taken.

• An employee who had been with the company about 20 years, talked virtually all the time, including times when nobody was around. He always insisted on having the last word and almost invariably would go off muttering disapprovingly when given an order. Twice in one day, his foreman's orders drew "I-know-my-job" retorts, which led to an exchange that culminated in discharge.

An arbitrator reduced the discharge to a three-and-a-half–month suspension, conceding that the employee, along with his extremely active tongue, apparently had a persecution complex, and his own special brand of "anything you can do I can do better." None of this was especially new to his fellow employees or supervisors. Although he had engaged in misconduct on the day of his discharge, his conduct on innumerable occasions in the past might similarly be characterized as objectionable. A slight variation in his 20-year theme should not precipitate anything so drastic as discharge, the arbitrator concluded (*Armour Agricultural Chemical Co.*, 40 LA 289).

*Disparaging Remarks*—Such remarks about a supervisor, management, or a company in general are not unheard of in employee conversation. Normally, such remarks, even if overheard by a supervisor, are not considered grounds for disciplinary action.

• After a company instituted a crackdown on previously tolerated practices, two employees were overheard making derogatory remarks about the company president. They were discharged for this and for failing to observe the newly instituted rules. On being terminated, one of the employees used profanity in directly addressing the president of the company.

Finding little to support the claim of rules violations, the arbitrator also found the case based on the derogatory remarks to be extremely weak. No one could show that such remarks were uncommon, that the statements were malicious in character, or that they affected morale and productivity. The only incident where the employer actually was confronted with disrespectful conduct was after he had fired these employees. Given that this occurred after their termination, it could not properly be used as grounds to sustain the discharge itself (*Top World*, 51 LA 1285).

● A worker was improperly discharged for criticizing management policies at a stockholders' meeting. The employee, who worked as a stock boy, was the son of a woman who owned 49 percent of the firm's common stock. When his mother became ill, the employee represented her at a meeting of the company's board of directors. During the meeting, the worker expressed several criticisms of management policies, as well as of the company's president, counsel, and accountant. Subsequently, the employer discharged the employee, contending that his "attitude toward work had changed considerably" and that he had begun to act more like a manager than an employee. While the employee was "vocal in his criticism" of company policies and "challenged the competence" of various employer officials, the arbitrator noted, he was "registering complaints and criticism not as an employee but as a representative of his mother." Consequently, the arbitrator ruled, the remarks were not proper grounds for discharge (*Hopwood Foods Inc.*, 74 LA 349).

## Mitigating Circumstances

Regardless of the type of abusive behavior displayed by the employee and its severity, arbitrators may reduce disciplinary penalties where the employer or management representatives have helped to create situations in which personality conflicts are more likely to flare up.

● An employee who had worked for a company 33 years without engaging in any insubordination became inebriated at the company Christmas party and threw the contents of a can of beer in the face of the industrial relations manager while letting loose with a stream of profanity. Management subsequently suspended the worker for 30 days for insubordination.

An arbitrator, however, overturned the penalty. The offense was not committed during working hours nor under the conditions of plant discipline, the arbitrator observed, and the employee's conduct appeared to be the result of consuming too much alcohol rather than being connected with the employment relationship. Furthermore, the arbitrator noted, despite prior incidents of drunken fights at the annual holiday party, the company continued to furnish free and unlimited liquor at the affairs, thereby running the risk of "predictable consequences" (*Hopper Paper Co.*, 30 LA 763).

● Another arbitrator decided that an employee was improperly reprimanded for expressing anger during a meeting with his supervisor, who had precipitated the altercation. The employee requested emergency leave to attend to a family crisis, but his supervisor wanted to know more details about the family emergency before approving the leave. When the employee refused to provide any more information, a heated argument ensued between the two men. Upset over the supervisor's attempts to elicit more details about the leave request, the employee became agitated and expressed himself in angry tones. Responding in a similar fashion, the supervisor pointed his finger at the employee and threatened to charge him with insubordination. Following the altercation, the employee was reprimanded for disrespectful conduct.

Finding that the supervisor had engaged in a pattern of harassment against the employee, the arbitrator reversed the employer's disciplinary action. The supervisor's "excited" response to the employee's remarks contributed substantially to the heated nature of the discussion, the arbitrator noted, holding that the employee's anger, although improper, was excusable. The supervisor's own "intemperate" conduct in dealing with a subordinate constituted unacceptable work place behavior (*Veterans Administration*, 75 LA 733; see also 81 LA 176, 81 LA 385, 90 LA 1302, 91 LA 482, 91 LA 905, 92 LA 28, 92 LA 340, 92 LA 521, 92 LA 871).

● An arbitrator ruled that just cause did not exist to discharge three non-English-speaking employees who allegedly were involved in a shop-floor confrontation with a supervisor. The altercation had resulted in a "charged atmosphere" at the plant after the collapse and death of a union steward immediately following a grievance meeting. The steward's death, and the language and cultural differences between management and the employees affected the clear interpretation of events, and the employer could not prove the employee's involvement in the incident, the arbitrator said (*Polycast Technology Corp.*, 97 LA 704).

• An arbitrator held that just cause did not exist to discharge an employee for fighting with his supervisor after being given a work assignment. Even though he conceded that he had struck the supervisor in the face and threatened to throw him from a catwalk, this was the employee's first offense in an outstanding 20-year work record. Moreover, the arbitrator said, the new, young supervisor's management style was harassing and provocative (*Ball-Incon Glass Packaging Corp.*, 98 LA 1).

• Another arbitrator found an employee's discharge for, among other things, his inability to control his aggressive behavior was too harsh. Even though the employee, a school custodian, had been suspended for aggressive behavior, instructed to control his anger, required to attend anger-management training sessions, and, in addition, his custodial work was below acceptable standards, the arbitrator held as mitigating the fact that the employee likely benefited from the behavior modification training, the sobering effect of a 21-month separation from his job following his injury in an auto accident, and his integrity and ability to perform the job (*Anchorage School District*, 105 LA 281).

• An arbitrator held an employee who suffered from depression mitigated his discharge, where the employee was very ill and had sought medical help but his physician had cancelled a scheduled appointment (*American National Can Co.*, 106 LA 289).

• An arbitrator upheld the termination of a worker who slugged his foreman, even though the supervisor had provoked the argument by calling the worker a term used in the plant as a derogatory way to refer to inexperienced, unskilled employees. According to the arbitrator, regardless of provocation, physical violence other than in self defense is universally condemned. At the same time, the arbitrator stressed, an employer should be obligated to do everything possible to end the use of "trigger" words or terms in the working environment (*Pioneer Finishing Co.*, 52 LA 1019).

## Union Activity

─────────────── **OVERVIEW** ───────────────

In cases involving alleged insubordination by union stewards or an alleged breach of plant rules, arbitrators generally look to see whether the offense was committed when the union representative was acting in official capacity or merely as a rank-and-file employee. If the steward is insubordinate as an employee, the penalty properly is the same as for any other employee under similar circumstances because the behavior will not constitute concerted protected activity under the National Labor Relations Act (92 LA 3, 63 LA 765, 62 LA 432).

If, however, the steward is "on business," the usual requirement of "obey now, grieve later," does not apply if the order given conflicts with the union's rights. This principle has even been extended to cases where union officials refused to obey orders in the good-faith, albeit mistaken, belief that the orders violated the contract.

No consensus exists among arbitrators, however, on whether management has a right to discipline a union official when he or she does not act in good faith, but rather, in knowing disregard of the contract and management's rights. One school holds that union officials have a blanket immunity from discipline by the employer for their official actions, regardless of good or bad faith, and that management's recourse is through the grievance procedure. The contrary view holds that evidence of bad faith destroys the shield that is usually accorded union officials.

─────────────── **SUMMARY OF CASES** ───────────────

### Grievance Investigation, Processing

If a steward, pursuant to the contract, seeks permission to leave his job to investigate a grievance, management cannot withhold permission unreasonably. It is not the supervisor's prerogative to decide whether or not the matter in dispute is a legitimate grievance and therefore subject to investigation.

• A union steward asked his foreman for a pass to investigate the discharge of a probationary employee. His foreman refused and referred him to the general foreman. The general foreman argued that the discharge of a probationary employee was not a grievable issue and told the steward to go back to his job or risk discharge. The steward refused and was fired.

An arbitrator later set the discharge aside, saying there "is a clear distinction between the case of a supervisor telling an employee to go back to his job, and a supervisor telling the union to stop investigating a grievance." When the duly authorized representative of the employer told the duly authorized representative of the union to stop investigating a grievance, the employer was issuing orders to the union, and it was the steward's duty, as a representative of the union, to insist on the union's rights. If the steward had been rough, rowdy, belligerent, or insolent in his attitude, some disciplinary action might have been warranted, but that was not the case here (*International Harvester Co.*, 16 LA 307).

• In another case, a union steward asked his foreman for permission to attend a meeting between two employees and an employer vice-president, but he was refused. The steward left his station at break time to attend the meeting anyway and was back at his post by the end of the break period but was nonetheless fired for insubordination. In reversing the discharge, the arbitrator noted that the steward had not been given reprimands for such conduct. The foreman who refused the employee permission to attend the meeting also admitted that he did not think the steward was guilty of insubordination (*General Fireproofing Co.*, 61 LA 389).

• A steward was, however, correctly suspended for refusing a repeated order to return to his workstation after being denied admittance to an injury-review meeting between a bargaining-unit employee and management, an arbitrator decided. The steward had no right to attend the meeting because no formal grievance had been filed, the arbitrator concluded (*Ethyl Corp.*, 96 LA 255; see also 95 LA 909, 90 LA 856, 88 LA 145).

• An acting union president who told an employee to refuse driving assignments was justly fired, according to one arbitrator. A truck driver also was acting as the local union's president when a dispute arose over a posting for another vacated driver's job. The successful bidder was an African American employee who grew concerned when he was not immediately placed in the new job. The company said while it was checking his driving record, a junior employee would temporarily fill the slot. Concerned that this was a smokescreen, the African American worker complained to the union, and the acting union president told the junior employee to stop driving, adding that if he did not, he could face union charges, lose his union card, and be fired. The company, however, fired the acting union president in response. According to the arbitrator, although he had operated out of unselfish, even laudable motives, "the method by which he sought to accomplish this goal was one that the collective bargaining agreement prohibited," and the termination was justified (*Linderme Tube Co.*, 116 LA 837).

## Leave for Union Business

Contract provisions for leaves of absence for union business vary greatly, and whether such leave should be granted depends not only on the particular contract clause, but also on the facts and context of each case, with particular reference to the good faith of both parties (*C & D Batteries*, 32 LA 589; see also 96 LA 60, 80 LA 201, 80 LA 1055, 78 LA 969, 76 LA 648, 75 LA 66, 71 LA 349, 71 LA 696, 64 LA 709, 58 LA 252, 54 LA 1130).

• The employer is entitled to enough information regarding the nature of the union business involved and the probable duration of the absence to permit it to make an intelligent choice as to granting or denying leave. Internal affairs of the union and union "secrets" need not be divulged (78 LA 8, 69 LA 831, 64 LA 1274, 50 LA 1140, 42 LA 632, 35 LA 873, 32 LA 589, 11 LA 569).

• Leave for union activity may encompass organizational activity outside the bargaining unit at a plant affiliated with the employer (80 LA 403, 74 LA 916, 74 LA 501, 74 LA 396, 64 LA 975, 58 LA 253, 50 LA 1140, 35 LA 873), but it does not include political activity (76 LA 648, 64 LA 1089, 37 LA 249, 8 LA 350, 5 LA 428).

• An employer may approve leave for union business on a conditional basis in certain circumstances (41 LA 739, 37 LA 475, 37 LA 249, 36 LA 400). Past practice has influenced arbitrators' decisions in granting leave for union business. (76 LA 1273, 75 LA 66, 70 LA 887, 43 LA 670, 15 LA 611, 14 LA 574, 11 LA 1074, 11 LA 569).

## Debates With Supervisors

Although a steward has the right to process a grievance energetically and may dispute a supervisor's decision, he may be subject to discipline if he becomes abusive to the supervisor.

• In an argument over a grievance, a foreman and steward exchanged angry words. The foreman then warned the steward that if he continued his display of bad temper "he had better punch his time card and leave." The employer subsequently issued the steward a letter of warning for his conduct.

In upholding the disciplinary action, the arbitrator said a "steward cannot be disciplined for actively pursuing grievances or presenting his arguments in a positive manner. A distinction must be drawn, however, between presenting arguments in a positive manner and being argumentative. There is a difference between attacking the logic of a decision and attacking the man who made the decision. Moreover, we cannot ignore tone of voice or attitudes. These may be just as important as the words used" (*Westinghouse Electric Corp.*, 38 LA 1226).

• Another arbitrator upheld the suspension of a union steward for using abusive and threatening language toward members of management.

Responding to a steward's request for permission to speak with a co-worker, a supervisor asked the steward what the two were going to discuss. According to the supervisor, the steward became angry at the question and replied with an obscenity. Later, a manager asked the steward to explain his reason for using obscene language. Denying that he had used such words, the employee contended that the supervisor was a liar. The manager then noted that other supervisors had made similar complaints about the steward and stressed to the worker that such abusive language was "uncivilized." The employee replied with a remark about what the manager could do, employing a crude analogy. Subsequently, the employee was suspended for three days for using abusive language toward members of management.

Acknowledging that "the right of the union steward to do his job properly must be protected," the arbitrator said that "mere militancy or zealousness on his part will not justify punishment, nor can a steward be limited to the language of polite society in fulfilling his role." On the other hand, "management cannot function properly if employees who are also union stewards can with impunity verbally insult and abuse members of management" (*Hobart Corp.*, 75 LA 907; see also 91 LA 482, 90 LA 462, 88 LA 512, 81 LA 1115, 81 LA 888, 88 LA 821).

• An employer had just cause to suspend a shop steward for making hostile remarks to a supervisor, according to an arbitrator. The employee in question worked at an automotive facility and had had a troubled relationship with his supervisor ever since his wife was killed in an auto accident involving the supervisor's brother. When the steward asked to speak to workers the beginning of a shift about an upcoming shutdown, the supervisor refused. The two got into a heated discussion, culminating with the supervisor's sending for plant security. The steward was suspended for 18 days for workplace hostility, and the union claimed he had been improperly disciplined for merely carrying out his union duties.

The arbitrator mused that the entire arbitration could have been avoided if the steward had merely been allowed to speak, a relatively common practice at this plant, especially given that the company otherwise displayed no anti-union animus. It was, however, the company's prerogative to stop the steward from speaking to the members at the start of their shift, the arbitrator concluded, denying the grievance (*Siemens Auto. Corp.*, 117 LA 398).

• Where another steward was discharged for using profane language during a joint labor-management meeting and "also threatened the employer's managerial control," the arbitrator disagreed with management's view of the incident and reinstated the employee. The employer conceded that the profane language alone would not have justified discharge in the context of the meeting but added that it drew the line at the steward's comment that he would tell management how to run its plant.

The arbitrator reasoned that although such outbursts are undesirable, they are also sometimes unavoidable. In the context of the meeting, the arbitrator concluded that there was no real threat to management's control because, despite the verbal threat, management was free to do as it pleased, subject to the grievance machinery (*Kaiser Engineers Inc.*, 63 LA 1051; see also 96 LA 56, 89 LA 361, 85 LA 716).

## Union Officer's Misconduct

An arbitrator held an employer did not have just cause to discharge a local union president who grabbed a security officer and used obscene language against another management representative in a dispute over how an outside union agent should have been escorted from the employer's premises. The arbitrator pointed out that the union president was a long-term employee, she was upset and acted impulsively, she did not assault or threaten the security guard after he asked her to remove her hand from his shoulder, she did not have a propensity for violence, and there was no evidence that the other employees would be reluctant to work with her if she were reinstated to her former job (*Army and Air Force Exchange Service*, 105 LA 332).

# *Misconduct*

# Damaging Company Property

## OVERVIEW

Indication of a person's deliberate intent to inflict damage is the primary factor weighed by arbitrators who are determining what kind of discipline is appropriate for the destruction or defacement of an employer's property. This consideration distinguishes vandalism or sabotage from mere negligence or carelessness, in which damage results not so much from a purposeful move to destroy as from a failure to follow procedures. (For a discussion of discipline for property damage due to gross negligence, see "Unsatisfactory Performance; Negligence.")

Thus, where malicious intent is proven, the actual dollar value of the damage takes on relatively little significance, and many arbitrators uphold the ultimate penalty of discharge even though the damage may be slight (94 LA 979, 92 LA 709, 77 LA 865, 73 LA 538, 72 LA 704). Conversely, absent evidence of a malicious intent and provided that the worker also is not guilty of gross carelessness, arbitrators generally will overrule discharge even though there may be considerable property damage (74 LA 257, 73 LA 98, 68 LA 1341).

## SUMMARY OF CASES

### Intent

To sustain discharge for malicious destruction of an employer's property, arbitrators generally require proof beyond a reasonable doubt that the worker willingly and knowingly engaged in the alleged act with full awareness of its consequences. Once this is established, however, they will uphold management's right to impose discipline as it sees fit, going on the theory, as one arbitrator explained, that management "is entitled to insist that employees respect the employer's property and to protect that property from abuse." According to the arbitrator, this management prerogative derives from the fact that "every worker's job is potentially threatened when employees engage in needless acts of vandalism against their employer's tangible property."

● Based on this reasoning, one arbitrator sustained the discharge of a worker caught tampering with the lock box fitted over the thermostat controlling the temperature in his work area. Although this was "not the most destructive

of acts," it reflected an "insensitivity to the underlying obligation of employment," the arbitrator declared, concluding the employer was justified in viewing the otherwise minor incident as a "willful act of property damage" that warranted termination (*National Car Rental System*, 72 LA 704).

● A worker caught using a hammer to bang on a soft-drink machine was properly suspended under a work rule prohibiting "intentional destruction of any property, tools, or materials of the company," an arbitrator held. The employee claimed that he had been handed the hammer "as a joke" during his unsuccessful attempts to retrieve his money from the nonfunctional machine and that he had used the tool without contemplating "any damage which might occur to the machine." Dismissing the worker's contention that he should not be disciplined because the element of intent was lacking, the arbitrator found that regardless of whether the employee thought the whole affair was a "joke," it was "plain that he was intentionally hitting the machine with a heavy tool" (*The Flexible Co.*, 48 LA 1227).

● An arbitrator ruled that an employee was properly discharged for hitting and breaking the glass face of a malfunctioning time clock where work rules provided for discipline for "damage to or destruction of" company property "through negligence or deliberate intent," even though the worker maintained that he had not intended to break the clock. Although granting that the worker "was frustrated and irritated, perhaps justifiably so in view of the history of malfunction of the clock," the arbitrator declared that "nevertheless, there was no justification for his action." The worker "intended to strike the clock, that deliberate act damaged company property, and his discharge was for proper cause," the arbitrator concluded (*National Services Industries Inc.*, 73 LA 538).

● Distinguishing "premeditated effort" from a "loss of restraint," another arbitrator overturned the discharge of a worker who broke the glass on a malfunctioning vending machine while trying to retrieve his purchase. Finding it "commonplace for human beings to bang on or kick a machine which does not deliver the promised goods," the arbitrator decided that the "provocation offered by the machine" plus the employee's otherwise clean work record militated against termination (*Goldblatt Tool Co.*, 74 LA 257).

● Another arbitrator ruled that just because a worker shook and kicked a cafeteria vending machine, the "assault" did not constitute a dischargeable offense because the machine was not damaged in the incident. Dismissing the employer's charge of "vandalism," the arbitrator pointed out that this label required the two elements of intent and damage. Here, however, even "if there was malice, there was certainly no defacement or destruction," he stressed. Furthermore, the employee's conduct was in accordance with "applicable mores," which hold that "vending machines are most imperfect creatures, subject to being physically abused without penalty when they malfunction," the arbitrator observed. In short, he concluded, the worker "commit-

ted no industrial offense, and the employer was entitled to administer no discipline" (*Cosden Oil and Chemical Co. Inc.*, 68 LA 1341).

● An employee was properly discharged for breaking a machine while making a "mockery" of following the tips a manager had given her to improve her performance. After being shown how to correctly place slats of wood on a conveyer belt, the employee exaggerated the procedures, finally pushing some sticks into the machine and breaking one of the chains. Upholding the discharge, the arbitrator noted that the employee had a history of unsatisfactory work and earlier had been transferred to the conveyer line as an alternative to dismissal (*Decorative Cabinet Corp.*, 17 LA 138; see also *Aluminum Co. of America*, 104 LA 260, where an arbitrator upheld the discharge of an employee who tampered with a vending machine because tampering triggered discharge under particular agreement).

## Vandalism

Vandalism as noted above combines the elements of intent and damage and therefore constitutes grounds for severe discipline, most arbitrators agree. On the other hand, arbitrators may overturn a discharge for vandalism if management has been lax in enforcing rules against drawing on the walls. The prime consideration here is whether the employee was aware that the action was prohibited.

● Discharge was too severe for an employee caught painting the words "peace, love, and brotherhood" on a door frame, an arbitrator decided, precisely because management had never warned employees that it would not tolerate graffiti. The employer also allowed scrawls and drawings to remain on the walls for extended periods of time, the arbitrator noted, pointing out that this inaction may well have contributed to the worker's lack of concern about a rule prohibiting this type of activity. Although management has the prerogative to decide what will be allowed to appear on its walls and what the penalties for infractions of the rules will be, these rights cannot be exercised arbitrarily and inconsistently, the arbitrator observed, concluding that the extreme penalty of outright dismissal was far too harsh a punishment for this particular, and first-time, offense (*Russell Stanley Corp.*, 66 LA 953).

● Where a prohibition was well communicated, management was justified in disciplining a worker for vandalism. In that case, the employer had experienced several acts of vandalism in its restrooms, including episodes in which workers caused toilets to overflow by deliberately stopping them up with rolls of toilet paper. The vandalism resulted in water damage to the walls and floor tiles in the restrooms. After the employer determined that a certain restroom was the primary target of the vandalism, it posted security guards in an adjacent storage room for surveillance. The guards stuffed a roll of toilet paper in one of the toilets and posted a sign on it saying "do not use." Later, an employee entered the restroom, removed the sign, and relieved himself. By the time the guards entered the restroom, the employee had flushed the toilet several times, causing it to overflow. Although the employee disclaimed any responsibility for the overflow, he was suspended for one week for deliberately damaging company property.

Finding that the employer's version of the incident was "consistent, cogent, and free of any significant discrepancies or incongruities," the arbitrator upheld the discipline. Pointing out that the employee did not offer to help clean up the mess when confronted by the guards, he concluded that the worker's denial of responsibility for the overflow displayed "a primary concern over culpability, fault, responsibility, and blame, rather than a primary concern over minimizing the damage" (*General Electric Co.*, 74 LA 161).

● An employee who painted over the word "No" on a company "No Parking" sign merited punishment, said one arbitrator, but not the five-day suspension he received. A security guard saw the employee spray-painting the sign one day after the employee had been warned not to park his truck in unauthorized spaces.

The employee, who denied committing the act, subsequently received a five-day suspension for destroying company property, based on the guard's testimony. Although painting the sign was "immature and inappropriate," the arbitrator said it did not rise to the level of "destruction." Nonetheless, defacing company property warranted some punishment, the arbitrator explained, ruling that the company's five-day suspension should be reduced to one day, with back wages to be paid for the other four (*Southern Indiana Gas and Electric Co.*, 112 LA 186).

### Sabotage

Sabotage is a particularly distasteful offense, arbitrators concur, in that it aims to deliberately subvert the employer's operations.

● Intentionally starting a fire to dramatize an allegedly unsafe working condition was sufficient cause for discharging an employee, an arbitrator decided.

On the day when an air pollution inspector was observing working conditions in another part of the plant, a worker deliberately started a fire at his workstation by throwing oil-soaked lead scraps into a vat filled with molten lead. The resultant fire shot flames four to five feet in the air. When the employee admitted starting the fire in order to get the inspector to take a look at conditions in his work area, he was discharged.

The arbitrator noted there was no dispute about the employee's actions or why he took them; however, he continued, "the 'good' motive to improve unpleasant or even unhealthy conditions of work is wholly disproportionate to the seriousness of this conduct." Furthermore, the worker's self-righteous attitude about what he had done could be reasonably interpreted as a harbinger of further hazardous acts, the arbitrator noted, concluding that, under these conditions, the employer was justified in discharging the worker (*F.E. Olds & Son*, 64 LA 726).

● Citing the "rights" of an employer "to manage its operation with care and concern for the safety of all its employees," another arbitrator upheld the discharge of a worker caught setting his work glove on fire in violation of a rule that prohibited sabotaging or willfully destroying company property. Finding management's version of the incident to be more credible, the arbitrator noted that "while the supervisor obviously lacks any incentive for making the charge," the worker, "who stands to lose, has every incentive for denying the charge."

With the evidence it presented, the arbitrator concluded, the employer "amply met its burden of persuasion" (*Cavalier Corp.*, 77 LA 865; see also *J.R. Simplot Co. and Teamsters Local 670*, 103 LA 865, in which an arbitrator upheld an employee's discharge for attempting to sabotage operations by throwing a wad of paper into an assembly line and stuffing fries into a batter machine, because these were acts of "sabotage").

● An employee was properly suspended for disconnecting wires from company speaker equipment, an arbitrator decided, finding that the action created a safety hazard in the plant. Displeased with the volume of music coming in over the public address system, the worker disconnected the wires in the speaker located next to his workstation. Maintaining that the action threatened the effectiveness of its communication system, management suspended the worker for "willful destruction of company property." Arguing that the action amounted to tampering with, rather than destroying, company property, the worker claimed that at most he should be given a written warning.

The arbitrator, however, found that pulling the wires from a speaker is more akin to destruction of property than to mere tampering. Furthermore, he noted, the employee's conduct posed the risk of serious property damage (*Mayville Metal Products Co.*, 64 LA 1239).

● A company had been plagued by frequent breakdowns of a conveyor, caused by foreign objects thrown into the works. Within a six-month period, there had been 43 such incidents. Employees were questioned about one of the breakdowns, which was caused by a small horseshoe-shaped object. One employee reluctantly admitted he had seen another

take such an object from a storage bin and put it in his pocket. Although this employee denied committing the sabotage, management fired him. Applying the test of "proof beyond a reasonable doubt," the arbitrator upheld the discharge. The credibility of the witnesses, the circumstantial evidence, and corroborating testimony indicated the guilt of the discharged employee, the arbitrator decided (*Aladdin Industries Inc.*, 27 LA 464).

● Management erred in firing a worker for sabotage where the evidence did not conclusively establish his guilt. One night outside the employer's premises, a security guard saw a man throw what looked to be a lighted object into a trash bin. A second guard also observed someone walking along a street just 35 feet from the bin shortly after the first guard called for assistance. Based on the guard's identification, an employee subsequently was discharged for attempted arson.

The arbitrator overruled the discharge, since the employee had an alibi for his whereabouts at the time of the incident, and because the first guard's identification was highly doubtful, given that he had made his observation from a distance of about 100 yards and the street was poorly lit (*Greyhound Lines-West*, 61 LA 44).

Conspiracy to commit sabotage also is a dischargeable offense; however, to be sustained, this allegation requires proof beyond a reasonable doubt that the employee was actively involved in planning the activity. Mere presumption of guilt, or superficial investigations, are insufficient for discharge.

● A manufacturing plant had been plagued by several incidents of sabotage, including a fire. Two employees admitted to setting the fire and implicated a third co-worker in the conspiracy. The co-worker was then indicted by civil authorities and discharged by the employer.

In reversing the discharge, the arbitrator ruled that the employer's action was premature because the indictment only raised a presumption of guilt, and the employer imposed the discharge penalty on the basis of doubtful information. Given that the co-worker was with the other two employees when they discussed setting the fire and knew the nature of the act but did nothing to prevent it, however, the arbitrator found him negligent and withheld back pay from the reinstatement order (*Donaldson Co. Inc.*, 60 LA 1240).

• An employer properly suspended all five workers on a crew after none would admit responsibility for sabotaging a piece of equipment, an arbitrator ruled.

After returning from their regular 20-minute lunch break, the crew reported that the machine they had been using was broken. Investigating the problem, a supervisor discovered that an electrical hookup was missing from a control panel. The supervisor decided that sabotage had occurred because the wire had been manually removed. When all the employees denied any involvement in or knowledge of the sabotage and none would admit tampering with the control panel, management suspended the entire crew.

The missing wire "was removed by some human agent," the arbitrator agreed, and "its removal constituted sabotage to the equipment." While acknowledging that the evidence implicating the employees was "entirely circumstantial" and the company did not consider "the nature of the involvement of individual crew members," he pointed out that the wire tampering could not be "explained reasonably except by assigning the blame to one or more members" of the crew. Even if all the crew members were not directly involved, all were "guilty of conspiring to obstruct the employer's investigation of the matter," the arbitrator decided (*Koppers Co.*, 76 LA 175).

# Discourtesy

—————————————— OVERVIEW ——————————————

Employees, particularly those involved in serving the public, are expected to be courteous and solicitous toward business patrons. As a general rule, arbitrators will uphold discipline in situations where employees are guilty of abuse toward either co-workers or members of the public with whom they come in contact, if the following conditions are met.

● The evidence convincingly supports the allegations of discourtesy (95 LA 771, 83 LA 224, 71 LA 805).

● Adverse consequences, such as "public embarrassment" or disruption of operations, clearly have resulted from the abusive behavior (98 LA 102, 95 LA 771, 94 LA 983, 93 LA 24, 82 LA 1186).

This section examines arbitration cases involving employees' discourtesy toward customers and members of the public as well as cases involving employees' complaints of discourteous behavior from supervisors. Discourtesy exhibited by employees toward supervisors generally constitutes insubordination and is discussed in that subsection.

—————————————— SUMMARY OF CASES ——————————————

### Due-Process Considerations

*Evidence of employee discourtesy—* Employee discourtesy toward an employer's business patrons is generally accepted by arbitrators as a just basis for management's disciplinary decisions; however, most arbitrators are careful to distinguish between "hearsay" evidence that an employee may be guilty of alleged abusive behavior and actual testimony that the misconduct took place. For example, one arbitrator approvingly cited as a "sound and good practice" for employers to have a "policy of obtaining written complaints" from customers that document the employee's guilt before taking disciplinary action (*Safeway Stores Inc.*, 64 LA 563).

● Discharge was improper for a bus driver who was accused of having attempted to kiss a female passenger while on duty, an arbitrator decided. Although the arbitrator acknowledged that the employer had "a most serious obligation for the health, welfare, and safety of its passengers," the arbitrator pointed out that

management based its case almost entirely on the testimony of a 17-year-old woman who was "unable to give dates or the description of passengers on the vehicle." Ruling that such testimony is "hardly the highest degree of proof," the arbitrator concluded that the company failed to produce evidence sufficient "to remove any reasonable doubt" as to what actually occurred (*Capital District Transportation Authority*, 72 LA 1313).

● Customer complaints about rudeness can provide sufficient cause for firing an employee, one arbitrator said. In the case at hand, a union filed a grievance when one of its members was discharged after a grocery store determined that she had acted with gross discourtesy to customers. Before meeting with the employee and her union steward, supervisors spoke to three customers who complained about the employee. Because neither the employee nor the union was permitted to review the complaints or contact the complaining customers, the union argued that this "hearsay" evidence could not be used to justify the employee's discharge. The arbitrator, however, upheld the discharge, finding that the union was given sufficient information regarding the substance of the charges. "No one will ever be able to be absolutely certain of what happened on these occasions," the arbitrator said, but the employee's long list of prior oral and written warnings and suspensions for discourtesy to customers showed that the employer had used progressive discipline in dealing with her, and that she was unable to respond to warnings and suspensions to correct her behavior (*Fred Meyer Inc.*, 117 LA 1063).

***Employee's past record***—An employee's record of displays of poor conduct toward business patrons may be sufficient cause for discipline.

• An arbitrator ruled that an employee was justifiably discharged for repeatedly insulting customers, because on two earlier occasions the employee had narrowly escaped termination for similar behavior. Reasoning that the employee's history was "rife" with incidents involving conduct that intimidated and embarrassed customers, the arbitrator decided that it was very "doubtful" that the employee would improve his conduct if given yet another chance (*Great Atlantic and Pacific Tea Co.*, 71 LA 805).

• Discharge was proper for an employee who failed to follow store procedures and displayed unbecoming conduct toward fellow employees and customers, another arbitrator ruled. Although the employee had been warned about her undesirable actions, the prevailing evidence showed that she disregarded the employer's regulations regarding proper behavior. Because the employee had been adequately warned that her continued flouting of company rules would result in dismissal, the arbitrator concluded that discharge was reasonable (*Goldman's Department Store*, 65 LA 592).

• An arbitrator decided that an employee was improperly discharged despite her history of rude, abusive conduct toward customers. Discharge was based on the receipt of several complaints, both oral and written, that detailed the employee's misconduct. The arbitrator refused to uphold the employee's claim that such complaints were "hearsay," explaining that "written complaints are clearly admissible for the limited purpose of showing that the company was receiving [customer] complaints" about the employee's attitude. Nonetheless, the arbitrator overturned the discharge because the employer failed to live up to its obligation to ensure "justice and due regard for the reasonable rights" of its employees. The employer's handling of the matter was deficient in two respects: first, the employer did not give the employee "an opportunity to explain her version of the incidents which resulted in the complaints by various customers"; and second, its failure to advise the employee that complaints were being lodged against her "lulled" her into thinking that the behavior was acceptable (*Apollo Merchandisers Corporation*, 70 LA 614).

## Degree of Discipline

Adverse effects resulting from an employee's discourtesy and the existence of clearly stated rules on employee behavior are important considerations in arbitral determinations about the severity of discipline.

• One arbitrator set aside discipline in a case where the employer contended that an employee violated an "unwritten" courtesy policy. Contending that this unwritten policy called for the "protection of confidential information" concerning patrons, the employer had suspended the employee for using improper language and talking in a "loud excited voice" about a movie celebrity who was on the work premises. Declaring that management had not "defined 'confidentiality' in terms of employee behaviors" nor "given proper advance notice of the rules," the arbitrator said that absent clearly promulgated policies the employer could justify the discipline only by showing that adverse "consequences" resulted from the employee's behavior (*Rochester Methodist Hospital*, 72 LA 276).

***Public-service employees***—Public-service employees are one group of employees whose day-to-day responsibilities involve the general public and who are expected to display courteous behavior, even though they themselves may encounter situations where members of the public are abusive. Particularly because such employees often work in an unsupervised capacity, arbitrators usually uphold the right of employers to discharge employees who are consistently unable to deal with people.

• "Public embarrassment" was sufficient cause to discharge an employee who cursed at a motorist after hitting his car and refused to give his name or driver's license number, an arbitrator found. It was "reasonable" for the employer, being "dependent on public goodwill and trust for its existence," to demand high standards from its drivers, and the employee's record reflected a pattern of careless and irresponsible behavior that warranted discharge, the arbitrator concluded (*Central Blood Bank of Pittsburgh*, 69 LA 1031; see also 65 LA 1098).

• A bus operator who physically ejected two passengers from his bus after an argument over transit rules was properly discharged, an arbitrator ruled, even though the employee contended that he had been provoked when one of the passengers hit him on the head. Finding that the employee's unsupervised job required him to interact with members of the public who might engage in "every conceivable mode of conduct," the arbitrator agreed that management could not depend on the employee to demonstrate reasonable and controlled behavior in his dealings with the public (*Metropolitan Atlanta Rapid Transit Authority*, 72 LA 723).

• An employee's accumulated record of rule violations, including several instances of documented discourtesy to passengers, properly prompted his discharge, another arbitrator maintained. Asserting that the company's business required "even-tempered, trustworthy drivers who consistently provide good service to their customers," the arbitrator decided that the employee had proved himself unreliable with respect to the firm's operating procedures (*Jacksonville Coach Co.*, 70 LA 432).

Other arbitrators have set aside or reduced discipline in cases where an employee's angry outburst was provoked.

• An employee who assaulted two teenage boys after they threw snowballs at his van was improperly discharged, an arbitrator ruled. Although the employee "unquestionably" should have "held his temper" rather than commit an "extremely poor act of judgment" that was "bound to reflect unfavorably upon the company," the arbitrator asserts that the employee clearly had been "provoked" by the assault. The fact of provocation did not excuse the employee's conduct, the arbitrator maintained, but it went "far to mitigate against the imposition of the most severe penalty at the company's command." The previous infractions of the employee "did not establish a record of such gravity" that the assault could be considered a "last straw," the arbitrator held, reducing the discharge to a 30-day suspension (*New Jersey Bell Telephone Company*, 68 LA 931; see also 57 LA 773).

*Patient care*—The care of patients is another area in which charges of discourtesy are frequent; however, employees who are responsible for the care and treatment of patients operate under slightly different circumstances from public-service employees, because their charges—those who are ill—may sometimes misinterpret actions or may be out of control themselves. As a result, arbitrators are careful to scrutinize the validity of charges filed by complainants, and will consult employees' past records to determine if there were previous instances of abusive or discourteous behavior.

• A nurse's aide who allegedly directed obscene language at a patient while lifting her abruptly from her bed was improperly discharged following a superficial investigation of the matter, an arbitrator ruled. Pointing out that the employee was tired after a "long and arduous" shift, the arbitrator decided that the discipline was "overly harsh." Although the employee "may have acted without the highest degree of care to which the patient was entitled," the arbitrator declared, her actions were not "maliciously intended," but rather were the "result of normal human frailty" (*Viewcrest Nursing Home*, 72 LA 1240; see also 53 LA 350).

• A state-owned hospital was not justified in discharging an employee for allegedly striking a mental patient during a scuffle, another arbitrator decided, because management had failed to establish that the employee had intentionally or maliciously abused the patient. Finding no evidence of prior sadistic behavior or improper treatment of patients by the employee, the arbitrator dismissed management's charges of premeditated abuse toward the patient and reduced the dismissal to a suspension (*Faribault State Hospital*, 68 LA 713).

• An arbitrator set aside discipline for an employee who was accused of abusing a mental patient with curses and threats. Saying that the complaints of "mental patients must be viewed with caution," the arbitrator found it "disturbing that management would elect to believe the testimony of three mental patients in preference to the testimony of its own personnel." Even those who are "well" sometimes misinterpret the actions of others, the arbitrator maintained, ordering the written reprimand removed from the employee's record (*Veterans Administration Medical Center*, 74 LA 830).

• An arbitrator upheld the right of management to discharge a nurse for refusing to medicate a patient and for extreme rudeness toward two other patients. Ultimately, the arbitrator said, it is the patient's well-being that is the primary concern of the employer. Because the employer had given the employee adequate chances over a three-year period to improve her discourteous behavior, the arbitrator decided, the discharge decision was justified (*Elizabeth Horton Memorial Hospital*, 64 LA 96; see also 91 LA 451, 83 LA 44, 81 LA 306).

### Internal Discourtesy

Dissension and fighting among the workforce can be the basis for discipline, particularly if such behavior is noticeable by business patrons or otherwise disrupts operations.

Where arguments among employees degenerate into brawls, employees properly are subject to discipline for fighting. (See "Insubordination; Abusive Behavior.")

• An employee's refusal to apologize to an African-American co-worker for using a particularly ugly racial epithet in her presence was sufficient grounds for a suspension, an arbitrator ruled. Although the employee claimed that she had not meant anything "racial," the arbitrator declared that her remark had a "racial bias which indeed is a form of discrimination," and the use of such a term was "socially undesirable and racially derogatory." The very fact that the African-American employee considered herself to be abused or insulted by the comment, the arbitrator said, was reason enough to uphold the discipline (*Memorial Hospital*, 71 LA 1252).

• In another case, an arbitrator decided that discipline was unjust for an employee who had been shot by his co-worker during an argument. The employer had allowed 11 months to pass before disciplining the employee for his part in the incident, waiting until a criminal trial had investigated the shooting incident. Finding that the delay in discipline was unreasonable, the arbitrator stressed that this decision does not mean that disciplinary action must be taken within a specified period of time. On the other hand, an employer may not wait an unreasonable length of time, pending criminal action against another employee, before notifying an employee of possible discipline (*City of Flint, Mich.*, 69 LA 574).

### Employer Discourtesy

Employees have filed grievances against employers for discourtesy.

• An employer violated its contractual obligation to promote a harmonious relationship between the company and the union by refusing to discipline a manager who verbally and physically abused an employee, an arbitrator decided. Although agreeing with the employer's argument that the union had no right to tell management how to discipline its supervisors, the arbitrator ruled that the foreman was guilty of abusive conduct. Management, the arbitrator concluded, was obligated to take steps to ensure that such conduct did not occur in the future (*San Antonio Packing Co.*, 68 LA 893).

Other forms of "managerial" discourtesy must fall within the realm of clearly unreasonable conduct in order to be considered violations of workplace policies.

● Casual remarks between supervisors about the behavior of a subordinate did not violate a contract provision requiring management and employees to show mutual respect for each other, an arbitrator decided. While emphasizing that "it goes without saying that criticism of employees is best left to private discussion," the arbitrator stressed that the supervisors had meant the remarks "lightly." He noted that "to call the situation disrespectful would be tantamount to ruling that supervisors cannot supervise"

(*Veterans Administration Hospital*, 71 LA 856).

● In a similar case, an arbitrator ruled that a manager was not disrespectful toward an employee during an interview in which he left the door to his office open and leaned back in his chair with hands behind his head. Disagreeing with the employer's contention that the "dignity and respect" policy applied only to relationships between employees and their direct supervisors, the arbitrator exclaimed that the employer certainly could not be suggesting that managers "could be ill-behaved toward employees other than those" over whom they had direct supervision. As regards the employee's allegations, however, the arbitrator found that she had failed to present any "objective facts" showing that the manager "intentionally" failed to conduct himself with "dignity and respect" during the session (*Veterans Administration Medical Center*, 75 LA 793).

# Dishonesty

## ————————— OVERVIEW —————————

Management would seem to be within its rights to fire an employee who has been dishonest, but in the real world, arbitrators frequently reduce the penalty. In such cases, arbitrators are often loathe to stigmatize an employee as "discharged for theft," given that that might render the worker permanently unemployable (*Commercial Warehouse Co.*, 62 LA 1015).

According to one arbitrator, when an employee is accused of criminal behavior, such as theft of property, the worker is likely to suffer, in addition to other sanctions, a "diminution" of reputation of the "severest sort" in the employment community. More than almost any other accusation, a theft charge greatly diminishes the accused worker's ability to find another job, the arbitrator pointed out, concluding that a higher degree of proof than the traditional civil standard of a "preponderance of evidence" was in order (*General Electric Co.*, 70 LA 1097).

The evidence required to support a discharge for dishonesty frequently is stated as "proof beyond a reasonable doubt," while a lesser degree of proof, such as "preponderance of the evidence," is accepted in cases that do not involve overtones of moral turpitude (71 LA 1109, 65 LA 1157, 65 LA 1091, 63 LA 849, 63 LA 648, 48 LA 891, 28 LA 65, 25 LA 906).

Because of this reluctance to label an employee a "thief," both management and arbitrators have a tendency to seize on some other violation of employer rules as justification for disciplinary action when, in truth, the real reason is the suspected dishonesty. This often results in cases where the penalty seems excessive for the offense that is the purported reason for disciplinary measures.

## ————————— SUMMARY OF CASES —————————

### Falsification of Job Applications

Arbitrators generally agree that discipline is warranted where it is shown that an employee falsified work records or employment forms; however, most arbitrators stipulate that the employee's falsification must consist of more than a mere oversight or lapse of memory. Usually, the falsification must be deliberate, and the person must have intended to defraud the employer.

• Arbitrators generally agree that after some reasonable period of time, falsification of an employment application should not operate as an automatic cause for discharge. Indeed, many arbitrators have ruled that a lengthy period of satisfactory employment should bar a subsequent discharge for falsification, provided that the facts falsified are not of such a nature as to endanger the present and future employment relationship (21 LA 560, 17 LA 230).

Arbitrators also have decided that the following standards should apply.

• Where falsification was deliberate and material to the employment and where no mitigating factors existed, a period of limitations was not applicable (91 LA 1261, 85 LA 834, 65 LA 1084, 60 LA 987).

• False statements on applications for employment create a dischargeable offense even if the employer's rules do not specify such conduct as cause for dismissal (55 LA 581, 43 LA 233, 42 LA 323).

● Misstatement as to the employee's medical history will justify discharge if the employee's physical condition, if known, would have disqualified the employee for the type of work for which he or she applied (*Scioto County Engineer*, 105 LA 876; see also 94 LA 249, 86 LA 640, 76 LA 520, 74 LA 354, 72 LA 1171, 64 LA 1260, 60 LA 1113, 55 LA 581, 39 LA 142, 36 LA 889).

● Failure to mention prior employers on an application may be cause for discharge because such information is material for the assessment of the applicant's qualifications (93 LA 124, 81 LA 158, 65 LA 797, 62 LA 389, 55 LA 581, 34 LA 143, 12 LA 207).

● If, however, failure to divulge names of former employers is used merely as an excuse, when the discharge is really for another reason, then the employer's disciplinary action may be overruled (60 LA 509).

● Misstatements as to whether or not an applicant's relatives work for the employer may be grounds for dismissal (73 LA 512, 71 LA 1168).

● Willful and deliberate falsification of a job application to conceal an applicant's prior workers' compensation claims—which would affect an employer's hiring decision—may be a dischargeable offense (91 LA 951).

● An employee's submission of false claims to a state employment services department in order to obtain unemployment compensation benefits to which he or she is not entitled may constitute a dischargeable offense if the false statements constitute fraud and theft under a particular contract; they were intentional and repeated; they served to raise significantly an employer's unemployment compensation contribution rate; or the contract's rules permit discharge for theft of employer property (*Leestown Co.*, 102 LA 979).

*Minor discrepancies*—Arbitrators have allowed for minor discrepancies on the application form under the theory that it is a natural tendency for employees to put their best foot forward in applying for a job. Some exaggerations or "puffing" are permitted. Another consid-eration used by some arbitrators is whether the employee would have been hired if he or she had disclosed the true information at the time. In other words, to discipline a person for minor discrepancies, they require that the truth about an individual's employment history, had it been known, would have served as a bar to the person's hiring.

● On his employment application, a worker replied "no" to the question "Have you ever had a back injury?" Four years later, in the course of treatment of an on-the-job injury, it was discovered that the employee had had back trouble off and on for 25 years. A discharge for falsifying the employment application was upheld. Although the arbitrator acknowledged that the employee may have answered the way he did because he did not regard himself as disabled, the arbitrator noted that this meant substituting the employee's judgment for that of the employer as to his qualifications for employment. And although the employer might also have concluded that the employee was not disabled enough to be disqualified for employment, it was entitled to have a full and accurate disclosure of all relevant health information in order to make a judgment (*Zia Co.*, 52 LA 89; see also 93 LA 381, 94 LA 690).

● On the employment application form, an employee checked "no" to questions asking if he had a skin disease or rash. Five months later he developed hand eczema, and the employer's physician referred him to a specialist. In relating his medical history, the worker told the specialist he had had the disease intermittently since he was 16 years old. The worker was subsequently discharged for lying on the application form. In overruling the discharge, the arbitrator noted that the employee honestly believed that he no longer had the condition at the time he applied for the job. The arbitrator concluded, however, that reinstatement should be probationary and terminable upon a disabling outbreak of the condition (*Springday Co.*, 64 LA 1129).

● An employee was improperly discharged for failing to mention on his employment record that he had been hospitalized, an arbitrator ruled. Although the employer's charge against the employee was valid, it was merely an excuse to fire the employee because of his heart condition, the arbitrator decided. Finding that the heart condition was insufficient to warrant discharge, the arbitrator ordered reinstatement, but without back pay (*Rockwell International*, 60 LA 869).

• One arbitrator held that the generally acceptable arbitral principle—that the falsification of material fact on an employment application provides just cause for summary discharge—is not applicable to the falsification of immigration-specific facts by alien applicants and employees, such as documents for the Social Security Administration and the Bureau of Citizenship and Immigration Services (formerly the Immigration and Naturalization Service) of the Department of Homeland Security. The rationale for this view is that these individuals and their U.S. employers face unique problems caused by extensive paperwork and processing backlogs. Alien employees must be given the opportunity to meet government requirements, the arbitrator cautioned (*Albertson's Inc.*, 102 LA 65).

***Delay in discovery of falsification and imposition of discipline***—One arbitrator has ruled that such delays may not preclude a finding of just cause for discharge for employees making false statements of medical history because an employer is permitted time to discover or obtain the necessary information from an employee's physician, to receive the necessary workers' compensation information, and to review the employee's personnel files for relevant information (*Ralston Purina Co.*, 102 LA 692).

## Disclosing Criminal Convictions

Failure to mention a criminal conviction in answer to a question requesting it is not necessarily grounds for dismissal. If the employee reasonably believes the conviction has been expunged from the public record, then his omission of the conviction is made in good faith, and discharge may be unjustified (*Kaiser Steel Corp.*, 64 LA 194).

• In another example, a worker was improperly discharged for "falsifying his application form" by not listing previous arrests, but as the arbitrator pointed out, even though both arrests were ultimately thrown out of court as illegal, the past cannot be erased, and the worker must share some of the blame for his discharge because he failed to make a frank disclosure on his job application. The arbitrator directed reinstatement but without back pay (*American Airlines Inc.*, 47 LA 119).

Other mitigating factors often lead to reversal or modification of disciplinary action where an employee has failed to mention a criminal history on a job application form.

• An employee who had committed armed robbery as a teenager 25 years earlier, answered "no" to a question on a job form concerning criminal convictions. In reducing his discharge to a short suspension, the arbitrator considered the employee's sincere belief that a "governor's proclamation" obliterated his conviction, the worker's 25-year history as a good citizen, and the employee's good work record (*American Stevedoring Corp.*, 65 LA 801).

• In consideration of a worker's good record and trouble-free period of employment, another arbitrator voided discharge for an employee who had falsified his job application form two years earlier. The employee had lied about the reason for leaving a previous job and had failed to mention that he had been arrested. The arbitrator directed reinstatement, but without back pay and with the charges and disciplinary suspension to remain a part of his permanent record (*Ward Mfg. Co.*, 46 LA 233; see also 77 LA 569).

• An arbitrator ruled discharge was too severe for an employee who allegedly gave a false "no" response to a criminal conviction question on an employment application. The employee reasonably believed that a youth-offender conviction had been expunged, and the evidence was conflicting as to whether the particular employer required "driving under the influence" convictions to be listed on an employment record, the arbitrator found, noting that there was no nexus between the employee's job and the remaining outstanding DUI conviction (*Freight-liner Corp.*, 103 LA 123).

● Where falsification is deliberate and relates to a material fact, and where the work record is poor, the employer may be justified in discharging the employee (93 LA 738, 91 LA 1193, 74 LA 176, 71 LA 1126, 71 LA 100).

● An employee was arrested on a gun possession charge that revealed a previous conviction he had omitted from his job application. The employer properly discharged the employee, an arbitrator ruled, because the worker deliberately concealed a prior felony conviction (*Houdaille Industries Inc.*, 65 LA 797; see also 81 LA 988, 81 LA 675).

● An arbitrator upheld an employee's discharge for deliberately failing to mention on his job application that he had been convicted of a crime and for omitting a gap in his work chronology for a period in which he was serving his jail sentence, even though the employee had a 14-month good work record with his current employer (*Trane Co.*, 104 LA 1121).

## Omitting 'Positive' Information

Although employees may be discharged for omitting information of a damaging nature from their application, discharge was not upheld in the rare instance where an employee omitted "positive" information.

● In this case, a utility man who did not list his bachelor of arts degree, masters degree, and completion of work toward a doctorate degree was improperly discharged, an arbitrator decided, despite knowledge of an employer's policy of not hiring people with a college education for "blue collar" jobs. Noting that the discharge merely was a pretext for getting rid of an "undesirable" employee, the arbitrator concluded that the falsification did not result in injury to the employer because the employee had demonstrated his competence on the job (*Hofmann Industries Inc.*, 61 LA 929).

## Falsifying Work or Time Records

Falsifying records by claiming credit for work not done is a serious offense that clearly justifies discharge. The falsifica-tion, however, must be deliberately intended to cheat the employer. Where there is doubt about that question, discharge may be set aside (102 LA 316, 96 LA 823, 95 LA 401, 84 LA 600, 83 LA 170, 81 LA 1004, 76 LA 213, 75 LA 45, 73 LA 1278, 72 LA 391, 71 LA 142, 63 LA 837, 62 LA 1015, 62 LA 934, 62 LA 14, 61 LA 363, 48 LA 891, 47 LA 966, 38 LA 1157).

● An employee who filled out his production record to reflect completion of a specified period of incentive work when in fact a portion of such period was spent training new employees was improperly discharged for dishonesty, an arbitrator ruled. Emphasizing that the employer's system for recording and distinguishing between "incentive" and "training" was confusing, the arbitrator concluded that the employer charged the employee with committing a crime but failed to prove the worker's guilt beyond a reasonable doubt (*H. R. Terryberry Co.*, 65 LA 1091).

● Two employees punched their time cards to reflect half-hour lunches when in fact they had taken two-hour lunches. In addition, one of the workers punched the card of the other, enabling the co-worker to leave early for deer hunting. Both employees subsequently were discharged by the employer. In reversing the discharge, but withholding back pay, the arbitrator found the unblemished work records of the employees to be mitigating factors. The employer had previously allowed employees to leave early without punching out, the arbitrator noted, concluding that the employer did not have a rule specifying discharge as the penalty for falsifying time records (*Great Atlantic & Pacific Tea Co. Inc.*, 63 LA 79).

● An employee was wrongly discharged for punching a co-worker's time card one half-hour early, an arbitrator ruled, which was done because the employee believed the co-worker was sick. The employee's action was devoid of any intention to cheat the employer, the arbitrator reasoned, emphasizing that the employer's past practice allowed employees to punch each other's cards (*Park 'N Fly of Texas Inc.*, 64 LA 1009).

● One arbitrator decided that a discharge for falsifying records was improper where the employer encouraged the employee's action. An auto mechanic had made a $120 repair estimate for a car that required only $9.50 in repairs at another shop and urged the need for repairs on another car that a state inspector later said were unnecessary. The employee was discharged, but the arbitrator reversed the employer's action because the employer had pushed its mechanics to sell repair services (*Fidesta Co.*, 64 LA 803).

## Falsifying Expense Accounts

Falsifying expense accounts to reflect costs not incurred by the employee may be grounds for discharge. In such cases, the employee is usually warned first by employer, then discharged for a subsequent violation. A satisfactory work record may not be considered a mitigating factor where the employee is a repeat offender or where he is evasive about answering questions concerning his conduct (81 LA 393, 75 LA 154, 75 LA 40, 64 LA 934, 64 LA 110).

## Falsifying to Obtain Health Benefits

False statements to obtain medical insurance or other health benefits may also serve as grounds for discharge. In cases where employees receive double benefits illegally by withholding information about their insurance sources, obtain benefits for persons not properly covered under plans by claiming they are family members, or make false reports of medical treatment for compensation, arbitrators have upheld discharge (96 LA 1090, 96 LA 644, 95 LA 46, 87 LA 160, 85 LA 643, 82 LA 604, 65 LA 623, 63 LA 768, 62 LA 493).

● An arbitrator held that an employer had just cause to discharge a 27-year employee for falsifying medical insurance forms to provide health coverage for his ex-wife. Falsifying records is a serious offense that almost invariably warrants termination for first occurrence, regardless of the employee's length of service, the arbitrator said (*Airfoil Forging Textron*, 106 LA 945).

● In this category, as in others involving conscious dishonesty or moral turpitude, the employer must meet the burden of proof beyond a reasonable doubt (*Dunlop Tire & Rubber Corp.*, 64 LA 1099; see also 89 LA 8, 95 LA 759).

## Deliberate Exaggeration of Medical Conditions

An arbitrator upheld the discharge of an employee who failed to put forth sufficient effort to perform a light-duty assignment, after having undergone surgery and months of therapy for a shoulder injury and a clavicle fracture. According to objective medical analysis, the employee's injuries had healed, but his doctors noted to the employer that the employee was deliberately exaggerating his complaints about pain and self-limiting his movements. He did not notify his employer when he was given restricted clearance to return to work and returned only when ordered to do so after the employer was notified the employee had been dropped from his rehabilitation program for lack of effort. His return lasted six months—he continued to complain of pain that was not reflected in his doctors' evaluation and refused job assignments. Finally, after having the employee's medical condition and ability to perform work reviewed at various times, the employer fired the employee after he failed to perform a light-duty assignment adequately (*Cramer Inc.*, 110 LA 37).

● Another arbitrator ruled that, even though a nondiscrimination provision in the parties' collective bargaining agreement referenced federal and state disabilities statutes, an employee who claimed to be disabled was not covered under the Americans with Disabilities Act, because both the employee and his occupational therapist testified that he could work and perform all major life activities. The arbitrator also noted that the Equal Employment Opportunity Commission dismissed as meritless a charge filed by the employee alleging discrimination (*Shell Oil Co.*, 109 LA 965; for an example that had a different outcome, see *City of Tampa*, 111 LA 65).

## Misrepresentation of Employer Statements

The discipline and/or discharge of employees for making statements that misrepresent an employer's point of view or actions are complicated by the fact that such actions relate to collective bargaining and are protected under, not only the particular contract, but also the external law of the federal National Labor Relations Act.

• In one particular case involving a union steward's alleged misrepresentation of, or false statements concerning, an employer's actions toward its Vietnamese employees, purportedly seriously compromising the employer's relationship and credibility with the employees, an arbitrator ruled that the steward's statements were such that they lost their protected status. Upholding the steward's discharge, the arbitrator cited the negative impact of the misstatements on the employer's reputation, as well as their potentially disruptive effect on plant operations, discipline, and labor-management relations (*Mid-West Chandelier Co.*, 102 LA 833).

### Theft of Employer Property

Generally, arbitrators believe that no employee needs a rule to warn that stealing employer property is wrong and that it constitutes a dischargeable offense (See, e.g., *Monsanto Co.*, 105 LA 923; *East Liverpool Board of Education*, 105 LA 161; see also 76 LA 1216, 76 LA 939, 76 LA 592, 76 LA 373). This is true even of items of relatively little value. Employers simply do not want to retain employees who demonstrate they cannot be fully trusted, and management is aware that small thefts can produce great losses if sufficient numbers of people are involved.

• Frequently, the claim will be made that the employee did not think an item was of any value to the employer or thought it had been thrown away or would be (*EMGE Packing Co.*, 61 LA 250). For that reason, it often is wise to have a clearly stated policy concerning the disposition of scrap, the equipment that may be used or borrowed, and the "sampling" of employer products by employees. Perhaps it will not be feasible to cover all possible contingencies, but an established procedure for clearing questionable items may save a lot of grief.

• Arbitrators tend to modify discharge penalties where the value of the stolen goods is relatively small and the employee's seniority is relatively long. Thus, discharge was deemed too harsh for taking two cents worth of crackers (*Spartan Stores Inc.*, 33 LA 40), theft of five beers by a long-service brewery worker (*Pabst Brewing Co.*, 29 LA 464), stealing a pair of coveralls by a seven-year employee with a good record (*Chrysler Corp.*, 24 LA 549), and pilfering building materials worth about $10 (*Peoples Gas Light and Coke Co.*, 44 LA 234; see also 77 LA 648, 71 LA 989).

• In one case, an arbitrator upheld discharge for theft of only $1.10, even though the employee had been with the employer 28 years and had a good record. The arbitrator said he might have imposed a lighter sentence if the employee had admitted his mistake. Instead, he had tried to get off the hook by inconsistent, evasive, and implausible statements and sometimes outright falsehood. Such conduct does not call for leniency, the arbitrator said (*Hawaiian Telephone Co.*, 43 LA 1218).

• An employee who had 12 years of service was properly discharged for stealing a package of ham, an arbitrator ruled. The employee had committed other thefts during the previous year, the arbitrator pointed out, emphasizing that her behavior had become so notorious in the plant that not only her employer, but her co-workers were concerned (*Manhattan Brand Food Products*, 62 LA 405).

• Stealing a can of tinned meat was sufficient cause for discharge, an arbitrator decided, even though the employee had five years of satisfactory service. The employee blatantly disobeyed a foreman's order to return the can of food that was the property of the employer's customer, the arbitrator concluded (*Kane Transfer Inc.*, 63 LA 858; see also 77 LA 133, 40 LA 533).

• An arbitrator held an employer had just cause to discharge an employee who had punched out another employee's time card to enable the other employee to receive overtime pay even though she had not worked the necessary hours, because the employee had committed a dischargeable infraction of "immoral conduct" in stealing and telling falsehoods (employee had denied to employer that she had performed the act), which was subject to immediate discharge under the parties' collective bargaining agreement (*Georgia-Pacific Corp.*, 104 LA 1212).

• Another arbitrator reinstated an employee who had been discharged for stealing a one-dollar bill, even though the collective bargaining agreement under which the employee was covered permitted his employer to discharge employees for theft of any kind. Finding mitigation in the employee's 20-year service, age, and the particular circumstances, the arbitrator held the employee's reinstatement was appropriate on terms that protected the employer's security interests. The employee's discharge was reduced to an extended suspension, provided he admitted responsibility in the incident and promised to abstain from all future misconduct; future infractions would subject him to immediate discharge (*East Liverpool Board of Education*, see above).

## Circumstantial Evidence as Proof of Theft

Circumstantial evidence may be sufficient to justify discharge for pilferage.

• In one case, an employee was seen secreting employer products on her person by a co-worker who notified a plant guard. The guard notified a supervisor, who directed her to recover the items from the employee; however, the employee and the guard were alone when the goods were recovered. The stolen items were returned to the processing line and so disappeared as evidence. The employee later denied the guard's testimony concerning the theft. In upholding the discharge, the arbitrator ruled that the testimony of the co-worker, the guard, and the supervisor was sufficient circumstantial evidence to prove the employee's guilt (*Max Factor & Co.*, 61 LA 886).

## Lie-Detector Limitations

In cases where management relies on lie detector tests to prove the guilt of an employee charged with pilfering, arbitrators may either prohibit the introduction of such evidence or admit it but require that the employer's allegations be corroborated by some other type of proof. Most arbitrators agree that lie detector tests are usually unreliable and that an employee cannot be discharged simply for refusing to submit to a polygraph examination (71 LA 1202, 70 LA 909, 70 LA 100, 68 LA 581, 64 LA 453).

• One arbitrator held that an employer improperly imposed indefinite suspensions, which were equivalent to discharges, on two employees for refusing to take a lie detector test. The employer had required its workers to submit to polygraph tests as part of a system for curbing thefts of employer property. Saying that it is uncertain whether polygraph tests record lies or only psychological changes caused by stress, the arbitrator maintained that the use of such tests raised serious constitutional questions about whether the employees' privacy rights were violated. Emphasizing that the employer had "extended" the use of lie detector tests by insisting that a refusal to submit would subject an employee to dismissal, the arbitrator concluded that the polygraph requirement was improper (*Art Carved, Inc.*, 70 LA 869).

• An employer improperly discharged employees who failed to pass a polygraph test to determine their involvement in theft of silver bars used by the employer, an arbitrator decided, where management claimed that the employees took the test voluntarily, but the employees believed that they had to take the test (*Bunker Ramo Corp.*, 76 LA 857).

• An employer properly discharged an employee for refusing to take a lie detector test that at the time he was hired he had agreed to take at any time during his employment if so requested, an arbitrator decided, where the motor vehicle registered in the worker's name had been found by the police to contain some $5,000 worth of employer property. Although the guilt or innocence of the employee in respect to the merchandise was not at issue, the question of whether the employer could require the worker to honor a written promise to submit to a polygraph test was, the arbitrator concluded (*Grocers Supply Co. Inc.*, 75 LA 27).

### Search-and-Seizure Procedures

Most arbitrators agree that the constitutional protections against illegal searches and the use of evidence obtained from such searches are not applicable to the workplace, particularly if the searching employer has probable cause to believe that a theft has occurred (66 LA 307, 51 LA 469, 50 LA 65).

• One arbitrator held that an employer was entitled to tighten up its security rules and begin inspecting the purses of female employees as they were leaving work. Despite the union's contention that the searches were an affront to the employees' dignity, the arbitrator concluded that management had a "paramount" right to search the purses because they might contain stolen property (*AMF/ Harley-Davidson Motor Co. Inc.*, 68 LA 811).

• Another arbitrator held that an employer did not have the right to search employees' lunch bags for stolen goods. The workers' privacy rights, the arbitrator declared, clearly included the right to be free from such searches (*Anchor Hocking Corp.*, 66 LA 480).

### Arrests for Thefts

What course of action should an employer take if an employee is arrested by the police and charged with theft of employer property? Management may be on dangerous ground in relying solely on actions by the police or what happens in court as a basis for discipline. Discharge or even suspension of an employee simply because he has been arrested for a crime connected with his work may be overturned by an arbitrator and is almost sure to be set aside and back pay ordered if the charges are dropped or the employee is acquitted (62 LA 901, 39 LA 1242, 39 LA 859, 35 LA 77).

• An employee was suspended from his job and arrested for theft after a search of his home by police and employer officials recovered employer glassware. Although the case was dismissed in court because the search warrant and the search were improper, the employee was still discharged by the employer.

In reversing the discharge, the arbitrator found a lack of direct evidence that the items recovered in the employee's home had been taken by him. The only evidence, the arbitrator noted, was the testimony of three persons, two of whom were admittedly hostile toward the employee (*Imperial Glass Corp.*, 61 LA 1180; see also 71 LA 1113).

• Where the employer has made an inquiry into the facts and has substantial evidence of guilt, discharge was upheld, despite the fact that criminal charges were dropped (76 LA 133, 61 LA 663, 44 LA 711, 38 LA 93, 32 LA 44, 31 LA 674).

# Dress & Grooming

## OVERVIEW

What is desirable or necessary by way of grooming and dress standards will vary greatly from employer to employer depending on the nature of the business and the type of work being performed by different employees. Therefore, the approach to setting and enforcing standards may range from a single code handed down by top management for all employees to separate codes for each employee group.

Management is concerned with an employee's appearance from the standpoint of the organization's public image, as well as from the standpoint of job safety and health factors, but employees often are opposed to broad company prohibitions or requirements regarding dress and grooming, considering them an infringement on their personal rights.

When ruling on the right of employees to determine their own clothing or hair styles, arbitrators usually point out that this right may be limited by the nature of the employee's job. Arbitrators generally are aware of the effect of changing times on dress and grooming habits, and unwarranted interference by management with an employee's preference for a particular mode of dress or hair length is prohibited. On balance, however, arbitrators recognize management's legitimate business reasons for regulating the personal appearance of employees.

In dealing with discipline for violation of dress and grooming standards, arbitrators make these points:

• The standard must be clear, unambiguous, and consistently enforced.

• The standard must be reasonably related to a business need of the company, although it is recognized that "business need" includes the need to keep employees from being distracted by outlandish or overly revealing attire.

• The standard must be reasonably attuned to contemporary mores and attitudes toward dress and grooming. As styles change, the standard may have to change.

## SUMMARY OF CASES

### Management Right To Establish & Enforce Reasonable Rules

The prevailing view among arbitrators is that an employer has the right to require employees to cut their hair, or to prohibit or change their dress, when, for example, there is a contractual right to adopt reasonable rules of conduct, the manner of dress reasonably threatens the employee's relations with customers or other employees, or when a question of safety is involved.

• An arbitrator held that an employer properly prohibited a PBX operator/receptionist of Mexican heritage from wearing nose jewelry, despite her contention that the jewelry was a reflection of her culture. The arbitrator ruled the employer's action was proper under a contractual provisions allowing it to "adopt reasonable rules of conduct" and requiring employees to be courteous and work for a "harmonious working environment." Furthermore, the arbitrator held that it did not violate a nonbias requirement in the bargaining agreement because federal civil rights laws do not protect an employee's ability to express his or her cultural heritage in the workplace (*Motion Picture & Television Fund*, 103 LA 988).

● An arbitrator ruled that an employer's policy requiring its drivers (who had public contact) to have conservative hair styles and be clean-shaven did not violate a bargaining agreement, even though other employees in the employer's workforce were permitted to wear long hair and/or beards. The employer had the discretion to establish and enforce dress and appearance codes consistent with its chosen public image, the arbitrator said, adding that the company had relaxed its hair-length policy over the years for its other employees who had no public contact (*Albertson's Inc.*, 102 LA 641).

● Most arbitrators hold that a reasonable relationship must be shown between the employer's image (or health and safety considerations) and the need to regulate employee appearance (55 LA 1020, 61 LA 645, 62 LA 357, 63 LA 467, 63 LA 1203, 63 LA 345, 66 LA 439, 70 LA 28, 77 LA 807, 91 LA 24).

● Whether or not any particular hair rule or dress standard meets the test of reasonableness depends on a variety of factors, including the nature of the employer's business and the degree of public exposure the employee encounters on the job (51 LA 292, 64 LA 376, 64 LA 783, 92 LA 1161, 93 LA 855).

● Most arbitrators agree that management's grooming standards must be clear, unambiguous, and consistently enforced (52 LA 1282, 62 LA 175, 63 LA 345, 64 LA 940).

In upholding the suspension of an employee who refused to cut his hair to conform with management policy, one arbitrator offered the following questions as additional criteria for determining discipline pursuant to grooming code violations:

▶ Did the bargaining agreement restrict, prohibit, or qualify the employer's right to establish grooming standards?

▶ Was the rule adequately communicated to all employees?

▶ Did the affected employees have an adequate opportunity to comply with the employer's grooming requirement?

▶ Was there sufficient evidence to establish that the employee's violation of the grooming code created a health or safety hazard or that it was injurious to the employer's public image (*American Buslines Inc.*, 64 LA 471)?

**The Public Image**

The employer's public image is a matter of concern, particularly where an organization offers services to the public or where the employee comes in contact with the company's customers. There is general agreement among arbitrators that the employer has a legitimate interest in the presentable appearance of employees who are visible to the public (*Albertson's Inc.*, 102 LA 641; see also 71 LA 22, 69 LA 141, 68 LA 31, 64 LA 471, 63 LA 467).

● One arbitrator pointed out that some other arbitrators may require management to present direct evidence that long hair, sideburns, mustaches, or beards have caused a loss of business or provoked complaints from the public. Other arbitrators, however, have been willing to accept an employer's reasonable business justification, even without empirical proof (*City of East Detroit*, 61 LA 485).

Following are some examples of arbitrators' rulings on "public image" issues.

● An employer had a right to require employees who were in contact with the public to present a favorable personal appearance by maintaining certain weight standards, an arbitrator found, in considering the discharge of an overweight flight attendant. Dismissing the argument that maintaining weight standards is more difficult for women than men, the arbitrator concluded that the employer enforced its standards in a reasonable manner and had given the employee an ample opportunity to lose weight (*American Airlines*, 68 LA 527; see also 75 LA 1273, 74 LA 1115, 74 LA 1017).

● An airline employer did not have the right to prohibit a male flight attendant from growing a neat beard, an arbitrator decided. The employer had argued that its no-beard rule was necessary to ensure that its employees promoted a conservative image, which, it claimed, was a business asset in a competitive industry. Rejecting this contention, the arbitrator held that management failed to prove that the employee's beard would damage the company's public image or its business activities (*Pacific Southwest Airlines*, 73 LA 1209).

• Another arbitrator ruled that a store owner improperly suspended a cashier and a checker for "unkempt" and "messy" hair that failed to conform to the firm's unwritten policy regulating employees' hair length. Although acknowledging that an employer may establish reasonable rules governing workers' appearance, the arbitrator decided that, given the type of work done by the two employees, the length of their hair did not interfere in any way with the efficient performance of their jobs. Furthermore, the arbitrator noted, the one or two customer complaints about the employees' hair length were "minor, vague, remote, and indefinite," and thus carried only "slight weight" (*Big Star No. 35*, 73 LA 850; see also 75 LA 798).

• An employer's desire to present a "clean shaven, clean cut image" to its customers was upheld by another arbitrator, who ruled that management had the right to prohibit all workers from wearing beards. In this case, the arbitrator explained, the no-beard issue was "pared to the bone by the absence of any hygienic overtones" because the grieving worker was not employed in the "delicatessen, the bakery, or other food preparation areas in the store." Although the company, absent "specific studies," could only claim, "somewhat empirically," that its clean-shaven image was "at least part of its touchstone of success as seen in its rising position in the market," the arbitrator decided, maintenance of this image formed a "reasonable" basis for the no-beard rule (*Randall Foods No. 2*, 74 LA 729; see also 77 LA 953, 77 LA 705).

• An employer had just cause to fire an employee who refused to put on his name badge, according to one arbitrator.

A 61-year-old bus driver worked 15 years for a series of owners of a passenger shuttle service at an international airport. When the latest in that series of owners took over, it implemented new rules and regulations on employee dress and deportment. Soon thereafter, the employee was subjected to discipline of increasing severity because of management concerns over his uniform and obedience to supervisors. After a series of incidents, he received a "last chance" deal brokered by his union to keep his job, but shortly thereafter, he refused an order to pin his name tag on his shirt and walked away from the supervisor who had ordered that he do so. The employee's misconduct was "clear and convincingly established" in the contract, the arbitrator said, noting that the rules specifically required name tags, and adding that the last chance agreement was unambiguous in requiring adherence to all lawful instructions (*Shuttlesport Inc.*, 117 LA 492).

## Safety & Health Considerations

Safety and health considerations may be valid reasons for an employer's restrictions on an employee's personal appearance; however, the employer must show a reasonable relationship between the application of the grooming standard and the health or safety factor. When employees' work involves the operation of machinery, arbitrators will generally uphold safety rules restricting the wearing of loose-fitting clothing, dangling jewelry, and long, unprotected hair, which might become entangled in a machine (74 LA 412, 69 LA 824, 62 LA 357, 61 LA 645).

• An arbitrator ruled that a fruit-processing employer properly discharged an employee for refusing to trim his long mustache because the employer's grooming rule was designed to protect the employer's products against hair contamination, rather than to regulate employee appearance (*Tree Top, Inc.*, 66 LA 8).

• A meat packing company's rule prohibiting the wearing of wigs and hair pieces in the plant for reasons of sanitation was upheld by an arbitrator on the grounds that such items fall into the same category as "street clothing," barred from the plant as a possible source of contamination (*Marhoefer Packing Co.*, 51 LA 583).

• In many cases involving no-beard rules, the safety issue is whether an employee should be required to shave off his beard before using a facial respirator or gas mask (69 LA 824, 68 LA 912).

• An African American employee who suffered from a skin condition, "pseudofolliculitis," which is common to his racial group and is aggravated by shaving, was ordered by management to shave his beard before using a respirator. Claiming that he should be allowed to test whether he could get a proper seal with the respirator before being required to remove the beard, the employee charged the employer with discrimination. Insisting, however, that the beard constituted a safety hazard because it prevented the employee from obtaining a good seal with the respirator, the employer maintained that any worker who had to wear special breathing equipment on the job should not have a beard, sideburns, or a moustache that might interfere with the proper functioning of the equipment.

The arbitrator, however, ruled that management improperly had refused to comply with the worker's request to conduct empirical tests of the respirator's sealing ability on bearded employees. Allowing the employer to apply its no-beard rule uniformly without conducting such tests, the arbitrator maintained, would effectively bar many African American males from rightful employment because of a skin condition specific to their race (*Niagara Mohawk Power Corp.*, 74 LA 58).

• An arbitrator decided that management improperly had relied on visual observation to determine that an employee's beard would prevent him from getting a positive seal with a fresh air mask. The employer's visual observation was insufficient in light of clear evidence that facial hair did not automatically prevent a positive seal, the arbitrator said, concluding that the proper way to determine if the employee could wear the mask safely over his beard was to conduct a test of the device's sealing ability on the worker (*Phillips Petroleum Co.*, 74 LA 400).

• The disciplinary action imposed on a firefighter, whose allegedly "long and excessively bulky" hair violated the department's grooming standards, was not upheld by an arbitrator, because the evidence failed to establish that the worker's hair interfered with the proper wearing of headgear or that the employee's hair style exposed him to added personal injury (*City of Los Angeles*, 66 LA 694).

Several arbitrators have ruled that an employer can, for safety reasons, ban facial hair for employees who wear respirators.

• A chemical plant issued a policy requiring employees to shave off beards that impair the proper seal required when wearing respirators. Their union argued the employer had failed to perform sufficient testing required by OSHA and unilaterally had issued the policy against bargaining-unit employees to protect itself from an OSHA investigation, while permitting other, nonunit, men who were not clean-shaven to enter the particular work area. The employer contended the policy was necessary to comply with federal regulations and to meet its contractual safety obligations.

The arbitrator prefaced his ruling by pointing out that labor-management relations were less than satisfactory and the employer might have performed more tests before implementing the policy. The employer was obligated under the parties' collective bargaining agreement to provide for employee health and safety and the union is obligated to cooperate, and the arbitrator noted the employer went to "considerable lengths" to determine if the policy were required under OSHA regulations. The arbitrator reasoned that he lacked authority to determine conclusively whether allowing beards would violate federal law, but because he was inclined to believe that it would be unlawful, he declined to put the employer in an untenable position by ordering it to rescind the no-facial-hair policy (*Dyno Nobel Inc.*, 104 LA 376).

• An arbitrator held that an employer properly issued a rule prohibiting facial hair in the area where a respiratory face mask was sealed, and therefore, it had just cause to fire an employee who refused to shave his beard.

Rejecting the union's contention that the employer's policy was brought about merely by its desire that employees be clean shaven and not by the desire to provide a safer workplace, the arbitrator pointed out that the evidence established that a better seal could be achieved between the face and the mask if the face was clean shaven. Even though a good seal could be achieved if a bearded employee had enough time properly to adjust the mask, the arbitrator concluded that in an emergency situation, time is of the essence, and additional time might be disastrous to the worker and fellow employees (*Hess Oil Virgin Islands Corp.*, 75 LA 771).

## Sex Bias in Appearance Rules

Besides the mass of arbitration cases arising from management attempts to regulate the wearing of beards, mustaches, sideburns, and long hair by male employees, there is the question of whether male grooming codes constitute unlawful sex discrimination.

• An arbitrator ruled that a necktie requirement imposed by one department head in a company was inconsistent with a contractual ban on sex discrimination, as well as with the employer's new, "swinging" public image. The union had protested that male employees in other departments were not required to wear ties and that the employer's dress policy had "gradually degenerated" into letting female employees wear anything they wished, including jeans, sweaters, tank tops, and other informal apparel. Observing that not only were female employees allowed to "go with the vogue," but the

company had launched a public relations campaign in which male employees were photographed wearing ties, turtleneck shirts, sport shirts, and "all sorts of attire," the arbitrator concluded, that the necktie rule was "arbitrary, capricious, and totally inconsistent" and that it was "predicated upon the personal taste of one department head" (*Union Tribune Publishing Co.*, 70 LA 266).

## Uniform Accommodations

Where employees are required to wear uniforms, accommodations may have to be made in certain circumstances, arbitrators have found.

• A public transit company, which furnished and paid for uniforms for its bus drivers, was required to either provide female employees with women's pants or to pay for those the drivers had special-ordered. On discovering that they were to be given men's uniform pants, most of the female drivers instead ordered comparable pants designed to fit a woman's body and equipped with a side, rather than front, zipper. When they were billed for the cost of the pants, the female drivers refused to pay. Saying that the women had, at the least, the right to expect to be provided with women's clothing, the arbitrator held that the employer's policy failed to meet the implied test of reasonableness (*Taylor Enterprises Inc.*, 67 LA 1285).

• Another arbitrator decided that a hospital employer, which required all operating room employees to wear pants for health reasons, had to allow a technician, whose religion forbade women to wear pants, the chance to design an alternative uniform rather than be transferred from the operating room (*Hurley Hospital*, 70 LA 1061; see also 75 LA 1300).

# E-Mail & Other Technology Issues

## OVERVIEW

For both employers and labor organizations, advances in technology have swiftly become a double-edged sword.

Employers have seen what havoc can occur when e-mail systems are used to infect computer systems with "viruses" and hackers breach "firewalls" designed to protect sensitive information from prying eyes. In response to these incursions, companies have installed increasingly sophisticated software to track down hackers and filter out unwanted e-mail. They also, however, have learned to use such software to keep an eye on employees' use of proprietary systems, especially workers' use of company e-mail and the Internet for purposes other than work.

Unions have latched onto the Internet as a swift and cheap means of communicating with workers and an efficient method of getting their message out to the public. Many labor organizations maintain sophisticated Web sites that provide a range of information—from salaries of chief executive officers to upcoming union activities and political campaigns. They use e-mail to communicate with workers, both those who are members and those the unions are seeking to organize. On the other hand, union leaders have begun to see technological advances as a method employers can use to erode workers' autonomy by keeping track of each keystroke to monitor productivity, reading employee e-mails, and checking up on their Web browsing habits.

For both employers and unions, new technologies can be both an effective tool or a dangerous implement. Employers want to keep private information private, but by the same token, they want to be able to find out what their employees are up to, how quickly they are finishing tasks, and whether they are spending their time working or checking sports scores on the Internet. Unions want to be able to use employers' e-mail systems to foster organizing and acquire lists of names of employees, while also shielding workers' communications from employers.

Because these are relatively recent developments in industrial relations, many legal questions remain unsettled and are only slowly working their way through the legal system. To avoid legal problems, however, employers should disseminate and adhere to written e-mail policies that make clear to employees that their e-mail communications are not private, that using the employer's e-mail system means they are using the employer's property, and that *all* workplace computer use is open to employer monitoring.

## SUMMARY OF CASES

### Misuse of Employer E-Mail

Employees may face discipline up to and including discharge for violation of an employer's policy or guidelines on the proper use of its e-mail system; however, employers would be wise to establish a clear and explicit policy on e-mail/Internet use before attempting to discipline employees for perceived misuses of these technologies.

• During a chemical company's audit of e-mail use, management discovered that 254 of 5,500 workers at a plant had saved, filed, and/or sent sexual and/or other inappropriate e-mails. Ultimately, 20 employees were terminated for violating the company e-mail policy, including 12 union-represented workers. In a grievance, the union contended that supervisory personnel were heavily involved in sending, receiving, and filing what the company considered to be inappropriate e-mail, and that the practice was well-known, tolerated, and widespread.

Rejecting the employer's argument that just-cause was not required for discharge under their contract, a three-member arbitration panel of the Federal Mediation and Conciliation Service said the fired workers were subjected to disparate treatment, noting that other employees who violated e-mail policy were given lesser discipline. The panel ordered the employees reinstated to their former positions or to mutually acceptable alternatives, but without back pay. It also ordered that the workers be given a refresher course on avoiding sexual harassment and about the proper protocol for use of company e-mail (*Dow Chemical Co. and IUOE Local 564*, Arbs. Barry Baroni, Frank Quinn, and Dianne Dunham Massey, FMCS No. 01-02581-3 4/1/02).

• In another case, an arbitrator upheld a nonunion employer's discipline of an employee for violating the company's e-mail policy by e-mailing an allegedly offensive newsletter to company offices in China, and in one issue, publishing an article in which he made offensive ethnic remarks. The employer later counseled the employee on this incident and other incidents involving his insensitivity about a variety of ethnic, gender, and diversity issues. The employee also was caught sending horse racing results through the employer's e-mail system and ordered to stop.

Still later the employer discovered that in two weeks' worth of the employee's e-mails, only 10 percent of the messages were work-related; the employer also found more racing results and newsletter references and ultimately fired the man. The arbitrator, however, reduced the employee's discharge to a suspension. He pointed out that the employer failed to define "serious misconduct" sufficiently at the time of the first infractions to give the employee adequate warning that he could be fired immediately for any subsequent offenses. The arbitrator ordered the employee reinstated under a last-chance agreement (*AlliedSignal Engines*, 106 LA 614).

• An employee should not have been fired for sending sexually graphic e-mail to a co-worker, according to an arbitrator who ruled on the case. A security department employee shared a computer with several co-workers, who all had separate company e-mail accounts. One day a female co-worker saw and was offended by a sexually graphic e-mail on another person's computer monitor that had been left on. After an investigation of the incident, the employee was terminated. Objecting to the discharge, the union contended that the employer's action violated the Electronic Communications Privacy Act. Moreover, the union said the employee was charged with violating a policy that he had never seen. The employer responded that the employee knew his actions violated the company's Internet and sexual harassment policies.

The employee's action did not justify termination, the arbitrator held, especially given that there was no evidence that the employee had been given a copy of the company policy on Internet usage before the incident. Although his actions did violate the company's sexual harassment policy, of which he was aware, other employees involved in receiving sexually graphic e-mail had received only suspensions, the arbitrator concluded, ordering the employee reinstated, but without back pay (*PPG Industries Inc.*, 113 LA 833).

• Finding that an insurance company's policy on the use of its e-mail system was "overly broad" and interfered with its employees' rights to join a union under the NLRA, an NLRB administrative law judge recommended that a representation election among insurance agents be set aside and a new election held (*The Prudential Insurance Co. of Am.*, N.L.R.B. ALJ, 22-RC-12173,11/1/02).

### 'Offensive' E-mails

• An employer improperly discharged an employee for sending and receiving inappropriate e-mails, an arbitrator decided. While investigating a worker's sexual harassment complaint, a consultant hired by a public utility discovered that approximately 75 employees had exchanged offensive e-mails. The consultant did find, however, that one of the employees had not exchanged any offensive e-mail at work after he had received a written warning for other misconduct, that he had sent the offensive e-mail only to his home account, but that he also had exchanged inappropriate e-mail with managers, including a district commissioner. After considering many factors, including the number of messages and the degree of explicitness, the employer fired the employee, the only union member discharged for violating the utility's e-mail policy.

The union contested the worker's discharge, claiming that the e-mail accounts of other implicated employees were not even investigated. Because of the employer's lax enforcement of its e-mail policy, the arbitrator said it did not have just cause to fire the employee. The employer also failed to follow progressive discipline mandated by the contract and arbitral common law, the arbitrator said, ordering the employee reinstated with back pay (*Snohomish Co.*, 115 LA 1).

### Use of Company Equipment to Criticize Employer

A written reprimand was unwarranted for an employee who used a company's e-mail system to express personal opinions about the employer's policy, an arbitrator determined.

A public high school librarian sent members of a regional association of librarians an e-mail message that used sarcasm to discredit the school district's proposed curriculum changes and sought help in trying to fight the proposals. In response, the employer issued a written reprimand to her for violating its e-mail policies.

The arbitrator agreed that the librarian had no inherent right to use the employer's computer and its e-mail system to express her personal opinions. In addition, he said, the employer could prohibit use of its equipment for purely personal activities without violating an employee's First Amendment rights under the U.S. Constitution. Nevertheless, he added, the school district could not discipline the employee because it had not established an explicit policy on workers' using its computer/e-mail system (*Conneaut School District*, 104 LA 909).

### 'Accidental' E-mail Distribution

An employer improperly fired an employee whose racy e-mail was transmitted over the company's computer system without his knowledge, ruled one arbitrator. A supervisor called over a refinery employee to show him a pornographic video e-mail, and with the supervisor's permission, he forwarded copies of the e-mail to co-workers. Unbeknownst to the employee, however, one of his colleagues sent it out on the plant-wide e-mail system, prompting management to fire him. The union grieved, charging that discharge was inappropriate, especially in light of the constant flouting of the company's e-mail policies by both management and bargaining unit workers.

The company violated the contract, the arbitrator found, because it lacked just cause to terminate the employee for his "accidental" and unintended violation of e-mail and harassment policies. There is a "tremendous difference" between posted policy and past practice, as evidenced by widespread use of e-mail by supervisors to send sexually charged jokes and other inappropriate messages, the arbitrator asserted, reducing the punishment from discharge to an unpaid three-day suspension (*Chevron Products Co.*, 116 LA 271).

# Gambling

_____ **OVERVIEW** _____

Gambling of some type occurs in most organizations, whether it be the relatively innocuous sports pool or lunch-hour poker game or the more serious organized "numbers" racket. In deciding on discipline for alleged on-premises gambling, arbitrators typically consider the following factors.

• Was the evidence connecting the employee to the gambling substantial and convincing? Arbitrators look to see if that evidence supports the charge that the worker engaged in the prohibited activity on company property and/or time (51 LA 707, 45 LA 247, 41 LA 823, 39 LA 859, 18 LA 938, 12 LA 699).

• Did the nature of the offense justify the penalty. For example, discharge may be appropriate where the employee previously had been disciplined for gambling but too severe in cases of first offense (95 LA 937, 95 LA 148, 86 LA 297, 52 LA 946, 49 LA 1262, 28 LA 97, 22 LA 210, 16 LA 727, 12 LA 21). Similarly, even though it may have tolerated sports pools or holiday turkey raffles, management may be warranted in cracking down on employees involved in illegal bookmaking or numbers operations (33 LA 175, 22 LA 210, 17 LA 150, 13 LA 253).

_____ **SUMMARY OF CASES** _____

### Rationale for Discipline

Management is within its right to promulgate and enforce rules against on-premises gambling, most arbitrators concur, because, as one employer put it, "organization and morale would be seriously affected" if such activity were permitted. As phrased by the employer in that case, "the evils which run concurrently with gambling, namely ill feeling, cheating, fighting, and the lure of 'easy money,' could disintegrate a highly productive workforce and reduce its efficiency beyond measure." If the "company and its employees are to reap the benefits of successful operation," that employer emphasized, "any factors which curtail industrial efficiency and production must be completely eliminated" (*Brown Shoe Co.*, 16 LA 461).

Based on similar reasoning, arbitrators have upheld discipline where the employer is able to show that the worker engaged in gambling on company premises, even though he may have been on his own time.

• A worker who engages in illegal activity on company property—even during his free time—is not carrying out his responsibilities as an employee, according to one arbitrator. Although management was unable to prove that the worker in this case was writing numbers on company time, the arbitrator upheld the discharge because the "numbers slips" found on the employee demonstrated that he was conducting his activities at the plant.

Dismissing the worker's arguments that the discharge was unwarranted because the activity took place "off-the-clock," the arbitrator declared that "during all times that an employee is on company property, he must be deemed to be an employee" and must "conduct himself properly in discharging his responsibilities as such employee." In short, the arbitrator concluded, the worker, while at the plant, "may not engage in illegal activities whether he does so on his 'free time' or not and whether he uses company property (i.e., a company telephone) or not in order to further his illegal activities" (*Jones & Laughlin Steel Corp.*, 29 LA 778).

• Another arbitrator sustained the discharge of an employee for running an illegal numbers racket on company property, despite evidence that he conducted the gambling on his own time. Because the gambling took place inside the plant, it was "inextricably bound up with his employment status," the arbitrator ruled (*Bethlehem Steel Co.*, 45 LA 646).

• An arbitration board overruled the dismissal of an employee who was arrested on company property with numbers slips in his possession and who subsequently pleaded guilty to a gambling charge. Dismissing management's allegations that the existence of the slips showed that the worker had engaged in the illegal activity on its premises, the board concluded that such possession did not constitute clear proof that "there had been gambling or accepting of wagers" by the worker on company property (*Jenkins Bros.*, 45 LA 247).

• Even if an employee is guilty of gambling on the employer's premises and on company time, if the employee is not forewarned that such an offense could prompt his termination, such a drastic sort of punishment is likely to be disallowed, as it was in the case of an employer who was fired for playing cards with his supervisors at the company's plant. A manager at the tire manufacturing facility received an anonymous phone tip one night that a "card game was on" at the factory. He called a supervisor who lived nearby, asking him to investigate the production office, which he did, photographing both the windows where the men were playing, and finally, the men themselves, as well as their bets on the table. After the investigation, the company fired the supervisors, who subsequently were allowed to resign, and the employee, a bargaining unit member.

The principle that discipline should be corrective rather than punitive, the arbitrator said, damaged the company's case. The two-year employee had an unblemished record, and the company handbook contained no proscriptions about gambling, In fact, both of the supervisors in question and many of the 900-member bargaining unit bet on Super Bowls, lotteries, etc., and the winners of these bets were posted at the time clock. Although gambling is a serious offense, "the fact that the supervisors were participants lent an aura of permissiveness to the gambling," the arbitrator asserted, ordering reinstatement for the employee with full seniority, but without back pay (*Yokohama Tire Corp.*, 117 LA 5).

## Nature of the Offense

*Organized Gambling*—Generally, organized gambling is viewed as a serious offense by arbitrators. Given that charges of criminal conduct may be involved, however, arbitrators will require that management meet stringent standards of proof to sustain a discharge decision. Thus, where an employee was apprehended with hundreds of dollars in small bills and change and a sheet of lottery numbers, an arbitrator upheld his discharge (*Bethlehem Steel Co.*, 45 LA 646).

• Another arbitrator decided that an employee's guilty plea to charges of illegal gambling on company property was just cause for discharge, because the employee's otherwise good work record did not outweigh the fact of his misconduct (*Jenkins Bros.*, 45 LA 350).

• The discharge of an employee for allegedly engaging in a numbers racket on company time and property was set aside by an arbitrator because management failed to meet its burden of proof. While agreeing with the employer regarding the "harmful effects of playing numbers," the arbitrator declared that he did not "believe an employee, especially one with long seniority, should lose his job for engaging in the numbers racket, unless there is substantial and convincing proof that the employee did so act," and stressed that "our system of justice and the recognized principles applied under it are based on the same belief" (*Chrysler Corp.*, 12 LA 699).

*Unorganized Gambling*—On the other hand, unorganized gambling meets with greater leniency from arbitrators.

• Employees involved in a "check pool" on company time and property were improperly discharged, an arbitrator decided, despite a work rule prohibiting on-premises gambling because the rule was established to guarantee that standards of "good conduct" were followed, it was not properly applied here given that the pool was not shown to be detrimental to these standards. In addition, management properly should have followed its own policy of issuing warnings for violations of conduct rules instead of terminating the workers for a first offense, the arbitrator said (*Black Diamond Enterprises Inc.*, 52 LA 945).

• A board of arbitration upheld the discharge of three employees caught playing poker. Dismissing the workers' protests, the board pointed out that management twice before had warned them about gambling on company time and property (*Brown Shoe Co.*, 16 LA 461).

# Garnishment

---- **OVERVIEW** ----

Garnishment, arbitrators acknowledge, creates numerous clerical and administrative burdens for employers, as well as involuntarily plunging them into the midst of an employee's personal financial difficulties.

This is especially true where an employee has incurred excessive wage levies, where arbitrators empathize with an employer's "natural wish to avoid the time, inconvenience, and expense of extra bookkeeping, extra accounting procedures, the necessity to file written returns with the attaching officer, as well as the additional trust liability for the funds that he [or she] is required to hold and his [or her] statutory liability for any failure to hold and to pay according to the instructions of the attaching officer" (35 LA 139).

On the basis of such reasoning, one arbitrator found that, "into the abstract, there is nothing unreasonable about an employer rule which provides that more than one garnishment within a year will constitute grounds for employee discharge" (63 LA 912). Another arbitrator, however, held that a rule that permits discipline for repeated garnishments is unreasonable (97 LA 444).

In practice, this right is bounded by several considerations, including federal and state garnishment laws that dictate the propriety of discipline for wage attachments.

The standard principles generally applied by arbitrators in garnishment cases mandate that a rule providing for discipline in such situations must be reasonably predicated on saving the employer from inconvenience, cost, liability, or the imposition of other serious burdens; it "must not be unreasonable" in terms of the penalty assessed for infractions; it must be applied without bias; and it "must be clear, unambiguous, and well-known by employees" (48 LA 1331).

Even when these principles are satisfied, however, arbitrators sometimes find that extenuating circumstances warrant discipline of lesser severity than discharge. Such mitigating circumstances, according to one arbitrator, may include situations where the employee lacked knowledge of the debt, had compiled an otherwise unmarred work record, arranged to discharge the debt through bankruptcy or resolved an imminent wage attachment through other means, or fell into debt because of income losses caused by chronic layoffs (63 LA 1157; see also 82 LA 1004, 57 LA 31).

---- **SUMMARY OF CASES** ----

### Rules and Warnings

Rules and warnings are two items that arbitrators typically look for in reviewing discharge for garnishment. Arbitrators are unlikely to disturb a discharge made in accordance with a garnishment rule that has been enforced consistently. Even if there is no specific rule dealing with garnishment, termination probably will be upheld if the employee has been warned and has failed to improve.

• An arbitrator ruled that an employer had just cause to discharge an employee who refused to make peace with the Internal Revenue Service, which had garnished his wages. The employee, who was unmarried, had submitted a tax form claiming 14 dependents, none of whom he had. In addition, the employee threatened to sue the employer if it withheld any money from his paycheck. The arbitrator upheld the discharge despite the employee's claims that he had made a tax protest that was protected by the First Amendment to the U.S. Constitution, and his contention that, under the federal Consumer Credit Protection Act, the employer could not fire the employee because his earnings were subjected to garnishment for any one indebtedness (*Las Vegas Building Materials Inc.*, 83 LA 998).

• An employer acted within its rights in discharging an employee whose wages were garnished three times in less than four years, an arbitrator ruled. The employee argued that the dismissal was unlawful, interpreting a labor secretary opinion letter to hold that if an interval between garnishments exceeds one year, discharge based on the second levy would constitute termination for one garnishment, an action prohibited (see above) by federal law.

The arbitrator, however, found that the law clearly was intended to protect only a "certain class of employees—those with only one indebtedness on which garnishments have been issued." The arbitrator stressed that it was "impossible to read into it any protection for the employee who has multiple garnishments for multiple indebtednesses," and pointed out that the employee had been counseled after the first garnishment, warned after the second that an additional levy would result in dismissal, and given a week in which to prove his claim that the third wage order was in error. The arbitrator concluded that "there was certainly nothing precipitous about management's action in this case" and that the dismissal

was entirely proper (*BBC Manufactured Buildings Inc.*, 77 LA 1132).

• An employer was justified in invoking a rule of conduct and discharging a garnishee who also had caused numerous delinquent credit complaints to be sent to the firm, despite management's repeated counseling. The employee protested that the termination violated the Consumer Credit Protection Act's prohibition against discharge for garnishment for one indebtedness, but the arbitrator found that the single garnishment was not the sole reason for the discipline. Rather, he stressed, "the cause of termination was a protracted record of financial irresponsibility" that had caused unreasonable demands to be placed on the employer. Under the circumstances, he concluded, federal law could not be construed so as to make the employee "invulnerable to consequences of unacceptable patterns of behavior" (*Continental Air Lines Inc.*, 57 LA 31; see also 77 LA 1132, 72 LA 850, 71 LA 832).

• Another arbitrator ruled that management had no right to fire an employee whose pay was garnished for three weeks in a row under one court order. Workers whose wages were attached were punished by warnings for the first two offenses and discharge for the third. In this case, the arbitrator held that three withholdings under one court order could not be considered three separate offenses (*Bagwell Steel Co.*, 41 LA 303; see also 78 LA 799, 71 LA 538).

• Another arbitrator upheld disciplinary action against a garnished employee, even though the employer had no rule concerning garnishments. In that case, the employee continued to receive notices of garnishment, despite counseling and verbal warnings from management. Eventually the employer issued a written warning, advising the employee that a "recurrence of two garnishments in one week will result in immediate termination." The employee subsequently was discharged for violating this provision.

Finding sufficient cause for discharge, the arbitrator ruled that management had acted fairly and objectively, particularly because it had attempted to assist the employee in his financial difficulties through counseling. Because the employee continued to show irresponsibility and created administrative expense for his employer, the arbitrator ruled, management was within its rights to fire him (*Lear Siegler Inc.*, 63 LA 1157).

● An employee's discharge was, however, not justified where the employer's warning to the employee about his garnishments was clouded by a conversation concerning an unrelated suspension, an arbitrator decided. In addition, the arbitrator noted, management had delayed a month before communicating with the union about the employee's possible discharge (*Virginia American Waterworks*, 63 LA 912).

● Discharge for excessive garnishment also was overruled by another arbitrator, despite 21 garnishments against the employee, because the employer admitted its rule on the matter was not usually applied in such instances and would not have been invoked except for other complaints against the employee, including poor attendance and criminal misconduct (*Rexall Drug Company*, 65 LA 1101).

***Repeated incidents of garnishment***—A past history of garnishment may justify severe disciplinary penalties, according to many arbitrators.

● A three-day suspension imposed on an employee for incurring eight garnishment orders in as many months "was not only reasonable but lenient as well," an arbitrator determined. The employee was a "chronic offender in the area of garnishments," the arbitrator noted, pointing out that one year previously, he had been given a one-day suspension for incurring five wage attachments. Furthermore, prior to the latest suspension, the employee had been warned by management that additional orders would result "in discipline up to and including discharge."

Nevertheless, the arbitrator stressed, the employee "made no effort to seek outside help in the form of personal bankruptcy or a trusteeship to take care of his financial problems" until the employer was faced with yet another garnishment

order. In view of the considerable progress the employee finally did make "toward getting his financial affairs in order," the employer "could have overlooked the last garnishment," the arbitrator noted, adding, however, that "it did not, nor was it required to overlook it." Based on the record as a whole, the arbitrator concluded, the employer's decision to suspend the employee "was not arbitrary, capricious, or unreasonable" (*Diem and Wing Paper Co.*, 72 LA 850).

● Over a period of four and a half years, an employee's indebtedness resulted in four separate court orders and two actual garnishments against his salary. Management counseled the employee several times about his financial problems and finally warned him that one more garnishment order would result in his discharge. When another order was issued, the employer terminated the employee, who protested that it was unfair for management to fire any employee for being in "a financial bind."

Upholding the discharge, the arbitrator noted that management "made every reasonable effort to counsel" the employee about his financial troubles and also conducted "an investigation to assure the validity and source of the encumbering debts." Despite the employer's "guidance and counseling," the employee "entangled" the employer "in the mesh" of his problems "throughout virtually the entire period" of his employment, the arbitrator observed. Just as "employees resist employer control and discipline for off-premises, nonwork related incidents," the arbitrator concluded, so "employers should have a corollary right to be free from measurable expense and involvement" in employees' personal problems (*Shawnee Plastics Inc.*, 71 LA 832).

● An employer properly discharged an employee who violated a plant rule by causing three garnishments to be served on the employer within 12 months. The rule was reasonable, according to the arbitrator, because the employer was not obligated to undertake the administrative burden of dealing with employees' financial problems outside the plant (*Federal Paper Board Co. Inc.*, 60 LA 924).

***Extenuating Circumstances***—Extenuating or mitigating circumstances sometimes lead arbitrators to reduce discharges for garnishment to less severe disciplinary penalties. In one case, for example, an arbitrator nullified an employee's termination for three wage attachments because of mitigating circumstances that included family illness (*American Airlines Inc.*, 47 LA 108).

● An employer improperly discharged an employee for incurring two garnishments, an arbitrator ruled, despite a work rule providing that more than one garnishment would constitute just cause for discharge without warning.

The termination "fell short of what was 'just,'" the arbitrator found, because of four extenuating factors: the employee had a good record; the garnishments resulted from debts that the employee had merely co-signed; management failed to inform the employee of possible programs for making voluntary wage deductions or to help him in any other way, as it had done with another employee in similar circumstances; and the employee had since "demonstrated his responsibility by diligently paying off debts on a business accountable to the creditors" (*Delta Concrete Products Co. Inc.*, 71 LA 538).

# Horseplay

_____ OVERVIEW _____

In determining how to handle incidents of horseplay or practical jokes on employer property, a distinction may be made between joking that involves only a remote possibility of injury and acts that involve a high risk of serious injury. Conduct of the latter type clearly warrants a more serious penalty even if disastrous consequences do not occur.

Saying that "horseplay is a 'first cousin' to willful intent to damage," one arbitrator said the following criteria set apart the more serious actions. If the acts are "premeditated, malicious, done with evil intent or with a bad motive or purpose, committed with an intent to wrong someone through actual or implied malice, done with the knowledge that it is likely to result in injuries or with reckless disregard of its probable consequences, then the "willful intent to damage" is likely to be established (*Ozark Lead Co.*, 69 LA 1227).

_____ SUMMARY OF CASES _____

### Severity/Degree of Danger

"Arbitral notice can be taken," one arbitrator maintained, "that horseplay exists" in any workplace "where a group of men is gathered together." "The real question is how frequent and how serious the horseplay is," he stressed, explaining that "there is a line between simply kidding around and dangerous and vicious acts" (*Erwin Mills Inc.*, 51 LA 225; see also 93 LA 580).

The distinction between relatively harmless horseplay and conduct that creates serious dangers is indicated in the following cases.

• For some time, employees had engaged in occasional horseplay when supervisors' backs were turned. Most often this took the form of blowing an employee's hat off with an air hose or throwing pieces of hard rubber used in shipping the employer's products. On one occasion when the rubber squares were flying, an employee who was struck in the head retaliated by sneaking up behind a coworker and dropping a lighted cigarette into the man's back pocket. After about five minutes, the employee entered a spray booth where highly combustible paints, lacquers, and solvents were used.

Fortunately, another employee noticed smoke coming from the victim's back pocket and stopped him. The prankster also dropped a lighted cigarette in the pocket of another employee who also managed to escape injury.

Refusing to set aside the employee's discharge, an arbitrator noted that his conduct showed a serious disregard for the personal safety of others. In allowing the first employee to walk into the spray booth, the prankster created a dangerous fire hazard. The second employee was working on a cutting machine at the time the "hot-seat" was administered. These incidents could not be considered in the same class with the throwing of rubber squares or the misuse of the air hose, the arbitrator concluded (*Decar Plastics Corp.*, 44 LA 921).

• A 30-day suspension was not too harsh for an employee who exploded firecrackers in the work area, an arbitrator ruled. Although the discipline was much more severe than what had previously been imposed for the same offense, the arbitrator observed that the employer had posted a notice that horseplay would not be tolerated in the plant because of the safety risks, and thus, it was justified in taking stronger action when the rule was violated again. An employee who indiscriminately shoots firecrackers in the presence of other people who are trying to work is showing contempt and disregard for the safety and well-being of his fellow workers, the arbitrator stressed (*Midland Ross Corp.*, 65 LA 1151).

● Returning from a work assignment, an employee spotted a snake on the road, which he proceeded to capture and bring with him to the job. There the worker was instructed by a foreman to find a container in which the reptile might be kept until the end of the shift. Holding the snake in front of him with two hands—a procedure that ensured, according to the worker, that co-workers could "get out of the way" if they so desired—he marched through various work areas until he finally located a can. Snake still in hand, he was preparing the container when a co-worker, who suffered from a heart condition, entered the room. Because he was "scared to death of snakes," the co-worker "left in a hurry," pushing other employees out of his way. Subsequently, the snake-wrangler was discharged for violating a work rule against "irresponsible behavior" on the job.

"That some people are frightened by snakes, even though the fear may be irrational, must be acknowledged and known to reasonable persons," the arbitrator declared. The employee's indifference to co-workers' possible fears—as exemplified by his "showy parade" through the workplace—indicated, the arbitrator decided, that he was "not willing to adhere to an appropriate standard of conduct"—which the arbitrator defined as "no more than the reasonable behavior of a responsible adult." Emphasizing the "real potential for injury or harm" created by the employee's behavior, the arbitrator concluded that the discharge "was for just cause and equitable under the circumstances" (*J.R. Simplot Co.*, 67 LA 645; see also 89 LA 297, 76 LA 339, 75 LA 592, 75 LA 305, 75 LA 290, 74 LA 785, 73 LA 912).

***Practical joke as 'gross misconduct'***—An arbitrator held that a grocery store had just cause to discharge a meat clerk, who, as a practical joke, gave a co-worker, who sometimes put jalapeno peppers on the employee's sandwiches, dog food under the guise of lamb. The co-worker did not get sick after eating the dog food, but a few weeks later, on learning what he had ingested, became nauseated and had trouble sleeping. The practical joker/employee was discharged for gross misconduct, as well as for violating several of the employer's work rules. The arbitrator upheld the discharge, holding that a prank that "goes against the grain" and was "glaringly wrong," exposed the co-worker to potential illness and potential physical harm because dog food is not intended for human consumption (*Ralph's Grocery Co.*, 105 LA 102).

If, however, the employer cannot show that an employee had any malicious intent or created a potential for serious injury or damage as a result of the horseplay, an arbitrator will be reluctant to uphold the ultimate penalty of discharge (*Ozark Lead Co.*, 69 LA 1227; see also 75 LA 672, 54 LA 281, 48 LA 1278).

● Discipline short of discharge was held warranted where an employee pulled back a supervisor's chair, causing her to fall. The employee's conduct showed a lack of judgment, the arbitrator found, but it was not shown to have been a malicious act. A ten-week suspension without pay, the arbitrator concluded, ought to be enough to impress upon the culprit that employees have an obligation to "conduct themselves as mature individuals rather than as lighthearted juveniles" (*Fisher Electronics Inc.*, 44 LA 343).

● In another case, an employer improperly discharged an employee for throwing a pie in the face of a management consultant, an arbitrator decided, where the employee mistakenly received the impression that the consultant generally was willing to participate in practical jokes. Pointing out that there was an excellent working relationship among plant personnel, including management at all levels and employees and union officials, the arbitrator noted that the reason for such an excellent relationship was in part due to the presence of room in the plant for a "little fun." Considering all the circumstances, the arbitrator concluded that the employee should be given another opportunity to demonstrate his desire and ability as an employee (*Clay Equipment*, 73 LA 817).

## Mitigating Circumstances

Aside from determining the degree of danger involved in an employee's actions, arbitrators will often take into consideration the worker's record of past performance and conduct, as well as management's responsibility in the situation, in determining the proper penalty for horseplay (96 LA 828, 91 LA 1402).

● Although an employer correctly maintained that it must impose severe punishment on violators of a three-times posted rule against horseplay, an arbitrator found, immediate discharge was too severe for a worker who smeared red ink on a machine handle. In lessening the penalty to a suspension, the arbitrator pointer out that the employee had five years' service with a good record, that he readily confessed to the transgression when asked about it, and that, although the offense was serious, it was not "sufficiently heinous to support a summary discharge" (*Southeast Container Corp.*, 69 LA 884).

● An employee who was prone to needling other employees had harassed a fellow worker all morning. In retaliation, the other man came up behind the grievant and grabbed him in a bear hug, placing most of his 265 pounds on the grievant's head and shoulders. The grievant thereupon drew a pocket knife and made a slicing motion toward the other worker, for which he was later discharged. In lessening the penalty to reinstatement without back pay, the arbitrator noted that the grievant's nearly perfect record of 19 years' service supported the conclusion that he is not a "chronically mean or vicious" person (*Erwin Mills Inc.*, 51 LA 225).

● The discharge of a worker whose horseplay actually resulted in injury to a fellow employee and could have caused

damage to equipment was overturned because of the worker's unblemished work and conduct record. "Adequate punishment" for the improper conduct, the arbitrator decided, was a disciplinary suspension without pay (*Butler County Mushroom Farms*, 41 LA 568).

● An employee was improperly discharged for dangerous horseplay, which, up until then, had been overlooked by management, an arbitrator ruled. The accumulation of a inflammable substance on surfaces in the employee's work area prompted occasional incidents of prankish pyromania, including employees' lighting the backsides of co-workers' uniforms and igniting the hangers on a conveyor belt that passed through the area. Although no employee had been disciplined for such antics before, one worker was terminated when his horseplay resulted in fire damage in an adjacent work area.

Concluding that the "use of any fire" in the area represented "a reckless disregard for the safety of persons and property," the arbitrator observed that management had taken "no action to stress the seriousness of this offense." Because the employer had not responded to prior misconduct, the employee had reason to expect that this latest fire would also be tolerated, the arbitrator concluded, holding that discharge was too harsh, under the circumstances (*Owens-Corning Fiberglass Corp.*, 70 LA 916; see also *Ogden Aviation Services*, 103 LA 198, where an arbitrator held that discharge was too severe a penalty for an employee who had engaged in horseplay because the incident lasted only several seconds, the act was not malicious, and such misconduct ordinarily would result only in a written warning).

● An employer was not justified in discharging a worker whose actions resulted in his own injury and created a safety hazard for others, an arbitrator ruled, where the employee had a mental and nervous disability that required treatment. Even though the employer had provided a three-month leave for psychiatric treatment, the arbitrator concluded, the arrangement had not ensured that the necessary reports and safeguards were in place for the employee's return to work, as had been done in the past when the employer encountered similar cases (*Foster Wheeler Corp.*, 57 LA 1171).

## Violation of Work Rules

An arbitrator held that an employer had just cause to issue a one-day suspension to an employee for engaging in horseplay—putting hot sauce on a co-worker's sandwich—even though two other employees involved in the incident only received written warnings. The arbitrator reasoned that the suspension was justified because the employee had violated the employer's work rules barring horseplay and abuse of property (*Snappy Air Distribution Products*, 104 LA 184).

## Horseplay As Harassment

An arbitrator dismissed an employee's contention that by approaching an African-American co-worker with a cloth bag on his head and asking, 'How do you like my do-rag? What it be," the employee merely was engaging in lighthearted horseplay. The arbitrator held the misconduct was definitely not horseplay, but rather constituted racial harassment, pointing out that the co-worker was the only African-American there, the grievant's language revealed his intent to ridicule speech or items of apparel stereotypically associated with African-Americans, and the employee was well aware that the co-worker previously had complained to the employer about colleagues' racist comments (102 LA 1179).

## Angry Response to Horseplay

An employer should not have fired an employee who lost his temper in response to a prank, an arbitrator decided.

After an employee began to drink soda from a straw, he realized that a medicated hand lotion had been applied to it. He tossed aside his soda and safety glasses and went to rinse out his mouth. The production line in the plant had started back up by the time he returned, and in the interim, another worker had had to fill in for him. Management fired the employee for violating several company rules, including damaging company property when he threw his soda and glasses, interfering with production by not being at his workstation, creating a safety hazard by throwing the soda, and littering the work area. In the employee's grievance, his union cited details of previous incidents of horseplay when nobody was fired, and challenged the employee's discharge. It also charged it was unfair that the employee who put the lotion on the straw was only given a five-day suspension for his role.

The arbitrator agreed with the union, saying that the company had overreacted in firing the employee. "Unexpectedly swallowing a foreign, peculiar tasting substance, and being taunted for doing so, understandably might not bring out the best in someone," he said, adding that soda could not be seen as a hazard when the employer had not acted similarly in the past to water from a water fight. In addition, the employer's claim that the employee's brief absence interfered with production was farfetched, given that those few minutes hardly made "for a case of job abandonment or interference with production," he concluded, reducing the discharge to a five-day unpaid suspension (*Whirlpool Corp.*, 115 LA 622).

## Horseplay of a 'Simulated Sexual Nature'

An arbitrator may permit horseplay of a sexual nature if the employer has tolerated such employee behavior in the past.

● In a case involving same-sex horseplay, an arbitrator overturned the discharge of two male employees for a male-on-male assault. The incident involved the alleged assault of a male summer employee by two male employees while he was working at a bottling plant. The two regular employees apparently called the summer employee into a warehouse where they turned off the lights, closed the door, and threatened him with sodomy—his pants and possibly his underwear admittedly were "tugged at" and allegedly pulled down. The summer employee, who quit a few days after the incident, complained to his supervisor and the regular employees were discharged.

The employer claimed the incident was the result of the summer employee winning some sort of verbal battle with one of the regular employees a few days earlier and added that, although same-sex horseplay was to be expected in an industrial setting, the incident was not a case of "sophomoric horseplay," but rather a "terroristic attack" meant to send a message. The arbitrator reduced the penalties to suspensions, claiming the discharges were without just cause because there was no clear evidence of any intent to consummate a sexual act, the employer had permitted horseplay even of a "simulated sexual nature," and its nonunit and supervisory employees had engaged in such behavior (*Coca-Cola Bottling Co.*, 106 LA 776).

### Rehabilitative Effect

Discipline short of discharge may be advocated for employees guilty of mild horseplay to see if they can learn from the disciplinary action and mend their ways.

● An employer was within its rights in disciplining a third-shift employee who was guilty of "teasing" his female co-workers by transferring him to the first shift, with attendant loss of his shift differential, an arbitrator said. For the action to have a rehabilitative value, the arbitrator pointed out, the employee should be given a chance to prove that he profited from the experience. Accordingly, the employer was directed to give him another chance to work on the third shift (*Sobel Metal Products Inc.*, 54 LA 835).

# Off-Duty Misconduct

## OVERVIEW

As a general rule, arbitrators hold that an employer may not discipline an employee for off-duty activities because "to do so would constitute an invasion of the employee's personal life by the employer and would place the employer in the position of sitting in judgment on neighborhood morals, a matter which should be left to civil officers" (*Menzie Dairy Co.*, 45 LA 283).

Nevertheless, although that particular arbitrator agreed that the "private life of an employee is beyond the reach of his employer," other arbitrators have pointed out that the effect of the off-duty conduct on an employee's job relationship may prevail over privacy considerations. Generally, management's right to fire a worker for off-duty conduct depends on the effect of that conduct on its operations.

Another arbitrator noted that management may be entitled to discipline employees for off-duty misconduct where "there is a direct and demonstrable relationship between the illicit conduct and the performance of the employee's job." The consequences of all other conduct is "to be left for correction or punishment by civil and moral authority," the arbitrator stressed, cautioning that even where the conduct results in "very substantial embarrassment to an employer," it "cannot be merely assumed that particular conduct ... is related to job performance" (*Internal Revenue Service*, 77 LA 19).

To support discipline for off-duty misconduct, management should be prepared to show that the employee's outside activity had a readily discernible harmful effect on employer operations. Thus, arbitrators will uphold discipline where the employer is able to prove the following.

- The conduct made the employee unable to perform the job satisfactorily and/or led others to refuse to work with him/her (96 LA 244, 95 LA 169).
- The misconduct jeopardized the employer's operations by, for example, creating publicity that harmed its public image (97 LA 585, 96 LA 1208, 96 LA 454, 96 LA 181, 95 LA 358, 95 LA 169, 91 LA 6).

Where an employer is unable to show a relationship or "nexus" between the misconduct and on-the-job performance or prove adverse effect to its business, arbitrators typically will rule against the discipline imposed for off-duty activities (*Central Illinois Public Service Co.*, 105 LA 372; see also 97 LA 801, 96 LA 325).

## SUMMARY OF CASES

### Off-Duty Misconduct on Company Premises

Generally, off-duty employees have an obligation to observe plant rules while on the employer's premises and may be sub-

ject to discipline for their misconduct even though the misconduct (which often will damage employee morale, discipline, or other legitimate employer interests) occurs while they are off duty and in a nonwork area of the plant (104 LA 180, 65 LA 1233).

## Adverse Impact

To sustain discipline for off-duty misconduct, arbitrators generally require that management clearly demonstrates how the incident has negatively affected the employment relationship (*Central Illinois Public Service Co.*, 105 LA 372 (fighting); 102 LA 1016 (illegal use, possession, or distribution of controlled substances); 78 LA 806 (verbal abuse of plant manager at employer picnic); 79 LA 1187, 76 LA 387 (possession/sale of cocaine); 76 LA 347 (theft); 74 LA 1293 (burglary); 74 LA 1084 (threatening foreman); 70 LA 756 (vandalizing supervisor's home); 69 LA 876 (shooting incident); 69 LA 507 (parking in "no-parking" zone near plant); 69 LA 379 (possession of heroin); 68 LA 1245 (shoplifting); 60 LA 172 (possession of stolen property); 57 LA 725, 56 LA 1221 (incest); 49 LA 117 (intoxication)).

● An arbitrator held that an employer had just cause to discipline a bargaining unit employee for assaulting a salaried employee during an off-duty incident in a bar, where the unit employee had called the salaried employee a "scab" for having worked in a unit job during a lockout that had occurred 15 months earlier. The arbitrator reasoned that the employer's labor relations had been affected by such name-calling and that a failure to discipline the employee for his role in the incident could cause the employer's salaried workers to be concerned if a future strike or lockout occurred. It also could give other unit employees the impression that attacks on salaried workers would not be taken seriously (*Central Illinois Public Service Co.*, 105 LA 372).

● An employer properly fired a store clerk after he fatally beat a 71–year-old woman who had intervened in an argument he was having with his wife on a downtown street. Although convicted of manslaughter, the employee argued that he should be allowed to continue on the job through the prison release program. The arbitrator, however, agreed with management that the employee's conduct was of such a brutal nature as to severely damage relations with customers and coworkers. Finding that the widely publicized assault would tend to create anxiety among fellow employees and hesitancy among customers about entering the store, the arbitrator decided that the fear of violence could be as harmful to a business as violence itself and therefore justified the discharge penalty (*Commonwealth of Pennsylvania*, 65 LA 280).

● Management properly issued a written warning to an employee whose parking infractions threatened the organization's "amicable relations" with area residents. Despite the existence of free parking facilities provided by the employer, a number of employees persisted in parking their cars on residential streets adjacent to the plant, thereby inconveniencing local residents. Attempting to cooperate with city authorities, the employer incorporated a parking ban into its work rules. Nevertheless, one employee continued to violate the ban and was issued a written warning.

The "neat question" in the case, the arbitrator pointed out, was whether or not the employer had "an exaggerated notion of how much supervision or influence" it could exercise over employees away from the job. An employee's off-duty activities often can serve as the basis for "very severe discipline," the arbitrator noted, if the employee's conduct makes it "difficult or impossible" for the employer to conduct its business. "The relations between a business enterprise and its neighbors" are "vital considerations" for an employer, particularly one located in a residential area, he stressed. "One of the facts of modern life," he continued, "is that shortages of parking spaces can lead to controversies which become virtual feuds." Thus, while the employee's decision to risk a parking ticket was "essentially his own business," his conduct also created a "serious problem"—the "wrath" and "antipathy" of local residents—for the employer (*Electronic Memories & Magnetics Corp.*, 69 LA 507).

● An arbitrator upheld the termination of an employee for off-duty misbehavior where the work entailed entering customers' homes. The arbitrator termed the employee a bad risk because of his association with disreputable characters capable of using to their advantage inside information on customers' residences and because of the employee's contempt for minimum standards of acceptable social behavior (*Gas Service Co.*, 39 LA 1025).

• Another arbitrator ruled that the discharge of an employee for after-hours behavior was fully warranted because the misconduct stamped him as an individual capable of resorting to violence and, therefore, potentially dangerous to co-workers (*Central Packing Co. Inc.*, 24 LA 603).

• An employer was justified in discharging three employees who were found guilty in court of possessing supplies that were part of another employer's shipment of goods. Finding that the employer's operations were closely linked to the theft area and that the employees previously were suspected of stealing employer property, the arbitrator decided that the discipline was for just cause. The employer's business interests were substantially harmed in view of the small size and close-knit character of the community, the arbitrator reasoned, emphasizing that the employees' reinstatements would have an adverse effect on the employer-employee relationship and, thus, were not warranted under the circumstances (*Inspiration Consolidated Copper Co.*, 60 LA 173).

• In another case, however, an arbitrator ruled that an off-duty shooting in self-defense was not sufficient grounds for termination. Although convicted of second-degree manslaughter, the power lineman was allowed to serve out his sentence on probation. The employer, however, terminated the employee, contending that his continued employment would have an adverse effect on the business because his duties required him to enter customers' homes.

Rejecting the employee's arguments, the arbitrator gave more weight to the testimony of several community leaders who attested to the confidence they had in the employee and their lack of objection to his coming into their homes on employer business. Such testimony, the arbitrator found, was convincing evidence that the employee's continued employment would have no adverse effect on the employer, whereas the failure to reinstate him might harm the organization's reputation. Because the primary reason for the discharge—adverse effect—had been disproved, the arbitrator concluded, the termination was improper (*Alabama Power Co.*, 66 LA 220; see also 78 LA 1311 (selling marijuana); 73 LA 1042 (vehicle damage); 71 LA 1004 (firing gun); 71 LA 82 (possession of marijuana); 68 LA 346 (fighting); 68 LA 254 (sexual affair with fellow employee); 44 LA 133 (bankruptcy)).

• Another arbitrator found that an employer had erroneously concluded that an employee's off-duty misconduct had tarnished its public image. After quarreling with his wife, the employee grabbed a shotgun and went into the woods behind his home. A short time later, a state police trooper was called to the scene, and upon arriving, ordered the employee to come out of the woods. As he emerged, the employee's shotgun discharged, grazing the trooper slightly. The officer arrested the employee and took him to jail. As a result of the publicity the incident received in two local newspapers, the employee was discharged; however, stressing that the publicity about the shooting was limited to two local newspapers that had not revealed the employee's association with the employer, the arbitrator ruled that the discharge was improper. The employee's work did not require him to deal with the public, the arbitrator found, and the employer's customers had no reason to fear the employee because of the incident or the newspaper publicity (*Valley Bell Dairy Co.*, 71 LA 1004).

• Two male employees were improperly suspended for "mooning" a woman, an arbitrator decided. After work, the two employees went to a cocktail lounge for a few hours. Later, as they headed for their car in a parking lot, they noticed a group of women "laughing" and "carrying on" behind them. One of the women blew a "rape" whistle, which the employees considered to be a "practical joke." In response, the employees dropped their trousers and exposed their buttocks to one of the women. The woman reported the mooning to the police, and, when management learned of the incident, it issued one-day suspensions to the employees for misconduct that adversely affected the "efficiency" of the employer's operation.

"There can be little doubt," the arbitrator asserted, that the employees' conduct was "sophomoric and foolish" and fell "substantially short of earning them a merit badge." He stressed, however, that an employer must have sensible "expectation concerning the conduct of employees on their own time," and may not "exaggerate unduly what the public may think of incidents having no bearing on their job." Under this standard, the arbitrator concluded, the employer had no basis for relating the "conduct of the two employees in this single and isolated occasion with the performance of their work" (*U.S. Internal Revenue Service*, 77 LA 19).

• An airline was not justified in discharging a service employee who, after completing his shift, won a $20 bet from fellow employees by "streaking" in front of the airport's terminal wearing only a ski mask, a T-shirt, and cowboy boots. Remarking that the employee's conduct apparently was not lewd and that it caused no morale problems among other employees, the arbitrator concluded that the alleged adverse publicity resulting from the employee's behavior could be considered no more than minimal (*Air California*, 63 LA 350).

### Effect of Arrest

As preceding examples demonstrate, arbitrators generally will not uphold a discharge for off-duty misconduct that is predicated solely on the employee's having been arrested for the incident. On the other hand, most will agree that management is justified in suspending an employee pending the outcome of trial on the charges. A suspension in such circumstances should not be considered disciplinary in nature, some arbitrators have

held, because it is unrelated to the final verdict as to the employee's guilt or innocence. Instead, the suspension should be viewed as an act of self-defense on management's part that is intended to eliminate a potential detriment to or impairment of the organization's business (48 LA 391, 45 LA 498).

• A university had just cause to fire a custodian who was arrested for possession of cocaine just one block from the school's campus, one arbitrator determined. When police arrested a longtime custodian for a university on cocaine possession charges, the school's administration learned from police reports that the employee had resisted arrest and exhibited mood swings and irrational behavior. Shortly thereafter, the university fired the custodian for violating its drug-free environment policy. He subsequently entered into a misdemeanor plea agreement and was placed on probation. Meanwhile, his union filed a grievance, claiming that the drug-free policy did not cover off-duty misconduct. Upholding the discharge, the arbitrator said the custodian, whose job put him in close proximity to the university's students, was arrested for possessing a controlled substance that he obviously intended to use. The fact that he was arrested off-campus was irrelevant, the arbitrator said, because there was a "tangible" relationship between the custodian's off-duty misstep and the university's obligation to maintain both a drug-free environment and an untarnished public image. In fact, the arbitrator asserted, the university was obligated to discharge the custodian because, based on his irrational behavior at the time of his arrest, the university could reasonably have assumed that he was a chronic drug user who would put students at risk (*Western Michigan Univ.*, 115 LA 628).

• Management was within its rights to establish a rule automatically subjecting employees to immediate suspension without pay if they were indicted or arrested for criminal activity, an arbitrator ruled. Rejecting the union's argument that the rule was unfair and unjust in that it convicted an employee before he had a chance to show his innocence, the arbitrator agreed with the employer that some of an employee's off-duty behavior could relate directly to the conduct of a business and therefore be subject to employer rules. According to the arbitrator, off-duty conduct that could be subject to management control included actions that would adversely affect employee morale, discipline, and other legitimate employer interests (*Virginia Chemicals Inc.*, 65 LA 760).

• An employee who was arrested for soliciting prostitution while off duty was justifiably fired, according to one arbitrator. When a deputy employed for 10 years with a Florida sheriff's office informed his superior that he had been arrested for soliciting prostitution, management put him in a restricted administrative assignment, and when its inquiry into the matter was completed, fired him. The employer said that individuals who serve as deputies must demonstrate "good moral character," adding that a prostitution solicitation charge could lead to the employee's decertification as a law officer. The union contended that the penalty was excessive and argued that the employee's long record of good service was a mitigating factor. A deputy sheriff who commits a moral character violation cannot claim to be of good character, the arbitrator said, although he agreed that the penalty was too harsh and admitted that he would have imposed a "lesser penalty" were the decision his to make. He rejected the grievance, however, saying that because there was no unfairness or disparate treatment, he could not intercede (*Broward County Sheriff's Office*, 115 LA 708).

• A driver-salesman arrested on a variety of obscenity charges should be suspended pending trial, or discharged if found guilty, or reinstated if proven innocent or if the charges are dropped. He should, however, be returned to a position that does not involve contact with customers, the arbitrator recommended. Suspension was clearly warranted in the case, the arbitrator held, because of the possible damage to the employer's image and good will if it continued to employ the driver. The duties of the job necessitated a close personal relationship with customers, he noted, stressing that the seriousness of the charge increased the risk of employer harm (*Menzie Dairy Co.*, 45 LA 283).

Such a suspension may be questioned, however, where a lengthy trial results in an extended loss of employment. In these types of cases, arbitrators often suggest that management would do better to conduct its own investigation of the incident and decide on the appropriate disciplinary action.

• Two employees were indicted for committing criminal acts of violence against nonstrikers during a strike. When they returned to work after the strike, the employer temporarily suspended them. The employees emphatically denied their guilt, and several months passed without a trial date being set.

A temporary suspension at the time they returned to work was justified, an arbitrator ruled, because the employer reasonably could conclude that their return at the time would disrupt plant operations. On the other hand, the suspension should not have continued beyond 60 days without the employer's making its own investigation and taking appropriate disciplinary action (*Plough Inc.*, 54 LA 541).

## Conviction Considerations

Arbitrators typically uphold discipline meted out to an employee whose off-duty misconduct results in a criminal conviction, especially where work rules provide for punishment in such cases. Thus, one arbitrator ruled that management was within its rights to discipline an employee convicted of possessing illegal drugs where negotiated work rules mandated discipline simply upon "conviction of a felony involving drugs." The employer did not need to investigate the case nor prove an adverse impact on its own reputation or the performance of its workforce because the rule was part of its contract with the union, the arbitrator said. Finding that off-duty possession and use of drugs was not as serious an offense as such misconduct on employer premises, however, the arbitrator decided that discharge was too harsh a penalty for the first-time offender and therefore reduced the discipline to a suspension (*Nugent Sand Co.*, 71 LA 585).

Arbitrators also will uphold a discharge where the conviction results in harm to the organization's image.

• A gas company employee convicted of embezzlement at his part-time job was properly discharged, an arbitrator ruled. The arbitrator noted the employer was "understandably concerned" about the risk of bad public relations, especially because its employees held a strong position of trust with respect to customers' homes. The fact that this particular employee did not have access to customers' residences was not known to the general public, the arbitrator pointed out (*New Haven Gas Co.*, 43 LA 900).

Where the court tempers the conviction by, for example, suspending part of the sentence or permitting a work release, arbitrators generally require that, absent compelling circumstances, management show similar leniency. Thus, arbitrators have warned, employers may not base a discharge on a conviction while ignoring the fact that the employee has received a suspended sentence with probation.

• Management improperly discharged an employee who was convicted of possessing marijuana but placed on probation, an arbitrator decided, dismissing the employer's contention that the disposition of the court was not relevant in light of the employee's confession of guilt to violating an employer rule against use of illegal drugs. Management, the arbitrator said, failed to present evidence that the employee's arrest had adversely affected its operations or the performance of co-workers, or that the reported drug activity had any impact on the employee's own performance, his record of attendance, or any other aspect of the employment relationship (*Indian Head Inc.*, 71 LA 82).

**Effect of Acquittal**

An acquittal, on the other hand, does not necessarily eliminate the possibility of discipline. Management may preserve its right to take disciplinary action against an employee who has been acquitted of the charges in a court hearing, subject to review within a mutually agreed-on forum.

• As one arbitrator declared, "in the absence of a contrary stipulation by the parties, determinations by other tribunals of issues arising on the facts are not binding on the arbitrators" (*Chrysler Corp.*, 53 LA 1279; see also 54 LA 541).

• Another arbitrator explained that, regardless of an employee's acquittal in a criminal trial, the finding of a disciplinary proceeding may establish that the employee did, in fact, commit the act in question. In such cases, the arbitrator said, "it matters not that the rigorous protection in the criminal law has saved the individual from criminal penalties because such fact does not constitute a bar to the employer's right to protect itself or its other employees" (*New York City Health & Hospital Corp.*, 76 LA 387).

• An arbitrator upheld the discharge of an employee for damaging employer property, even though a jury had acquitted the employee of the criminal charge of malicious destruction of property. The arbitrator held that the jury's action did not foreclose him from making his own judgment on the evidence presented to him, observing that he did not know what evidence or arguments were presented in the criminal action, which rules of law were applied, and which elements of evidence persuaded the jury to reach the verdict it did (*Chrysler Corp.*, 53 LA 1279).

• An employer justifiably denied back pay to an employee who was fired after being found guilty of child abuse even though he was later cleared on appeal and reinstated, an arbitrator ruled. The employee, a teacher's aide at a private school for students who have learning and behavioral disorders, was accused by a student's parents of inappropriate behavior toward their daughter. The school investigated and learned only that the employee had given the girl his phone number at his second job but nonetheless put the employee on paid administrative leave. The investigating agency found credible evidence of child abuse and when the school learned that the employee had been placed on the state's register of sex offenders, he was fired. Subsequently, the employee was cleared on appeal and reinstated without back pay, prompting his union to file a grievance over the back-pay issue. Although the union knew about the employee's appeal, it never told the employer, the arbitrator noted, adding that "given the presumption of child abuse which cloaked the grievant," it was the union's duty to inform the employer. Rejecting the grievance, the arbitrator said the employer properly acted on the information it had at the time. The fact that the employee was cleared on appeal, he added, was "insufficient to warrant back pay" (*Park Forest Academy*, 115 LA 879).

● If, however, an employer has agreed to base its disciplinary decision on the outcome of a trial, it may not ignore an acquittal to which it objects. "It is essential to good labor-management relations," one arbitrator stressed, "that grievance settlements not be disturbed in the absence of conclusive showing of changed conditions" (*Standard Oil Co.*, 13 LA 799).

● Following the "logic behind the reasoning," an arbitrator ruled that city management improperly discharged a police officer for "unbecoming" conduct after it had agreed to return the officer to the payroll if he were acquitted of morals charges. Management later said that the agreement was not a binding contract because "essential elements" of the contractual process were missing and that, in any event, the settlement had been made by the former chief of police, who had retired prior to the officer's acquittal. Rejecting these arguments, the arbitrator found that at the time the agreement was made, the since-retired police chief had full authority to settle grievances and impose discipline, and that the city could not now renege on that settlement. Furthermore, the arbitrator pointed out, "even though given ample opportunity," city managers were unable to show "any conclusive change in the circumstances

which would permit them to rescind the agreement" (*City of Pontiac, Mich.*, 77 LA 765).

## Off-Duty Sexual Misconduct

An employer may be presented with a difficult decision when an employee is convicted of criminal conduct that is regarded as immoral or repugnant by society. On the one hand, there is the threat to employee and/or customer relations that may be presented by returning the employee to the job. On the other, the argument may be made that punishment of the employee should be left to the courts and that the employee should not be placed in "double jeopardy" by loss of employment as well.

● In resolving this dilemma, arbitrators tend to weigh the employee's past record against the threat of a recurrence of the misconduct. Thus, an employee who pleaded guilty to a charge of taking indecent liberties with a nine-year-old girl and who spent about eight months in a state mental hospital was given a conditional reinstatement. The employee's record of 16 years' employment without prior incident was cited as some indication that he could continue as a satisfactory employee, while the fact that he had been a factory employee was seen as minimizing any adverse affect on the morale or efficiency of other employees, as well as the public at large. Citing the employee's lack of public contact, the arbitrator noted that his ruling might have been different had the employee been a retail clerk in a toy store (*Armco Steel Corp.*, 43 LA 977).

● Some of the considerations to be weighed in such cases were reviewed by an arbitrator who ordered the reinstatement of an employee who sought to return to his job after serving a nine-month jail sentence for a morals charge at a motion picture theater. The arbitrator noted that the employee had a 37–year, unblemished work record; the nature of the offense did not impair the employee's ability to perform his job; the underlying psychiatric problem that led to the offense did not, in itself, render the employee unfit for further employment; and aside from supposition, it was not shown that either supervisors or fellow employees would be subjected to resentments or tensions impairing the department's operation if the employee were to be reinstated (*United States Steel Corp.*, 41 LA 460).

Many factors may serve to mitigate the effect of an employee's off-duty misconduct of a sexual nature.

● An employer discharged a male police officer who allegedly had engaged in an off-duty, illicit affair with a civilian under investigation on the basis that his affair "obstructed official business." An arbitrator overturned the officer's discharge, holding that the employer had no right to intrude in his private life, given its commitment in the bargaining agreement to take disciplinary action only in cases of "serious" off-duty misconduct. The arbitrator also held there was no indication that the officer's affair "obstructed official business" and noted that, in order for him to sustain the discharge, the employer would have to have developed a formal, written notice that consorting with the woman during the investigation was a dischargeable offense (*City of Toronto*, 102 LA 645).

● Another arbitrator found that an employer wrongly discharged a police officer who had been convicted of fourth-degree sexual misconduct and indecent exposure in an incident involving a 14-year-old babysitter. The arbitrator reinstated the employee with back pay, noting that there were no complaints of misconduct issued while the officer was on duty; he was remorseful and committed to resolving his pedophilia, as evidenced by his enrollment in a treatment program; and the director of the program testified that the officer did not pose a threat to society and had an encouraging prognosis (*City of St. Paul*, 101 LA 265).

● In another case, where an airline purser was arrested once in an altercation arising from his taking pictures of nude males in a hotel room, an arbitrator converted a discharge to a 90–day suspension. When the employee subsequently pleaded guilty to criminal charges involving the photographing of a nude minor, a discharge penalty was upheld. The cumulative effect of these incidents exposed the airline to potential damage, the arbitrator said, noting that "some people may be given pause" in riding planes "under the control of persons who are so inept at managing their own affairs" (*Northwest Airlines Inc.*, 53 LA 203).

## Social 'Transgressions'

Certain cases labelled as "misconduct" involve no criminal activity, but rather represent transgressions of societal "taboos." In such cases, arbitrators generally require that management conclusively demonstrate how the employee's private affairs can have a negative impact on the employment relationship.

● "In this age of so-called enlightenment and permissiveness, it would be difficult to assess the impact that the private lives of fellow employees have on the workforce," an arbitrator declared, overturning the discharge of an employee who had an affair with a co-worker. Upon learning that the employees, both married, had become intimately involved, management gave them the option of resigning or being fired. While the man chose to resign, the woman refused to accept the ultimatum and was subsequently discharged for conduct unbecoming an office employee. Reinstating the employee, the arbitrator dismissed the employer's contentions that the discharge was necessary in order to protect the organization's good name. Agreeing with the employee that her private life had no adverse effect on the organization or on her job performance and finding that the employees were "consenting adults," the arbitrator concluded that the "punishment did not fit the crime" (*Operating Engineers*, 68 LA 254).

● An employer erred in discharging two married employees for "unbecoming conduct" after catching them in an embrace. Interpreting the phrase to mean "conduct that is so open and notorious that it affronts fellow employees or customers and is carried on while the employee is on duty," the arbitrator decided that this definition did not agree with the facts of the case. The transgression "did not occur on the employer's time, did not affront any customer, and was not the subject of complaint by a fellow employee," he pointed out, concluding that the discharge was too severe (*Williams Bros. Markets*, 64 LA 528).

• An employer that dismisses an unwed pregnant employee also is likely to encounter legal problems. The courts have held that discharging an employee, married or not, for pregnancy is unlawful sex discrimination under Title VII of the 1964 Civil Rights Act, given that pregnancy is a condition unique to women. An employer's claim that its action stemmed from abhorrence of premarital sexual activity was rejected by an appeals court, which held the employee involved was discharged not because of her sexual conduct but because she was pregnant and unmarried. Making a distinction between wed and unwed pregnancy when applying employment policies, the court decided, had no rational relationship to the normal operation of the employer's business (*Jacobs v. Martin Sweets Co.*, 6th Cir., 1977, 14 FEP Cases 687).

**Traffic/Moving Violations**

An arbitrator held that an employer's work rule that mandated discipline of drivers for off-duty driving violations was unreasonable, where the driver who incurs an off-duty traffic violation that does not impair the employee's license or his/her ability to drive for the employer, may find his/her job in jeopardy. In addition, the nexus between off- and on-duty driving conduct should be determined on a case-by-case basis, the arbitrator said (*Coca-Cola Bottling Co. of Mid-America Inc.*, 101 LA 576).

• In such a case-by-case basis, one arbitrator held that an employer did not violate a bargaining agreement, which provided that an employee's personal life is not an appropriate concern of school board, when it disciplined a school bus driver for a careless driving citation she had received while off-duty. The arbitrator said that in this case, the driver's motor vehicle records were relevant to the performance of her job as a school bus driver, regardless of whether the moving violation occurred on or off the job (*Orange County*, 108 LA 216).

# Outside Employment/'Moonlighting'

## OVERVIEW

Moonlighting, i.e., holding a second job during an employee's off-time, can be just cause for discharge or discipline, particularly if there is a provision in a labor contract that allows an employer to terminate an employee for engaging in outside employment.

Although employees may argue for their rights to do as they please during off hours and to use their skills and knowledge to augment their incomes, outside employment may interfere with an employer's need for full productivity during working hours and loyalty from employees.

For example, outside employment may be a cause for disciplinary action in the following situations.

• If the issue of dishonesty is raised, such as when an employee fraudulently takes a leave of absence in order to work on the outside job, an employer might be able to legitimately take action against the person (*Flamingo Hilton Hotel/ Casino*; see also 104 LA 675, 91 LA 1261, 91 LA 647, 90 LA 16, 83 LA 48, 67 LA 606, 66 LA 177).

• If the outside employment adversely affects the employee's primary job through poor performance, absenteeism, or tardiness, there also may be sufficient cause for discipline. Additionally, arbitrators generally uphold discipline where the second job causes a worker either to neglect routine job duties or to refuse to carry out regularly scheduled overtime (89 LA 1062, 66 LA 1071, 66 LA 177, 62 LA 779).

• A conflict of interest may arise between the outside employment and the employee's primary job. This is particularly damaging to the primary employer when the secondary company is a competitor, and trade secrets or special skills are involved (104 LA 312, 94 LA 841, 87 LA 1140, 86 LA 1073, 85 LA 286, 82 LA 1259, 74 LA 1066, 73 LA 164, 72 LA 855, 71 LA 762).

In all of the above situations, an important consideration in determining the kind of discipline warranted is whether or not the contract or a "reasonable" management rule or policy expressly forbids outside employment or business ventures (*Flamingo Hilton Hotel/Casino*, 104 LA 675, involving alleged violation of contractual clause prohibiting "gainful employment" while on a leave of absence).

## SUMMARY OF CASES

### Dishonesty in Moonlighting

Just cause for discharge usually is found where an employee falsely claims sick leave in order to work on a second job. Such cases usually are treated as instances of misconduct akin to dishonesty rather than as simple absenteeism.

• A worker was properly discharged after having been discovered plowing a field of corn for spring planting while on sick leave, an arbitrator ruled. The employee's activities during his period of sick leave constituted a business venture for profit that was prohibited by the bargaining agreement, the arbitrator ruled, noting that the employer had a clearly stated rule that did not permit leaves of absence for the "purpose of any other employment or business venture" (*Farmland Foods*, 67 LA 606).

• Another arbitrator held that an employer properly discharged an employee who had admittedly lied when he denied working at another company during a period when he was on sick leave because of injuries sustained in an automobile accident. The arbitrator found that the employee's continued absence, although he was able to work, caused scheduling difficulties and loss of production during a critical season. The employee's dishonesty, the arbitrator declared, "showed a clear intent to deceive the company for the purpose of obtaining a personal benefit" (*I. B. Goodman Mfg. Co.*, 62 LA 732).

• An employee may be able to escape discipline for working elsewhere while on sick leave if no intent to cheat is involved. Just cause for discharge was held to be lacking where an employee took a second job involving light work while recuperating from a heart attack. The employee had sought to return to his primary job, but both his doctor and the company doctor had recommended against it, and the company also turned down his request for lighter work. The employee's failure to notify the company of his other job and his denial at one point that he was working was held to constitute at most bad judgment, rather than dishonesty (*American Bakeries Co.*, 43 LA 1106; see also *Mercoid Corp.*, 63 LA 941).

• An arbitrator set aside the discharge of an employee who rode a tiger in a novelty animal exhibition while on leave for an occupational back injury. Reasoning that the worker could have injured himself anew during the stunt, the employer contended that he should have obtained its written permission to engage in the off-duty employment. Based on a description of the event, however, the arbitrator found that the tiger-riding activity posed no "foreseeable risk" of injury to the employee and concluded that it was unreasonable for the employer to consider such activity as detrimental to either itself or the employee (*Randle-Eastern Ambulance Service*, 65 LA 394; see also *Rock Hill Printing and Finishing Co.*, 64 LA 856).

• The discharge of an employee who was found tending bar at a local tavern while on sick leave was set aside by an arbitrator on the basis of testimony from the tavern owner and the employee that they were old friends, the employee was not compensated, and he often used the tavern as a "second home" (*Standard Brands Inc.*, 52 LA 918).

## Working for Competition

Arbitrators generally concede that management has the right to bar employees from working for a competitor during their off hours. Such employment not only gives the competitor the benefit of experience provided by the full-time employer, it frequently does so at bargain-basement prices. At the same time, the worker may unintentionally harm the primary employer by divulging trade secrets or such proprietary information as new designs or sales figures.

• An employer has the right to establish a rule against working for a competitor, one arbitrator decided. In applying such a rule, a company is not required to establish beyond doubt that the employee's moonlighting has damaged its business or led to a financial loss, the arbitrator said, maintaining that management can take action against the offending employee where it "reasonably" infers that the outside employment might lead to disclosure of information or the use of special skills (*Ravens-Metal Products Inc.*, 39 LA 404; see also 96 LA 526, 71 LA 762).

Arbitrators insist that employers inform their workers through clearly established rules that any outside employment is forbidden. Even when the evidence is clear that a worker has broken a rule against outside employment, many arbitrators require that management allow the employee a chance to relinquish the secondary job before enforcing a final decision to fire the worker.

- After learning that two of its workers had accepted part-time employment with a competitor, the employer gave them a formal warning that any further activity of that sort would be cause for discharge. Although ruling that the employer was justified in barring the outside work, the arbitrator considered the warnings in this case unjustified. The employer had the right to forbid the outside employment, the arbitrator said, but it could not impose discipline concurrent with giving notice of its policy (*Mechanical Handling Systems Inc.*, 26 LA 401; see also *Phillips Petroleum Co.*, 47 LA 372).

- An employer that required all employees to disclose any moonlighting activities improperly discharged a worker for failing to reveal his part-time job with a competitor because the employer had terminated the worker without giving him a chance to resign from the second job. Other employees in similar situations, the arbitrator noted, had been allowed an opportunity to relinquish their outside interest before any disciplinary action was invoked (*William Feather Co.*, 68 LA 13).

- Discharge was improper where an employee was not given a reasonable opportunity to disengage himself from a business that his primary employer considered a conflict of interest, another arbitrator ruled. Although the employer contended that the worker's part ownership in a local bar competed with its retail business, the arbitrator decided that the employer had failed to prove that the bar was a competitor. If the employer's interest in the operation competed with his primary job, the arbitrator noted, then the employer should have allowed the worker a chance to give up his ownership interest in the bar (*Albertson's Inc.*, 65 LA 1042; see also 96 LA 1).

### Direct Competition

Arbitrators agree that management has the right to discharge an employee when the worker's off-duty activity con-

stitutes direct competition because the business is similar to that of the employer (57 LA 1258, 55 LA 1044, 53 LA 1176).

- Workers soliciting business for personal gain while on company time should be liable for discipline, arbitrators agree. "It is an established rule of employment law," one arbitrator said, "that an employee may not use for his own benefit and contrary to the interest of his employer, information obtained in the course of the employment." Ruling that an employer had "just cause" for discharging workers who were soliciting business for private gain on company time and working in competition with the employer, an arbitrator stressed that "no employee needs to be told that if he is soliciting company customers on company time and property for a competing business, that he runs a great risk of losing his job" (*Alaska Sales and Service Co.*, 73 LA 164; see also *Jacksonville Shipyards Inc.*, 74 LA 1066).

- Another arbitrator converted a discharge to a disciplinary layoff where the employee had been siphoning business from his employer. In this case, the employer had a specific rule forbidding employees to solicit during working hours with the intent of obtaining work ordinarily performed by the company. Nevertheless, noting such mitigating factors as the employee's good record and the absence of any evidence that the employer had actually lost money, the arbitrator held that giving the worker a second chance would benefit both the company and society (*Heinrich Motors Inc.*, 68 LA 1224; see also *Patton Sparkle Market*, 75 LA 1092).

### Other Conflicting Employment

Even where the second job is not with a direct competitor, management still may claim that it inherently conflicts with the employee's responsibilities and obligations to the primary employer.

- An arbitrator ruled that a wholesale distributor of cigarettes would be justified in discharging a salesman if the worker did not divest himself of his interest in a private vending machine business serving the employer's retail customers.

Pointing out that the employee's outside business activity created a conflict of interest, the arbitrator concluded that the employer's legitimate business interests required that the company be able to discharge the employee so long as the worker refused to terminate "those outside, but closely related, business activities, which caused economic harm to the employer" (*Phillips Brothers Inc.* 63 LA 328).

Such conflict-of-interest issues often are also raised by employers in the publishing industry. Here are some examples of how arbitrators have ruled in these cases.

- An arbitrator determined that an employee violated an employer prohibition against outside activities that created a "clear conflict of interest," by writing and publishing a book about the employer, based on his work as an investigative reporter covering a story on the employer's financial problems. In addition, even though the employee had permission to use his story without restrictions on writing a book, the arbitrator said, the journalist commented on the employer in a derogatory fashion, thus violating the employer's rules (*United Press International Inc.*, 94 LA 841).

- A publisher had the right to give one of its reporters a choice between his job with the paper and an outside job as editor of a union weekly that espoused political views contrary to the newspaper's editorial policy (*Niagara Falls Gazette*, 41 LA 899).

- A publisher did not show just cause for discharging two circulation managers for operating a local beer tavern. The arbitrator rejected the company's contention that a bias against beer existed in a large segment of the community, noting that the sole test of community morals is that which has been crystallized by statute or ordinance into positive mandate. Given that dealing in beer production or sales is a legal business, the employees were not engaged in activities of a detrimental nature to the newspaper (*Memphis Publishing Co.*, 48 LA 931).

- A publisher did not have the right to order one of his advertising salesmen

to quit a night job in a local department store, notwithstanding the publisher's contention that other advertiser-stores might view it as a conflict of interest. As a remedy, the publisher was directed to make the employee whole for wages he lost by relinquishing his part-time employment (*Lowell Sun Publishing Co.*, 43 LA 273).

- A publisher had the right to fire its drama critic for accepting outside work as a press agent for a summer theater and allowing her name, which was also the name of her column in the newspaper, to be used in promoting the summer theater (*Tribune Publishing Co.*, 42 LA 504).

## Other Adverse Interference

Moonlighting that does not involve working for a competitor or otherwise conflict with the primary job usually is not regarded as just cause for discharge, in the absence of contractual prohibition on outside employment.

- On the other hand, a company was held to be within its rights when it adopted a rule prohibiting the holding of a second full-time job, on the ground that this would have a natural and obvious tendency to interfere with an employee's work (*Goodyear Tire & Rubber Co.*, 41 LA 1126).

- An arbitrator held that an employer properly issued a written reprimand to an auxiliary engineer who published an article in a newspaper that suggested the employer had an atrocious safety record, despite the claim that the employee's action was entirely without malice (*San Diego Gas & Electric Co.*, 82 LA 1039).

- An employer had just cause for discharging a worker who took three days off to harvest his corn crop despite a specific order to report to work, an arbitrator decided. The need to harvest and the potential economic loss if he failed to so, the arbitrator ruled, did not excuse the worker's failure to fulfill his obligation to the employer. Furthermore, the arbitrator decided, management had the right to discipline without giving written warning because the employee had blatantly refused to carry out its specific instructions (*Dryden Manufacturing Co.*, 66 LA 1071).

• In the course of preparing reprimands about an employee for spoiled work, management stumbled onto the fact that he was moonlighting. The reprimands were changed to a discharge when the employee refused to give up his second job. An arbitrator set aside the discharge because management had insufficient backing for its conclusion that it was injured by the worker's other job. Although his two jobs allowed him only about five hours of sleep a day, his foreman saw no signs that the employee was suffering from lack of sleep and instead had given him rapid promotions. There also was no showing that he was less efficient or spoiled more work than nonmoonlighters (*United Engineering & Foundry Co.*, 37 LA 1095).

• Another arbitrator reinstated a worker who had been discharged for excessive absenteeism on the condition that he stop working in any outside business for one year. On several occasions, the employee had failed to report to work because of arm and neck pains. When management discovered that he was working at a garage on the days he had called in sick, it terminated the worker. Although finding that the worker's outside venture had interfered with his regular job by causing him to be excessively absent, the arbitrator concluded that the worker's prior satisfactory job performance and length of service warranted his receiving a second chance (*Microdot Inc.*, 66 LA 177).

• An arbitrator held that an employer improperly discharged a flight attendant whose "Bohemian" lifestyle and work as a professional artist were described in a magazine feature article that identified him as working for the employer. Even though the employee failed to get the required pre-publication review, approval, and permission from the employer, the arbitrator pointed out, neither the employee's artistic endeavors nor the article constituted work "detrimental to, or in conflict with, the company's interest" (*Trans World Airlines Inc.*, 93 LA 167).

# Sexual Harassment

———————————— **OVERVIEW** ————————————

Sexual harassment in the workplace occurs whenever unwelcome gender-based conduct affects an employee's job. Two types of sexual harassment are actionable under Title VII of the 1964 Civil Right Act: "quid pro quo" (literally, "this for that," denoting that sexual favors have been demanded in return for purportedly allowing the victim to remain in a job or advance in the company) and "hostile environment." The two types of sexual harassment are not necessarily mutually exclusive and can occur together. As a practical matter, distinguishing between them is necessary only when determining the extent of an employer's liability.

Sexual harassment also occurs when submission to the advances or requests is "a term or condition of an individual's employment." It is not necessary that the object of the harassment be a subordinate of the harasser; harassment of co-workers, including the creation of a "hostile" work environment, is also sexual harassment, as is harassment of clients or customers of the employer or other nonemployees, such as independent contractors and others.

Arbitrators have readily accepted the principle that sexual harassment violates a collective bargaining agreement's prohibition against sex discrimination, and more commonly, that an employee who engages in sexual harassment may properly be disciplined for just cause.

Generally, arbitrators must enforce the intent of the parties in a collective bargaining agreement, rather than enforcing external law—specifically, definitions and standards contained in Title VII. When there is no conflict between external law and the terms of a bargaining agreement, arbitrators are free to examine external law in interpreting the agreement.

Alternative dispute resolution also is being used more often in the mediation of sexual-harassment charges filed against employers. Many employers argue that mediation can save money by avoiding costly litigation, can help the parties maintain workplace morale, and can avoid the airing of charges and counter-charges in public.

Arbitrators considering cases of discipline for sexual harassment must determine whether the employee's misconduct actually was sexual harassment, and whether the discipline imposed was appropriate. In making the first determination, many arbitrators rely on the Equal Employment Opportunity Commission's 1999 "Guidelines on Discrimination Because of Sex," which define sexual harassment as encompassing "unwelcome sexual advances, requests for sexual favors, and other verbal or physical conduct of a sexual nature" that have the "purpose or effect of unreasonably interfering with an individual's work performance or creating an intimidating, hostile, or offensive working environment."

If an employee's conduct were, indeed, sexual harassment, the arbitrator must then decide whether the discipline was justified. To make this determination, arbitrators may consider whether:

- the victim's testimony was credible;
- the incident was reported to management;
- the harassment interfered with the victim's job performance or adversely affected the employer's operations;
- the behavior created an intimidating, hostile, or offensive working environment;
- the victim suffered any diminution in job status because of a refusal to submit to or tolerate the sexual overtures; and/or
- the alleged harasser was aware of the employer's policies prohibiting sexual harassment. It should be noted that even if there is no shop rule against sexual harassment, one line of arbitral authority states that because sexual harassment is inherently impermissible, employers may discipline employees for harassment relying only on the "unwritten law of the shop."

[**Note:** Arbitration of sexual-harassment issues generally arises from grievances challenging the discharge or discipline of an employee for misconduct based in whole or in part on alleged sexual harassment of another employee rather than complaints of alleged victims of such harassment.]

## KEY DECISIONS—

***Types of harassment***—Sexual harassment constitutes a form of sexual discrimination under Title VII of the Civil Rights Act of 1964. As was stated above, the EEOC and the federal courts have recognized two distinct types of sexual harassment: "quid pro quo" and "hostile environment" harassment.

- "Quid pro quo" harassment occurs when an aspect of a person's job is conditioned on his or her accepting the sexual advances or conduct of another worker (usually a manager or supervisor).
- "Hostile environment" harassment occurs when an employee is subjected to a pattern of unwelcome, sexually related conduct in the workplace that creates a hostile, intimidating, or offensive work environment. It should be noted, however, that sexually harassing conduct need not be of a specifically sexual nature, it need only be gender-based.

Sexually hostile environment can be created by:
- discussing sexual activities;
- telling off-color jokes;
- unnecessary touching (including among members of the same sex);
- commenting on physical attributes;
- displaying sexually suggestive photographs, calendars, magazines, etc.;
- using demeaning or inappropriate terms, (e.g., "Babe");
- using indecent gestures;
- sabotaging the alleged victim's work product;
- engaging in hostile physical conduct;
- granting job favors to those who participate in consensual sexual activity; and/or
- using crude or offensive language.

***Defining sexual harassment***—Although Title VII has prohibited employment discrimination on the basis of sex since 1964, it was not until 1976 that a court interpreted that prohibition as extending to sexual harassment (*Williams v. Saxbe*, D.D.C., 1976, 12 FEP Cases 1093).

* Sexual harassment is *not* gender specific—men as well as women can be its victims ( *Showalter v. Allison Reed Group*, D.R.I., 1991, 56 FEP Cases 989). It occurs in a wide variety of forms, including touching, pressure for sexual favors, suggestive looks or gestures, sexual joking or teasing, the display of offensive sexual materials, gender baiting, hazing, and retaliatory discharge. Title VII forbids any harassment in which one, some, or all of the employees of one sex suffer significantly unfavorable treatment on the job because of their gender.

*'Quid pro quo' harassment*—Quid pro quo harassment occurs when an individual is forced to choose between suffering an economic detriment and submitting to sexual demands. This kind of harassment was the first type of gender discrimination recognized by the courts (29 CFR 1604.11(a); see, e.g., *Barnes v. Costle*, D.C. Cir., 1977, 15 FEP Cases 345).

* In one case, an employee was reprimanded and eventually terminated for refusing to submit to her supervisor's sexual demands (*Williams v. Saxbe*, D.D.C., 1976,12 FEP Cases 1093, *rev'd and remanded on other grounds sub nom. Williams v. Bell*, D.C. Cir., 1978, 17 FEP Cases 1662, *on remand sub nom., Williams v. Civiletti*, D.D.C., 1980, 22 FEP Cases 1311).

* In another case, the employee's job was abolished after she refused to submit to her supervisor's sexual advances (*Barnes v. Costle*, D.C. Cir., 1977, 15 FEP Cases 345).

* In still another case, the employee was discharged when she refused her supervisor's sexual advances (*Miller v. Bank of America*, 9th Cir., 1979, 20 FEP Cases 462).

By its very nature, quid pro quo harassment can only be committed by a supervisor or a member of the company's hierarchy who has the power to confer or withhold a tangible job benefit. Employers are strictly liable to employees who suffer economic harm as a result of such harassment if the harasser had actual authority to alter the victim's work conditions regardless of whether the employer actually knew of the harassment.

*Hostile environment harassment*—To establish that a sexually hostile environment exists, complainants must show that they were subjected to unwelcome gender-based harassment that affected a term, condition, or privilege of employment in that it was sufficiently severe or pervasive to alter the conditions of the person's employment and create an abusive working environment, the U.S. Supreme Court ruled (*Meritor Savings Bank v. Vinson*, U.S., 1986, 40 FEP Cases 1822).

"Title VII affords employees the right to work in an environment free from discriminatory intimidation, ridicule, and insult" whether based on sex, race, religion, or national origin, the court declared. Sexual harassment that "creates a hostile or offensive environment for members of one sex is every bit the arbitrary barrier to sexual equality at the workplace that racial harassment is to racial equality. Surely, a requirement that a man or woman run a gauntlet of sexual abuse in return for the privilege of being allowed to work and make a living can be as demeaning and disconcerting as the harshest of racial epithets," the court insisted, quoting from *Henson v. City of Dundee* (11th Cir., 1982, 29 FEP Cases 787).

## SUMMARY OF CASES

### Hostile Environment Harassment

*Verbal and Visual Harassment*—Arbitrators routinely support decisions to discipline employees for sexual harassment in the form of unacceptable, unwelcome, vulgar conduct, including the following:

- sexual, crude, or suggestive language directed at a co-worker (*AMG Industries*, 106 LA 322) in which a male employee was discharged for making sexually loaded remarks on an employer intercom about a female employee;
- Sexual jokes and propositions (*International Mill Service*, 104 LA 779; see also *Safeway Inc.*, 105 LA 718);
- obscene sexual gestures (*Can-Tex Industries*, 90 LA 1230);
- unsolicited, directed, and sexually suggestive physical contact with a co-worker (*Safeway Inc.*, 105 LA 718);
- intentionally entering a women's restroom with a female co-worker present (*Porter Equipment*, 86 LA 1253);
- a male employee's exposing himself to several female co-workers (*Eureka Co.*, 101 LA 1151);
- spreading lies about the sexual activities of a co-worker (*Social Security Administration*, 81 LA 459);
- sexually explicit queries (*Steuben Rural Electric Corp.*, 98 LA 337);
- offensive allusions to a female (independent contractor) instructor's torso on an anonymous course-evaluation form (*Michigan Dept. of Transportation*, 104 LA 1196);
- verbal abuse of a gay co-worker where an employer policy incorporated the language of a city ordinance prohibiting harassment based on "sexual or affectional preference" (*Food and Commercial Workers Local 88*, 99 LA 1161);
- a female employee's harassment of a male supervisor by sending him love letters containing "graphic verbal commentaries" about his body (*American Protective Services Inc.*, 102 LA 161);
- a gay employee's explicit recounting of his sexual encounters and his threats and propositions to three male co-workers (*Hughes Aircraft Co.*, 102 LA 353); and
- other conduct creating a hostile work environment (*Anaconda Copper Co.*, 78 LA 690).
- On the other hand, a male employee's repetition of an off-color joke to a female employee whose father complained to management after he was asked to explain the joke does not constitute sexual harassment, one arbitrator ruled, because the joke was impersonal and therefore not offensive to that particular employee (*Ralphs Grocery Co.*, 100 LA 63).

### Nonvulgar, Unwelcome Sexual Advances

Arbitrators have upheld discipline of employees for sexual harassment in cases in which the employees make unsolicited, amorous advances toward other employees where the advances are persistent and annoying, even where the conduct is not crude or physical.

In these types of cases, arbitrators are required to distinguish between harmless, ineffectual romantic conduct and obsessive-compulsive neurotic behavior.

- An employer did not have just cause to discharge a male employee for sexual harassment after he touched the breast of a female co-worker, one arbitrator found. After a brief, personal discussion in the office of the female co-worker, with whom he had an allegedly flirtatious relationship, a male physician's assistant hugged the woman and touched her breast. Although the two employees disagreed over precisely what happened, the female worker did not immediately file charges over the incident. A few weeks later, however, she filed a formal sexual harassment complaint against the male employee, and he was fired. His union protested the discharge, claiming that it was excessive discipline for a single incident of inappropriate touching. Ordering the male worker reinstated with back pay, the arbitrator said a single incident of unwelcome, intimate contact did not rise to the level of sexual harassment and was insufficient to warrant discharge. According to the U.S. Supreme Court, "hostile environment" sexual harassment must be deliberate, "repeated," and unwelcome before it would warrant discharge (*U.S. Department of Veterans Affairs*, 115 LA 198).

### Harassment of Customers, Clients, and Other Nonemployees

Employees not only are prohibited from sexually harassing their fellow employees, but also must not harass nonemployees with whom they come into contact as part of their job. The following types of sexual harassment of nonemployees have been found improper:

- making offensive comments to a passing individual city resident. (*City of Rochester*, 82 LA 217);
- making sexual advances toward the teenage daughter of a customer (*Pepco*, 83 LA 449);
- making sexually oriented jokes and comments to clients (*County of Ramsey*, 86 LA 249);
- making sexual propositions to customers (*Nabisco Food Co.*, 82 LA 1186);
- making crude and offensive sexual remarks to a female bartender and her mother during the delivery of a product (*Lohr Distributing Co.*, 101 LA 1217); and
- making unwelcome advances, asking offensive questions, and making comments of a sexual nature toward nonemployee, independent contractors (*Dayton Newspapers Inc.*, 100 LA 48).

### Seriousness of Offense/Proper Discipline

One arbitrator developed five criteria for determining the seriousness of the sexual harassment.

- Did the employer have a written anti-sexual harassment policy in place when the incident occurred? Was it specific enough to make employees understand what constitutes sexual harassment, and what the consequences of infractions of the policy would be? Was the sexual harassment policy adequately disseminated to employees?
- Did the employer have an effective procedure for employees to use in alerting management of sexual-harassment complaints? Was the work environment such that it discouraged employees from making formal or informal complaints?
- Did management know, or should it have known, of the sexual harassment that occurred?
- Was the sexual harassment committed by the employee's supervisor on whom the employee was dependent for employment, work assignment, promotion, performance evaluation, and/or salary increases?
- What was the personal relationship between the person accused of harassment and the person(s) considered to be his or her victims?
- In one case, an arbitrator held that an employer did not have just cause to discharge two male employees who were accused of sexually harassing another male employee. The two employees allegedly had called the summer employee into an office, turned out the lights and closed the door, "tugged at" his pants and underwear, and threatened him with sodomy. The employee, who quit a few days after the incident, complained the next day to his supervisor, and the two employees were fired. Reducing the discharges to suspensions, the arbitrator noted that there was no clear evidence that the two male workers intended to consummate the sexual act and that the employer previously had tolerated—and supervisors had engaged in—horseplay of a "simulated sexual nature" (*Coca-Cola Bottling Co.*, 106 LA 776).

### Need for Written Policies

Lack of a written anti-harassment policy can make justifying discharge for sexual harassment more difficult for an employer.

• A female employee claimed that during an evening work shift, a male co-worker repeatedly (25 to 30 times) propositioned her and made many other sexually suggestive remarks. The harassment was so persistent and upsetting, the woman said, that she felt ill and had to leave work early. She complained to management, and the man was fired. Subsequently, the union filed a grievance on his behalf.

The arbitrator disagreed with the man's claim that he had done nothing wrong, finding that he did sexually harass his co-worker, unreasonably interfered with her work, and created a hostile work environment. The employer had to do something, the arbitrator said, adding, however, that there were mitigating factors; significantly, the employer's lack of a written policy on preventing sexual harassment, the lack of sensitivity training on the subject for the employees, and the absence of any warnings of the consequences of engaging in such behavior. Because of these mitigating factors, the arbitrator ordered the male employee's discharge reduced to an unpaid disciplinary layoff (*Commercial Printing Co.*, 115 LA 393).

## Relevance of Past Harassment

A unique problem that has arisen involves whether evidence of past sexual harassment offenses by the alleged harasser should be relevant in arbitration of current sexual harassment cases.

• One arbitrator considered it relevant to the extent that it established a pattern of conduct that was consistent with the accusations of the current sexual harassment victim (86 LA 254).

• In another case, however, an arbitrator found that the employer had improperly considered prior incidents of alleged sexual harassment in deciding whether the employee was guilty of current charges (86 LA 681).

• An arbitrator ruled that an employee was improperly suspended for allegedly filing a false sexual harassment claim against a co-worker. The arbitrator said that although the alleged victim (who previously had been raped) may have ex-

aggerated one claim and incorrectly stated a second, she had not done so intentionally intending to deceive or defraud (92 LA 653).

## When Discipline Is Justified

Many arbitrators, relying on EEOC guidelines to determine whether misconduct was sexual harassment, have upheld an employer's disciplinary action against the harassing employee. For example, discharge has been sustained where:

• the employee's harassment created an intimidating, hostile, and offensive working environment (105 LA 371), where a leadman intimidated and assigned to undesirable jobs female employees who refused to comply (88 LA 791), the employer violated EEOC guidelines on sexual harassment (89 LA 27) by writing "obscene" comments on a magazine (94 LA 289);

• the employee adversely affected production with repeated obscene gestures and comments to female co-workers (93 LA 721);

• the employee's profanity damaged the employer's public image (93 LA 25);

• the employee engaged in persistent and continued sexual advances that created an offensive working environment and interfered with job performance by causing co-workers to lose work time (97 LA 957);

• the employee knowingly violated an employer policy barring sexual discrimination (*International Mill Service*, 104 LA 779, where a male employee's sexual jokes and propositions directed at a female employee created a hostile work environment in violation of the employer's policy barring sex discrimination, and where the employer also displayed a poster stating the policy);

• the employee failed to respond to corrective discipline for obscene name-calling and gesturing (78 LA 985); and

• the employee, whose record reflected prior incidents involving physical touching, threatened to rape a co-worker (74 LA 1281, 75 LA 592).

• Arbitrators also upheld the lesser penalties imposed by employers where the misconduct has involved touching a female co-worker, (80 LA 133, 81 LA 459) or physical restraint (75 LA 592).

Following are details of specific cases of sexual harassment in which arbitrators have upheld the employer's penalty for the misconduct.

• An arbitrator held that a federal agency had just cause to issue a one-day suspension to a male employee who crossed the line from "friendly" to "indecent" in his interaction with female employees. The arbitrator ruled it is friendly to compliment a female employee by telling her she looks particularly pretty, but it is unacceptable in an office environment to tell another employee who is not a personal friend that you are attracted to her. It is "unavoidable and healthy" that one's eyes should be drawn to a sexually attractive person, the arbitrator commented, but is unacceptable to stare deliberately to the point that the other person feels uncomfortable (*Norfolk Naval Shipyard*, 104 LA 991).

• Just cause existed to discharge a female employee (and union steward) under a rule against sexual harassment for writing anonymous letters that accused a female co-worker of sexual infidelity with her supervisor, an arbitrator concluded. The letters were examined by a handwriting expert, who definitively established that the employee wrote them. The employee was "incontestably guilty" of harassment that was calculated to "bring disrepute" to the co-worker and "create domestic disharmony," as well as "a psychologically repressive work environment," the arbitrator pointed out. Although not "unmindful" of the employee's 32 years of service and exemplary record, the arbitrator said it was not a mitigating factor in this case because the misconduct was not only "heinous," but also "in most respects more serious than other forms of sexual harassment" prohibited by the employer (*Schlage Lock Co.*, 88 LA 75; see also *American Protective Services*, 102 LA 161, where a female employee wrote unsolicited, anonymous love letters to her supervisor that contained "graphic verbal commentaries" about his body, in violation of her employer's sexual harassment policy).

• A 20-day suspension was appropriate for an employee who "bluntly solicited" a female co-worker, an arbitrator ruled. The employee on several occasions, both on and off the job, told the co-worker that he wanted to have oral sex with her. The co-worker did not respond to the employee's advances, would "hide" from the employee when he came to her work area, reported the incidents to her supervisor, and submitted a written statement to the employer detailing the misconduct. Management suspended the employee for "disruptive harassment" for his "unceasing efforts" to win the co-worker's submission.

The arbitrator concluded that the misconduct "interfered" with the co-worker's job performance, adding that the facts "established to a degree of certainty one rarely encounters" a hostile, abusive, and intimidating work environment. The employer had a legal obligation to take "immediate and appropriate corrective action," the arbitrator pointed out (*Veterans Administration Medical Center*, 87 LA 405).

• An arbitrator held that an employer had just cause to discipline a leadman who violated the employer's sexual harassment policy, which required him to stop situations that are, or might be interpreted to be, sexual in content and to report them to a supervisor. The employee was looking at a "girlie" magazine that had been brought to work by another employee and neither attempted to stop other employees from looking at the magazine, which was explicitly sexual in content, nor reported to a supervisor its presence in the workplace (*American Mail-Well Envelope*, 105 LA 1209).

## When Discipline Is Reduced

In some cases, however, arbitrators found misconduct constituting sexual harassment but held that the penalty assessed by the employer was inappropriate because of mitigating factors or because the employer failed to properly investigate the harassment complaint, failed to give the employee adequate notice of the prohibition, or failed to give the employee a chance to defend him- or herself before the discipline was imposed.

Some mitigating factors that have prompted lesser penalties include:

- seniority (80 LA 19);
- a good work record and the absence of past disciplinary problems (71 LA 54, 83 LA 571, 85 LA 11);
- evidence that the misconduct amounted to an isolated incident that was not likely to recur at any time in the future. (79 LA 940);
- the harassing employee's attitude (85 LA 11);
- the harassed employee's attitude (95 LA 1097);
- the quality of proof of the employee's guilt and the thoroughness of the employer's investigation (*Vista Chemical Co.*, 104 LA 818);
- an employer's failure to address sexual harassment specifically in policies and procedures; to follow progressive discipline procedures; or to provide proper supervision to limit "shop talk," joking, teasing, or ridicule (86 LA 1017, 88 LA 1292, 95 LA 510);
- the nature and amount of horseplay, obscenity, etc., prevalent in a given workplace (94 LA 1217); and
- the fact that supervisors/employer agents also engaged in harassment of a particular employee, thus purportedly conveying a message to employees that sexual harassment would be tolerated (*Metropolitan Transit Committee*, 105 LA 300).

Specific cases in which arbitrators have reduced the penalties imposed by employers include the following.

- Discharge was reduced to a written notice of violation of an employer's policy against sexual harassment for a male employee who continued to send letters, flowers, and gifts to a female co-worker despite her protestations. The arbitrator refused to apply the "reasonable woman standard" in determining whether there was just cause for discharge, holding that the arbitrator's jurisdiction is limited to determining whether just cause exists under the terms of the collective bargaining agreement, unless the employer can establish that the arbitrator is also bound by public policy. Public policy does not mandate discharge for sexual harassment, the arbitrator stated—it merely requires that the hostile work environment be eliminated (*KIAM*, 97 LA 617).

- An employer had sufficient cause to discipline, but not to discharge, a male police officer who sexually harassed a female co-worker, the arbitrator found. The male officer, who had worked 17 years for the city of Boston, was fired after he was accused of sexual harassing a female subordinate who accused him of unfastening her bra straps while the two were parked in a city van. Although the officer denied the allegations, after an investigation, he was fired. Management believed the female officer's allegations and under the parties' labor agreement, violators of the sexual harassment policy were subject to discipline, up to and including termination. The union contended that discharge was excessive, given the officer's 17-year, discipline-free employment record. The employer had just cause to discipline the male officer, but not to discharge him, the arbitrator said, given that the contract did not require such a drastic punishment, especially for a first offense. The arbitrator ordered the officer reinstated but without back pay, effectively suspending him for one year without pay (*City of Boston*, 116 LA 906).

- For 22 years, a male employee had worked as a cutter/grinder for a tool manufacturer before being laid off. He later found work at a local library as a technician, but over a period of time, he engaged in a variety of lewd actions, offending a number of different people, and prompting his termination. The local grieved, arguing that the worker's evaluations had been superior, and that he had never been terminated before or ever been accused of sexual misconduct. The arbitrator pointed out that his actions were "clearly inappropriate, manifestly unprofessional, and totally unacceptable," but added that they did not constitute sexual harassment *per se*. He noted that the employee, when confronted, had apologized for unintended hurt he had caused and appeared to genuinely believe the actions were inoffensive. The grievance was upheld, the arbitrator said, restoring the man's seniority but giving him no back pay; in addition, he was ordered to undergo sensitivity training before his reinstatement (*Dayton, Ohio, and Montgomery County Library*, 117 LA 71).

● Discharge was too severe a penalty for an employee who deliberately entered a ladies' rest room and told a female occupant that he "always wanted to know what it looked like," one arbitrator concluded. Although the employee displayed "poor judgment," the arbitrator said, the incident did not justify dismissal of an employee with 14 years' seniority, especially because there was "nothing immoral about the employee's conduct" (*Perfection American Co.*, 73 LA 520).

● Discharge was reduced to a seven-month suspension for an employee who allegedly pinched a female co-worker's breast while making a "kissing" sound. Although the employee denied harassing the female employee, the arbitrator credited the woman's testimony, pointing out that she displayed no bias or bad feeling against the male employee. Mitigating circumstances in the case, the arbitrator said, included the following: the employee's 28 years of employment; his reasonably good work record with the employer; the absence of past disciplinary problems in the employee's record; and the female employee's failure to report the incident when it occurred. The arbitrator warned, however, that the reduction in the penalty "should not be construed to lessen the seriousness of the conduct," nor be understood in any way to relieve the employer of its duty to protect employees from sexual harassment (*Dayton Power and Light Co.*, 80 LA 19).

● Discharge was reduced to a three-month suspension for one employee, and a six-day suspension was reduced to three days for another, by an arbitrator who found that the department involved was "a disruptive place to work largely because of poor supervision, leadership, and general discipline." Supervisors themselves participated in the teasing and ridicule that was rampant in the department, the arbitrator noted, so the disciplined employees were" not alone in the problem," and "they cannot be held solely

responsible" (*New York Air Brake Co.*, 74 LA 875).

## Employer's Burden of Proof

Some arbitrators equate sexual-harassment disciplinary cases as any other disciplinary case involving misconduct, without specifically mentioning a burden of proof, appearing to require the employer to establish sexual harassment by a preponderance of the evidence (87 LA 405, 88 LA 1292).

● Other arbitrators, however, hold that an employer must prove that the disciplined employee engaged in sexual harassment by "clear and convincing evidence" (*Vista Chemical Co.*, 104 LA 818, in which an arbitrator held that proof that an employer justly discharged a male employee who allegedly harassed a female employee must be by "clear and convincing evidence" and that arbitrators must impose a strict-scrutiny approach to charges of sexual harassment in connection with the "clear and convincing evidence" standard).

● Still other arbitrators require that an employer prove sexual harassment "beyond a reasonable doubt" (85 LA 11, 85 LA 15).

● In one case, an arbitrator justified his using the beyond-a-reasonable-doubt standard by saying that a charge of sexual harassment clearly involves an accusation of moral turpitude, carrying an enormous social stigma, and that it is not overly dramatic to say that in some cases an employee's life is on the line—a marriage, a parental relationship with children, a standing in a community, relationships with other employees, etc. In addition, once the employer has proved beyond a reasonable doubt that the employee is guilty of sexual harassment, the company must still establish that the discipline imposed is "just and sufficient" (*King Soopers Inc.*, 86 LA 254).

## Harassment of Nonemployees or While Off-Duty

Employees who harass customers or clients may be disciplined if the conduct adversely affects the employer's reputation and customer relations or damages the employee's effectiveness.

• A telephone repair technician was properly discharged for making obscene and harassing telephone calls to a customer, an arbitrator concluded, even though the employee was off-duty when the calls were made. Because of the nature of the company's business and the need it has for public confidence in the integrity of its repair personnel, the arbitrator concluded the employer "would not be responsible to the public" if it permitted the employee, in light of his misconduct, "to enter upon the premises of a customer to provide telephone service" (*Southern Bell Telephone & Telegraph Co.*, 75 LA 409).

• A deliveryman was properly discharged for making "sexual propositions" to customers to whom he delivered the employer's product, an arbitrator concluded. The deliveryman had been barred from making deliveries at several retail stores because of his behavior and had already been subjected to progressive discipline. The misconduct harmed the company's reputation and interfered with its business, the arbitrator pointed out, and had consequences for other employees. Because the deliveryman was barred from some stores, delivery route rotation was disrupted; other drivers complained of coolness from customers with whom they had always had good relations; and one driver was threatened by an outraged husband with a gun. "A delivery man is the company's representative," the arbitrator pointed out, and "has a special duty to be courteous and honorable in his dealings with customers" (*Nabisco Foods Co.*, 82 LA 1186).

• An arbitrator found that a sales representative's harassment of a female employee at a sales conference dinner constituted sexual harassment. A female employee alleged that a sales representative poked and eventually kissed her in trying to find out the room number of another woman. A second female employee alleged that earlier the sales representative had grabbed her buttocks and responded with obscenities when she asked him to leave her alone. The sales representative eventually went to the room of a third female employee, where he allegedly grabbed the woman's roommate, pulled her on top of him, and passed out on the bed. When the employer discharged the sales rep for sexual harassment, the union argued that the conduct occurred when the employee was off-duty. The employer maintained the dinner was a company-sponsored event and therefore work-related.

An arbitrator upheld the discharge, holding that the conference was held to further the employer's business interest and therefore the off-duty standards were not applicable. To permit lack of supervision to void a discharge would enable the offending employee to escape accountability for his or her own misconduct, the arbitrator reasoned (*Superior Coffee and Foods and Teamsters Local 848*, 103 LA 609).

### Conflicting Testimony

Sexual harassment cases often require an arbitrator to resolve conflicts in the testimony given by the alleged victim and the accused, and even within different statements made by the victim.

• An arbitrator upheld the suspension of a male employee accused of improperly touching a female employee, despite inconsistencies between the woman's oral and written accounts of the incident. Noting that the woman might have been so traumatized by the experience that her recollection of it was clouded, the arbitrator ruled that the inconsistencies in her versions of what happened did not undermine the basic truthfulness of her charges (*Fisher Foods Inc.*, 80 LA 133).

• An employee's false allegation of sexual harassment by her supervisor did not insulate her from punishment or make a valid case that she was fired in retaliation for making the claim, an arbitrator ruled. The worker, who had a poor record and had received numerous warnings about her lax attention to her job, had been overheard telling a co-worker that she was going to "get" her supervisor. She accused him of sexual harassment, but when the matter was investigated, there was unanimous praise for the man, who had never had any complaints brought against him. By contrast, the employee had a history of fighting, making racial slurs, and sleeping on the job. The company fired her for dishonesty, specifically for making the false allegations of sexual harassment, and the union objected, arguing that she believed she had been harassed and warning that firing someone for making a false statement on this issue would have a chilling effect on legitimate complaints of sexual harassment.

The arbitrator determined that even if that were the effect of the decision, it was taken for good reason, and the employee's termination was in no way retaliatory. Such dishonesty, he asserted, "is commonly regarded as a first-offense dischargeable violation." Furthermore, although the employer cited only the false statements as a reason for the discharge, the totality of the employee's work record, as well as her demeanor at the arbitration hearing, disqualified her "from continuing to work with others," the arbitrator concluded (*Mrs Baird's Bakeries Inc.*, 114 LA 59).

● An employee was properly discharged for embracing and kissing a co-worker, an arbitrator concluded, even though there were no witnesses and the two employees told completely different stories. The arbitrator found the disciplined employee "to be a thoroughly unbelievable witness," and thus accepted the victim's version of the incident. "Employees have the right to be safe from abusive actions and it is the duty and responsibility of the company to give them this protection and further, to discipline and even discharge those employees

whose misconduct justifies such a penalty," the arbitrator concluded (*Care Inns Inc.*, 81 LA 687).

## Delay in Filing Complaint As Bar to Arbitration

Arbitrators have ruled that delays in filing a sexual harassment complaint may not be a bar to arbitration.

● Even where the allegedly harassed employee failed to complain the first time the harassment occurred, she later left the employer, and the only remedy sought was that the "sexual remarks and verbal abuse stop." The arbitrator found that grounds for a grievance existed as long as the employee found the workplace hostile because of the actual sexual harassment or the threat of embarrassment. Moreover, the arbitrator said, public policy not only favors arbitrability as opposed to the forfeiture of rights, but also favors the resolution of sexual harassment complaints (*Burnett & Sons*, 102 LA 743).

● In another case, an arbitrator ruled that an employee's delay in filing a sexual harassment complaint should be attributed to "harmless error," because sexual harassment victims may not complain immediately as a result of the embarrassment, humiliation, and stigma attached to filing such a complaint—the underlying thinking that the harassed individual provoked or encouraged the improper conduct. The arbitrator reasoned the employee should not lose standing to make the complaint that resulted in the arbitration (*George Koch Sons*, 102 LA 737).

# Sleeping & Loafing

## OVERVIEW

Generally, an arbitrator will uphold an employee's discharge for sleeping on the job only if the sleeping is recurrent and/or there is some exacerbating factor (*Basin Electric Power Cooperative*, 91 LA 443; *Coca Cola Bottling Co.*, 111 LA 577). If, however, the employer has a work rule that makes sleeping on the job a firing offense or there is an established practice that makes it so, then arbitrators will usually sustain a termination based on only one incident (98 LA 183, 86 LA 430, 81 LA 1263, 77 LA 1143, 74 LA 115).

In addition, discharge for a first offense is generally regarded as justified if the employee's sleeping would create any danger for other workers, to persons in his or her care, or to the employer's equipment (81 LA 955, 76 LA 232, 76 LA 18, 73 LA 705).

Ultimately, however, the employer has a heavy burden to prove that the employee was in fact sleeping. An employer must not only prove that an employee was actually asleep (rather than just resting his or her eyes), but also must show that the employer's rule against sleeping has been applied fairly and consistently. Discrepancies in applying a no-sleeping-on-the-job rule will give the arbitrator reason to overturn a discharge (95 LA 452, 91 LA 30, 90 LA 1053, 88 LA 991, 64 LA 77, 61 LA 686, 27 LA 512, 27 LA 137, 19 LA 380, 14 LA 907).

In the opinion of one arbitrator, sleeping-on-the-job cases fall into three categories: (1) the worker who is ill or tired for a good reason and who involuntarily drops off while trying to work; (2) the worker who has been out whooping it up while off duty and who yields to the need for sleep during working hours; and (3) the worker who makes preparations, hides out, and goes to sleep as a regular practice. Employees in the last group deserve the severest discipline, the arbitrator advised.

## SUMMARY OF CASES

### Penalty for Sleeping

Generally arbitrators have held that where an employer has strictly enforced a no-sleeping rule, the discharge of a worker for violating it is fully justified, at least in principle. In the absence of a specific rule, arbitrators seem to choose a penalty after considering the degree of responsibility of the worker's job and the circumstances under which he or she was found asleep.

• In one case, a maintenance man was found asleep on a blanket in a remote section of the plant. His shoes were off and an alarm clock was set to wake him just before the end of his shift. His preparations for sleeping, together with the fact he had been moonlighting, suggested to the arbitrator that sacking out on the employer's time was a habit with him. The arbitrator concluded that his conduct put him into the class of offenders who, with premeditation, hide out to sleep; such behavior gives the employer much more leeway to terminate the employee for a first offense (*Collins Radio, Co.*, 30 LA 121).

***Discharge for first-time offense—***
Sleeping on the job long has been a dis-

chargeable first-time offense in a broad range of industries and employment situations. For example, one arbitrator ruled that an employer had just cause to discharge a long-term employee for sleeping on the job, even though the employee had a good service record, where the employer had issued a reasonable plant rule providing that a first-time offense of sleeping on the job constituted a dischargeable offense. The arbitrator reasoned that any employer has the right to expect that their employees stay awake while at work in order to perform the jobs for which they are paid (*Manley Brothers*, 105 LA 442).

• An arbitrator found that sleeping while hazardous work was in progress was grounds for firing an employee, even though it was the first time he had been disciplined for sleeping on the job (*PPG Industries*, 110 LA 372).

• An arbitrator decided that discharge was too severe a penalty for a worker who was not feeling well and was found sleeping when no work was available. The arbitrator distinguished between this instance and that of sleeping while an unattended machine was running, and thus reduced the penalty (*Nestle Co.* 45 LA 524; see also 94 LA 340).

## Sleeping During Break

Can a worker be disciplined for sleeping during lunch breaks or rest periods? The answer to this question may depend on whether the worker took steps to make sure that he would wake up before the break was over. In these types of cases, making preparation for a nap by setting an alarm clock is a good thing, an indicator that the employee has every intention of not overstepping the rules and only sleeping during his or her break.

• In one instance where an employee took such measures and had good intentions, his discharge was overruled. An employee usually ate at his workstation, but on a day when he had a headache, he told his group leader he was going to lie down in the rest room and asked the leader to come and get him in 15 to 20 minutes. After about 15 minutes, a foreman discovered him, and he was fired for sleeping on the job with an intent to deceive.

In light of all of the circumstances, an arbitrator decided the employee should be reinstated with back pay. Because he told the group leader where he was going, he obviously was not trying to hide anything. Moreover, he was entitled to a break and had not been away from the job more than the permissible length of time. Finally, his machine was not in operation when he left it so there was no risk of damage to the employer's products (*Kawneer Co.*, 30 LA 1002).

If, however, the circumstances show that a worker might have remained asleep throughout the rest of his shift, an arbitrator likely will uphold the disciplinary action taken by the employer.

• A three-day suspension as discipline for sleeping on the job was too harsh a penalty for an otherwise good worker, one arbitrator ruled. An employee was assigned to light duty because his doctor discovered that the man had rheumatoid arthritis. He generally worked independently while on these light-duty assignments, and one day, he worked through his scheduled break time and took his break later. After completing his assignments, the employee took a nap in the break room, was discovered, and later was suspended for three days because he did not have his supervisor's permission to go on break at that time. The union argued that the employee was sleeping on his break time and also asserted that the employee was taking medications that made him drowsy. The arbitrator noted that there were several mitigating factors that rendered the punishment too harsh: the employee, by choosing to sleep in the break room, was clearly not trying to hide (a worse offense than merely snoozing); the employee had been with the company for several years and had a good work history; and his sleeping posed no threat to other workers. The employee also was authorized to determine the order in which he performed his daily tasks, the arbitrator said, reducing the suspension to just one day (*AAA Plumbing Pottery Corp.*, 115 LA 351).

## Proof of Sleeping on Job

Can a worker be disciplined for sleeping on the job merely on the basis of impressions someone gets by observing him from a distance? Most arbitrators agree that there must be convincing evidence that the worker was asleep (83 LA 468, 81 LA 1009). As always employers need to carefully assess the information on which they base a disciplinary decision and not jump to conclusions.

• An employee had begun his assignment of holding the brake of an overhead crane during a grinding operation when a foreman and several other people walked up. Seeing the worker's head nodding and his eyes shut, the group concluded he was sleeping. Although the worker's foreman arrived 10 minutes after the grinding began and found the worker awake, the employer dished out a two-week suspension. The worker admitted he had been drowsy, but he said his eyes were shut only because they were smarting from the oil and brake fluid in the crane cab. The union contended that from the 25- or 30-foot distance from which the worker was observed, no one could tell whether he was really asleep. Finding discipline unjustified, he said the witnesses only assumed the worker was asleep, because they were not close enough to be sure (*John Deere Ottumwa Works*, 27 LA 572).

• A supervisor discovered an employee lying on a pile of plastic-covered bags on the roof of the plant, after the worker had been paged on a public address system twice and had failed to respond to the call. Although the worker explained that he was merely resting to relieve a toothache, he was nevertheless fired for sleeping on the job.

In overturning the discharge, the arbitrator ruled that the burden of proof was not met by the employer. Noting that the supervisor testified that the employee's eyes were open and he was lucid when he was found, the arbitrator concluded that there was no evidence that the employee had actually prepared the "bed" on which he was resting, leaving in doubt the "premeditated" nature of his action (*Costal Resin Co.*, 61 LA 686; see also 71 LA 1041).

## Mitigating Factors

In determining whether an employer's disciplinary penalty for sleeping on the job is warranted, arbitrators may consider mitigating factors including the employee's inadvertently or accidentally falling asleep, the employee's work record, or any medication or temporary physical discomfort that may have caused the worker to fall asleep (95 LA 1006, 91 LA 443, 86 LA 1096, 81 LA 1200, 77 LA 1200, 76 LA 643).

• An employee was discharged for sleeping on the job and for verbally abusing a supervisor who tried to awaken him. The employee thought the supervisor was a lower-level employee; however, after learning the identity of the supervisor the worker apologized for his behavior. Finding that the employee's conduct caused no harm and that he did not realize that he was insulting a supervisor, the arbitrator ruled that the employee's work record and lack of prior disciplinary action were sufficient reasons to warrant reinstatement (*Union Carbide Corp.*, 66 LA 702).

• An employee who had taken codeine for a toothache was hit in the groin by a valve arm he was polishing, and knocked to the floor. To relieve the pain, the worker laid down across some packing boxes in a corner of the shop. He was soon approached by a foreman who suspended him for sleeping on the job. The worker was later discharged.

In reversing the discharge, the arbitrator found that the employer's contention that the lights had been turned off in order for the employee to escape detection was at best doubtful, if not altogether false. The sleepless night the employee spent because of a toothache was considered a mitigating factor the arbitrator ruled, concluding that the foreman summarily suspended the worker without any investigation into his reasons for falling asleep (*Crown Cork and Seal Co.*, 64 LA 734).

• An employer properly discharged an employee for sleeping on the job even though it was caused by various medical problems, including obesity, an arbitrator decided, despite the fact that the worker did not intentionally go to asleep to avoid working. Noting that the presence of an employee who is asleep at work is not conducive to an employer's public image, the arbitrator pointed out that an employer had the right to expect the employee to present himself "fit for work." Finding that the employer attempted rehabilitative measures and progressive discipline to correct the employee's behavior, the arbitrator concluded that under the circumstances discharge was warranted (*City of Iowa City*, 72 LA 1006).

**Sleep apnea**—Arbitrators are split as to whether a diagnosis of sleep apnea should mitigate an employee's discharge for sleeping while at work. One arbitrator ruled that a post-discharge diagnosis of sleep apnea was not mitigating, whereas another arbitrator ordered an employee with the sleep disorder reinstated after he was terminated for sleeping, even though the worker had not followed recommended treatment.

• After several incidents of an employee's apparently dozing off while at work, including one in which his error caused a power blackout, a power-facility employee was counseled and agreed to be examined by a neurologist chosen by the employer. No special medical problems were detected but he was told to contact the neurologist if his sleep problems persisted. Based on the neurologist's report, the employer notified the employee that further incidents could lead to termination.

The employee was subsequently discharged after he was observed falling asleep on three occasions. The employee filed a grievance after a post-discharge diagnosis of sleep apnea. The union contended the employee's misconduct was caused by a medical condition (misdiagnosed by the employer physician) and was involuntary. The employer maintained that the discharge was for just cause, noting that the employee knew of work rules on inattentiveness and that his job was in jeopardy, yet he declined offers of help and failed to seek medical evalua-

tion of his condition until after he was fired.

The arbitrator found that, despite the post-discharge diagnosis of sleep apnea, the employee's discharge was for just cause given the nature of his job. The arbitrator noted that the union failed to show that it was the employer's—and not the employee's—responsibility to determine the cause of his problems and the worker did not seek medical help until after he was terminated. The employee was at fault, the arbitrator concluded, because, contrary to the doctor's instructions, he had failed to keep the neurologist informed of any recurrences of his problem (*Texas Utilities Electric Co. Production Div.*, 103 LA 152).

• In another ruling, an arbitrator ordered a plant cook who had been discharged for falling asleep during a break reinstated, despite an employer rule against sleeping on the job. The employee had been diagnosed with sleep apnea but had not followed recommended treatment to control the sleep disorder, the arbitrator noted; however, his conduct had not harmed the employer (*EG & G Mound Applied Technologies*, 102 LA 60).

**Last-chance agreement**—An employee found sleeping on duty was properly discharged, an arbitrator ruled, despite the fact that his *Weingarten* rights were violated, because he had signed a last-chance agreement stating that next incident of sleeping on the job would result in his discharge (*Maui Pineapple Co.*, 86 LA 907).

## Aggravating Factors

Just as employers should take into account any mitigating factors in crafting a penalty, they may also look to exacerbating factors for "ammunition" in selecting a harsher punishment.

• In one case, an arbitrator decided that an employer had just cause to fire an employee for a first offense of sleeping on the job. When a health care worker at a 14-bed residential treatment center that specialized in treating depressed and schizophrenic patients was found sleeping in a lounge chair in the center's secluded, darkened living room, the employee was fired for violating a company rule against on-the-job snoozing. The union asserted that this first offense did not warrant such a final punishment. The arbitrator noted that all cases of sleeping on the job are not equal; in this instance, the employee's misconduct should be elevated to a "much higher level" because his work was in a mental health facility where many patients were at high risk of harming themselves or others. Given this heightened standard, the employer was free to dispense with progressive discipline (*Horizons of Michigan*, 115 LA 1672).

● Another arbitrator held that a health care facility employee's first offense of sleeping on duty was serious enough to warrant discharge, noting that the employer did not abuse its discretion under the parties' contract or act arbitrarily when it interpreted the contract to provide that sleeping on the job carried with it a mandatory penalty of discharge (*Central Illinois Public Service Co.*, 105 LA 372).

**Penalty for Loafing**

Is discharge too severe a penalty for the first offense of loafing on the job?

Although an employer may feel that once employees are found guilty of loafing, they have lost their value as an employee, an arbitrator may reduce a discharge penalty and give the employee another chance.

● An employer's charges against an employee were that he loafed on the job and as a result of his loafing, his work area was not cleaned properly, and he neglected to tend to a bin, which overflowed and caused economic losses to the employer. The employer stated it had previously realized that he was deficient in his duties and had reinstructed him. When he failed again he was discharged.

The employee was ordered reinstated with back wages, less two weeks' pay for a disciplinary layoff. The arbitrator found that the employer had reinstructed the employee in his duties but had not specifically warned him that his job was at risk at the time of that reinstruction, as was customary. The arbitrator also found that the irregularities complained of were no greater than those of other employees who had been reprimanded or laid off but not discharged (*International Minerals & Chemical Corp.*, 4 LA 127).

# Strike-Related Activities

## OVERVIEW

Work stoppages may present a wide range of disciplinary situations, including the following.

*Unlawful job actions, such as contractually prohibited slowdowns or wildcat strikes*—In such circumstances, discipline is warranted by the sole fact of the walkout or slowdown and may be applied either to all participants or only to those who initiated or prolonged the job action (102 LA 1115, 97 LA 1006, 96 LA 294, 93 LA 1097, 90 LA 24, 89 LA 1226, 89 LA 1257, 89 LA 880).

*Offenses committed during an authorized strike*—Although discipline may not be invoked for a lawful work stoppage, any misconduct that occurs during the walkout is grounds for punishment, provided that there is concrete evidence to support the charges and absent any mitigating factors (94 LA 929, 90 LA 969, 90 LA 502, 89 LA 126, 87 LA 394, 87 LA 188).

*Misconduct following a settlement*—Hostility engendered during a strike may continue after the return to work, most frequently in the form of intimidating behavior toward strikebreakers. Although many arbitrators agree that such misconduct justifies discipline, others hold that a lesser punishment than would be exacted for similar behavior under normal circumstances is most appropriate, given that "human emotions do not always respond to command."

The following discussion examines in greater detail how arbitrators view these types of situations and the factors they consider in weighing discipline imposed for strike activities.

## SUMMARY OF CASES

### Unlawful Work Stoppages & Slowdowns

In cases of work slowdowns, arbitrators tend to uphold discipline even though, as one arbitrator noted, the employer may not be able to present "direct evidence and proof of concerted activity." In such situations, the arbitrator stressed, "the employer is required only to establish a prima facie case based on circumstantial evidence which would lead the reasonable person to conclude that the employees' action were more probably concerted." At that point, "the burden of coming forward with evidence to rebut such prima facie presumption shifts to each employee because each employee would be best able to produce substanti-

ating or corroborating evidence to support any contrary contention."

• In one case, the arbitrator decided that management had established a probable case for its allegations that a group of 21 employees was involved in an unlawful work stoppage when none of the workers could provide any alternative explanation for failing to report for work on the day in question. Accordingly, he concluded, the employer was justified in issuing disciplinary layoffs (*Longview Fibre Co.*, 69 LA 1182).

• Three-day suspensions were appropriately levied against employees who engaged in a group "sick-out," another arbitrator held, precisely because the workers could not support their claims of illness with medical certificates. Although the employees argued that doctors' statements properly were required only in case of an extended illness, the arbitrator ruled that management was within its rights to demand the documentation and impose discipline for lack thereof because it legitimately suspected the workers of "abusing the sick leave privilege" (*Barbers Point Federal Credit Union*, 76 LA 624).

● A worker was properly discharged for limiting her production, an arbitrator decided, finding that her work record and working conditions indicated that the decline in production was caused by a "deliberate slowdown." Stressing that management had imposed the ultimate penalty of discharge only as a last step in a series of progressive disciplinary measures, the arbitrator rejected the worker's claim that her 33 years of service militated against discharge. Although agreeing that "long service with a good record weighs heavily in favor of an embattled employee," the arbitrator concluded that, nonetheless, "no union, company, or arbitrator can always and forever shield an employee from a contractual result of an act of pure folly in a context where the ultimate result was known or should have been known to the individual employee" (*Martinsburg Mills Inc.*, 48 LA 1224).

● Long service has, however, led other arbitrators to overturn discharge for work slowdowns. For example, citing the worker's extensive record of satisfactory performance, one arbitrator converted a dismissal for a deliberate slowdown to a four-week layoff (*Reed Roller Bit Co.*, 29 LA 604; see also *Armour & Co.* 8 LA 1).

*Honoring picket line*—Refusing to cross a picket line also may be grounds for discipline where such action leads to a violation of contract provisions banning interference with work performance or operations.

● Based on the no-strike clause of its collective bargaining agreement, an employer was justified in suspending workers who refused to cross another union's peaceful picket line to perform their duties, an arbitrator decided.

Although the employees argued that the no-strike agreement did not apply, the arbitrator ruled that their refusal to perform their duties was, in fact, a work stoppage in violation of the contract provision that specifically stated there would be "no strike, work stoppage, slowdown, or any other interference with or impeding of work." By agreeing to this provision, the employees had waived their statutory rights to refuse to cross a picket line, the arbitrator found, concluding that their actions warranted two-day suspensions (*Monongahela Power Co.*, 64 LA 1210).

● Another arbitrator held that management properly disciplined its inspectors for reporting late to their assignments because they had honored an informational picket line. The parties' bargaining agreement specified that employees were "responsible for not taking sides or personally becoming involved in an industrial dispute between the management and the employees of the official establishment or plant to which they are assigned." Rather, in such cases they were to report to work "as scheduled" unless "otherwise directed by their supervisor."

There was "no question" that the employees were aware of both the contract provision and their assignments yet "voluntarily" chose to honor the picket line and thus report late, the arbitrator declared, finding the employees "guilty as charged." As for the propriety of the discipline, the penalty imposed was a one-day suspension for "failure to follow instruction to report as scheduled," the arbitrator noted, stressing that "had the agency so desired, the charge could have been that of engaging in an unlawful activity—a strike—with the statutory penalty of discharge." When "weighed against the offense committed," the arbitrator concluded, the penalty was not too severe (*U.S. Dept. of Agriculture*, 75 LA 36).

● Despite the existence of a no-strike/no-slowdown agreement, an arbitrator reinstated a worker discharged for honoring a picket line set up by another union at the worksite. The controlling factor in this case was a second contract provision that barred disciplinary action against an employee who "refuses to go through or work behind any primary picket line, including primary picket lines at the company's place of business." Finding that the picket line was an extension of one set up at the company's wholly owned subsidiary and thus was properly classified as a "primary" line, the arbitrator ruled that the employee's actions were protected from reprisal (*Coca Cola Bottling Co.*, 72 LA 73; see also 89 LA 1227, 84 LA 5, 72 LA 706, 69 LA 1024).

**Wildcat strikes**—Wildcat strikes are grounds for severe discipline, arbitrators overwhelmingly agree, absent any indication that the workers were prevented from reporting to the job through "duress, coercion, intimidation, or the like." Declaring that "willing participation in a work stoppage is among the most heinous of industrial offenses," one arbitrator stressed that dismissal in such circumstances would not be "too severe" a penalty or one that would "shock the conscience" of an arbitrator.

Accordingly, that arbitrator ruled that management was justified in dismissing 132 workers who refused to end a wildcat strike in the face of union officials' instruction to return to the job. Finding no evidence that any of the employees were prevented from showing up for work, the arbitrator concluded that each thus was "an employee responsible" for the unauthorized strike as defined under the contract and appropriately subject to the agreement's provision authorizing discharge for unlawful work stoppages (*American Air Filter Co.*, 47 LA 129).

● For practical purposes, however, most employers do not go to the extreme of discharging all wildcat strikers. As one arbitrator explained, "a company that is the victim of an unlawful strike cannot be expected to 'cut off its nose to spite its face' by firing all participants" (*Charles Mundt Sons*, 46 LA 982).

● Most arbitration cases dealing with wildcat strikes involve selective discipline, with the issue under debate whether an employer properly could and did discipline only certain strikers or

whether in doing so it acted in an arbitrary, capricious, or discriminatory manner. Especially where the employer has selectively applied the discharge penalty, some arbitrators may require clear proof that the workers thus disciplined deserved being singled out because they were either instigators of unlawful activity or at least more active in it than other employees. Absent such evidence, the dismissals may be overturned (67 LA 1250, 61 LA 148).

● Other arbitrators do not set such strict "rules" and will uphold the propriety of selective discipline under a wider range of circumstances (93 LA 1097, 77 LA 505, 66 LA 626, 63 LA 677, 61 LA 896, 55 LA 1159, 53 LA 75, 53 LA 45).

● "No agreement provision and no obligation to justice compels the company to discipline in every case of employee misconduct," one arbitrator declared. "Inequality of treatment in disciplinary matters does not amount to unjust discrimination if there are rational grounds for distinguishing between those to be disciplined and those not to be disciplined," the arbitrator maintained, stressing that "it is only where the grounds for distinction are irrational, arbitrary, or whimsical that disciplining of some employees and not others may be looked upon as unjust and discriminatory" (*Ford Motor Co.*, 41 LA 609).

● Management properly charged all wildcat strikers with five absences each under its absence control program, regardless of the actual amount of time an individual worker spent off the job and despite the union's contention that disciplinary measures should be governed by the parties' no-strike agreement rather than the absenteeism program. Both the "literal application of the terms" of the absentee policy and a strict assessment of discipline for violating the no-strike clause "would have resulted in the termination of the majority" of its employees, management pointed out, with the result that the organization would have suffered the "same detrimental effect on production as the unauthorized work stoppage itself."

Finding it a "fundamental prerogative of management to select the form and extent of disciplinary action as long as it is not specifically restricted from doing so by the agreement, as long as cause is demonstrated, and as long as equal treatment is accorded," the arbitrator agreed with the employer that it had "discretion to apply the absentee policy as it chooses in the context of a wildcat strike, whether the application be literal, something less stringent than literal application, or no application at all" (*Kennecott Copper Corp.*, 77 LA 505).

● In another case, however, management erred in discharging four of 26 wildcat strikers. Although acknowledging the employer's right of discretionary punishment in such cases, the arbitrator pointed out that the discipline should be applied to a "representative group" rather than be levied in a completely arbitrary manner. If the company had conducted a thorough investigation, the arbitrator noted, it would have found that other employees had greater responsibility for the walkout and were more deserving of discipline (*Homer Laughlin China Co.*, 67 LA 1250).

## Use of Selective Discipline

***Instigation of work stoppage or slowdown***—The instigation of a work stoppage/slowdown by an employee, as noted above, generally is regarded as one justification for the application of selective discipline.

● Holding that the initiators of a walkout bear a heavier responsibility for the misconduct than other strikers, an arbitrator sustained management's move to suspend only the first employees to leave work. The arbitrator found that the selective discipline was further justified in that the company could not have given all 800 workers disciplinary layoffs without shutting down the plant (*Goodyear Atomic Corp.*, 27 LA 321).

● Three employees were properly discharged for attempting to prevent co-workers from reporting to the job and inciting a wildcat strike to protest what they considered to be prior unjust discipline, an arbitrator ruled. Rejecting the employees' contention that the stoppage was justified because management had failed to respond to their legitimate grievances, the arbitrator upheld the employer's argument that the workers had flagrantly violated the contract. Stressing that one of the most serious and disruptive acts an employee can perform is to lead a wildcat strike, the arbitrator concluded that in inciting the unlawful activity, the workers knew they had embarked on a dangerous course of action (*National Mine Service Co.*, 69 LA 966; see also *Warner & Swasey Co.*, 65 LA 709).

● Another arbitrator ruled that a worker was properly dismissed for causing an unauthorized work stoppage following a dispute with his supervisor. Any disagreement "with company policy or the actions of his supervisors" should have been pursued "through the grievance procedure," the arbitrator ruled, declaring that an employee who "disregards the contractual dispute settlement mechanisms and engages in self-help subverts the fundamental nature of the collective bargaining relationship." Because the worker "knowingly caused a work stoppage" in violation of the contract, the arbitrator concluded, the discharge was warranted (*Traverse City Iron Works*, 76 LA 21).

● An arbitrator held that an employer had just cause to discharge a union steward for violating a collective bargaining agreement's no-strike provisions, despite his contention that he had not engaged in the work stoppage. The arbitrator ruled that the steward clearly had assumed the leadership role in the work stoppage by speaking to union members on the day of the event; a claim of being discriminated against, or singled out, because of his union membership was not supported; approximately 18 co-workers acted with him in refusing to perform the assigned work until required OSHA certificates were posted; and his entire course of conduct indicated an intent to obstruct the normal operations rather than to raise legitimate safety concerns (*National Maintenance & Repair Inc.*, 101 LA 1115).

● Yet another arbitrator reinstated five workers who were discharged for organizing an unlawful strike because the contract's no-strike clause failed to specify, and management had not warned them that they could be dismissed for their actions. Besides failing to make clear the range of discipline possible, management officials "stood or sat idly by while employees around them argued about walking out" and some supervisors even "actively encouraged the walkout" (*Superior Switchboard & Devices Division*, 75 LA 1107; see also 96 LA 294).

● Where the evidence did not support management's allegations that an employee had attempted to incite a walkout, an arbitrator ordered the worker's reinstatement. Not only was the crewman who made the accusations an unreliable witness, the arbitrator pointed out, but also there were no signs of job desertion to corroborate the story (*Payne & Keller Inc.*, 70 LA 114).

*Union leadership*—Union leadership may be a basis for selective discipline in cases where union officials have not carried out their responsibility of promoting adherence to a contract's no-strike/no-slowdown clause. Arbitrators consistently have held union leaders to a higher standard of responsibility than the rank-and-file in such cases. "A shop steward's duty in the face of an unauthorized work stoppage is well settled," an arbitrator declared, explaining that "not only should he make a determined effort to prevent the stoppage before it begins, but upon its development must actively and unequivocally attempt to bring an end of the stoppage at the earliest possible moment." The arbitrator added that "only in this way can the steward comply with his responsibility to uphold the integrity of the contract and its orderly processes for dispute settlement" (*United Parcel Service Inc.*, 47 LA 1100).

● Other arbitrators similarly have stressed that union officials have "an especial obligation to refrain from committing overt acts designed to encourage others to walk out or stay out." Pointing out that such officials have been "chosen to be custodians of the agreement, guardians of its rights, and monitors of its obligations within the prescribed procedures," one arbitrator concluded that

"hence, if they engage in overt acts which flout the agreement's most solemn obligations, they engage in a specific class of acts which set them apart from the rank and file" (*Mack Trucks*, 41 LA 1240).

● Declaring that union officials "must give more than 'lip service' to their obligation" to prevent unlawful work stoppages, an arbitrator ruled that an employer properly imposed more severe discipline on union delegates than on rank-and-file workers for participating in a stoppage. The contract specified that "in the event of an unauthorized slowdown, boycott of overtime, or any other form of strike," union officials were to "immediately notify participating employees that the conduct is in violation of the agreement" and "instruct participating members to resume normal operations at once."

Nevertheless, the arbitrator found, the union delegates not only failed to honor this pledge but even went so far as to encourage the members in their recalcitrance by actively taking part in the work stoppage. Rejecting the delegates' contention that complying with the contract provision would have meant acting "as double agents," the arbitrator pointed out that one "can't have his cake and eat it too." Having accepted the honor of the titled delegate position and the accompanying leadership, the arbitrator concluded, the officials "must accept the responsibilities of the position" (*New Jersey Bell Telephone Co.*, 77 LA 1038; see also 68 LA 618, 49 LA 27, 43 LA 608, 41 LA 732).

● On the other hand, where union officials have attempted to prevent or halt a work stoppage without success or where they are not contractually bound to take such affirmative action, arbitrators have overturned discipline selectively levied against them (64 LA 1210, 64 LA 425, 55 LA 1159).

● An employer improperly suspended a union steward for demonstrating "negative leadership" by standing outside the plant gate rather than reporting for work during an unlawful job action, an arbitrator decided. Although the steward came to the plant on all three days of the unlawful strike, he went home after being unable to get through the blocked entrance, the arbitrator found. Observing that the steward had not carried a picket sign and had never before been disciplined during his eight years of employment, much less involved in an unlawful strike, the arbitrator concluded that the charges against him were "arbitrary and unjust" (*Powermatic/Houdaille Inc.*, 65 LA 1245).

● A union official who eventually tried to halt a wildcat strike was improperly discharged, an arbitrator decided. In light of the official's initial participation in the unlawful action, the arbitrator decided, a one-year probation was in order (*Cyclops Corp.*, 45 LA 560; *Quanex*, 73 LA 9).

● An arbitrator held that a union did not engage in an unlawful work stoppage when 23 employees refused to work in response to confusion over an employer's newly published policy change. The arbitrator ruled that there was no evidence of employee concerted activity and it was not clear that employees had acted with one mind. Also, the arbitrator pointed out that there was neither a classic sit-down strike nor an absolute refusal to work by all employees (*Virgin Island Telephone Corp.*, 101 LA 273).

## Misconduct During Lawful Strikes

Even where a work stoppage is lawful, employees may be justifiably disciplined for misconduct committed in association with the strike. Recognizing that the term "misconduct" covers a multitude of offenses, from taunting strikebreakers to assaulting supervisors, several arbitrators have outlined general criteria by which the propriety of discipline may be judged. In addition to deciding whether the evidence is sufficient to support the allegations, arbitrators will pose such questions as the following.

● "What is the extent of participation? In any mob situation the degree of involvement of the individual in any action is important."

● "What was the nature of the violence? This has both quantitative and qualitative aspects. Participation in several incidents is more serious than in only one. Some actions are more reprehensible than others. Shouting insults and shoving are of a different order from striking a person."

● "Was the violence provoked? To the extent that the violence is retaliatory and defensive, it is less culpable than if undertaken as an act of aggression."

● "Was the violence premeditated or undertaken on the spur of the moment? Premeditated violence is the more inexcusable."

● "What will be the impact of the punishment? Discharge is more of a penalty for an old man than a young one; for a long service employee than a short service employee."

● "Was the disciplinary action discriminatory? A company is under some obligation to treat persons similarly situated in a comparable, although not necessarily identical, manner (*Cudahy Packing Co.*, 11 LA 1138).

Expanding on these guidelines, another arbitrator has determined that reviews of strike misconduct also should be influenced by the following considerations.

● "How serious was the offense in terms of injury to persons or damage to property?"

● "Were remedies at law available and were they involved?"

● "Was the conduct destructive of good employee-employer relations?"

● "Was the conduct destructive of good community relations?"

● "Will the discipline restore good relations, or is it the result of a spirit of vindictiveness?"

● "Was the conduct such that the employee could be reabsorbed into the work force" (*J.R. Simplot Co.*, 64 LA 1061)?

● A striking employee who verbally and physically abused a supervisor at a local social club was justifiably discharged, an arbitrator ruled. The employee's behavior was particularly blameworthy in that the incident occurred away from the picket line and thus was not the result of "inflamed group passions," the arbitrator found. Reinstating the worker in the face of the damage to the employer-employee relationship, the arbitrator concluded, would be a "visible and highly public vindication" of the abusive behavior (*General Telephone Co. of Kentucky*, 69 LA 351; 92 LA 578).

● An employer was justified in discharging a picketing striker for "streaking," "mooning," and using racial slurs against replacements, under a strike settlement agreement authorizing dismissal only for picket-line misconduct "that would be considered serious under normal working conditions." The arbitrator rejected the worker's arguments that even if he were guilty of the allegations, such behavior was not so serious as to warrant discharge. Rather, finding that "any one of these three actions would constitute misconduct if engaged in within a plant operating normally," the arbitrator specified that "any would create a major disturbance, interrupt production, upset plant discipline, and bring opprobrium to the company." Furthermore, while the use of racial epithets alone "might or might not be considered serious enough to warrant immediate discharge within a plant," the arbitrator stressed, "occurring on a picket line such language can only be calculated to injure the company, its standing in the community, and to reflect discredit upon the public relations image of the company and union alike" (*H & L Tooth Co.*, 66 LA 1020).

● An employer had just cause to fire a striker who threw screws at company vehicles, even though his discharge letter mentioned only "cans and rocks," not screws, said one arbitrator. When a "general helper" at a metals plant walked the picket line with fellow union members, he was seen by a hired guard "dropping screws" onto an exit driveway in front of an 18-wheel truck leaving the plant. Days later, a manager took photos of the strikers, which were shown to the guard, who identified the employee as the striker he saw depositing screws. Weeks later, the company fired the employee for "throwing cans and rocks at outbound vehicles, which endangered drivers and the public." The union challenged both the letter and the guard's testimony. Although the union focused on the fact that the compa-

ny's letter made "no mention" of screws, but only "cans and rocks," the arbitrator said the case hinged on the credibility of those involved and upheld the penalty meted out by the employer (*Merchants Metals Inc.*, 117 LA 1).

● An arbitrator upheld an employer's discharge of a strike shift leader who on four occasions taunted and threatened drivers who were crossing a picket line and then repeatedly lied about his misconduct, even though the incidents constituted only 15 minutes of a three-year strike (*Bayou Steel Corp.*, 108 LA 513).

● A striking employee was, however, improperly discharged for tire-slashing because management failed to "continue and complete a comprehensive investigation of the matter sufficient to establish the employee's culpability." Although "circumstantial" evidence suggested that the worker may have been responsible for the damage, it did not meet the "burden of proof" standard for upholding the dismissal, the arbitrator concluded (*Collins Foods International Inc.*, 77 LA 483; see also *McDonnell Douglas Astronautics Co.*, 74 LA 726).

***Mitigating factors***—Mitigating factors also may lead an arbitrator to reinstate a worker discharged for picket line misconduct.

● Citing a "satisfactory" work history, one arbitrator reduced to a six-month suspension the termination penalty levied against a worker for throwing ball bearings through the window of a guard house during a strike. Furthermore, although the company argued that the employee was a "rabble rouser" whose return to the workforce could "create the possibility of discord and hostility rather than enhance a peaceful, working relationship," the arbitrator found no evidence "of prior acts of hostility toward the company nor damage to company property that would tend to justify the apprehension of the company were he to be reabsorbed into the workforce." Management's "stated objective for the disciplinary action"—deterrence of future such incidents—could be better accomplished "by a lengthy suspension without pay and accompanied by a stern reprimand," the arbitrator concluded (*Charter International Oil Co.*, 75 LA 929).

• Finding that the misconduct was not so "grave" as to prevent the employees' being "reabsorbed into the workforce," an arbitrator reduced to lengthy suspensions the discharges imposed on two employees for strike offenses. The first employee, who threatened a contractor performing work at a picket site, deserved a four-month disciplinary layoff, the arbitrator decided, while the second, who kicked in the side panel of a company pick-up truck, warranted a five-month suspension (*General Telephone Co. of Kentucky*, 69 LA 351).

• An employer that chooses to continue to operate its plant during a strike, regardless of the fact that such action historically invites violence, may not be justified in discharging employees for picket line misconduct, according to some arbitrators. In two similar cases, arbitrators reduced dismissals to disciplinary layoffs, based on the theory that a company that elects to "continue operations and engage replacements" during a strike "cannot escape a share of responsibility for the militancy and aggressiveness of the strikers." Violence usually occurs only when management decides to utilize strategies of replacing striking workers and/or deploying armed guards, one arbitrator noted, deciding that by taking on the historical "inevitability" of violence in pursuing such options, an employer is guilty of "contributory negligence" that militates against outright dismissal (*Washington Scientific Industries Inc.*, 67 LA 1004 and *J.R. Simplot Co.*, 64 LA 1061).

## Post-Strike Misconduct

"Strikes are not fought," one arbitrator has pointed out, "without leaving a residue of bitterness and defeat, or arrogance and pride, in their participants." Frequently these emotions take shape in acts of misconduct by returning workers directed at those individuals who crossed the picket line during the strike—management officials, outside suppliers, and, especially, new employees taken on as replacements. Particularly where returning

strikers are warned against harboring grudges, arbitrators are likely to agree that hostile behavior justifies disciplinary action.

Unless the offense is of an extremely serious nature, however, arbitrators generally will not sustain a discharge for post-strike misconduct, deciding, rather, that a disciplinary layoff is more appropriate punishment. The reasoning underlying many arbitral decisions in these cases is similar to that applied to cases involving misconduct that occurs during strikes and work slowdowns.

• "By continuing its operations during a bitter and acrimonious strike, and settling on terms extremely disadvantageous to the union, the company encouraged hostility and bitterness among its employees, and cannot complain if, in the first 10 days following defeat, some of their anger spilled over, embarrassing several who supported it." With this assertion, an arbitrator reduced to a disciplinary warning the discharge penalty management had levied against a flight attendant for spilling food and beverages on and refusing to utilize the services of other employees who had worked during a strike. Although he noted the attendant's "breach of professional courtesy of self-control," the arbitrator declared that the slow process of building up post-strike cooperation "is not aided by humiliation, or by a unilateral imposition of terms and conditions of employment." The "spirit" of the back-to-work agreement, which "indicated an intention to forgive strike-related actions and restrict antagonisms to the past," should be applied here, the arbitrator stressed, concluding that in the "absence of prior discipline, and given the nature of the circumstances," punishment should be "minor" (*Continental Airlines*, 77 LA 368).

• Although "some form of discipline" was warranted, discharge was too severe for a returning striker who directed abusive language toward new hires taken on as strike replacements, another arbitrator ruled. Upon returning from a six-month strike, the workers repeatedly referred to the new-hires as "scabs" and made threatening remarks to them. Management "counseled" the worker for his abusive language but took no action until the employee arrived at work one day wearing a T-shirt with a caption that made obscene reference to the strike breakers. Citing this latest incident in an intimidating "course of conduct," the employer discharged the worker. The arbitrator, however, reduced the penalty on the grounds that " 'counseling' does not suffice for disciplinary action intended to correct the misconduct and apprise the employee of the seriousness of his actions." Absent explicit warning that discharge would result if the employee continued to intimidate the new hires, the arbitrator concluded, suspension was a more appropriate discipline (*Chromalloy American Corp.*, 72 LA 838).

● An employer was justified in disciplining an employee for making inflammatory remarks immediately following a strike, an arbitrator decided. During the month-long work stoppage, the employer's trucks were operated by drivers from another company. On the day following strike settlement, one of the drivers was having difficulty starting a truck when an employee laughed and said he hoped the truck blew up. Later, management found that the truck would not start because the gas tank had been filled with water. Although there was no evidence connecting the worker to the sabotage, management issued him a five-day suspension for making a serious threat at a time when tension was still "high."

Agreeing that the statement was indeed "inflammatory and threatening," the arbitrator pointed out that in making such comments on the first day back at work, the employee naturally stirred up the driver's concern and apprehension. Although the comment was "further magnified by the fact that an act of sabotage had taken place," the arbitrator continued, the worker should be disciplined only for the totality of his "actual involvement" in the post-strike misconduct. Ruling that the five-day suspension was excessive in light of the just cause standard, the arbitrator ordered that the discipline be reduced to a two-day layoff (*Emery Industries Inc.*, 72 LA 110).

● Five employees who engaged in post-strike "staring" tactics against replacement workers were properly suspended, an arbitrator decided, because the employees had been sufficiently warned about and directed to stop the harassment (*La Crosse Telephone Corp.*, 65 LA 1077).

# Workplace Violence

## ———————— OVERVIEW ————————

Tensions, misunderstandings, and jealousies can strain relationships in the workplace and lead to heated disputes and fights among the employees or between them and their supervisors. Because these disturbances can destroy workplace harmony and impair efficiency, management frequently tries to forestall such behavior, either through disciplinary measures or other, less punitive actions (e.g., mediation, peer counseling, etc.).

Stories about workers who have injured or killed co-workers or supervisors are are nothing new, but the perceived increase in the frequency of such incidents has prompted employers to take the threat of workplace violence seriously, leading some of them to institute so-called "zero-tolerance" policies. Some of these policies are geared toward preventing actual mayhem by making even the threat of violence a dischargeable offense. Others, however, target a variety of behaviors, some of which do not actually involve physical violence, but rather are believed to lead to a general lack of civility that makes violence less shocking and hence, possibly more prevalent. Those broader policies aim to put a stop to all manner of misconduct, including general harassment, bullying, and overall "uncivil" behavior. In recent years, arbitrators have been seeing more and more cases that spring from violations of these zero-tolerance policies (see below for details).

In cases involving fighting or aggressive misconduct, arbitrators generally agree that, absent mitigating circumstances, management has the right to invoke disciplinary penalties, including discharge, in order to minimize workplace disruptions (97 LA 356, 94 LA 773, 94 LA 767, 94 LA 610, 88 LA 418).

Where fighting occurs, arbitrators have reduced discharges to less drastic penalties when it is shown that the violence was provoked. In such cases, one arbitrator said, an employer reasonably could discharge the employee who provoked the assault without discharging the one who finally resorted to violence to protect himself (*Goodyear Decatur Mills*, 12 LA 682; see also 98 LA 1).

## ———————— SUMMARY OF CASES ————————

### Considering All Factors

Fights on the job are a serious matter, one arbitrator asserted, emphasizing that, in order for a discharge to satisfy the "just cause" requirements, all relevant factors surrounding the fight must be considered (*Harshaw Chemical Co.*, 46 LA 248; see also 92 LA 871).

In determining the propriety of discipline meted out to employees involved in fighting, arbitrators usually consider the following:

- the length of service and the overall work record of the employee (*Dorsey Trailers Inc.*, 60 LA 1305; see also 102 LA 377, 93 LA 1277);

- whether the employee's misconduct consisted of a single, thoughtless blow or a series of deliberate acts

(*American Motors Corp.*, 51 LA 945; see also 102 LA 377);

- whether the blow was struck with a dangerous instrument, a clenched fist, or an open hand, etc. (*Polysar Inc.*, 91 LA 482, 81 LA 569, 66 LA 1005, 60 LA 917);
- the effect of the employee's "breach of shop etiquette" on the morale, safety, and work habits of other employees (*C-E Building Products Inc.*, 60 LA 506);
- the presence or absence of mitigating factors, such as provocation (*Bethlehem Structural Products Corp.*, 105 LA 205; see also *Boeing Co.*, 51 LA 1153, 76 LA 1249, 76 LA 244), discrimination, or a failure by management to take preventive action (*Zinsco Electrical Products*, 65 LA 487); remorse shown by the grievant (*Clow Water Systems Co.*, 102 LA 377), or the employees' good work/attendance records, contributions to plant operations, lack of disciplinary problems (*Zeon Chemicals Kentucky*, 105 LA 648); and
- whether the incident indicated that the employee has vicious tendencies, is seriously emotionally unstable, or has dangerous propensities toward such conduct (*Pioneer Rubber Co.*, 53 LA 283; see also 75 LA 12).

## Zero-Tolerance Policies

In recent years, some companies have determined that the only way to stem an apparent increase in workplace violence is to make any kind of fighting a dischargeable offense.

- An employer justifiably fired an employee for fighting with a co-worker, a panel of arbitrators found. The 12-year employee, a clerk for an airlines, got into an argument with a co-worker. When he approached the co-worker later in the day, the argument deteriorated into fisticuffs. Because fighting was cause for immediate discharge, the employee was fired, but the union asserted that he was only defending himself from an assault, a statement that was refuted by numerous witnesses. The company had an "obligation to maintain a safe workplace" and was justified in punishing fighting with severe discipline or discharge, the panel

said. Finding that the evidence clearly showed the employee's misconduct and knowledge of the zero-tolerance policy, the panel upheld the discharge (*American Airlines Inc.*, 116 LA 161).

- An employee's threatening a co-worker and acting out in self-destructive ways justified an employer's firing him under its zero-tolerance policy. The employee, who had been with the company for nine years, threatened a colleague who refused to move from a seat in the break room at a table where the employee had left his drink. He took off toward his work area, slammed his fist into a nearby tool locker, and had to seek first aid when his hand swelled. Shortly thereafter, other maintenance employees told their supervisors that they felt unsafe because of the man's violent outburst. The company fired the employee, claiming he had violated its zero-tolerance policy on violence. The union fought the discharge, claiming the employer's policy did not mandate firing someone for violating policy, adding that the employee was under psychiatric care and taking prescribed, anti-psychotic medication to resolve anger management problems. Upholding the firing, the arbitrator found that although the employer's policies on workplace violence did not *require* termination in each case involving threats of violence, the totality of circumstances gave the employer just cause to discharge the worker (*Whirlpool Corp.*, 115 LA 33).
- In another case, an arbitrator found that an employee who threatened to kill his boss could not be fired because the employer did not demonstrate that there was a genuine danger. A bus driver returned from a three-day suspension (for straying from his route) and allegedly issued a threat in the presence of the company safety director, saying that he would kill his supervisor. The company had a zero-tolerance policy with regard to violence and fired the employee the next working day after company officials were told of the incident. The employee later denied making any threat, and his union argued that the employer's delay in responding showed that the threat was not taken seriously and therefore was not

covered by the zero-tolerance policy. Calling the employer's account of the events more credible, the arbitrator nonetheless pointed out that the safety director's failure to notify company officials of the incident for an entire work day, as well as her failure to call the policy or take any action whatsoever, undermined the employer's claim that the threat was genuine. The zero-tolerance policy could not be applied to the threat in question, the arbitrator concluded, ordering the employee reinstated but without back pay (*Ryder/ATE*, 111 LA 1039).

## Abusive Language/Threatening Conduct

Mere cursing or the use of abusive, obscene, or vulgar language in and of itself is not sufficient basis for discipline of an employee, arbitrators generally hold (97 LA 750, 95 LA 302, 95 LA 543, 90 LA 1302, 81 LA 1077, 81 LA 1051).

Much depends on the manner and spirit of the language used, as well as the general tenor of the workplace. Such language may be used to lend color to one's remarks, or it may be designed to goad someone into a fight.

● In deciding whether cursing and using threatening language warrants discipline, a test used by many arbitrators is whether the conduct violated reasonable job decorum so as to cause apprehension or reaction in another employee that might hamper production (95 LA 1021, 95 LA 895, 77 LA 1259, 75 LA 288, 75 LA 258).

● Certain kinds of abusive language and threats are sufficient to warrant discipline or discharge, arbitrators have found in a number of cases (88 LA 512, 88 LA 418, 85 LA 1011, 81 LA 865).

● An employer properly discharged an employee for threatening to blow up a plant and the home of the assistant manager after the manager chastised him for insubordination, an arbitrator ruled, despite the fact that the employee's threat was made in the heat of anger (*D & D Poultry*, 81 LA 553).

● An arbitrator ruled that there was just cause to suspend a local union president for directing obscenities, abusive language, and falsehoods at his supervisor and accusing management of lying and being "out to get" employees. Although the local president's remarks were made during a union-management meeting, where his actions would normally have been considered "protected activity" under the National Labor Relations Act, the arbitrator said the conduct was so "egregious and disrespectful" that it lost NLRA protection (*Trans-City Terminal Warehouse Inc.*, 94 LA 1075; see also 92 LA 3, 90 LA 585, 81 LA 821).

● An employer had just cause to discharge a female employee who threatened a co-worker, an arbitrator found. A 14-year employee of a power company had a mental breakdown and began seeing a psychiatrist. She told the psychiatrist she had suicidal thoughts and felt the urge to harm her supervisor and several co-workers. The employee subsequently took medical leave, and within a few weeks her physician pronounced her well enough to work half-days. She followed that schedule for about a month, but then told a colleague that she would kill a male co-worker if he did not stop disturbing her. Upon learning of the remark, the employer provided 24-hour security for the co-worker and the employee's supervisor. Also, heeding the advice of the employee's psychiatrist to take her threats seriously, it fired the female employee. The union filed a grievance, contending the employee's abrupt discharge violated due process provisions of the collective bargaining agreement. The company, however, was only following the psychiatrist's advice by providing 24-hour security and ultimately firing the employee, the arbitrator said (*Alabama Power Co.*, 116 LA 157).

## Assessing Aggression

Determining who was the aggressor and apportioning penalties in accordance with degrees of responsibility are other important issues arbitrators face in these cases.

● One arbitrator ruled that an employer improperly discharged an employee who was involved in a fight with a co-worker in the lunch room. The fight began after an argument between the workers in which both used obscenities. After an incomplete investigation, management decided to discharge both employees, on the mistaken belief that they were equally responsible for the altercation, the arbitrator observed. Emphasizing that the evidence clearly established that the co-worker was the aggressor, the arbitrator stressed that that person had no right either to strike the employee or to grab her purse, which the co-worker allegedly believed contained a dangerous weapon (*Affiliated Hospitals of San Francisco*, 64 LA 29).

• An employer did not have just cause to discharge an employee who pulled a knife during the course of an argument with a co-worker after the co-worker taunted the employee with racial slurs and dared him to use the knife, an arbitrator ruled. Pointing out that the co-worker provoked the fight, the arbitrator ruled that the employer had engaged in disparate treatment by not disciplining the co-worker. Noting that the employee had a good work record during his nine years with the employer, the arbitrator concluded that the employee pulled the knife because he was frightened, not because he was being aggressive (*Welch Foods Inc.*, 73 LA 908).

## Off-Duty Fights

Ordinarily, employees are not subject to discipline for misconduct committed off company premises; however, arbitrators often make an exception to this "rule" if an off-duty fight is specifically job related, particularly when the fight is between a rank-and-file employee and a supervisor.

• One arbitrator held that an off-duty fight between two employees during a poker game was not just cause for discipline absent any harm to the employer. "No evidence takes this case outside the general rule that off-duty indiscretions do not permit discipline," the arbitrator ruled, emphasizing that there was no proof whatsoever that the employees were unable to work together after their off-duty altercation or that any other employee refused to work with either of them (*Honeywell Inc.*, 68 LA 346).

• In upholding the discharge of an employee for a violent assault on another employee, an arbitrator cited the following circumstances as warranting action by management: the attack occurred very near the plant at a place where other employees were known to be present; it occurred during the scheduled working day; it stemmed from activities inside the plant that were a part of the employment relationship; and other employees could have been expected to become involved, and did. The attack had a disruptive effect on plant operations, morale, and efficiency, the arbitrator concluded (*Victorian Instrument Co.*, 40 LA 435).

• Other arbitrators have noted that the employer has an obligation to maintain order and safety on its premises, which includes more than just the plant. Therefore, discharges have been sustained for assaults that take place in employer parking lots and against employees leaving the employer premises (29 LA 820, 30 LA 948, 50 LA 407).

## Mitigating Circumstances

In rare circumstances, discharge may be considered too severe a penalty for assault, particularly if the worker is "acting under substantial provocation." In one case, for example, an arbitrator ruled that management lacked just cause to discharge an employee for striking a co-worker who used "abusive and provocative" racial slurs (92 LA 521, 92 LA 340, 92 LA 28, 87 LA 877).

• An employee's medical or psychological condition may or may not mitigate an arbitrator's discipline (90 LA 1137, 89 LA 432, 83 LA 966).

• In another case, an arbitrator held that an employer was not justified in discharging an employee who struck a co-worker with a two-inch pipe. The co-worker had called the employee "bad names," the arbitrator noted, and had threatened him with a piece of timber. The employee faced a real threat, the arbitrator pointed out, adding that in trying to avoid the encounter, the employee had twice walked away before starting to fight.

"It should be obvious that an employee suffering an unprovoked attack should not be expected to calmly keep his hands by his side while being clobbered," the arbitrator asserted, maintaining that when fighting is a "reasonable self-defense" mechanism, it does not constitute just cause for discharge. Finding that the employee's conduct was provoked, but that his self-defense measures were excessive under the circumstances, the arbitrator reduced the discharge to a two-month suspension (*Central Foundry Co.*, 63 LA 731; see also 95 LA 519).

• Mitigation also may be found in the failure of management to head off an impending conflict, such as where it knows of bad blood between employees and fails to take readily available steps to keep them apart (*Zinsco Electrical Products*, 65 LA 487).

• An arbitrator held that an employer did not have just cause to discharge its non-English speaking employees who allegedly were involved in a confrontation with a supervisor on the shop floor, where the altercation resulted from a "charged atmosphere" on the floor immediately after the collapse and death of a respected union steward. In addition, the arbitrator ruled that language and cultural differences between the employees and management precluded a clear interpretation of events (*Polycast Technology Corp.*, 97 LA 704).

### Violation of No-Firearms Rule

Arbitrators generally agree that management has the right to forbid employees from possessing firearms on employer property (*Interstate Brands Corp.*, 104 LA 993).

• On the other hand, arbitrators may be unwilling to uphold an employer's disciplinary action against the employee who brings a gun into the plant where the employer has not promulgated or posted rules prohibiting such conduct (69 LA 613, 64 LA 291); where a no-firearms rule has not been consistently enforced in the past (77 LA 845); or where there is insufficient evidence that the employee possessed a firearm (77 LA 1018).

• An arbitrator held that an employer lacked just cause to discharge an employee for possessing a firearm on company property. The arbitrator admitted that the employer's disciplinary policy listed employee possession of firearms as an offense requiring discharge for a first offense, although management could impose a lesser penalty. Furthermore, the arbitrator held, the bargaining agreement stated that employee possession of a firearm on employer property was an offense that "may," but not "shall," result in the employee's discharge. The arbitrator ordered the employee reinstated, but without back pay because although the gun was unloaded and the employee was merely showing it to people, some sort of discipline was called for (*Interstate Brands Corp.*, 104 LA 993).

• A truck driver, involved in an accident, was found to be carrying a loaded gun and subsequently was discharged. The arbitrator decided that discharge was not for just cause, given that the company rule against gun-toting was never made clear to the employees or enforced (*American Synthetic Rubber Corp.*, 46 LA 1161; see also 43 LA 568).

# *Substance Abuse*

# Intoxication & Alcoholism

## OVERVIEW

Although arbitrators generally agree that a run-of-the-mill drinking problem must be addressed by some sort of discipline, the more serious issue of alcoholism is usually regarded as an illness and as such, is seen as distinct from simple misconduct caused by an employee's having a "few too many" drinks. Instead, in such cases, arbitrators often deal with the problem through counseling and other alcohol treatment programs. If it appears that the employee is making a good-faith effort at rehabilitation, reinstatement may be ordered or the penalty may be reduced.

The following discussion of grievances that arise over intoxication and alcoholism include:

- arbitrators' standards in assessing such cases;
- employers' need for a policy concerning alcohol use and intoxication;
- safety considerations triggered by workplace intoxication;
- proper evidence of alcohol possession and intoxication;
- rehabilitation and discipline of alcoholic employees; and
- off-duty drinking and drinking during holiday seasons.

## SUMMARY OF CASES

### Arbitrators' Standards

Three arbitration models are used most often to decide arbitration cases involving intoxication/alcoholism:

1. the straightforward application of the traditional corrective-discipline model;

2. a rejection of the corrective-discipline model in favor of a therapeutic model (drug therapy, psychotherapy, behavior therapy, or a combination of therapies); and

3. a modification of the corrective-discipline model.

In cases involving the use and possession of intoxicants, arbitrators typically sustain a penalty of discharge for drinking or drunkenness in these situations:

- frequent absenteeism caused by drinking;

- drinking on the job combined with other misconduct such as serious improper behavior or falsification of employment records;

- drinking at work that results in a person's inability to do his or her job;

- drunkenness or drinking that has a definite destructive effect on the employer's business and/or the morale of other employees; and

- chronic alcoholism with no sign of efforts at rehabilitation.

When such factors are not present, and where drinking on the job is a first offense, the penalty of discharge often is reduced to some lesser disciplinary measure. In addition, long, continued service usually is recognized as a factor in an employee's favor when determining the appropriate penalty for intoxication.

### Need for Company Rules

Not every incident of intoxication on company property demands that the employee involved be treated as a sick person rather than be disciplined for misconduct. Several arbitrators have pointed out that rules against consumption or possession of alcohol while on company property or company time obviously make good sense, as do rules against employees' reporting to work while inebriated.

● Generally, unless there is other evidence that the on-premises intoxication or drinking is part of a pattern that suggests alcoholism, management is free to treat the matter as a simple violation of company rules (90 LA 960, 89 LA 838, 81 LA 630, 81 LA 449, 81 LA 318).

● In one case, an employer's plant rule forbidding employees to possess or drink alcohol on company premises provided adequate justification for firing an employee for consuming a can of beer and keeping unopened cans of beer in his vehicle, an arbitrator ruled. The employer's method of communicating the ban on alcohol also was appropriate, and the employee was aware of the rule, the arbitrator found. The first-offense discharge was not excessively harsh because management consistently applied the same penalty to other employees who committed similar offenses (*AMF Lawn and Garden Division*, 64 LA 988; see also *Arvin Industries*, 96 LA 1185; *General Telephone Company of California*, 77 LA 1052).

## Safety Considerations

Generally, arbitrators uphold an employee's discharge for intoxication where the employee's behavior endangers other employees or damages equipment. The degree of danger or the attitude of the employee toward rehabilitation also are factors in determining if discharge should be reversed.

● One arbitrator ruled that an employer was justified in discharging an alcoholic employee who vandalized a supervisor's home, car, and travel trailer. Although the arbitrator acknowledged that alcoholism is a disease, he emphasized that the interests and welfare of the employee had to be balanced against the interests and welfare of other employees and the company. Reinstating the employee would likely be seen as "tolerating, if not condoning, destruction of a supervisor's property by employees, thereby inhibiting supervisors in the performance of their duties." Even though the employee subsequently sought treatment for his illness and apparently was progressing satisfactorily, the arbitrator concluded that the "extreme vandalism" and the "associated trauma" experienced by the supervisor and his family weighed against reinstating the employee (*NCR*, 70 LA 756).

● An employer properly discharged an alcoholic who worked in an underground mine where even brief lapses in basic mine safety practices could lead to serious injury or death, an arbitrator decided. Finding that the risks involved in the employee's occupation made his return to work inappropriate, the arbitrator rejected the suggestion that if the employee returned to his job, he would continue in rehabilitation (*Asarco Inc.*, 76 LA 163).

● A heavy equipment operator was properly discharged for intoxication when he drove his road grader off the road and into a creek, injuring himself and damaging the grader. Although the employee claimed that he was an alcoholic and was willing to undergo rehabilitation, the arbitrator pointed out that whether or not the employee's intoxicated condition was the result of alcoholism, he "should have recognized his condition and the danger it presented." Instead, the employee went ahead to operate dangerous equipment, thereby "deliberately jeopardizing" his safety, as well as the safety of his fellow employees and the equipment itself, the arbitrator noted. "Under these extreme circumstances, the company has an unchallengeable right to punish such conduct severely as a deterrent to ensure that it will never happen again," the arbitrator concluded (*Freeman United Coal*, 82 LA 861).

● Another arbitrator, however, ruled that an employee who was drunk while on duty and fell over the edge of the barge on which he was working was improperly discharged despite management's claims that the accident "severely jeopardized" the employee's life and the safety of others. Noting that the employee admitted he had an alcohol problem, became an active member of Alcoholics Anonymous, stopped drinking, and had no prior disciplinary or poor performance record, the arbitrator reduced the discharge to a 60-day suspension (*Ohio River Co.*, 83 LA 211).

## Evidence of Intoxication

Where an employee is disciplined for alleged intoxication, a dispute often arises as to whether the evidence regarding his state of sobriety is sufficient to allow the employer to take action. In some instances, an employee's refusal to take a sobriety test enables him or her to evade termination for drunkenness, but in others, the arbitrator will see such obstinance as suggesting guilt.

• Mere opinion evidence is not sufficient proof of a drunken condition. The evidence must be specific in describing various details of appearance and conduct so that it is clear that the person accused was in fact under the influence of alcohol (85 LA 1127, 85 LA 251, 83 LA 1323).

• Supervisors who have no medical training nevertheless are capable of recognizing when an employee is intoxicated or under the influence of alcohol if they objectively compare an employee's normal demeanor and work habits with those at the time his or her sobriety is questioned (*Dayton Walther Co.*, 77 LA 1064).

• Results of breath/blood-alcohol/urinalysis tests may be accepted as conclusive proof of intoxication. Arbitrators differ over whether management is required—or allowed—to give a blood test in order to prove intoxication because such tests might cause undue delays and disrupt production (*Charleston Naval Shipyard*, 54 LA 145; see also 90 LA 286).

• Despite detecting the odor of alcohol on an employee, an employer lacked just cause to fire him for violating its drug-alcohol policy, according to the arbitrator hearing the case. When the employee, an aircraft mechanic, came into work smelling of alcohol, his supervisor sent him home for the day. One week later, the mechanic was promoted to crew chief, but shortly thereafter, he was given a written warning for having reported to work smelling of alcohol, exhibiting aggressive behavior, and arriving at work a half-hour late—at which point he was sent to a clinic for a blood-alcohol test. The mechanic countered that he had not been drinking on the day in question. Two weeks later, however, he again reeked of alcohol and was fired. His union protested, claiming that the employee's blood test was negative for alcohol and that the employee showed no signs of impairment. The arbitrator said the employer's decision to send the employee home on two separate occasions and to require drug-alcohol testing was a prudent response; however, the employer lacked just cause to fire the employee merely for smelling of alcohol because he showed no signs of mental or physical impairment, breakdown, or defect in conduct or job performance. Finally, the arbitrator pointed out that the drug-alcohol test came back negative, prompting him to order the employee reinstated with back pay. He did, however, also order the employee to get a professional alcohol abuse assessment within 30 days (*DynCorp*, 114 LA 458).

• An arbitrator reinstated an allegedly intoxicated employee after ruling that the employer mishandled his blood test. A medical group's laboratory failed to follow procedures, the arbitrator found, reducing the discharge to a 90-day suspension and ordering the employee sign a last-chance agreement requiring him to attend and successfully complete an alcoholic rehabilitation program and provide written proof that he was attending Alcoholics Anonymous meetings. Failure to do all of the above, the arbitrator cautioned, would result in termination (*Pacific Motor Trucking*, 86 LA 497; see also 87 LA 972).

• An arbitrator reinstated a delivery driver who was discharged for refusing to submit to a blood test. A supervisor smelled alcohol on the driver's breath, and when the driver admitted to drinking a beer at lunch—after having two traffic accidents that day—the supervisor asked the employee to submit to a blood test. The driver refused to take the test and was discharged for insubordination. Overturning the dismissal, the arbitrator pointed out that the employer could not fire the employee for insubordination because he was not warned that his refusal to undergo the test would be an admission of intoxication or that it would result in his dismissal (*Signal Delivery Service*, 86 LA 75).

• Another arbitrator overturned the discharge of an employee who was not given a blood test even though management judged him to be intoxicated after observing his unusual "walking and talking patterns." Noting that "a person is not intoxicated until or unless a certain quantity of alcohol or other substance is found in one's blood," the arbitrator said a blood test "quite clearly" was in order in this case. "To discharge a person for suspected but unconfirmed intoxication is to discharge unjustly," the arbitrator observed, concluding that no one knew if the employee had been under the influence because he was never tested (*Durion Co.*, 85 LA 1127).

• A print shop employee was unjustly discharged for intoxication without proof that he was in fact drunk, said an arbitrator. After the employee's supervisor smelled alcohol on his breath, the employee admitted that he had had two beers before reporting for his shift. The employee was discharged even though he would not take a blood test as requested. The arbitrator reversed the discharge because of "insufficient evidence" to prove that the employee was intoxicated. The arbitrator did not, however, award the employee back pay, deciding that in not taking the blood test, the employee was "forestalling an independent evaluation of his condition, which was reasonably suspect" (*Foote and Davis Inc.*, 88 LA 125).

• Another arbitrator upheld the discharge of an employee who was fired for drinking but did not take a sobriety test. The discharge was upheld on the basis of witness testimony without reliance on the sobriety test, when the arbitrator found that the testimony clearly showed that the employee was intoxicated on the day of his dismissal. In fact, the arbitrator noted, refusal to take a sobriety test has been held to constitute an implied admission of guilt (*Cal Custom/Hawk*, 65 LA 723; see also 77 LA 1180, 76 LA 1005, 76 LA 144).

### Evidence of Alcohol Possession

When plant rules clearly forbid the possession of alcoholic beverages on company property, management may use the discovery of an open container of alcohol to support the discipline of an employee. Merely observing an open bottle of alcohol does not necessarily prove that the employee is in possession of the alcohol, arbitrators have held.

• An arbitrator reduced the penalty against a truck driver who brought an open can of beer into a compulsory company meeting. Finding the employee's suspension too harsh, the arbitrator noted that the employer had a "demonstrated practice" of providing beer for employees; consequently, the employee was not flagrantly defying management authority by walking in with the open can of beer (*Keebler Co.*, 88 LA 183).

• An employer had just cause under its no-alcohol policy to fire an employee who kept several bottles of wine in his locker for two weeks, an arbitrator ruled. Based on an anonymous tip, supervisors at a facility inspected an employee's locker and found three bottles of cooking wine, two of which had been opened. The employer learned that the bottles were samples that the company's research kitchen discarded and that were later retrieved by the employee. After an investigation, the employee was discharged for violating company rules against theft and possession of alcoholic beverages on company property.

His union filed a grievance, arguing that the 20-year employee did not intentionally steal company property. The arbitrator agreed, noting that he had not intended to deprive the company of anything of value, his conduct did not constitute dishonesty, and it would be "unduly harsh" to characterize his actions as theft. In addition, she wrote, the employer had not proved that the employee's failure to request permission to take the wine home constituted a serious violation of employer policy. Nonetheless, she said the employee, without obtaining his supervisor's permission to do so, kept the wine in his locker, which constituted "possession" of alcohol and enabled management to fire him under the no-alcohol policy (*Heinz USA*, 115 LA 1161).

• A lack of evidence prompted the reinstatement of an employee who was fired after the company security guard discovered him squatting behind a car in the company parking lot. The guard also found a Styrofoam cup hidden behind the rear tire of the car and after examining its contents, concluded that it was filled with some kind of alcohol. Although no analysis was ever made to determine the cup's contents, the company fired the employee, an action the arbitrator found was not justified because the company failed to show that the employee did anything wrong, even though the circumstances created some suspicion that the employee may have been drinking (*Kast Metals Corp.*, 65 LA 783).

## Alcoholism as Mitigator

While some arbitrators have been reluctant to mitigate the discipline of alcoholics (*Armstrong Furnace Co.*, 63 LA 688; see also 75 LA 901), other arbitrators are willing to give the alcoholic employee the benefit of the doubt, and are inclined to reinstate the alcoholic whenever there seems to be a possibility of recovery (*Charleston Naval Shipyard*, 54 LA 145; see also 56 LA 527, 56 LA 789).

## Rehabilitation or Discharge?

The application of progressive discipline may not correct alcohol-related performance problems; it may, however, be instrumental in warning employees that they have a serious problem that requires counseling or rehabilitation. If an employee voluntarily seeks treatment for alcoholism, an arbitrator may consider such a move as a mitigating factor when evaluating the employee's job performance or attendance record. (This is especially true in light of the Americans with Disabilities Act, which makes that crucial distinction between an alcoholic who blunders along and keeps drinking and one who seeks treatment. )

The burden generally is on the employee to show that he or she has taken meaningful, affirmative action to deal with a drinking problem. Where there is convincing evidence that a discharged employee has taken such positive steps, an arbitrator may order reinstatement, often conditioned on the employee's successful completion of an alcoholism rehabilitation or counseling program and on whether the employer knew of the employee's alcohol dependency at the time of the dismissal.

● A drunk crew-leader fired for urinating on a co-worker should be reinstated if, among other conditions, he completes an alcoholic treatment program and apologizes to the co-worker, the arbitrator ruled. After an off-duty evening of beer drinking, the employee urinated on a co-worker at night in a motel room they shared while on assignment cleaning toxic waste tanks. The union said the worker, despite admitted periodic blackouts, had been employed for 20 years without complaint. The company knew of his drinking but took no corrective action, and he therefore was entitled to a warning instead of dismissal. Acknowledging how "disgusting and repulsive" the employee's actions toward the co-worker had been, the arbitrator said the blackouts were exceedingly worrisome, especially in such a hazardous occupation. The company was right to remove him from the workplace, but termination was not necessarily appropriate for someone with his long record of service without discipline, the arbitrator concluded, ordering the man reinstated after he completed an alcohol abuse rehabilitation program at his own expense and apologized to his colleague (*K & D Industrial Services Inc.*, 112 LA 820).

● Another arbitrator reinstated an alcoholic employee even though his employer had "sufficient just cause" to fire him for "excessive absenteeism and tardiness" prompted by his addiction. The arbitrator noted a number of mitigating factors, including that: the employer knew that the employee's poor attendance record was the result of his alcohol-abuse problems; other alcohol-dependent employees were given second chances to improve their records; the employee had a "lengthy and more-or-less satisfactory" job performance record; and the employee's recognition that he was an alcoholic and had taken self-help measures to control it (*Youngstown Hospital Assoc.*, 82 LA 31).

● An arbitrator ruled that an employer improperly discharged an employee for "unsatisfactory attendance" when the employee was absent for an extended period because of his admission to a hospital alcoholism-treatment program. Before admitting himself to the hospital, the employee had participated in two alcoholism programs that had failed to cure his addiction. The employee's "bootstrap decision" to deal with his problem directly by seeking treatment at the hospital was an acceptable reason for being absent from the job, the arbitrator ruled, pointing out that the employee had acted in a "positive manner" in response to the employer's warnings that he must "overcome his personal problem" (*Warner and Swasey Co.*, 71 LA 158).

● In another case, however, an arbitrator ruled that a company was not required to reinstate an excessively absent employee when he successfully completed an alcohol rehabilitation program because he had not disclosed his alcoholism until after he was discharged. Finding that because there was nothing in the labor agreement "exculpating an employee from his actions due to the fact that it is subsequently learned that they were due to chronic alcoholism," the arbitrator ruled that although the employee was "on the way to fully resolving his alcohol abuse problems," he has "no right to require this company to reinstate or rehire him" (*Bemis Co.*, 81 LA 733; see also 90 LA 399, 86 LA 430).

*Past Practice*—Where an employer's past practice has been to refer employees suspected of abusing alcohol to an employee assistance program in lieu of termination, the employer is obliged to do so, even if the employee's intoxication is substantiated by a blood-alcohol test and the parties' collective bargaining agreement gives the employer the right to either discharge or discipline employees in such situations, one arbitrator ruled (*Georgia Pacific Corp*, 108 LA 43).

### Refusal to Undergo Rehabilitation

Despite the increasing recognition that alcoholism is an illness and must be treated as such, arbitrators have held that management has the right to discipline an employee for drinking on the job, if the employee refuses to even attempt rehabilitation.

● One arbitrator decided that an employer had just cause to discharge an alcoholic employee who refused to continue participating in a treatment program. Rejecting the employee's argument that he had agreed merely to enroll in the program, not to complete it, the arbitrator said that it would be "absurd" to expect any beneficial results from treatment that was started but not finished. The arbitrator also noted that while in the program, the employee refused to cooperate to the point that he had been asked to leave the institution. Deciding that management had taken all "reasonable" measures to help the employee deal with his "acute and chronic" alcoholism, the arbitrator ruled that the dismissal was warranted (*National Gypsum Co.*, 73 LA 228).

● Another arbitrator emphasized that even though alcoholism is an illness, it is an illness that only the patient can "cure." The discharge of an alcoholic was upheld where the employee had been given repeated opportunities to bring his drinking problem under control and had failed too often for the arbitrator to conclude that all would be well if only he were given another chance (*Caterpillar Tractor Co.*, 44 LA 87).

### Conditional Reinstatement & 'Last Chance' Agreements

Arbitrators, as a solution in giving an employee a second chance, typically reduce an employee's discharge to a conditional reinstatement. The extent to which arbitrators may properly set the terms of the reinstatement is subject to debate—in terms of both therapeutic protocols and arbitration processes. Some arbitrators have gone so far as to recommend the medication the employee should take. Other arbitrators find that they are making or interpreting clinical decisions that should be left up to clinicians.

Often employers and employees, as part of a substance-abuse policy, will reach a bargain wherein the substance abuser will be reinstated with the under-

standing that he or she goes into a rehabilitation program and remains drug-free
for the duration of his or her employment, with the knowledge that any violation of this agreement will result in immediate termination.

• An arbitrator upheld an employee's discharge after he had been reinstated under a last-chance agreement for
misconduct stemming from alcohol abuse.
The agreement stipulated that any violation of company rules would be considered violation of his one-year probation,
and that any such violation could not be
grieved under a collective bargaining
agreement. The employee was discharged for violating a safety work rule,
even though he had completed a rehabilitation program required by the last-
chance agreement (*Gaylord Container
Corp.*, 97 LA 382; see also 87 LA 973, 65
LA 803, 56 LA 319).

The arbitrator posed five criteria for
determining the validity of a last-chance
agreement:

• Was a union representative
present when the employee signed the
agreement?

• Are its requirements reasonable?

• Did the employee sign it of his or
her own free will?

• Did the employee understand its
provisions?

• Was the probationary period of
reasonable duration?

• An employee was discharged for
just cause after he failed to attend counseling sessions required under a last-
chance agreement, according to the arbitrator. The employee was fired for chronic
tardiness, which he later blamed on an
alcohol problem, prompting the company
to reinstate him with the understanding
that he must sign a last-chance agreement. When he failed to abide by the
agreement, which required that he attend
treatment sessions for one year, he was
fired. Objecting to the discharge, the
union argued that the employee failed to
attend counseling because he was not notified about his next appointment and
when a certified letter was sent to his
home, the employee was hospitalized.
The company was within its rights to ter-

minate the employee, the arbitrator said,
adding that the employer took proper
steps to keep the employee apprised of
his status (*Fort James Corp.*, 113 LA
742).

## Employee Assistance Programs

Although some observers have seen
the emergence of a concept that every
employer has the duty to aid alcoholics
and drug addicts, the primary instrument
for dealing with these problems has been
the voluntarily created Employee Assistance Program, run by an employer, a
union, or jointly.

• In arbitration, the most salient
question posed by the EAP movement is
whether the employer who has or recognizes an EAP, or even promulgates a
policy on alcohol rehabilitation, incurs an
obligation to allow the employee to try
rehabilitation before imposing discipline.

## Off-Duty Drinking

Under normal conditions, the consumption of alcohol after working hours
does not have a direct impact upon the
employer-employee relationship and
therefore is not subject to discipline (97
LA 801).

• One arbitrator upheld the discharge of an employee for violating a new
amendment to a no-drinking rule that
had been extended to meal-time drinking
off company property. The arbitrator
pointed out that the union had led the
company to believe that it saw an "evil" in
lunch-hour drinking and would support
the company in an effort to do something
about it (*International Pipe and Ceramics Corp.*, 44 LA 267).

• Discharge was too severe a penalty
for an employee who drove after drinking
alcohol and then backed his van into another vehicle in a company parking lot, an
arbitrator determined. An employee of a
city housing authority backed a van out of
a space in the agency's lot, slightly scrap-
ing the bumper of a co-worker's car. The
five-year employee was suspended pending the results of a blood-alcohol test,
which later showed a .02 blood alcohol
concentration. He was then fired for violating the employer's drug and alcohol

policy, which the union protested, saying there had been no proof the man was impaired. The employer did not have just cause to fire the employee for the "driving under the influence" incident, the arbitrator held. The damage to both vehicles was very minor, the parties' collective bargaining agreement failed to set a minimum blood-alcohol level for being under the influence, and the employee's blood-alcohol level was calculated at a lab's minimum threshold for impairment, the arbitrator pointed out. In addition, the employee showed no signs of intoxication at the time of the accident and had a clean record. The arbitrator ordered the worker reinstated with back pay under a last-chance agreement (*Las Vegas Housing Authority*, 112 LA 259).

• An employee who had been with a company for 25 years and had an obvious drinking problem was justly dismissed for off-duty drinking. After issuing several written warnings about his use of alcoholic beverages, the company finally discharged him for being drunk on company property. Subsequently, the company agreed to take him back if he promised to stay off alcohol, attend AA meetings regularly, and follow doctor's orders. Nearly a year later, the employee was observed by company officials drinking beer in a tavern while off duty. As a result, he was discharged, which the arbitrator found was acceptable given the man's employment history and attitude, which indicated that he did not intend to improve his conduct in regard to the use of alcohol (*Emge Packing Co.*, 52 LA 195).

## Holiday Drinking

During the holiday season, some arbitrators take a more liberal view of no-drinking rules and make allowances for employees who are caught drinking alcoholic beverages on the job.

• An arbitrator decided that an employer properly suspended a truck driver for drinking alcoholic beverages during a warehouse party on the last working day before Christmas, and for breaking a lock on a plant gate while attempting to retrieve his vehicle. The arbitrator held, however, that management was not justified in completely barring the employee from ever driving a company truck again. The "core" question, the arbitrator stressed, was whether the employer's disciplinary action fit the entire picture. Although conceding that the employee "slipped and slipped rather badly" by acting irresponsibly at the Christmas party, the arbitrator noted that, in a "candid moment," most people would admit that they had engaged in similar conduct. "If we were all angels at all times," the arbitrator concluded, "we would sprout wings and fly up to Heaven" (*Ashland Oil Inc.*, 59 LA 292).

• Another arbitrator similarly decided that an employer was not justified in discharging an employee who was caught drinking whiskey at work on the last day before a Christmas shutdown. A supervisor had observed the employee, amidst co-workers, drinking from a pint-size bottle filled with a whiskey-colored liquid. Although condemning the conduct of the employee, the arbitrator maintained that "justice tempered with mercy" should be the standard for reviewing discipline in such cases. Stressing that the employee had a long, "unblemished" work record and that drinking on the last day before the Christmas holidays was "customary" on the job, the arbitrator concluded that the discharge should be converted to a suspension (*Wagner Electric Corp.*, 57 LA 10).

# Drug Abuse

_____ **OVERVIEW** _____

Arbitrators generally support management's view that an employee's posses-sion or use of drugs, especially on company time and premises, is a serious offense. Increasingly, however, arbitrators require management to show that an employee's involvement with drugs has had a harmful effect on some aspect of the employment relationship. When evaluating a situation involving an employ-ee's use of illegal drugs—or prescription drugs, for that matter—arbitrators must deal with some questions that are similar to those they encounter in alcohol/intoxication cases. Once an employee admits to having a drug "problem" and shows a willingness to seek treatment, the employer's response likely will have to change, as it accommodates the person's disability. Employers do not, as arbitrators' rulings have shown, have to put up with unproductive, drug-using employees who balk at treatment and are not willing to work with the employer to deal with their drug abuse.

In determining the proper penalty for drug-related offenses, arbitrators focus on issues that include whether:

● a drug-abuse policy has been established and clearly communicated to employees;

● employees' use or possession of drugs had, or was likely to have, a negative effect on workplace safety;

● the drug involved was a controlled substance or a prescription drug properly used by the employee;

● discipline was based on sufficient evidence of drug use, especially when management uses witnesses and polygraphs to support its case;

● discipline meted out for drug involvement was on a par with that given to employees involved in alcohol-related offenses;

● use of drugs took place while the employee was off-duty; and

● the employee was arrested or convicted on drug charges, and whether the media attention given the drug arrest or conviction has an adverse impact on the employer business or reputation.

_____ **SUMMARY OF CASES** _____

### Enforcement of Drug-Abuse Policy

As with other types of offenses, arbi-trators will generally uphold discipline for drug use where management has for-mulated a rule prohibiting it, communi-cated the rule to employees, and consis-tently applied discipline in a nondiscriminatory manner.

● An employer was justified in dis-charging two employees who admitted to smoking marijuana on the job under a plant rule prohibiting the sale, use, or possession of alcohol and drugs on em-ployer premises, an arbitrator held. The arbitrator pointed out that the employees had acknowledged that they were aware of the rule, which, he added, "had been consistently administered." Finding no "mitigating or extenuating circumstances," the arbitrator declared that nothing in the case warranted the conclusion "that the discharges were not completely justified" (*Pepsi-Cola Bottlers*, 68 LA 792).

• Citing management's failure to ensure that employees understood its prohibitions against using or being under the influence of intoxicants on its premises, an arbitrator overturned the discharge of an employee who had brought marijuana into the plant. "To be a basis for proper disciplinary action against an employee," the arbitrator pointed out, "a rule must be reasonable in nature, clearly published, and it must be known to the employee." Although employees were given copies of the rules, the arbitrator noted, there was no follow-up to ensure that they had read them. "It is a risky assumption," the arbitrator pointed out, "for a firm to give rules to employees in a written form and expect them to read and understand them without some type of follow-up to confirm reading and clarity of understanding" (*Ethyl Corp.*, 74 LA 953).

• An employer that previously had been lax in enforcing its rules against reporting to work under the influence of drugs improperly terminated 25 employees for smoking marijuana during their lunch break, an arbitrator found. After the employer had asked local police to help it end workplace drug use, the police raided the employer parking lot, arresting or citing 50 employees. Management then discharged 25 of them for violating its drug policy. Overturning the discharges, the arbitrator pointed out that the employees had been "readily observed smoking marijuana at the same time and place" day after day. The employer's inaction with respect to enforcing its rules against drug use, the arbitrator concluded, had resulted in the employees' viewing the parking lots "as sanctuaries for this relaxation" (*Lockheed Corp.*, 75 LA 1081).

• An arbitrator held an employer had just cause to discharge a senior corrections officer after he tested positive for cocaine use and failed to report to work, despite the 19-year employee's contentions that there was no proof he had used cocaine while at work or that it impaired his ability to work. The arbitrator asserted the employee was the third person in the chain of command at the prison, his use of cocaine compelled the conclusion that he illegally acquired and used it, and there was reason to conclude his drug use had an adverse impact on his job performance. The arbitrator concluded that the escalating problems of excessive absenteeism and apparent cocaine use were linked and together constituted just cause for severe discipline (*State of Delaware*, 104 LA 845).

• An employer's zero-tolerance drug policy was interpreted too rigidly in the case of an employee who was terminated for testing positive for drugs after he suffered a minor worksite injury, according to one arbitrator.

The employee had worked for the company for 32 years when he informed his supervisor that a metal particle had become lodged in his eye while at work. supervisor referred him to a clinic where he had to consent to a post-accident drug test. While at the clinic, the employee admitted that he had recently smoked marijuana on his days off, and when he returned to work, management fired him on the spot. The union protested the employer's action, saying the discharge exceeded what was required by the company's drug policy and pointing out that the worker's right to confidentiality had been violated. The arbitrator agreed, stating that the penalty was unjustified and excessive. The employer lacked reasonable cause to suspect the employee of drug use, especially in light of his "quality" work record, the arbitrator found, ordering him reinstated with back pay (*Simmons Co.*, 112 LA 164).

## 'Last-Chance' Agreements

Often employers and employees, as part of a substance-abuse policy, will reach a "bargain" wherein the substance abuser will be reinstated with the understanding that the employee undergo rehabilitation and remain drug-free for the duration of his or her employment. Any violation of that agreement will result in immediate termination.

• In one case, an employer agreed to finance, under an employee assistance program, the rehabilitation of an admitted substance abuser, who committed to finishing the rehabilitation program, staying drug-free while participating in the program, and forfeiting his job if he violated either provision. An arbitrator found the agreement to be fair and reasonable and said the last-chance agreements had been fully explained to employees as part of the employer's substance-abuse policy. Given all these factors, the arbitrator upheld the employee's discharge for testing positive for cocaine after having missed several rehab meetings (*Diesel Recon Co.*, 96 LA 1123).

• An arbitrator ruled a last-chance agreement violated the due process rights guaranteed an employee under a collective bargaining agreement. The employee had failed to provide a urine sample after he had signed an agreement authorizing an employer to require unannounced drug and alcohol tests at its discretion, and the employer had rejected a union request to arbitrate the termination, citing a section of the agreement providing that "no grievances, claims, arbitration, or lawsuit will be filed" if the employee were discharged. The arbitrator called the termination "arbitrary," agreeing with a union claim that the last-chance agreement ran counter to the labor contract which forbade the waiver of procedural due process protections (*Monterey Coal Co.*, 96 LA 457).

• Another arbitrator ruled that an employee was properly discharged under a last-chance agreement even though his agreement authorized termination "without recourse to the grievance procedure." The employee was required to test for drugs during work hours based on an admitted drug dependency, and had tested positive for a substance such as valium, and had failed to inform his employer of valium, prescription from a physician who was not a regular doctor (*Kaydon Corp.*, 89 LA 377).

## Safety Considerations

Generally, arbitrators are stricter in upholding discipline levied against employees who are using drugs at work or whose use of drugs outside the worksite impairs their job performance if the impaired employee would endanger other employees or the public.

• A city bus driver who had been involved in an accident while on her route was justly dismissed after a blood test and urinalysis revealed the presence of habit-forming drugs in her system, an arbitrator concluded. Although lacking "absolute proof" of the employee's drug use, "to allow an employee who has taken drugs to continue to drive a bus would pose a danger to the public," the arbitrator said, and "it is unthinkable" that such an employee should be allowed to continue in the job (*Washington Metropolitan Area Transit Authority*, 82 LA 150).

• A police dispatcher who admitted to using cocaine off the job was properly dismissed, said an arbitrator who declared that "it is incompatible with the functions of a police communications dispatcher to have a person employed in the role admittedly taking cocaine or other controlled substances." Moreover, because a person in that job "receives telephone calls from the public regarding possible life-threatening situations which must be rapidly analyzed," the arbitrator said, the job requires "full concentration of the dispatcher's faculties while in the performance of their duties and the use of controlled substances such as cocaine impairs that function" (*San Francisco Police Department*, 87 LA 791).

• A chemical plant employee whose job was not "in a sensitive area" was unjustifiably discharged for smoking marijuana on the premises, an arbitrator held. Arguing that its business required alert employees, management insisted that an employee under the influence of drugs could "cause an erroneous mixture of chemicals" that might result in "explosions or fires." The arbitrator, however, pointed out that the employee worked "in the boiler house, unloading and shoveling coal," rather than in a sensitive area where there would be the "possibility of dangerous mistakes" (*Hooker Chemical*, 74 LA 1032).

• Another arbitrator held an employer's discharge of an aircraft engine assembler who failed two drug tests was in violation of the parties' collective bargaining agreement. The arbitrator ruled the employer lacked evidence that the employee violated the contract's "peculiar" language explicitly prohibiting employee drug use/possession "in the workplace," "while performing work," and "during working hours." Although the discharge of an employee in a safety-sensitive job for a second drug-test failure is usually acceptable and might be deemed appropriate in other employment contexts, the arbitrator said, the positive test results cannot be equated with proof that the employee used or possessed drugs while he was at work or that he was in an impaired physical condition while performing his safety-sensitive job. The arbitrator noted that he had no "roving commission" to implement either federal policy against drug use or any particular level of aviation safety concern, regardless of how clearly justified either might be (*Textron Lycoming*, 104 LA 1043).

## Nature of Abused Drug

If an employee's performance is adversely affected by a prescription drug—as opposed to an illicit substance—arbitrators often will nonetheless enforce management's disciplinary action.

• An employee who arrived at work impaired by prescription drugs was justly discharged, an arbitrator found. Both observations of the employee's behavior and medical analyses showed that the employee "was impaired and unfit for active duty when he showed up" for work, the arbitrator said. Even if all of the substances detected in the urine and blood screens were prescription drugs, "the taking of these simultaneously constitutes abuse" and defies common sense, he concluded (*Citgo Petroleum*, 88 LA 521).

• An employee was properly given a three-day disciplinary layoff when management determined that he reported to work under the influence of drugs, an ar-

bitrator decided. The employee objected to the discipline, claiming that the drug was valium and that it had been prescribed for him by his physician. Upholding the layoff, the arbitrator ruled that whether the employee's behavior was adversely influenced by his "taking medicine as prescribed or using drugs without benefit of prescription is not relevant to the fact that the employee was under the influence and therefore a risk in the workplace" (*FMC Corp.*, 80 LA 1173).

## Witnesses to Drug Involvement

When employers have disciplined employees for drug involvement, based on the testimony of witnesses to the employees' drug use or possession, arbitrators look for corroborative evidence of drug involvement before enforcing disciplinary measures. Generally two types of witnesses are available to management: undercover agents, or supervisory employees and co-workers.

*Undercover Agents*—When employers who have mounted anti-drug campaigns in their workplaces hire undercover agents to detect drug use and possession, arbitrators usually weigh the testimony of the undercover witness in light of his expertise and the other evidence presented, including contrasting testimony from the accused employee.

• An arbitrator overturned the discharge of an employee that was based on the unsupported testimony of an undercover agent. Noting that "the accused must always be given the benefit of substantial doubts," the arbitrator asserted that "dismissal for alleged criminal conduct may not be upheld when the sole evidence supporting the charge is the uncorroborated testimony of an undercover informant." Corroboration could include samples of the drugs allegedly used by the employees, laboratory analyses, photographs, or tape recordings, the arbitrator pointed out (*Pacific Bell*, 87 LA 313; see also 97 LA 271, 95 LA 813, 83 LA 580).

• Two employees were unjustly discharged for alleged drug use, an arbitrator concluded, noting that management's only evidence consisted of reports from an undercover agent that "were filtered down to the employer management by and through the agent's supervisor." In the arbitrator's opinion, without "some type of corroboration," of the agent's reports, which might have been either "direct or circumstantial," the employee's testimony must be "superior." To allow a job to be "damaged or tarnished or taken away by uncorroborated and unsubstantiated evidence," the arbitrator maintained, "would be to allow an employer to act arbitrarily and capriciously and unreasonably in many instances" (*Pettibone Ohio Corp.*, 72 LA 1144).

● Another arbitrator ruled that an employer, relying on evidence of an undercover detective, properly discharged four employees for possession and use of marijuana on employer premises. The testimony of the detective was "firsthand information where the incidents testified to were backed up by reports written daily," declared the arbitrator. Moreover, the undercover detective's "demeanor, the impression that his testimony was truthful, his memory, his perception," and his prior experience as a police officer shows that his testimony was "accurate and credible," the arbitrator concluded, ruling that the discharges were for just cause (*Consumer Plastics Corp.*, 88 LA 208).

*Supervisors or Co-Workers*—Management personnel or co-workers also may testify regarding an employees' drug use or possession. In such cases, arbitrators will consider the strength of the testimony based on what the witness claims to have seen—or smelled.

● An arbitrator upheld the discharge of four employees who were witnessed by four supervisors smoking a marijuana cigarette among them. Concluding that the "chain of circumstances pointing to the guilt of the grievants goes far beyond conjecture and suspicion," the arbitrator observed that the four witnesses testified that, in addition to smelling the "pervasive and unmistakable odor of marijuana," they observed the employees deeply inhaling the smoke as they passed the marijuana cigarette back and forth while and looking "suspiciously from side

to side before lighting or inhaling from the cigarette" (*Cascade Steel Rolling Mills Inc.*, 78 LA 753).

● An employer had just cause to dismiss an employee after two supervisors discovered her smoking what they thought was a marijuana cigarette in the women's locker room, an arbitrator said. The supervisors testified that they found part of a marijuana cigarette on the floor of the locker room, which smelled of marijuana smoke (*Dobbs Houses Inc.*, 78 LA 749; see also 88 LA 633, 75 LA 642, 75 LA 597).

● An arbitrator overturned the discharge of an employee whom a supervisor discovered in the employer's exercise room, which smelled of marijuana. Management must show "good and sufficient evidence to support the charges of drug use," the arbitrator said, but in this case, the supervisor was not able to say irrefutably that the odor he smelled came from the employee's smoking in the exercise room. Because "significant doubt" remained as to the employee's guilt, the arbitrator ruled, to uphold the employer's position would be tantamount to shifting the burden of proof to the employee, making him guilty until proven innocent (*Owens-Corning Fiberglas Corp.*, 86 LA 1026).

## Polygraphs Evidencing Drug Abuse

Just as arbitrators often find reason to suspect the reliability of management witnesses who attest to an employee's drug involvement, so too do they sometimes doubt the evidence of lie-detector tests introduced to substantiate drug charges. When presented with the results of polygraphs, arbitrators often require corroborative evidence before upholding discipline for drug use or possession.

● An arbitrator reinstated an employee who was fired after a polygraph examiner told the employer that he believed the employee had been "deceptive" about his drug use. arbitrators and courts have consistently held a "jaundiced view" of both the polygraph process and the "admissibility of the results" of a polygraph exam, the arbitrator asserted. Employers that want to make use of polygraph results have been advised to make sure that the test is administered by a qualified examiner, closely follows the incident in question and is taken voluntarily, the arbitrator said. At the time of this polygraph, the arbitrator noted, the employee was taking prescribed medication that, according to his doctor, could have affected the results of the exam. The employer failed to "take the total circumstances under enough consideration," nor did the polygraph evidence alone support a conclusion that warranted termination, the arbitrator held (*Houston Lighting & Power*, 87 LA 478).

• An arbitrator upheld the terminations of several employees who had been discharged for on-the-job drug and alcohol use based on the uncorroborated testimony of an undercover agent who "passed" a polygraph test. The arbitrator accorded "significant weight" to the fact that the agent's testimony was supported by the polygraph results, while all the accused employees refused to submit to the test (*Georgia Pacific*, 85 LA 542).

### Equal Treatment for Abusers

Arbitrators sometimes will compare the discipline given to drug abusers with the discipline the employer has levied against alcohol-abusing employees, often overturning or softening discipline given drug abusers if they have been treated more harshly.

• In the case of three employees discharged on their first offense of smoking marijuana on employer premises, the arbitrator found that the employees were indeed guilty of violating the employer's drug and alcohol policy. The arbitrator, however, noted that the employer regularly applied progressive discipline—not automatic dismissals—for employees' first offense in using alcohol on employer property. The arbitrator held that "alcoholism in industry, and as a social problem, is far more debilitating, costly, and destructive than marijuana. There is no rational or reasonable basis for treating them as distinct. Therefore to treat alcohol abuse with progressive discipline and treat drug abuse with immediate discharge is improper" (*Mallinckrodt Inc.*, 80 LA 1261).

• Two bus employer employees who smoked marijuana on the roof of their office during work hours were properly discharged rather than offered counseling through the employee assistance program, as an alcoholic bus driver had been offered, an arbitrator ruled. Even though the EAP had been designed to treat both alcohol and drug-abuse problems, the arbitrator declared that the employer had not treated the two cases disparately because the bus driver was an admitted alcoholic, while the dismissed drug users "denied they had a drug problem and maintained that they were recreational users" (*Central Ohio Transit Authority*, 88 LA 633).

### Off-Duty Drug Use

In cases that involve discipline meted out for employees' off-duty behavior, arbitrators will consider the relationship between the off-duty behavior and the employee's job and what effect that behavior has on the person's working life.

• One arbitrator held that "discharge for misconduct away from the place of work has no basis unless the behavior harms the employer's reputation or product; or the behavior renders the employee unable to perform his duties or appear at work; or the behavior leads to the refusal of other employees to work with the employee" (*General Telephone Co. of Calif.*, 87 LA 443; see also 88 LA 425).

• One arbitrator upheld the discharge of an employee whose use of illegal narcotics outside of work interfered with his job performance. The arbitrator ruled that the employee's "drug-induced" condition "rendered him unfit to perform his work," and therefore, the employee violated "the contractual prohibition against the use of illegal narcotics." Even though there was no evidence to show that the employee used the drugs while on duty, the arbitrator concluded that "the employer acted within its contractual right when it discharged" the employee "without opportunity to rectify or change his offending behavior" (*Lick Fish and Poultry*, 87 LA 1062).

• An employee was justly discharged when he reported to work under the influence of drugs he took while off-duty, decided an arbitrator. Management noticed the employee arrived at work "walking like he was somewhat in pain" and appearing "droopy-looking." After a urinalysis revealed the presence of drugs in his system, the employee admitted to using marijuana over the previous weekend and was subsequently discharged. The arbitrator reasoned that because the employer's policy prohibited employees from reporting to work while "under the influence of drugs," the employee was justly disciplined although his use of marijuana had occurred while he was off-duty (*Houston Power and Light*, 87 LA 478).

• An employer improperly discharged an employee for smoking marijuana off the premises during his lunch break, another arbitrator held. The arbitrator noted that "an employee's lunch period is generally considered his own time and the employer's control and responsibility is even further weakened because the grievant was six blocks away from the plant." Given these circumstances, the arbitrator concluded, "it is difficult to believe that any harm or danger specifically accrued to the plant or other employees" through the employee's actions (*Gamble Brothers*, 68 LA 72).

## Arrest on Drug Charges

Because arrest does not prove that an employee actually has committed any crime or engaged in behavior that endangers the reputation of his employer or the safety of his co-workers, arbitrators are reluctant to uphold discipline against employees arrested on—but not convicted of—drug charges.

• An employer unjustly suspended an employee without pay after his arrest in connection with local drug trafficking, said an arbitrator. "We have not regressed to the point where the presumption of innocence until proven guilty is abandoned," insisted the arbitrator. The employer was "precipitous" in suspending the employee, said the arbitrator, stressing that no charges had been levied against the employee and a "real investigation" had not been conducted by the

employer (*Times Mirror Cable Television*, 87 LA 543).

• Another arbitrator ruled that the dismissal of an employee arrested on charges of cocaine possession was proper, even though the charges were dismissed. An employee who managed a community center was fired after his arrest for possession of cocaine. Pointing out that police arrest "is not a basis for determining guilt," the arbitrator nonetheless upheld the employee's dismissal, finding that the employee's position required "great contact with the community, where success is based on trust and leadership," and that the community center "would suffer and that its programs would be undermined if a facility manager who had had drug involvement were reinstated" (*Wayne State University*, 87 LA 953).

## Conviction on Drug Charges

Adverse effects on operations, other employees, and the employer's position in the community may give an arbitrator sound arguments, when supported by strong evidence, for upholding a discharge in cases involving an employee who has been convicted on drug charges. When a court tempers the sentence by, for example, suspending part of it or permitting a work release, however, arbitrators generally require that management show similar leniency.

• An arbitrator ordered the reinstatement of an employee convicted of possession of marijuana because the court put the employee on probation. Stressing that the "conviction and probation order must be taken as a whole," the arbitrator ruled that management erred in relying only on the conviction to terminate the employee. As long as the probation order remained in force, the employee had the right to "continue in service and work with seniority rights unimpaired" (*Port Terminal Railroad Assoc.*, 60 LA 430).

• An employee whose sentence for unlawful delivery of marijuana was suspended was entitled to conditional reinstatement by his employer, absent "specific and compelling evidence" that his conviction was "harmful to the interests of the employer or other employees," ruled an arbitrator. Although management argued that the employee "could be a destructive influence on other employees," that his "continued employment would be damaging to the employer's reputation," and that the reinstatement might "cause other problems, such as absenteeism and tardiness," the arbitrator dismissed these objections as "either hypothetical or speculative" (*Intalco Aluminum Corp.*, 68 LA 66).

● An arbitrator upheld the discharge of an employee convicted of three off-premises drug-dealing felonies and sentenced to a four-year prison term and who generated extensive publicity about the case and was identified as worker for the employer. The arbitrator said common sense alone should be enough to tell the employee that a drug conviction could result in discharge, even though the employer had no formal rule prohibiting illicit off-premises drug activity. Also emphasizing the severe, adverse impact that the publicity of the event had on the employer, the arbitrator added that her continued employment and presence in the workplace would have further negative impact on the employer (*Haskell of Pittsburgh*, 96 LA 1208).

● An arbitrator ruled that the indirect harm caused by customer reading of an employee's drug arrest was sufficient to warrant his discharge even without direct evidence that the employer's reputation was damaged (*Delta Beverage Group*, 96 LA 454).

● A discharge was reduced to a suspension where news accounts of an employee's drug arrest did not identify his employer, and the person's co-workers expressed no reluctance to work with him (*Mobil Oil Corp.*, 95 LA 162).

● An arbitrator upheld the dismissal of an employee who was fired after his employer learned of his conviction for selling cocaine. The arbitrator rejected the employee's argument that he was unjustly discharged, given that the sale took place neither on employer premises nor on employer time.

Rather, the arbitrator ruled that just cause existed for the discharge "because of the impact of the arrest on the employer's product, its reputation, employee safety, plant security, and production and discipline." Specifically, the arbitrator said, in light of the employee's conviction for selling marijuana two years earlier, the employer further has just cause that the employee "may continue using drugs" and "may attempt to sell drugs to other employees" (*Martin-Marietta Aerospace*, 81 LA 695; see also 76 LA 387, 68 LA 697).

# Drug Testing

## OVERVIEW

As drug testing becomes an increasingly popular method of discovering or confirming that employees are using drugs, the number of issues that arbitrators must address in drug-testing grievances also increases.

Among the drug-testing issues that concern arbitrators are whether:

- an employer may impose a drug-testing policy;
- an employer may demand that an employee be tested at random or for just cause;
- the results of a drug test proved that an employee's work performance is impaired;
- testing procedures unjustly invaded an employee's privacy; and
- samples were carefully tested and protected against tampering and adulteration.

## SUMMARY OF CASES

### Imposing Drug Testing Unilaterally

Employers that unilaterally impose a drug-testing policy on their unionized workforce often encounter objections from the labor organization, which argues that because neither employees nor their representatives had a role in creating the policy, it is unreasonable in light of existing contract provisions. Arbitrators, however, are divided over whether management may impose a testing policy without employee input.

- Unilaterally promulgating a drug-testing program was within management's traditional rights, an arbitrator ruled. When a truck driver continually refused to sign a form acknowledging his receipt and awareness of his employer's drug-testing policy, the employer discharged him. Objecting to the discharge, the union argued that the implementation of a drug and alcohol testing policy was a subject for bargaining, and that because the policy was instituted unilaterally, the driver was right not to comply. Upholding the discharge, the arbitrator ruled that "there is no question but that the employer had the right to implement this drug and alcohol test policy. It is clearly an exercise of management's right and

was an integral part of the employer's responsibility to maintain safety, efficiency, and discipline in the workplace" (*Concrete Pipe Products*, 87 LA 601).

- Another arbitrator held that a testing policy, imposed without union input, was unfair. After an employer implemented a substance abuse policy, the union objected, arguing that the policy constituted new work rules, and therefore, as set out in the contract, required union-management negotiation. Calling the employers' policy "improper," the arbitrator held that although "there is no doubt that there is more drug abuse in our present day society," the employer "cannot overlook a contractual clause" that demands negotiations on rule making (*Hobart Corp.*, 87 LA 905).

- One arbitrator declared that a drug-testing policy implemented unilaterally was unreasonable because it failed to treat employees "fairly and equitably" as the contract required. The testing policy was objectionable, said the arbitrator, because it mandated testing for employees whose work had no bearing on safety and who did not work with the public, provided that uncooperative employees could be charged with insubordination, dictated the testing method to be used despite the availability of many methods, did not allow employees to test a portion of their sample by a lab of their choosing, and did not mandate that the employer verify positive test results with a confirmatory test (*Bay Area Rapid Transit*, 88 LA 1; see also 95 LA 729, 94 LA 393).

## Employer's Right to Test

Typically, testing policies call for testing employees either randomly—i.e., without any suspicion that they use drugs—or for just cause, where management claims that it has sufficient reason to suspect drug use and require the employee in question to undergo a drug test.

*Random testing*—In a minority of cases, arbitrators will sanction an employer's use of random testing. Reasons for upholding such policies include public interest and safety, as well as the employee's history of drug use.

● In one case, an arbitrator held that a refinery did not violate a collective bargaining agreement when it implemented a random drug and alcohol testing program, where the employer had bargained in good faith before implementing the program, established a need for the policy (18 of 184 bargaining unit employees had documented substance abuse problems and had been involved in 22 incidents over a 15-year period), and an earlier reasonable cause testing policy apparently was not successful (*Atlas Processing Co.*, 106 LA 172).

● An employee subject to a last-chance, conditional, return-to-duty agreement in which he agreed to submit to random, comprehensive drug screening was properly discharged when he tested positive for cocaine and and other substances after he reported to work in an excited condition, threatening to kill his wife. The employee's being under the influence of drugs on plant property was a dischargeable offense, the employee did not show that the testing procedures were inadequate, and he could not prove that anyone had tampered with his specimen, the arbitrator said, upholding the penalty (*Koppers Co.*, 94 LA 363).

● A drug-testing policy implemented at a nuclear power plant was reasonable, declared an arbitrator. The policy called for the periodic and random testing of all personnel who were granted unescorted access inside the plant's security fence. Opposing the policy, the union argued that the test's "random administration without probable cause offends all concepts of reasonableness and fairness." While "random testing without probable cause is abhorrent to any fair-minded person," the arbitrator replied, "the disasters at Three Mile Island and Chernobyl give eloquent testimony to the disastrous effects of human error" that could occur at this power plant. Although "there is something inherently offensive about this type of testing," the arbitrator concluded, "the balancing of public interest favors the imposition of the rule" (*Arkansas Power and Light*, 88 LA 1065).

● In the case of a hospital nurse who admitted to having used drugs in the past, an arbitrator ruled that her employer had just cause to request the nurse's consent to random drug testing in light of her history and a proven lack of persistence in seeking rehabilitation. Pointing out that there is "no 'certain' cure for addiction to mood-altering chemicals," the arbitrator upheld the testing order, noting that the risks and probabilities of the nurse's resuming drug use "must be evaluated in the context of the job responsibilities," which could involve life-threatening situations for her patients (*Deaconess Medical Center*, 88 LA 44; see also *Rothe Development Inc.*, 106 LA 97 and 96 LA 596, 95 LA 7, 94 LA 399, 91 LA 1385, 91 LA 1186, 91 LA 363).

● An arbitrator held that an employer had just cause to discharge an employee who tested positive for amphetamines during an off-work, random drug test, even though it would have been more appropriate for the employer to administer the test while the employee was at work. The man in question had previously been suspended for taking drugs and had been given a second chance, under which the employee was put on indefinite probation and was required to undergo random drug testing and rehabilitation (*BHP Coated Steel Corp.*, 105 LA 387).

*For-cause testing*—When management can furnish arguments that there was a sufficient reason to test an employee, arbitrators more willingly uphold discipline that results from a positive drug test. Factors arbitrators consider in these just cause determinations include the following.

• *Safety*—Although claims that drug testing is an integral part of maintaining employee and public safety in a potentially hazardous industry can help an employer justify its policy (e.g., in public transportation, see 82 LA 150), safety claims may not always override other labor relations concerns. In one case, an explosives manufacturer, arguing that working while "impaired due to drugs is extremely dangerous" in a munitions plant, instituted a drug-testing program that called for random testing of employees. Under its testing policy, the employer discharged an employee for a positive urinalysis, but the employee argued that the random testing policy was unjust. Overturning the discharge, the arbitrator held that, despite the employer's safety concerns, "the taking of a person's urine without any suspicion that she may have been under the influence of drugs is highly invasive of personal privacy" (*Day and Zimmerman Inc.*, 88 LA 1001; see also 91 LA 213).

• An arbitrator held an employer had just cause to discharge an employee who failed a drug test after he lacerated his hand and was taken to an urgent care facility. The employer's drug testing policy, which required the testing of employees who are involved in accidents requiring off-site medical care, was reasonable where the employees worked in the vicinity of large, potentially hazardous industrial equipment and the policy's distinction between minor and serious accidents provides a reasonable basis to test, the arbitrator ruled (*Jefferson Smurfit Corp.*, 106 LA 306).

• *Suspicion of Employee Drug Use*—In light of observations by management that an employee was "unsteady,

staggering, swaying, and disoriented; that her eyes were glassy and her speech slurred," an arbitrator maintained that the employee was properly discharged for refusing to take a drug test, given that the purpose of a drug test is "to confirm whether or not an employee is under the influence" of drugs as suspected (*American Standard*, 77 LA 1085; see also 97 LA 850, 97 LA 343).

• *Possession of Drugs on Employer Premises*—In another case, an employer forbade employees from bringing alcohol or drugs on employer property. After marijuana was discovered in an off-duty employee's car parked on employer premises, they requested that he take a drug test. Finding that the employee was not obligated to submit to the test, the arbitrator declared that the grievant was not driving his car as an employee. Therefore, the arbitrator said, "the employer representatives were not entitled to instruct him to submit to testing for any purpose" (*Texas Utilities Generating Co.*, 82 LA 6).

*Off-duty drug testing*—Off-duty scheduling of drug testing may not violate a collective bargaining agreement, one arbitrator ruled.

• Pursuant to a new bargaining agreement, a school board conducted three random drug and alcohol tests of employees who operated board-owned vehicles. Each time, the board randomly selected the employees to be tested and scheduled the tests between the employees' morning and afternoon work. The employees generally were compensated for one-hour of straight time for taking the test. Notification of a third test, unlike the prior tests, was given to employees on the morning of the test. The employer denied requests by two employees for reimbursement of income allegedly lost from outside employment due to the employer's failure to give advance notice. The union filed a grievance, claiming that the employer violated the agreement by failing to reimburse employees for lost wages due to the scheduling of the test during work time.

Nothing in the bargaining agreement restricted the employer's right to conduct random drug/alcohol testing and nothing in the contract obligated the employer to give advance notice of such tests, the arbitrator said. Further, the agreement does not require that the employer reimburse employees for wages allegedly lost from other employer because they had to undergo the tests, the arbitrator added (*Wooster City Board of Education*, 102 LA 535).

● An arbitrator ruled that an employee who was reinstated after completing a drug treatment program should not have been placed on permanent suspension after he failed a random drug test on a day he was off work because the reinstatement agreement did not supersede provisions of the parties' collective bargaining agreement, which did not prohibit off-duty drug use (*New Orleans Steamship Assoc.*, 105 LA 79).

*After OSHA-reportable accident—* An arbitrator held an employer had just cause to discharge an employee injured in a workplace accident who tested positive for marijuana after he came on company property to collect his workers' compensation check, where the employee had not undergone a drug test since he had experienced the OSHA-reportable accident and he was aware that he could be tested once he returned to company property. (*Solar Turbines Inc.*, 104 LA 1070)

● An arbitrator held an employer had just cause to discharge an employee who failed a drug test after he lacerated his hand and was taken to an urgent care facility. The employer's drug testing policy, which required the testing of employees who are involved in accidents requiring off-site medical care, was reasonable where the employees worked in the vicinity of large, potentially hazardous industrial equipment and the policy's distinction between minor and serious accidents provided a reasonable basis to test, the arbitrator ruled (*Jefferson Smurfit Corp.*, 106 LA 306).

## Employee's Access to Treatment

An employer did not treat an employee fairly when it fired him for failing a drug test without giving him a chance to attempt rehabilitation, as others had received, according to the arbitrator.

The employer had been plagued by workplace accidents that it believed were caused by drug use among its 300 employees. Management had reason to suspect one of its employees of drug use after several episodes involving his girlfriend and mother, both of whom also worked for the employer. One day, when the employee reported for his night shift, he was interviewed about drug use and ordered to take a drug test, which revealed cocaine in his system. He was suspended and told he would be fired unless he named other employees who used or sold drugs at the plant. When the employee refused to name names but asked to be admitted into a drug treatment program (as provided for in the contract) the employer fired him.

The union grieved, arguing that 29 other employees who had asked for the rehabilitation option had been able to take advantage of the program, along with getting a "last chance" agreement that enabled them to keep their jobs. The arbitrator agreed with the union and said the employee should be evaluated and if possible, rehabilitated "in the same manner as previous employees" (*Interforest Corp.*, 117 LA 1121).

## Contractual Obligations

An employer's decision to discharge an employee for refusing to submit to a drug test may be successfully challenged if the employer has failed to follow its contractual obligations.

● An employer improperly discharged an employee who refused to take a blood test after being accused of smoking marijuana, an arbitrator ruled. A manager observed the employee smoking what appeared to be a marijuana cigarette. After the employee refused the manager's request to submit to a drug test, the employee was fired. While the employer had reasonable grounds to order the drug test and to discipline the employee for his refusal to take the test, the arbitrator pointed out, under the collective bargaining agreement, two written warning notices are required before an employee may be discharged or even suspended. Accordingly, the arbitrator ordered the employee reinstated (*Warehouse Distribution Centers*, 90 LA 979).

***Just-cause standard***—An employer policy that provides for the automatic discharge of employees who fail random drug tests violates a collective bargaining agreement that requires any discharge to be for just cause, an arbitrator ruled. In agreeing to a just-cause standard, the arbitrator said, an employer promises to consider an employee's employment record and/or any other mitigating factors or extenuating circumstances prior to determining if the employee should be discharged (*Alaska Dept. of Transportation*, 108 LA 339).

### Proof of Impairment

An employee may argue that basing discipline on a positive drug test is unjust because the test does not sufficiently prove that the employee was impaired by drug use. Generally, arbitrators agree that drug testing alone does not provide scientific proof of impairment.

• An employee argued that he was unjustly dismissed after a drug test, arguing that his job performance was unimpaired. The arbitrator, however, ruled that the employer acted in a "fair, reasonable, and contractually permissible manner," by discharging the employee. The employer's policy permitted it to dismiss employees who were found using drugs, the arbitrator noted, and finding the positive test result to be sufficient proof of drug use, ruled that the employee was justly dismissed (*Indianapolis Power and Light Co.*, 87 LA 826).

• While a positive drug test was "not conclusive" evidence that an employee was under the influence of marijuana, along with the positive finding, an employer had enough other evidence to justify the employee's dismissal, an arbitrator decided. Moreover, the employee also "admitted use of marijuana," the arbitrator added, which "violated a known safety rule," and thereby endangered his co-workers; and "was absent without notifying management" (*Georgia Power*, 87 LA 800).

• Another arbitrator found that an employer unjustly discharged an employee after a supervisor observed the employee's erratic behavior, the cause of which turned out to be cocaine in the employee's system. The arbitrator noted that even though the employer had shown via a blood test that the employee was using drugs, without "proof of either the inadequacy of work performance, intoxication, or the creation of a risk of harm, the proof that an employee used cocaine is insufficient to constitute just cause" for discharge (*Kroger Co.*, 88 LA 463; see also 88 LA 91).

### Employee Privacy

Depending on the particular circumstances involved in a case, when an employee is asked to undergo a drug test, an arbitrator may decide that certain drug-testing procedures overstep the privacy employees should enjoy.

• An employee who refused to submit to urinalysis in the presence of a nurse was unjustly discharged, an arbitrator held. Because the employee would have had to undress fully to provide the specimen and was refused a request for a robe, she refused to submit to the test and was fired. Because the employee would have had to undress completely, the arbitrator maintained that the presence of the witness was "more than usually embarrassing," and the refusal to allow her to wear a robe "made the conditions of the test unreasonably onerous" (*Union Plaza Hotel*, 88 LA 528).

• A drug-testing program that permitted an official to observe an employee urinating and required employees to report all prescription medicines they were taking was unreasonable, an arbitrator decided. The policy was implemented over objections of the union, which called the procedures an invasion of privacy. Finding that the plan's prescription-reporting requirement was "vague and unreasonable," the arbitrator said if it is possible for an employee to alter a urine specimen, then the "circumstances or location should be changed rather than requiring observation of urination." The arbitrator ordered the parties to negotiate the testing procedures into a "reasonable form" (*Sharples Coal Corp.*, 91 LA 1065; see also 95 LA 393).

## Chain of Custody/
### Laboratory Issues

Challenges to drug testing are sometimes based on employees' claims that the testing procedure was unsound or careless and therefore that the test results are unreliable. Where such arguments have been made, arbitrators note whether the employers have guarded the sample well and tested it thoroughly.

• An arbitrator rejected an employee's claims that his suspension based on a positive drug test was unjust because the employer could not prove that it maintained a careful "chain of possession" regarding the specimen. The employer exercised "due care" in securing the sample and properly identifying it as the employee's, the arbitrator noted, adding that greater requirements for proper identification of the sample "might well result" in a program that would be impossible to carry out (*Union Oil Co. of Calif.*, 87 LA 297).

• Overturning the discharge of an employee whom management thought was under the influence of alcohol while at work, an arbitrator noted that the employer did not follow the sample-handling procedures it had established in concert with the union. The procedures required that an employer and union representative together mail an employee's blood sample to the laboratory for testing. In this case, however, the nurse gave the sample to the employer representative, who took the sample home and kept it overnight in his refrigerator, and then mailed it to the lab the next morning without ever notifying the union (*Holliston Mills*, 60 LA 1030).

• Another arbitrator pointed out that one crucial evidentiary test for workplace substance abuse is the analysis of medical tests. In upholding the discharge of an employee, the arbitrator commended the "very careful and thorough" testing procedure implemented by the employer, which included requiring the employee to undergo both blood and urine tests, and submitting the samples to two separate, professional and independent labs, each of which corroborated the positive findings of the other (*Citgo Petroleum Corp.*, 88 LA 521; see also *Dravo Lime Co.*, 105 LA 54).

# *Unsatisfactory Performance*

## Incompetence

_____ OVERVIEW _____

Incompetence, unlike mere carelessness, generally is not treated as a disciplinary problem because the usual remedies of warnings and suspensions are inappropriate and nonproductive when the employee is, in truth, unable to do the work.

As one arbitrator explained, in this type of situation, "an employee is not guilty of fault or wrongdoing," and, consequently, does not warrant "discipline" as such. There is, however, a "class of nonculpable reasons which will ultimately support discharge, not because the employee is necessarily guilty of fault or wrongdoing, but, rather, because the essence of the employment relationship is so impaired that it is not reasonable to require an employer to continue that relationship." Specifically, this class includes "inability to perform the work with reasonable efficiency," because, "if permitted to go on, this would impair the employer's ability to make a profit, to grant wage increases in future negotiations to good productive employees, and, indeed, an employer's very ability to provide jobs."

Whenever a nonculpable cause of termination arises, however, an employer must first warn the employee of possible consequences and work with the employee "to try to correct or remove the thing that is destructive to the employment relationship," the arbitrator stressed. If it becomes clear "that the cause that impairs the employment relationship is chronic or of long-standing" character and that "there is no reasonable prognosis that the cause can be removed within a reasonable period of time," then "nondisciplinary termination" is warranted.

Accordingly, the arbitrator upheld the discharge of an incentive rate worker who consistently failed to produce enough pieces to earn minimum wages. Pointing out that the employer had counseled and warned the employee for more than a year about her inefficiency, the arbitrator declared that the employer should no longer be "forced to supplement her wage beyond the work given in exchange" (_Florsheim Shoe Co._, 74 LA 705; see also 91 LA 293).

Other arbitrators similarly have upheld termination for incompetence where an employer repeatedly had counseled the employee about the problem (97 LA 378, 96 LA 556, 91 1347, 91 LA 1014, 91 LA 593, 76 LA 254). This emphasis on counseling also underlies arbitral decisions to sustain "nonculpable" discipline short of discharge where the reprimand or suspension is designed to function as a warning to the employee (74 LA 274, 73 LA 385).

• Discipline is likely to be overturned, however, where an employer cannot substantiate allegations of incompetence; has neglected to give the employee proper training or supervision necessary for learning how to do the job correctly, or has failed to give the employee adequate warning and an opportunity to improve poor performance (97 LA 1196, 97 LA 1145, 97 LA 1045, 97 LA 931, 97 LA 549, 97 LA 12, 96 LA 957, 92 LA 850).

Even where the worker clearly is incompetent, an employer may be able to serve its own best interests in terms of hiring expenses and workforce morale by reassigning the employee, where possible, to another job that is within his or her capabilities.

## SUMMARY OF CASES

### Failure to Meet Production Standards

The employer, one arbitrator pointed out, "has regularly been held to be entitled to set production standards and discharge an employee for failure to meet them provided the standards are fair and reasonable" (*Allied Employers Inc.*, 65 LA 270; see also 95 LA 182, 92 LA 862, ).

● Stressing that "maintenance of high efficiency is important to the profitability of the employer and the continued jobs of the employees," an arbitrator declared that "continued low production" on the part of any one worker "cannot be condoned." In this case, the employee had been warned several times about his "low production" but continued to work at a pace that was vastly "inferior" to that of even temporary employees, the arbitrator noted.

In view of these circumstances, the employer's decision to suspend the worker for three days was "neither arbitrary nor capricious," the arbitrator declared, but rather "could be viewed as lenient." Cautioning the employee that the employer was using "progressive discipline" in an effort to drive home the lesson, the arbitrator emphasized that unless he "immediately" improved his "deportment," he could "expect to be discharged without any hope of reinstatement" (*Lash Distributors Inc.*, 74 LA 274).

● A worker was properly terminated for "substandard" performance after he botched four separate work assignments in a row, an arbitrator decided. Several supervisors testified that the employee was "consistently the worst performer in the entire workforce," and even co-workers admitted that they had had to help rectify the employee's mistakes, the arbitrator pointed out, ruling that the termination was "reasonable and for just cause" (*Pet Inc.*, 76 LA 292).

When an employer resorts to discharge for an employee's failure to meet production standards, an arbitrator judging the reasonableness of the action may consider the adequacy of the employee's training, supervision, and equipment provided to do the job, and the weight of production records, work sheets, or work samples submitted by the employer to establish the worker's incompetence.

● Arbitrators also agree in theory that an employer has the right to tighten work standards and require better performance, even if this is a break from past laxness. To bring about such a reversal of past practice, however, an employer may have to do more than merely exhort employees to do better. Discipline of workers who continue to produce at the old standards may not be upheld if the new standards have not been clearly defined and communicated to the employees (12 LA 527, 8 LA 282).

● The production standard that is set must be reasonable, as one arbitrator said in upholding termination of a substandard worker in large part because output norms were based on a "thoroughly standardized" work measurement system that had been "applied in a thoroughly professional way by a licensed and authorized practitioner." With this "valid measurement" demonstrating that the employee's output level was less than half normal capacity, the employer had the right to discharge her, the arbitrator concluded, notwithstanding the fact that it had continued to employ the worker beyond the probationary period (*Northern Telecom Inc.*, 65 LA 405).

● As another arbitrator noted, the probation clause with regard to discharge simply means that an employer is not prohibited from terminating an employee, as long as it defends "its actions on the basis of other parts of the contract" (*Sager Lock Works*, 12 LA 495).

• An employee who had passed his probationary period in a higher-level job was justifiably discharged for improper work performance, an arbitrator ruled. Dismissing the union's allegations that the employee should never have been promoted to the position because he lacked the necessary "ability and education," the arbitrator found that the worker had performed competently throughout his probationary period. Fitness for the job, the arbitrator pointed out, was not confined to "technical or practical qualifications only," but included "responsibility and reliability" as well. Agreeing with the employer that the employee's problem was "not a matter of competence but of negligence and disregard of warnings," the arbitrator concluded that the worker had "disqualified himself for continuation in the employer's employ" (*Admiral Paint Co.*, 60 LA 418).

• An employer should have demoted, not discharged, a registered nurse for her poor job performance, according to the arbitrator in the case.

The employee, an RN, had worked for many years as a lower-level nurse for a county; after passing her RN test, she was promoted to a different nurses' station, where she was "counseled" a number of times and suspended for two weeks. Eventually she was discharged. Most of the discipline was for the employee's alleged negligence in dispensing medication, although none of her mistakes resulted in serious harm to anyone. The union argued that mitigating circumstances, such as poor supervision and inadequate training, could explain the employee's poor performance. The arbitrator agreed that termination was too harsh a penalty for the employee's errors, although the errors could not simply be attributed to a lack of training. Adding that she believed the employee was simply overwhelmed by the new position, the arbitrator ordered the RN reinstated but demoted to her previous job classification (*Santa Clara County*, 113 LA 1148).

## Inadequate Training or Equipment

Generally, an employer has an obligation to give an employee adequate training and proper equipment before disciplining the worker for incompetence. On the other hand, arbitrators have held that employers are not required to maintain an indefinite training program for employees, or absolve them of all responsibility for equipment.

• An arbitrator held an employer improperly discharged a bilingual Russian emigre who was a state economic assistance worker for poor work performance because the employer had neglected to give her special training that would emphasize her need to understand cultural differences and tasks associated with her job (*County of Hennepin*, 105 LA 392).

• An employer properly removed a worker from a training program when, after seven weeks of instruction, she had been unable to "master even the most rudimentary facets" of the job, an arbitrator decided. The arbitrator dismissed the worker's arguments that the training program was "too short" and that the employer was obligated to keep her in the program for "whatever length" of time was necessary to make her "sufficiently competent" in the job. On the contrary, the arbitrator held, in today's "industrial era of highly educated and compensated workers," companies cannot afford to "allow an employee an almost indefinite time in which to become sufficiently qualified to properly and safely handle a specific job." In any case, he declared, the worker's "lack of mechanical aptitude was the primary factor in her failure in the training program, not the make-up of the training schedule" (*Allied Chemical Corp.*, 75 LA 1101).

• An arbitrator upheld written reprimands issued to a group of workers for restricted output, notwithstanding the employees' contention that they had done "the best they could" with "faulty equipment." Even granting that there had been equipment problems, the arbitrator stressed, the employees were culpable because they had neglected their "duty" to advise their supervisor of the faulty machinery and thereby wasted the opportunity to get it repaired without "significant loss of production" (*Wallace-Murray Corp.*, 73 LA 385).

• An employer properly discharged a chemical operator for failing to check a vacuum breaker while pumping hydrochloric acid from one storage tank into another, resulting in the collapse of the tank and loss of 400 gallons of acid, an arbitrator decided. Arguing that he did not receive proper operating instructions on the pumping process and that a frozen valve was the cause of the incident, the employee insisted that he had not been negligent.

Finding that the employee was trained by another operator to check the breaker, the arbitrator ruled that the worker committed a serious operating error that resulted in the tank's collapse. Pointing out that the employee's poor work record indicated that he previously had been warned on at least two occasions that his operating errors would subject him to discharge, the arbitrator concluded that the worker was "seriously remiss" in his duties (*Neville Chemical Co.*, 74 LA 814; see also 72 LA 81).

• An arbitrator held a 23-year employee who was "on loan" to a department as a mechanic was unjustly discharged for unsatisfactory job performance, given that the employee had not received adequate training for his new position, proper supervision during a trial/probationary period, or appropriate job assessments and evaluations as outlined under a performance improvement plan imposed on the employee by the employer (*Peoples Natural Gas*, 105 LA 37).

## Proof of Incompetence: Sales Records

• Arbitrators may be hesitant in approving discharges for inefficiency based on sales records. Unlike the output of most production workers, the work records of salespeople are subject to several factors beyond their control. These include different areas and customers, competition, product changes, and prevailing business climate. Arbitrators agree that these other factors must be considered before using a poor sales record to justify a discharge. Where an employer failed to show that a decline in ice cream sales was the driver/salesman's own fault, for instance, the man's discharge was overruled (*Russell Creamery Co.*, 21 LA 293; see also 98 LA 112, 96 LA 274.

• Another arbitrator ruled that an employer was justified in discharging a department chief because of his low sales record. Although the worker argued that the drop in sales was the result of economic conditions, the arbitrator decided that the true cause of the decline was the worker's "lack of application or lack of sales ability," as evidenced by the fact that his sales record "averaged only about two thirds that of his assistant" and "ranged as low as approximately one-third." Absent evidence that the assistant was a "super salesman," the arbitrator declared the discrepancy could only be explained by the employee's unsuitability to the job (*Allied Employers Inc.*, 65 LA 270).

# Negligence

## OVERVIEW

There is a consensus among arbitrators that undue negligence, carelessness, or wanton disregard for the employer's property or operations provides just cause for discipline (97 LA 1029, 97 LA 542, 95 LA 1016, 92 LA 1143, 91 LA 1284, 91 LA 1162, 91 LA 286).

Although an employer probably should not have a flat rule of "one strike and you're out" when it comes to employee negligence, the employer does not have to wait until major damage is done or all materials are ruined before resorting to discharging a negligent employee. The decision in each case should be based on a careful consideration of the alleged negligent act and related factors. One arbitrator suggested that these points should be considered:

- the possibility of the act's recurrence;
- the attitude of the erring employee, in particular the desire and ability to learn from the mistake (98 LA 188, 97 LA 162, 92 LA 1214);
- the actual and potential injury involved;
- the influence of the discipline on other employees;
- the effect of the mistake on the parties with whom the employer deals, such as customers or the government; and
- the employee's length of service (37 LA 953; see also 95 LA 435, 93 LA 1236, 50 LA 571).

## SUMMARY OF CASES

### Gross Negligence

To sustain a discharge for one-time carelessness or a first offense, management usually must be prepared to prove that the employee was guilty of gross negligence—that is, an almost willful disregard of what is being done and an almost complete inattentiveness to the job when the person had the opportunity to foresee the likely consequences (97 LA 1029, 97 LA 542, 94 LA 21, 91 LA 1284, 91 LA 1162).

- An employer properly discharged a worker for gross negligence after she "panicked" in an emergency situation, despite eight weeks of training in emergency procedures. Instead of simply shutting off the valve that fed gas to a heater where the flame had gone out, the worker ran for help. Meanwhile, the gas continued to build up, causing an explo-

sion that resulted in considerable damage to the heater.

The arbitrator dismissed the worker's arguments that the discipline was too severe because she had had only one week's experience in the job she was assigned to at the time. The employer had a right, following its "thorough training" in safety procedures, to assume that all employees were "well versed and familiar with the proper safety procedures," the arbitrator declared. Moreover, the employer was justified in insisting on "competent and careful adherence to its procedures," the arbitrator noted, especially where the correct response to the emergency entailed "simply shutting off a valve." Stressing that the employee's "failure to adhere to the simple safety procedures in this case resulted in extensive damage to the charge heater and perhaps more important, potential harm to fellow employees," the arbitrator concluded that termination was justified (*Hess Oil Virgin Islands, Corp.*, 72 LA 81).

• A hospital employee who mistakenly released the wrong body to a funeral home should have been suspended, not fired, said one arbitrator. The employee failed to follow the company's policy for identifying a body before releasing it and was discharged for negligence. The union objected, claiming that only one other employee under the current agreement had been discharged for the same offense. That employee, unlike this one, had a disciplinary history, but in this case, although proper procedure was not followed, there was some dispute as to whether this employee was entirely responsible for the mix-up or whether another worker also was involved. The employee's conduct was not grossly negligent or willful, the arbitrator concluded, ordering the employee reinstated with back pay less a five-day suspension (*UPMC Presbyterian*, 114 LA 986).

• A worker who failed to follow established procedures while pumping out a tank, thereby causing the tank to collapse and 400 gallons of hydrochloric acid to be lost, was properly terminated, another arbitrator ruled. Despite earlier warnings—after other incidents—that another operating error would subject him to discharge, the arbitrator stressed, the worker showed "little, if any, positive response" to the employer's efforts to "mold him into an acceptable employee." Given the magnitude of the latest incident, the arbitrator decided, management was justified in its actions (*Neville Chemical Co.*, 74 LA 814).

• An employer properly discharged a payroll clerk for careless errors that resulted in overpayments exceeding $1,200 in a single month. Considering that the employee had received special training following an earlier discovery of errors, and that it was apparent then that she knew how to perform her job properly, the arbitrator found just cause for her discharge (*Greyhound Lines Inc.*, 67 LA 483).

• A drill press operator negligently misdrilled a number of holes in an aircraft part he was working on, and then attempted to cover up the mistake by discarding the part, which was worth about $800. When the part was later discovered, the worker was discharged for his poor work and for failing to report the mistake to his foreman. Upholding the discharge, the arbitrator pointed out that the employee was well aware of the employer's stringent rule on reporting mistakes, which had been designed to guard against defective parts being used in the finished passenger airplanes. He not only did not report his mistake, the arbitrator found, but apparently went so far as to conspire with his supervisor to deceive management in order to keep his job (*Rohr Industries Inc.*, 65 LA 982).

• An arbitrator overturned the discharge of a machinist who had made a costly error because of the employee's four-year blemish-free work record. Although management argued that the mistake amounted to gross negligence and warranted immediate dismissal, the arbitrator ruled otherwise because the error did not involve willfulness or recklessness or a wanton disregard for life, health, or property. Rather, he said, it amounted to a good-faith oversight on a simple step in a complicated process, something that could have happened to anyone. Although it was a serious error, this type of first offense does not warrant discharge, the arbitrator decided, especially considering the employee's past record, his honesty in reporting the mistake, his tenure, and his sense of responsibility. Instead, the arbitrator concluded, a two-week suspension was more appropriate (*Ingalls Shipbuilding Corp.*, 37 LA 953; see also 97 LA 386, 96 LA 585).

• An employee was improperly discharged for negligence after the company car he momentarily had left unattended was stolen, another arbitrator decided. Whereas the employer based the discharge decision on a work rule against leaving a running vehicle unattended, the arbitrator found that management did not address this issue "on a regular basis." Consequently, he said, "the employer was as much at fault" in the situation as the employee. In light of the worker's past record of failing to follow established procedures, however, the arbitrator concluded that a lengthy suspension was in order (*Servair Inc.*, 76 LA 1134).

• Management improperly disciplined two workers in a case of "group responsibility," an arbitrator decided. Because an operation that normally was performed by one of two workers was not carried out, the employer incurred several thousands of dollars in damages. It then disciplined both of the workers. Overturning the penalties, the arbitrator came out strongly against holding an entire crew responsible for performing a task that management had not specifically assigned to any one individual. Such a practice would carry discipline to the extreme by permitting punishment of a group whenever individual responsibility could not be pinpointed, the arbitrator declared, pointing out that responsibility for assigning duties rests with the supervisor (*International Nickel Co. Inc.*, 44 LA 376).

## Neglect of Duty or Responsibility

Neglect of duty (inattention to responsibilities or ordinary negligence) may be distinguished from gross negligence in that the inattention is less intentional and, for the most part, results in less severe repercussions or involves minimal expense. Although arbitrators are unlikely to sustain terminations for isolated incidents of this type, they generally will uphold less drastic penalties, provided that these are imposed in accordance with established policies and that there is "clear and convincing evidence" to support the charge (97 LA 66, 97 LA 60, 95 LA 873, 93 LA 302).

• In one case, an arbitrator ruled that management had "failed to meet its burden of proof," prompting the arbitrator to overturn a suspension imposed on a worker who allegedly was sleeping while on emergency duty that involved monitoring communications channels. Although the worker, by his own admission, had been lying down, the arbitrator noted, management acknowledged that he could have been watching television in this position, albeit somewhat awkwardly.

The arbitrator also dismissed allegations that the employee and his co-workers were neglecting their duties by watching television because the employees were specifically instructed only "to monitor the radio and telephone and to respond to emergency situations."

Although management declared that watching television while on duty is "a transgression of common sense rules of the workplace," and "detrimental to the departmental morale and discipline," the arbitrator found that the issue at hand had "nothing to do with either the inherent evils of television or the shaping of departmental discipline." Rather, he said, the question to be resolved was whether the workers were neglecting the specific duties that had been assigned to them. The employer was unable to demonstrate that the workers had missed any "emergencies, telephone calls, or radio communications," the arbitrator therefore concluded that the suspensions were improper (*City of Cleveland*, 71 LA 1041).

• An employee was properly disciplined for neglect of duty after he failed to monitor several government contracts, which resulted in overpayments by the employer. Failing to find one "scintilla" of evidence supporting the employee's claim of extenuating circumstances, the arbitrator ruled that management was justified in deciding to discipline the worker. The penalty was too severe a punishment, the arbitrator decided, given that management's policies specifically stated that an official reprimand was the appropriate discipline in such cases (*General Services Administration*, 75 LA 1158).

• An airline mechanic, whose negligence while performing a routine inspection risked damaging an aircraft engine, was properly penalized by a written reprimand. After examining the air intake section of the engine, the mechanic conducted a "test run" of it. Hearing a "funny sound," he immediately cut the engine off and then noticed bits and pieces of shredded material floating in the air. These were later discovered to be the mechanic's own wallet and papers, which he had left inside the engine. The employer issued a written reprimand for the employee's failure to "maintain his given responsibility." Protesting the reprimand, the employee claimed that he would not purposefully leave something in the engine intake and pointed out that the engine was not damaged.

It was clear that the employee did "leave his wallet in the air intake," the arbitrator said, so "it must be recognized that he demonstrated a lack of care for the work in question." The fact that "no actual damage occurred to the engine" was irrelevant, the arbitrator stressed, because the "same inattention" that caused the employee to leave his wallet in the engine's air intake could result in his leaving behind another object that would cause damage. Although the arbitrator accepted the employee's argument that he did not purposely leave his wallet "to be destroyed," he concluded that the employee's discipline was warranted (*Air Force Department*, 76 LA 315).

### Habitual Carelessness

Arbitrators generally uphold management's right to discharge employees with records of chronic carelessness over a period of time, regardless of the causes for the carelessness or whether the culminating incident, standing alone, was sufficient to justify termination (96 LA 609, 94 LA 1080, 74 LA 1008).

• An employee who persisted in her poor work habits was properly discharged, an arbitrator decided. The worker's responsibilities included answering telephone calls from customers and performing routine clerical duties. She consistently carried on personal conversations rather than taking business calls, was frequently absent from her work area, and took inordinate lengths of time—up to nine months in one case—to process invoices, thereby causing the employer to lose substantial discounts for timely payments. Finding that the employee made no attempt to improve her performance despite verbal and written warnings from her supervisor, the arbitrator ruled that management was under no obligation to keep on a worker who "did not diligently apply herself" to her job (*General Electric Co.*, 74 LA 1278).

• Another arbitrator upheld the discharge of an employee for "gross and habitual" carelessness. Although the employee argued that he had not had time to correct his behavior before being terminated, the arbitrator found that management had properly applied a "series of progressive disciplinary measures." The worker had received a total of nine warnings and five disciplinary letters for carelessness and poor performance within a five-week period, the arbitrator pointed out, stressing that the employee "knew he was getting close to discharge" (*S & T Industries Inc.*, 73 LA 857).

• An arbitrator sustained the termination of a worker who did not perform efficiently and had a record of discipline for excessive tardiness. Although management could have terminated the worker for a previous incident, it had suspended her instead, the arbitrator noted. In light of the fact that this "leniency was not improving the employee's work habits," she concluded, management was justified in discharging the worker (*Trojan Luggage Co.*, 76 LA 324).

• An employer was justified in discharging a mill worker who negligently caused the dumping of thousands of pounds of industrial paint, considering the worker's "repeated and admitted violations of safety rules either by deliberate action or by gross negligence." The arbitrator, pointing out that lesser discipline had failed to change the worker's conduct, concluded that "he was not a safe employee for other employees to work with" (*W. C. Richards Co.*, 64 LA 382).

### Accidents & Accident-Prone Workers

Management has the right to fire an employee who is "accident-prone," one arbitrator said, if it can show that the worker meets the definition of one who has "a greater number of accidents than would be expected of the average individual under the same conditions" or who has "personality traits that predispose to accident[s]." This determination can be made, however, only after the employer explores the possibility of whether this predisposition can be corrected, the arbitrator cautioned.

In the case at hand, management based its allegations on the fact that the worker filed inordinate numbers of insurance claims for on-the-job injuries. Reviewing the nature of the claims, the arbitrator found that the evidence suggested that the employee "had only a propensity to file claims in instances where most employees would have been satisfied with receiving merely first-aid treatment." If this were true, he noted, "a conclusion of accident proneness would be unjustified, although a reason for warning" would exist.

The arbitrator suggested that management suspend the worker for a "significant period" and when her returned to work, warn her that "while she should report all accidents, she should not exaggerate them." This technique "would shed light on whether her propensities might be remedied," he explained, whereas "without such experience, it is not clear that she was sufficiently 'accident prone' to warrant discharge as too burdensome an employee" (*Georgia-Pacific Corp.*, 52 LA 325).

• Another arbitrator has argued that industrial discipline, particularly the supreme penalty of discharge, should not be based on the notion that an employee merely is "accident prone." Workers may unluckily be involved in series of accidents for which they are completely blameless, the arbitrator observed, while others, who act recklessly, somehow escape accidents. According to the arbitrator, it's not the former group that deserves discipline, but the latter. Using this reasoning, the test for discipline is not whether the employee was involved in accidents, but whether he or she is so careless and inefficient as to justify the conclusion that he or she is not a safe and competent employee (*Interstate Bakeries Corp.*, 38 LA 1109).

Driving accidents are special cases— the dangers implicit in careless operation of a vehicle typically weigh heavily in an arbitrator's decision on the propriety of discipline imposed on a vehicle operator whose driving judgment is questionable. "Arbitrators are ordinarily reluctant to disturb disciplinary discharges," one arbitrator noted, "if it means the return to the highway of an employee who may be dangerous to himself, to others, and where the legal and financial interests of the employer are potentially at stake."

Thus, the arbitrator pointed out, discharges have been upheld where: the employee-driver had been involved in numerous accidents and/or had a poor past record, the operation involved the transportation of dangerous materials, or the worker was guilty of gross negligence or willful and wanton conduct. On the other hand, the arbitrator continued, discharge has been overturned where the alleged negligence was not conclusively proven; the employee's error presented no danger to the public; the negligence was ordinary, rather than gross, in nature; or special conditions, such as bad weather, made the accident not entirely the worker's fault.

• In the case at hand, the arbitrator ruled that discharge was too severe a penalty for a worker who was involved in an accident on the worksite, even though he previously had received a three-day suspension for damage to employer property that resulted from another driving accident. Taking into account the weather conditions and the terrain, the worker's actions were "not so clearly negligent and so clearly in disregard of legitimate employer production or performance expectations so as to warrant discharge," the arbitrator found.

Furthermore, the worker's record of "one prior minor accident in no way is comparable to the pattern of cases where discharge has been sustained because of a great number of accidents" caused by negligence. Finally, "in making his ill-fated attempt," the arbitrator concluded, the worker "did not so substantially misjudge the danger so as to make his continued employment a grave hazard to the employer" (*Kaiser Sand & Gravel Co.*, 50 LA 571).

• A warning was appropriate for a truck driver who had run his tractor-trailer into the rear of another employer vehicle, an arbitrator ruled. The worker argued that slippery road conditions had caused him to plow into the other vehicle when it suddenly stopped, and that in any event, he should "simply have been advised in writing that an accident had occurred and that he should drive carefully in the future." The arbitrator, however, found that the employee was "an experienced, veteran truck driver" who should have known "the degree of care he was required to use in the operation of his vehicle." Deciding that it was the worker's carelessness, not the road conditions, that had caused the accident, the arbitrator agreed with management that the employee was guilty of "hazardous and negligent" driving that warranted a written reprimand (*Hoerner Waldorf Champion International Corp.*, 75 LA 416).

• A forklift operator was properly discharged for causing an accident that injured a co-worker, an arbitrator ruled. The employee was driving a forklift truck when he collided with another truck driven by a co-worker. In the accident, the co-worker suffered a deep gash to his forehead that required several stitches. After conducting an investigation, the employer concluded that the employee had been speeding and had failed to yield the right of way to the co-worker's vehicle.

Consequently, the employee was discharged for gross negligence and disregard for safety. The arbitrator decided that the evidence proved that the worker was driving carelessly, without due regard for his own safety or that of his fellow workers. Furthermore, the employee had been warned about his unsafe driving in the past, the arbitrator observed, concluding that in light of the circumstances, the penalty was not too severe (*Economics Laboratory Inc.*, 77 LA 73).

## Disability

————————————— OVERVIEW —————————————

In most cases involving physical disability, an employer's right to discharge, transfer, or lay off an individual depends on whether the employer has good reason to believe that the person cannot perform satisfactorily or without undue hazard to the employee or co-workers. This determination, in turn, depends on an evaluation of medical evidence, job requirements, and the work environment. The mere fact of disability, taken alone, generally is not sufficient to support a personnel action, especially if the disability has been of long standing.

Discrimination against the handicapped is forbidden by the Americans with Disabilities Act of 1990 (42 U.S.C. § 12101 et seq.), the Rehabilitation Act of 1973, and by state fair-employment-practice laws. Additionally, some cases of disability discrimination have been decided on in light of constitutional guarantees, such as the right to due process.

The ADA prohibits discrimination in employment, public services and transportation, public accommodations, and telecommunications services against qualified individuals who have disabilities. This chapter solely focuses on Title I of the ADA, which bans disability discrimination in the workplace in companies that employ 15 or more people.

*What Is Prohibited* — Title I of the ADA prohibits covered employers from making employment decisions that discriminate against qualified individuals with disabilities.

● Covered employers must reasonably accommodate known physical and mental limitations of an otherwise qualified applicant or employee with a disability. An exception exists for employers that can show that the accommodation would impose an undue hardship on their business operations.

● Employment agencies, labor organizations, joint labor-management committees, and state and local governments also are covered by the law, as enacted by Congress. In 2001, however, the U.S. Supreme Court said Congress exceeded its power under the Constitution by extending the ADA to cover state employees. The court found that states are immune from lawsuits by state employees for damages under Title I of the ADA.

## KEY DECISIONS—

In one case an arbitrator reinstated a worker who was discharged because he was "industrially blind," largely because it appeared that the employee had made an amazing adjustment to his disability and had worked for years without mishap (*United Gas Improvement Co.*, 40 LA 799; see also 94 LA 513).

When an employer can support its allegations with clear and convincing evidence, arbitrators typically uphold the action (96 LA 1003, 76 LA 1233, 75 LA 122).

At least one arbitrator has held that where there is little danger to others, it is up to the employee to decide whether to continue working with a life-threatening physical disability (*Interwoven Stocking Co.*, 39 LA 918).

Arbitrators will, however, generally uphold an employee's removal from a job when the employee's disability might somehow endanger the employee or his or her co-workers (*Boeing Co.*, 106 LA 650).

## SUMMARY OF CASES

### Conflict Between Accommodation of Disabilities and Contracts

The Americans with Disabilities Act and the Rehabilitation Act accord certain rights to disabled workers who meet particular standards relating to the seriousness and permanence of their alleged disabilities.

There always have been workers with disabilities, and labor and management commonly have worked together to accommodate such employees. Nevertheless, what constitutes reasonable job accommodations under the ADA may conflict with the seniority provisions of an existing labor agreement. To avoid potential conflicts, both unions and management should consider negotiating procedures that will ensure compliance with the ADA without contravening the contract.

● In one case, an arbitrator ruled that disability accommodation pursuant to ADA and the Rehab Act breached the seniority of another worker.

As part of a reduction in force, an employer eliminated a clerk position in its tool room. One of the remaining clerks, who was close to early retirement, was given a temporary tool-room position. She otherwise would have been laid off because she was medically restricted from handling the chemical used in other jobs that were available. The employee whom she displaced was transferred to another area even though he had seniority.

The union contended that the transfer violated seniority provisions of the collective bargaining agreement, adding that the ADA and the Rehab Act do not permit an accommodation for one employee that would violate another employee's se-niority rights. The employer contended that failure to accommodate the disabled clerk would have violated federal law.

The arbitrator ruled that the employer had in fact violated the collective bargaining agreement's seniority provisions, adding that even if the clerk were considered "disabled" under ADA, the employer had no obligation to accommodate her in violation of the agreement. The arbitrator ordered the employee reassigned to the temporary position with back pay (*Olin Corp.*, 103 LA 481).

● Another arbitrator ruled in a similar way that an employer's light-duty accommodation policy violated a collective bargaining agreement's seniority provisions. A bargaining unit was divided into labor grades based on skill levels, and tasks were assigned to employees according to their classification. The union and the employer cooperated on creating temporary light-duty work assignments and had negotiated a memorandum outlining procedures for filling those jobs, requiring selection be based on bidders' job performance and seniority. "All things being equal," the memo stated, job vacancies would be filled with the most senior bidder who had the appropriate skills and abilities.

Shortly thereafter, however, the employer began bumping certain employees to accommodate other, less senior employees who needed light-duty work. The employer maintained that it was free to do so because seniority was not an "absolute entitlement" to specific job tasks, asserting that the phrase "all things being equal" in the memo gave it authority to consider physical ability in assigning jobs. The union protested, claiming the job assignment violated displaced employees' seniority rights.

To permit an employer to displace workers from jobs won through hard-earned seniority rights would cripple the seniority system negotiated by the parties, the arbitrator said. A vacancy does not occur whenever the employer finds it "convenient or economical" to bump an employee out of a bid position and place an injured worker in the slot, the arbitrator stressed. If the employer wished to acquire the power to unilaterally bump workers out of their positions, it had to negotiate that right with the union, the arbitrator stated (*Thomson Consumer Electronics Inc.*, 103 LA 977).

## Reasonable Accommodation

Employers must offer employees who have "qualified" disabilities reasonable accommodation. Factors for determining if an employer has provided a bona fide disabled employee reasonable accommodation include the provision of necessary assistance and training, as well as offering such employees alternative positions that conform to the reasonable accommodation standard. In addition, nondiscrimination provisions of collective bargaining agreements are designed to ensure that an employee's right to work is not denied because of a disability. Arbitrators, however, have set limits to such reasonable accommodation.

● An arbitrator held that an employer offered a reasonable accommodation to an employee who had injured his knee by giving him a position in a painting department and not cutting either his pay or benefits.

The employee had rejected the employer's offer, claiming he was unable to climb stairs because of his disability and was allergic to certain chemicals used in the painting department. The arbitrator held that the employee's inability to climb stairs occurred only during repetitive stepping on equipment and not during occasional climbing to get to his work space and noted that the employee had climbed stairs at home without further damaging his knee. Also, the arbitrator found the employee failed to provide medical evidence of his alleged paint allergies (*Riester and Thesmacher Co.*, 107 LA 572).

## Medical Evidence

Conflicting medical views of a person's disability often are at the center of disability cases and how employers should accommodate such employees. The general view seems to be that an employer is entitled to rely on the opinions of its own doctors, as long as it gives the employees an opportunity to rebut those views before a final decision is reached.

● Where there are differences between an employer doctor's conclusion and that of an employee's doctor, an effort should be made to reconcile the difference by, for example, having the two doctors discuss the matter. Where conflict persists, however, greater consideration is given to the physician who has done the most extensive examination or who is more qualified in the treatment of the injury in question.

Additional factors that are considered by arbitrators when they consider conflicting medical evidence include the following:

● the employer's decision must be based on bona fide nondiscriminatory expert opinions and advice;

● the personal testimony of a medical witness who is subject to cross-examination generally is entitled to more weight than mere written reports where there is no difference in the degree of expertise possessed by the medical witnesses who are testifying; and

● in the absence of contract provisions, management is allowed to make its decision on advice from its own medical consultants as long as the advice is fair and impartial—it need not submit such advice to outside experts for their consideration (*Hospital Service Plan of New Jersey*, 61 LA 947).

An arbitrator ruled that an employer properly transferred a partially disabled employee to light-duty status because the employer had adequate medical evidence that the employee should be transferred to such an assignment. In addition, the arbitrator said, the employer had the legal obligation to transfer the worker to light duty in order to protect the person's own safety and health, as well as the safety and health of the person's colleagues (*ITT Automotive*, 105 LA 11).

## Raised Physical Requirements

Can an employer stiffen the physical requirements for various jobs and then discharge employees who fail to meet them? Unless there is a definite change in the nature or conditions of a job, workers may not be discharged for failing to meet physical requirements that are higher than those they met when they were hired for the job, according to most arbitrators.

• One employer, suspecting that poor eyesight on the part of some employees was causing them to produce a lot of defective work, set up a new vision-testing program. In some cases, the visual requirements for jobs were raised. Several workers could not pass the new tests for their jobs and were discharged. The arbitrator decided that the discharges were not for good cause under the contract and ruled that the workers could keep their jobs as long as they continued to meet the standards in effect at the time they were hired. The arbitrator suggested, however, that there was nothing to prevent the employer from applying higher visual standards to future placements (*Connecticut Telephone & Electric Corp.*, 22 LA 632; see also 97 LA 175).

## Workers' Compensation Claims

In some instances, employers have tried to justify personnel actions on the grounds that the employees' medical histories indicate they are likely to become disabled, thereby making the employer liable for future workers' compensation claims.

At least one arbitrator has held that an employer may rightfully refuse to hire on this basis. In that case, the applicants were rejected because they refused to sign waiver forms relieving management of liability in a workers' compensation case. Noting that other applicants all had previously filed workers' compensation claims, the arbitrator found that the employer had reason to believe that they were "at least partially disabled." The

employer was legitimately concerned that the workers would "aggravate their medical problems while performing their jobs," the arbitrator pointed out.

By requiring the waiver, management was "essentially informing" the trio that it had "no desire to assume any of the risk of such further aggravation," and that they would be working "at their own risk," the arbitrator explained, concluding that it "legitimately refused to hire" the applicants when they chose not to sign the release (*Rust Engineering Co.*, 76 LA 263).

Where workers have been on the payroll for some time, however, arbitrators generally agree that management may not use workers' compensation claims worries to justify discharge.

• A truck driver who had five years' seniority received treatment under a contractual health and welfare plan for back pains, which, it turned out, were caused by congenital malformation of the lower spine. Following treatment, the worker applied for reinstatement, but management refused, claiming it had no obligation to risk the possibility of future absenteeism and claims for workers' compensation. The arbitrator, however, held that the risk to the employer was outweighed by the worker's interest in his job, which he had performed competently over a period of years. There was no certainty, he pointed out, that the worker would have further trouble with his back. Even if he did, his condition would not pose an immediate hazard either to himself or to other employees, the arbitrator commented. Finally, he noted, the worker's doctor had stated that he could safely return to his job (*Bethlehem Steel Co.*, 29 LA 476).

• An employee who had sustained 20 injuries during the previous four years of his 18 years of employment was called into his supervisor's office and told that because he had received workers' compensation payment totaling 100 percent disability, he was considered totally disabled by the employer and would be discharged. The arbitrator, however, failed to find any medical evidence that employee could not perform his job or that he was a safety hazard to himself or others. Noting that the employee was allowed to return to work without any restrictions following two major injuries, the arbitrator reinstated him (*Quality Electric Steel Castings Inc.*, 62 LA 1157).

● Discharge was overturned where an employee had already collected workers' compensation for a back injury deemed 16 percent "permanent partial disability." In that case, the worker had had back surgery and then returned to his job, which called for heavy lifting. After the employee was at work for eight weeks, the employer was informed of the man's medical status and thereafter decided to discharge him to prevent the possibility of further injury.

Despite the employer's apparent good faith, the arbitrator found a lack of clear, thorough medical evidence, complicated by the employee's eight-week return to the job with satisfactory results. Because there was no guarantee that the employee's reinstatement would not create a risk to himself or others, the arbitrator reduced the discharge to a suspension, pending further medical evidence (*Newkirk Sales Co.*, 61 LA 1144).

## Insurance Costs

In some instances, an employer's insurance employer may object to the continued employment of a disabled employee or may threaten to raise its premiums substantially if the employee is retained. One arbitrator indicated that management is not obligated to pay substantially more for insurance to accommodate a handicapped employee (*Hiller Chevrolet-Cadillac Inc.*, 37 LA 629).

● According to another arbitrator, however, the insurance carrier should not be permitted to dictate which employees should be fired and for what reasons. This would make the negotiated restrictions on discipline virtually meaningless, he said (*Expert Dairy Service Inc.*, 45 LA 217).

● Insurability at normal rates was an implied condition of continued employment for a truck driver, an arbitrator decided. According to the arbitrator, the employer had the right to expect that it would not be exposed to unreasonable risk or expense in the employment relationship. Nonetheless, the arbitrator continued, in the present case, management was under a continuing obligation to provide the disabled employee with any available work that did not involve an insurance problem (*J.A. McMahon Co. Inc.*, 44 LA 1274).

● Yet another arbitrator ruled that an employer could not discharge an obese employee who had high blood pressure, even though it previously had had to pay a $33,000 damage award to the family of another worker who suffered a heart attack on the job. Although the employer's doctor had recommended the discharge, the arbitrator found that the employee was not a serious industrial risk (*Great Atlantic & Pacific Tea Co.*, 41 LA 278).

## Obesity & Hypertension

Where marked obesity is accompanied by high blood pressure or other attendant physical conditions that affect an employee's fitness for work, arbitrators have upheld management's denial of work to the employee.

● An employee whose various obesity-related problems caused him to fall asleep on the job was discharged for just cause, an arbitrator decided. The employee had been hospitalized after he repeatedly fell asleep on the job.

When he returned to work, management warned him about the necessity of conforming to a special diet in order to improve his condition, but he slipped back into his "errant behavior" of staying up late and consuming "excessive" amounts of junk food. He again started falling asleep on the job, and when management's counseling and minor discipline failed to put him on the right track and stop the problem, the employee was fired on the grounds that he was "unfit for work."

The employer not only assisted the employee when it learned of his problems, the arbitrator noted, but also "took him back to work, counseled him, and followed a consistent program of progressive discipline which should have had the effect of being both rehabilitative in nature and a deterrent" to his bad habits. Despite management's "reasonable and accommodative efforts," the worker himself "did little to mitigate his medical problem." The employer had "a right to expect" the employee to present himself "fit for work," the arbitrator decided, concluding that the worker's repeated failures to take advantage of the opportunities given him militated against his reinstatement (*City of Iowa City*, 72 LA 1006).

• In other circumstances, however, where the overweight condition has not interfered with an employee's work in the past, an employer may not say "you're too fat for me." Thus, an employee who had two years of service was ordered reinstated, despite her obesity and high blood pressure, where her condition had not affected her job performance in any way (*Magnavox Co.*, 46 LA 719).

• Another arbitrator held that an employer improperly denied reinstatement to two women on the ground that their obesity was deleterious to their health.

The employer's concern for their health should not be converted into "an essentially paternalistic attempt to regulate an employee's personal life," he said. A similar disqualification, he noted, could be levied against cigarette smokers on the theory that smoking may result in shortness of breath that could impair employee efficiency. On the other hand, the arbitrator upheld the employer's refusal to reinstate one of the workers who suffered from nervousness, hypertension, and dizzy spells, as well as obesity (*Mutual Plastics Mold Corp.* 48 LA 2).

• An employee suffering from hypertension was properly discharged after requesting his second extended medical leave within one year, an arbitrator ruled. In this case the employee had already taken a six-month leave and had been warned by the employer that a recurrence could result in discharge. Nevertheless, the employee filed for a second leave. In the absence of a "just cause" provision in the collective bargaining agreement, the arbitrator concluded that the "reasonable discharge" was suffi-

ciently backed by the circumstances (*American Broadcasting Companies Inc.*, 63 LA 278).

## Mental Illness

Although recognizing an employer's natural hesitancy about re-employing a person who has a mental illness that may intermittently recur, arbitrators have refused to uphold discharges where there was medical evidence that the employee had recovered to the extent that his return to work would not involve an undue risk to himself or to others. Management may not assume that such a risk exists from the bare fact that an employee has been treated for mental illness (61 LA 121, 28 LA 333, 26 LA 295).

• In cases involving immoral or socially reprehensible conduct resulting from mental illness, arbitrators may direct reinstatement on evidence that the illness has been cured. These awards have been based in part on the assurances that the employee's fellow workers have no objection to his reinstatement (24 LA 229, 22 LA 1, 15 LA 42).

Arbitrators, however, generally will uphold discharges where there is evidence that the worker's continued employment presents a substantial risk to co-workers.

• An employee suffering from schizophrenia was properly discharged for grabbing, shoving, and screaming at a co-worker, an arbitrator agreed.

The worker had been hospitalized and diagnosed as a paranoid schizophrenic shortly after being hired. When he returned to the job, management tried to place him only in low-stress situations. Nevertheless, the employee was hospitalized two more times but again returned to work after being released. Several years later, the employee began exhibiting hostile and aggressive behavior on the job and claimed he was being picked on by co-workers.

After shoving and choking a general foreman, the employee was suspended, but later was allowed to return to work. One night as employees were clocking out, he grabbed a co-worker, pushed him against the wall, and began shouting at him. Management then decided to fire the employee although it understood that his behavior was induced by the illness.

The arbitrator noted that the psychologist had found that the employee was suffering from a "schizophrenic illness" that caused him to "manifest paranoid thought processes focused primarily on the work situation." The medical evidence also indicated that returning the employee to work would likely trigger repeat behavior, the arbitrator observed, upholding the dismissal (*Wilcox Co.*, 75 LA 122; see also 92 LA 1291).

● Another arbitrator held that an employee who suffered from bipolar disorder (i.e., manic-depression) was discharged with just cause because his explosive behavior could not be controlled even though it might be regulated through medication under close medical supervision (*Rohm and Haas*, 104 LA 974).

● In yet another case, an arbitrator ruled that an employer had just cause to discharge an insubordinate employee who, as a result of a car accident, was prone to outbursts, had various cognitive deficits, and lacked normal workplace inhibitions. Considering the nature of the employee's disability and the fact that he was on medication that could not control his behavior, the arbitrator sustained the employee's discharge, concluding that the employer was not required to retain an employee who was "so disabled as to demonstrate incapacity to consistently carry out his required job." The arbitrator noted that he would have considered placing the disabled worker on sick leave until his disability had been treated had it been claimed that the employee's condition was subject to cure or control (*National Linen Supply*, 107 LA 4).

## Epilepsy

In several cases involving the employment of epileptics, arbitrators have ruled against discharge because of the mere existence of the disability without clear evidence of a safety hazard did not justify such a drastic response.

● An arbitrator reinstated an employee who had epilepsy and who was discharged after seven accident-free years with an employer. Management had fired the employee after an Occupational Safety and Health Administration staffer commented that epilepsy "constituted a dangerous condition." During his employ, the worker had suffered two seizures on the job, neither of which resulted in injury to the employee himself, his co-workers, or the employer's operations. According to the worker, his seizures always were preceded by at least five minutes warning, which alerted him to the impending seizure and enabled him to find a place to lie down until the seizure was over. In addition, the employee consistently refused to operate forklifts or climb ladders, and regularly took medicine that helped to control the frequency of seizures.

Citing medical testimony that the employee could work safely in the plant, especially given the warning of an oncoming seizure, the arbitrator pointed out that the worker had adapted remarkably well, even to the point of enlisting the aid of his co-workers in making adjustments to his work situation. Although sympathizing with the employer's concerns over safety issues, the arbitrator gave more weight to the worker's accident-free record. The discharge represented the "elevation of safety to a sacred cow," the arbitrator declared, maintaining that to terminate a seven-year employee because of the possibility of future accident would convert concern with safety to "callousness." The time to decide whether or not the worker's continued employment constituted a hazard, the arbitrator concluded, would be when and if an injury resulted from his condition (*Samuel Bingham Co.*, 67 LA 706).

● Discharge was upheld, however, in the case of a crane operator who passed out and fell during his seizures. Hazards to himself and others existed in his continued employment, the arbitrator noted, pointing out that impartial medical experts had advised the employer against retaining the worker. Not only were there no other jobs at the plant for the worker to perform safely, but he also lacked a long and satisfactory record, the arbitrator observed (*Acme Galvanizing Inc.*, 61 LA 1115).

• An employer was justified in refusing to let an employee who had suffered epileptic seizures return to his former job, even though medical evidence indicated his condition was under control. The employee had been a lineman for a utility employer when he began having seizures. After lengthy treatment, he was cleared by his physician to return to his former job. The employer's doctor, however, believed that he would still be a "hazard," so he was kept in the lower-rated job. Despite conceding that medical evidence showed the employee was physically able to perform lineman's work, the arbitrator upheld the employer's decision not to put the employee back on a job that involved unusual hazards (*Gulf State Utilities Co.*, 45 LA 1252).

• Discharge may be upheld even if the employee has not been examined by a physician. Where an employee had two seizures while at work, his employer acted reasonably in discharging him out of fear of possible injury to himself and others, an arbitrator ruled. Medical testimony, given by a private doctor who had not examined the employee, failed to show that the seizures could be fully controlled in the future, and there was no other job at the plant to which the employee could be transferred, the arbitrator concluded (*Weber Manufacturing Co. Inc.*, 63 LA 56).

### Allergies

Arbitrators have ruled that employers may lawfully discharge employees who develop permanent allergies while on the job if the employer has taken all feasible steps to accommodate the employee's condition.

• An employee who monitored and sampled nitroparaffin chemicals was diagnosed as having a permanent allergic reaction to the chemicals in the form of "contact dermatitis" on her hands. The employer provided the employee with special glove liners, but the dermatitis worsened and she was transferred out of the bargaining unit and given light clerical duty. She later returned to work after being issued special gloves, but her allergy again grew worse and she was discharged for being unable to perform her job. Her union grieved her discharge, claiming the employer had not provided required protective devices or attempted to change the chemical sampling procedure, and had violated the labor agreement, which had incorporated provisions of the ADA.

Denying the grievance, the arbitrator said that the employer had given the employee every manner of protective device as required under the agreement. Noting that the employer did not violate the ADA, the arbitrator held that the employee was not protected under that law because she was not a "qualified individual with a disability" whose condition substantially limited her major life activities. In addition, the arbitrator concluded, the employer was not required to transfer the employee from her production and maintenance unit to a job that had no risk of chemical exposure (*Angus Chemical Co.*, 102 LA 388).

### Job Reassignments

When presented with clear evidence that an employee's disability interferes with job performance or poses safety hazards, arbitrators will sustain a reassignment to another position where the disability can be better accommodated, especially if this action is an alternative to discharge.

• "Removing an obviously disabled man from a place of unusually hazardous exposure for him" is "the 'right' thing" to do, an arbitrator explained, adding, however, that the outright firing of a disabled employee is doing the "right thing in the wrong way." Rather, management should reassign the worker to a more accommodating position, the arbitrator stressed. In this case, no such position was currently available, the arbitrator decided, so the worker properly should have been put in layoff status (*Vulcan Mold & Iron Co.*, 40 LA 1266; see also 92 LA 1228).

• An employer properly reassigned a crane operator to another job when, following an accident, it discovered that the employee had "zero depth perception," an arbitrator decided. Dismissing the employee's argument that the accident was caused by the poor condition of the crane, the arbitrator stressed that regardless of whether this allegation were true, "the requirement of good depth perception for anyone operating the crane is a reasonable requirement," but "particularly if the crane is in poor condition" (*Foster Wheeler Corp.*, 54 LA 871).

• Management was within its rights to demote an employee whose heart condition prevented him from competently performing his job duties, another arbitrator ruled.

Following his return to work after a heart operation, the employee was allowed two trial periods to build back up to normal output levels. Evaluations showed, however, that he was not performing satisfactorily, and the worker was demoted to a lower position. Although the worker charged that he had not been given a fair opportunity to show what he could do, the arbitrator agreed with management that he had had ample time to demonstrate his abilities and that the evaluation process had been fairly conducted. With supervisory and production reports showing that other employees were outperforming the worker by as much as two to one, the arbitrator stressed, the demotion was justified (*Haven-Busch Co.*, 74 LA 1205).

• An employee whose right leg had been amputated was properly restricted to driving an automatic transmission truck, even though, as the worker claimed, there was "no evidence that his physical handicap presented a safety hazard" warranting the ban his driving a vehicle that had a manual transmission. Although the worker's safety record was "commendable," the arbitrator agreed, this record was compiled primarily while he was driving trucks that had automatic transmissions.

The employer's conclusion that the worker was not qualified to use a manual clutch, the arbitrator observed, was based solely on safety concerns. Management need only show that there is a "minimal increase in risk" to establish a logical basis for its restrictions, the arbitrator stressed, concluding that the employer was justified in preventing the employee from driving any company vehicle that had a manual transmission (*Des Moines Asphalt and Paving Co.*, 76 LA 1233).

• As one arbitrator noted, although an employer "certainly" may be able to redesign a particular job to conform to a worker's medical limitations, it need not, absent specific contract provisions, create a "special job" for a disabled worker (*Data Transportation Co.*, 75 LA 1154).

• Supervisors were not required to "make work" for an employee to do when medical restrictions prevented him from performing his normal duties, an arbitrator stressed. The employee's obesity placed great strains on his back muscles, making it difficult for him to bend, stoop, or lift objects that weighed more than 10 pounds. Although management attempted to assign work to him that fell within these narrow limitations, the arbitrator noted, the employee "was frequently not cooperative," and "largely determined" on his own to apply "pretty stringent" interpretations of how the restrictions applied to a particular assignment management asked him to perform.

Whereas, at one time the worker "was willing to hose down an area," on another occasion he insisted that he could not perform this type of work. As a result, the supervisors "were beginning to run out of things" for the employee to do, the arbitrator pointed out.

Declaring that an employer is not obligated to keep on the payroll a worker who is unable "to perform enough useful productive work to warrant his continued employment," the arbitrator ruled that management would be justified in discharging the employee if he failed to take advantage of a last-chance opportunity to reduce his weight to optimum levels and be able to resume his job duties without restrictions (*Reynolds Metals Co.*, 71 LA 1099).

• In another case, however, an arbitrator held that an employer violated a collective bargaining agreement and the ADA when it discharged two "patient escorts." New technology had made the escort positions obsolete, and the two employees had sustained on-the-job injuries, but rather than accommodating their disabilities by reassigning them to training for other available jobs for which they might have been qualified, the employer had fired them, the arbitrator said (*Johns Hopkins Bayview Medical Center*, 105 LA 193).

---

**Part 3**

# Safety and Health

# Safety

## OVERVIEW

Arbitrators generally acknowledge that management has the right to issue and enforce safety rules but caution that such rules must be reasonably related to the purpose of ensuring a safe and healthful workplace.

Discharge for the infraction of a safety rule may be justified where an employee has persistently disobeyed safety regulations in spite of progressive discipline. Serious infractions, particularly those that endanger other workers, may subject the employee to immediate discharge.

Safety rules must be uniformly enforced. When there has been a past practice of not enforcing a safety rule, arbitrators have overturned discipline because it is not equitable. In some cases, an employer's failure to comply with safety rules or regulations has been regarded as a contractual violation.

Employers also may be held liable for violations of bargaining agreements that are supposed to ensure safe working conditions.

## SUMMARY OF CASES

### 'Reasonableness' of Rules

Safety rules must be "reasonable," arbitrators have held—i.e., they must have a relationship to the employee's safety in the workplace. Arbitrators have rejected management's unilateral promulgation of rules that are only peripherally related to workplace safety.

• An employer's rule forbidding employees to wear certain types of clothing while walking between the plant gates and the shop area was unreasonable, an arbitrator concluded. The walkway between the gates and the shop was a "supposedly safe pedestrian walkway," noted the arbitrator. The rule thus appeared, the arbitrator said, "to be an unreasonable interference with the personal freedom of the employees to come and go from and to their work places without unreasonable regimentation."

Other parts of the employer's rule, relating to wearing beads and finger rings, the arbitrator decided, should be referred to the labor-management committee for further consideration, following which the employer "may impose a reasonable rule as to beads and finger rings realistically limited to such times and occasions as when the employee is, in fact, involved in or near moving machinery" (*Babcock & Wilcox*, 73 LA 443; see also 94 LA 1047).

### Reasonable Application of Rules

However reasonable a safety rule may be, it may be overruled by an arbitrator if it is applied in an unreasonable fashion.

• A blanket employer rule against the wearing of beards, which was based on beards' preventing a proper seal being made between a full-face respirator and the employee's face, was pronounced "arbitrary and unreasonable" by an arbitrator. "The employer certainly has the right and obligation to promulgate reasonable safety rules and to enforce them," acknowledged the arbitrator, but the "established need for respirator use or a reasonable probability of emergency use are the underpinnings which give the beard prohibition validity," the arbitrator noted, ordering the employer "to rescind the overly broad beard policy and return to a previous policy, under which any beard prohibition draws its essence from the need to wear a respirator" (*Allied Chemical Corporation*, 74 LA 412; see also 92 LA 492, 92 LA 1214, 91 LA 987).

## Progressive Discipline

Safety rules may be enforced through progressive discipline, just as any other reasonable workplace regulations, arbitrators have concluded.

• After sustaining a number of injuries as the result of failing to wear proper safety equipment and failing to observe appropriate safety precautions, a worker was progressively disciplined and finally discharged. An arbitrator upheld the discharge, observing that the employer's system of rules provided "for progressive disciplinary actions for successive violations of the rules and regulations, which include safety regulations." The arbitrator concluded that "the safety rules requiring the use of protective equipment are reasonable," and added that because they are reasonable, and because the collective bargaining agreement "specifically permits the establishment of rules and regulations, it is the duty of all employees" to abide by these rules (*Vulcan-Hart Corp.*, 78 LA 59; see also 98 LA 357, 96 LA 609, 96 LA 931, 94 LA 152, 94 LA 178, 94 LA 777).

## Past Practice

If management fails to enforce a safety rule, especially over a period of time, the rule may be considered moot, and the employer may not penalize employees for violating the rule unless management notifies employees of its intent to resume enforcement.

• An arbitrator overturned the discipline of an employee who had failed to use a safety belt as prescribed by a seat belt regulation that management had allowed to lie dormant for at least 20 years. "In fairness, and desire to promote favorable employee relations," maintained the arbitrator, "the employer should have given notice of its intent to enforce seat belt usage and the nature of discipline to be administered for noncompliance." In the absence of "such previous warning," the arbitrator concluded that "the employer's action lacked equitability" and should not be enforced (*U.S. Army Corps of Engineers*, 86 LA 939).

## Uniform Enforcement of Rules

Safety rules also must be uniformly applied to all employees exposed to the same risks—supervisors as well as line workers—arbitrators have concluded.

• An arbitrator reprimanded an employer for not requiring its supervisory employees to wear the same protective equipment that the workers were required to wear during periods when they were exposed to the same risks. The arbitrator noted that the bargaining agreement specifically stated that "all levels of supervision of the employer, the employees, and the union will cooperate fully to promote safe practices, health conditions, and the enforcement of safety rules and procedures." When supervisors "are exposed to the same risks but do not observe the same safety rules that line employees are required to observe," the arbitrator said, the supervisors "are clearly violating" the agreement. "Such a violation by a foreman may not only endanger the foreman himself," observed the arbitrator, but "it may also endanger employees with whom he is working" (*Noranda Aluminum Inc.*, 78 LA 1331).

• An arbitrator reduced a written warning and a 90-day proscription against driving an employer's trucks to a written warning for an employee who drove a tractor-trailer erratically and unsafely, in violation of a reasonable safety rule that authorized both warnings and disqualifications as penalties, because two previous rule violators were not disqualified from the same task (*Seaway Food Town*, 94 LA 389).

## Employee Knowledge of Safety Rule

In upholding discipline for employees' failure to follow employer workplace safety requirements, arbitrators often must first discern whether the employee was aware of the safety rule before he or she committed the violation.

• An arbitrator held that an employer did not have just cause to discharge an employee for not wearing a protective face shield while pumping chemicals because the employer failed to prove it expressly alerted the employee to a "supposed" general rule requiring face shields when handling any chemicals. No documents distributed to employees contained such a rule, a training video communicated the opposite message by showing employees handling chemicals wearing only goggles, and no supervisor notified the employee of the rule, the arbitrator pointed out (*Cone Mills Corp.*, 104 LA 833).

**Ensuring Safe Working Conditions**

An arbitrator found that a state school board did not violate a collective bargaining agreement that ensured every effort would be made to provide safe working conditions when it assigned an unaccompanied, female teacher to supervise a study hall in an isolated auditorium. The arbitrator's based the decision on a number of factors including the following: teachers who had previously supervised the study hall by themselves had not complained to the employer; the teacher's infrequent unlocking of a door between the study hall and an adjoining classroom to provide quick exit/access for help was inconsistent with her claimed concern for her safety; less than 20 percent of disciplinary referrals issued by the teacher for a particular period were issued for disruptive behavior; and the school provided security when classes began and generally had increased security at the school (*Washington Local Schools Board of Education*, 104 LA 1185).

# Smoking Policy

———————————— **OVERVIEW** ————————————

Generally, arbitrators will uphold an employer's right to impose a "reasonable" smoking policy—restricting smoking to specific areas in the workplace or banning smoking entirely in the interest of safeguarding both life and property—and they likely will sustain discipline for violations. Mitigating factors have, however, been taken into consideration in reversing discipline in some smoking-related cases.

Arbitrators tend to reverse discipline if management has permitted violations to go unpunished in the past. Employers would be wise to remember that consistently and equitably applied rules are the best defense against having discipline overturned.

Employers' no-smoking smoking policies may be considered part of the "terms and conditions" of employment and as such, are a subject for mandatory bargaining. Employers that try to impose smoking controls unilaterally, in violation of their collective bargaining obligations, may face unfair labor practice charges under the National Labor Relations Act.

———————————— **SUMMARY OF CASES** ————————————

### Smoking Not Contractual Right/Working Condition

One arbitrator ruled that an employer's no-smoking policy was not unreasonable, arbitrary, or capricious, but in fact was based on sound, accepted medical evidence about the dangers of smoking as well as economic data on its associated costs. The employer's rule was reasonably related to its effort to provide a safe and healthful workplace, the arbitrator said, adding that, particularly in an industrial setting, employees do not have a right to smoke anywhere and anytime. Smoking is neither a contractual right nor a "working condition," but rather, a privilege that an employer may or may not grant. The employer's particular work rule was appropriate, in light of the fact that employees were given adequate notice when it was established; the rule treated all employees, visitors, and vendors equally; and the employer instituted the rule by offering employees access to smoking cessation programs (*Timkin Co.*, 108 LA 422).

● An employer's implementation of a total ban on employees' using tobacco did not violate its collective bargaining agreement, an arbitrator found. The company initially announced that using tobacco products would be banned in all the employer's buildings. The union filed a grievance, claiming the tobacco-free workplace policy violated the parties' bargaining agreement and asserting that workers should be allowed to continue to smoke outdoors during breaks. The arbitrator sided with the employer, stating that the company-wide ban on tobacco did not violate any provision of the contract. The employer had a right to adopt a tobacco-free rule in order to help accomplish a legitimate management objective of improving the overall health of its workforce and reducing substantial costs associated with employees' using tobacco. The premises-wide ban also was appropriate, the arbitrator said, because the building-wide ban had proved to be unenforceable. In addition, employees were given adequate notice of the policy, they were offered smoking cessation classes and products, and the ban did not discriminate against any unit employees, the arbitrator concluded (*Plasti-Line Inc.*, 114 LA 1240).

## Smoking in a Restricted Area

Fire or other hazards posed by smoking have been considered by arbitrators to be adequate justification for no-smoking policies and for discipline meted out to those who disobey such policies.

• An airline employee who, after being ordered to extinguish her cigarette in a no-smoking area, lit another a short time later was properly discharged, an arbitrator concluded. While observing that smoking in prohibited areas was not "expressly provided as a cause for discharge," the arbitrator pointed out that there are certain "critical areas," such as the aircraft fueling site, where smoking is perilous and "constitutes legal malice" (*Gladieux Food Services Inc.*, 70 LA 544).

• In another case, an employer did not engage in "surface bargaining in its negotiations with a union over attempts to revise an existing smoking policy, an arbitrator decided. Several years earlier, a different arbitrator had ruled that an employer's no-smoking-indoors policy that authorized smoking only in ventilated rooms at various facilities was invalid. The arbitrator had ordered the employer to reopen employee smoking areas, remove smoking-related employee disciplinary notices, and bargain with the union to attempt to develop a systemwide smoking policy that took into account the physical hazards of workers' having to go outside to smoke, especially in bad weather. The parties could not agree on a plan, and the union filed a grievance accusing the employer of "surface bargaining," essentially refusing to bargain in good faith.

Even though the previous order dealt with the issue of finding a solution to bargaining unit members' having to go outside to smoke, that did not mean that that original arbitrator had directed the employer to expand its smoking facilities beyond what existed prior to the award, the arbitrator said. Furthermore, the employer's refusal to make counterproposals or suggest compromises did not constitute a refusal to bargain, he said. Finding no evidence that the employer engaged in dilatory tactics, made unreasonable demands, or engaged in other tactics that would constitute "surface bargaining," the arbitrator rejected the union's grievance (*Regional Transportation Dist.*, 115 LA 1703).

## Mitigating Factors

Management also has a duty to consider mitigating factors in smoking cases. As with other types of disciplinary actions, a too-hasty response from management over an employee's infraction of the rules may prompt an arbitrator to overturn whatever disciplinary measures the employer took.

• Returning from a break, an employee entered a room clearly marked as a no-smoking area and "inadvertently" lit a cigarette; realizing his mistake, he quickly tried to extinguish it. A supervisor who saw the employee putting out the cigarette and exhaling "a cloud of smoke" fired the employee on the spot, but an arbitrator overturned the discharge. Although the arbitrator acknowledged that management "forcefully and convincingly" demonstrated "the hazard of an open flame" in the no-smoking area, he observed that "consideration must be given to mitigating circumstances." The employee had an "exemplary" record, the arbitrator pointed out, adding that the employee was "horrified" by his unconscious act of lighting the cigarette and thus did not have the "guilty mind" required to intentionally commit the dischargeable offense of smoking in the restricted area (*Converters Ink*, 68 LA 593).

## Justified No-Smoking Policies

Arbitrators have upheld the unilateral imposition of a no-smoking rule in certain cases:

• where the rule is deemed reasonable and justified by safety, health, and bona fide business requirements;

• where a balance has been struck between the rights and interests of smokers and nonsmokers; and

● where the policies are not overly burdensome, unreasonable, arbitrary, or capricious.

● Interpreting a contract that allowed an employer to promulgate "reasonable rules and regulations," an arbitrator upheld an employer's no-smoking policy because it struck a balance between smokers' and nonsmokers' rights; it was not overly burdensome, unreasonable, arbitrary, or capricious; and the smoking areas provided for smokers were sufficient to accommodate the number of smokers who wanted to use them during specified times (*Tomkins Industries*, 112 LA 281).

● After a discarded cigarette caused a fire, an employer unilaterally decided to limit smoking to lunch and break times only, and solely in two designated areas. An arbitrator upheld the rule, finding that banning smoking at workstations for safety reasons was "not unreasonable." The employer "established the possibility of a fire being caused" in work areas, the arbitrator noted, and presented "valid safety concerns" to justify smoking prohibitions. Similarly, restricting smoking to break times was not unreasonable, given management's concern about the "impact on production" of a policy that would permit employees to leave their workstations whenever they desired to smoke (*Morelite Equipment Co.*, 88 LA 777).

● After 14 years of restricted smoking, the hospital imposed a no-smoking policy with the support of 78 percent of its employees and on the recommendation of a labor-management task force. At the same time, a state law banning smoking in hospitals was passed that would go into effect the following year. A hospital's no-smoking policy is reasonable because the issue was not addressed in its labor agreements and most of the employees favored implementation, an arbitrator decided. Moreover, he cited management rights clauses in two relevant labor agreements permitting management to set "reasonable rules and regulations" and the fact that the unions representing the hospital's employees had ample opportunity for redress through grievance

and arbitration but did not file any objections in a timely manner (*Methodist Hospital*, 91 LA 969; see also *Norris Plumbing Fixtures*, 104 LA 174).

● During the term of a collective bargaining agreement, the employer implemented a no-smoking policy that banned smoking in work areas. The union charged that the employer had unilaterally altered "the conditions of employment," and thus was required to bargain over the change. Refusing to impose a duty to bargain, the arbitrator said an employer may impose a workplace ban on smoking without engaging in bargaining. The employer has a "legal obligation to maintain a safe working environment," the arbitrator held, citing the Surgeon General's report in which experts said "ambient tobacco smoke in the workplace" constitutes a health hazard. Employers are lawfully obligated to eliminate "toxic agents" from the workplace; therefore, a total ban on smoking during working hours was "appropriate," he concluded (*Central Telephone Co. of Nevada*, 92 LA 390; see also 104 LA 174, where an arbitrator held that an employer had an absolute right to impose a smoking ban, citing the health risks of both primary and secondary smoke).

● Another arbitrator determined that an employer's complete ban on smoking in all employer facilities was reasonable. The ban was acceptable even though 50 percent of the workforce smoked because smoking in the workplace was a privilege and not a statutory or contractual right, and the union failed to prove that smokers suffered serious hardships as a result of the rule change (*Wyandot Inc.*, 92 LA 457).

**Unilateral implementation of smoking policy change**—Recognizing a sharp increase in societal concern over the health risks of secondhand smoke, arbitrators increasingly have allowed employers to impose bans on smoking in large sections of the workplace without first bargaining over the change in policy.

● An employer unilaterally promulgated a new plant rule that restricted smoking to the lunch room during rest and lunch periods. Upholding the employer, the arbitrator maintained that revision of the plant's smoking rule was a reasonable exercise of management's reserved rights. In this case, the arbitrator said, management was "not guilty of bad faith or intent on being unreasonable" because it had a "legitimate business interest and purpose in restricting the smoking privilege to the lunch room." Adding that "smoking is not a practice or working condition that the employees are dependent upon," the arbitrator concluded that the rule change was "within the permissible scope of management's prerogative" (*Sherwood Medical Industries*, 72 LA 258; see also *Akron Brass Co.*, 101 LA 289; and *Tomkins Industries*, 112 LA 281).

### Unreasonable Smoking Bans

If a smoking policy is found to be unreasonable and not justified by safety, health, or business needs, arbitrators may overturn the policy although in recent years, smoke-free workplaces have become the norm.

● An arbitrator held than an employer's no-smoking policy violated language in a collective bargaining agreement that gave employees the right to smoke at any time. The no-smoking policy would have permitted smoking only in outdoor areas during two 10-minute approved breaks and lunch periods. Before the policy was implemented, the parties negotiated a new contract, and the new contract retained a provision that employees could smoke when they wished, provided they did so in designated areas. After the no-smoking policy took effect, an employee filed a grievance, claiming the policy violated the bargaining agreement.

The arbitrator stated that the no-smoking policy violated the contract, because the contract clearly permitted an employee to smoke any time he or she wished and the policy limited employee smoking to break times and designated areas, all of which were outside the plant. In addition, the arbitrator said, under the contract, an employee would be required, in effect, to get supervisor approval to leave the plant to smoke a cigarette. The arbitrator concluded that the policy

would have nullified contractual language and thus could not be upheld (*Hobart Corp.*, 103 LA 1089).

● An arbitrator ruled that an employer's ban on smoking only in its administration building was unreasonable, noting that no one had objected to smoking in that building and that in another, adjacent building, management allowed employees "to make their own arrangements." The arbitrator also rejected management's contention that it was obliged to protect the public from the hazards of smoke in the administration building. No such protection was provided for visitors to other buildings, therefore the no-smoking restriction was "not reasonable," the arbitrator said (*Union Sanitary District*, 79 LA 193).

● An employer's decision to prohibit smoking by employees in nearly all areas of the workplace was not justified by either health or business needs, an arbitrator ruled. Although he agreed that the "relationship between health and cigarette smoking is direct and proximate," the arbitrator concluded that the rule did not clearly benefit nonsmokers, because the work area was well-ventilated, whereas the smoking restriction tended to produce heavier amounts of smoke during breaks. Furthermore, the arbitrator reasoned, there was no proof that cutting down the consumption of cigarettes during working hours directly benefited employees' health, thereby reducing absenteeism or increasing the "longevity of good employees" (*Schien Body & Equipment Co. Inc.*, 69 LA 930).

● An employer's total ban on smoking "on employer premises" was unreasonable and invalid because it included "adjacent areas" such as grounds and parking lots, an arbitrator ruled. Tobacco smoke quickly dissipates outdoors, the arbitrator said, and employees smoking in their cars have little discernible effect on the health and safety of others (*VME Americas Inc.*, 97 LA 137; see also 96 LA 506, 96 LA 403, 96 LA 122, 95 LA 1163, 94 LA 894, 93 LA 1255, 93 LA 1070, 88 LA 329, 83 LA 529).

● An arbitrator held an employer's unilateral implementation of a no-smoking policy that ended a 20-year practice of using outside smoking areas violated a collective bargaining agreement, where the agreement provided that any "privilege," (e.g., smoking) not addressed in the contract and enjoyed by employees would continue, and the contract contained no management rights clause (*Cross Oil & Refining*, 104 LA 757).

● An arbitrator held that a no-smoking policy at a manufacturing facility violated a bargaining agreement and past practice, where the history of smoking at the particular facility established a term or condition of employment over which the employer was obligated to bargain, and the union involved successfully had challenged the employer's earlier attempt to ban smoking in a break room (*Basler Electric Co.*, 94 LA 888).

● An arbitrator ruled that an employer's unilateral in-plant smoking ban was improper because there was no employer discussion of the ban with the health committee before the employer implemented the rule, and the contract required all safety and health investigations to be conducted jointly (*Lincoln Brass Works*, 102 LA 872; see also *Raybestos Products Co.*, 102 LA 46, in which a plant-wide smoking ban was found to be in violation of a contract, under which smoking was permitted if the "cleanliness of the plant" was maintained).

## Smoking Rule Violations

Whether an employer has just cause to discharge employees who violate plant smoking rules depends on the context of the violation and the mitigating circumstances of the particular case.

● One arbitrator held that a violation of a no-smoking rule warranted a suspension rather than discharge. A 30-year employee of a chemical employer was observed with a lit cigarette in his hand while he was repacking hydrochloric acid into a 55-gallon drum. Smoking was prohibited near hazardous materials under the employer's safety rules, violators were subject to discharge, and the employee was fired immediately. The union objected to the discharge, maintaining that the chemical was classified as nonflammable on an Occupational Safety and Health Administration "material safety data sheet." The union also noted that the plant's heating system contained two overhead heaters that had gas pilot lights with exposed flames.

Reducing the discharge to a suspension, the arbitrator pointed out that although the employer had discretion under its safety rules to fire an employee, this particular discharged was arbitrary and capricious. Smoking in the facility may have been hazardous, the arbitrator acknowledged, but the employer could hardly justify immediate termination for smoking in the same area where exposed heater pilot lights burned (*Van Waters & Rogers*, 102 LA 609).

● Another arbitrator determined that an employer did not have just cause to fire an employee for leaving work without authorization to smoke a cigarette under a rule that prohibited smoking in unauthorized areas and/or times. The arbitrator concluded that the restriction on times at which an employee was allowed to smoke in an unauthorized area did nothing to promote the rule's stated objectives of protecting the health of nonsmoking employees and barring employees from smoking near combustible materials (*Barnstead-Thermolyne Corp.*, 107 LA 645).

● Another arbitrator upheld the immediate discharge of an employee who carried a lighted cigarette into a plant. The employee's conduct violated the employer's no-smoking rule by creating the type of safety/fire hazard that the antismoking rule intended to eliminate, the arbitrator concluded, noting that the rule specifically subjected violators to discharge (*Century Products Co.*, 101 LA 1).

# Acquired Immune Deficiency Syndrome

## OVERVIEW

Acquired Immune Deficiency Syndrome, a life-threatening bloodborne viral disease, has sparked widespread medical and legal concerns and raised numerous questions regarding the treatment of employees or job applicants who have been infected by Human Immunodeficiency Virus, known as HIV, or have full-blown AIDS.

Generally, the problems that have arisen in the workplace have been in one of two forms: either an employee who has HIV/AIDS files a grievance over the way he or she is treated or other employees refuse to work with people who are HIV-positive or who have HIV/AIDS.

Under the National Labor Relations Act, employees may refuse to work if they can present an ascertainable, factual reason that their safety or health is endangered. NLRA protection has not been found to extend to an employee's refusal to work with a person who has HIV/AIDS because of the overwhelming medical evidence that indicates fears of contracting HIV/AIDS through normal workplace contact are unreasonable. If an employee who has HIV/AIDS is covered by a collective bargaining agreement, the contract's provisions generally determine matters of sick leave, health benefits, or any disciplinary action that is to be taken. Specific mention of HIV/AIDS is still unusual in labor contracts, however, and many cases of discrimination against HIV-positive individuals end up in the courts rather than being heard by an arbitrator.

HIV/AIDS is a protected disability under the Americans with Disabilities Act of 1990, which adopted the definitions for disability contained in the Rehabilitation Act of 1973. Moreover, the statute makes special provisions for food handlers, providing that only those persons who have contagious diseases that can be transmitted through food may be transferred to other jobs or denied positions as food handlers if no other reasonable accommodations can be provided.

The federal Rehabilitation Act may prohibit discrimination against persons with HIV/AIDS, according to a number of labor law attorneys. The Department of Justice has taken the position that people infected with the AIDS-causing virus are protected handicapped individuals under Section 504 of the Rehabilitation Act, even if they do not manifest symptoms of the disease. The Office of Federal Contract Compliance Programs has taken the position that all conditions related to HIV/AIDS are covered handicaps under Section 503 of the Rehabilitation Act. These determinations are based in part on current scientific evidence that HIV/AIDS cannot be transmitted via the kind of casual contact that occurs on the job.

Guidelines for dealing with employees who have HIV/AIDS or may be at risk for the disease were issued in late 1985 by the Centers for Disease Control of the U.S. Department of Health and Human Services. The guidelines recommend against the imposition of employment restrictions and routine medical screening of food service, personal service, and most health care employees who have or may be at risk of developing AIDS.

The Occupational Safety and Health Administration standard for occupational exposure to bloodborne pathogens is designed to protect all employees who in the course of their work could reasonably be expected to come into contact with human blood or other potentially infectious material. Under the rule, employers are required to use a combination of engineering and work-practice controls and to provide personal protective clothing and equipment to shield employees from occupational exposure to bloodborne diseases or potentially infectious body fluids. Employers also must provide hazard warnings, conduct information and training programs, make hepatitis B vaccinations available, and keep medical and training records.

A majority of state and local Fair Employment Practices agencies also have determined that HIV/AIDS is a protected handicap under their current handicap laws, and several jurisdictions have adopted laws specifically prohibiting HIV/AIDS discrimination. Testing employees involuntarily for the AIDS virus is prohibited in some jurisdictions, and strict confidentiality of the results of voluntary tests is required.

## SUMMARY OF CASES

### CDC Guidelines Superseded

Individuals should not be barred from work or prohibited from using telephones, office equipment, toilets, showers, eating facilities, or water fountains simply because they have HIV/AIDS, according to Centers for Disease Control guidelines.

The laws prohibiting discrimination against persons who have HIV/AIDS may, at times, conflict with other laws, such as those protecting public health. They also may create problems of the same sort caused when people with any disability file a grievance that must be dealt with in light of an existing collective bargaining agreement.

• A nursing home discharged a health care employee who tested positive for antibodies to the AIDS virus. The employer argued that it was following a state law requiring nursing homes and certain other facilities to establish a written policy "for the control of communicable disease." The employer's policy specifically stated that any employee who had a communicable disease would be "suspended until a negative report is received." The employee questioned whether the state law covered HIV/AIDS and also argued that the nursing home should have followed CDC guidelines, both to reduce the risk of spreading the AIDS virus and to determine what to do when an employee tested positive for HIV.

HIV/AIDS is a communicable disease covered by the state law, an arbitrator decided, adding that "given the severity of the risk" of contracting HIV/AIDS, the employer was correct in following "the explicit requirements of state law." The CDC guidelines, the arbitrator said, "are not adequate or appropriate" and "even with the guidelines in place, the possibility of transmission exists," the arbitrator maintained. Discharge, however, was improper, the arbitrator said. The appropriate step, as required by the employer's own policy, would have been to "continue the employee on medical leave, and then to suspend him until he no longer had a communicable disease." While declining to award back pay because the employee was not eligible to return to work, the arbitrator did direct the employer to pay certain medical bills and to allow the employee to continue health care coverage (*Nursing Home*, 88 LA 681).

### Refusal to Work with HIV/AIDS Carrier

An employer may not discharge an employee for refusing to work with persons suspected of carrying the HIV/AIDS virus, an arbitrator ruled if the employer contributed to the employee's fears.

• A prison guard was fired for refusing to conduct pat searches because he feared he would contract HIV/AIDS from inmates who showed symptoms of the HIV virus. An arbitrator ordered the discharge reduced to a lesser penalty, even though a refusal to perform assigned job duties would ordinarily merit termination. In this case discharge was too severe because the employer was "at least partly responsible" for the employee's "exaggerated fear of contracting the disease." A mitigating factor, the arbitrator said, was an "inaccurate" memorandum from the employer that warned against the sharing of personal items, thus implying that HIV/AIDS could be transmitted through casual contact. That memorandum, the arbitrator stressed, "reinforced" the employee's fears and contributed to his reluctance to believe correct medical information about the way HIV/AIDS is transmitted. The arbitrator ordered reinstatement, without loss of seniority, but declined to award back pay (*Minnesota Department of Corrections*, 85 LA 1185).

## Medical Record Disclosure Duties

Most states have privacy laws and restrictions protecting the confidentiality of medical information. Some collective bargaining agreements, however, require the disclosure of medical information to their members for their protection.

• Where a contract called for prison guards and their union to be informed about inmates who had or were "medically suspected" of having a communicable disease, the employer was obligated to notify the union and the guards of inmates who tested positive for HIV/AIDS. The problem arose when an inmate died of AIDS, and some 20 other inmates requested confidential HIV/AIDS tests because they had engaged in homosexual relations with the deceased inmate. Several inmates tested positive, but the union

was not given their names because of the confidentiality promised them.

The arbitrator concluded that "a realistic and meaningful interpretation" of the contract requires the employer to release the names of the inmates testing positive. "The obvious purpose" of the contract section, the arbitrator observed, "is to alert the bargaining unit employees (guards) to the need for special caution in dealing with inmates who can subject them to the risk of contracting diseases such as AIDS" (*Delaware Department of Corrections*, 86 LA 849).

## 'Environmental Differential Pay'

Employees were not entitled to environmental differential pay, an arbitrator ruled, because the work was not performed "with or in close proximity to micro-organisms." An arbitrator ruled that night maintenance staff who cleaned a federal medical center site where the AIDS-causing HIV was stored and studied were not entitled to environmental differential pay allowed by federal regulations for duties involving either "high degree hazard" (8 percent differential), or "low degree hazard" (4 percent). The work was not performed "with or in close proximity to micro-organisms" so as to involve "potential personal injury" or "potential for personal injury."

Moreover, according to the arbitrator, the federal medical center did not violate its duty to provide a "safe and healthful workplace free from recognized hazards" and to comply with applicable laws and regulations when it permitted the maintenance employees to clean the room in which the HIV virus was kept. There was no evidence of any violation in procedures, and the federal inspectors' "notice of unsafe or unhealthful working conditions" resulted from an investigation that had occurred several weeks after the completion of the HIV research (*Veterans Admin. Medical Center*, 94 LA 169; for more on *environmental differential pay*, see *Tennessee Army National Guard*, 109 LA 693).

# Part 4

# *Seniority and Its Application*

# Calculating Seniority

## OVERVIEW

Generally, seniority is based on an employee's length of service, although a collective bargaining agreement may provide for exceptions, such as so-called "superseniority" for union officers and stewards, denial of seniority for probationary employees, and loss of seniority in whole or part under specified circumstances. (Superseniority is a kind of special seniority that is not based on length of service; it supersedes normal seniority and is seen as a way of protecting shop stewards from layoff so that a union maintains a core group of knowledgeable officials to handle grievances.)

Because seniority, length of service, and their concomitant rights are created by the collective bargaining agreement, it is necessary for arbitrators to look first to the agreement's language in determining the seniority status of employees. In the absence of a definition of seniority in the contract, the term is "commonly understood to mean the length of service with the employer or in some division of the enterprise" (*Curtiss-Wright Corp.*, 11 LA 139).

An employee's relative seniority status in the company usually depends on three basic considerations—when seniority begins to accumulate, the effect of changes in work assignments on seniority, and the effect of interruptions in employment on seniority.

## SUMMARY OF CASES

### Seniority Starting Date

In the absence of language to the contrary, arbitrators generally hold that seniority begins to accumulate from an employee's date of hire rather than the effective date of a collective bargaining agreement. Problems may arise, however, where formerly separate operations are merged or new businesses are acquired.

*Original hiring date*—Seniority normally is regarded as beginning on the date a person is hired, not the date on which seniority rights were won.

● A part-time employee promoted to full-time status is entitled to seniority from the date of hire, not the date of promotion, an arbitrator ruled. Although the contract excluded part-time employees from some benefits, it was amended to establish a part-time seniority list and specifically defined seniority as beginning on the hiring date. Thus, the arbitrator

concluded, the employer's past practice of counting seniority only from the date of full-time employment was overridden by the agreement (*Columbus Retail Merchants Delivery*, 65 LA 825; see also 97 LA 1011, 94 LA 11, 93 LA 1297).

● An arbitrator held that an employer improperly laid off several employees with greater unit seniority and retained long-service workers who had come into the unit from nonunit jobs, even though the employer contended that flexibility in its operations demanded use of the date of employment as the basis for seniority, rather than the date of the employees' entry into the unit. Reversing the employer's action, the arbitrator ruled that seniority rights under the contract were based on date of entry into the unit (*Elmar Electronics Inc.*, 64 LA 912).

*Change of ownership*—The extent to which seniority rights survive a change in ownership depends on the specific circumstances of a given case. If a new owner simply takes over from the former owner, the employees usually will retain their seniority rights based on their original dates of hire. A more problematic situation is created when the change in ownership is accompanied by a merger of the newly acquired employer with an existing bargaining unit.

Some arbitrators feel that it would be unfair to the new owner's other employees if those in the newly acquired operation carried their seniority rights intact after a merger of operations. Other arbitrators are equally insistent that it would be unfair to strip the workers at the newly acquired facility of seniority rights they have earned. Some arbitrators have tried to dovetail seniority rights in the interest of fair play for both groups of workers.

● Going by the letter of the sales contract, under which the buyer agreed to assume the labor obligations of the seller, the buyer honored all accrued seniority rights of the seller's workforce. The union that represented the buyer's own workforce argued that equity dictated a decrease in the newly-acquired workers' seniority. On employee benefits, the arbitrator decided, the buyer had to honor full seniority, but on competitive status, a full-seniority transfer would work an unfair advantage on the buyer's own workers. To balance these considerations the arbitrator fashioned this formula:

● the seller's workers retained full benefit seniority;

● those who transferred with two or more years' seniority retained one-half their competitive-status seniority; and

● those who transferred with less seniority went to the bottom of the merged competitive status seniority list (*Country Belle Cooperative Farmers*, 48 LA 600; see also 66 LA 1029).

**Seniority in plant merger**—When an employer merges two plants that had separate seniority lists, a new single list must be created, by considering length of service, relative positions on the separate lists, or both.

● One arbitrator weighed these factors equally, reasoning that going by

length of service alone would be unfair to workers in the plant where length of service was relatively low. By the same token, dovetailing the two lists according to workers' relative positions on the separate lists would be unfair to those in the plant where length of service was relatively high. The arbitrator, therefore, set up two numerical lists—one based on length of service, the other based on a person's position on the separate seniority lists. Then he figured what each worker's average position was on the two lists and determined the worker's position on the combined seniority list (*Moore Business Forms Inc.*, 24 LA 793).

● Another arbitrator decided that the most equitable method for determining seniority was to make a pool of the combined jobs resulting from a merger, with each group getting a proportionate share of it. In the case at hand, the transferred work accounted for 41.3 percent of the surviving jobs, or 70 percent of what the transferred workers had contributed before the merger. Thus, the arbitrator credited the transferred workers with seven-tenths of their seniority at the midpoint date of the transfers (*Sonotone Corp.*, 42 LA 359).

● Under a multi-employer agreement that confined seniority rights to the worker's "plant," an arbitrator gave seniority preference to workers in relation to the types of operations they formerly performed at two merged plants. Those whose work was similar at both plants should be assigned from both seniority lists in the proportion that such workers at each plant bore to the total number of workers at both plants, the arbitrator directed (*Superior Products Co.*, 42 LA 517; see also 90 LA 1252, 72 LA 458, 71 LA 476).

**Employees hired the same day**— Most arbitrators give equal seniority to employees hired on the same day.

● When a union urged that seniority for workers hired the same day should be computed according to the order of their physical examination, an arbitrator ruled that seniority should not be measured in units of less than one day (*Standard Oil Co. of Ind.*, 3 LA 758).

• Another arbitrator concluded that tossing a coin was the only way to resolve a dispute involving two workers who had equal seniority. The contract fixed seniority "from the date of issuance of the union card." Two women were transferred into the unit on the same day and were issued union cards on the same day. Because both women enjoyed the same seniority rights, the arbitrator arrived at the coin toss as the most equitable method for deciding which one would be laid off (*McCall Corp.*, 49 LA 183).

*Delayed challenges to seniority*— Arbitrators differ as to how long an employee retains the right to challenge his standing on the seniority list, unless the contract specifically limits this period. Absent such a restriction, one arbitrator said that an employee has a right to complain about the continuation of an error in the list at any time.

• In this case, an employer gave an employee credit for too much seniority in his department, and the error went unchallenged for nine years. Another employee filed a grievance asking that the error be corrected so that he could move up a notch on the seniority list. The employer rejected his request on the basis of a contract provision stating that grievances must be filed within 30 days of the occurrence of the events involved. The time limit did not apply in this situation, the arbitrator said, because if it was a contract violation to give a man extra seniority credit in the past, it also was a violation to continue giving him the extra credit. The arbitrator ruled, however, that the preference given to the other employee in the matters of promotion, demotion, and layoffs was beyond challenge (*Bethlehem Steel Co.*, 23 LA 538).

• Another arbitrator, however, held that if a posted seniority has gone unquestioned for a long period of time, the errors cannot be corrected even though there is no "statute of limitations" in the contract (*Creamery Package Mfg. Co.*, 31 LA 917).

*Challenging the seniority of others*—An employee may challenge another's seniority date, one arbitrator ruled, where employees have the right to file grievances over the interpretation and application of the contract and the contract describes the method of computing seniority. In these circumstances, the arbitrator said, the incorrect listing of a seniority date was a contract violation that any employee can protest (*Republic Steel Corp.*, 18 LA 907).

*Responsibility for seniority error*— Responsibility for an error on a seniority list rests with the party who prepared it.

• An employer prepared a seniority list, considered final and binding when a copy was given to the union. The list was incorrect, but according to the arbitrator, the union was not jointly responsible for the mistake. The rule that the list was final and binding applied only to a correct list, and because the employer had the sole responsibility for preparing the list, it also had the sole responsibility for any errors, he concluded (*Bethlehem Fabricators Inc.*, 41 LA 6; 85 LA 774).

## Units for Seniority

Seniority units are defined by the collective bargaining agreement, either specifically or by interpretation. A seniority unit may be employer-wide, multi-employer, or departmental. It also may be based on the bargaining unit, an occupational group or classification, or on a combination of these groups.

• Seniority rights may be acquired in one unit and exercised in another. For example, seniority may be based on service with an employer, but its exercise may be limited to the employee's particular department. Similarly, seniority rights may be based on different units for different aspects of the employment relations. For instance, departmental seniority may prevail for layoff and recalls, while employer-wide seniority determines vacation and pension rights (97 LA 470, 97 LA 132, 96 LA 1211, 96 LA 670, 93 LA 1192, 91 LA 763, 91 LA 605).

• The accrual of seniority may vary for different classifications of employees. For example, an arbitrator held that an employer's two-track seniority system for regular and temporary employees was acceptable (*Hazelwood Farm Bakeries*, 92 LA 1026).

***Where unit not specified***—If the seniority unit is not clearly specified, arbitrators are inclined to assume that employer-wide seniority was intended, particularly if this fosters operational efficiency.

● A contract specified that "accepted rules of seniority" would apply to layoffs and that acquisition of seniority would begin on the first day of employment, regardless of classification. Company-wide seniority was held to govern. If, as urged by the union, classification seniority were to apply, the employer would lose the flexibility afforded by the contract, because of the seasonal nature of the work and the varied skills of the employees, the arbitrator decided (*Great Lakes Homes Inc.*, 44 LA 737).

### Work-Assignment Changes

When seniority is not on an employer-wide or bargaining-unit basis, provision must be made for employees who transfer from one seniority unit to another. Under the most restrictive approach, the employee loses his seniority in his old job, and starts from scratch in his new one. More often, however, the employee retains or even accumulates seniority in his old job—at least for a long enough period to afford protection in case things do not work out in the new job. A third approach permits the employee to carry seniority previously acquired over the new job.

● Some contracts may be very specific regarding the seniority rights of employees promoted to supervisory positions and later returned to the unit. In cases where the contract specifically excludes the period as supervisor from the seniority calculation, the employer's only defense in granting seniority may be a denial of the employee's supervisory status (*Chrysler Corp.*, 65 LA 544; see also 75 LA 1077, 70 LA 1217).

● In the absence of contract clauses specifying the seniority rights of employees who are promoted to supervisory positions, arbitrators are divided on the seniority status of such employees if they later are demoted and returned to the bargaining unit. Some arbitrators have held that supervisors continue to accumulate seniority after promotion unless the contract specifically states otherwise (70 LA 1246, 62 LA 1013, 43 LA 228, 34 LA 285, 31 LA 137, 25 LA 595).

● Other arbitrators, however, have ruled that seniority is strictly a contractual right and may not be accumulated after promotion (32 LA 892, 31 LA 859, 31 LA 200).

● Still others have held that an employee forfeits all his or her seniority when promoted because the person in effect has voluntarily resigned from the unit (27 LA 30, 26 LA 898, 40 LA 388).

● There is more apparent agreement among arbitrators that supervisors who have never been in the unit are entitled to no seniority credit on demotion (41 LA 583, 33 LA 150, 32 LA 274, 29 LA 828).

### Employment Interruption

***Layoffs and leaves***—Seniority generally is retained or accumulated, at least to some extent, where absence is caused by illness, layoff, or other leave of absence. In one case, however, an employee was properly denied seniority for the eight months of his layoff, one arbitrator decided, where the relevant contract language stated that "seniority is continuous service with the employer, compiled by time actually spent on the payroll, plus properly approved absences." The contract also listed exclusive reasons for seniority to be "broken." In upholding the employer's denial, the arbitrator ruled that the layoff was a period spent off the payroll and not an approved absence. Furthermore, the phrase "broken seniority" was taken to mean a complete loss of seniority, the arbitrator concluded, rather than a gap in its calculation (*Firestone Tire and Rubber Co.*, 61 LA 136; see also 75 LA 297, 72 LA 609, 72 LA 240).

● Does an employee retain his seniority when he takes a job with another employer? One arbitrator ruled that other employment during a leave of absence does not terminate seniority in the absence of a clause forbidding the taking of outside work (*Goodyear Tire & Rubber Co.*, 5 LA 234; see also 72 LA 663, 63 LA 941).

● Another arbitrator ruled, however, that an employee may not accumulate seniority simultaneously with two employers and that an employee forfeited his employee status during a layoff by working for another employer (*Fairchild Engine & Airplane Corp.*, 3 LA 873).

**Military leave**—Seniority generally accumulates during leave for military service because this is required by federal (and often state) laws governing reemployment rights of veterans (75 LA 696, 63 LA 750).

**Effects of unauthorized absence**—If an employee has a good reason for being absent, most arbitrators will protect the worker's accumulated seniority even though his absence is unauthorized—unless, of course, the contract specifically provides for forfeiture.

● An employee was absent for one week without permission at Christmas time. On his return, the employer claimed it was rehiring the employee so that his seniority would begin at the day he was rehired. The arbitrator agreed with the employer that granting or denying leave was a management prerogative that could not be questioned unless employer action was unreasonable or discriminatory. In this case, however, the arbitrator ruled that because the absence was for good cause, there should be no break in the employee's seniority (*Pittsburgh Metallurgical Co. Inc.*, 12 LA 95).

**Refusal of recall from layoff**—An employee who refused an offer of recall from layoff was improperly deprived of seniority, an arbitrator ruled. The employee had refused reinstatement on the night shift because employment during that shift would conflict with his religious obligations, and the employer denied seniority to the worker, arguing that the contract clearly provided for seniority denial in such cases. Overturning the employer's action, an arbitrator ruled that the employer had violated Equal Employment Opportunity Commission guidelines that require an employer to accommodate the religious needs of employees where no undue hardship to the employer will result (*American Forest Products Corp.*, 65 LA 650).

**Loss of superseniority**—When union officials leave office, one arbitrator held

that their superseniority end. There was no reason, the arbitrator held, why benefits and privileges that union officials acquire by virtue of superseniority should continue after they are out of office (*Rockwell Spring & Axle Co.*, 25 LA 174; see also 97 LA 792, 75 LA 263).

**Termination of probationary status**—Where an employee is serving a probationary period and that period is defined as a certain number of working days, one arbitrator said, he achieves status as a regular employee the moment he clocks out on the last day of his trial period.

● Under the provisions of one employer's contract, all new employees had to serve a 30-day probationary period before they could become regular employees and begin to accrue seniority. During that period the employer could fire an employee without being subject to the contract's "just cause" restriction. One employee clocked out on his thirtieth day of work and received a telegram that evening notifying him that he was fired. The arbitrator concluded that the employee had become a regular employee at the time he left work and was covered by the "just cause" provision of the contract, noting that because seniority began to accrue at the conclusion of the probationary period, full status as an employee was also achieved at that time (*Lyon Inc.*, 24 LA 353).

**Computing probationary period**—Many questions arise in determining when a new employee completes probation and acquires seniority status. Small variations in contract language may make the difference in answering this question.

● Under a contract providing probation "for the first month" of employment, an arbitrator held that an employee who worked less than a month, was discharged, was rehired 17 days later, and worked another three weeks, had completed her probationary period. Given that the periods of employment were separated by only 17 days, the arbitrator decided that the employer had an ample opportunity to judge the employee's suitability for the job (*Kreisler Industrial*, 27 LA 134).

• A contract that defined the probationary period in terms of "continuous employment" led an arbitrator to decide that the employer could require a rehired probationer to serve a completely new probationary period (*Armstrong Cork Co.*, 23 LA 366).

• An agreement indicating an employee would be on probation until he "performed work" on 30 days within any three-month period led an arbitrator to hold that days on which an employee had been sent home because of bad weather could be discounted in figuring his probationary period. It might have been different, the arbitrator noted, if the agreement had stated the probationary period in terms of time employed (*Bethlehem Steel Co.*, 27 LA 300).

• In an agreement defining the probationary period as 45 "working days of actual service with the employer," an arbitrator decided that the employer could not exclude overtime or weekend work from the calculation of seniority, even though the employer and the union had reached an informal, verbal agreement providing that only straight time would be included (*Hoover Ball & Bearing Co.*, 64 LA 63).

# Order of Layoff

—————————————— **OVERVIEW** ——————————————

Broadly speaking, layoff procedures fall into three categories:
- layoffs are based solely on seniority;
- seniority determines the order of layoff, assuming the senior employees can do the available work; and
- seniority governs only if ability or other factors are equal.

Applying procedures in the first category usually poses no serious problem, but procedures in the other two categories are fruitful sources of grievances.

Among other problems discussed in this section are those relating to the exceptions made to seniority rules and those presented by layoffs that are meant to last only for brief periods of time.

—————————— **SUMMARY OF CASES** ——————————

**Seniority versus Ability**

*Contract requiring equal ability*If a contract states that seniority governs layoffs where ability is "equal" an arbitrator is likely to hold that this means "relatively or substantially equal," but not "exactly equal." Ability, arbitrators reason, cannot be measured precisely.

- In one case an arbitrator ruled that an employer violated the contract by retaining a junior mechanic and laying off a senior one on the ground that he was not equal in skill and ability because he had never worked on certain machines that the junior man had. The arbitrator stated that, as a general rule, employees within the same classification should be deemed to have relatively equal ability and skill for layoff purposes, especially when their duties are the same. In view of this, he ruled, the senior employee should have been the one retained (*Poloron Products of Pa.*, 23 LA 789; see also 73 LA 128).

*Employer's right to determine ability*—Arbitrators have frequently held that where a contract makes "fitness and ability" a factor to be considered along with seniority under one of the modified seniority clauses, but is silent as to how and by whom the determination of qualifications is to be made, management is entitled to make the initial determination,

subject to challenge by the union on the basis that the decision was unreasonable, or capricious, arbitrary, or discriminatory (96 LA 1069, 92 LA 926, 85 LA 1069, 79 LA 106, 77 LA 313, 76 LA 142, 75 LA 910).

- Some arbitrators have placed the burden of proof on the employer. They have held that management must give definite evidence that a junior employee clearly and demonstrably has greater ability in order to retain him in preference to a more senior worker (*Flexonics Corp.*, 24 LA 869).

- Where an employer properly laid off a part-time journeyman meatcutter rather than a head meatcutter, even though the journeyman had greater seniority, an arbitrator, in deciding whether the employer or the union must show that the senior employee was not qualified, stated that the employer must explain why it has not followed the seniority rules. In the absence of evidence presented by the employer, the contract's seniority provisions will be given full effect (*Shop Rite Foods Inc.*, 63 LA 60).

*Factors in measuring qualifications*—When contracts make seniority controlling in layoffs, what factors should be taken into account in determining employees' qualification?

• Where a contract said seniority would govern if "ability to perform the work" was relatively equal, the only thing that should be measured was the ability to perform the particular job at stake (*Bethlehem Steel Co.*, 24 LA 820).

• Where a contract said seniority would govern provided ability and skill were relatively equal, a junior worker could be retained on a job in preference to a senior worker who required a much greater amount of supervision in performing the job (*Copco Steel & Engineering Co.*, 12 LA 6).

• In a case where the contract specified that seniority was to govern when management decided the abilities of two employees were "substantially equal," an arbitrator ruled against management's retaining a junior employee instead of a senior worker on the grounds that the employer's criteria for measuring qualifications were too narrow. The arbitrator found that the employer made its decision on the basis of only one of many functions the workers performed; that there was nothing in the contract to allow the employer to judge an employee on the basis of that one function; and that the employer had never made performance of that one function a condition of continued employment (*National Broadcasting Co.*, 61 LA 872).

• When senior male workers were demoted to "outside gang" work before junior women, an arbitrator upheld the employer's action based on the implied contract criterion of "qualifications" to do the work. The work was heavy physical labor the two women could not do, the arbitrator ruled, adding that a general distinction between men and women would be invalid, although the use of objective standards in assessing candidates was permissible (*Morton-Norwich Products Inc.*, 62 LA 1241).

• In another case, where a contract provision clearly required senior employees to have "ability to do work" if moving into an open job at the employer's other plant, an employer properly laid off senior employees at who failed to pass a test that would have qualified them for jobs at another plant that were being held by junior employees (*Metalfab Inc.*, 65 LA 1191).

• Where a contract stated that in the event of a layoff, employees would be laid off in order of seniority, provided that "remaining employees are able to perform the available work," an employer properly determined that workers who would replace a senior inspector were not able to do the job. Noting that the employer was under considerable pressure to improve quality control from a client that provided a major part of its business, the arbitrator concluded that the quality control manager's limitation of replacements to employees who previously had worked under him as inspectors because they would be familiar with his methods, was a credible requirement in light of the critical nature of the work (*R.J. Tower Corp.*, 73 LA 933).

*Use of merit-rating plan*—Merit-rating plans (or performance reviews) involve essentially documenting supervisory opinion concerning various aspects of the "fitness and ability" of an employee. A merit-rating plan may include the following: quantity and quality of work; knowledge of the job; ability to learn; initiative; acceptance of responsibility; ability to direct others; safety habits and accident record; attitude toward co-workers and management; attendance; and personal characteristics such as moral character, physical condition, and appearance. Other factors may include the degree of pertinent experience and training, special conditions of the job, and honors such as incentive awards or other special achievements (*U.S. Dept. of the Interior*, 53 LA 657; see also 74 LA 486).

• An arbitrator upheld an employer's basing ability measurements on a unilateral merit-rating plan, ruling that the plan could be used because it included factors properly related to measurement of ability and skill and there was no evidence that the factors were rated incorrectly (*Merrill-Stevens Dry Dock & Repair Co.*, 17 LA 516).

• Where a merit-rating plan used such factors as cooperation, safety habits, personal habits, and attitude toward superiors, another arbitrator ruled that the employer could not use it to determine workers' relative ability for purposes of layoff. Because these factors were not the same as ability to perform a job, he reasoned, the plan was an unfair measure of ability (*Western Automatic Machine Screw Co.*, 9 LA 606).

• An employer decided to lay off a senior man with a low efficiency rating, based on a report that compared the relative efficiency of workers in a department. Because this was the first instance of the use of tests, the arbitrator held that they were improper. They could be used in the future, however, provided that the ratings conform with rules that were the norm for such procedures and the workers were told about management's intentions (*McEvoy Co.*, 42 LA 41).

*Point system*—An arbitrator held that an employer's use of a point system did not violate a collective bargaining agreement's seniority provisions and was not implemented in bad faith or arbitrarily, where seniority under the contract was defined as including an employee's ability, qualifications, and aptitude to perform a job, and length of service in descending order governed layoffs because the employer used the same factors for each employee (*Wilson Trophy Co.*, 104 LA 529).

## Exceptions to Seniority in Layoffs

Exceptions often are made to the strict application of seniority in layoffs. The most common exceptions are:

• superseniority granted to union stewards and other representatives to ensure that workers remaining on the job during a layoff will continue to have union representation;

• superseniority rights accorded to management to permit it to select key employees for retention during a layoff without regard to the usual seniority rules. Management-designated employees—sometimes equal in number to union representatives with superseniority—may be exempted from the operation of seniority. Employees who have special skills who cannot be spared without impairing efficiency also may be exempted; and

• the lack of any seniority rights for probationary employees, permitting management to designate individual probationers for layoff without regard to their hiring dates.

## Superseniority for Union Representatives

Although arbitrators have liberally construed contracts' superseniority clauses in order to ensure the fullest possible union representation, arbitrators also have balanced this with the view that superseniority benefits are limited to those rights and privileges expressly stated in a collective bargaining agreement. In addition, substantial limitations on superseniority for union representatives have emerged under the National Labor Relations Act.

• The National Labor Relations Board has ruled that superseniority clauses, which are not, on their face, limited to layoff and recall, are presumptively unlawful (*Dairylea Cooperative*, 219 N.L.R.B. 656, 1975, 89 LRRM 1737).

• The NLRB has continued to invalidate superseniority clauses applied to union officers who do not have "steward-like" grievance-handling responsibilities—e.g., union negotiating committees and union executive-board members (*Gulton Electro-Voice Inc.*, 266 N.L.R.B. 466, 1983, 112 LRRM 1361).

• Where the major purpose of the superseniority clause is to allow for efficient administration of the contract, arbitrators have permitted layoff of union stewards when, for example, a work group was reclassified (*Textron Inc.*, 83 LA 931), or when a temporary layoff did not impede a union's ability to administer a contract (*Almet/Lawnlite Inc.*, 87 LA 624).

Under a union contract giving top seniority on a plant-wide basis to the bargaining-unit chair, must an employer retain a steward when there is no work available for the employee and the employer has retained only a few bargaining-unit employees? Many arbitrators say that under such an all-inclusive clause the union representative must be kept on the job as long as even one bargaining-unit employee is still working.

• In one case arising under such a clause, the arbitrator held that a shop chairman clearly had top seniority rights in the entire shop under all circumstances. He said that the superseniority given union representatives under collective agreement is not related to their functions as productive workers but stems from their special status in administering the agreement (*Freed Radio Corp.*, 9 LA 55).

• In another case, an employer violated a contract's provision recognizing union officers' right to top seniority, an arbitrator held, when it refused to recall employees who were elected to union offices during their layoff caused by lack of work. Although superseniority has the effect of pushing all employees to a lower position on the seniority list, it does so whether the employees are union members or nonunion members, the arbitrator pointed out, adding that the benefits of having union officers and grievance committeemen who are not subject to as much turnover serve as a protection for nonunion members as well as union members (*Keller Industries Inc.*, 63 LA 1230; see also 100 LA 414, 90 LA 257, 89 LA 221, 81 LA 1242).

• Express contractual restrictions against the transfer of union representatives during a reduction in force from a department or shift that they had been representing, have been upheld by arbitrators (73 LA 13, 64 LA 1080).

• Where a bargaining agreement's superseniority clause was ambiguous and the employer had never interpreted it as granting superseniority, an arbitrator ruled that an employer properly laid off a union steward during a business slowdown, where the employer was laying off employees strictly on the basis of seniority (*Curtis Sand & Gravel Co.*, 96 LA 972).

• An employer was allowed to reduce the workweek of union officers who held superseniority. The arbitrator found that the employer merely was staggering his work schedule to spread available jobs among the workforce, which did not constitute a layoff despite the reduced hours (*Wilcox Crittenden Co.*, 43 LA 1046; see

also 74 LA 719, 72 LA 96, 70 LA 49, 66 LA 1289).

## When Representatives Are Unable to Do Work

Under a contract that gives top departmental seniority to shop stewards and also, in another article, provides that seniority applies in layoffs if employees are able to do required work, do shop stewards have the right to be retained even if they cannot do the work? Most arbitrators have held that union representatives must be kept on regardless of their ability so long as other employees are still working in their departments. The purpose of a superseniority clause, they have noted, is to protect union representation during reductions in force. If stewards were laid off before other employees, the clause would be nullified and the purpose would be defeated, these arbitrators have observed (*Luders Marine Construction Co.*, 2 LA 622; see also 97 LA 792).

• An arbitrator ruled, in a case where superseniority rights conflicted with recall subject to ability to perform the work, that an employer's assessment of relative ability is irrelevant and outweighed by a superseniority provision where the retained steward can perform the work at an acceptable level (*U.S. Steel Corp.*, 85 LA 1113).

• Other arbitrators have decided that all sections of a contract article must be read together to determine the intent of the parties. So where a contract within the same article provides for superseniority for shop stewards and then limits the application of seniority by the ability factor, it is all right to lay off shop stewards who cannot perform the required work (*Roberts-Gordon Appliance Corp.*, 8 LA 1030; see also *United States Time Corp.*, 23 LA 379).

• Where a contract provided for recall based on a "employer's operational requirements as well as seniority and ability," and a union steward had no experience in a particular, relevant job classification, an arbitrator ruled that an employer did not violate contractual superseniority provisions when it failed to recall the steward to a classification that he had never held (*Siemens Energy & Automation Inc.*, 91 LA 598).

## Rights of Alternate Union Officers

According to one arbitrator, superseniority for union stewards does not extend to their alternates. The arbitrator decided one employer had a right to lay off an alternate union committeeman on the ground that the benefits attached to the position rather than the worker, and alternates were not covered by the superseniority clause. There was nothing wrong with the employer's extending the benefits to alternates if it wished, he said, but the union did not have the right to insist upon such extension (*Kidde Manufacturing Co.*, 40 LA 328).

## Superseniority No Guarantee of Particular Job

Under a contract that gave stewards top seniority in the area in which they served, was a steward entitled to retain his particular job during a force reduction?

● Some arbitrators have held that a clause of this type simply gives a steward preferred seniority in the area that he serves—a division, a department, or the plant. It does not give him the right to remain in his own job (18 LA 780, 13 LA 628, 17 LA 291).

● Unless otherwise specified in a contract, superseniority ends when the union official vacates the protection and privileges of his or her office. An arbitrator ordered an employer to transfer a former union president, when he vacated his job as union president, from a job that he had during a layoff because of superseniority to a classification for which his experience and regular seniority qualified him. The contract implied that the superseniority entitlement to the position ceased when the employee vacated the protected union office. In addition, the senior employee on layoff was qualified for the job in question, the arbitrator found (*Lockheed Aeronautical Systems Inc.*, 94 LA 137).

## Superseniority for Employee without Regular Seniority

Under a contract that permitted an employer to grant superseniority to a certain number of employees of its own choosing, one arbitrator ruled that an employee who had no regular seniority was not disqualified for such superseniority.

● One contract provided that an employee acquired seniority after he had worked 30 days. It also allowed the employer to retain on its "working force" a certain number of employees "without regard to their seniority." When management laid off one man with seniority while keeping another who had not yet worked 30 days, the union protested; superseniority, it argued, could not be given to a worker who had no seniority at all.

The arbitrator sided with the employer. The employee, he pointed out, was a member of the workforce even though he had not worked 30 days. In the arbitrator's opinion the phrase, "without regard to their seniority" meant that seniority was not a factor at all (*Bethlehem Steel Co.*, 28 LA 808).

## Employee with Security Clearance

Can seniority rules be deviated from in order to retain a junior worker who has a security clearance where government-contract work requires such a clearance? One arbitrator held that an employer could not do this in a case where it was responsible for the fact that only the junior worker had been cleared.

The employer had full knowledge of its contractual obligations, the arbitrator said, and could have avoided the problem if it had obtained clearance for the senior worker instead of the junior one. The only way the employer could have got around its "self-imposed predicament," the arbitrator suggested, would have been to lay off somebody who had not yet achieved seniority status. Then it could have assigned the senior worker to that job, at his regular wage rate, until his security clearance came through (*Webcor Inc.*, 32 LA 490).

## Layoff of Probationary Employees

Under most contracts, probationers must be laid off before employees with seniority are dropped.

● One arbitrator ruled that an employer properly retained probationary employees who were qualified to perform the duties of their electrical tester jobs, instead of permitting their displacement by more senior employees, given that the senior employees lacked the qualifications to do the work (*Eaton Corp.*, 65 LA 671).

● An employer had the right to retain a probationary employee who had experience in operating certain machines, instead of recalling laid-off senior employees who did not have the ability to run the machines, an arbitrator held, because under the contract the employer was entitled to keep the employee on the job if he was qualified (*Bellows International*, 65 LA 1280; see also 68 LA 1032).

● Arbitrators usually have said that probationers do not have to be laid off in any specific order. In cases where unions have questioned management's procedure in laying off such employees, the arbitrators have held that it need not have been according to length of service because the new employees had acquired no seniority (6 LA 760, 14 LA 963).

### Layoff of Probationary Apprentices

Under a special apprenticeship agreement, one arbitrator determined that an apprentice was immune to ordinary reductions in force even if he was still on probation. He reasoned that it would frustrate the purpose of apprenticeship to make any apprentice subject to layoff by seniority in the absence of such a requirement in the agreement (*California Metal Trades Assn.*, 27 LA 105).

### Layoff of Handicapped Employee

Under a contract giving handicapped employees transfer rights regardless of seniority, do they have any special protection against layoff? One arbitrator ruled that once a handicapped worker had exercised his special privilege of transferring without regard to seniority, he had no further special protection. Unless the contract specifically provides otherwise, the arbitrator said, handicapped employees must be treated just like other employees during a layoff (*John Deere & Co.*, 22 LA 383).

### Temporary versus Indefinite Layoffs

For temporary or emergency layoffs, an employer often is allowed more leeway in selecting employees for layoff than in the case of indefinite layoffs.

In the absence of contract clauses making layoff rules inapplicable to temporary layoffs, some arbitrators have held that ordinary layoff procedures must be followed even where the lack of work lasted only a few hours (21 LA 400, 30 LA 441) or one or two days. (64 LA 256, 59 LA 984).

● The more common view, however, is that the frequently cumbersome seniority rules need not be followed in the case of a brief temporary layoff (61 LA 506, 43 LA 1092, 41 LA 970, 12 LA 763, 4 LA 533).

● In the case of layoffs caused by emergency breakdowns or other conditions beyond the control of the employer, arbitrators generally disregard seniority rules applicable during ordinary layoffs. Examples include: a three-day layoff caused by an acute gas shortage (*Atlantic Foundry Co.*, 8 LA 807); a temporary shutdown caused by a breakdown in equipment (*United Engineering and Foundry Co.*, 31 LA 93); and an eight-day layoff precipitated by a heavy snowfall (*Riverton Lime & Stone Co.*, 8 LA 506).

● Where it was not shown that application of seniority rules would cause a hardship, an arbitrator ruled seniority should have been followed during an emergency layoff. The arbitrator found nothing in the contract to authorize the employer's unilaterally established rule that layoffs did not include periods of less than three days (*Yale and Towne Mfg., Co.*, 40 LA 1115; see also 74 LA 844).

### Temporary Layoffs for Taking Inventory

Does layoff for the purpose of taking inventory have to follow seniority provisions? Arbitrators have ruled both ways on this question. Some have said that seniority must be applied to any period of slack work, no matter what the reason.

● An employer closed down its plant for two days to take inventory. Certain production employees were called in to assist, but the selections were not all made in accordance with seniority. The contract was silent on the exact point but did provide that seniority would govern in case of layoffs.

The question was whether the shutdown constituted a layoff subject to seniority provisions. The arbitrator ruled that the shutdown actually "constituted a slack work period resulting in layoffs of employees within the meaning of the agreement." Therefore seniority had to be considered, and the employer erred in laying off workers who had more seniority than some of the employees put to work to take inventory (*Warren City Mfg. Co.*, 7 LA 202; see also 65 LA 471).

● In another case an arbitrator held that a shutdown for inventory purposes was only a temporary cessation of operations and not really a layoff. Therefore, he said, management could select any people it wanted to help take inventory, and the remainder of the workforce could be laid off without regard to seniority (*Caterpillar Tractor Co.*, 7 LA 555; see also 74 LA 89).

# Layoff Notice & Pay

———————————————— **OVERVIEW** ————————————————

Various problems may arise when an employer agrees to give either advance notice of layoff or pay in lieu of notice, but most center around two main issues. These are whether management is excused from both notice and pay under particular circumstances, and the form of the notice and to whom it should be given. Beyond collective-bargaining provisions, layoff-notice arbitration decisions may be affected by state plant-closing statutes as well as by the federal Worker Adjustment and Retraining Notification Act.

Some collective bargaining agreements provide for payment of a separation allowance to employees who are laid off or who lose their jobs for other reasons.

## KEY DECISIONS—

If a contract requires advance notice of layoffs, arbitrators generally hold that a layoff notice must be clear, specific, and directed to the individual attention of the employees affected. Thus, one arbitrator ruled that a notice requirement was not met by an employer's repeatedly telling a union at their regular joint meetings that there was a possibility of a layoff without making any effort to notify each employee of the prospect of losing his or her job (*Phillip's Waste Oil Pick-Up & Road Oiling Service Inc.*, 24 LA 136; see also 61 LA 494).

• Similarly, a general notice to the union of an impending layoff without identifying those to be laid off does not satisfy a requirement of written notice in advance of a layoff. The purpose of an advance notice requirement is to give employees an opportunity to look for other work, so the employer is required to list those employees to be affected (*Donaldson Co.*, 21 LA 254).

• Even where the layoff is as short as five days, an arbitrator ruled that a general notice to the department that some employees will be laid off was insufficient. If layoffs are to occur, the arbitrator emphasized, the affected individuals must be specifically told in advance that they are to be laid off (*Anaconda Aluminum Co.*, 65 LA 498).

*Exceptions for Emergencies*—Many contracts require notice in advance of layoff except in emergencies. What is considered an emergency? Such occurrences as machine breakdowns, fire, and inclement weather generally are recognized as circumstances beyond management's control. Other situations that have been looked upon by arbitrators as emergencies outside of management's control and therefore excusing the failure to provide advance notice include: (1) a strike affecting supplies, (2) an unforeseen materials shortage, (3) snowstorms, (4) unexpected business or financial crisis, and (5) gas shortages requiring plant shutdowns (73 LA 1127, 67 LA 699, 66 LA 909, 62 LA 962, 50 LA 290, 49 LA 1140, 12 LA 726, 5 LA 295).

• If a contract does not provide for exceptions to a layoff notice requirement, is management still bound to give notice or pay except in emergencies? Arbitrators have ruled both ways on this. Some have held that in the absence of a written exception in the contract, employers must meet notice requirements even in emergencies (29 LA 706, 18 LA 227).

• Other arbitrators have taken the view that a clause requiring notice applies only to situations where management reasonably can give notice—and management is not obligated for pay in lieu of notice when an emergency prevents it from giving notice (*International Harvester Co.*, 14 LA 134).

## SUMMARY OF CASES

### Receipt of Notice Required

Under a contract stating that an employee "shall receive" advance notice of a layoff, one arbitrator has ruled that merely "sending" a notice was not enough to relieve the employer of reporting-pay liability.

• An employer sent telegrams to employees who were being laid off. One employee did not get the word, although he was at home at the time it should have been delivered. He reported for work as usual the next day. The employer denied his claim for reporting pay, saying that its obligation was met by sending a correctly addressed telegram.

The word "receive," the arbitrator pointed means that more than the sending of a message is necessary. The contract, he said, recognized this, for it used "shall be notified" instead of "shall receive notice" in another provision. Although the employee had a telephone, no attempt was made to reach him by this means. Thus, the arbitrator reasoned, all reasonable efforts were not made, and the employee was entitled to pay (*Douglas & Lomason Co.*, 28 LA 406; see also 88 LA 594).

### Penalties for Notice Violations

When an employer fails to give employees proper or timely notice of layoffs, as provided in a bargaining agreement or under state or federal law, and if the employer also fails to give an adequate written explanation for its lack of notice, it may be held liable, for example, for pay in lieu of notice.

• An employer that notified a union and employees of layoffs on the morning that the layoffs were implemented was found liable to affected employees for two days' pay in lieu of notice. The arbitrator ruled that the contract clearly required two days' advance notice of layoff to union or immediate written explanation for the lack of notice. Because the employer did not furnish a written explanation until the union requested it three weeks later, he said, there was no emergency (*York International Corp.*, 93 LA 1107; see also 86 LA 866).

• An arbitrator held that an employer must compensate night-shift employees for four hours' reporting pay because it failed to notify the employees of layoff until after they had reported for work on the day of the layoff, despite the employer's claim that the employees were not scheduled to work on the day of the layoff and that it notified the employees' union two days earlier. The notification of layoff given the union does not constitute adequate layoff notice to employees, the arbitrator said, noting also that the contract required the employer to issue layoff notices 48 hours prior to the layoff and during work hours (*Fritz Co.*, 101 LA 507).

• Employees, who had 15 minutes' notice of "termination of employment" caused by a plant closure and sale, were not entitled to payment in lieu of a three-day notice or to continued insurance coverage required in case of layoff, an arbitrator ruled, because they were discharged, not laid off. The mere existence of a contract does not guarantee a continuation of employment or of employment-related benefits, and in addition, the issue of a procedure for the continuation of benefits in the event of closure or sale was never discussed by either party (*Hausman Steel Corp.*, 93 LA 813).

• An arbitrator ruled that an employer that failed to comply with a two-week notice of termination requirement when it sent a letter of termination to employees that provided only one-week notice, need not pay a compensatory remedy because the losses were minimal (*Independent School District No. 721*, 82 LA 1323).

• An arbitrator held that an employer was not required to give laid-off employees two-weeks' notice, where a strike settlement specifically waived all "work guarantee" (*Safeway Stores Inc.*, 85 LA 51).

• An arbitrator said that 46 days was adequate notice of an intent to permanently close a plant, where a letter agreement required 90-days' notice "if circumstances permit." The union had all the information that it needed for bargaining four months before the formal notice, and there was no evidence that the requirement guaranteed 90 days of employment or that a waiver of the time limit could only occur under circumstances outside the employer's control (*Commonwealth Aluminum Corp.*, 89 LA 1097).

## Computing Notice Period

When a contract requires advance notice a certain length of time prior to the layoff, can nonworking days be counted as days of notice? At least one arbitrator has ruled that they cannot. He noted that one purpose of advance layoff notice is to allow the union time to try to find other employment for the laid-off workers. This purpose, he said, would be defeated if nonworking days could be counted in the notice period (*Hoke Inc.*, 3 LA 750).

• An arbitrator ruled that an employer had to pay eight hours wages to employees laid off without the required one day's notice, despite the employer's contention that he could not give notice because employees' were not in the plant due to a vacation shutdown. The arbitrator said that a vacation shutdown was like a weekend, and if employees were to be laid off they should have been notified at or before the start of work on the last day before the weekend (*Magnavox Co.*, 64 LA 686).

• Another arbitrator ruled differently, where 24-hour notice was required before layoffs, and an employer told workers at 3:30 p.m. on Friday that they would be laid off effective 6:00 p.m. Saturday. Because Saturday was not a scheduled working day, the union maintained that the workers should have been given a full working day as notice period. Rejecting the union's position, the arbitrator found that the "24 hours notice" merely meant 24 hours following posting of layoff notice, adding that there was no clear past practice governing Friday layoff notices (*White Metal Rolling and Stamping Corp.*, 65 LA 771).

## Layoff Shorter Than Notice Period

Some contracts provide for notice a specified length of time in advance of layoff or pay for the same period in lieu of notice. Are workers entitled to pay for the full notice period when they're laid off, without notice, for a shorter period of time? A state arbitration board held that employees laid off without advance notice were entitled to pay for the full period, even though they were laid off a shorter time.

• A contract said that workers would not be laid off without a week's notice or a week's pay in lieu of notice. The workers were given no advance notice when they were laid off for two days. The union claimed the employer owed them a week's pay, but the employer claimed it had not been possible to give advance notice. The arbitration board conceded that application of the contract provision seemed harsh because the layoff lasted only two days, but it pointed out that it would not have seemed so if the layoff had lasted longer. The employer's obligation under the contract was clear and unqualified, the board ruled; therefore, one week's pay was owed each worker (*General Baking Co.*, 28 LA 621).

• The fact that a contract provides for two weeks' notice of layoff or pay in lieu thereof does not necessarily mean that employees not given two weeks' notice must be granted a full two weeks' pay, according to one arbitrator.

A contract provided for two weeks' notice of layoff or pay in lieu of notice for employees with six months' service. The employer made a general layoff with only a few days' prior notice. Some employees lost less than two weeks' work, but the union claimed the full two weeks' pay in lieu of notice in addition to their regular earnings for any work done within the period. An arbitrator ruled that the most reasonable interpretation of the provision was that employees were entitled to "pay in lieu thereof" only for layoffs from work that fell within the two weeks after notice was given. In other words, he said, they could expect to receive only their regular pay for the two weeks following the layoff notice, including pay for both time worked and layoff time (*Phillip's Waste Oil Pick-Up & Road Oiling Service Inc.*, 24 LA 136).

### Notice for Temporary Layoff

An employer attempted to avoid a contract requirement providing for two week notice in event of layoff by claiming the provision only applied in cases of permanent layoff, and that his three-day notice was sufficient because the layoff was only temporary. In overturning the employer's action, however, the arbitrator read no such distinction in the contract language. A layoff is a layoff whether it is permanent or temporary, the arbitrator said, and if a distinction were to be made between the two, it should have been made explicit in the contract (*International Paper Co.*, 60 LA 447; see also 73 LA 573).

● An employer violated its collective bargaining agreement when it reduced the workweek for all bargaining-unit members rather than lay off less-senior employees, an arbitrator determined. When customer orders dropped dramatically, a manufacturer laid off 29 bargaining-unit members, then asked union leaders to consent to proposals that ultimately would keep everyone working but shorten the workweek for as long as customer orders remained low. Despite union opposition, the employer imposed the changes, reducing the workweek from 40 to 32 hours for three weeks. It then laid off another 29 workers, but as orders picked up brought back all but five

of the laid off employees to work full-time.

The union grieved, charging that the employer violated the contract by not laying off junior employees in favor of full-time work for more-senior members. The arbitrator held that the layoffs were in fact governed by seniority and that the union and members should have been given a three-day notice before reductions of more than three work days were instituted. Moreover, in previous plant shutdowns, work was assigned to the most senior employees who wanted it, and past practice buttressed the union's position, she said, awarding back pay to all affected members (*Northwest Automatic Prods. Inc.*, 117 LA 465).

● A company violated its labor agreement when it temporarily laid off employees, even though it was for legitimate business reasons, an arbitrator decided. At an adhesives plant, some employees were temporarily laid off for a few days in November and again for a few days in December because of slow sales. The union argued that the company could not implement two layoffs for the "same continuous cause." Under specific contract provisions, the arbitrator stated that for layoffs of less than seven days, the employer could lay off employees by seniority within their shift and classification and need not adhere to plantwide seniority in making the layoffs. Such action could not, however, be taken repetitively to cover additional layoffs caused by the same continuous cause, she added, ordering the company to identify any laid-off employees who could have exercised their plant-wide seniority to avoid layoff and compensate them for any pay lost because of their second layoff (*Cytec Fiberite*, 116 LA 568).

### Where Notice Is 'Impossible'

An employer that had agreed to give three days' advance notice of layoffs, "except where such notice is impossible," violated the contract when employees were laid off without any advance notice because of lack of work. The arbitrator ruled that because the word "impossible" was not explained, it should be given its ordinary definition and only an emergency of major proportions would release the employer from its obligation of giving notice. Decline or even cessation of orders did not qualify as such an emergency, the arbitrator concluded (*Mobil Chemical Co.*, 50 LA 80).

## Notice of Layoff Caused by Wildcat Strike or Slowdown

When a layoff is made necessary by an unauthorized and unexpected work stoppage by employees in other departments of the plant, most arbitrators excuse employers from giving layoff notice or pay.

● A slowdown has been held to be a situation that relieved an employer of the notice requirements. Under a contract that required advance notice of a layoff except in emergencies, one arbitrator held that there was an emergency within the meaning of the contract when an employer had to lay off several workers on short notice because of a work slowdown in one department. The arbitrator said the employer was justified and did not have to give the workers layoff pay because the layoff was neither planned nor desired by the employer (*Lone Star Steel Co.*, 28 LA 465).

# Bumping & Transfer to Avoid Layoff

## OVERVIEW

Seniority rights lose much of their meaning if senior employees do not, when faced with layoff, have the right to claim jobs held by their "juniors." At the same time, employers often oppose such bumping rights because it impairs efficiency. As a result, bumping questions give rise to many grievances.

Even where the right to bump is expressly spelled out in a collective bargaining agreement, problems may arise. For example, may an employee bump only in his or her own department, or anywhere in the plant? May he or she displace an employee who has less seniority, or only the least senior employee? May an employee claim a higher-rated job if the employee is qualified for it? Does an employee have the right to a trial period to prove that he or she can do the work?

In general, arbitrators have held that bumping rights are implied by a contract providing for the application of seniority when the workforce is being reduced. They have further ruled that, in the absence of explicit contract language to the contrary, an employee may displace any employee down the ladder who has less seniority, not merely the least senior employee (91 LA 710, 87 LA 1107, 84 LA 1001, 76 LA 1017, 76 LA 773, 75 LA 1163, 74 LA 584).

In addition, where a contract contains a provision that gives senior employees the right to bump junior employees in a layoff but specifies that ability and experience, in conjunction with seniority, will be determining factors in making layoff decisions, arbitrators have ruled that the employer may allow those senior employees without training to bump junior employees with training (98 LA 333, 98 LA 209, 86 LA 54, 85 LA 24, 84 LA 1001, 84 LA 952, 84 LA 604, 83 LA 205, 82 LA 313, 82 LA 1205).

## SUMMARY OF CASES

### Plant-Wide Seniority Implies Bumping

If a contract provides for a plant-wide seniority system to be applied in layoffs, most arbitrators agree that bumping rights are implicit, even though they are not specifically mentioned. Such an interpretation, they say, means that an employee whose job is discontinued may displace a junior employee in an equal or lower classification provided he can perform the junior employee's job (76 LA 899, 14 LA 938, 13 LA 843, 8 LA 816).

● Not all arbitrators will conclude that bumping rights exist when not mentioned in the contract. At least one has ruled that no such rights exist unless stated in clear and unambiguous terms in the agreement (*Norwalk Co.*, 3 LA 535).

### Bumping Rights under Plant-Wide & Departmental Seniority

When a contract provides for both plant-wide and departmental seniority, is an employee facing layoff permitted to bump to any job in the plant held by a junior employee? Under such a provision, whether bumping rights are expressed or implied, many arbitrators have ruled that departmental seniority should be applied first so that the senior employee would bump to a lower job in his or her own department. Plant-wide seniority, they say, should apply only when there are no jobs remaining within the employee's department (38 LA 939, 30 LA 472, 3 LA 205).

• An arbitrator found that under a system establishing seniority by both plant and department, the bumping rights of senior employees was limited to low-classification jobs or positions within the department over which the employee maintained posted job rights. The bumping and layoff procedure had not been reduced to a detailed written agreement, so the company argued that it was valid on the basis of past practice. The arbitrator concluded that the union failed to show the existence of a contradictory practice (*United States Steel Corp.*, 65 LA 283).

• A dispute arose as to whether an employee with company-wide seniority could displace a junior employee, who had job-site seniority. The employer would not allow the bump, claiming the contract called for job-site seniority in cases of bumping.

Although agreeing with the employer, the arbitrator nonetheless found that the contract language was inconsistent on whether job or company seniority should govern. He therefore based his decision on a combination of factors, including past practice and the union's concession that it would not have taken the same position had the grievant never worked at the same job-site (*American Building Maintenance Co.*, 62 LA 1027).

### Bumping Limited to Choice of Classification

Under a contract permitting an employee, during a layoff, to bump a man with less seniority in any department if he had the ability to do the work, one arbitrator ruled that the senior employee's choice was limited to picking a classification. Management had the right to decide which job within the classification he could fill, the arbitrator ruled (*Fulton-Sylphon Co.*, 2 LA 116; see also 84 LA 952).

• Under a similar provision, another arbitrator held that an employee could choose the job he liked best within a classification because of nonwage factors.

Under one contract, an employee slated for layoff could displace a man with less seniority in any department, provided the employee had the ability to do the job. An employee whose shift was discontinued bumped to a work crew on another shift. He requested one job on the crew but was given another. Both positions were within the same job classification and paid the same wage rate, and the company argued it had a right to decide which one the employee should have.

An arbitrator, however, found that the employer was wrong. The fact that the two jobs carried the same rate did not mean there was nothing to choose between them, he said; nonwage factors made one seem more desirable to the employee. Moreover, the arbitrator pointed out that past practice had been to post particular jobs on the crew for bidding. Thus, he concluded that the employee should be given the job he wanted (*Dayton Steel Foundry Co.*, 29 LA 191; see also 76 LA 399).

### Bumping Limited to Particular Job

Under a contract providing that an employee subject to layoff was entitled to bump the employee with the least seniority in the employee's occupational group, one arbitrator held that an employee was limited to bumping into only one job—that held by the least senior employee in the same job grouping. Because the employee was not able to do that particular job, the employer was justified in laying her off, the arbitrator ruled, even though employees with less seniority were kept working. He said that the contract clearly would not permit her to bump into just any job held by an employee with less seniority (*Ford Motor Co.*, 1 LA 462).

• A laid-off employee was not entitled to select the particular job on which to exercise her bumping rights where the contract referred to ability to do "required" work and willingness to accept the "work proffered." The arbitrator said that the element of choice was in the hands of the company rather than the employee (*United Screw & Bolt Corp.*, 42 LA 669).

• Under a contract simply making seniority the governing factor in layoff, but not mentioning bumping rights, another arbitrator decided that an employee facing layoff could bump any junior employee in an equal or lower classification. The employee was not limited to bumping only the most junior employee, the arbitrator said. If that were the intent of the parties, they should have said so in the contract, he reasoned (*Warren Petroleum Corp.*, 26 LA 532).

## Ability as a Factor

Where a contract allows bumping if the senior employee is capable of performing the job of a junior employee, who is to decide on the ability of the senior employee? Most arbitrators hold that management has the right to determine ability. The union can challenge management's decision through the grievance procedure, but has the burden of proving that management's judgment was wrong, arbitrary, or capricious (75 LA 1001, 41 LA 148, 22 LA 53, 6 LA 786).

- An arbitrator ruled as unreasonable, arbitrary, and capricious, and an unconscionable bargain by the employer, a collective bargaining agreement's bumping clause that required employees to have 30 days' experience in the new positions and to demonstrate that employer records show such experience (84 LA 571).

- It was the employer's past practice that dictated that senior employees were permitted to exercise bumping rights only if they could perform posted jobs without training. The arbitrator honored management's practice despite the union's contention that the junior employee whom the employee wished to bump was performing "menial" tasks, because both the employee and the chief steward admitted that the junior employee could have been performing more complex tasks in that job (*Morton-Norwich Products Inc.*, 61 LA 494).

*Qualifications as factor*—An arbitrator held an employer properly refused to allow two employees to bump into positions they had held during three temporary shutdowns, where the parties' collective bargaining agreement limited bumping rights to employees who are "in

the company's opinion" qualified "at the time" to perform the available work. The arbitrator found the two positions into which the employees wished to bump recently had been combined and the job duties expanded to encompass the use of new technology and the grievants' quality of work during the temporary assignment to the jobs verified the employer's conclusion that the employees were not qualified to use the requisite new technology, policies, and procedures (*Worldsource Coil Coating*, 102 LA 17).

- A maintenance worker who lacked skills was properly laid off in a "sound business decision," according to one arbitrator. When two workers classified as general maintenance mechanics were let go, the union protested and came to an agreement with the company to rehire the more senior worker. The other worker, who had 35 years with the company, was rehired briefly and then laid off again. The union objected that the work of general maintenance mechanics was being given to skilled maintenance mechanics and to a supervisor, and that the worker's age was a factor in his layoff. The company, however, said the union lacked "the courage and candor" to tell the worker his job had been sacrificed to save another's. Although the arbitrator rejected the company's claim that the earlier agreement reached without arbitration covered this dispute, he decided that the company's layoff of the worker did not violate its contract. He was sympathetic to the worker's plight, the arbitrator said, but "management must be allowed to exercise its inherent right to operate its facility in the most productive and efficient manner possible" (*White Consolidated Industries*, 114 LA 1031).

*Skills test*—An arbitrator ruled a university violated a collective bargaining agreement when it required bumping clerical employees, whose positions were eliminated in a reduction in force, to undergo a skills inventory test, although the university properly used the test for promotional and bidding purposes. The arbitrator held seniority usually is the main determining factor in reductions in force; the university did not notify the union it planned to use the test for bumping; and an employee's failure on the test could mean a qualified employee could be refused to be permitted to bump into a position the employee previously had performed successfully (*Central Michigan University*, 102 LA 787).

**Need for Trial/Break-In Periods**

Several arbitrators have ruled that senior employees are entitled to a reasonable *trial period* in order to demonstrate their current ability (96 LA 1069, 93 LA 1028, 82 LA 655, 82 LA 213, 88 LA 1112, 85 LA 1069, 85 LA 24, 83 LA 977, 82 LA 751, 82 LA 213, 81 LA 1248).

• Other arbitrators, however, have ruled that senior employees whose qualifications are questionable are not entitled to a trial period in a layoff situation, but, instead, are entitled to a reasonable break-in period (82 LA 751, 82 LA 721, 81 LA 1100).

• Another arbitrator stressed that a "trial period" is not to be equated with a "training period." A trial period, the arbitrator said, emphasizes a successful bidders's ability at the beginning of a period, provides criteria for determining a bidder's ability to perform in a new position, and is followed by an automatic progression in classification on satisfactory performance; whereas, a training period emphasizes prerequisite ability on the completion of a program (93 LA 1028; see also 82 LA 655).

• Still another arbitrator held that an employer may require testing to determine a senior employee's qualifications for a position to which the employee wishes to bump. (91 LA 710).

• To qualify for retention during layoff, other arbitrators have held that senior employees must be able to perform the necessary jobs after a reasonable break-in period, and are not entitled to any instruction or training (96 LA 105, 61 LA 72, 23 LA 584, 11 LA 667, 7 LA 526).

• Some arbitrators go even further and hold that the senior employee, in order to exercise his bumping rights, must possess the ability to perform the job in question without benefit of any training or trial period (67 LA 282, 65 LA 901, 44 LA 694, 44 LA 24).

**Efficiency as a Factor**

Under a contract requiring a senior employee to be able to do another employee's job efficiently in order to bump the employee, can it be assumed that the senior employee is not qualified just because he has never done the job at that company? One arbitrator has ruled that such an assumption is not justified. He suggested that an employer, in judging an employee's ability to do the work efficiently, is obligated to take into consideration the employee's entire work record, including jobs the employee had at other firms.

• During a force reduction at one company, a milling machine operator was not permitted to bump a junior employee who operated an engine lathe. The contract said employees would be given preference in layoff in accordance with their length of service, "subject to their ability to perform the work in question, it being understood that efficiency is a necessary requisite." Because the employee had never operated the lathe, the company argued, he could not do the job efficiently. The union, though, pointed out that the employee had had 12 years' experience at his trade and had operated engine lathes at other employers.

An arbitrator sided with the union. Under the contract, he said, the company could not deny the employee the job unless it could prove he could not do it efficiently. This it had failed to do, the arbitrator noted, even though checking on the employee's performance at the other firms where he claimed he had run a lathe would have been a simple matter (*Cobak Tool & Mfg. Co.*, 30 LA 279; see also 96 LA 681, 96 LA 189, 96 LA 117).

• In another case, where the contract said the employee doing the bumping could do so only if "seniority to be exercised is greater than the seniority in that classification of the employee to be displaced," a truck driver who had sought to bump a less senior garage serviceman, was refused the move by the company. In upholding the company's refusal, the arbitrator noted the grievant's lack of experience as a garage serviceman (*Jenkin-*

*Guerin Inc.*, 64 LA 703; see also 94 LA 1190).

## Upward Bumping

Can an employee about to be laid off bump a junior employee in a higher-rated job classification? Arbitrators have ruled both ways on the issue of upward bumping. Where arbitrators have upheld the right of a senior employee to bump into a higher-rated classification, one or more of the following reasons were used.

• The collective bargaining agreement does not expressly prohibit upward bumping. (91 LA 221, 62 LA 192).

• The layoff provisions of the agreement are broad (44 LA 694, 30 LA 886, 20 LA 394, 14 LA 502).

• Upward bumping does not conflict with the agreement's promotion provisions (29 LA 439, 12 LA 738).

• Past practice of the parties either supports or does not prohibit upward bumping (62 LA 192, 44 LA 694, 21 LA 214).

• One arbitrator decided that where the contract stated that both ability and seniority were determining factors in bumping, "present rather than potential" ability was called for. Where the senior employee had the required ability, junior employees—including those in higher-rated jobs—had to be laid off first during a reduction in the workforce (*Greater Louisville Industries*, 44 LA 694).

• Another arbitrator denied an upward bump, although he admitted there was nothing in the contract to prohibit it, because he was not convinced the employee seeking the move could perform the higher-rated work. The arbitrator found that the employee could perform only about 20 percent of the job he sought, and that the contract did not provide for the training he would need to successfully carry out the duties that were being performed by a less senior employee. Because the employee failed to meet the burden of proof that he could perform the job at the time he sought it, the grievance was denied (*United Telephone Co. of Ohio*, 60 LA 805).

• Other arbitrators have decided that bumping upward amounts to promotion. When a contract neither permits nor prohibits upward bumping but makes the promotion clause separate from the layoff provision, layoff is no occasion for promoting employees to higher-paying jobs, these arbitrators have ruled (71 LA 295, 25 LA 417, 23 LA 789, 15 LA 891).

• Where a contract provided that all promotions to higher classifications should be given to the most senior qualified employee who bids for "the vacancy," an arbitrator denied an upward bump. The employee, a senior mechanic, who had received a layoff notice tried unsuccessfully to bump into a higher-rated classification of station mechanic. The desired job was held by another employee who had less seniority than the employee.

In upholding the employer's refusal to grant the upward bump, the arbitrator stated that there was not a single reported arbitral decision extending permission, approval, or even toleration of upward bumping as a means of achieving a promotion in violation and defeat of the specifically agreed promotion requirements of a collective bargaining agreement (*K.L.M. Royal Dutch Airlines*, 60 LA 1053).

• Ambiguity in the bumping procedures or contrary past practice also can limit the right of senior employees to bump. When an employee sought to bump into the top mill crew job, the company refused to promote him. Historically, it contended, employees had never been permitted to bump into top jobs that they actually had not performed. According to the arbitrator, established past practice and failure of the contract to provide a training period for bumping supported the company's right to turn down employees whom it determines are unqualified (*Empire-Reeves Steel Corp.*, 44 LA 653).

• Other arbitrators have denied the right of a senior employee to bump into a higher-rated classification (85 LA 47, 84 LA 1069).

One or more of the following reasons were used.

• A layoff may not be used as a means of achieving a promotion. The rationale here seems to be that a promotion can be sought only when a vacancy exists; promotions must be governed by the promotion clause of a collective bargaining agreement; and because upward bumping would result in a promotion in violation of the promotion requirements of the contract, it cannot be permitted (76 LA 899, 72 LA 719, 71 LA 295).

● Evidence indicated that past practice prohibits upward bumping, or there is an indication that past practice allows it (44 LA 653, 30 LA 815, 30 LA 1, 23 LA 220).

● The bargaining history indicates an intent to preclude upward bumping (24 LA 261).

● Although the collective bargaining agreement would permit upward bumping, it does not require that it be permitted. Therefore, without a showing of practice by the parties, the arbitrator cannot sustain a claim to upward bumping (38 LA 128, 30 LA 815).

## Right to Second Bump

If an employee fails to qualify on the first job the employee bumps into, does the employee have the right to try out on another job held by a junior employee? Arbitrators are generally agreed that no second bump need be allowed when the contract is silent on the matter.

● An employee slated for layoff was given the choice of bumping into a job held by a junior employee, as required under the contract. She chose a job she had never before performed; after a week's trial she was informed that she lacked the ability to do the job satisfactorily and was then laid off. The union protested, saying that she had not been given time enough to become familiar with the new job and that, even if her disqualification was proper, she should have been offered an opportunity to bump into another job rather than been laid off.

Ruling that the layoff was proper, the arbitrator found that the employee had been given a reasonable opportunity to demonstrate her ability in the job and that she was not entitled to bump into another job, because the contract did not provide for repeated bumping. The arbitrator decided that the employee herself

was largely responsible for her poor selection of a job to bump into, because she had purposely passed up a job she knew she was capable of doing (22 LA 53, 12 LA 391).

## Right to Bump at Will

Can employees use their accumulated seniority to bump whenever they wish into jobs occupied by employees with less seniority? Most arbitrators hold they cannot. They limit bumping rights to a situation where an employee is moved out of his job as in a layoff.

● An employee bid on a job and was awarded it on the basis of his seniority and qualifications. A year later because of advancing age he attempted to exercise his seniority to bump or "roll" into an oiling job. The company allowed this and the employee was discharged when he was unable to handle any of the available jobs offered him. The employee protested the discharge, claiming that the bumping right did not apply to such a situation. The contract provided that in layoffs the last one in would be the first out.

The arbitrator agreed that "this necessarily implies that a senior employee can 'roll' a junior employee when the former's job is abolished." But the arbitrator limited that right solely to such a situation. He ruled that advancing age was not reason enough to permit an employee on his own initiative to pick out a job held by a junior employee and bump him. The arbitrator pointed out that "the company could not operate efficiently if an employee were free to 'roll' a junior employee at any time he or she desires to do so" (*Anchor Rome Mills Inc.*, 9 LA 595).

● Under a contract stating that employees with seniority could bump into more desirable jobs, another arbitrator ruled that they could do so any time they desired. He said if the parties had meant to limit bumping rights only to situations when vacancies occurred, they should have said so in the contract (*Continental Oil Co.*, 8 LA 171).

## Responsibility for Initiating Bumping

Who is responsible for seeing to it that the bumping provisions of a contract are carried out—the employer, or the employee and the union? Does the company have to start the bumping machinery in a layoff or should the senior employee put in a claim for the job to which he is entitled? When the contract did not specifically spell out the procedure, some arbitrators held that it was up to employees to claim their rights.

• One employee, a crane follower, had been laid off for five months, when he was recalled as a punch helper. A week later, he bid for and was awarded a job as a rivet heater being held by a junior employee. He also put in a claim for back pay to the time of his layoff, claiming he should have replaced the junior rivet heater at that time.

The arbitrator agreed with the employer that the employee had some obligation to be diligent in asserting his rights, either by himself or through his steward. If he did not do so, he should not be permitted to collect back pay from the company, for that would mean that the company was paying twice for the work—once to the man laid off, and once to the man who kept the job (*General American Transportation Corp.*, 15 LA 672).

• In another case, an opposite decision was reached where an employee was bumped from his job by a senior employee, and did not realize that he had a right to another job that he had previously bid for but turned down. Three weeks later the employee was informed of his right to the other job, and so he filed a grievance when the employer refused to bump him into it.

The arbitrator rejected the company's argument that the employee had waited too long after being bumped before filing the grievance. Remarking that the employee could not have known of his right despite reasonable diligence, and so could not have filed the grievance before the company informed him of it, the arbitrator decided that the grievance was timely filed and proper, because it was filed one day after the employer refused to bump the employee into the desired job (*Dayton-Walther Corp.*, 64 LA 645).

## Right to Refuse Downgrading

When a contract is silent on the matter, can an employee elect to be laid off rather than downgraded during a reduction in force, or can the employer discharge him if he refuses to accept a lower-rated job? According to one arbitrator, in the absence of contract language requiring employees to take available work or be discharged, they have the right to choose layoff.

• Two employees' jobs were eliminated during a reduction in force, and they were offered lower-rated jobs on the basis of their seniority. They refused to take the jobs and were discharged. The company said the discharges were for just cause because the men had refused the only work available to them.

The arbitrator, however, decided that the right of senior employees to bump into or to take lower jobs was not the same as a requirement that they take such jobs. In the absence of clear contract language requiring them to take available work or be discharged, the arbitrator concluded that they were free to request layoffs and subsequent rehire in line with their seniority. He ordered the company to change the separation status of the employees from discharge to layoff (*Caterpillar Tractor Co.*, 23 LA 313).

• Employees may continue to elect layoff rather than demotion, despite the introduction of a supplemental unemployment benefit plan, an arbitrator held, where this right of election had existed in the past (*United Engineering & Foundry Co.*, 47 LA 164).

# Worksharing

## OVERVIEW

During a period when work is in short supply, a reduction in the workweek may seem like a palatable idea to an employer; the union, however, may see things slightly differently. Particularly in situations where a collective bargaining agreement provides supplemental unemployment benefits, a union is likely to favor layoff for the few, while maintaining normal working hours for the many.

Arbitrators generally seem to agree that if a contract does not address worksharing and requires that seniority be followed in reducing the workforce, an employer may not shorten the workweek in lieu of making layoffs. If management could telescope the workweek on a whim, they reason, seniority rights would not mean much.

## SUMMARY OF CASES

### Management's Right to Shorten Workweek

If the contract contains no specific provisions relating to worksharing, is the employer free to cut the workweek in order to spread available work among the largest number of employees? The answer to this question depends on the interpretations placed on other types of contract clauses. If the agreement states that seniority must be followed in cutting the workforce, an arbitrator is likely to hold that management may not shorten the workweek in preference to making layoffs.

• One employer, relying on a clause recognizing its right to "curtail production," chopped a day off of the regular workweek for all employees. An arbitrator decided the workweek reduction was a contract violation. The agreement, he noted, stated that force reductions were to be made in order of seniority. If management could cut the workweek to four days, it could make further reductions, he pointed out, and seniority would not mean much (32 LA 244; see also 95 LA 482, 92 LA 1094, 90 LA 922, 90 LA 301).

• Another employer also reduced the workweek to four days when business was bad. The contract with the union dictated that "either the hours per day or the days per week could be reduced by mutual agreement" with the union. Although the union rejected the employer's worksharing proposal, management shortened the workweek anyway.

Arguing that it had the right to reduce the workweek, the employer maintained that union approval was needed only for the form of the reduction—i.e., either hours per day or days per week. The arbitrator rejected this argument and ruled that the employer's action violated the employees' seniority rights. The worksharing had to be by mutual consent, the arbitrator reasoned. Given that there was no consent by the union, the employer's alternative was layoffs by seniority, the arbitrator concluded (*Aro Corp.*, 55 LA 859; see also 73 LA 810).

• An arbitrator ruled that an employer could not institute one- and two-day plant-wide layoffs, because such "share the work" programs were in violation of a clear seniority layoff clause governing reductions in the workforce. The arbitrator rejected management's contention that a separate clause granting permission to lay off all employees due to "changes in customer requirements" was applicable, because the clause concerned only "unforeseen, unpredictable, unplanned and unanticipated conditions," which the present situation—a slow business period—was not (*Tecumseh Products Co.*, 65 LA 471).

• Clauses stating that the regular workweek shall consist of so many hours and so many days generally have been held not to prevent management from cutting the workweek instead of laying employees off.

One employer reduced the normal workweek from 40 to 35 hours by scheduling five seven-hour days when business slowed down. The union argued that this was a violation of a contract provision stating that the regular workday would be eight hours and the regular workweek five days. The arbitrator disagreed, saying that this provision did not establish a guaranteed eight-hour day, five-day week but was merely a statement of the normal operating schedule for purposes of figuring overtime. Nothing in the contract prohibited the employer from shortening the regular workweek, the arbitrator concluded (22 LA 473; see also 96 LA 445, 96 LA 117, 89 LA 1313, 81 LA 502).

• An employer had the right to maintain its two-shift system during an economic downturn, an arbitrator decided, even though the system resulted in frequent scheduling of less than eight-hour workdays, where the contract clearly stated that the employer "shall have no responsibility or obligation to furnish any minimum number of hours of work per week or per day to its employees" (*Dixie Container Co.*, 65 LA 1089).

• An employer had the right to reduce the workweek to 35 hours, an arbitrator ruled, where the contract gave management the unlimited right to schedule production. The reduction was reasonable during a temporary business slowdown, the arbitrator concluded, rejecting the union's argument that a reduction to a 32-hour workweek was the only exception to the "regular 40-hour week" (*Rex Chainbelt Inc.*, 52 LA 852).

• In another case, although the union argued that junior employees should have been laid off so that senior employees could work a full 40-hour week, the arbitrator ruled that the contract clearly gave the employer the right

to divide work equally in the event of insufficient demand (*Industrial Garment Mfg.*, 65 LA 875).

## Layoff Before Worksharing

Many arbitrators believe that it is only fair that regular employees or those with seniority should be kept on a regular workweek as long as possible. Therefore, they agree that probationary or short-service employees should be laid off before the workweek is reduced (*Western Automatic Machine Screw Co.*, 12 LA 38; see also 88 LA 594, 68 LA 838).

• The point at which layoffs should stop and cutting hours should begin may be found in the specific language of the contract. One agreement stated that when it became necessary to make layoffs involving employees with two or more years of service, operations would be reduced to a single shift or to a 32-hour week before further layoffs were made. An arbitrator held that this clearly required the employer to lay off all employees with less than two years' service before reducing the workweek to 32 hours (*Aetna Ball & Roller Bearing Co.*, 22 LA 453).

• Where the contract did not provide the answer, one arbitrator said that employees should be laid off until the work group was reduced to a "reasonable minimum." When it reached the point where a further reduction in the workforce would have impaired the standard of quality set for the group, then the employer could reduce the workweek, he said (*Bloom-Ease Inc.*, 12 LA 941).

## Worksharing Before Layoff

A contract may call for a reduction in working hours before any layoffs can be made.

• One agreement required a reduction in the workweek to 32 hours before employees were laid off. The employer claimed it could make layoffs to eliminate the night shift instead of reducing hours as long as the volume of work did not drop enough to justify instituting a 32-hour week. An arbitrator ruled that the employer could not lay off employees as long as there was enough work to keep everybody working for 32 hours or more per week (*Babcock Printing Press Corp.*, 10 LA 397).

• Another employer could not discharge permanent employees for lack of work, but had to reduce hours of individual employees in order to comply with the contract that stated that "all work of any classification in any shop shall be equally distributed among the employees of that classification without discrimination." The arbitrator reasoned that the provision was intended to apply to decreases in available work, as overtime distribution was addressed in a separate provision. The entire structural thrust of the contract, he concluded, was toward the worksharing principal, and it would take explicit contract language to justify other conclusions (*Wilshire Mfg. Jewelers*, 49 LA 1079).

• Where the contract permitted employee layoffs according to seniority after the workweek was reduced during four weeks in the year due to lack of work, and the employer laid off maintenance employees for two days on the basis of their seniority after it had reduced the workweek in their department to four days a week for four weeks, an arbitrator upheld the employer's actions, despite the union's contention that the contract's "hours" provision guaranteed a 40-hour week. Such a construction would prohibit layoffs and render the contract language meaningless, the arbitrator ruled, rejecting the union's argument that layoffs could not cover portions of weeks, but only full weeks (*Arcata Graphics*, 65 LA 785).

• An employer had the right to reduce hours of all employees, including union officers, in a department for lack of work. The contract granted union officers superseniority in layoffs, but also stated that a "reduction in hours of work or a staggering of work schedules of employees is not a layoff requiring the application of" seniority. Although the slips given employees when their hours were reduced stated that employees were being "laid off", the slips also contained the dates upon which employees were schedule to return to work. Because the other facts indicated that the employer's action constituted staggering of work schedules, with sharing of available work among all employees, according to the arbitrator, this was not a "layoff" as defined in the contract (*Wilcox Crittenden Co.*, 43 LA 1046).

## Worksharing Instead of Layoff

A special agreement gave one employer the right to reduce the workweek for up to six weeks, instead of the original two weeks provided for in the contract. The union had sought the agreement to avoid layoffs, and this purpose was spelled out in the document and agreed to by management. However, when business slacked off, the employer still laid off employees, charging that no employer would agree not to resort to layoffs regardless of a decline in business. An arbitrator, however, disagreed with the employer, citing the clear, unambiguous language of the bargaining agreement calling for worksharing in lieu of layoffs (*Allen Group Inc.*, 64 LA 1085).

## Group Affected by Worksharing

Can hours be cut for one group of employees while other groups are still operating on a full schedule? Where a contract with a provision for worksharing specifies that the shorter workweek shall apply to a single classification or department, or to the whole plant, an arbitrator will undoubtedly require strict adherence to the contract language.

• One contract stated that when work slowed down in any department, hours should be reduced to 32 a week for 30 days before any layoffs were made. The employer reduced the workweek for one class of employees within a department, but not for others. The arbitrator said this action was a violation of the contract because all classes of employees within the department should have been put on a shorter week. Employees whose hours were cut were awarded pay for the time they lost (*Mueller Brass Co.*, 3 LA 271).

• Another employer "transferred" three employees out of their department and into lower-rated jobs while others in the original department continued to work overtime, although the labor agreement prohibited layoffs of regular employees until hours were reduced to 40 per week. The arbitrator overturned the transfers, finding them to be outside the scope of management rights. The moves were actually layoffs from the department, the arbitrator concluded, and the employees should not have been moved while others were on overtime (*Bartelt Engineering Co.*, 51 LA 582).

• An employer had the right to schedule a four-day workweek for employees in its manufacturing department during a time period in which a regular workweek was scheduled for employees in its parts depot and export departments, an arbitrator decided, where the contract gave the employer the right to schedule four-day workweeks upon compliance with certain requirements.

Pointing out that the manufacturing employees on the four-day workweek were not on layoff but on a contractually permissible shortened workweek, the arbitrator concluded that the fact that the depot and export employees were not placed on four-day workweek did not convert the scheduling change into a reduction in force that required application of layoff procedures (*Hyster Co.*, 66 LA 523).

# Recall From Layoff

————————————— OVERVIEW —————————————

A vast majority of collective bargaining agreements require that recalls from layoffs be accomplished in reverse order of layoff; thus, many recall problems automatically are eliminated when the order of layoff is determined.

Disputes, however, frequently arise over such questions as an employer's right to give physical examinations on recall, whether an employee can continue on layoff rather than accept an undesirable job, and an employer's obligations regarding recall notices.

Arbitrators usually have held that management has the right to require employees to take physical exams when they return to work after an extended layoff. Arbitrators also have said, however, that an employer may not set higher physical standards for returning employees than for those who are already working for the company.

————————————— SUMMARY OF CASES —————————————

### Seniority or Ability in Recall

Under a contract that contained a seniority clause but was silent on applying seniority to recall, one arbitrator ruled that a senior employee should be recalled if able to perform the required work. Management should not bypass a senior employee able to handle the work just because a junior employee could do a better job, even though the contract did not outline the recall procedure, the arbitrator ruled (*Laher Battery Production Corp.*, 11 LA 41).

• In a case where recall was to be made by seniority and ability, but qualifications were not explicitly mentioned in the recall clause, an arbitrator decided that ability to do the work was an implied factor in the contract. Additionally, the arbitrator ruled that a training period for senior employees to gain full familiarity with certain equipment, which junior employees were already capable of handling, was also implied. Thus, when work for laid off employees became available, the arbitrator concluded that the employer was obligated to recall senior employees who required some training, over junior employees who had in fact trained on the complex machines prior to layoff (*Thiokol*

*Corp.*, 65 LA 1265; see also 95 LA 467, 94 LA 158, 82 LA 1007, 76 LA 932, 76 LA 699, 76 LA 575, 76 LA 540).

• An arbitrator ruled that, despite the fact that a senior employee was not recalled, an employer had the right to recall a junior employee to do shop work in addition to repair work on a railroad crane that he was recalled from layoff to do. The junior employee had done most of the original work on the crane when it was custom-built for a customer and the customer had specifically requested the employee to do the repair work, the arbitrator reasoned (*T. Bruce Sales*, 81 LA 481; see also 93 LA 553).

• An arbitrator held that an employer, determining the order of recall for two employees who had identical departmental seniority, was required to recall the employee who had been laid off twice over a one-week period, rather than the other employee, who had been laid off once and recalled (*Jacksonville Shipyard Inc.*, 82 LA 90).

### Ability, Skill, and Efficiency as Factors in Recall

Under collective bargaining agreements making seniority the controlling factor in recall situations, where ability, skill, and efficiency were equal, arbitrators have ruled that senior employees did not have to be given a break-in period to become proficient on jobs where junior employees had already proved themselves the most efficient through past performance. The arbitrators upheld the recall of the junior employees in preference to the seniors.

• An arbitrator held that an employer's refusal to recall a senior typesetter from layoff because he lacked the proper computer skills to operate a newly installed desktop (computer) publishing system was not arbitrary, capricious, or discriminatory. The former employee had claimed that the employer had discriminated against him by failing to offer him the same computer training as was offered to junior employees, but the parties' labor contract gave the employer the right to have "sufficient qualified employees" to perform necessary work "on all shifts at all times," the arbitrator said, adding that the grievant also failed to practice on a computer on his own time or take outside computer courses, as contractually required and as other, more junior employees had done (*Type House + Durograph*, 102 LA 225).

• A contract provided that in recall after layoff, seniority would govern if ability, skill, and efficiency were equal. When two junior employees were recalled to their jobs, the union protested that there still were five employees on layoff who had more seniority and were qualified to do the work; two of these five should have been recalled, the union argued. An arbitrator upheld the employer. Although the five senior employees might have done the work proficiently after a break-in period, he found that *at the time of recall*, the junior employees were the most efficient on the jobs in question. In light of the fact that the contract made seniority controlling only where efficiency already was equal and made no provision for a training period, the arbitrator concluded that recall of the junior employees was proper (*Curtis Companies Inc.*, 29 LA 50).

• Another contract provided for the recall of a laid-off employee on the basis of seniority "so long as he can do the job in a reasonably efficient manner." A dispute arose when a junior employee who was operating a new machine, and who was the only qualified one to do so, went to work on a less advanced machine while the new one was being repaired. A laid-off senior employee of the same classification argued that he should have been recalled from layoff status to work the older machine, which he was capable of working.

The arbitrator disagreed, however. Although the junior employee was not operating the new machine during the period in question, the arbitrator found that operating the new machine was an important part of the employee's duties because he was to continue working on it once repairs were completed. Furthermore, the arbitrator concluded there was no past practice that supported the senior employee's arguments (*Eagle-Picher Industries Inc.*, 65 LA 1108).

• An arbitrator held that an employer violated a collective bargaining agreement when it recalled 15 employees for salvage work but did not honor the seniority provisions of the collective bargaining agreement. The parties' contract provided that laid-off employees would be recalled to work on the basis of seniority; it also defined "seniority" as the "length of service and the ability to step into and perform the work of the job at the time the job is awarded." The arbitrator ruled that a number of laid-off senior employees who met the rehire criteria had been passed over for job openings in favor of less senior workers (*Sunnyside Coal Co.*, 104 LA 886).

## Physical Exams on Rehiring

Can laid-off employees be required to take a physical examination upon return to work? Arbitrators generally agree that, in the absence of a specific contract ban on the practice, management may require employees returning to work from extended layoffs, strikes, or leaves of absence to have new physical examinations (22 LA 632, 11 LA 364, 8 LA 1015).

• An employer should follow a consistent practice in the use of medical exams. When an employer bypassed a senior employee because of his past medical record, an arbitrator said it was acting improperly. It should have based his recall on present medical information, as it did with other employees, the arbitrator concluded (*National Lead Co.*, 42 LA 176).

## Physical Standards on Rehiring

Most arbitrators have ruled that an employer may not set higher physical standards for employees returning from layoff than are applied to employees still on the job.

• An employee about to be recalled from layoff was found by the employer doctor to have blood pressure higher than that permissible for new employees, although within the range allowed for persons already employed by the employer. Accordingly, the employee was denied recall.

An arbitrator ruled that the employee was entitled to recall, pointing out that the contract contained no provision for denial of recall rights to a laid-off employee whose physical condition would have been acceptable if he were still working for the employer (*Allegheny Ludlum Steel Corp.*, 25 LA 214).

• An employer had no right to deny recall to a dump-truck driver who had lost his left hand and forearm in an accident while on layoff, an arbitrator ruled. The employee had been fitted with a prosthetic device that enabled him to pass driving tests and drive a tractor, the arbitrator found, and so he should be given the same opportunity of recall as others. More rigorous standards could not be used by the employer, the arbitrator maintained. But if the doubts about the employee's safety and fitness for the job that prompted the recall denial were to materialize later, then the employee's employment could be affected just as any other employee's, the arbitrator concluded (*Murphy Construction Co.*, 61 LA 503).

• An employer had no right to refuse to reinstate a laid-off electrician on the basis of a doctor's report, according to another arbitrator. Although the employer admitted that it gave recalled employees "more tolerant treatment" in medical exams than new hires, the arbitrator found that this employee was given the same examination as that given new employees. Further, the refusal to reinstate the employee was based on the possibility of future recurrence of back trouble, not on his present condition. Therefore, the employer was ordered to rehire the employee (*Weatherhead Co.*, 42 LA 513).

• In one situation, even though an employee's physical condition was the same at the time of recall as it was upon layoff, an arbitrator held that the employer could refuse to put him back to work to protect his health.

A 300-pound man with a heart murmur was denied recall because the employer medic said it would endanger his health to work. An arbitrator upheld the employer's action. The fact that the man worked until he was laid off was no sign he was not endangering his health all that time, the arbitrator said; it merely indicated the employer did not know about his condition. When it found out, it had every right to refuse to recall him in order to protect his health, the arbitrator concluded (*Potter Press*, 26 LA 514).

## Worker with Superseniority

An arbitrator ruled that union stewards who had superseniority over employees/assemblers, whom they represented, were not entitled to be recalled ahead of the assemblers (recalled to work in a certain department), because the stewards' jurisdiction did not extend to the particular department (*Textron Inc.*, 83 LA 931).

• If an employee is elected to union office while on layoff and thus acquires superseniority, is he entitled to immediate recall? One arbitrator has held that an employer need not recall an employee in such a case until there is a job opening for which he or she can qualify. The purpose of superseniority, he remarked, is to ensure continuity in the administration of the contract, not to make jobs for union representatives (*Queen City Industries*, 33 LA 794; see also 75 LA 263, 75 LA 261).

• An arbitrator held an employee who was elected to a grievance committeeman position while on layoff was not entitled to recall ahead of more senior employee, where the relevant collective bargaining agreement granted superseniority to committeemen only for layoffs (*Amerimark Building Products*, 104 LA 1066).

## Recall of Job Steward

When employees are recalled to a job, must their "job steward" be recalled as well? An arbitrator ruled in the affirmative when the question arose in a construction case.

• Two carpenters were assigned to a construction project, and the union properly assigned a third employee as the project's job steward. After the carpenters' work was suspended to allow plumbers and electricians to work at the site, one of the original carpenters and another later returned, but the union steward was denied recall. The employer defended its action by arguing that it was a specialty contractor required only to have a "shop steward" who served as steward for all jobs with less than three men, and that the union's insistence on a shop steward implied its waiver of a job steward. The arbitrator disagreed, finding no provision in the contract to require the shop steward to perform all the functions of a job steward and nothing to substantiate the employer's claim of the union's implied waiver (*Master Builders Assn. of Western Pennsylvania*, 63 LA 664; see also 74 LA 987).

## Refusal to Accept Lower-Rated or Different Job

Can employees refuse to accept a recall notice to a lower-rated job without jeopardizing their seniority rights? If there is nothing in the contract to the contrary, most arbitrators hold that employees can refuse notices to lower-rated jobs without loss of seniority (*Service Conveyor Co.*, 9 LA 134).

• It has been held that employees do not have to accept recall to perform a job different from that held prior to layoff under a contract allowing employees to choose between layoff and transfer.

An employee was laid off when his department closed for vacations and maintenance. During his layoff he refused an offer of a job in another department, saying he preferred to wait for recall to his own department. When his department reopened, however, employees with shorter service were recalled ahead of him. The employer said that he had waived his right to recall by refusing the other job.

The arbitrator decided that, because the contract permitted employees to take a layoff instead of a transfer to another department, an employee could refuse an offer of a job in a different department without losing his right to be recalled to his own department in line with his seniority (*International Harvester Co.*, 22 LA 773).

## Refusal to Accept Recall to Part-Time Work

A laid-off employee did not lose seniority when he rejected a recall for two-days' work per week, an arbitrator ruled, because full-time employees were guaranteed a 40-hour week, and the employer's practice was to interpret "guarantee" to mean that employees were entitled to 40 hours' work for any week in which they worked (*S & S Meat Co.*, 97 LA 873).

## Recall to Lower-Rated Job

When a laid-off employee does accept recall to a lower-rated job, at what rate should he be paid? One arbitrator ruled that recall to a lower-rated job is the same as a transfer, and accordingly is governed by contract provisions relating to transferred employees.

• A employer's contract provided that an employee transferred to a lower-rated job would continue to receive his former rate for 15 consecutive working days. An employee recalled from layoff to a lower-rated job received his old rate for only five days, whereupon he claimed that he was entitled to the old rate for 10 additional days.

The union, pointing to a contract provision that a recalled employee must accept the job offered or lose seniority, argued that because the employee did not have the option of refusing the lower-rated job he had in effect been transferred by the employer. The employer based its case on a past practice of not treating recalls to lower-paying jobs as transfers.

The arbitrator ruled in favor of the union. The word "transfer" as used in labor agreements, he pointed out, means a shift or change from one job to another; no one claimed that such a move would not have constituted a transfer if the employee had not been laid off, the arbitrator noted. In his opinion, the layoff did not change the picture (*National Can Corp.*, 25 LA 177).

• Although another arbitrator upheld the right of employees to refuse recall to a lower-rated job, he did not agree that acceptance of a lower-rated job when recalled is the same as a transfer (*Service Conveyor Co.*, 9 LA 134).

• In another case, the arbitrator did not dispute the employer's right to put the employees in lower-rated jobs when work in their former classification was not available at the time of recall, but he did insist that they be paid at their former, higher, rate. The arbitrator based his decision on a contract clause requiring the "regular rate of pay" for employees working at lower-rated jobs for the employer's "convenience," and on the employer's past practice (*Allen Group Inc.*, 65 LA 114).

• An arbitrator decided that a laid-off bakery sales clerk was not entitled to retain her wage rate following her placement in an apprentice position that initially carried a lower wage rate. Despite the union's claim of a past practice consisting of one prior instance in which a clerk who was placed in the same type of position retained his bakery clerk rate of pay, the arbitrator ruled that that single instance, under the circumstances, was insufficient to show an established past practice (*Ralph's Grocery Co.*, 71 LA 692).

## Recall After Strike

When a contract provides for observance of seniority in layoff and recall, do recalls after a strike have to be made according to seniority? According to some arbitrators, layoff and recall provisions in a labor agreement do not apply to recall after a strike.

• A plant's production and maintenance employees struck for 12 days. As soon as the employees agreed to come back to work the employer drew up a schedule for resuming operations and notified employees when to report.

The union claimed that the recalls were not made strictly according to seniority as provided for in the contract. The employer argued that the contract was not applicable to this situation. It pointed out that operations had to be started up bit by bit and that not all employees could be rehired together.

The arbitrator ruled that the contract "was obviously not drafted to deal with a situation like this one. This situation did not involve any layoffs and hence did not involve rehiring after layoff." Therefore, the arbitrator ruled for the employer that production could be resumed bit by bit and that employees could be called without regard to strict seniority rules (*Swift & Co.*, 8 LA 295).

• Another arbitrator likewise allowed an employer to recall junior strikers before senior strikers. The arbitrator found that the employees were not in "layoff status," so the contract provision that called for seniority to govern in the case of recall from layoff did not apply (*Yoder Brothers Inc.*, 62 LA 476).

• Another employer retained a new hire instead of recalling a senior striker, and also failed to recall an employee with 29 years seniority until after Thanksgiving holidays. The arbitrator supported the employer's actions, because in the first case it was not clear that the employer was under any obligation at the end of the strike to follow seniority during the two or three weeks' delay in starting of regular work; secondly, there was no evidence that the employer was obligated to recall employees out of their classification and the employee was recalled as soon as work was available in his classification (*Borg-Warner Corp.*, 61 LA 234).

• Where an employer's employees went on strike and the employer hired replacements, an arbitrator reinstated senior strikers after the employer refused to do so. The arbitrator ruled that the contract that had continued in force during the strike did not restrict its seniority clause to employees who were working, nor did it exclude employees not at work. However, although the arbitrator ordered back pay for employees who were refused work while junior replacements were employed, he recognized the right of the employer to determine the number of available jobs for the returning employees (*Tarcon Inc.*, 64 LA 955).

• An arbitrator ruled that an employer was obligated to apply a contract's seniority provision in its recall of strikers, subject only to special agreements by the parties first to recall employees in certain key departments. The arbitrator reasoned that recall was an "increase of working force," which the contract stated was subject to seniority, and found no agreement by the parties to ignore seniority in the recalls (*Orscheln Brake Lever Mfg. Co.*, 63 LA 736; see also 75 LA 113).

### Refusal to Recall Senior Employee with Poor Record

Can a laid-off senior employee be refused recall as a form of disciplinary action for such an offense as poor attendance? If a contract requires that employees be recalled to work in line with their seniority, one arbitrator has ruled, such other factors as a poor attendance record do not justify a denial of the employee's right to be recalled.

• While the high-seniority employee at one employer was on layoff, a temporary job came up and was filled with a man holding lower seniority. Management supported its action on the ground that, among other things, the senior employee had a record of several unexcused absences.

In rejecting the employer's justification of its refusal to recall that employee, the arbitrator decided that the employee's absenteeism was an extraneous issue. The employer should not have considered the employee's attendance record in considering his recall, said the arbitrator, because this was something that should have been disposed of at the time the absences occurred. Such an offense, he said, should not be made the basis for denial of job opportunities for the indefinite future (*Cleveland-Cliffs Iron Co.*, 24 LA 599).

### Recall for Overtime

Is an employer required to recall a laid-off employee to perform overtime work in the department? At least one arbitrator has ruled no.

• An employee who had been laid off during a cutback in the workforce discovered that people in other classifications were performing overtime work that he had performed prior to the cutback. He filed a grievance charging that he should have been the one to perform the overtime.

In upholding the employer's position, the arbitrator found that the employee's seniority rights extended only if a recall or hiring added to the number of employees in his former classification. Emphasizing that a basic right of management is the right to determine the size of the workforce, the arbitrator concluded that it would violate this right to order the employer to rehire the employee (*Avco Corp.*, 63 LA 288).

### Failure to Send Proper Recall Notice

What constitutes proper notice of recall from layoff? If the contract specifically requires that laid-off employees be notified of recall by a certain means, most arbitrators say that method must be used without exception. If the employer does not give the proper notice, these arbitrators say, it may not take away the employees' seniority and re-employment rights.

• An arbitrator held that an employer's telephone call to a laid-off employee did not trigger recall, stressing that, under the collective bargaining agreement, the employer was required to notify laid-off employees by certified mail (*Manville Forest Products Corp.*, 92 LA 681).

• One employer's contract required that laid-off employees be recalled by registered letter and that they report within five days after receiving notice. Instead of sending registered letters, however, the firm sent the union steward a request that he tell employees to come to the plant for rehiring. One employee who was not notified by the steward and who did not report within the five-day period was permanently laid off.

The arbitrator decided the employee had not been notified of recall in the manner prescribed by the contract, that is, by registered letter; neither had she been contacted in any other way by the employer. Accordingly, the arbitrator ordered her reinstated with full seniority and back pay starting with the fifth day after she should have been notified (*Ohmer Corp.*, 13 LA 364).

## Failure to Receive Recall Notice

When is an employee's failure to receive notice a valid excuse for not reporting? Some arbitrators have held that an employee is entitled to back pay and full seniority when the employee's failure to receive recall notice was not his or her fault, even though the employer had met its notice requirements.

• One employer complied with the contractual requirement that employees be notified of recall either by letter or telegram by mailing a notice to the apartment house where an employee lived. Through some slip of the post office, the notice was sent to the wrong apartment and the employee failed to report on time. The employee lost his seniority for failing to report on time after the recall. The arbitrator found that although the employer had met its obligation, the employee failed to receive the notice through no fault of his own. Under these circumstances, the arbitrator decided, the employee had not been properly notified of recall and was, therefore, entitled to back pay and full seniority (*Levinson Steel Co.*, 23 LA 135).

• In another case, the contract required the employee to respond to a recall notice within 72 hours, except on weekends and holidays, or lose rights to recall. After one telegram was allegedly ignored by the employee, a second telegram was dispatched, notifying the em-

ployee to report back to work the next day. Because the employee was out of town, however, he did not find the telegrams until later. When he did report for work he learned that he was discharged for failure to respond within 72 hours of the first notice. In overturning the discharge, the arbitrator found it reasonable for the employee to have expected the second telegram to grant him a second 72 hours, which expired on the afternoon of the day he reported for work. Even though the employee could have avoided the discharge by requesting leave, checking his mail, or calling the dispatcher, the arbitrator conceded, the critical issue was the status of the second telegram (*Ameron Inc.*, 64 LA 517).

• If it appears that an employee has intentionally avoided receiving a recall notice or ignored it and its requirements, arbitrators are likely to uphold an employer refusal to rehire him (*Blackmer Pump Co.*, 20 LA 238).

• If an employee fails to give a contractually required notice to the employer of his desire to return to work from layoff, an employer may be justified in not rehiring the employee, if the employer does not act in a discriminatory manner when sending the recall notice (*Challenge-Cook Bros. Inc.*, 65 LA 533).

• An employer was not obligated to compensate employees for time they lost when their recall was delayed because the recall letter the employer mailed was not received by them, an arbitrator ruled, notwithstanding the union's contention the employer should have used certified mail in the recalls. Pointing out that the recall procedure provided for in the contract did not specify the type of mail that had to be used by the employer in administering the recall process, the arbitrator concluded that management's obligation to use reasonable means in notifying employees of their return to work was satisfied with the employer's practice of using a two-step procedure of telephone and regular mail, followed, if necessary, a week later by certified mail (*Warren Molded Plastics Inc.*, 76 LA 740).

• An arbitrator ruled that an employee's failure to respond to an employer's recall notice within 24 hours, per the collective bargaining agreement, constituted a voluntary quit. The arbitrator dismissed the union's contention that the employee was unfamiliar with the contract's notice/voluntary-quit provision. The arbitrator held that it was the employee's responsibility to know the terms and conditions of the bargaining agreement, and pointed out the employee had been laid off and recalled many times (*Stroh Brewery Co.*, 92 LA 930).

## Rehiring Employee Who Has Lost Seniority

When a contract gives preference in hiring to former employees, one arbitrator has said, the same employment standards cannot be used in judging them as are used for other job applicants. He held that former employees should be given the inside track when their qualifications are as good or better than those of other applicants.

● One agreement stated that "preference will be given in employment to those former employees who lost their seniority as a result of layoff and who apply for employment." When one women in this category applied for employment, she was rejected on the ground that she did not meet the employer's employment standards. The employer later gave two reasons for the rejection: (1) the employee's personnel record had been marked "do not rehire" at the time she lost her seniority and (2) a check with her former supervisor at the time she applied for employment showed he still did not want her back.

An arbitrator said the firm did not give the employee preference in accordance with the contract. Instead, she was disqualified on the basis of absolute standards. The preference clause, the arbitrator explained, did not give ex-employees an absolute right to available jobs, but it did give them the inside track where they were as good or better than other candidates. Here the employer did not attempt to compare the employee with other people applying for jobs at the same time. Management, the arbitrator decided, had to give the employee proper consideration the next time a job opening occurred (*Libby, McNeill & Libby*, 30 LA 309).

## Reverse-Order Recall Inapplicable to Short-Term Shutdown

An arbitrator determined that an employer that shut down operations to do equipment repairs and laid off all employees for five days did not violate a collective bargaining agreement when it recalled certain junior employees before recalling more senior employees whose crew was on a regularly scheduled day off. Reverse-order recall, which normally would be standard, did not apply in this case because all the employees were laid off at the same time, and recall by seniority would have negated other contract provisions. In addition, work time and time off would balance out among the various crews very quickly because the junior employees soon would be on their regularly scheduled day off while the affected senior crew worked, the arbitrator concluded (*Asarco Inc.*, 102 LA 795).

# Part 5

# Leave of Absence

# Paid Sick Leave

## OVERVIEW

Most employees are covered by collective bargaining agreements that provide some protection against wage loss that is caused by illness. This may take the form of sickness and accident insurance or paid sick leave. Some agreements provide for both, such as where paid sick leave covers the waiting period before sickness and accident insurance takes effect.

In addition, a majority of employers permits unpaid sick leave for employees who are not covered by paid sick leave or by insurance plans or who have exhausted their paid leave or insurance benefits.

Sick-leave provisions may be negotiated into a bargaining agreement, or a sick-leave plan or policy may be implemented unilaterally by an employer. Arbitrators recognize an employer's legitimate concern in preventing the abuse of sick-leave claims and will uphold reasonable rules regarding employers' requiring the documentation of illnesses, employee health care claim forms, and systems for policing sick-benefit plans, provided they are not arbitrary, capricious, or discriminatory. Whether an employee's absence from work constitutes sick leave is of critical importance in most cases.

## SUMMARY OF CASES

### Eligibility Rights

Arbitrators generally view sick leave as a right employees have earned. This means that an employer cannot establish new conditions for eligibility other than those prescribed by the contract or past practice.

The following cases illustrate this point.

• An employer could not require an employee who had been absent for six weeks to submit to a physical exam in a workplace where the contract specifically stated that examinations would only be required of employees who were absent for at least 90 days (*Buckeye Forging Co.*, 42 LA 1151).

• An employer could not deny sick pay to an employee just because he did not file a claim for it until five months after his illness (*Republic Oil Refining Co.*, 16 LA 607).

• A supervisor in one department could not require that employees provide the names of their doctors to qualify for sick leave for "lengthy periods" because the rule was never communicated to employees and was both vague and disparately enforced (*Milwaukee Area Dist. Bd. of Educ.*, 65 LA 383).

• An employer could not deny pay to employees with chronic illnesses despite the employer's claim that the illnesses barred them from offering a fair return for their salaries (*United States Steel Corp.*, 63 LA 549).

Arbitrators came to very different conclusions in the following cases.

• An employer had the right to ask the nature of illness or injury of employees before granting sick leave because the labor contract enumerated the type of conditions that qualified for sick leave with pay and contained a method for submitting sick-leave forms (*Willoughby-Eastlake City School District, Bd. of Education and Teachers*, 75 LA 21).

• An employer properly denied sick pay to employees who refused to authorize access to medical records prepared by their personal physicians (*Noland, Lloyd, Foundation Inc.*, 74 LA 1236).

### Effect of Used Sick Leave on Credits Under New Plan

Can sick leave already taken be counted against the credits employees have coming to them under a new sick-leave plan? If there is no restriction in a new plan, it is usually considered prospective in nature, without any retroactive effect, and arbitrators will hold that employees start with a clean slate.

• An employer adopted a plan that provided for paid disability leave for a specified number of days during any 12–month period. Under this plan, the employer said, benefits paid to employees in the 12–month period preceding the effective date could be deducted from the total for which they qualified under the new plan. The firm maintained that the 12–month period referred to in the contract did not necessarily mean the period starting with the effective date of the new plan, given that the plan merely continued and modified a plan was already in existence.

The arbitrator, however, ruled that in the absence of any definition of "12–month period," the usual interpretation that a newly adopted plan is prospective must apply. The new plan, he said, could not work retroactively by charging previously paid benefits against employees' credits (*Timken-Detroit Axle Co.*, 21 LA 196).

• Usually service acquired with an employer before a sick leave plan goes into effect can be counted toward eligibility. One arbitrator noted that it is general practice to base sick leave eligibility on total service, not just on service acquired after a plan becomes effective (*Holga Metal Production Co.*, 19 LA 501).

### Sick Pay During Layoff

Under a contract basing sick-leave rights on length of service, what happens to an employee's credits that are already built up if he or she is laid off?

• Generally, if the contract provides for retention of seniority during layoff, arbitrators hold that sick-leave rights

also are retained. In at least one situation, however, where an arbitrator found no clause that preserved continuity of service during layoff, he decided that employees had no right to sick-leave credits acquired before being laid off (*O'Brien-Suburban Press Inc.*, 18 LA 721; see also 23 LA 459).

• Another arbitrator denied sick leave to an employee who sustained an on-the-job injury during a temporary recall from layoff. The arbitrator based his decision on contract language that specified sick pay would be given only if the employee were unable to perform his or her scheduled work because of illness or injury. In this case, the employee returned to layoff status and had no scheduled work that would fall into the category of work he was unable to perform, the arbitrator found. Furthermore, there was no contract provision requiring sick pay during layoff, and no evidence of a clear past practice requiring sick pay under such circumstances (*American Bakeries Co.*, 64 LA 450).

### Sick Pay During Strike

When strikes or other unusual circumstances occur, questions may arise as to the continued eligibility of employees already on sick leave when work interruptions take place.

• One arbitrator vetoed an employer's denial of sick pay to an employee who was on leave when her union called a strike. The employer, he said, had gone too far in assuming that the employee would have refused to work if she had been well (*Outboard Marine & Mfg. Co.*, 11 LA 467).

• Another arbitrator ruled that an employee was not entitled to sick pay when most employees were off duty because of a strike by another union. The arbitrator reasoned that the purpose of a sick-pay provision is to pay an employee not because he or she is sick but because the employee's illness prevents the employee from working. If no work is available, the employee is not entitled to sick pay, the arbitrator concluded (*Trans World Airlines*, 41 LA 312).

• In another case, an arbitrator granted sick leave only in the case of employees who were excused prior to the strike and whose excuse had been extended into the strike period. Other employees were denied sick leave during the strike, regardless of whether they actually were ill (*County of Santa Clara*, 65 LA 992; see also 72 LA 776, 73 LA 981).

## Sick Pay During Temporary Shutdown

When an employer closed down because of a hurricane, it refused to grant sick or injury pay to those employees who had been out on such leave at that time. It asserted that they had no right to benefits on a day on which they would not have been able to work even if they were well. The arbitrator, however, held that they were entitled to the pay because the primary cause of their unemployment continued to be their illness or injury. Neither injury nor sick benefits were geared to work done by able-bodied employees; if this were the case, he reasoned, then those on leave could claim extra pay if able-bodied employees worked overtime (*Eastern Air Lines Inc.*, 41 LA 801).

## Disability or Sick-Leave Pay?

Receipt of workers' compensation may pose some problems under sick-pay provisions. If the clause does not specifically call for the deduction of workers' compensation from sick pay, an arbitrator may award full or supplemental sick pay to an employee who also is receiving workers' compensation (*Republic Oil Refining Co.*, 16 LA 607; see also 27 LA 90).

• One arbitrator held that an employer had no right to deduct disability payments from sick-leave pay when past practice had been to grant the full amount of both benefits. He found nothing wrong with an employee's receiving benefits in excess of his regular wages. Sick leave pay was a negotiated benefit to which the employee had a right, the arbitrator said (*Mohawk Airlines Inc.*, 39 LA 45).

• An arbitrator ruled that an employer had no right to deprive an employee of sick-pay benefits by discharging him, despite the finding by three doctors that the employee had a severe disability

and could receive disability benefits from Social Security. The contract provided for sick-leave payments for up to 52 weeks, and the employee contended that he was entitled to the payments. Finding no specific evidence that the employee, despite his disability, could not return to his job at the end of 52 weeks, the arbitrator awarded full sick-leave benefits (61 LA 1188).

• Another arbitrator rejected an employee's claim to sick pay in addition to workers' compensation on the ground that nothing in the contract indicated the parties intended to have any sort of supplemental arrangement. To order the employer to make such payments would have the effect of amending the contract, he said (*Babcock & Wilcox Co.*, 22 LA 456; see also 71 LA 1118).

*Waive right to workers' comp as condition of reinstatement*—Can an employer demand that an employee waive the right to workers' compensation as a condition of reinstatement after sick leave? Arbitrators have expressed divergent views on this subject, as is illustrated below.

• One arbitrator, in ordering the reinstatement of an employee who had a hernia, decided that the employer could require him to sign a waiver of all compensation claims that might stem from his condition (*Consolidated Vultee Aircraft Corp.*, 10 LA 1950; see also 25 LA 216).

• Another arbitrator, however, stated that waivers cannot be required if such a requirement is in effect a contract modification. (*Royal McBee Corp.*, 23 LA 591).

## Falsifying Sick-Leave Claims

Where there is evidence that an employee falsified his claim of illness, an arbitrator would probably uphold discipline of him unless the sick-leave policy or plan itself specifies how abuses are to be handled.

• An arbitrator upheld a two and one-half week suspension of an employee who reported in sick and was discovered the next day operating a tractor on his farm. Although the employee had been ill the day before and was still suffering from his ailment, the arbitrator found he was not too sick to work because operation of the tractor was considerably more strenuous than his duties as a television engineer (*Station KMTV*, 39 LA 324).

• In another case, however, discipline was overturned by an arbitrator where an employee admitted that he had performed outside "remunerative work" while drawing benefits under a sickness and accident plan. The plan itself specified that the penalty for engaging in such work, where not detrimental to a speedy recovery, was forfeiture of benefits, not discharge, the arbitrator noted (*Corn Products Co.*, 44 LA 127).

• Similarly, an arbitrator held that an employer was not justified in discharging an employee who falsified his time card to claim sick leave improperly. The contract's sick-leave provisions said the employer could reduce or eliminate sick-leave privileges if abuses were found, the arbitrator noted. Thus, management should have invoked these remedies instead of resorting to discharge. (*Central Illinois Public Service Co.*, 44 LA 133).

### Sick Pay for Overtime

Where a contract defined a "normal work day" as eight hours, one arbitrator held that an employee regularly scheduled for a longer than normal work day could not collect sick pay for the overtime he was used to working. The clause involved called for one day of sick leave after a year's service, two days after two years, and so on. The parties split over whether a "day" under the clause was the usual work day or the normal day as defined by the contract. The arbitrator reasoned that the parties had some definite notion of the price tag when they negotiated the sick-leave clause. So he thought it likely that they were thinking in terms of a normal day. Thus, the arbitrator held, the employee was entitled to sick pay for just the regular eight hours, not for the overtime (*Bell Aircraft Corp.*, 26 LA 558; see also 76 LA 1261, 72 LA 1201).

### Sick Pay During Vacations

When an employee became ill just before his scheduled vacation, the employer charged his absence to extended vacation pay. The arbitrator said that this was not proper. He held that problems arising from absenteeism because of illness occur whether or not employees are scheduled for vacations, so that circumstance should not affect the employer's responsibility to pay for sick leave (*U.S. Steel Corp.*, 44 LA 615).

• On the other hand, payment of both disability and vacation benefits was not required by an arbitrator, despite the employer's history of having done so. The contract "precluded payment of disability benefits if wages were received." The arbitrator said that a past practice could not modify the application of clear contract language (*Westinghouse Electric Corp.*, 45 LA 131).

### Sick Pay During Leave of Absence

One arbitrator ruled that employees on leaves of absence are entitled to sick pay. In that case, the employee continued to accrue seniority and earn holiday pay while on leave. Thus, the arbitrator decided he was still on the "active payroll" despite the employer's contention that sick pay was only provided for employees actually laboring on a day-to-day basis. Because the contract specified sick pay for all employees on the active payroll the arbitrator awarded the sick pay (*Freightliner Corp.*, 63 LA 834).

• Another arbitrator ruled, however, that an employee on sabbatical leave was not entitled to use her accumulated sick leave because sick leave was not a "fringe benefit" under the collective bargaining agreement, which said that professional employees should receive one-half of their regular salary, plus "all fringe benefits" included in their contract (*Allegheny Intermediate Unit*, 82 LA 187).

### Job Rights after Absence for Illness

Can an employee returning from sick leave bump a man hired to replace him? Under contracts with seniority provisions, most arbitrators uphold the right of an employee returning from sick leave to exercise his seniority to get his former job back.

• When a senior employee returned from approved sick leave, an arbitrator ruled that the employer had to take him back even though it had hired a replacement on his job. The arbitrator reasoned that the returning employee's job had not been eliminated, so he was entitled to the same protection as he would have received had he not been on leave. Therefore, he was entitled to displace the junior employee and get his job back, the arbitrator concluded (*Everett Dyers & Cleaners*, 11 LA 546; see also 17 LA 548).

• Even under a contract that had no provision for sick leave but did have a seniority clause, an arbitration board decided that an employee who had been absent because of illness was entitled to his job under the contract. The employer refused to take him back, but the board found no evidence that he had quit or had been discharged. On this basis, the board said that he should still be considered an employee, even though the employer had hired a replacement. The board reasoned that when the absent employee returned to work, the employer had one too many employees. Therefore, the arbitrators ruled, the layoff provisions of the contract should apply and whichever of these two employees had the most seniority should get the job (*Don Lee Broadcasting System*, 1 LA 571).

• Under a contract stating that an employee on sick leave would be returned, if qualified, to his or her old job or one like it, an arbitrator ruled that an employee who was unable to do his old job was not entitled to any job he could do. The employee was a lineman for an electric employer and was recovering from tuberculosis. His own doctor said he could work in any job that did not involve climbing or heavy lifting. The employer decided this ruled out lineman work and similar jobs and so refused to rehire him. The arbitrator upheld the employer, stating that the contract did not require the employer to give the man any job he could perform. He also noted that reinstatement under this contract depended on the employee's being qualified (*Southern California Edison Co.*, 26 LA 827).

### Effect of Sick Leave on Eligibility for Automatic Increase

Should time spent on sick leave be counted in fixing the date on which an employee becomes eligible for an automatic increase? In the absence of a contract provision on the matter, some arbitrators have ruled that employees do not have to be given credit for time spent on sick leave in determining their eligibility for length-of-service raises. They have observed that automatic wage increases are designed to reward employees for increased proficiency that comes from continued experience on the job. Job proficiency cannot be gained on sick leave, they noted (*Bell Aircraft Corp.*, 17 LA 230; see also 18 LA 847).

### Sick Leave for Family Illness

When most employees claim sick leave, it is because they are sick. Is an employer required to grant sick leave, rather than personal leave, for an employee when his children are sick? One arbitrator ruled yes.

[**Note:** This is an area of changing law; more and more employers also are recognizing child care (or elder care) as time that can be charged against an employee's sick leave.]

• An air traffic controller for the Federal Aviation Administration was absent because two of his children were ill. The employer, however, refused a request for sick leave and charged the employee's day off against his personal leave. Overturning the employer's decision, the arbitrator found that the employer's job required alertness, perception and concentration, and the employee was incapable of working at his full ability because of his children's illness. The contract had a clause granting sick leave to an employee who was "incapacitated" and the arbitrator concluded the employee was indeed incapacitated by stress and sleep deprivation (*Fort Worth Air Traffic Control Center*, 64 LA 45).

### Doctors' Opinions

Although management may have the right to require a doctor's statement as proof of illness, arbitrators disagree as to whether such certificates may be required in all instances.

• One arbitrator held that it was unreasonable for an employer to require a doctor's certificate in all cases of sick leave because such a rule imposed a hardship on many in order to punish a few who abused their sick-leave privileges (*General Baking Co.*, 40 LA 387; see also 90 LA 262).

● Another arbitrator held just the opposite, deciding that a rule requiring a doctor's certificate for each day of sick leave taken was reasonable (*Federal Services Inc.*, 41 LA 1063).

● In a similar ruling, an arbitrator decided that an employee's refusal to submit a doctor's certificate, even though his illness was genuine, relieved the employer of its obligation to pay him for his leave (*Philips Petroleum Co.*, 45 LA 857).

● In yet another case, an arbitrator ruled that an employer did not violate a bargaining agreement's sick-leave provision when it required a union employee whose sector had been losing membership to reschedule his sick leave or to get a doctor's statement indicating the need for immediate surgery (*Indiana State Teachers Assoc.*, 104 LA 737).

### Type of Certificate Required

The type of medical certificate to be accepted by management has also been an issue before arbitration.

● An employer refused to grant sick leave when a notice from the employee's doctor read simply, "Treated for bronchitis. Return to work 4–22–74." Although the employer claimed the notice did not provide specific language that the employee was incapable of working, the arbitrator ruled that in ordering the employee not to return to work until a certain date, the doctor implied that the employee was incapable of working before that date (*United States Steel Corp.*, 64 LA 540; see also 75 LA 97).

### Requiring Physical Exams on Return

Whether an employer can require an employee returning from sick leave to get a medical clearance is another issue on which arbitrators are divided.

● One arbitrator held that an employee returning from a long illness did not have to obtain a medical release from his doctor because the contract said nothing about such a release (*Inspiration Consolidated Copper Co.*, 7 LA 86; see also 28 LA 554).

● Another arbitrator balked at requiring an employee to consent to an employer examination where she had complied with the contractual requirement that she obtain certification for work from her own doctor, and where the contract did not provide for an employer doctor's evaluation (*MGM Grand Hotel*, 65 LA 261).

### Conflicting Doctors' Opinions

When the employer's physician is of the opinion that an employee is unsuited for his or her former job but other doctors hold a contrary view, can an employer refuse to reinstate the employee? In one case, finding a preponderance of the medical evidence in the employee's favor, the arbitrator ordered the employee's reinstatement.

● When a railroad conductor sought to return to work after a six-month absence caused by a heart condition, the employer barred him on the basis of an examination by the plant physician. Though his personal doctor reported that he had fully recovered, a third physician noted that a job requiring less strain would be better. The employee then was examined by the state hospital's work-evaluation unit, whose findings were favorable. Still he was unable to get his old job back.

The arbitrator said the case for reinstatement was supported by the largely positive evidence, especially the findings of the work-evaluation unit. Because he believed the employer was motivated by concern for the employee's welfare, however, he denied back pay for the period prior to the work unit's findings (*U.S. Steel Corp.*, 38 LA 395; see also 73 LA 1060).

● An employer violated the collective bargaining agreement by firing an employee who was absent for four days and did not bring in his doctor's note until he was healthy enough to return to work, said one arbitrator. The contract between the union and the employer stipulated that workers reporting to work after three days "without proper cause or notice" to management were considered to have quit and would be fired. The employee had missed four days but had phoned management each day to report his illness and visited his physician for a written note explaining the cause. When he returned to work at the start of his shift, the plant manager told him it was too late for a doctor's excuse and that he had been terminated because he failed to provide the written excuse within the first three working days of his absence. The union objected, arguing that by informing management immediately of his illness, phoning in daily to update the situation, and returning with a physician's note, the employee satisfied all requirements of the contract.

The contract clearly did not require documentation from a physician within the first three days of an absence, the arbitrator said, adding that it did require employees to be in daily contact with managers over the cause of their absence,

as the employee had done. The company also had given no examples of past practice with regard to firing workers in such situations, he said, ordering reinstatement with full restoration of seniority and all earnings and benefits lost as a result of the termination (*Can-Clay Corp.*, 117 LA 1019).

• Another arbitrator did award back pay to an employee at half the wage, when the employer and union doctors could not agree on whether the employee who was recovering from drug addiction was capable of returning to work. Although the contract provided that in case of stalemate the two sides mutually were to appoint a third doctor to decide the issue, they did not take any steps to do so. The arbitrator found that the employee became "re-employable" sometime during the course of the disagreement, but because the exact date was uncertain and both parties were at fault, only half-pay was awarded (*Air Carrier Engine Service Inc.*, 65 LA 66).

# Personal Leave

―――――――――――――― OVERVIEW ――――――――――――――

The vast majority of employers have a policy of granting employees leaves of absence without pay where it is necessary for personal reasons. At least in the case of leave for illness, many employers feel that they have nothing to lose by such a policy, if the employee is a good employee and will have to be absent anyway, it is better to make some provision for getting the employee back on the payroll in regular fashion than to take the chance of permanently losing a valuable worker.

Usually, however, employers want to reserve the right to decide each case of personal leave on its own merits. For this reason a company will phrase its leave policy in very general terms: "Leave will be granted for good cause," or "Management will approve a reasonable request for leave." The theory is that management holds the reins and can grant or deny a leave request at will.

Of course this is not always the case. Employees have long memories, and if leave is granted in one case and denied in another, a feeling that management is being unfair may spring up and create morale problems. In other words, if an employer grants a certain type of leave—e.g., maternity leave—in a few cases, it has, in effect, established a policy of granting this type of leave, and except for unusual circumstances, will have to continue to do so for morale purposes.

Except as restricted by the collective bargaining agreement, an employer has the discretion to grant or deny leaves of absence for personal reasons. Unless management acts in an arbitrary or unreasonable manner in passing on a request for leave, an arbitrator is unlikely to disturb its decision.

Most agreements specifically make provisions for unpaid leaves of absence for sickness, and most companies probably would grant such leave for a limited period of time even if not required to do so by contract. In most cases, arbitrators also will enforce leave rights based solely on past practice.

Issues relating to *funeral/bereavement leave* and *leave for jury duty* also are discussed in this chapter.

―――――――――――― SUMMARY OF CASES ――――――――――――

### Good Cause for Leave

Although admitting that an employer has the right to grant or deny leaves of absence under most contracts, arbitrators insist that employers apply this right reasonably and without discrimination. Sometimes arbitrators will disagree with an employer's judgment as to whether the reason for leave was good cause.

● In one case a contract specified that leaves of absence "shall be granted for reasons acceptable to employer and union." It also stated that seniority could be broken for three days' absence without good cause. An employee requested leave during the Christmas holidays for the purpose of securing a home for his mother. When the employer disapproved his leave, he took off anyway. Upon his return to work he was considered a new employee by the employer and thus lost his seniority rights. The arbitrator recognized the employer's right to grant or deny leaves of absence; however, he believed that in this instance management had been unreasonable. Because the employee had asked for leave for a good cause, the arbitrator ruled, he was entitled to reinstatement with full seniority (*Pittsburgh Metallurgical Co. Inc.*, 12 LA 95; see also 76 LA 673, 75 LA 953, 75 LA 131, 74 LA 1284).

● In another case, when a union failed to show the employer had discriminated against an employee in denying her leave to attend a religious function, an arbitration board held that the employer's judgment could not be questioned (*Union Oil Co.*, 3 LA 108; see also 73 LA 1146, 71 LA 937).

● Another arbitrator determined that an employer did have the right to inquire into the general nature of an employee's absence when he requested personal leave. When one employee was absent in order to see another man's wife, his two-day suspension was upheld despite the claim of absence for "personal reasons" (*Fairbanks Morse Co.*, 47 LA 224).

### Falsifying Reasons for Leave

Where there is evidence that an employee falsified his reasons in a leave request, an arbitrator probably will uphold the employer's right to discipline him.

● An employee requesting leave gave his foreman a telegram stating that his mother, who was in another city. was seriously ill. His foreman told him to see the general foreman at the end of the shift. The employee worked out his shift without protesting the delay and received permission to take a leave of absence. Furthermore, he told the foreman that he definitely would be back to work on a certain date. The foreman became suspicious of the employee's nonchalance about the delay and his willingness to set a date for his return, so the employer hired an investigator, who discovered that the employee's mother was not seriously ill and that the employee actually was

taking time off to attend a convention that was being held in the city where his mother lived. The employee was discharged on his return.

At the arbitration hearing, the employee admitted that he knew his mother was not seriously ill but simply old and worried about her son. Although he did attend the convention from time to time, he insisted the primary purpose of the trip was to see his mother. The arbitrator decided the employee had, in any event, misrepresented the reason for the leave. The employee should have explained that his mother simply wanted to see him instead of saying she was ill, and the discharge was upheld (*International Harvester Co.*, 14 LA 980).

● An employer properly disciplined an employee for claiming sick leave after being denied personal leave, according to one arbitrator. Throughout the employee's 11-year tenure, the employer had had problems caused by taking excessive leave. The employee had requested an unpaid day of leave for the day before Thanksgiving but her request was denied. In spite of the denial, the employee failed to report to work for any of the three days preceding Thanksgiving. When she returned to work on the following Monday, she submitted a request for sick leave for the three days missed and included a note from a podiatrist saying she had been under his care for a week. Her supervisor suspended the employee for 10 days. The arbitrator said her purported ailment was part of "a back-up plan" in case her personal leave request was denied. Because she used three days of sick leave to get herself "a week and a day off," an appropriate remedy would be another week off without pay," he said, reducing the employer's discipline to a five-day suspension (*North Royalton City School District*, 116 LA 1275).

### Regulating Leave Through Workforce Requirement

Where an employer has both a contract and past practice that outline procedures for granting leave, can it add the requirement that the workforce be maintained at a certain minimum level?

- An employer had a clause in the labor contract providing for leave to enable employees to cover "emergencies" that arose outside of scheduled vacation time. The employer, however, unilaterally determined that the workforce had to be at certain levels before such leave would be granted. The employer justified this unilateral condition as being a corollary to its reserved right to determine the manpower levels on various shifts. The arbitrator disagreed, ruling that the new requirement was improper. Past practice had allowed employees to determine what constituted "emergencies," which was undefined in the contract, and the employer had always acquiesced, the arbitrator noted. Furthermore, the arbitrator reasoned that enforcing the workforce-level requirement would result in a "chilling effect on exercise of the employees' rights under the contract" (*City of River Rouge*, 65 LA 1105).

## Seniority Protection During Indefinite Leave

If an employer grants an employee a leave of absence and then reinstates him without loss of seniority, if the union claims this is unfair to other employees, can it force management to reinstate the person as a new employee?

- In one case, where the contract contained no leave clause but did contain a seniority clause, an arbitrator held that the union could prevent management from giving an employee seniority credit while on leave. An employee wanted to work on his farm and asked for an indefinite leave of absence. The employer granted his request. Over a period of a year the employee returned to work only for a few days. At the end of the year the employer put the employee back on full-time duties when he requested it. The union complained that the employee should be treated as a new employee within the meaning of the contract, but the employer answered that the employee had been on an indefinite leave of absence and was merely returning from his leave. Although there was no leave provision in the contract, the seniority clause provided for the accumulation of seniority when a person was on sick leave or layoff.

The arbitrator reasoned that if there was no limit placed on the length of leaves, an employer could defeat the seniority clause by granting leaves up to two or three years in duration. He stated that the seniority clause had to be given a reasonable interpretation in order to carry out its meaning and concluded that the clause governing seniority could not be read so as to protect the employee's seniority (*National Gypsum Co.*, 2 LA 566).

## Promotion Rights During Leave

If a contract bases promotion on seniority, is a senior employee who is on leave when a vacancy comes up entitled to a chance at the promotion after he returns? Some arbitrators feel that unless the contract specifically waives seniority rights during leave, management is required to reopen the bids after the return of a senior employee.

- An employee was on a leave of absence when a higher-paid job for which she was qualified was given to another less-senior employee. The employee contended that her seniority had accumulated during her absence and that she was entitled to the promotion when she returned. The employer based its refusal on the wording of the layoff clause reading: "In case of a layoff, if the employee next in line for return to work is not available, he then forfeits his right to the job."

When the case went to arbitration, the employee who had been absent was ordered promoted to the higher job. The arbitrator stated that because there had been no question raised as to the employee's ability or physical fitness, he could not hold otherwise. He refused to apply the "layoff" clause to a situation where the employee was on an authorized leave instead of being laid off. The "leave" clause provided for the retention and accumulation of seniority during leave, and the "seniority" clause stated that seniority was the controlling factor in promotions, the arbitrator emphasized, concluding that because the employee had seniority, she should be promoted (*Curtiss-Wright Corp.*, 9 LA 77).

## Accrual of Leave Rights

When an employee voluntarily quits the employer, is he entitled to compensation for leave he has accrued during the year, or may leave rights only be granted at the end of a year, like a bonus? One arbitrator has said that personal leave is a form of additional compensation that employees earn upon putting in each day's work, and to which they are entitled upon quitting.

• When some employees voluntarily quit, the employer withheld the personal leave pay they had "accrued" during the year. Management contended that the leave time was being earned for use in the following year and, therefore, was not an earned right until then. For support, the employer showed, and the union agreed, that new employees—those in their first year of employment—get no leave, but draw on that year for leave during the second year. Furthermore, the employer argued that leave was a working benefit and that when the employees quit, they gave up the rights they could only use incidental to continued work.

The arbitrator disagreed with the employer's contentions. Citing contract language providing that "any employee who leaves employment with the employer prior to the end of the calendar year shall be paid for all personal or sick leave time accrued at his regular rate at the time he leaves employment," the arbitrator concluded that leave is an additional "fringe benefit" that is earned every day, and to which employees are entitled when they quit (*Gunther-Nash Mining Construction Co.*, 65 LA 767).

## Paid Funeral Leave

Arbitration cases involving funeral-leave provisions have turned on the precise wording of the funeral-leave or "bereavement" pay clause. Arbitrators in general appear to lean toward the strict interpretation of such clauses.

• Where a collective bargaining agreement explicitly stated that a certain number of days of paid leave would be allowed to attend the funeral of a member of the employees's "immediate" family, arbitrators have held that such a leave provision includes attendance at the funeral and necessary travel time but excludes absences to aid bereaved relatives or to attend to the estate (*National Uniform Service*, 104 LA 981; see also 80 LA 1305, 73 LA 115, 73 LA 96, 70 LA 830, 67 LA 536).

• Where the contract language used is "pay for lost time" or "paid leave of absence" although attending the funeral of a family member, arbitrators generally have denied such pay when the employee was already on vacation or otherwise not scheduled to work (79 LA 82, 75 LA 1076, 75 LA 845, 70 LA 950).

• In some cases, however, an arbitrator may favor a broad interpretation on that portion of a funeral-leave clause that specifies the family members or relatives for whose funeral the leave provisions apply—e.g., consanguinity or close affinity. Where a contract listed "brother" among other members of the family, an arbitrator, emphasizing the close relationship between an employee and his stepbrother, ruled that the stepbrother constituted the employee's brother under the contract (*Foremost Dairies*, 43 LA 616).

• An arbitrator ruled that half-brothers were included in the word "brother," for purposes of a contract's funeral-leave clause, despite an employer's claim that the employee's half-brother was not represented to the community as part of the employee's family unit. Several dictionaries and the state legislature defined brother to include half-brothers, the arbitrator pointed out, and the "family-unit" test should not be applied when there is a blood relationship or where a contract lists relatives covered (*Hartman Electrical Manufacturing*, 92 LA 253; see also 95 LA 455, 76 LA 1107, 71 LA 874, 71 LA 473).

• Other arbitrators have leaned toward a strict interpretation of funeral/bereavement-leave relationship clauses (*Northville Public Schools*, 104 LA 801 and *National Uniform Service*, 104 LA 981; see also 96 LA 115, 89 LA 1285, 87 LA 1042, 86 LA 1132, 83 LA 1153).

*Past practice*—Of course, past practice may be relevant to an arbitrator's decision. In a case where a contract contained no funeral-leave clause but did provide for maintenance of working conditions, an arbitrator held that an employer was required to continue an established practice of granting up to three days of funeral leave (*Commercial Motor Freight*, 34 LA 592; see also 104 LA 801, 53 LA 1215).

● Another arbitrator held that a school employee was properly denied bereavement leave to make funeral arrangements for his wife's stepfather and to attend the funeral, despite his union's contention the employer had granted such leave in the past. The arbitrator ruled that the parties' collective bargaining agreement allowed for bereavement leave only for the death of a member of an employee's "immediate" family, defined as including only a "father, mother, spouse, sister, brother, father-in-law, mother-in-law, or child." The arbitrator pointed out that although the employer had granted such bereavement leave once before, it was in fact based on an employee's misinformation and the employer's failure to check past records (*Northville Public Schools*, 104 LA 801).

● Yet another arbitrator ruled that an existing funeral-leave policy that did not include payment of such benefits during any period of paid absence from work, had carried over into a new contract provision covering paid funeral leave (*Food Employers Council*, 45 LA 291).

● Employees were not entitled to funeral leave to attend the funeral of their grandparents-in-law, where the contract expressly stated that funeral leave would be granted to attend the funeral of a member of an employee's "immediate family," and the parties included specific examples of included or permissible in-laws in the definition, an arbitrator determined (*National Uniform Service*, 104 LA 981).

***Length of funeral leave***—The usual provision is for "up to three days" funeral leave. Arbitrators generally agree that funeral leave is not intended solely for allowing travel time to attend out-of-town funerals, but that it also can serve the additional purpose of enabling the employee to assist with funeral arrangements. With this view, arbitrators are inclined to permit employees to have the choice of which three days to take off.

● An arbitrator found that an employee who requested Thursday, Friday, and Monday as bereavement leave, was not entitled to be paid for Monday under a contract that granted three "consecutive days" of bereavement leave, because "consecutive" means following one after the other, not "consecutive regular work days" (*Gulf Printing Co.*, 92 LA 893; see also 96 LA 1029, 96 LA 574, 94 LA 519, 94 LA 33, 92 LA 893, 89 LA 385, 89 LA 179, 84 LA 137).

● An employee took off Monday, Tuesday, and Wednesday to attend the Wednesday funeral of a relative. The employer only granted leave for Monday, however, claiming that the contract language granting "up to three days funeral leave" meant up to three days following the death, which had occurred the previous Friday. The arbitrator disagreed, finding that no provision in the contract supported the employer's claim that leave centered around the death rather than the funeral. The arbitrator decided that because the leave was "funeral leave" rather than "death leave," the word "days" must center on the event of the funeral (*W.G. Bush & Co.*, 65 LA 608).

● Some arbitrators have emphasized that the "up to three days" language should not be construed as a guarantee of three days' funeral leave. Thus, one arbitrator refused to allow paid leave for an employee to use on the day after the funeral, which was spent in assisting relatives in their travel plans. This did not qualify as time spent either in attending or arranging for the funeral, the arbitrator held (*Trane Co.*, 53 LA 1108; see also 73 LA 115).

● Another arbitrator also sided with the employer and restricted funeral pay. The contract provided leave pay for up to three "consecutive days," provided that "pay shall be allowed only for time absent from regularly scheduled working hours on Monday through Friday." Two grievances arose under this clause. In one, an employee took off from Tuesday through

Friday to attend a Sunday funeral, and the arbitrator limited pay to Friday. In the second instance, the employee took off Wednesday through Friday for a Saturday funeral and the arbitrator awarded pay only for Thursday and Friday. The arbitrator reasoned that the clear, unambiguous language calling for pay only for three consecutive workdays prior to the funeral outweighed the union's argument of contrary past practice granting more liberal pay (*FMC Corp.*, 64 LA 1300).

• One arbitrator granted four days of funeral leave, despite a contractual limitation of three days, where the employee's sister and brother-in-law had both died, and the contract provided for three days off for the funeral of the former, and one day off for the latter. The employer argued that there was no provision allowing "pyramiding of leave" for multiple funerals; however, the arbitrator found that the parties had negotiated the clause to enable employees to deal with the immediate problems connected with funerals, and in this case the employee spent the four days driving to and from the funerals, which were a substantial distance away (*Federal Glass Co.*, 65 LA 787; see also 72 LA 337).

*Scope of funeral leave*—Is an employee whose vacation is interrupted by a funeral entitled to be paid for funeral leave? Several arbitrators have held that this is a subject that should be decided by negotiation rather than by arbitration.

• One employee took his two-week vacation to go on his honeymoon. His mother died after the wedding, so he canceled his plans and attended to the details of the funeral and mourning services that followed. The employer granted a two-day unpaid extension of his vacation, but denied funeral-leave pay. The language of the funeral-leave clause tied benefits to loss of working time, the arbitrator said, and because the employee suffered no such loss, he was not entitled to funeral-leave pay (*Maui Pineapple Co., Ltd.*, 46 LA 849).

• Night-shift employees were entitled to the same funeral leave provisions as day-shift employees. The contract did not make any distinction between differ-

ent types of employees, the arbitrator held, so the employer could not arbitrarily introduce different treatment of night- and day-shift employees (*Lehigh Portland Cement Co.*, 47 LA 840).

*Proof of attendance*—An employer need not extend funeral-leave pay until proof of attendance has been submitted. When an employer discovered that an employee had not been to a funeral as claimed, it refused to grant him any pay. The arbitrator disallowed the union's claim of "automatic" payment for funeral leave and said that the employer had the right to establish a procedure for determining whether employees met the contract requirement of funeral attendance (*Borg-Warner Corp.*, 47 LA 691).

*Funeral leave during strike or shutdown*—Is an employer obligated to pay funeral leave to employees who are on strike, or who attend a funeral during that strike?

• At least one arbitrator said the employer did have to pay striking workers who attended a family funeral during the job action. The arbitrator found that work was available, and that the employees could have worked had they reported to the employer. Therefore, because funeral pay is compensation for time not worked due to attendance at a funeral, and given that the employees did in fact attend the funeral, the arbitrator concluded that the presence of the strike was inconsequential (*U.S. Pipe & Foundry Co.*, 65 LA 111).

• An arbitrator ruled that two employees were entitled to funeral-leave pay even though they were attending the funeral at a time when the employer's plant was closed because of severe weather and other employees were laid off. The employer argued that to grant the employees funeral leave pay would put them in a more advantageous income position than had they been available for work during the period when the plant was closed. The arbitrator found, however, that once the maximum three days of paid funeral leave provided by the contract had been granted, any subsequent work stoppage occurring because of conditions beyond the employees' control could not empower the employer to diminish the funeral leave pay (*Hillerich & Bradsby Co.*, 70 LA 950).

## Jury-Duty Pay

The vast majority of reported arbitration decisions deal not with an employee's right to a leave of absence for jury duty, but with the resultant pay problems under pertinent contract language on jury-duty pay differential. In the absence of such a provision, arbitrators have held that the employer is not required to pay jury-duty benefits to its employees (69 LA 1102, 38 LA 113).

Because jury-duty contract provisions are designed to provide competent jurors through the removal of the monetary loss that would otherwise accompany jury service, arbitrators have ruled that employees who are called for jury duty although on vacation or layoff are not entitled to jury pay (51 LA 1288, 76 LA 170, 65 LA 264, 50 LA 852, 39 LA 50).

*Computing jury-duty pay*—What is the basis for figuring jury-duty pay? One arbitrator has held that such pay should be computed on the basis of the hours an employee would have worked rather than on the contractual minimum workday.

• A contract required the employer to pay the difference between a "full day's pay" and the amount an employee received for each day he served on a jury. When an employee was paid the difference between his jury-duty rate and the six-hour daily contractual guarantee, he complained that he ordinarily worked more than six hours a day and so should be paid more.

Both the contract language and its interpretation in the past led the arbitrator to decide that the parties' intent was to prevent employees from losing pay although serving on juries. He therefore computed the pay on the basis of the hours the employee's replacement worked, minus the time the replacement spent on other jobs, plus overtime pay for the overtime hours of work the jurist actually would have performed, less the $6 daily jury-duty rate (*American Bakeries Co.*, 40 LA 1195; see also 98 LA 343, 76 LA 170, 74 LA 865, 74 LA 10, 73 LA 448, 72 LA 1057).

*Jury-duty pay for shift workers*—Under a contract providing pay for working time lost because of jury duty, is management required to pay employees on late shifts who cannot work because of daytime jury duty?

• A contract called for payment of the difference between regular earnings and jury pay when it was necessary for an employee to be away from this work because of jury duty. An employee on the night shift demanded pay when he took off from work for three days because he had to be in court by 9:00 a.m. and his shift did not end until 8:00. The employer maintained it did not have to pay the employee for time lost because the jury duty occurred outside his regular workday. An arbitrator decided, however, that the employee was entitled to pay under the contract. He lived 11 miles from the plant, and the court was 35 miles from his home. Under the circumstances, the arbitrator concluded that it was necessary for the employee to be away from his work if he was to arrive at court on time and in proper condition to fulfill his obligation as a juror (*Ozark Smelting & Mining Co.*, 27 LA 189).

• In another case, employees on an 8 a.m. to 4 p.m. shift did not have to report to the courthouse until 1 p.m. The employer refused to compensate them for morning hours, holding that the employees could have worked. The arbitrator disagreed with the employer, noting that the purpose of jury-duty benefit is to permit employees to have whatever time is necessary to serve on jury duty without any financial, physical, or emotional hardship (*Leve Brothers Co.*, 65 LA 867).

• An arbitrator held that an employee was entitled to jury-duty pay under one contract, even though he could have worked his regular shift although on jury duty. The employer had agreed to pay the difference between an employee's wage loss and the amount he received for jury duty. It turned down one employee's claim because he was on the second shift—from 4 p.m. to 12:30 a.m., on the assumption that he could have worked although serving on the jury if he had wanted to. The employer also pointed out that the employee had not proved that he had done more than report to the courthouse each morning.

The arbitrator reasoned that the purpose of jury pay is to ensure that an employee is willing to accept jury service by doing away with the monetary loss they would otherwise sustain. Requiring a man to work his regular shift after doing his civic duty, said the arbitrator, would defeat that purpose (*Greenleaf Mfg. Co.*, 32 LA 1).

***Computing overtime/jury-duty pay***—Arbitrators are split on whether jury duty should be counted as "time worked" in computing overtime in a week in which an employee spends one or more days on jury duty and other days on the job for a combined total of more than 40 hours. Several arbitrators have held that jury duty does not count as time worked and that therefore employees are not entitled to overtime premiums when their combined hours on the job and on jury duty exceed 40 per week (63 LA 899, 52 LA 575, 52 LA 357).

• Others have held that this in effect penalizes the employee for serving on the jury and that a more equitable policy would be to count jury duty as time worked in computing overtime (55 LA 510).

***Jury pay during suspended operations***—Is an employer required to pay jury leave when operations at its plant are suspended? The issue arose in one case where a snowstorm shut down a facility, and the employer refused to grant jury pay to employees serving on jury duty at the time. The arbitrator found management's decision acceptable because jury pay was based on the availability of work the employee could perform had he not served on the jury. In this instance, there was no available work because of the snowstorm, so there was no obligation to provide jury pay, the arbitrator concluded (*FMC Corp.*, 65 LA 264).

# Leave for Union Business

_____ **OVERVIEW** _____

Provisions in collective bargaining agreements that allow employees leaves of absence to conduct union business vary greatly, and whether such leave should be granted depends not only on the particular contract clause, but also on the facts and circumstances of each case, with particular reference to the good faith of both parties.

Although the internal affairs of the union and union "secrets" need not be divulged, the employer is entitled to enough information regarding the nature of the union business involved and the probable duration of the absence to permit an intelligent choice as to granting or denying leave.

One arbitrator, stressing that the term "union activities" is not unlimited, held that arbitrators must determine whether "the nature of a particular activity is an appropriate basis for absence" based on the twin ideas of "reasonableness and undue burden" (91 LA 1317).

Under some collective bargaining agreements, arbitrators have approved the action of management in granting leave on a conditional basis. In some cases, past practice of the parties and industry practices also have influenced or determined the arbitrator's ultimate decision.

Questions that might arise when leave for union business is considered include:

• Should there be a limit on the number of employees allowed to be on leave for this purpose at any one time?

• What should be the maximum duration of the leave—hours, days, months, or longer?

• Is the leave permitted for any union business? One arbitrator defined normal union business as activities falling within two broad areas: those performed by the union as bargaining representative of the employees; and those performed on behalf of the union as an entity; political activity; and bargaining in another plant. Another arbitrator raised a third category—peripheral "activity on behalf of bargaining-unit employees not arising out of the bargaining relationship."

• Does management have the right to require the union to explain the purpose of the leave before it is granted?

• What procedures should be followed when employees return from union leave?

• Does management have the right to deny union leave for certain reasons, such as a compelling business need?

• Do employer benefits accrue while an employee is on union leave?

• Should a distinction be made between business for a local union and business for an international?

## SUMMARY OF CASES

### Frequent Short Absences Not Allowed

Under a contract permitting leave of absence for union business, most arbitrators agree that union officials do not have the right to leave their jobs at frequent intervals to attend to union affairs. These arbitrators uphold management's right to insist that union officials tend to their jobs regularly or demand that they take extended leave if their frequent absences interfere with production. Some arbitrators hold that an employer can discipline union officials for leaving their jobs too often.

• When one union representative left his workplace to post union notices after the employer had refused him permission, he was suspended. The union claimed that the employer could not discipline him because he was on leave for union business. The arbitrator upheld the employer's action on the ground that the union leave clause did not allow a union representative to leave his job for frequent short periods of time to transact union business in the shop. He said the clause was clearly intended to permit absences for more extended periods outside the plant. Thus, he ruled the employee was properly disciplined (*Ampco Metal Inc.*, 3 LA 374).

### Unlimited Union Leave Permitted

When a contract placed no limit on the length of leave for holding union office, one arbitrator held that the employer had no right to terminate such leave.

• An employee received a leave of absence to take the position of full-time staff representative with the international union. After two years, the employer notified him that it was cancelling his leave and expected him to report back to work. When he did not, he was fired. Management claimed that it was unreasonable to expect it to grant union leave for eternity, when seniority and pension rights were accruing all the time. Whether this was equitable or not was beside the point, the arbitrator said. The

contract stated that union leaves "shall be available" in reasonable number. The parties' failure to place any time limitation on union leave clearly indicated to the arbitrator that no such limitation was intended (*Blaw-Knox Co.*, 41 LA 739).

• A local official should not be allowed to devote too much employer time to union business, an arbitrator ruled. Although the contract granted the employee paid time off for union business, it was not "carte blanche permission to spend as much employer time as he pleased on union business," the arbitrator held. He further said that having full-time union officials on the employer payroll could smack of unlawful domination of the union by management (*Pratt & Letchworth*, 48 LA 1345).

### Area of Union Business

Can "union business" be interpreted as applying only to local union affairs? Under a contract providing for leave to be granted for union business, arbitrators are likely to rule that an employer may not limit this privilege to business involving just the local union. One arbitration board reasoned that there are many cases where an employee would be called upon to perform work for an international of which the local union was a member. It said that the union business may in no way involve the local union. Thus, the board ruled, the meaning of "union" in the leave provision could not be restricted to the local union (*Robertshaw-Fulton Controls Co.*, 11 LA 1074).

### Content of Union Business

Few contracts specifically cover all instances that may be considered "union business" in the leave provisions. Distinguishing between what is and what is not "union business" is further complicated by the varied nature of union activities.

• At least one arbitrator ruled that serving on a political action committee was not "union business" under a contract that permitted leave for the purpose of transacting union business or representing the national union. He said that the employer rightly denied an employee's request for leave to serve on a union political action committee. He decided that the contract was intended to provide leave for the purpose of taking care of business for the union in its role of bargaining agent and to represent the national union in the traditional ways (*Anchor Duck Mill*, 5 LA 428).

• Another arbitrator agreed with an employer who refused to permit an employee to take leave to negotiate a contract between the union and another employer. The employee was a union president, and he had requested time off under a clause stating that "the business representative of the union or his agent designated in writing is to be considered a member of the shop committee and may sit in on any and all meetings." The arbitrator found, however, that the contract did not contemplate time off for union representatives to negotiate a contract with third-party employers (*Leonetti Furniture Mfg. Co.*, 64 LA 975.

• An employer improperly refused to give the members of a negotiating committee a second day off to complete a review of a newly negotiated contract, an arbitrator ruled. Notwithstanding the employer's contentions that the contract did not provide time off for committee members and that management was only required to consider request for time off in a fair and reasonable manner, the arbitrator decided that two days to review the agreement was not unreasonable if a careful job was to be done (*Hyde Park Foundry & Machine Co.*, 71 LA 349).

• Where a contract's part-time leave provisions allowed reasonable time for elected union representatives to attend conventions or conferences of the union, an arbitrator held that an employee/union official should be granted leave to attend a legislative affairs conference. The arbitrator said that conferences might well include a meeting between union representatives and members of the state legislature (*Le Roi Mfg. Co.*, 8 LA 350; see also 74 LA 501).

• An arbitrator held that a public-sector employer violated a collective bargaining agreement by refusing to grant a local union president an unpaid leave of absence to lobby the U.S. Congress during a union's "lobby week." According to the arbitrator, lobbying was considered an integral part of labor relations in the public sector, the employee held an important union post and played a significant role in the lobby week; he had no essential tasks required during the leave time he requested; he notified the employer and informed management about the events in question; and the issues to be discussed were of mutual concern to both parties (*U.S. Army Corps of Engineers*, 104 LA 30).

• A federal agency did not violate its collective bargaining agreement when it denied two union officials the use of leave for union business when they were working on normal union representational activities, an arbitrator found. On two occasions, the president and vice-president of a union local, both of whom were employees of a regional office of the Department of Veterans Affairs, asked for "partnership time" to account for hours spent on union representational activities during work hours. The employer denied their requests and forced them to take annual leave. The arbitrator agreed with the employer and pointed out that the contract clearly stated that the expected partner in such activities was either labor or management, not a member of the bargaining unit, adding that the hours these officials spent in the union office could not be called "partnership time" (*Dept. of Veterans Affairs*, 115 LA 1432).

**Personal Leave for Union Business**

Some contracts do not have specific clauses granting leave for union business and instead include—either implicitly or explicitly—union business as a reason for taking personal leave. However, employees may sometimes experience difficulty in justifying leave for union business under these circumstances.

• A teacher sought a paid half-day emergency leave to attend a union-sponsored meeting. The employer, however, contended that meeting did not meet the criteria of "personal and compelling" reasons specified by the contract as justification for "emergency leave." The arbitrator sided with the employee. Noting that past practice had established a very liberal application of the personal leave clause, which was the precursor of the present clause, the arbitrator pointed out that when the former clause was "dovetailed" into the new clause, the negotiators understood that the prior leave practices would not be affected (*Lake Holcombe Joint School Dist.*, 63 LA 1096).

## Organizational Work

Can an employee claim union business leave to engage in organizational work for the union at another employer? Under a contract granting leave to a union officer "to perform his duties as an executive officer of the union," an arbitrator ruled that an officer was entitled to time off for proper union activities that the officer was required and authorized to do. Applying this test, the arbitrator held that organizational work authorized by union members was a proper occasion for leave. The fact that the employer disapproved of the organizing was irrelevant in the arbitrator's view (*Telex Inc.*, 35 LA 873).

## Picketing As Union Business

One arbitrator has ruled that a union business leave clause does not give a large number of employees in a plant the right to leave in order to picket at the place of business of another employer. He reasoned that if the union could, by merely submitting a written request, create mass absenteeism it would hamper the general operation of the plant and thus defeat the right of management to direct its affairs and working forces. He further stated that the "leave" clause had not been intended to apply to late reporting or temporarily absent employees but had been intended to refer to those on extended periods of absence (*Chrysler Corp.*, 11 LA 732.

• An arbitrator ruled that a school board was acting within its rights when it denied teachers leave to picket another school. Their contract permitted up to 25 days off during the school year for attending "official sessions" of their union.

The teachers claimed that besides picketing, they were surveying the strike scene to evaluate strategy and public relations factors in the strike. The arbitrator, in denying the teachers' grievance for back pay, reasoned that the clause was designed to permit employees to participate in the internal union affairs, and not to support external business affecting an outside party (*Jackson Public Schools*, 64 LA 1089; see also 76 LA 648).

## When Union Refuses To State Nature of Union Business

Is a union obligated to give a reason for a request for leave for union business? Where a contract specified that leave would be granted to permit employees to engage in labor activities, one arbitrator ruled that the employer had the right to ask the union the purpose of any leave it requested. In order for the employer to determine whether the leave was for bona fide labor activity, it would have to know the nature of the union business, he reasoned. If the union refused to give the reason, then the employer was not obligated to grant the leave, the arbitrator decided (*Carter Carburetor Corp.*, 11 LA 569).

• Another arbitrator held that an employer may not inquire into the nature or location or the business to be performed. Doing so, he reasoned, would amount to prying into the internal affairs of the union.

The arbitrator listed three questions that management reasonably may ask an employee requesting leave—(1) whether the employee holds a union office that entitles him to leave, (2) whether the leave is to be used for official duty, and (3) how much time off is required (*Telex Inc.*, 35 LA 873).

## Leave for Rival Union Business

Leave to work for a union other than the contracting union is not permitted under a "union activity" clause, one arbitrator ruled, although it may be permissible to grant such leave requested under some other clause in the contract.

• A clause in the contract provided for leave of absence to local union representatives "chosen by the union" and to employees "elected to a full-time position with the union." Another clause provided for leave of absence for "good and sufficient reasons." An employee was granted leave to attend to his duties as an officer of a rival union. Upon his return to duty, the contracting union claimed that the employee had lost his seniority rights as his leave was unauthorized under the contract terms. The employer contended that the employee was on authorized leave under both the "leave for union activity" clause and the "leave for good and sufficient reasons" clause.

In his decision the arbitrator was critical of the employer's action in permitting leave to work for a rival union. The arbitrator felt that the employer's action had violated the spirit of the contract as to what were "good and sufficient reasons." However, because it had not violated the letter of the contract, he upheld the employer's granting of the leave.

In its attempted application of the "leave for union activity" clause, the employer was held in error. The arbitrator stated: 'Beyond any conceivable doubt, these two sections were included in the contract solely for the benefit of members of the contracting union . . . when acting for the union" (*Swift & Co.*, 6 LA 422).

## Discipline for Taking Unauthorized Leave

One arbitrator ruled that where an employee in good faith requests leave and, in the face of a rejection by management, takes lave anyway, he is not subject to discipline. Union business leave, the arbitrator reasoned, is for the benefit of the union and not of the individual employee. To say that an employee is personally liable if he mistakenly goes on leave, he added, would be like saying that a supervisor is personally liable if he mistakenly discharges or suspends an employee.

The employer's recourse in such cases, according to the arbitrator, is to file a grievance against the union to test whether a good-faith absence comes within the scope of the union business leave clause. If it is found not, an employee taking leave under similar circum-

stances thereafter would be subject to discipline, the arbitrator said. The arbitrator held, if an employee acts dishonestly or in bad faith in claiming the leave privilege, he is subject to discipline (*Telex Inc.*, 35 LA 873).

## Effect of Long Leave on Pension Benefits

Where an employee takes a long-term union leave and then returns to active employment for a couple of years before his retirement, is he entitled to count the years of his union leave in computing his pension benefits? One arbitrator has ruled yes.

● An employee was actively employed by an employer for 23 years, and then took a 22–year union leave. He returned to active employment with his employer for two years before electing to retire. A dispute arose when his employer refused to consider the leave as "credited continuous service" under the pension plan. The employer argued that the leave should be excluded because during that time the employee was not really an employee under the contract definition of "employee" as any person who was "working" under the collective bargaining agreement. This individual, the employer continued, was a full-time officer of the union and received his compensation from it for his services.

The arbitrator decided to credit the leave period under the pension plan. He based his award on the contractual intent of parties to include those individuals on approved leave as "employees." Also, the parties carefully delineated conditions that would disqualify employees from participating in the pension plan, the arbitrator noted, but did not include approved leave. Thus, the arbitrator reasoned that they did not intend for approved leave to be a cause for disqualification (*Western Textile Products Co.*, 64 LA 709; see also 68 LA 101).

## Effect of Leave on Automatic Increase/Promotion

Is an employee who takes time off to accept a full-time union job entitled to automatic increases he would have received if he had not taken leave? One arbitrator held that an employee was entitled to such increases where the contract provided for reinstatement without loss of seniority following union leave (*Spartan Aircraft Co.*, 28 LA 859).

• A company justifiably refused to promote a senior employee who was also a union activist because he would have had to be absent from work every week to carry out union duties, an arbitrator found. The employee, who served as treasurer of a union local, was rejected by his employer for a team leader position at the company, even though he had more service time than two other employees who were hired. The union argued that other team leaders had been allowed leave to meet military reserve obligations or to fulfill National Guard duties. The company contended that the employee's weekly absences were too much to warrant promotion; as for the military leaves of absence, the employer pointed out that public law mandated time off for reservists and National Guard members.

The employee's absence rate was a justifiable reason for the company not to promote him, the arbitrator found, noting that the leader position required regular availability, and the union officer could not meet that requirement (*USS*, 113 LA 475).

### Time Spent Handling Grievances

Although an employer may challenge, in specific cases, the amount of time claimed by union officials for grievance activity, the employer may not unilaterally set a limit on such time.

• When the number of hours spent on grievance settlement increased greatly, the employer limited the amount of time allowed, excusing his failure to negotiate the matter on a ground that it was a reasonable measure designed merely to return to a previous practice. The arbitrator dismissed this as contrary to the contractual obligation to pay for all time reasonably and actually required for handling matters under the contract (*Goss Co.*, 44 LA 824).

### Leave to Attend Arbitration Proceeding

Is an arbitration hearing part of the paid grievance time allowed union offi-

cials? It depends on the time and circumstances of the hearing and the individual contract.

• An arbitrator ordered an employer that required employee/witnesses to request vacation or holiday time for time off to prepare for an out-of-town arbitration hearing to continue its past practice of excusing a reasonable number of employees to prepare for arbitration, subject to last-minute personnel needs in work-related emergencies (*Texas Utilities Mining Co.*, 87 LA 815).

• A contract required an employer to pay "for all time spent during working hours investigating and adjusting grievances and complaints." A number of stewards attended arbitration hearings and gave testimony regarding various grievances. Their requests for pay for time spent at the proceedings were turned down by the employer. The employer said that the stewards were necessary participants in grievance adjustment, but not in arbitration hearings. The argument was upheld, and the stewards were not paid, as the time did not qualify for payment under the terms of the contract (*Consolidated Industries Inc.*, 43 LA 331).

• For years, a chief steward walked through the plant at the start of each work day to permit the employees to make known any grievance they might have. Although it had not objected before, the employer began refusing to pay for these visits unless the chief steward first requested and received permission to do so. The contract gave the steward the right to reasonable time off to investigate grievances "upon notice and approval" by management. According to the arbitrator, the practice followed by the steward for years without objection from the employer was the same as notice to and approval by the employer and was not subject to unilateral change by the employer (*American Saint Gobain Corp.*, 46 LA 920).

• One arbitrator has held that handling grievances need not even involve the negotiated grievance procedures. In that case, employees who gave depositions during working hours in a suit arising under Title VII of the Civil Rights Act were denied compensation for the time they took off from work to file the depositions. The employer, who was alleged to have violated the Act, required the employees to take the time off without pay, contending that they were not "processing their grievances" under the contract clause that provides pay for "processing grievances;" however, the arbitrator awarded back pay. Emphasizing that the employees had a right to elect to take their grievance to court rather than to use grievance procedures negotiated in the contract, the arbitrator concluded that they were "processing their grievances" through the court, and were entitled to back pay (*Wallace Silversmiths Inc.*, 64 LA 1110).

• An arbitrator held that an employer did not violate a contract requiring it to grant leaves of absence for "good and sufficient cause," when it refused to grant leave to an employee to participate in an arbitration hearing (*Youngstown Vindicator Printing Co.*, 88 LA 17).

• One steward took time from the job to discuss his own grievance with the union attorney. The employer docked the steward for the time he left work early, but the arbitrator ordered back pay for that time. The arbitrator reasoned that the contract included the steward's own grievance in the phrase "formal grievances," which stewards could take employer time to process. It also appeared that he had prior approval from the employer to do so, the arbitrator concluded (*County Sanitation District, Los Angeles*, 64 LA 521).

• Arbitration is merely the last step of the grievance procedure and, as such, is governed by the grievance language of the contract, one arbitrator said. Thus, the contract clause granting time off for grievance investigations entitled the local union president to accompany an industrial engineer on a union requested time study, the arbitrator decided, despite management's objection (*Hupp Corp.*, 48 LA 524).

• In one case, an employer issued two-day suspensions to employees who took time off to testify at arbitration hearings at the union's direction, instead of obeying employer orders to report for work. The employer argued that the union had failed to provide adequate notice for the leaves as required by the contract, and therefore they were not valid. Although the arbitrator agreed in part with the employer, he reasoned that the employees were innocently caught in a tug-of-war battle between the union and the employer, and so he reduced the suspensions to only one day (*United Engineering Co.*, 64 LA 1274).

## Arranging Leave

_____ OVERVIEW _____

In setting its policy on leaves of absence, management really has two separate and distinct problems: short-term absences, usually caused by illness or other unavoidable reasons for failing to report for work; and longer absences, for which employees can plan in advance, and that may be granted for any one of a dozen different reasons.

For short-term leaves, most employers merely require that the employee notify the employer that he or she is going to be absent. Notice must be given within a specified time, usually the first day or the first morning of the absence. Disciplinary penalties are specified for failure to make proper notification.

For long absences, or short-term leaves that are avoidable, employers usually require advance notice and approval from the proper management official before the leave is taken (94 LA 761, 74 LA 1185, 72 LA 1258, 72 LA 544, 72 LA 541, 72 LA 133).

If an employer has followed a lax policy in arranging and granting leaves, an arbitrator is not likely to be too sympathetic if management suddenly decides that an employee should be fired because he or she was a bit too casual about arranging for his or her leave.

_____ SUMMARY OF CASES _____

### Oral or Written Grant for Leave of Absence

Employers often require that authorization for leave of absence be put in writing. Despite this requirement, employers sometimes grant oral requests for leaves of absence. In such instances the question arises as to whether the employee was on an authorized leave.

• An arbitrator is likely to decide that management has given up the right to discipline an employee by giving oral permission to be absent. An employee was absent on an extended leave after obtaining oral permission from management for the leave of absence. The employee, on returning to work, was notified by the employer that he had lost his seniority rights because the leave authorization had not been put in writing. A contract provision stated that management "agrees that leave shall be in writing and a copy thereof sent to the union." The arbitrator held that the leave was autho-

rized and that the employee did not lose his seniority rights, finding that the provision on a written leave request was for the protection of the employer (*Gem Electric Mfg. Co. Inc.*, 11 LA 684).

• The fact that a contract provides that employees who request leaves of absence for a period of more than six days must make application in writing does not preclude finding that an employee who orally requested time off for one day was on "leave of absence."

An employee, the fourteenth member of a work crew, requested time off to visit a friend. Under the contract, the employer agreed to guarantee 13 men on the crew and to replace the fourteenth if an employee took leave. The union, on the other hand, agreed to absorb the work of the fourteenth member if his or her absence were due to sickness, accident, or absenteeism. Both parties agreed the absence was excused, but the employer referred to it as an excused "absence," and the union as "leave."

The arbitrator, in holding for the union, ruled that the contract implied that a leave of absence for a period of less than six days would not be reduced to writing. There is a clear difference, he said, between "absenteeism" and being off duty with permission (*Emge Packing Co.*, 15 LA 603).

• An employer unjustly penalized an employee for absenteeism after she missed a day of work to attend a court-ordered hearing on her divorce, an arbitrator determined.

The employee, who worked from midnight to 8 a.m., received a court order notifying her that the date had been set for the pretrial hearing on her divorce. The employee gave the employer's human resource administrator a copy of the order and asked for leave for her next shift in order to comply with the order and attend the hearing. The HR administrator denied the employee's leave request and told her that she would be assessed points under the collective bargaining agreement's absenteeism policy if she missed work to attend the hearing because the policy did not cover domestic court appearances. Her union filed a grievance, contending that the court appearance was covered under the policy, which allowed leave for employees to comply with "court issued summons." The employer "acted arbitrarily and capriciously" in rejecting the employee's court order, the arbitrator said, ordering the employer to remove the points assessed against the employee under the absenteeism policy (*OleTex Inc.*, 116 LA 1001).

## Oral Discussion with Management

If management wants to make sure that leaves will be granted only after formal authorization, it should make this requirement fairly specific in its contract or personnel policy. Otherwise, an employee may claim that he was granted a leave of absence when the employer intended no such thing.

• An employee contracted tuberculosis and was told by his doctor to take a long rest. The personnel director told him not to worry and that everything would be fine. The employee considered the statement a grant of a leave of absence and was gone for more than a year. When he returned, he discovered he had been discharged. The arbitrator ordered payment of half the wages the employee would have earned from the date he applied for reinstatement until the date of the award. He reasoned that the employer's liberal policy in respect to leaves of absence for illness strongly suggested that the employee had been granted a leave of absence. The words of the personnel director, he said, in the light of all the circumstances, must be construed as an oral grant of leave (*Morey Machinery Co. Inc.*, 9 LA 570).

## Reasonable Notice for Leave of Absence

Several questions may arise when the term "reasonable notice" is used in a contract provision on leave. Who determines what is "reasonable" and what is not "reasonable"? What length of time can be considered "reasonable"?

Unless the agreement says otherwise, the union probably can demand an equal voice in answering such questions.

• A contract provided that "reasonable notice" should be given to the proper employer official before an employee could leave his or her job. The employer, without consulting the union, posted a new rule that stating that "reasonable notice is deemed to be 48 hours." An employee requested permission for immediate absence for a few hours and left the workplace when the request was denied. When the employer disciplined the employee, the union contended that he was on legitimate leave and should not have been disciplined. The arbitrator found that the employer had no right to set a specific period of time without first obtaining the union's consent. When the "reasonable notice" clause was inserted in the contract, he said, it became a proper subject for bargaining and management could not unilaterally fix its meaning (*Ampco Metal Inc.*, 3 LA 374; see also 71 LA 70).

## Notice to Employer to Return to Work

Contract clauses covering leave sometimes provide for notice to the employer when an employee intends to return to duty. Unless the contract terms are very specific, confusion may arise as to the proper timing of the notice.

• In such an instance one arbitrator held that an employee had a "reasonable" time to submit his request for rehire. A union official was absent for several years on an authorized leave of absence for union business. Once those union duties were completed, he waited 12 days before submitting a request for rehire to the employer. The employer refused on the ground that he had not given the contractually required notice—i.e., immediately after his release from union duties. The employer also argued that the "increasing forces after layoff" provisions in the contract required an employee to report for work within five days after he was recalled from a layoff. The union argued that the "leave-for-union-activity" clause merely required the employee to notify the employer one week before he was ready to go back to work.

The employee was ordered reinstated with seniority and back pay. The arbitrator held that the "increasing forces after layoff" clause had no application in fixing the period of time required for giving notice at five days. He stated that a careful examination of the leave clause failed to reveal any requirement about a fixed period of time for giving the rehire notice, and therefore, a "reasonable" period should be allowed. The arbitrator concluded that 12 days was not too long a period of time in this instance (*Armour & Co.*, 10 LA 140).

### Reinstatement After Leave of Absence

If any employee requests reinstatement after an extended authorized leave of absence, how much time does management have to reinstate the employee?

• In the absence of specific policy to cover the situation, an arbitrator held in one instance that the employer had a "reasonable" time. Two weeks, however, was "unreasonable." An employee who was absent for six months on authorized leave requested reinstatement to his former position. Management delayed

two weeks before he was put back to work. In answer to the employee's claim for two weeks' salary, the employer stated that it was entitled to at least several weeks' notice before placing the employee because the nature of its operations required that much time to plan work and set up schedules.

It seemed to the arbitrator that it would be unfair to require the employer to put the employee back to work on the same day he decided to return to work. Because the employee had been absent for six months, the employer should have been allowed a reasonable opportunity to find out where he could best be used. Because of the nature of the operation, the arbitrator concluded that the employer should have found out in one week where best to place the employee (*Crawford Clothes Inc.*, 12 LA 1104).

• Another employer was also unjustified in delaying by one week the reinstatement of an employee on leave who returned a day late from an overseas trip when he missed a connecting plane flight, an arbitrator ruled. The employee did in fact fail to notify his employer of the delay—an unapproved extension of leave—but this was insufficient cause to justify placing him on an alternate work schedule that commenced one week later, the arbitrator decided. The employer's action amounts to a suspension prohibited by a just-cause provision, the arbitrator maintained, because there was no evidence that the employee was not back from the trip or that he was not able and willing to resume his work (*Potlatch Corp.*, 63 LA 816).

• An employee who had been injured on the job was held by an arbitrator to be entitled to her former position even though she had been out for more than a year, because she had obtained a medical certificate approving her return. She had been told by the employer that she could return to her job when such a condition was fulfilled. The arbitrator ruled that the contract provision permitting leave of absence for one year only was not applicable, because it was not intended to apply to forced absence for on-the-job injury. The employee had neither requested nor received formal leave of absence, and the employer, in describing conditions for the reinstatement, had not mentioned time limits (*Texlite Inc.*, 48 LA 509).

● Another arbitrator upheld an employer's delay in reinstating an employee on sick leave when the employer's physician erroneously reported that the employee had a hernia. The employer waited until another physician reported that the employee was in fact fit to return to work before he was reinstated. The arbitrator found the employer's action reasonable in light of the first physician's diagnosis and rejected the union's argument that that doctor might have resented the employee's earlier criticism of him, and therefore, deliberately altered his report (*Philco-Ford Corp.*, 62 LA 351).

### Extension of Leave

If an employer requires employees on leave to renew the leave at definite periods, can it discharge an employee who does not get a leave request in before the expiration of the leave period?

● An employee requested an extension of his leave of absence two days after his original leave had expired. The contract required that such leave be renewed every six months. Another provision of the contract stated that an employee was deemed to have quit, with subsequent loss of seniority, if the employee failed to report for work for three consecutive working days and had not been granted a leave of absence. The union argued that the seniority-protection clause applied in this case because the employee had been absent only two days beyond the termination of his leave. The employer took the position that the renewal had not been requested within the six-month time limit and therefore the employee had not complied with the contract.

The arbitrator held that the only logical construction that could be placed on the six-month renewal qualification was that the request for renewal of leave must be made before the expiration of the original period. He also stated that the three-day seniority-protection clause, for actively employed workers absent without leave, had no application to absentees overdue from leaves of absence (*Campbell, Wyant, & Cannon Foundry Co.*, 1 LA 254).

### Canceling Leave

If management has the sole right to grant or deny leaves of absence, can it also cancel leaves that have been authorized?

● Undoubtedly, the right to deny leave extends also to the cancellation of leave already granted; however, this probably should be handled by notifying employees and giving them a chance to return to work, not by unilaterally changing their status from "on leave" to "quit." An employee on the day shift was told that the employer was moving her to the night shift in order to avoid laying her off. For personal reasons she could not work nights. She orally requested a leave of absence, which was granted. While she was on leave, the employer marked her record "quit." The employee entered a claim for vacation pay and the employer answered that she was a "quit" and was not entitled to payment.

A majority of an arbitration board decided that the employer had the right to deny the employee the leave. The board said, however, that the denial should have been made when the request was made. The majority pointed out that it was entirely possible that the employee, given the choice of her job or the night shift, might have changed her decision. The board held the employer's action in changing from approval to disapproval without notifying the employee was unfair (*Anchor Rome Mills Inc.*, 9 LA 497).

# Maternity/Parental/Family Leave

## OVERVIEW

Many unions have negotiated maternity or pregnancy disability leaves for their members; however, interpretation of these contract clauses often involves reference to other leave provisions, such as general leave, parental leave, family leave, or sick leave, or consideration of the employer's past practices. In addition, a number of laws, both federal and state, affect maternity leave policies.

Paternity leave, a form of parental leave available to men, although usually unpaid, may consist of the right to use sick, personal, or vacation days on the birth or adoption of a child.

The federal Family and Medical Leave Act of 1993 requires employers that have 50 or more employees to give eligible employees up to 12 weeks of unpaid, job-protected leave annually:

- to care for a newborn or newly placed adopted or foster child;
- to care for a seriously ill child, spouse, or parent; or
- for the employee to recuperate from his or her own illness.

The FMLA does not supersede state or local laws that may provide more extensive family- or medical-leave rights. Currently, a number of states and territories have maternity-leave provisions that cover private- or public-sector employees or both, and many states maintain some form of family leave provisions for private- or public-sector employees or both.

Although arbitrators are generally reluctant to look past a labor contract to complicated bodies of law, many do refer to anti-discrimination law when considering maternity leave cases. As one arbitrator pointed out, "applicable provisions of state and federal law impress themselves upon the labor contract and not only may, but must, be given consideration in any arbitration proceeding which arises thereunder" (*Wausau District Public Schools*, 64 LA 187).

The Pregnancy Disability Amendment to Title VII of the 1964 Civil Rights Act makes disparate treatment of pregnant women for employment purposes illegal. Therefore, employers must treat pregnancy and childbirth in the same way as they treat other disabilities. In addition, government contractors must provide time off for childbearing purposes in certain circumstances under Executive Order 11246, which is more generous to employees than is Title VII. E.O. 11246 requires that the employee be reinstated to the same or an equivalent position, whereas Title VII mandates only that the person receive equal treatment and does not require reinstatement.

State pregnancy leave laws also may have even more stringent requirements for employers, including provisions for a minimum length of leave and for reinstatement to the same or an equivalent job. A majority of states make some provision for employees to take leave for disability resulting from the birth of a child with the understanding that the employee will be reinstated to the same or similar job when she returns to work.

Maternity leave, however, generally is without pay once regular sick leave and vacation leave have expired (95 LA 1042). Typically, maternity leave will not be allowed unless authorized by a state statute or by a collective bargaining agreement (89 LA 105).

## SUMMARY OF CASES

### Arbitral Considerations

Collective bargaining agreements vary widely in the types and amounts of leave offered to covered employees. Because of this variation, arbitral interpretations of maternity leave clauses have been affected by the presence or absence of other leave clauses, as well as by the exact wording of contract provisions.

In addition to contract language, arbitrators frequently consider the following factors:

- the employer's past practice;
- whether the pregnancy created a disability;
- whether the employee was laid off prior to or during the period of disability;
- what accommodations, if any, were appropriate for a pregnant employee;
- whether there was discrimination against or bias in favor of pregnant employees;
- whether maternity leave is appropriate for adoption; and
- whether insurance coverage should continue during an unpaid leave.

### General Leave Clauses

Many contracts allow employees to apply for leaves of absence—usually unpaid—for various purposes. Whether general leave may be used for maternity purposes depends on several factors.

- The presence of a general leave clause gives the company the right to grant or deny maternity leaves, according to one arbitrator. In reviewing an employer's agreement, the arbitrator found nothing that would qualify such a right, and noting a distinction between sickness and pregnancy, concluded that the employer could grant sick leave without being compelled to also grant maternity leave (*American Stove Co.*, 8 LA 779).
- Another arbitrator held that an employer that had granted maternity leave in the past under a general leave clause had to continue to do so. The arbitrator added that management must administer the general leave clause fairly and justly in the interests of all employees and the company (*General Electric Manufacturing Co. Inc.*, 11 LA 684).

### Paid Sick Leave Clauses

Although most contracts have a clause granting paid sick leave to employees, the term "sick" is rarely defined. The result is a number of contradictory decisions that vary with the specific contract language and facts of the case.

- Where a contract provides for unpaid maternity leave and for paid sick leave, an employee may not take paid sick leave for maternity purposes, an arbitrator ruled. Arbitrators may not "go behind the contract language to probe for an intent other than the one disclosed by a simple reading of the provision as supported by practice," the arbitrator pointed out, and because the contract differentiated between sick and maternity leave, the arbitrator should as well (*Millinocket School Committee*, 65 LA 805).
- In another case, an arbitrator held that an employer properly denied an employee's request to use sick leave to care for her recently adopted child because the employee's adoption-related absence was not one of five authorized uses of sick leave allowed under the existing collective bargaining agreement. Instead, her absence was covered under a contractual provision granting unpaid parental leave to employees who are adopting a child who is younger than five (*Columbia Local School District*, 100 LA 227; see also 97 LA 383).
- An arbitrator determined that it was illegal for an employer to maintain an administrative regulation that required employees to choose either unpaid child-

rearing leave, or paid sick leave, but not both. The provision in the contract for unpaid leave for child-rearing did not preclude an employee from using paid sick leave for the period of time that she was physically disabled because of pregnancy, the arbitrator held (*Sweet Home Central School District*, 71 LA 1102).

● A contract provided that pregnant employees were entitled to prenatal and/or infant care leave, to be granted on request and used in conjunction with sick leave. The contract also provided sick leave for a period of disability due to pregnancy, and contained, in the prenatal/infant care section, the provision that the "sum of such leaves will not exceed four months." From these provisions, an arbitrator concluded that an employee was entitled to four months of prenatal or infant-care leave, in addition to sick leave for the period of her disability, despite the employer's contention that the "sum of all leaves" included the sick leave (*West Side Credit Union*, 77 LA 622).

● A female employee was not entitled to use a "sick leave bank" to cover the post-delivery care of her child, an arbitrator ruled, explaining that the contract allowed workers to use the sick bank only if they were incapacitated by a "severe" sickness or injury. The employee claimed that breastfeeding her child after delivery constituted "sickness," but as the arbitrator pointed out, breastfeeding is not a sickness, and even assuming that it is, it clearly was not among those examples of "extraordinary physical problems" that the contract addressed for purposes of using the sick bank (*Cheektowaga Central School Board of Education*, 80 LA 225).

### 'No Discrimination' Clauses

Many contracts include clauses prohibiting discrimination on various grounds. These clauses may be useful to arbitrators in discerning whether a contract requires paid maternity leave. The effect of such a provision is to refer an arbitrator to definitions of discrimination formulated by the EEOC and the courts.

● Under a contract that provided unpaid maternity leave and paid sick leave

for "personal illness," an employer may not deny sick leave pay to an employee because of a pregnancy-related disability, an arbitrator ruled, despite the employer's past practice of never granting sick leave to employees taking maternity leave. A contractual nondiscrimination clause prohibiting discrimination "with respect to any term or condition of employment," and a state law prohibiting sex discrimination, were deciding factors, the arbitrator noted (*Muskego-Norway School District*, 71 LA 509).

### Contract Language Changes

Even a relatively minor change to a collective bargaining agreement's language can end up by forcing an employer to provide benefits, a number of arbitrators have concluded.

● When an employer agreed to a new contract that moved a provision for a "pregnancy leave of absence" into the clause covering "sick leave of absence," it committed itself to providing paid sick leave rather than unpaid pregnancy leave, an arbitrator ruled, pointing out that the employer's intentions during contract negotiations were irrelevant (*Scottscraft Inc.*, 64 LA 279).

● Although an exclusion of maternity benefits was removed from the benefits clause of a contract, an employer was not required to pay benefits for maternity-related leave, an arbitrator decided. "The omission from the collective bargaining agreements of the earlier exclusion of 'maternity' and the silence of the agreements with respect to an obligation to pay such benefits are hardly the stuff from which a binding contractual obligation can be erected," the arbitrator said (*Chromalloy Division*, 71 LA 1178).

### Employer's Past Practice

A number of decisions have hinged on the employer's past practice of either granting or not granting paid maternity leave, especially where the contract is silent or ambiguous on the subject. Some arbitrators find past practice "fairly conclusive" (*Walled Lake Consolidated Schools*, 64 LA 239), while others find it a "unilateral pronouncement by management," and hence, "not controlling" (*Kaiser-Permanente Medical Care Program*, 64 LA 245).

● Under a teachers' contract providing unpaid "parental leave" for up to one year after the birth of a child, an employer could not unilaterally limit the leave to half a year, an arbitrator found. The employer had agreed to the clause in several different agreements, and had, over a period of years, denied only one other request for a full year's leave. In that case, the leave requested did not coincide with the school year, but spread over parts of two different school years. The case at hand, however, involved a request for leave for one school year, the arbitrator noted, and was refused because of "the general dissatisfaction" of the school board with long leaves. Whether or not this "dissatisfaction" was justified, the arbitrator said, the board could not reject the teacher's leave request without showing the request to be "inappropriate" (*Ankeny Community School District*, 77 LA 860).

### Disability and Layoff Issues

A pregnant employee's right to disability benefits and the effect of a layoff on a pregnant worker are two other issues where arbitrators have varying determinations.

● Under an insurance plan agreement that provided accident and sickness benefits for disabled employees in a doctor's care, a pregnant employee certified as disabled by her physician was entitled to benefits, an arbitrator concluded. The employee had previously suffered two miscarriages, and her physician recommended that she cease doing any work that involved lifting, pulling, pushing, or straining of any kind. The employer initially paid disability benefits to the employee but then decided that the payments were made incorrectly. The employee was placed on unpaid personal leave from February until June, when benefits were reinstated to cover the period of hospitalization, delivery, and recovery. The arbitrator concluded that, because the insurance plan's description of disability did not specifically exclude pregnancy-related conditions from coverage, the employee should have been paid benefits in the same fashion as any other employee suffering from a temporary disability (*Caterpillar Tractor Co.*, 79 LA 1070).

● An employee who was partially disabled because of pregnancy, but who was able to do light work at the time of a layoff, and who later became completely temporarily disabled, was not entitled to disability benefits, an arbitrator decided, based on the contract's exact terms and the company's past practice. Had the employee been disabled at the time of the layoff, she would have been eligible for benefits, the arbitrator pointed out, but her absence "was not because of her partial disability, but because no work was available, i.e., she was on layoff," the arbitrator said (*Hormel Fine Frozen Foods*, 75 LA 1129).

● An employee who was placed on layoff while she was on maternity leave, and who was replaced by a less senior employee, had to be reinstated with back pay to her former position, an arbitrator concluded. By refusing to reinstate the employee when she expressed her desire to return from maternity leave, the employer "constructively discharged" the worker "without any semblance of just cause," the arbitrator noted (*Pipe Fitters Union Local 636*, 75 LA 449).

### Accommodation Concerns

An employer may lawfully require a pregnant employee to take leave when her pregnancy adversely affects her ability to work, but it first must accord to that employee the same opportunities that other temporarily disabled workers are given to perform modified or alternative tasks.

● A pregnant employee who was unable to perform the various physical tasks required by her job and who was denied a transfer to a light-duty position was the victim of sex discrimination, an arbitrator decided. The worker had requested a transfer to another department and then asked to be assigned to a light-duty position in her own department. When her requests were refused, the employee asked for and was granted sick leave. She was without income during her pregnancy after she had exhausted both her sick leave and vacation benefits. Noting that a male employee was assigned to light duty following an operation, the arbitrator asserted that the pregnant employee "faced an employment situation where she was not accorded fair and equal treatment." The arbitrator concluded that the "weight of the evidence clearly supports" the employee's contention that "for whatever reason, intentionally or unintentionally," the worker had been a victim of sexual discrimination (*Cities Service Co.*, 87 LA 1209).

### Discrimination in Favor of Pregnant Employee

At least one arbitrator has concluded that the Pregnancy Disability Act prohibits discrimination in favor of, as well as against, pregnant workers.

● An employer who involuntarily reassigned a female employee, rather than either of two pregnant employees ahead of the reassigned worker on the involuntary assignment schedule, violated the Pregnancy Disability Act, an arbitrator concluded. Under the law, "a difference in sex is not necessary for pregnancy discrimination to occur," the arbitrator notes, adding, "all that need occur is for a woman affected by pregnancy to be treated differently" from other persons. The arbitrator stressed that one of the pregnant women was scheduled to return from maternity leave before the date of the assignment, that the other would have been in her fifth or sixth month of pregnancy, and that neither of the pregnant workers was disabled and unable to perform the assignment (*National Weather Service*, 83 LA 689).

### Demotion and Discharge Decisions

An employer may demote or discharge a pregnant employee if it has a legitimate nondiscriminatory reason for the action, according to several arbitrators.

● Upholding an employer's right to determine if its workers are qualified for their jobs, an arbitrator ruled that an employee was properly terminated when,

following treatment for a difficult pregnancy and other physical disabilities, she demonstrated that she was unable to perform all her duties. Although medical reports from a number of doctors who treated the employee seemed to "lean in favor" of the worker, they in fact only "add confusion and make one wonder if the later 'clean bill of health' is justified," the arbitrator maintained, adding that, in any case, employers must not be "handcuffed" by doctors' statements in trying to determine if an employee is qualified for a job (*National Standard Co.*, 85 LA 401).

● An employer improperly terminated an employee for failing to return to work at the expiration of maternity disability leave, an arbitrator decided. The worker initially had requested and been granted a leave of absence without specifying an exact return date, but later, at management's request, she submitted a new leave form on which she specified both the beginning and end dates of her pregnancy disability leave. First, it would be "most unfair," the arbitrator said, "to hold an employee to exactness about [a] date when there is no exactness possible in predicting either the birth date or the date of recovery." Second, if the employer was "misled" about the employee's return date, "it was the employer's own fault." Management relied on information that was "the result of the employer's insistence on the completion of an ambiguous form under confusing circumstances" and "failed on numerous occasions to protect its interest by making reasonable and logical inquiry" (*Cooperative Optical Services*, 86 LA 447).

### Reinstatement to Position

Reinstatement of a pregnant worker to her job or a comparable position following maternity leave is not required by Title VII, unless that is the policy for all employees on disability leave, but individual states may enact laws that grant more protection than the federal statute with regard to requiring reinstatement. In addition, some unions have negotiated contracts that require employers to give reinstatement priority to employees who are returning from maternity leave.

• In one case, a teacher who had been on maternity leave for one school year notified the school district that she intended to return to work. She bid on seven open positions for which she was qualified. The contract provided that employees returning from maternity leave would "enjoy an unequivocal preference over employees requesting transfers, most teachers being reemployed by the School District, and newly hired persons," the arbitrator notes, yet this teacher was not interviewed for any of the seven positions but was instead reassigned to her previous job.

Meanwhile, five of the seven vacancies were filled by employees lower on the priority list. Noting that the school district "undeniably failed" to give the returning teacher the priority to which she was entitled, the arbitrator pointed out that "she should have been considered for most, if not all, of the seven vacant positions she sought." Thus, the school district must assign her to one of those positions (*Decatur School District*, 86 LA 841).

### Maternity Leave for Adoption

Employers that have a maternity leave policy may be required to extend the leave to employees who become parents through adoption.

• Emphasizing that "our society places great value on adopting children," one arbitrator has held that a maternity leave policy should not be interpreted to preclude situations "where the family unit is increased by adoption rather than natural birth." The employer's policy allowed up to six months of sick, annual, or unpaid leave, or a combination of the three, for "maternity reasons." When an employee sought a three-month leave without pay to care for her newly adopted daughter, management told her that she would have to first use all her annual leave.

The arbitrator decided, however, that the "maternity reasons" acceptable for leave under the policy should include the "care of an adopted child during the initial period of adjustment when the adopted child becomes a member of the new household or family." Previous maternity leave grants had not been "solely confined to the actual delivery period," but had made "allowances for the mother to be with her new child" following the baby's arrival at home (*Office and Professional Employees*, 71 LA 93).

• Employees who adopt children are eligible for maternity leave under a contract that granted up to one year of "maternity" leave at the request of the employee, according to another arbitrator. The case arose when an employer granted personal, rather than maternity, leave to an employee who adopted a baby. The arbitrator noted that the length of the leave "establishes the fact" that the parties' object was to provide substantial time for child-rearing. An adopted child requires the same amount of care as an infant raised by its natural mother, the arbitrator reasoned, so an employee who adopts a child is in no less need of a maternity leave than one who gives birth. Had the contract provided time off for "childbearing," the employer might have been permitted to restrict the leave to pregnant employees, but leave provided for maternity purposes should be granted to any employee who needs to perform the "duties" of "motherhood," the arbitrator determined (*Ambridge Borough*, 81 LA 915).

### Other Maternity Leave Issues

Other issues that arbitrators may be required to decide include the following.

• *Unmarried Employees' Rights*— When an unmarried employee sought maternity leave benefits in one plant, management dismissed the worker instead of granting her leave. An arbitration board then ordered the company to reinstate her and grant her leave, reasoning that there was no association between her conduct and her job (*Crane Co.*, 12 LA 592; see also *Allied Supermarkets Inc.*, 41 LA 713).

• *Insurance Coverage During Unpaid Leave*—An employee on an unpaid maternity leave was entitled to have her insurance premiums paid by the employer under a contract clause that provided insurance for "employees," an arbitrator ruled. The contract between the union and the employer provided for unpaid leave after employees had exhausted their sick leave; in the past, the employer had continued insurance coverage even after the worker had begun the unpaid leave. Because the contract clause is ambiguous, in that it does not define "employee," the arbitrator concluded that past practice required continuation of insurance coverage (*Greensburg Salem School District*, 76 LA 241).

● *State-Law Effects*—In at least two cases that arose before the Title VII amendment was enacted, employers were ordered to pay sick leave benefits for maternity-related medical disabilities in accordance with state law, which prohibited any discriminatory practice (*Apollo-Ridge School District*, 68 LA 1235; *West Allis-West Milwaukee Joint City School District 1*, 68 LA 644).

## Paternity Leave

An employer's refusal to allow an employee to use accrued sick leave to take time off to care for his wife after the birth of their child violated a collective bargaining agreement, according to the arbitrator hearing the case.

A police officer wanted to use 90 hours of accrued sick leave to care for his wife after childbirth. The employee submitted Labor Department forms stating that his wife would require hospitalization, as well as two to six weeks of spousal care after the birth. The employer twice denied his leave request, and ultimately, the employee used 91 hours of vacation time to tend to his wife.

The union contested the employer's actions, arguing that they violated the city's past practice, a view the arbitrator accepted. The employer also violated the collective bargaining agreement by trying to alter the interpretation and application of the sick leave provisions as applied to family illnesses, he said. Both the FMLA and the state's family leave statute allowed employees to take up to 12 weeks of leave per year to care for a spouse who had a serious health condition, he pointed out. In addition, the municipal administrative code specifically provided that employees could use accrued sick leave to care for a spouse who was not well, the arbitrator said, ordering the employer to credit the employee for his lost vacation leave (*Moses Lake*, 114 LA 745).

# Part 6

# *Promotions*

## Posting of Vacancies & Bidding

———————————————— **OVERVIEW** ————————————————

Arbitrators generally recognize that in the absence of a contract provision limiting an employer's rights in filling vacancies, the employer has the right to determine whether a vacancy exists and whether and when it will be filled (*Mid-Central/Sysco Food Services Inc.*, 103 LA 872, 98 LA 222, 97 LA 1197, 96 LA 1007, 96 LA 553).

When, however, duties associated with a job vacancy are reassigned and continue to be performed by employees in other jobs, arbitrators will examine whether an employer has intentionally avoided following the contractually required procedures for filling jobs (see, e.g., *Atlas Inc.*, 102 LA 364; see also 97 LA 196, 88 LA 614, 85 LA 449, 85 LA 290, 84 LA 390).

Moreover, contractual provisions dealing with the posting of vacancies, but not specifically requiring management to fill vacancies, have been narrowly construed by arbitrators. In one case, for example, a contractual provision for posting of "permanent vacancies" was held to apply only if the employer decided a vacancy existed. In this instance, the employer had decided that there was no need to replace a promoted employee. Thus, no vacancy existed, the arbitrator concluded (49 LA 74; see also, 46 LA 1027, 44 LA 161).

Even where a job has been posted for bidding, this does not necessarily guarantee that a vacancy exists and will be filled. For example, in one case an arbitrator upheld an employer's permitting a successful bidder to withdraw his bid and return to his original job, even though the latter had, in turn, been posted for bid (52 LA 894, 43 LA 951).

It is well established that management has the right, unless clearly restricted by the agreement, to decide whether or not to fill temporary vacancies occasioned by absences caused by illness, vacations, etc. (96 LA 1007, 90 LA 577, 85 LA 1190, 85 LA 290, 55 LA 19, 43 LA 395, 41 LA 492).

———————————————— **SUMMARY OF CASES** ————————————————

### Job Postings

*Violation of contractual posting requirements*—Arbitrators commonly examine whether an employer intentionally reassigned job duties associated with a vacancy in order to avoid posting requirements under a contract.

• An arbitrator interpreted a contract clause requiring the posting of a vacancy where there was an increase in the normal complement of a classification as applying only where an employer had determined that a vacancy did in fact exist. Infrequent transfer of employees to assist in the department did not prove that a vacancy existed, the arbitrator held (*Homestake Mining Co.*, 88 LA 614).

• An arbitrator ruled that an employer violated a wage agreement by failing to post 12 jobs after it changed shift hours from 10 a.m. through 6 p.m. to 7 a.m. through 3 p.m. The employer had on three occasions posted jobs subject to less substantial shift-time changes, the arbitrator pointed out, and posting the jobs would give senior employees an opportunity for assignment to a more desirable shift (*U.S. Steel Mining Co.*, 97 LA 196).

• An employer violated the contract when it filled a night shift opening with a day shift volunteer and did not post either job for bidding, an arbitrator found.

An electrical technician and steward in the local union filed a grievance when the employer permanently transferred a co-worker from day to night shift without posting the position he left. The company claimed that the co-worker volunteered to take the place of a bargaining unit member who went on medical leave and eventually was assigned full-time to the rotating night-shift job. When the employee on sick leave returned, he asked for and was transferred to the job vacated by the co-worker.

The arbitrator noted that although it was true that the company treated the two moves as a simultaneous exchange of jobs, it still had to follow the contract requirement that "permanent transfers shall be posted for bidding." As soon as the company permanently moved one worker out of a shift, it created a vacancy in that job, the arbitrator pointed out, noting that the union said it was not seeking to undo the transfers, but wanted only a prospective remedy. The arbitrator upheld the grievance and ordered the employer to fill vacancies in the future through plant-wide bidding consistent with contract requirements (*Dakota Gasification Co.*, 117 LA 777 ).

**Posting new jobs**—Generally, when a contract provides that job vacancies must be posted, the employer is required to post all such vacancies, including newly created jobs.

• An arbitrator held that an employer violated the contract when it transferred an employee to a job that it had failed to post. Regardless of the employer's claim that it had to create the position to accommodate an employee's request for a transfer, the contract required that "new" and "open" jobs be posted, the arbitrator found (*Rogers-Wayne Metal Products Co.*, 92 LA 882).

• An employer did not create new jobs in a manner that required the jobs to be posted or placed for bidding, an arbitrator ruled, when, during a process of reorganization, the employer created a new work group and changed the proportion of duties assigned to employees in the group. Pointing out that the changes in duties, benefits, and working conditions were not of such a magnitude to constitute a new job classification, the arbitrator concluded that the employer's "traditional prerogative" to change work within a given job classification was reaffirmed by the comprehensive management rights clause in the contract (*United Telephone Co. of the Carolinas*, 71 LA 244).

**Temporary vacancies**—Some arbitrators have held that temporary vacancies do not have to be posted or filled in accordance with seniority. They reason that to apply this requirement to every brief vacancy would be a handicap and a detriment to the efficient management of the business (88 LA 614, 84 LA 36, 70 LA 1275).

• Relying on past practice, another arbitrator decided that an employer had the right to hire college students during the summer for unskilled work, even though the union claimed that the jobs should have been treated as temporary vacancies available to all employees. Noting that there was no past practice of having the work performed only by helpers, apprentices, and journeymen, the arbitrator pointed out that there was no evidence that the temporary students did any work that they were prohibited from performing (*Central Illinois Public Service Co.*, 72 LA 874).

• An arbitrator rejected an employer's claim that its management rights clause permitted it to fill temporary vacancies without posting the jobs. The agency had filled a team leader position with an acting team leader appointment for an unknown duration. In light of a specific clause requiring job postings, the "ceiling problems" of the agency were irrelevant, the arbitrator reasoned. Had the agency awarded the job to the grieving employee, its personnel would not have increased, the arbitrator concluded (*Office of Economic Opportunity*, 63 LA

692; see also 96 LA 1007, 90 LA 577, 85 LA 1190, 85 LA 290).

*Job originally filled 'temporarily'*— One arbitrator approved management's failure to post a temporary vacancy, as well as its subsequent appointment of the acting replacement to permanent replacement. The employee was originally appointed to replace an employee on a short-term sick leave, and because the contract specifically exempted vacancies of 60 days or less from the posting requirement, the employer acted within the agreement, the arbitrator found. Later, when it became apparent that the vacancy would become permanent, the employer posted the job but could not find a qualified candidate, the arbitrator noted. Given that the employee in the acting position had demonstrated his competence, his appointment as a permanent replacement was proper, the arbitrator concluded (*Wm. Powell Co.*, 63 LA 641).

*Job posting or transfer*—An employer violated the requirement to post a job opening when it promoted a junior employee over a senior employee to fill that vacancy, an arbitrator ruled. The employer maintained bid lists from which it selected candidates for promotions as jobs became available. When a group leader's job became vacant, the employer examined its bid list, and found no qualified candidates. It therefore allowed the supervisor to select the most qualified candidate. The union charged, however, that when no qualified candidates were to be found on the bid list, the employer should have posted the vacancy.

Agreeing with the union, the arbitrator ruled that there was a contractual requirement to post jobs when bid lists had been exhausted. As a remedy, the arbitrator ordered the job to be posted but denied the union's requested remedy of promotion of a particular senior employee to the job because it was not clear that the employee would have bid for the job (*Whirlpool Corp.*, 63 LA 1122).

• In another case, an arbitrator upheld management's temporary transfer of a retiring employee's duties to other employees. The duties were transferred to two other employees during a comput-

erization process, and the arbitrator found that management had the right to make such temporary transfers to the employees who were in lower classifications. To ensure that the transfers were only temporary, however, the arbitrator ordered the employer to return the lost position to the unit within 90 days following bidding procedures as required by the contract (*Ohio Brass Co.*, 62 LA 913).

*Job posting versus assignment to supervisor*—When a bargaining unit employee retires, can the employer decide not to replace him, and instead assign his duties to his supervisor? An employer who attempted to do this lost the arbitration proceeding to the union. The arbitrator based his decision on the union recognition and seniority clauses, which led him to conclude that the duties of the retiring employee should remain in the bargaining unit. Because the retirement created a permanent vacancy, the job should have been posted, the arbitrator decided (*Stanray Corp.*, 63 LA 332; see also 73 LA 1250, 70 LA 182).

*Previously posted jobs*—What is the employer's obligation to post another job vacancy notice after it has already done so, but without successfully recruiting from its employees? According to one arbitrator, the employer still has a responsibility to post the job even though it will probably do no good.

• An employer posted a notice of a job opening for an experienced crane operator. The employer already had one employee working the crane, but wished to train another. After reviewing the bids from its employees, the employer found no qualified candidates, but a few months later, the crane operator left the employer and a new, experienced crane operator was hired. The union complained that the job opening should have been posted again, and the arbitrator agreed. The contract language explicitly required job openings to be posted; however, because the employer's earlier attempt to recruit a crane operator had been unsuccessful, it was clear that no one was actually disadvantaged or hurt by the contract violation, the arbitrator concluded (*Consolidated Diesel Electric Co.*, 65 LA 1074).

## Posting Requirements

*Information required on job notice*— Under a contract provision where the practice had been to name specific jobs in posting vacancies, one arbitrator decided that the employer could not suddenly decide to list only the classifications of job vacancies, rather than specific jobs. He said the practice of posting particular job openings by name had to be continued (*Lion Oil Co.*, 25 LA 549).

• An arbitrator held that, under a contract, an employer's steel division must identify the specific machine by number, rather than merely stating the category of a machine, when posting vacancies in a particular occupation. The contract required an indication of "specific equipment involved," the arbitrator pointed out, substantial differences existed among machines within some categories, and the employer's job postings had included machine numbers for 26 years (*Riblets Products Corp., RPI Div.*, 93 LA 1049).

*Notices to be posted uniformly throughout plant*—Even though a contract did not require posting of vacancies, an employer whose practice was to post jobs in some departments had to post them in all departments, an arbitrator ruled. Failure to post job openings in certain departments, he said, unfairly prevented employees from exercising their seniority rights (*National Malleable & Steel Castings Co.*, 4 LA 175; see also 67 LA 354).

*Notice to union*—When a contract requires management to notify the union of its compliance with posting requirements, how much notification is necessary? One arbitrator ruled that management properly discharged its duty when it informally notified the union through its local chairman about its decision to reject employee applicants as unqualified prior to its hiring of an outsider. Although the union argued that the employer improperly waited until after the hiring to meet with the union committee, the arbitrator decided that such a meeting was not required by a strict reading of the contract (*Semling Menke Co.*, 62 LA 1184; see also 73 LA 516).

## Bidding

*Bidding procedures/sufficiency of bid*—Arbitrators must also rule on whether an employer has followed a bidding procedure outlined in a contact, and whether an employee's bid meets the requirements for a particular job (91 LA 605).

• An arbitrator held that an employer violated a contact by awarding a second-shift die-setting position to a senior qualified bidder, instead of another employee. The senior bidder had been awarded the same position on the third shift 83 days earlier, the arbitrator pointed out, and the contract expressly restricted an employee from bidding on another job for at least 90 days after he or she had begun work in a position into which he or she previously had bid. In addition, the agreement did not make seniority a sole controlling factor in job-vacancy awards, the arbitrator noted (*PSW Industries Inc.*, 97 LA 155).

*Bidding in same classification*—Under the promotion provisions of a contract, can an employee bid for a job in the same classification as his own? Arbitrators have generally held that, in the absence of a specific definition in the contract, "promotion" means a movement to a higher classification, not a lateral movement to a job that the employee thinks is more desirable (30 LA 550, 24 LA 723, 23 LA 159, 21 LA 707).

*Bidding downward*—Can an employee bid for a job in a classification lower than his own? When a senior employee asked to fill a temporary vacancy in a job rated below his own, the employer had the right to refuse him, an arbitrator ruled. The arbitrator said that the employee could not assert seniority rights to downward transfer unless a local practice to that effect existed, which he found was not the case (*Bethlehem Steel Co.*, 44 LA 457).

• An arbitrator held that a contract contained no language permitting downward bidding. Therefore he disallowed an employee's use of seniority to get a lower level job (*Pittsburgh Plate Glass Co.*, 44 LA 7).

● Additionally, another arbitrator upheld management's refusal to permit a downward bid. The arbitrator reasoned that the employer's right to "arrange" its employees had not been expressly restricted by the contract with respect to "downbids," and that management therefore could reject a downbid request when it adversely affected operations (*Longview Fibre Co.*, 63 LA 529; see also 83 LA 685).

● Other arbitrators have come to the conclusion that senior qualified bidders have a right to a job, even though it is in a lower classification. In one case, even though the bidding clause made some reference to promotions, the arbitrator decided it did not restrict movement to promotions alone (69 LA 822, 41 LA 329, 40 LA 1305).

*Supervisors' bidding rights*—Can a supervisor bid for a job that opens up in a bargaining unit? Where a contract permitted an employee to continue to accumulate seniority for a year after transfer out of the bargaining unit, an arbitrator ruled that a supervisor who was once in the unit could bid for a job in the unit. Because the supervisor still had seniority, the arbitrator held that he had the same bidding rights as other employees (*Owens-Corning Fiberglas Corp.*, 29 LA 578).

● In a case where a supervisor was not, and never had been, a member of the bargaining unit, an arbitrator said he had no right to bid on a posted job. Although the bidding clause referred to "employees," the arbitrator decided it clearly referred to members of the bargaining unit. Because supervisors were not members of the unit, they could not accumulate seniority under the contract, and thus had no right to bid (*Boardman Co.*, 41 LA 215).

*Trainees' bidding rights*—Can a trainee bid for a job other than the one for which he or she is being trained? Under certain circumstances, one arbitrator ruled yes.

● Three industrial trainees bid for jobs out of the job categories for which they were being trained. The employer refused to consider the bids, claiming that they were abusing the job-bidding system. The arbitrator, however, found that the job-bidding clause in no way limited the rights of the employees to bid provided they had "potential capabilities for the job." In the case of two of the employees, the arbitrator found evidence that they were in fact qualified for the jobs, and therefore held that management's decision violated the contract.

The third trainee had held his job for less than two months. The arbitrator said he would not overrule management's action in his case because of the brief period of employment, despite the argument that the employee lacked interest in his job (*Black Clawson Co.*, 64 LA 175).

● Transferring a new hire into a different job before he was eligible to bid on it was a contract violation, held one arbitrator. A mining company had a labor agreement that provided for a bidding process to fill job vacancies. After the company posted a classified job notice for an oil truck driver and no employees bid on it, it transferred a unit driver who was 53 days short of working six months at his new job, as required by the contract. The local filed a grievance, claiming that a "security clause" in the contract required members to wait six months before being eligible to bid on a job vacancy. The employer replied that no one had bid on the job opening, so it was free to transfer employees at will, a practice the company said it often used over the years without complaint by the union.

Ruling for the union, the arbitrator ordered the driver to complete the remaining 53 days at his job before bidding on new jobs. He reaffirmed the contract's security clause by requiring that in the future both the union and company had to agree in writing to hire a covered employee if contract bidding rules were to be bypassed (*Arkhola Sand & Gravel Co.*, 115 LA 837 ).

*Right to trial period*—Are employees who bid on new jobs entitled to a trial or training period in which to learn the job? Some arbitrators have ruled that employees must be given a reasonable opportunity, under adequate supervision, to learn how to perform the work, while others

have held that an employee should be removed from the position if he or she cannot "grasp" the details of the job.

● A senior applicant for a higher-
rated job was entitled to a trial period on
the job, an arbitrator ruled, where the
contract stated that a senior bidder for a
job shall be given an opportunity to demonstrate with "normal supervisory instructions" his or her qualifications to
perform the job. Although the employee
may not have been entitled to a training
period under the contract, the arbitrator
concluded that "normal supervisory instructions" could not be interpreted to
require that the senior applicant be able,
ready, and willing to take over, without
training or indoctrination, and fulfill all
the job duties with the usual and normal

supervision required by employees who
have long since adjusted to a routine performance (*John Deere Chemical Co.*, 42
LA 443; see also 73 LA 1218, 72 LA 1238,
71 LA 1171, 71 LA 733).

● A trial period was properly denied
in a case where the employer hired an
outsider for a particular job, after rejecting all in-house candidates. The union argued that candidates should have been
given a 30–day trial period before being
rejected, but the arbitrator noted that the
contractual requirement of a trial period
extended only to those actually hired or
promoted to new positions, and not to
candidates for those positions (*Semling-
Menke Co.*, 62 LA 1184; see also 73 LA
937, 73 LA 935, 73 LA 20, 71 LA 479).

# Bases for Promotion

## OVERVIEW

The right of management to promote employees is frequently qualified by seniority provisions in a labor contract. While unions may tend to overemphasize seniority and de-emphasize merit and ability as the basis for promotion, management often emphasizes a supervisor's personal judgment of an employee's ability and places less emphasis on a worker's seniority.

If the contract states that promotion decisions must be based on "fitness and ability" as well as seniority but is silent as to who determines what "qualified" means, arbitrators often conclude that management is entitled to make the initial determination. The union, however, retains the right to challenge the employer's decision on the ground that the employer's determination either was unreasonable based on the facts, or else was capricious, arbitrary, or discriminatory (98 LA 26, 97 LA 86, 97 LA 41, 96 LA 338, 96 LA 100, 95 LA 206, 94 LA 905, 94 LA 435, 93 LA 660, 93 LA 589).

This right to determine ability may be held by management either as a residual management right or as a necessary adjunct to the right to manage the plant and direct the working force (52 LA 889, 40 LA 697, 38 LA 132).

## POINTERS—

• Arbitrators usually let an employer's judgment stand in the selection of employees for promotion, unless it can be shown that the employer ignored the terms of the contract or acted in an arbitrary manner.

• In making promotions to supervisory positions, the employer normally has a free hand.

• If no present employee is qualified to perform a vacant job, the employer ordinarily has the right to hire from the outside.

## SUMMARY OF CASES

### Determining Qualifications

An employer, arbitrators have held, has the right to judge, weigh, and determine the necessary qualifications of the respective applicants so long as the methods used are fair and nondiscriminatory (*Lockheed Aircraft Corp.*, 25 LA 748; see also 75 LA 2, 75 LA 494, 74 LA 1023, 74 LA 811, 73 LA 632).

The qualifications compared must relate directly to the requirements of the job in question (*Pittsburgh Steel Co.*, 21 LA 565).

### Factors For Promotion

*Seniority as a crucial factor*—Where primary emphasis is on seniority in determining promotion rights, arbitrators have held that a better-qualified employee may not be given precedence over a senior employee capable of doing the work. To pass over a senior employee, an employer must be able to show that the employee is not capable of doing the job. If seniority is controlling, the employer cannot ignore seniority and promote the "most-qualified," "best-qualified" bidder, or even a bidder whose qualifications are "substantially equal" to those of a senior bidder (*Kansas City Power & Light Co.*, 104 LA 857, where an arbitrator held an employer could not promote a junior employee based on an ability test results; see also 97 LA 968, 96 LA 976, 96 LA 670, 90 LA 1020).

● An employer was not allowed to promote a Grade C electrician to a Grade B vacancy for which a Senior Grade B man was available, despite the employer's contention the senior employee took an unreasonably long time to perform certain tasks and sometimes wasted time. The arbitrator held the senior employee was reasonably capable of performing the higher-rated work, even though he was deficient in some of the qualifications that would make him an employee of the highest caliber (*American Monorail Co.*, 21 LA 589).

● Where contracts require promotion by seniority if "merit and ability are approximately equal," arbitrators will consider those other relevant factors (also, see below under specific categories) (96 LA 338; see also 94 LA 562, 94 LA 266, 90 LA 562, 89 LA 1288, 89 LA 1035, 88 LA 420, 86 LA 111, 85 LA 393).

**Burden of proof**—Where seniority is a determining factor only when ability is relatively equal, arbitrators have held that management has the burden of proving, when challenged, that it determined ability correctly, not merely that it did not act in an arbitrary, capricious, or discriminatory fashion. It must be shown that the selection was "reasonable," as well as free from arbitrariness, favoritism, or bias (44 LA 283, 42 LA 1093).

● One arbitrator ruled that the employer's burden of proof extended to showing that: (1) the standards for comparison of job bidders' qualifications were established in good faith; (2) the standards were not patently inadequate; (3) the standards were applied fairly and impartially; and (4) a decision favoring a junior employee was not clearly unreasonable (*Atlas Powder Co.*, 30 LA 674).

**Experience as a factor**—Experience has a definite place in determining comparative fitness, ability, and qualifications. And the experience factor need not be limited to prior experience of the job in question. Arbitrators have upheld giving preference to a junior employee where the experience of the junior employee is more closely related to the work involved than the experience of the senior employee (93 LA 233, 84 LA 23, 83 LA 960, 83 LA 317).

● Under a contract providing that seniority would govern provided qualifications were equal, an employer was justified in promoting a junior employee with two years experience in the particular field over a senior employee with only 10 days experience, an arbitrator ruled. The union did not attempt to argue that the senior employee was as qualified as the junior one, but relied on a clause providing that seniority would govern if the senior employee could perform the job. However, even under this clause, the arbitrator concluded that it was doubtful that the senior employee could have qualified for the job within 10 days, given that this was only as long as the traditional trial period for new jobs at the plant (*Greif Brothers Corp.*, 64 LA 1219).

● Under a contract making seniority controlling in promotion where ability to perform the work and physical fitness are relatively equal, one arbitrator said that proved ability, not potential ability, was the test for selection. Even if potential ability is about the same between two bidders, he held, management can promote the junior man if he alone can step in and take over the job immediately.

In this case, two jobs had opened up in a plant and the employer posted notices of the vacancies in accordance with its general policy. The employer made promotions on the basis of a person's ability to perform work, physical fitness, and seniority where the first two factors were equal. The employer assigned two junior employees to fill the vacancy of weighman, truck sales, bypassing several applicants having greater seniority. The arbitrator ruled for the employer. He pointed out that under the ability clause the employer had the right to select the junior employee with demonstrated ability, as proved by experience on the job, rather than one who had never actually performed the job and had never demonstrated the particular skills that the job called for (*Pittsburgh Limestone Corp.*, 6 LA 648; see also 50 LA 445).

• Under a contract requiring that a vacancy be filled by the employee with most seniority where skill and ability are equal, the employer was not justified in promoting an employee with less seniority, even though he had experience in the other departments. The arbitrator reasoned that this experience was fully balanced by the senior bidder's higher educational accomplishments (*Lockheed-Georgia Co.*, 49 LA 603; see also 72 LA 1167).

• Where the contract called for promotions to be awarded to "qualified senior employees," an employer improperly failed to promote the most senior employee, an arbitrator ruled. Management argued that the senior employee did not meet her supervisor's requirements. However, the arbitrator noted that the evidence showed that the supervisor had told all four promotion candidates that they would "do quite well," and that he "wished he could employ all four," but had only one vacancy (*Clinch Valley Clinic Hospital*, 64 LA 542; see also 75 LA 1024, 74 LA 266).

*Aptitude/ability as a factor*—Under a contract making seniority and aptitude factors in promotion, an arbitrator held that an employer could not refuse a senior employee a promotion on the ground that he was not able to perform the job at the time. Choosing a junior man for the promotion was not justified even if he was the only one able to perform the job, the arbitrator said. There was no reason to think the senior men could not have learned it. "Aptitude," the arbitrator said, means the potential to learn a job, and the bidder with the highest seniority should have been given a trial period to determine whether he had the aptitude (*Vulcan Mold & Iron Co.*, 29 LA 743).

• An arbitrator held an employer's promotion of a junior bidder to a lead person position did not violate a collective bargaining agreement that specified jobs should be awarded to the bidder with the greatest seniority who had the required

qualifications. Even though the junior and senior bidders for the job were virtually equal in critical skills, the arbitrator found the senior bidder lacked certain important qualities: the ability to work well with supervision and a superior attitude toward quality (*Spontex Inc.*, 105 LA 254).

• An arbitrator held an employer's promotion of a 13-year employee over a 17-year employee for a leader position did not violate a collective bargaining agreement, where the employer had rated the less senior employee higher in initiative, as well as communication and interpersonal skills (*Nordson Corp.*, 104 LA 1206).

*Education as a factor*—Arbitrators generally agree that employers may consider an employee's education when deciding whether or not to promote the employee (96 LA 201, 94 LA 463, 88 LA 1035, 86 LA 943, 82 LA 851).

• An arbitrator held that under a contract that provided that where skill, work record, and ability of bidders are equal in the judgment of the employer, seniority shall prevail, an employer properly awarded a posted job of plant engineer to a junior employee who had performed the duties of the job for eight months to one year prior to the job posting and had B.A. and M.A. degrees, instead of awarding the job to a senior employee who had never performed the job duties (*South Central Rural Telephone Cooperative Corp.*, 81 LA 594).

*Poor attendance record as a factor*—An arbitrator held an employer properly denied a senior employee a promotion to a team-leader position based on his poor attendance record because the employee worked for the employer two days per week and a union for three days per week. The arbitrator reasoned the position required a high degree of regular attendance and the employee's record with the employer was poor as a result of his dual status, and there was no evidence the employee was willing to make himself available to work full time as a team leader (*USS-Minnesota Ore Operations*, 101 LA 124).

*Determining 'ability'*—Arbitrators differ on the problem of what factors can be taken into consideration in determining "ability" to do a job. Thus, one arbitrator has expressed the view that management must confine its determination to whether the employee is capable of handling the job at hand; how he gets along with other people, his attendance record, and other considerations do not count (*McQuay-Norris Mfg. Co.*, 1 LA 305).

Some arbitrators, though, are inclined to give management more latitude.

• One arbitrator upheld the employer's rejection of a union steward for promotion. The contract gave management a free hand in judging the ability and qualifications of employees; as long as it honestly believed another man could do the job better, the arbitrator ruled, its judgment could not be upset. Taking note of quarrels between the steward and management representatives, the arbitrator saw no evidence of anti-union discrimination because the quarrels had no direct connection with union business (*Norwich Pharmaceutical Co.*, 30 LA 740; see also 98 LA 134, 98 LA 117, 85 LA 721, 73 LA 1215, 72 LA 752).

If a contract requires that both seniority and individual ability be taken into account in making promotions, arbitrators usually will not substitute their own judgment of employees' ability for management's. Most of them seem to try to strike a balance between management's right to judge ability and employees' seniority rights. Generally they uphold the employer's judgment unless it is found to be discriminatory, arbitrary, or erroneous. They rule that it is the union's responsibility to prove that management's judgment was faulty.

• One arbitrator upheld the employer's choosing of a junior applicant due to his superior overall job experience. The contract did not indicate the order of importance of the three factors—seniority, ability, and previous experience—in job assignment; thus, he overruled the union's contention that these criteria are in descending order of importance (*Reliance Universal Inc.*, 50 LA 397).

• Another contract required the employer to recognize seniority as a determining factor in promotion only if "consistent with the ability to perform the required work." In this case, the employer first promoted, but then terminated the trial periods of senior employees who, it argued, were clearly not qualified. The employees took nine days to complete a four-day electrical wiring job, then caused the flooding of a basement floor through negligence and finally connected a ground wire to a live circuit, the employer maintained.

Despite the union's argument that the employer improperly assigned the employees to work with other trainees instead of with experienced electricians, the arbitrator upheld management's decision. The union's proposal was self-defeating because the contract required that job applicants have a minimum of one year's experience in the field, the arbitrator reasoned, agreeing with management that the trial period clearly demonstrated the employees' incompetence (*ICI United States Inc.*, 65 LA 869; see also 74 LA 962).

***Probationer versus senior worker—*** Even where seniority was only a secondary factor, one arbitrator ruled that management could not promote a probationer who had better qualifications. The contract stated that in selecting employees for promotion, three factors would be considered—seniority, ability, and physical fitness: Where the last two factors were relatively equal, seniority would govern.

The employer had no authority to promote the probationary employee, the arbitrator said, even though he was the best qualified of the bidding employees. The reason was that he had no seniority, and in the arbitrator's opinion the agreement required that a man possess all three promotion elements in some degree to be considered for promotion. As long as employees with seniority had bid for the job, the arbitrator concluded, the probationer was not eligible (*Borden Chemical Co.*, 32 LA 697).

***Selection for training leading to promotion—***If a contract provides that promotion will be based on seniority where ability is equal, can management choose a junior employee for special training leading to a promotion? One arbitrator ruled that without a clear understanding with the union beforehand an employer had to follow seniority in selecting employees for training that would lead to promotion.

• An employer decided to give special training in inspection procedures. Although it admitted that the ability of two candidates for the training was equal, the junior employee of the two was picked. After completing the course, she was assigned to a newly created higher-rated job. When the senior employee protested, the employer consulted with the union and agreed to give the senior employee the special training. However, after finishing the course she was denied the disputed job on the ground that its requirements had changed in the interim.

The arbitrator maintained that in this case the employer was under an obligation to show the union at the outset that it genuinely needed flexibility in developing the new job and was not trying to bypass seniority rules. Because management failed to do this and let the matter drift, the arbitrator ordered the employer to pay the senior employee the earnings she lost by not being selected initially for the special training (*Purolator Products Inc.*, 25 LA 60).

• In another case, an arbitrator held that requiring a high school education or its equivalent was a reasonable requirement for promotional training, but that a 30-year age cutoff for bidders was too low. The educational requirement was sustained because it related to the need for mathematical ability on the job. Because the contract referred to age 65 as retirement age, the arbitrator said that employees completing the training course could have enough years of useful work left to repay the employer's investment, even if the employees were older than 30 (*Ball Bros. Co.*, 46 LA 1153).

*Promotion of union official*—Can an otherwise qualified union representative be denied promotion on the ground that the time he spends on union affairs during working hours limits his ability to do the job? Unless past practice has been to restrict the promotion of union officials

engaged in their duties during the working day, an employer cannot deny promotion to an employee who is otherwise qualified on the basis of his seniority and ability, one arbitration board said.

• Two employees at an employer were promoted to leadman jobs ahead of a union steward who had more seniority and more than enough ability to do the work. The employer justified its action in bypassing the steward by saying that although he was qualified for the job in every respect, he spent too much time on union business to be able to do the leadman's job satisfactorily.

A board of arbitration decided that only the presence of an established past practice limiting the promotion of union representatives could justify the bypassing of the union steward. They found no such practice at the employer and accordingly decided that the steward should have received the promotion (*Douglas Aircraft Co.*, 23 LA 786).

• When an employee who had shown her ability to perform a job was denied the position because she could not devote full time to it due to her union duties, an arbitrator said the employer had unfairly discriminated against the union. He further said that if employees "find that their union positions are handicaps in obtaining preferred job assignments, it will become practically impossible for the union to attract the leadership it needs to carry on its work" (*American Lava Corp.*, 42 LA 117; see also 72 LA 1151).

*Compulsory promotion*—Must an employee accept a promotion to a vacancy for which he is eligible against his own wishes? Under one contract stating that a promotion shall be given to the senior eligible employee in the department, an arbitrator held that all this required was that the employer offer the vacant job to the senior employee. He was not obligated to accept it, and if he turned it down, the arbitrator ruled, it should have been offered to the next senior qualified employee (*Electro Metallurgical Co.*, 20 LA 281).

• Another arbitrator decided that if the right to waive a promotion is not spelled out in the contract, management normally has the right to make promotions regardless of employee desires. This is true, he noted, provided the employees' job security and seniority are not jeopardized (*Gisholt Machine Co.*, 23 LA 105).

## Promotion To Supervisory Position

*Employer's right to select supervisors*—Most arbitrators agree that management has the exclusive right to select its supervisors without union interference. They limit the application of contract clauses dealing with promotion to those jobs covered by the union contract or that fall within the bargaining unit. And they specifically point out that because supervisory positions are not within the bargaining unit management has the sole and exclusive right to fill them as it sees fit (52 LA 1183, 52 LA 463, 40 LA 321, 6 LA 16).

• When management ignores seniority to promote a highly qualified employee to a supervisory position over a more senior, but unqualified, employee, it can expect the arbitrator to rule in its favor, absent any explicit contract language that would give the union valid grounds for complaint (*SCM Corp.*, 58 LA 688).

• When the contract does contain explicit language governing promotion to supervisory positions, management is more open to challenge from the union. One such contract provided that the employer "will normally promote its own men in accordance with seniority and qualifications to supervisory positions." When the employer selected for promotion the most junior employee out of 45 applicants, while passing over two long-term employees with supervisory experience, the union protested, and the arbitrator ruled against the employer.

The arbitrator rejected management's argument that the junior employee's "ambition" was so great a qualification that it compensated for his extremely short length of service. Furthermore, the arbitrator found little evidence to support management's claim that the employee had sufficient "drive" for the job and that more senior employees lacked this

"drive" (*British Overseas Airways Corp.*, 52 LA 165).

*Retention of duties after promotion to supervisor*—Is an employer permitted to have an employee who is made a supervisor perform the same work he did while in the bargaining unit? One arbitrator ruled that because an employee's duties while in the unit were largely supervisory in nature, an employer could assign him the same work after he became a supervisor. Because his duties were largely supervisory, the arbitrator found no merit in the union's argument that work was being taken from the bargaining unit. He said that the union should have objected earlier when the employee was assigned the duties while still in the bargaining unit, not when he became a supervisor (*Chrysler Corp.*, 23 LA 247).

• An arbitrator approved management's transfer of some of an employee's old duties from the bargaining unit to his new job as a supervisor. The arbitrator found that the duties the employee carried with him to his new job were supervisory in nature, and that those functions not supervisory in nature had in fact been transferred to other employees remaining in the bargaining unit (*Crown Zellerbach Corp.*, 52 LA 1183).

## Promotion or New Hire

*Passing over qualified bidder*—Unless the contract shows an intent to give employees preference over outsiders, one arbitrator has held that management is not required to promote from within.

• One union filed a protest when management hired an outsider to fill a designing job. A draftsman already working for the employer wanted the job, and the union claimed he had the necessary ability. Given that the contract stated that promotions were to be based on seniority and ability, the union argued, the inside man was entitled to be promoted.

There was some disagreement as to the adequacy of the draftsman's qualifications, but the arbitrator said this aspect of the case was irrelevant in any event. The important thing, he held, was that the contract placed no restriction on outside hiring. The contract only outlined the procedure to be followed if the employer decided to fill a job through promotion, the arbitrator noted. If the parties had intended to give present employees preference over outsiders, the arbitrator concluded, they should have said so in the agreement (*Chrysler Corp.*, 32 LA 988; see also 85 LA 190, 85 LA 73, 84 LA 956, 84 LA 952, 72 LA 719).

• Where a contract required consideration of unit employees on the basis of seniority and qualifications, an employer could not hire outside where several unit bidders were qualified to fill a vacancy. The arbitrator reasoned that the posting provision would be meaningless if the employer could hire from the outside or promote from within as it pleased, rejecting qualified unit applicants (*The Burdick Corp.*, 49 LA 69).

• A city violated its recognition clause, an arbitrator ruled, when its department of public works hired new employees instead of promoting from within to fill new street-sweeper machine-operator positions. The arbitrator reasoned that when the city hired the new employees, they became part of the bargaining unit, and hence subject to past practice. In this case, the past practice that had developed in the department's promotional training program dictated that new sweeper operator's jobs should go to certified operators with the greatest seniority. Thus, although the actual hirings may have been proper, the placement of new hires in the operator's jobs was not, the arbitrator concluded (*City of Milwaukee*, 65 LA 833; see also 75 LA 511, 73 LA 1218).

***Hiring from outside when bidders lack ability***—If a contract requires the employer to fill vacancies on the basis of seniority, assuming capacity to perform the work, can an employee be hired from the outside to fill a job? Most arbitrators rule that under such a provision an employer can hire from the outside to fill a vacancy when no present employee is capable of performing the job.

• To fill a vacancy on a maintenance job an employer posted notice of the vacancy for bids. Of the twelve employees

that bid, eleven agreed that they lacked the qualifications for the job; the twelfth was noncommittal and failed to press his claim. Under these conditions the employer hired a new employee to fill the vacancy. The union opposed this action arguing that one of the bidders should have been given a trial period on the job.

The employer replied that it had always been its policy to bring in men from the bottom and train them and then upgrade them to top skills rather than bring new men in at the top. But in this case, the employer pointed out, there was no one available to upgrade who would be able to handle the job and in such an exceptional case it was necessary to resort to outside hiring.

The arbitration board ruled that "the circumstances warranted the employer, in this case, from all the evidence, in departing from its usual and commendable procedure of upgrading and giving full opportunity to men within its own plant." The board found that because the bidders were not qualified for the job the employer was justified in filling the job by new hire (*Atlantic Foundry Co.*, 8 LA 807; see also 96 LA 1105, 82 LA 1273, 40 LA 403, 31 LA 267).

• An arbitrator upheld an employer's outside hiring when none of the four in-house bidders for a millwright's position could attest to their qualifications when asked to do so. The union argued that senior employees were to be given preference for all job openings provided they could learn to perform work within a reasonable period of time. However, the employer had proved his need for a millwright who could immediately perform complex duties, the arbitrator noted, pointing out that none of the in-house bidders would have been proficient even after several months (*Kerns Desoto Inc.*, 64 LA 1125).

• When an employer's determination that in-house candidates are unqualified to fill a vacancy is made in good faith, he may not even be required to interview them for the position, an arbitrator has ruled. (*Walker Mfg. Co.*, 62 LA 1283).

***Hiring outside applicant who has more training/ability***—Under a contract requiring that promotions be based on length of service, training, and efficiency, one arbitrator ruled that previous training could not be a requirement for promotion to an apprentice job. He said that an employer could not hire a new man in preference to a senior employee merely because the senior employee had not graduated from a vocational school.

• One employer selected an outside applicant for an apprenticeship instead of promoting an employee to it. After deciding that the apprenticeship itself was a training program, an arbitrator awarded the vacancy to the untrained employee instead of to the outsider who had completed a vocational training program.

To deny an employee the opportunity to enter the apprenticeship program, the arbitrator said, would nullify the purpose of the program. According to the arbitrator, the selection of an apprentice should be made on the basis of length of service and efficiency, without regard to the training factor. The employer, he said, could not have both an apprenticeship program and a requirement that applicants have prior training (*Hershey Estates*, 23 LA 101).

# Measurement of Ability

## OVERVIEW

In the absence of a contract provision for the method to be used or the factors to be considered in determining ability, management has been permitted (or required) to use a variety of methods and to consider a number of factors, including: the use of performance or aptitude tests; a trial period on the job; reliance on a merit rating plan or on the opinion of a supervisor; consideration of production records, disciplinary records; or absenteeism, education, experience, physical fitness, age, and potential for further advancement.

Arbitrators have held that an employer is entitled to use any method at its disposal to determine ability, as long as the method used is fair and nondiscriminatory (*Ohio Department of Transportation, State of*, 103 LA 225 and *Bowater Inc.*, 103 LA 1000; see also 93 LA 874, 93 LA 961, 90 LA 1103).

Any test used to screen job applicants should be designed to measure qualities that have been shown to be related to performance on that particular job. Tests that are not validated for job-relatedness not only are wasteful, but also may violate fair-employment laws if they end up screening out minority groups.

## SUMMARY OF CASES

### Written Tests as Measure of Ability

Whether or not an arbitrator approves the use of a written test to determine employees' ability in making promotions seems to depend largely on the weight the contract gives to seniority in filling vacancies.

If a contract makes seniority the governing factor when fitness and ability are equal, many arbitrators allow the employer to require employees seeking promotions to take written tests. Under this kind of clause the employer has to measure the relative or comparative ability of candidates for a job, and an objective written test is a fair way to do this, these arbitrators hold (*M. A. Hanna Co.*, 25 LA 480; see also 97 LA 244, 97 LA 86, 96 LA 17).

● A frequently expressed view is that an employer may use tests to aid in deciding whether an applicant meets the job requirements, but that the test results may not be relied on to the exclusion of other considerations (29 LA 262, 29 LA 29).

● An employer could use two aptitude tests in judging an employee's qualification for a job, even though the tests were never used in the past and the contract did not expressly permit them. The employer promised that the tests would not be used to pass or fail an applicant, but only as additional criteria in judging an employee's qualification; and despite the employer's decision regarding the applicant, the individual would have the right to redress under the grievance procedure (*Union Carbon Co.*, 49 LA 465; see also 47 LA 552).

● One arbitrator said an employer could use such a test if it were fairly applied and management did not use minute differences in scores to deny promotion to senior employees (*Stauffer Chemical Co. Inc.*, 8 LA 278; see also 49 LA 589, 41 LA 902).

● If a contract states that all vacancies shall be filled by the senior applicant provided he has the ability and physical fitness to perform the job, an arbitrator may rule against the use of a test.

One arbitrator held that this kind of clause did not permit the employer to promote an employee because he was better qualified for the job than employees with more seniority. The arbitrator ruled that, because the senior employee had to be given the job if he or she could do the work satisfactorily, the employer could not base promotion on the results of a written test (*Marquette Cement Mfg. Co.*, 25 LA 127; see also 41 LA 856).

• Arbitrators generally uphold management's right to use tests that have been specifically designed to determine an employee's ability to perform a certain job. However, they also hold that aptitude tests not directly related to the work in question properly should be used by management only in the selection of new employees, in counseling employees, or in other general uses. But such general tests should not be used as a standard for denying a senior employee a promotion (52 LA 633, 43 LA 1184, 41 LA 1025, 34 LA 46, 31 LA 1002).

• In a ruling against the use of a general aptitude test for promotions, one arbitrator said that "men were denied promotions not for lack of ability to perform the work but for lack of ability to pass written tests having little or no relationship to the jobs sought." It is quite conceivable, he said, that the employer's best bricklayer could not pass a written test on bricklaying. He gave these ground rules.

• If a job does not require the ability to read and write, no written test whatever may be given.

• If a job requires ability to read and to copy words and figures, a written test must be limited to testing ability to read and copy words and figures.

• If it requires simple arithmetic, the test must be only of simple arithmetic (34 LA 37).

• An arbitrator held that an employer improperly imposed testing requirements on two candidates for reclassification to master mechanic, where they had spent the required time in lower classifications and stated that they met other agreed-upon qualifications, and, moreover, neither had been disciplined on a

matter of competency, and the employer's past practice had been to presume the competency of otherwise-qualified candidates absent such discipline (*Palm Iron & Bridge Works*, 97 LA 681).

## Screening Resumes Prior to Test

An arbitrator held an employer's screening of resumes to eliminate applicants prior to a written test did not violate a collective bargaining agreement, despite a provision in the parties' agreement requiring promotion based on fitness as determined by competitive examination and to give "strong consideration" to qualified workers (*City of St. Petersburg*, 104 LA 136).

## Number of Required Tests

How many tests should an employee be required to take while being considered for a promotion?

• After a senior employee obtained a low qualifying score on a state-sponsored aptitude test, the employer gave him the employer's exam as well. The union charged that the employer was not determining qualifications in a "uniform manner," and that because specific pass and fail grades were not released by the state, the employee should have been awarded the job as the senior man.

The arbitrator upheld management's second test for the employee. Given that the state test was deficient as a selection criterion, and because the employer test was directly related to the requirements of the job, it was proper for management to act as it did, the arbitrator ruled (*International Steel Co.*, 64 LA 1093).

## Refusal to Administer Test

When a written test is properly used to screen job bidders, may an employer refuse to administer the test to employees who have failed it in the past? One arbitrator has ruled no.

• An employer refused to administer a test to a job bidder for a newly created position because the applicant had failed the test when it was given as a requirement for other promotions. Management argued that allowing the employee to retake the identical test whenever new job postings were made would enable the employee to pass the test because of his familiarity with the questions rather than because of increased knowledge gained through experience or education.

The arbitrator reasoned that the tests were not given to ascertain an applicant's knowledge of the subjects on which he is being tested, but rather to determine his aptitude to learn. Therefore, the arbitrator concluded, all employees who bid on jobs that require them to pass tests should have the opportunity to take the required tests after they have signed bids and before the jobs are awarded (*Dayton-Walther Corp.*, 65 LA 529).

## Testing and EEOC

Although arbitrators may be more inclined to permit the use of general aptitude tests for new hires, EEOC looks with equal disfavor on the use of such tests for hiring and for promotions. In either case, EEOC has said (with Supreme Court approval) use of the test may be justified only if it can be shown that success on the test is statistically correlated with success on the job.

## Oral Exam/Interview to Determine Qualifications

In a situation where the contract does not specify any method to be used to determine employees' qualifications for promotion, one arbitrator has said that an employer has the right to use any method it sees fit, including oral examinations and interviews. But the test should be related to the skill and knowledge required for the job and otherwise not be unfair or unreasonable.

● A contract required the employer to consider for promotion only those employees "who are deemed qualified to do the work." When a job opening occurred in the top classification in one department, one employee in the department was given an oral test by the foreman to determine whether he was qualified for the job. He failed to pass the exam and was denied the job. The union took the matter up as a grievance, arguing that the test was unfair because there was no prescribed standard exam and no written job description on which the test could be based.

The arbitrator upheld the employer's action. Because the contract did not specify a particular method for determining whether an employee was qualified for promotion, he said that it was okay to use an oral exam. Furthermore, he found that the test was a fair one, partly because all employees then in the job had previously passed the same test (*Hammarlund Mfg. Co. Inc.*, 19 LA 653).

● Another arbitrator held an employer improperly promoted a junior employee on the basis of a subjective oral interview (*Madison Metropolitan School District*, 103 LA 652).

## Physical Tests to Determine Ability

Because arbitrators are more likely to uphold the use of the tests that are clearly reflective of the work to be performed than tests that have little relation to the job, physical tests may be easier to defend as a basis for determining ability in manual jobs.

● An employer denied a black female employee a promotion after she failed the physical exam for the job. The union argued that the employer violated the contract that called for promotions to be based on "ability, physical fitness, and continuous service."

The arbitrator upheld management's action. The employee was properly denied the promotion, the arbitrator said, because she failed to meet the requirements of the job—i.e., passing the physical exam. Because there was no evidence that the exam reflected racial or sexual discrimination on the employer's part, the grievance was dismissed (*United States Steel Corp.*, 65 LA 626; see also 96 LA 1033, 76 LA 432, 75 LA 148).

## Merit Rating & Efficiency Rating as Measures of Ability

Some arbitrators have upheld management's right to use the results of a formal merit rating plan in selecting employees for promotion.

● Under a contract requiring the promotion of the senior employee where ability was relatively equal, one arbitrator said that one employer's merit-rating plan was an acceptable method of measuring relative ability (*Acme Steel Co.*, 9 LA 432).

## Aptitude Tests as Prerequisite to Trial Period

Is an employer justified in requiring bidders for better jobs to pass aptitude tests before being given a tryout on the job? Where training employees for better jobs is an expensive process, arbitrators are likely to uphold the use of tests to screen out applicants who cannot show the aptitude that would warrant the expense of a tryout, even though as senior employees, they would have first bid for the jobs. But the tests should be objective and should measure, as far as possible, the aptitude for the jobs involved (*United Rayon Mills*, 14 LA 241; see also 90 LA 1282).

● Where a contract specifically provided for a trial period, an arbitrator ruled that the employer had no right to turn down the senior bidder for a job simply because she had failed a mathematical test (*National Seal Co.*, 29 LA 29).

● An employer was overruled when he sought to administer a mechanical-aptitude test to the senior employee before granting him a promotion under a contract clause awarding promotions on the basis of seniority. The employer unsuccessfully argued that the test was proper in light of the employee's lack of experience at the new job. The arbitrator voided the test requirement and awarded the job to the employee subject to his successful completion of a reasonable trial period (*Monarch Tool Co.*, 65 LA 150).

● An employer was held to have violated the contract when it promoted a junior employee to a new position of electrical trainee on the ground that he was the only applicant who passed a written test showing extent of electrical knowledge. The arbitrator ruled that the test used was not a fair measure of ability to perform the job because the position was created to give employees a chance to develop electrical skills (*Vulcan Materials Co.*, 49 LA 577; see also 49 LA 1160).

● Another arbitrator approved management's use of a test to select candidates for an electrical training program. The arbitrator found the test a valid reflector of probable success in the training program, and noted that the contract left management free to determine qualifications for the program. The selected employee was junior to a passed-over applicant, but because the contract did not specifically make seniority a factor, this was irrelevant, the arbitrator added (*International Steel Co.*, 64 LA 1093).

● An employer did not violate a contract when it administered an aptitude test to applicants for a training program, another arbitrator ruled, emphasizing that the test would screen out those who had little likelihood of learning the complex skills taught in the program. The arbitrator concluded that the test was fair and reasonable, administered without discrimination, and validated to meet government requirements (*Celanese Piping Systems Inc.*, 64 LA 462).

## Trial Period to Test Ability

When is a senior employee entitled to a chance to prove himself on a job for which he is bidding? Arbitrators' awards suggest that a trial period may be in order, in appropriate circumstances, under two common types of promotion clauses.

*Seniority Controlling if Bidder Able to Perform Work*—The first is a provision that makes seniority determining in promotions if the senior bidder is able to perform the work.

● Under one contract providing that seniority should govern in promotions if the senior employee "has the competency for the job," an arbitrator held that a senior employee should have been given a breaking-in period to prove he was able to do the job. The employer had passed over the senior man and promoted a more competent junior employee who was able to do the job without a breaking-in period because of his past experience. This was immaterial, the arbitrator said. He pointed out that the contract required the employer to promote the most senior applicant who was competent, not the most competent applicant. Thus, the senior employee should be given a trial period to prove whether he could perform the job, the arbitrator ruled (*Beaunit Mills Inc.*, 16 LA 667).

***Seniority Controlling if Ability of Bidders Relatively Equal***—The second type of promotion clause is one that makes seniority controlling where ability is relatively equal. When an employer has no objective measure of relative ability under such a provision, some arbitrators say that a trial period is the best way to clear up any doubts about the ability of the senior bidder.

• In one case, when a hoist-operation job opened up, the supervisor gave it to an employee in preference to an older man with more seniority. His reason was that he felt the latter employee was too old to handle the job. An arbitrator pointed out that this employee was strong and rugged and his supervisor's doubt as to his ability did not justify bypassing him for promotion. Given that the supervisor's decision was based on such a weak assumption the arbitrator said the employee should be given a chance to prove his ability on the job. He concluded that although a trial was not necessary in all cases it should not be denied where there was a reasonable doubt of ability and where it would cause no serious inconvenience (*Ford Motor Co.*, 2 LA 374).

### Trial Period versus Training Period

If a contract provides a trial period for promoted employees and makes seniority a factor in promotion, must management give the senior applicant for a job a trial period even though he is not qualified for the job?

According to one arbitrator, there is a big difference between a *trial* period and a *training* period. A trial period must be granted only after an employee has been selected for promotion, he said, and this rules out those who do not have the necessary qualifications.

• Besides granting a 12-day trial period to employees who were promoted to higher-rated jobs, one contract said that seniority would be the determining factor in promotion, "all circumstances being reasonably equal." When the employer

bypassed the senior bidder for a job requiring some special preparation and experience, the union lodged a complaint. It conceded the junior man was qualified and that the senior man was not, but it argued that the latter should have been given an opportunity to prove he could handle the job.

The arbitrator disagreed. The contract did not entitle the senior bidder to a period of on-the-job training, he said. Management was essentially correct in arguing that the trial period became available only after an employee had been selected for promotion. However, the arbitrator warned, management must be prepared to justify the denial of a trial period to a senior bidder (*Colonial Baking Co.*, 34 LA 356; see also 74 LA 962, 73 LA 937, 39 LA 336).

### Length of Trial Period

How long a period of training should an employee be allowed to show that he can perform a higher-rated job? To a large extent, the answer to this question depends on the job to which the employee is being promoted.

• In one case, an arbitrator held that five weeks was not long enough to provide an adequate measure of an employee's ability as a crane operator and awarded him an additional two weeks (*Lukens Steel Co.*, 18 LA 41; see also 71 LA 1171).

• An arbitrator ruled that three months was a reasonable period in which to determine whether an admittedly qualified employee had the proper temperament for the higher-rated job of floor inspector (*Seeger Refrigerator Co.*, 16 LA 525; see also 75 LA 1101, 73 LA 935).

• It has been held that if a trial period for promoted employees is established, it should be well defined and applied equally to all employees (*Consolidated Water Co.*, 23 LA 427).

### Past Performance as Measure of Ability

Arbitrators' decisions suggest that an employee's record of on-the-job performance should be regarded as a key indicator of ability.

• Under one contract providing for job transfers based on seniority where knowledge, training, and ability were substantially equal, an arbitrator held that a supervisor's preference could not overrule evidence of a senior employee's on-the-job ability. When two employees bid for a maintenance mechanic job, the junior man was promoted on the basis of the supervisor's judgment of knowledge, training, and ability. The arbitrator found that the senior employee had performed the job satisfactorily in the past and this was more objective evidence of ability than the supervisor's opinion. On the ground that their work experience showed that the two men were relatively equal in skill, knowledge, and ability, the arbitrator concluded that the senior man should be promoted (*Plymouth Cordage Co.*, 27 LA 816).

● Failure to make the grade during a previous trial on a job is enough evidence that an employee is not capable of handling the job, according to one arbitrator. In such an event, he said, an employee is not entitled to a second trial period (*Republic Steel Corp.*, 3 LA 761).

## Lack of Interest as Measure of Ability

Can a senior employee be bypassed for promotion because he shows lack of interest in his work? Arbitrators have ruled that "lack of interest" cannot be considered in measuring ability, particularly where it seems to be temporary and not consistent with the employee's usual attitude.

● A contract required that the senior employee be given preference in promotions where abilities were equal. In filling the job of "Job Foreman," the employer bypassed a senior employee on the ground that he showed a "lack of interest" in his work. The union filed a grievance arguing that because the abilities of the two men were equal the senior employee should have gotten the job. The arbitrator agreed with the union contention. He ruled "that interest in work or lack of interest in work is a matter of incentive to exercise ability or capacity and is not one of the norms for measuring ability." The arbitrator then went on to point out that this lack of interest in the present case was a temporary condition apparently contrary to the employee's customary attitude so far as could be determined from his total job history. Therefore, because abilities were equal, the arbitrator held that the senior employee should have been given the promotion (*Ford Motor Co.*, 7 LA 324).

● Another arbitrator upheld management's decision to pass over for promotion a senior employee whose performance in his present job was only marginal, who had been demoted from four other positions, and who had declined to take a job-related test to demonstrate his ability. The arbitrator reasoned that because management had a responsibility to determine whether the employee was qualified for the promotion, the union's argument urging him to ignore the employee's past record could not be upheld (*United States Steel Corp.*, 64 LA 639).

## Sex Discrimination in Weighing Ability

Arbitrators generally acknowledge that a female employee has the right to bid on a job traditionally held by male employees. Yet, many arbitrators, in determining whether an employee's job classification has been adversely affected because of sex discrimination, have refused to encroach upon management's recognized rights to judge employment qualifications and to determine job content (67 LA 833, 67 LA 23, 66 LA 180, 66 LA 1276, 62 LA 1294).

● In one case, an arbitrator ruled that an employer did not discriminate against a senior female clerk-stenographer when it failed to promote her to senior accounting clerk. The job, instead, was awarded to a male applicant in the accounting department who had five years of experience in the accounting field. Finding that the employer properly determined that the qualifications of the two applicants were not "reasonably equal" and that the female employee did not have "sufficient" ability to fill the job, the arbitrator held that no discrimination occurred (*Missouri Utilities Co.*, 68 LA 379).

• Another arbitrator held that an employer violated a contractual anti-discrimination clause when it disqualified a female employee because she could not perform the job's required duties. Noting that the employer had engaged in a pattern of sex discrimination that made it impossible for the employee to receive a fair training period, the arbitrator observed that the dispute displayed "classic socio-psychological motives" in terms of male resentment of the "real competition" represented by the female employee (*Braniff Airways Inc.*, 66 LA 421).

---

# Transfer

## OVERVIEW

Collective bargaining agreements seldom provide special procedures applicable to the general subject of permanent transfer; however, sometimes special transfer rights are given to disabled or older employees.

Temporary transfers present a different problem; in the absence of specific contract language, arbitrators usually have upheld the right of employers to assign employees to new and different tasks on a temporary basis, as long as those transfers do not violate seniority or other contractual rights. An important consideration in such cases often is whether the agreement contains a management clause that recognizes the employer's right to direct the workforce.

A transfer may take various forms, including requirements by employers that employees rotate among jobs within their classification, move from one shift to another, move from one job to another in a different classification at the same level, or move to a new machine or a new location on the same job.

Although some bargaining agreements make the right to transfer employees subject to other conditions in order to protect employees' seniority or other contractual rights, arbitrators generally require that any restrictions placed on the right to transfer be clearly stated in the agreement. Several arbitrators have held that an employer's right to transfer employees is not contingent on the employees' willingness to be transferred (*Crescent Metal Products*, 104 LA 724; see also 73 LA 372).

Various justifications have been accepted by arbitrators in upholding transfers required by management, including:

- business needs—e.g., reduction in work, technological changes (94 LA 632, 76 LA 516, 67 LA 702, 66 LA 671, 62 LA 1200);
- the employee's presence in a given job creates some undue hazard for him or herself or other employees (92 LA 833, 64 LA 24);
- a breakdown in machinery makes it necessary to transfer an employee to another job or another machine (*Eagle-Picher Industries Inc.*, 65 LA 1108);
- incompetence (62 LA 798, 45 LA 229); or
- personality clash (79 LA 203, 69 LA 1138, 67 LA 509, 67 LA 271).

## SUMMARY OF CASES

### Permanent Transfer

Permanent transfers may be made at the employer's insistence (*Small Business Association*, 66 LA 1017), the employee's request (67 LA 509, 64 LA 316), or on the advice of a supervisor. Whether a permanent transfer stems from an employer's decision or from an employee's request, the procedures involved with respect to measuring the employee's ability to perform the job and to apply seniority rules are similar to those used in cases involving promotions.

*Transfer to another plant or locality*—An arbitrator found that an employer violated a contract when it moved a junior employee into another employee's millwright job on a roller-plant "A" crew and transferred the other employee to a vacant leader-shift position on bearing-plant "D" crew without his consent. The contract required that out-of-occupation transfers—i.e., from millwright occupation to leader-shift occupation—be made by reassignment of the most junior employee when such transfers are not needed to fill vacancies not filled by bidding or voluntary transfer (*Timken Co.*, 97 LA 146; see also 91 LA 1377, 91 LA 181, 90 LA 1252, 89 LA 1101, 89 LA 201, 81 LA 382).

• An auto manufacturer was not bound to transfer employees from plants where certain models were discontinued to plants that still assembled those models. Because the same type of work was done at both plants, the arbitrator said, the "operations" had been transferred. Thus, the employer was not obligated by the contract to transfer the employees, he concluded (*Chrysler Corp.*, 43 LA 349).

• An arbitrator ruled that the permanent closure of a warehouse did not require the absorption of displaced employees by the parent employer. The arbitrator found that because the contract did not include the warehouse employees as part of the "company," the contract's seniority clause, for job-transfer purposes, excluded the warehouse employees (*March Wall Products*, 45 LA 551).

• An arbitrator held an employer did not violate a contract when it transferred a senior employee to a job in another building and assigned a junior employee to work on the employee's machine, even though the employer had not established a past practice of involuntary reassignment of the employee and his replacement by the junior employee, where: the contract gave the employer the right to assign its workforce and there was nothing in the contract providing for seniority entitlement to preference in performance of a particular task or in selecting a machine within a given classification (*Crescent Metal Products Inc.*, 104 LA 724).

***Transfer into and out of bargaining unit***—An arbitrator ruled that an employer did not violate a bargaining agreement when it temporarily transferred a bargaining-unit employee to perform nonbargaining-unit work on a voluntary basis, because the work in question was not bargaining-unit work (*Delfield Co.*, 96 LA 448; see also 97 LA 1035, 97 LA 48, 91 LA 181, 90 LA 228, 85 LA 511, 83 LA 458).

***Unit attrition by transfer***—Seniority need not prevent the transfer of an employee whose job performance is not satisfactory while retaining more able junior employees in the same classification, an arbitrator ruled. This was done as part of a general movement to streamline a telephone employer's desk unit. Because the general policy was aimed at upgrading the unit's performance level, the arbitrator felt the employer was justified in considering ability as well as seniority (*Southwestern Bell*, 45 LA 229).

***Transfer to job employee cannot handle***—Assuming management has an unrestricted right to transfer employees within occupational groups, can an employee complain if he or she is transferred to a job that the employee cannot perform, and then discharged for lack of qualifications?

• Arbitrators generally agree that where management is given the right to transfer personnel, it must be exercised reasonably. One arbitrator, for example, felt that transferring an employee to a job at which she had no prior experience and that she lacked the physical ability to do was unreasonable. The employee, he said, should not have been fired for failure to qualify for the job after a short trial period (*Curtiss-Wright Corp.*, 11 LA 139).

***Transfer for health reasons***—Can employees be transferred against their wishes for the purpose of protecting their health? In the absence of a specific contract restriction on transfers of this nature, it is likely that an arbitrator would uphold management's right to make such transfers where it is apparent that they are made in good faith, are not for discriminatory purposes, and are supported by reasonable medical findings.

• An employer transferred to a lighter (and lower-paying) job an employee who had undergone two operations. It did so on the advice of its plant physician, who said the employee could not safely handle his regular, heavy work. The employee wanted his regular job, however, and produced a note from his own physician saying he could return to work.

The arbitrator held that the transfer was proper. He declared that "management had an obligation to avoid exposing employees to undue hazards to their health or safety and that this obligation created a right, under a management-rights clause, to transfer an employee if his presence in a given occupation created an undue hazard for himself or others." The arbitrator considered it important that no discriminatory purpose was apparent in this case, that there was no question of bad faith, and finally, that the recommendation of transfer was made by the plant physician, who was more familiar with the types of work involved than the employee's personal doctor (*International Shoe Co.*, 14 LA 253).

• A machine operator, who was involved in an accident while operating a ground-controlled crane, was properly removed from the job, an arbitrator decided. A test revealed that the employee had zero depth perception, the arbitrator observed, pointing out that there was no provision in the contract that barred the employer from requiring relevant physical examinations. Moreover, it was the employer's practice to remove employees from jobs because of medical considerations, the arbitrator concluded (*Foster Wheeler Corp.*, 54 LA 871).

• An employee who developed a skin rash, she claimed had been caused by certain cleaning compounds used in her work, was not entitled to be transferred to other work where she would not come in contact with the compound, an arbitrator ruled. Rejecting the contention that the employee was not attempting to exercise special privilege, but was merely attempting to provide the employer with a honest day's work for an honest day's pay in a nonhazardous situation, the arbitrator pointed out that there was no contract provision allowing employees to shift

around to fit their physical needs. Although such shifting may be good business, that is not the same thing as a requirement under the contract, the arbitrator concluded (*Eaton Corp.*, 73 LA 729).

**Worker bumped by returning veteran**—What are the job rights of an employee who is transferred after the veteran whom he or she replaced returns to work? In the absence of a specific contract provision on the subject, one arbitrator decided that an employee transferred to make room for a returning veteran has the same rights as an employee on layoff.

• When a veteran returned to his old job, the man who had been hired to replace him was transferred to a lower-paying job in another department. Another employee was given the first vacancy that occurred in the veteran's department on the basis of his plant-wide seniority. The union filed a grievance, arguing that the transferred employee had first crack at the job in his old department because of his greater departmental seniority.

The arbitrator noted that the contract was silent on the subject of veterans' reemployment rights. Under a draft law, however, an employer simply is required to reinstate a returning veteran, the arbitrator pointed out; it can do as it pleases about his replacement. In the arbitrator's view, the employer had the option of either continuing operations with a larger-than-normal workforce or laying off the replacement. If it took the second alternative, the layoff would be no different from another, the arbitrator said. Given that the contract in this case specified that departmental seniority would govern layoff and recall, the arbitrator concluded that the veteran's replacement was entitled to the job in his old department, just as he would have been had he been laid off (*Mead Corp.*, 22 LA 292).

**Transfer when union business interrupts work**—If a union official is frequently called from the job to tend to union business, can the official be transferred to a job where his or her absences would not interfere with production? One arbitrator has said that such a transfer is not discriminatory in itself.

• A union officer employed as a dispatch clerk was needed on her job regularly because she determined work schedules for other employees. When union business required her to keep interrupting her production work, the employer ordered her to trade jobs with another woman, where ultimately her pay and working conditions were the same as in the clerk's job. The union protested that the transfer violated a contract clause prohibiting discrimination against union members. The employer did not violated the contract's nondiscrimination clause, because the transferred officer's new pay and working conditions were the same as before, and, moreover, the new job permitted her to carry out her union business (*Oliver Corp.*, 15 LA 65).

**Limitation on transfer of union officials**—Is a provision that shop stewards may not be transferred without their consent limited only to transfers outside of a bargaining unit? One arbitrator said that such a provision could not be given such a narrow interpretation.

• When the chief shop steward at one employer was transferred first to the second shift and later to the third, the union protested that the employer violated the clause prohibiting transfers of stewards without their consent. The employer claimed that the clause referred only to transfers outside the bargaining unit. Upholding the union, the arbitrator found that a movement from one shift to another was a transfer within the general meaning of the word (*Midland Rubber Corp.*, 18 LA 590).

• An arbitrator ruled that an employer was not required to transfer an employee from the second shift to the first shift just because he was elected chief steward. Although the contract implied that the chief steward should be on the first shift, the arbitrator said, it did not say that he must work the first shift or that the employer must transfer his work from one shift to another. The employer allowed the chief steward to have unlimited access to the plant, the arbitrator held, which was all that was required of it (*Chrysler Corp.*, 42 LA 1018).

• As for shifting departments, an employee's right to serve as a shop steward in his or her "home" department was not limited by the employer's right to transfer him elsewhere. Thus, an employer was forced to recognize a welder as steward for his home department despite the fact that he had been transferred to another department. Because the employer's power to assign could have eliminated a desirable union candidate, this right should not be construed to narrow the privilege of selection. Likewise, the right of selection does not bind the employer to transfer an employee back to his home department, for the purpose of representation, without prior negotiation (*New York Shipbuilding Corp.*, 44 LA 924).

• Union officials holding superseniority may not be transferred from the units they represent. Superseniority is designed to provide continuity of representation for the units in which the officials are elected, to allow the officials to police the contract in their departments, and to make them readily available to unit members and supervision (*New York Shipbuilding Corp.*, 43 LA 741).

**Shift transfers**—If a contract is silent on the matter, do employees have a right to chose their shifts on the basis of their seniority? Most arbitrators feel that, in the absence of a specific contract provision permitting it, employees may not exercise their seniority to transfer to a shift of their choice. One union claimed that senior employees could bump juniors on more desirable shifts. It argued that seniority should be applied to shift transfers as well as governing layoffs, recalls, and demotions under the contract. The arbitrator, however, decided nothing in the contract gave senior employees the right to displace juniors on other shifts (*Kuhlman Electric Co.*, 19 LA 199).

• An arbitrator decided that an employer violated its contract when it transferred an unwilling, senior paintmaker-helper who was an employee on the first shift to a position on a newly created second shift. The union had argued that junior employees who previously held the paintmaker-helper classification should have been transferred, instead of the senior employee.

Although the employer contended that management had the right to assign employees to shifts and that no employee was guaranteed a daytime job when he was hired, the arbitrator, nevertheless, ruled that the employer's right to transfer employees from one shift to another was based on the contract's seniority provisions. Because there were other qualified employees who had less seniority than the transferred senior employee, the arbitrator concluded that the employer was obligated to transfer the junior employees first (59 LA 574).

● An arbitrator ruled that an employer improperly transferred junior employees, during a reduction in the workforce, to yard crews that worked the Monday through Friday shift, instead of transferring senior operators and material handlers whose transfer to the yard crews could have enabled them to work their normal scheduled days in addition to working and receiving premium pay (*Koppers Company Inc.*, 67 LA 752).

● Another arbitrator ruled that an employer's transfer of an employee from a day shift to a swing shift was improper where the parties' collective bargaining agreement provided that all employees "shall work standard workweek" unless by "mutual agreement" (*Public Utility District No. 1 of Clark County*, 103 LA 404).

*Lateral transfers*—Seniority entitled a qualified employee to a lateral transfer, regardless of relative ability. So long as the man had the basic ability to perform the job, he was entitled to it over a newly hired man. The fact that he was "efficient" or "badly needed" on his present job should not stand in the way of his transfer.

● A turret-lathe operator requested a transfer to a new tape-controlled tracer lathe, where the operator's job carried the same rating but offered greater opportunity for promotion. In rejecting the transfer request, the employer said the employee was "one of our most efficient operators on assignments that require the full capabilities of trained operators." Under the contract, seniority, skill, and ability were made the determining factors in passing on transfer request.

The contract did not mention "efficiency" as one of the factors to be considered, the arbitrator noted. An able employee should not be penalized for his ability by denying his seniority rights (*Steel Products Engineering Co.*, 47 LA 952).

● An arbitrator has held that lateral transfers should not be denied simply because the job does not pay more than the previous one. If it offers a better chance for advancement, it should be considered a "promotion" and follow normal contractual procedures for promotion and lateral transfers (*Picker X-Ray Corp.*, 42 LA 179).

**Temporary Transfers**

*Temporary versus permanent transfer*—In light of the fact that management usually retains an unrestricted right to make temporary transfers to fill short-term gaps in the workforce, arbitrators frequently are asked to pass on the distinction between "temporary" or "permanent" transfer where the contract contains no definitions. The dividing line often is set at a week or two (36 LA 767, 23 LA 581).

Where contracts specify the time limit on temporary transfers, a common ceiling is 30 days.

*Worker's right to refuse transfer*—When a contract does not spell it out, do employees have a right to refuse temporary transfers to other jobs? Where the assignment was to lower-rated work, an arbitrator ordered an employee reinstated, holding that management went too far in terminating his employment for refusal to accept a transfer (*Great Atlantic & Pacific Tea Co.*, 1 LA 63; see also 7 LA 459).

● Another arbitrator ruled that an employee must accept a temporary transfer unless the contract specifically spells out his right to refuse it (*Phillips Oil Co.*, 18 LA 798; see also 73 LA 497).

● In a related group of cases, arbitrators have upheld employee refusals to accept transfers regarded as "unreasonable." For example, an employer was held to have acted unreasonably in asking glaziers to do temporary work as painters (3 LA 782).

*Temporary transfer to higher-rated job*—Is an employee transferred temporarily to a higher-rated job entitled to the regular pay for that job? If the pay practices for temporary transfers are spelled out in the contract, there is no problem. But at least one arbitrator has held that, even when the contract is silent on the matter, management is obligated to pay the rate for a higher job to a man who temporarily fills the job. He reasoned that it is inherent in a classification system that an employee should receive the higher rate if he performs a job in a higher classification (*Tide Water Oil Co.*, 17 LA 829; see also 63 LA 487).

*In-grade transfer to temporary job*— In the absence of contract provisions and any established past practice, can a temporary job be assigned to an employee from another classification rather than to one in the same grade? Reasoning that a case has to be decided on the basis of logic and equity where no other guides are available, one arbitration board ruled that a man in a helper classification has more right to a temporary helper's job than an employee from another classification. They said that fairness dictated that the employer give the helper the job because losing it meant a loss of pay. As long as the employer failed to show that there was an unreasonable administrative burden involved, the arbitrators ruled, the job should have gone to the helper (*National Carbon Co.*, 23 LA 263).

*Voluntary transfer to lower-paying job*—At what wage rate must an employee be paid who is given a choice of taking work on a lower-paying job to avoid layoff or for some other reason? Most companies make clear that where an employee is required (for employer convenience) to take a lower-paying job, the employee receives a regular rate for the period; but where an employee voluntarily accepts a lower-paying job, as in a force reduction, the employee receives the rate of that job. Most arbitrators have upheld this practice, even where no clear distinction was made between voluntary and required transfers (76 LA 1017, 76 LA 854, 76 LA 516).

*Part 7*

# *Vacations*

# Vacation Eligibility

## OVERVIEW

Generally, arbitrators have held employees enjoy no inherent right to a vacation. Any vacation rights that an employee may have arise out of a collective bargaining agreement (66 LA 160, 65 LA 745, 59 LA 1245, 48 LA 965, 44 LA 1045), or evolve out of a well-established employer practice. Arbitrators have recognized the twofold nature of the vacation benefit: time off from work and pay (87 LA 932).

Even though a vacation policy is spelled out in detail in the contract, numerous questions may arise when it comes to determining the rights of individual employees. The most common disputes relate to employees who are not actively at work during the vacation season—e.g., employees on layoff—and those whose employment is terminated prior to their vacation.

Furthermore, employee absences affect vacation eligibility. The types of absences that may be held to break vacation eligibility include:

- layoffs for slack work;
- time lost during a strike;
- time lost after a strike, before return to work;
- time lost because of illness;
- time lost because of occupational injury;
- leaves of absence for union business;
- leaves of absence for personal reasons;
- leaves of absence for "civic" or military reasons; or
- chronic absenteeism.

## SUMMARY OF CASES

### Effect of Layoff

If an employee has met all the regular requirements for a vacation, there is little doubt that he is entitled to vacation pay if he is laid off before the vacation season rolls around. The usual practice is to treat vacation rights, once earned, as a vested benefit.

- Where a contract stated that an employee would be entitled to a paid vacation provided he had a specified amount of service and was "in the employ" of the employer on April 15, an arbitrator ruled that the employer was wrong in denying vacation pay to employees who were laid off before April 15 after meeting all the other requirements for a paid vacation (*Botony Mills Inc.*, 27 LA 1).

- Employees who were laid off because of plant closings late in the year assumed the status of employees on indefinite layoff who would be eligible for vacation pay for vacation earned in the year of layoff, an arbitrator decided. Despite a contractual provision that stated that an employee must have been actively employed at some time during the calendar year to be eligible for vacation benefits during "that calendar year," the arbitrator ruled that the applicable provision was a clause that entitled employees to vacation if they were laid off for an indefinite time (*Continental Can Co.*, 76 LA 1212).

- It may be a different story if the contract says employees must be "on the payroll" as of a certain date. Some, though not all, arbitrators have held that when an employee is laid off he ceases to be on the payroll for vacation purposes (23 LA 298).

• Although a laid-off employee generally is entitled to previously earned vacation-pay rights, it does not follow that the time he spends on layoff will be credited toward meeting the service or work requirements for future vacations. The general rule is that vacation pay "is associated with work and does not accrue during periods of unemployment or layoff unless the agreement so provides expressly or by necessary implication" (67 LA 997, 64 LA 791, 64 LA 641, 64 LA 103, 34 LA 170).

### Eligibility Based on 'Service' & 'Employment'

Many contracts base vacation eligibility on a certain amount of "service." Management's reasoning often is that "service" means actual work, and that therefore, layoff time should not be counted in figuring vacation eligibility. On the other hand, employees will argue that their "service" has not been broken while on layoff because "service" is synonymous with "seniority." This latter view has been upheld in arbitration.

• Under a contract requiring a certain number of "years' service" for vacation eligibility, the employer maintained that "service" meant being on the job. Therefore, it argued that a three-week layoff period should be deducted in calculating "service," with the effect that a laid-off employee would not be eligible for a vacation until a year and three weeks had passed. The union's position was that "years of service" was the same as seniority.

The arbitrator noted that the contract made seniority dependent on "length of continuous service," and that in this connection "service" never was considered broken by layoffs. Therefore, the union's position was upheld as "the one ordinarily adopted," because the agreement failed to set forth specific work requirements for vacation eligibility (*St. Louis Smelting & Refining Co.*, 28 LA 219).

• When a contract bases vacation eligibility on "employment," some arbitrators hold, this too is the same as seniority. If a laid-off employee has a right to recall on a seniority basis, then his employment is not generally thought to be ended by layoff, one arbitrator noted. Thus, he reasoned, laid-off employees who fulfilled the conditions that qualified them for recall were entitled to have their layoff periods counted as employment in determining vacation credits (*Hanchett Mfg. Co.*, 28 LA 235).

• One arbitrator ruled that laid-off employees who continued to accumulate seniority were not entitled to vacation benefits under a contract provision entitling employees to vacation as a reward for "satisfactory service," or under a provision granting employees "earned vacation." Emphasizing that the vacation provisions laid down an actual work requirement before an employee became eligible for vacation benefits, the arbitrator concluded that the provision pertaining to "earned vacation" negated any automatic accrual of employment benefits during a layoff (*Frye Copysystems Inc.*, 65 LA 1249).

• An employee who had several years of service with an employer was not entitled to include her 10-month layoff as part of "length of service" for vacation purposes, an arbitrator decided, because there was a long-standing practice of not including layoff as part of length of service (*National Cash Register Co.*, 64 LA 103).

### Effect of Strike

In the absence of contract language requiring a different result, arbitrators are unlikely to permit employees to benefit in the accrual of vacation credits during time spent on strike, because vacation benefits as deferred wages are part of the pay received for working for an employer (79 LA 1294, 70 LA 636, 66 LA 745, 53 LA 784, 49 LA 55, 45 LA 512, 42 LA 102).

• Many arbitration cases turn on the question of whether the strike is an "excused absence" depriving or not depriving, depending on the particular contract, employees of vacation credits (74 LA 1061, 49 LA 113).

• Other cases have involved contracts basing vacation pay on some qualifying phrase such as "hours worked" or "time worked" (68 LA 447, 38 LA 1236); "years of service" (66 LA 745, 43 LA 1); "continuous service" (63 LA 1235, 53 LA 170, 34 LA 428); "employment" by the employer (49 LA 1180, 27 LA 251); being in "the employ" of the employer (33 LA 837); or "scheduled working days" (62 LA 415, 47 LA 319, 33 LA 638).

• Arbitrators have interpreted these phrases as requiring the actual rendering of services for vacation eligibility, and as excluding time spent on strike. Therefore, they distinguish between the bare retention of employment status and the actual performance of services that fulfill the eligibility requirements (33 LA 837, 27 LA 251, 22 LA 466).

A strike may raise several questions regarding vacation eligibility.

• Are employees who fail to return to work at the end of the strike still entitled to claim vacation benefits?

• Given that vacation benefits usually are considered an earned right, those who quit during a strike generally are entitled to claim their vacation pay if they have otherwise met the eligibility requirements. Vacation benefits may be denied, however, if strikers who terminate fail to meet notice requirements for resignation.

• Does time spent out on strike count the same as working time in determining service requirements for vacation eligibility?

• Where vacation eligibility is tied to "continuous service," arbitrators generally rule that time spent on strike should not be counted in computing continuous service (42 LA 929, 48 LA 213, 47 LA 319, 47 LA 1164).

• One arbitrator ruled that an employer had the right to deduct the time that employees spent on strike against the employer in determining the employees' vacation eligibility date under a side letter incorporated in the contract, stating that credit for vacation eligibility would not be earned during time spent on strike. According to the arbitrator, there was evidence that during negotiations on the side letter the parties decided that strike time would be treated as layoff time, and the union had agreed that layoff, except for certain months of a grade period, would affect vacation eligibility dates (*George Banta Co. Inc.*, 74 LA 388).

• In another case, an arbitrator ruled that an employer properly reduced its employees' vacation benefits to reflect the work time that was lost as the result of a strike. The contract entitled employees to receive vacation benefits based on their continuous service with the employer during specified dates, the arbitrator reasoned, pointing out that by linking the words "continuous" and "service," management clearly intended that employees must comply with such a requirement in order to get vacation benefits (*Ohio Power Co.*, 63 LA 1235).

• Teachers who continued a two-week-old strike through the first three days of their scheduled one-week vacation were not entitled to vacation pay for the three-day period, an arbitrator decided. The striking teachers failed to meet the school's requirement that they be in a paid status for at least one of the five working days immediately preceding a vacation in order to be eligible for the pay, the arbitrator maintained, concluding that the regulation was consistent with the contract (*Hawaii Dept. of Education*, 62 LA 415).

• One arbitrator ruled that taking part in a strike, even though it was in violation of the contract, was not in itself cause to deprive employees of vacation credits. In the arbitrator's view, the strikers would have forfeited vacation credits if management: (1) had fired them before the vacation credits accrued or (2) had notified them that their return to work would be conditioned on a waiver of vacation credits (*Marathon Rubber Products*, 6 LA 238).

### Strike versus Lockout

Where a contract provided vacations for employees in "continuous service" for a specified period of time, the arbitrator held that the time employees spent on strike could not be counted in computing "continuous service" but the time they were locked out could be counted. He reasoned that the lockout was voluntary on the part of the employer and prevented employees from accruing the "continuous service" required for vacation eligibility. The strike, however, did not come within the exceptions to the vacations provisions, so it must be considered as a break in service (*Denver Upholstered Furniture Mfrs.*, 42 LA 929).

## Strike as "Excused Absence"

One arbitrator held that time spent by the employees on strike did not constitute "excused absence" within the meaning of a contract provision. The strike was "legal" in that it violated no law, but the arbitrator doubted that it was "excused" by the employer, and further, such an interpretation would require the employer to "subsidize the strike" (*Motor Car Dealers Assn. of Kansas City, Mo.*, 49 LA 55).

## Effect of Absences

Some contracts deal with the effect of absences on vacation eligibility by fixing a cut-off point of a designated number of absences after which the right to vacation benefits is affected. For example, it might be specified that "an employee's vacation pay will be prorated, if during the vacation-eligibility year, he was absent for more than 60 days regardless of the reasons for the absences.

In the absence of such a provision, arbitrators tend to adopt a cut-off rule of their own under which they may ignore absences of relatively brief duration but may disallow or prorate vacation pay where lengthy absences are involved.

## Absence for Military Service

Special rules apply where an absence is caused by an employee's entering the military service or meeting military training obligations. Such absences generally must be counted as time worked.

● An arbitrator ruled that an employee who worked as a part-time oven-man for 10 and one-half months prior to entering military service was entitled to include the time that he spent in the military as "continuous employment" to be

counted in determining the length of vacation that he earned under a contract entitling employees to an annual vacation after having one or more years of employment (*Vie De France Corp. and Bakers, Local 118*, 74 LA 449).

## Absences for Illness or Injury

Do employees who are absent because of illness or other disability lose their right to vacation pay?

In the absence of specific language in the contract, an employer may or may not have the right to deny an employee vacation pay while he is out sick or because of an injury. In deciding such cases an arbitrator may look to the general contract language on vacation pay rights or to the employer's past practice.

● In one case an arbitrator ruled that an employee who sustained an injury in an automobile accident was entitled to receive contractual sickness and accident benefits in addition to vacation pay, notwithstanding the employer's contention that the simultaneous payment constituted "double compensation," which was not intended by the contract. Because the agreement neither expressly nor implicitly denied an eligible employee the right to receive both sick and vacation benefits simultaneously, the arbitrator upheld the double payment (*Airco Inc.*, 62 LA 1056; see also 91 LA 1083, 71 LA 460).

● Even where an employee's absenteeism was partly his own fault because of excessive drinking, an arbitrator held that he was entitled to vacation pay because there was proof that he also could not work because of an injury (*Chicago & Harrisburg Coal Co.*, 2 LA 57).

● Where a contract provided that "time lost for illness" would not affect vacation pay, an arbitrator ruled that an "injury," even though occurring on the job, was not "illness" for purposes of computing these benefits (*Modecraft Co.*, 44 LA 1045; see also 85 LA 967, 74 LA 1061).

## Leaves of Absence

Generally, where there is no controlling contract provision, arbitrators uphold the employer's right to deny vacation benefits to employees who have been on leave of fairly long duration.

## Absence for Union Business

Does time spent on union business count as time worked for purposes of vacation eligibility? In some cases, arbitrators have ruled that it does not.

• Under a contract, eligibility for vacation benefits hinged on a work requirement of 1,400 hours in a vacation year. The local's president was 64 hours shy of the requirement. The union pointed out that up to 340 hours of leave could be credited toward satisfying the vacation work requirement; and absence for union activity was leave time under the contract. Because the officer had spent more than 64 hours on union affairs, it added, he had a right to vacation benefits. The employer replied that elsewhere in the agreement a distinction was made between "excused union activity" and "authorized leave of absence." Hence it denied the president had been on leave. The arbitrator upheld the employer's position, saying that if union activity had been meant to be a leave of absence there would have been no reason for making the distinction cited (*American Air Filter Co. Inc.*, 39 LA 942).

• Where a contract's vacation clause required employees to have been "continuously in the service of the employer" as of the eligibility date, an arbitrator upheld the employer's refusal to grant vacation to an employee who had been on union business leave for six months. The arbitrator reasoned that "continuously in the service" meant "continuously available to the employer," which the man on leave was not (*Chamberlain Co. of America*, 8 LA 755).

## Maternity Leave

How does maternity leave affect an employee's vacation rights? At one plant where the vacation clause called for a year's "continuous employment," those who took an enforced six-month pregnancy leave forfeited their eligibility for that year, an arbitrator ruled. Workers on maternity leave were not "continuously employed in the employer's plant" during the year, and in this sense were "laid off." The union had argued that pregnancy

was not an "illness" or a "layoff" that would interrupt an employee's continuous service for vacation purposes. The sense of the vacation provision, he found, is that benefits are a reward for actual continuous employment (*Clean Coverall Supply Co.*, 47 LA 272).

## Effect of Termination

The tendency to treat vacation pay as an earned right generally means that an employee who has met all of the eligibility requirements for a paid vacation is entitled to claim his vacation pay if he is terminated prior to taking his vacation.

• What if he has met all of the eligibility requirements except a requirement that he be on the payroll as of a certain date? After an extensive review of prior court and arbitration decisions, an arbitrator concluded that the principle was well settled in industry, generally, that employment on the specified date is not a condition of eligibility for vacation pay and therefore that termination prior to that date does not disqualify the individual for the vacation pay to which he is otherwise entitled (49 LA 837; see also 71 LA 781).

This principle is followed fairly closely in cases where the termination is involuntary, such as in the case of a shutdown or disability retirement.

Exceptions may be made, however, where the termination is voluntary such as a quit or a voluntary retirement. In such cases, the employer's past practice may be decisive.

• A contract's clause provided that after having completed six months' service, employees would be allowed 10 working days' vacation with current pay during the following six months, and that employees who had completed one year would be allowed 15 working days' vacation during the following 12 months with current pay. When an employee quit one month after her anniversary date with the employer, the employer claimed she was only entitled to a vacation balance of two days and two and three quarters hours, because the other 15 days she demanded were credited on the first anniversary and not "earned" until completion of two years' service.

The arbitrator, however, awarded the other 15 days of vacation to the employee after finding that the history of the contract's language and the bookkeeping methods used by the employer for the past 20 years revealed that that was the norm at the company (*Columbia Typographical Union*, 63 LA 507).

• A union was out of line, an arbitrator ruled, when it attempted to win for quitting employees the entire vacation benefit that they would have been entitled to had they worked a full year since their last vacation. The employer was correct in awarding the vacations on a pro rata basis, the arbitrator decided, rejecting the union's argument that vacations were fully vested from the start of the vacation year. The right to accrue vacation benefits during the year was recognized by the contract and confirmed by past practice, the arbitrator concluded (*Wire Sales Co.*, 62 LA 185).

### Effect of Discharge

In the absence of specific language of disqualification, arbitrators generally hold that an employee who otherwise meets the requirements for vacation pay is not disqualified by virtue of his being discharged before he takes his vacation.

• An employee discharged for chronic absenteeism was ruled eligible for vacation pay where the contract did not cover the situation. The arbitrator decided that to permit the disqualification would amount to an amendment of the contract (*Weaver Mfg. Co.*, 19 LA 325).

• Discharge for cause was held by another arbitrator not to disqualify an employee under a contract that did not specifically bar payments under such a condition (*General Foods Corp.*, 18 LA 910).

• An employee discharged for negligence was not held disqualified for terminal vacation pay under a contract that specified only that resignations or discharges for rule infractions would relieve the employer of its obligation to make vacation payments, an arbitrator decided (*Byerlite Corp.*, 12 LA 641).

• At least one state court has ruled that employees discharged for striking in violation of a no-strike clause were entitled to vacation pay earned prior to the strike (*Pattenge v. Wagner Iron Works*, Wis. Cir. Ct., 1956, 38 LRRM 2615).

### Effect of Permanent Shutdown

Are employees entitled to vacation pay when they are terminated because of plant shutdown?

• Arbitrator have generally held that previously acquired vacation credits are earned, or additional wages, payable even if a permanent plant closing takes place before the vacation actually becomes due (76 LA 1212, 13 LA 804, 12 LA 860).

• Some arbitrators have held that employees idled because of a shutdown were entitled to vacation pay, even though the agreement expired before the eligibility date.

In one case an arbitrator noted that the employees had been laid off when the plant was closed and the contract stated that a man was not terminated until he had been on layoff for two years. Thus, he said, the employees were still in the employer's employ and their earned rights survived the contract's expiration (*Botany Mills Inc.*, 27 LA 1).

• In another case an arbitrator held that employees who lost their jobs in a plant shutdown had pro rata vacation pay coming to them because they were terminated through no fault of their own. The fact that the contract had expired before the vacation eligibility date was immaterial, he said (*Brookford Mills*, 28 LA 838).

### Death of Worker Before Vacation or Eligibility Date

When an employee dies before receiving the vacation that is due him, are his survivors entitled to the vacation pay? Where no set rule has been developed on this problem, arbitrators seem to consider what other circumstances do or do not break an employee's vacation eligibility.

• Even where a contract disqualified employees who quit, retired, or were discharged from receiving vacation pay, an arbitrator held that "death" was not an implied exemption as maintained by the employer. In awarding accrued vacation benefits to the survivors, the arbitrator stated that to hold "death" as a disqualification would be to alter the contract (*Pittsburgh Steel Co.*, 43 LA 860).

• Where the contract required an employee to work at least 1,000 hours in one year in order to be eligible for a vacation the next year, and also provided that "if an employee shall have earned a vacation but dies before such vacation has been taken, the vacation pay shall be paid to his widow," an arbitrator ruled that the widow was entitled to that pay, even though the employee died in December of the year before he was to take the vacation. The arbitrator rejected the employer's argument that no pay was due the widow because vacation pay went only to those still on the payroll as of January 1. Nothing in the contract specified that, he said, and the employee had worked his 1,000 hours (*Clinton Corn Processing Co.*, 41 LA 513).

• An employer was required to pay vacation pay to the widows of two employees who had performed no work in the year in which their vacations would have been taken. The contracts, he noted, destroy vacation eligibility only upon quit, discharge, or retirement. He held that it would be improper to modify the contract to add "death" (*Pittsburgh Steel Co.*, 43 LA 860).

• Where a contract provided for vacation rights to be forfeited if employment was terminated prior to January 1 of the vacation year, the arbitrator upheld the employer that had consistently denied benefits to survivors of employees who died before January 1. The arbitrator maintained that giving the language its normal meaning, death must obviously be held to terminate the employment relationship (*Bethlehem Steel Corp.*, 47 LA 258).

### Vacation Rights of Retirees

Whether vacation pay is due employees who retire voluntarily prior to the vacation season often depends upon past practice and the wording of the contract, and particularly upon whether the contract fixes a specified date for determining vacation eligibility.

• A contract's vacation pay eligibility requirements were: being on the payroll on Jan. 1; having at least one year continuous service as of Jan. 1; and having worked for the employer in 26 of the 52 weeks immediately preceding Jan. 1. An employee who met the second and third requirements but who retired before January 1 sought vacation pay.

In upholding the employer's denial of vacation pay, the arbitrator said the employer was entitled to enforce the requirement of being on the payroll as of January 1 in this case, even though it might not be entitled to do so in cases of involuntary terminations, such as those due to shutdowns or disability retirements (*Rex Chainbelt Inc.*, 49 LA 646).

• In a case where the contract did not have a vacation eligibility date, an arbitrator directed the payment of vacation pay in one year to an employee who had retired the prior year. The employee prior to his retirement had met the dual contract requirements of having worked at least 800 hours in the current vacation year and of having at least six months service as of the prior calendar years (*B & T Metals Co.*, 50 LA 205).

• An arbitrator awarded a retiree vacation pay earned through the time of his retirement, despite a contractual requirement that he establish his participation in the pension plan to be eligible to receive other pension benefits. The arbitrator reasoned that because the parties' contract granting unpaid vacation pay to "any employee who retires" was without limitation or qualification, the employer's denial of the pay was a violation of the contract (*Rexall Drug Co.*, 63 LA 965).

• Another employee who scheduled his two-week vacation before the start of his retirement, but who instead went on sick leave through the retirement date, was not entitled to vacation pay, an arbitrator ruled, because the contract required vacation pay or holiday pay to be used before sick leave (*Kentucky Utilities Co.*, 64 LA 737).

### Successorship and Vacations

Is a successor employer required to consider time employed by the original employer when calculating employees' vacation time? If the successor employer assumes the labor-management relationship of its predecessor, the answer probably will be yes.

• One arbitrator found a successor employer liable and listed the following reasons for his decision: the successor employer hired all of the predecessor's employees in the bargaining unit; the employer operated in the same manner and at the same location as the predecessor; the change of ownership did not create a hiatus in operations; and the successor employer's contract contained substantially the same provisions as the old contract (*A.B.A. Diesel Parts & Service Co.*, 62 LA 662).

• A successor employer obligated itself to pay vacation pay to its predecessor's employees, an arbitrator ruled, when it wrote a letter telling employees of their continued employment and that they would be permitted to take one or two weeks of "vacation" depending on their seniority (*Zenetron Inc. and Radionic Workers, Local 5*, 74 LA 861).

# Vacation Scheduling

## OVERVIEW

Vacation scheduling involves a balancing of the employer's interest in scheduling vacations in such a way that it best meets the needs of the business against the employee's interest in taking a vacation at the most desirable time (*Houdaille Industries Inc.*, 61 LA 958).

In one case an arbitrator elaborated some general guidelines that may be followed in striking this balance. "Absent specific contract language, it is generally understood in industrial relations that a vacation is an earned equity and is generally to be taken in terms of the employee's preference, subject to the exigencies of the employer's production and maintenance requirements. Where the contract is silent on the specific policy or procedure to be followed, it must be assumed that the employee will request his vacation at a time suitable to his own preferences and that his preference will be honored to the degree that employer requirements will permit. However, where the contract is silent, it must also be assumed that managerial discretion is greater than in those cases where contract language puts the burden on management to show need for the employee to take his vacation at a particular time" (*Hubinger Co.*, 29 LA 459).

According to another arbitrator, in the absence of a specific contrary provision in the contract, an employer has an unrestricted right to schedule vacations and, in fact, to refuse to grant any vacations at all. Vacation rights are "creatures of the contract," he explained, stressing that the scheduling of vacations involves considering both the requirements of the employer and the wishes of the individual employee whenever practical (*Berkeley-Davis Inc.*, 65 LA 742).

## SUMMARY OF CASES

### Arbitrator's Vacation Formula

Faced with the problem of how employees' desire to choose the time for their own vacations can be reconciled with management's need to maintain efficient operations, one arbitrator came up with a formula. It was based on a contract providing that vacations would be granted at times most convenient to employees with consideration given to maintaining production:

(1) Management establishes a quota system indicating the weeks available for vacations and the number of employees needed to work those weeks. By December 1 it must publish a vacation schedule for the following calendar year based on this quota system.

(2) Employees must indicate four vacation choices by December 10. They may split their vacations, but the minimum period is one week.

(3) Because vacation priority is based on seniority, a list is set up by assigning varying numbers of points to the various seniority groups. The employer must post the list by December 15. If an employee has to settle for his or her second or third vacation choice, the priority points are doubled or tripled the next year.

(4) The employer must publish a vacation replacement list showing whether it plans to hire replacements or will rely on overtime by present employees to maintain production.

(5) A vacation grievance committee is set up to resolve employees' complaints on schedules and replacements (*Mansfield Tire & Rubber Co.*, 32 LA 762).

## Vacation During Sick Leave

If an employee is out on paid sick leave when his or her regular vacation period arrives, is the person entitled to another vacation period at a later date? Sick leave and vacation leave are entirely different privileges, according to an arbitration board, so the employer should reschedule the vacation period of an employee who is on sick leave during that person's regularly scheduled vacation (*Derby Gas & Electric Co.*, 21 LA 745; see also 25 LA 94).

● Where an employee was on sick leave when his scheduled vacation came up and his vacation could not be rescheduled, an arbitrator held that he was entitled to vacation pay in addition to sick pay (*Tenneco Oil Co.*, 54 LA 862).

## Vacation During Shutdown

Many companies have a practice of scheduling vacations each year during an annual plan shutdown. In lieu of such a practice, however, management may run into trouble if it tries to require employees to take their vacations during periods of layoff caused by lack of work, particularly where the layoff is for an indefinite period. An arbitrator pointed out that some correlation between vacations and what otherwise would be layoffs is not only permissible, but desirable.

● One arbitrator held that management could not require employees to take their vacations during a period of indefinite layoff where to do so would destroy the substantive features of a vacation. According to the arbitrator, "a vacation is a period of rest between periods of work. A layoff is a period of anxiety and hardship between periods of work. The tremendous difference lies in the assurance of the vacationer that he will return to work at the end of his vacation and the equal assurance of the employee on layoff that he does not know when he will return to work" (*Ford Motor Co.*, 3 LA 829).

● Even where a shutdown for lack of work is for a definite period, arbitrators have overruled attempts to require employees to take their vacations during that period. Usually such decisions arise in cases where management previously promised to give some consideration to employee preferences in scheduling their vacations. The reasoning is that those employees who do not choose to take their vacations during the shutdown are deprived of their opportunity to state their preferences by the unilateral scheduling of vacations during the shutdown (97 LA 578, 96 LA 445, 93 LA 107, 81 LA 254, 48 LA 1018, 32 LA 776, 31 LA 462).

● In another case, a contract stated that each employee must schedule his or her vacation in advance at a time acceptable to the employer. When the employer had to shut down for two months because of a lack of orders, it claimed authority to require all employees to take their vacations at that time. The arbitrator overruled the employer's action, reasoning that those employees who did not choose to take their vacations during the shutdown were deprived of their opportunity to specify what times they wanted. Moreover, the right given the employer to allot vacation periods in order to ensure "orderly operation of the plant" may allow management to spread out vacations to avoid too many replacements at one time, but "orderly" is not synonymous with "economical" or "efficient," the arbitrator said (*Koppers Employer Inc.*, 42 LA 1321).

● An arbitrator found that an employer was not free to join the trend toward plant shutdowns for vacation because the contract bound the employer to "endeavor to comply" with vacation requests. Although the arbitrator acknowledged the gradual changes in factory conditions, such as increased vacation tenure and a larger workforce, he still maintained that in planning a shutdown, the employer was "in fact endeavoring not to comply with requests" (*Welch Grape Juice Co.*, 48 LA 1018).

● On the other hand, an employer had the right to schedule one vacation shutdown during the summer months, an arbitrator ruled, under an oral agreement giving the employer the right to schedule not more than one summer vacation shutdown per year per department. Rejecting the union's contention that the employer failed to secure contract language recognizing management's right to schedule vacation shutdowns, the arbitrator concluded it was not necessary to obtain such contract language in light of the employer's long-standing past practice of scheduling vacation shutdown for legitimate business reasons, the oral agreement, and the absence of limiting language in the previous agreement (*Lynchburg Foundry Co.*, 76 LA 554).

● Moreover, in the absence of contract language or binding past practice, management has the inherent right to fix employee's vacation time, an arbitrator ruled. The employer in this case decided it no longer could afford the disruptions that accompany individual vacation scheduling, and it unilaterally designated the week of July 4th for a plant-wide vacation shutdown. The arbitrator overruled union objections based on past practice, finding that the union had never participated in past disagreements over vacation schedules (*Vogt Mfg. Corp.*, 44 LA 488; see also 30 LA 225).

## Workers' Desires versus Efficient Operations

Under a contract that allows employees to choose the vacation periods they want subject to requirements of the business, the employer must have real and valid reasons for denying them the period they ask for (94 LA 309, 77 LA 633, 67 LA 709, 59 LA 268).

● When one employer turned down an employee's request for a specific vacation period because it overlapped with that requested by another employee, an arbitrator ruled against this action. Although the contract provided that the "needs of the business must be considered in scheduling vacations," the arbitrator found that both employees' being gone at the same time would not necessarily conflict with efficient operations. To turn down a request for a given vacation time, the arbitrator said, management should show that a vacation at that time would adversely affect production, safety, or general employee relations (*Tin Processing Corp.*, 15 LA 568).

● Another arbitrator ruled that management could not make a blanket denial of all vacation requests for a certain week, even though the contract made employees' requests for vacations subject to operational requirements. The employer had announced in advance that no vacations would be given during Christmas week. In the arbitrator's view, the employer violated the vacation clause requiring it to make every effort to meet the desires of employees in scheduling vacations. Also, it had failed to show that absolutely no one could be spared, the arbitrator noted (*Bethlehem Steel Co.*, 30 LA 899).

● In other cases arbitrators have upheld management's right to reshuffle vacation schedules in order to meet the needs of its business.

In one case, establishment of a "one-man, one-week" vacation rule, under which only one employee in a department could be on leave at any given time, was upheld by an arbitrator as a proper exercise of management's right to ensure the orderly operation of its plants (*U.S. Steel Corp.*, 46 LA 887).

● Where a contract gave the employer the right to schedule vacations throughout the year, an arbitrator upheld management's right to allot vacations to eligible employees over the full year on an equal basis, thereby eliminating the "summer bulge" of vacations (*Laclede Steel Co.*, 54 LA 506).

● Another arbitrator ruled that management could refuse to schedule vacations during months when peak business was expected, even though that business did not materialize. The contract said management would fix vacations according to the employees' wishes "in so far as practical" and "in accordance with the needs of the business." In the arbitrator's view, this gave the employer the sole right to limit vacation-time selection, as long as heavy business forecasts were reasonable (*Westinghouse Electric Corp.*, 40 LA 972).

● In a case where it had been a practice for two years to commence vacations on a Monday, an arbitrator held that the employer could continue this practice. The contract gave the employer the right to schedule vacations in the interest of plant efficiency. The union wanted each employee's vacation to start after his regular days off. But the arbitrator said that, by starting vacations on Monday, the employer was justifiably exercising its right to increase efficiency and avoid costly premium payments (*Sinclair Refining Co.*, 12 LA 193).

• Another arbitrator decided that a utility employer properly postponed and rescheduled the vacation of one member of a three-man maintenance crew, because the second member was out of town at the time and the third member would have been left alone to perform work normally done by all three (*United Telephone Co.*, 64 LA 906; see also 73 LA 813, 73 LA 687, 73 LA 48).

### Vacation: Workers versus Foremen

Where a contract gave employees their choice of vacation dates in seniority order, the employer was obligated to give employees vacation preference over foremen where the two conflicted, as long as there was no operational problem, the arbitrator stated. Because nothing indicated that management assigned the vacation weeks to foremen on the basis of anticipated production needs, he concluded that foremen had to take second choice (*Air Reduction Chemical & Carbide Co.*, 42 LA 1192).

• Adoption of an extended vacation plan did not give an employer the right to abandon a past practice of allowing employees and foremen to work out the schedule, one arbitrator decided. Although the employer may set the total number of employees who may be on vacation at one time, it may not determine when particular employees shall be off. Rather, it is bound by past practice and must permit foremen and employees to work this out among themselves, subject only to the limits of plant manpower needs (*Reynolds Metals Co.*, 43 LA 1150).

### Extended Vacations

In a grievance against an employer's refusal to grant an employee his pre-ferred vacation period, an arbitrator provided several observations and principles for the scheduling of extended vacations in the steel industry.

• Subject to the employer's right "to ensure orderly operation of the plants," extended vacations should be granted "at times most desired by employees." To implement this plan, a procedural agreement was adopted permitting the employer to establish plant and unit quotas and allowing employees to select vacation periods within these quotas in order of seniority.

• (1) The employer is not bound to continue quotas used in a prior year. (2) He is bound to honor vacation selections on the basis of seniority within separate lines of progression. (3) He may continue to schedule vacations by calendar quarter, because this had permitted most employees to receive time off during preferred summer quarters. (4) Exceptions should be made in special cases of hardship, where granting of employee's request would not interfere with production (*Armco Steel Corp.*, 45 LA 120).

• Another arbitrator asserted that the employer may not give employees entitled to regular vacations priority over extended vacationers. The employer may require an employee to take his vacation during a period other than the one he requested, only when its decision is related to the need to maintain orderly plant operation (*Pittsburgh Steel Co.*, 42 LA 1002).

### Work During Vacation

Under a contract allowing management to request employees to work during their vacations, at least one arbitrator has held that this gives the employer the right to *compel* employees to skip their vacation.

• At the end of the first week after a return to work from a strike the employer issued vacation checks to all employees instead of scheduling free time. The contract specified that: "Under unusual circumstances, the management may request certain or all of the employees to work during their vacation, but in such event the employees will be paid their regular pay in addition to their regular earnings." The union contended that under this clause, management might only request, not compel, employees to work during their vacations. It argued that "request" would require the employee's approval.

The arbitrator ruled otherwise, stating that the obvious intent of the contract was to give management the right to require work under unusual circumstances. Furthermore, it was held that the definition of "unusual circumstances" must be left largely up to the employer. The arbitrator found no abuse of that discretion (*Maxwell Bros. Inc.*, 5 LA 449).

## Changing Vacation Schedules of Transferred Employees

An employer's imposition of limits on the vacation schedules of transferred employees violated a collective bargaining agreement, an arbitrator found.

● Employees at a baking employer selected their vacation times, by seniority, in December and January for the upcoming vacation year. One year, the employer denied vacation requests of two employees who had voluntarily transferred into another department, citing a provision in the collective bargaining agreement that limits the number of employees in each department who can be on vacation at one time. It eventually let the employees have their vacation choices, but notified the union that in future employees who took voluntary transfers would only be allowed to pick the unselected vacation weeks available in their new departments.

The issue is not whether past practice or clear contractual language determines the outcome, the arbitrator explained, because vacation selections are made in conformity with the contract when they are made. The question is whether employees who already have selected their vacation within the contractual limitations can be required to lose their choice upon transfer to another department, the arbitrator said. Noting this question was not covered by the contract, the arbitrator found that allowing voluntarily transferees to take their selected vacation times with them is a binding practice on the parties, and may not be changed unilaterally by the employer (*Schmidt Baking Employer and Bakery, Confectionery*, 104 LA 574).

● Another arbitrator ruled that an employer's contractual right to designate vacation schedules did not permit it to grant vacation times according to shift seniority, where the contract provided only for seniority in job classification and in employment (*Baltimore Sun Co. and Baltimore-Washington Newspaper Guild Local 35*, 103 LA 363).

● The denial of an assistant town clerk's request for a vacation during election season was upheld in *Town of Trumbull and State, County, and Municipal Employees Local 1303-180* (99 LA 173). The contract did not deal with the timing of vacations, only the amount of vacation employees were entitled to, the arbitrator said, and vacations were prohibited during election season by past practice.

# Vacation Pay

## OVERVIEW

Frequently, arbitrators are called on to settle disputes over vacation pay, even though the contract usually specifies the method for computing the benefit. Some of the issues an arbitrator may have to resolve include the following.

- What happens when an employee works at more than one rate?
- Do "incentive employees" get their base rate or full incentive earnings?
- Are overtime, shift, holiday, and other premium rates and bonuses included or excluded?
- What is the effect of a retroactive wage increase?
- If employees work a different workweek from the plant's scheduled workweek, which one is used as a base?
- Is the *date* on which vacation pay is computed clear?
- Is it the employee's anniversary date, the eligibility date, or the date the vacation is actually taken?

## SUMMARY OF CASES

### Inclusion of Incentive Pay

Should employees' incentive payments be included in vacation allowances paid them?

Incentive bonuses usually are considered by employees as a part of their earnings. Thus, if vacation payments are based on "current hourly earnings" arbitrators most likely would hold that incentive pay must be included.

- An employer agreed that: "The rate of vacation pay per week shall be the same as the current hourly earnings for a full scheduled workweek as worked the previous two months prior to June 1st."

In spite of this language, which had appeared in various contracts, the employer contended that vacations were payable on the basis of "base rate." It argued that the "base rate" had been used in the past, and that the wage-incentive payments at the plant never entered into calculations or discussions regarding vacations.

The arbitrator ruled against the employer, using this line of reasoning: The terms "base rate" and "current hourly earnings" have well established and quite different meanings. The first refers to a minimum rate, the second to actual earnings of an employee. There was no reason here for ruling that the two terms were identical. Therefore, vacation pay should "be calculated on the basis of 'hourly earnings' to include incentive bonuses over and above base rate and on the basis of the workweek 'as worked' by the several employees entitled to vacation pay" (*Schneider Metal Mfg. Co.*, 4 LA 100).

- Under a contract basing employees' vacation pay on "gross earnings" of the preceding year, a lump sum paid to employees to "buy out" an old incentive plan in favor of a new one must be included in computing employees' vacation pay. The arbitrator ruled that the written contract must prevail and that the ordinary meaning of "gross earnings" encompasses payment (*Johnson & Johnson*, 49 LA 841).

### Inclusion of Overtime Earnings

Under a contract that excludes overtime earnings from vacation pay, does this mean all earnings during overtime hours or merely the premium rate for the overtime?

- One arbitrator held that it was clear that an employer was not obligated to base vacation pay on any earnings over 40 hours (*Webster Tobacco Co. Inc.*, 5 LA 164).

Even where a contract is silent on whether overtime premiums should be included in figuring vacation pay, chances are that an arbitrator will not require the employer to include them.

• Under one such agreement that based vacation pay on average hourly earnings, defining such earnings to include regular day rates, incentive rates, and shift premiums, an arbitrator ruled that overtime pay did not have to be included because it was not specifically mentioned in the definition (*Kensington Steel Co.*, 17 LA 662).

### Inclusion of Shift Premiums

Should shift differentials be included in vacation pay that is based on "regular rate"?

• At least one arbitration board gave an affirmative answer to this where the employees worked regularly on second or third shifts (*Hans Rees' Sons Inc.*, 10 LA 705).

• It has been held that where shift premiums have not been included for a period of years, this past practice should prevail (*Bell Aircraft Corp.*, 9 LA 65).

### Inclusion of Holiday Pay

Under a contract that bases vacation pay on "straight-time earnings," should holiday pay be considered part of earnings?

• Although management may feel that employees can hardly have "earnings" while they are off work because of a holiday, at least one arbitrator has required holiday pay included under such a vacation clause.

He held that the parties agreed in effect to treat employees eligible for holiday pay as though they had come in and worked on the holiday. He declared that:

"Holiday pay cannot fairly be said to be similar to a shift bonus, overtime bonus, or a Christmas bonus. On the contrary, holiday pay more closely resembles vacation pay because both are paid at straight-time rates rather than bonus rates." It was concluded that holiday pay

should be included in figuring "earnings" (*Master Weavers Institute*, 11 LA 745).

### Inclusion of Vacation Pay

Under a contract providing vacation pay equal to a specified percentage of earnings for "hours worked" during the preceding year, must vacation allowances paid in that year be included in figuring total earnings?

• According to one arbitrator, such allowances need not be included in computing earnings unless it can be affirmatively shown that the parties intended them to be. Standing alone, he said, the words "hours worked" can refer only to hours actually worked during the year (*John Deere Spreader Works of Deere & Co.*, 20 LA 670).

• Another arbitrator ruled that the employer violated the contract that stated that "employee's gross earnings for the 52 weeks prior to January 1 of the vacation year shall be the basis for computing vacation pay" by excluding the prior year's vacation pay. Even though the employer has been computing vacation pay in the same way for ten years, the method was incorrect and constituted a continuing violation of the contract (*Huffman Mfg. Co.*, 49 LA 357).

• Vacation pay that an employee received in 1974 was part of his "gross annual earnings" for that year for purposes of computing his vacation pay for 1975, an arbitrator ruled, where the contract entitled the employee with specified length of service to vacation and vacation pay at the rate of a certain percentage of his "gross annual earnings." Despite the employer's contention that the phrase "gross annual earnings" was ambiguous and that past practice should be considered in resolving the ambiguity, the arbitrator concluded that the contract language established the parties intent to consider the total "earned" amount, which included employees' vacations and holidays (*Canada-Ferro Company, Ltd.*, 66 LA 572).

### Inclusion of Other Pay

Most other forms of pay for authorized leave time usually are included by arbitrators in vacation pay computations.

● One arbitrator held that vacation, holiday, bereavement, and jury duty pay must be included in computing an employee's average straight-time earnings for the previous year for the purpose of computing vacation pay.

After an extensive review of prior decisions, the arbitrator concluded that the "almost consistent trend of arbitral authority is that all monetary benefits paid to an employee pursuant to the provisions of a collective bargaining agreement and incidental to his employment relationship are to be treated as earnings and included in the employee's earnings for the purpose of vacation pay. Any exceptions from the generally accepted meaning of the phrase 'straight-time earnings' should be expressly set forth by specific contract language" (*Ridge Machine Co.*, 53 LA 394).

## Where Employee Works at Two Rates

If a contract bases vacation pay on the employee's "regular rate," what is his regular rate if he has worked on two or more jobs paying different rates throughout the year? Arbitrators have interpreted such provisions in different ways.

● Where a man had been permanently transferred to a lower-rated job, an arbitrator held that he was properly given vacation pay at that lower rate under a clause that based vacation pay on the rate of the employee's regular job. The contract defined "regular job" to mean that to which an employee is regularly assigned or the job he is working on immediately prior to his vacation, whichever is higher. The arbitrator said that the lower-rated job was his regular job because he had been permanently assigned to it a week before his vacation (*Olin-Mathieson Chemical Corp.*, 24 LA 116).

● Where an employee was working at a job only temporarily, or where the employee's work required frequent shifts from one job to another, some arbitrators have held that such employees should be paid vacation benefits at the rate they received the majority of their time during the preceding year (*Hiram Walker & Sons Inc.*, 5 LA 186).

## Effect of General Wage Increase

When a new contract is negotiated that increases pay rates, should the old or new and higher rates be used in figuring vacation pay?

Unions may insist that rates *in effect at the time the vacation is taken* should be the basis for computing vacation pay, while management will argue that the vacation has been *earned* at the old rate.

Here again, where the contract is unclear, arbitrators tend to be guided by the employer's past practice.

● After reviewing prior awards, one arbitrator concluded that "thus, in all cases that have come to the attention of the arbitrator here, the unanimous view has been that where the contract language is not clear, the long established past practice must be followed" (*Sweden Freezer Inc.*, 43 LA 471).

Where there is no past practice, an arbitrator may conclude that the parties must have intended that the rate prevailing at the time of vacation is the one that should be used.

● An employer and union negotiated a new contract during May. This new agreement granted substantial wage increases, effective June 15. The employer distributed vacation pay on June 27, using old rates although it recognized the new vacation benefits as to length of service, overtime, etc. Its position was that pay rates in effect when the vacations were earned were the ones to be applied.

An arbitrator disagreed. He declared that when the parties drew up their new contract it was far more likely that they were thinking of the vacations just ahead of them than of the next year's vacations. Furthermore, the new rates were to be effective for two years, and if the parties had meant to use a different rate for vacation purposes, they would have said so, according to the arbitrator. It was concluded that the rate prevailing at the time of the vacations should be used (*Lynch Corp.*, 9 LA 115).

● Where a contract based employees' vacation pay on their hourly rate on May 1 of current year, an employer was not required to include in its employees' vacation pay a cost-of-living adjustment that became effective in the pay period beginning on May 13, 1974, an arbitrator decided, despite the union's contention that the wage increase was delayed by management because of clerical problems. Although the union may have intended to have the May 1 date include the cost-of-living allowance for May in the vacation pay calculations, the arbitrator found that it did not communicate that position to the employer during contract negotiations, nor did it make any other communications or actions supporting that intention (*Milwaukee Press & Machine Co.*, 65 LA 549).

A compromise system of pay may also be worked out by an arbitrator faced with the question of whether old or new rates should govern.

• An employer and union signed a new contract in April retroactive to March 31, which provided for a wage increase and a completely new vacation plan. Many employees would have received less vacation under the new plan, so the parties agreed that the year's vacations would be figured under the old contract. There was no discussion, however, as to rates of pay for vacation time, so the question was submitted to the arbitration board to determine whether the old or new rate be applied in figuring vacation pay.

The arbitrators held that it was the responsibility of both parties to bring up the matter of applicable pay rates and to secure an agreement on the matter. Given that neither party met this responsibility, it was concluded that it would be fair "for the parties to ... share equally the benefits and penalties of their failure to fix the rates at a point half way between those originally sought by the union and those sought by the employer" (*Crosley Motors Inc.*, 8 LA 1024).

### Effect of Retroactive Increase

When a wage increase is agreed to after vacations have been taken, and the increase is made retroactive to a date preceding the vacation, should the extra pay be included in the vacation pay? At least one arbitrator has said it should.

• "As a general rule, when a wage increase is made retroactive," the arbitrator held, "it applies to all hours for which employees have been paid during the retroactive period. That rule is applicable whether such hours are those of holidays, vacations, or hours of work" (*Pioneer Alloy Products Co. Inc.*, 5 LA 458).

### Effect of Annual Improvement Increase

Must an annual improvement factor be added to an employee's vacation pay if the increase goes into effect while he is on vacation?

• In the absence of any contract provision on the subject, one arbitrator ruled that such an increase must be incorporated in pay for any part of a vacation that falls after the effective date of the increase (*Ford Motor Co.*, 17 LA 512).

### Effect of Strike

Can time spent on a strike be excluded in computing vacation pay?

The answer usually turns on the past practice of the parties or upon the wording of the contract.

• Where a contract based vacation pay on "time worked," an arbitrator held that management had a right to deduct strike time (*Modecraft Co.*, 33 LA 1236).

• An arbitrator ruled that economic strikers were not entitled to vacation-benefit accrual, despite a claim that the employer had not reduced the accrual for leaves of absence and that the NLRB stated in an unfair-labor-practice decision that a "leave of absence is, under the plan, the same as a strike." The NLRB, the arbitrator found, did not state that strike time was to be treated as a leave of absence and made no determination that vacation benefits accrued during the strike.

In addition, the arbitrator noted the employer had prorated vacation accruals for leaves of absence, and vacation pay is a form of compensation that is not earned on strike. The arbitrator added that the retroactive application of the contract applied to vacation-benefit accrual, despite the claim that the retroactive application was solely for the purpose of health-insurance-premium payment because the contract did not specifically restrict the application of the effective date to select provisions (*Murphy Oil USA Inc.*, 92 LA 1148).

• An employer had the right to reduce the vacation benefits of employees to reflect their absence from work that was caused by a strike, an arbitrator decided, where the contract granted employees vacation with pay following completion of a specified period of service, because the parties intended "service" to mean "service rendered" or "worked" (*Reichhold Chemicals Inc.*, 66 LA 745; see also 63 LA 1235).

• Under a contract providing that the anniversary date of each employee shall be his most recent date of hire by the employer and that his eligibility for vacation pay shall be computed from such date, an arbitrator held that an employer did not have the right to deduct time lost because of leave of absence, layoff, and strikes from the total years of service for purposes of computing employees' entitlement to vacation pay (*Blue Box Co.*, 61 LA 754).

• Where the contract was *silent*, an arbitrator was persuaded by a past practice of allowing full vacation pay in strike situations (*Mobil Oil Co.*, 42 LA 102).

• Past practice worked to managements' favor in a case where the employer, in figuring out weekly vacation pay, followed the practice of dividing the employees' earnings in the past year by 52 weeks. In view of this practice, the arbitrator saw nothing wrong in using the 52-week divisor in a year when the employees had lost six weeks' earnings because of a strike (*Blaw-Knox Co.*, 47 LA 1164).

## Effect of Workers'
## Compensation Payments

Arbitrators' views vary on whether an employee is entitled to both vacation pay and workers' compensation benefits.

• An employee who received 15 weeks' pay for working and 30 weeks' pay from workers' compensation during one year was not entitled to vacation pay for

that year, according to one arbitrator. The contract provided that employees had a right to vacation pay if they had worked for the employer for one year, and received 40 "paychecks" within the year. Considering the union's unsuccessful attempt to include reference to workers' compensation checks, the arbitrator maintained that "paycheck" meant a check for work done (*Ohse Meat Products Inc.*, 48 LA 978).

• Employees were not entitled to have included in computation of their vacation pay time they were absent from work because of injuries received on the job, for which they were compensated under state workers' compensation law (*Modecraft Co.*, 44 LA 1045; see also 83 LA 969).

• Employees who failed, because of an industrial accident, to accumulate contractually specified straight-time hours of work were entitled to vacation pay on the basis of actual hours worked, an arbitrator ruled, despite receipt of workers' compensation during the vacation period (*Solar Chemical Corp.*, 56 LA 99).

• An employee who was awarded total disability under workers' compensation was entitled to vacation benefits for 400 weeks during which he was to receive the workers' compensation benefits, an arbitrator ruled. Pointing out that the employee who continued to receive benefits from the employer was considered as being on the employer "payroll," notwithstanding the fact that he was not on the "active payroll," the arbitrator concluded that there was nothing in the contract to support the employer's claim that its vacation obligation was restricted to the year the employee sustained the injury (*Thomas Industries Inc.*, 61 LA 627).

## Quit or Retirement Before Eligibility
## Date

Where a contract stated that employees must have a certain period of service and must have worked a certain number of days "prior to August 1 of the vacation year," to be eligible for vacation pay, the arbitrator ruled that those who fulfilled the requirements but left the job before

Aug. 1, were entitled to vacation pay. It is a generally recognized principle in industry that under this type of vacation clause employment on a specific date is not a condition of eligibility for vacation pay (*Telescope Folding Furniture Co.*, 49 LA 837; see also 83 LA 1092).

● An employee whose last day of work was December 30, 1975 and who was placed on retirement on January 1, 1976 was not entitled to vacation pay for 1976, an arbitrator ruled, under contract provisions granting vacation pay to employees who were on the payroll on the beginning of the vacation year and who have worked during the vacation year. The contract defined the vacation year as constituting the period from January 1 to December 31. Despite the union's contention that the employee was on the payroll for the period ending January 4 and therefore was "on the payroll on the beginning of the vacation year," the arbitrator concluded that the employee did not work during 1976 and thus failed to meet the requirement that an employee must have worked during the vacation year to be eligible for vacation benefits (*Westvaco*, 67 LA 128).

● Employees who elected to retire before the period set for taking vacations were not entitled to vacation pay, an arbitrator decided, under a contract stating that an employee who quits or is discharged for cause shall not be eligible for vacation or vacation pay (*York Wall Paper Co.*, 69 LA 431; see also 91 LA 795, 84 LA 863).

### Effect of Plant Shutdown

Employees who were terminated as a result of an employer's voluntary shutdown of the plant are entitled to pro-rata vacation pay for the time worked prior to the shutdown, an arbitrator ruled, even though the contract required a minimum number of hours worked as eligibility. He reasoned that vacations are additional wages and no longer considered merely periods of rest. Therefore, vacation benefits already earned under the unexpired contract cannot be completely annulled by the shutdown (*National Plumbing Fixture Corp.*, 49 LA 421; see also 87 LA 1109, 85 LA 979, 51 LA 400).

● An arbitrator held that an employee on his layoff was not entitled to request a deferment of lump-sum payment for vacation or sick-leave benefits until the expiration of his three-year recall rights or upon request for payment of benefits, under a contract that provided for the deferral of benefits to a month selected in the next calendar year by an employee who retires (*Sacramento, Calif.*, 82 LA 996; see also 82 LA 686, 82 LA 193, 81 LA 1268, 81 LA 556).

### 'Actual' or 'Normal' Workweek?

Some contracts spell out what a "normal" workweek is, and then in the vacation clause they base vacation pay on the "workweek." If, under such a contract, a plant has actually been operating on a schedule longer or shorter than the normal workweek, which period should be used in computing vacation pay—the actual or the normal week? Decisions have gone both ways in solving this problem.

● It has been held that the workweek as defined in the contract is the one to be used, even when management has been basing vacation pay on the actual workweek in the past (*Dunkirk Radiator Corp.*, 1 LA 249).

● At least one arbitrator has held that the number of hours actually being worked by employees was the proper base for vacation pay. The contract in this case based vacation pay on the "scheduled workweek in the previous calendar year" and also defined the "normal" workweek as 40 hours long. Reasoning that "scheduled" refers to a time established in advance and consistently adhered to, the arbitrator decided that vacation pay should be based on the six-day week actually worked because the employees usually expected to work on Saturdays unless otherwise notified. He found that 65 percent of the time they did not receive such notice. For this reason he ruled that the six-day week was the "scheduled" workweek (*Cemenstone Co.*, 9 LA 41).

### Individual versus Plant Workweek

Where different employees work a different number of hours per week, another common problem in computing vacation pay arises—whether the workweek of each employee or the standard workweek for the whole plant should be used. Arbitrators have held that the plant's workweek is the one to be used to avoid confusion.

• Under a contract basing vacation pay on the "weekly hours worked by the employer in a majority of the workweeks of the vacation year," the union contended that the weekly average of actual hours worked by all employees should be used in computing vacation pay. An arbitrator upheld the employer's view that the number of hours scheduled for the whole plant should be the base. He reasoned that the word "company" in the clause refers to a whole and not isolated parts of the operation. The union's position, he said, would cause much confusion and destroy the meaning of established work schedules (*G. C. Hussey & Co.*, 5 LA 446).

• In another case an arbitration board decided that the exclusion of overtime payments from vacation pay pointed "to a definite workweek in the plant as a whole" (*International Harvester Co.*, 9 LA 35).

### Effect of Changes in Workweek

Where the length of the workweek has varied from time to time during the vacation year, which period should be used in figuring vacation pay?

• One arbitrator held that the workweek in effect at the time the vacation is taken is the proper one (*General Controls Co.*, 12 LA 852).

• Under a contract that specified 48 hours as the base for figuring vacation pay, an arbitrator held that the employer could not reduce vacation benefits to 40 hours' pay just because the workweek had been reduced to 40 hours (*Kempsmith Machine Co.*, 5 LA 520).

# Part 8

# *Holidays*

# Eligibility for Holiday Pay

———————————— OVERVIEW ————————————

Holiday pay does not exist as a matter of law (53 LA 1165), as one arbitrator said; or as another held, "There is no inherent right to holiday pay, and none exists except as set forth in the labor agreement" (46 LA 102).

Therefore, although holiday pay is recognized as an earned benefit, pay for holidays not worked is usually conditioned upon an employee's compliance with certain, contractually stated work requirements. Most collective bargaining agreements, for example, require both a stipulated minimum period of service, and work on designated days surrounding the holiday, before an employee is entitled to holiday pay.

It is generally agreed that the purpose of "surrounding-days" work requirements is to prevent employees from "stretching" holidays (53 LA 1206, 49 LA 468, 48 LA 1101) and to ensure a full working force on the day before and the day after a holiday (46 LA 102, 40 LA 673).

Thus, a significant consequence of the work requirements clauses, according to one arbitrator, is that the "failure of an employee to comply with them as a condition precedent to holiday pay operates to disqualify him from receiving such benefit" (*Motch & Merryweather Machinery Co.*, 51 LA 723).

Arbitrators have upheld management decisions not to award holiday pay to employees who fail to meet such work requirements, despite employees' claims that they were absent through no fault of their own (91 LA 345, 69 LA 604, 69 LA 189).

In cases where employees claim that an illness prevented them from meeting the holiday work requirement, eligibility for holiday pay may depend on whether the employees are able to provide a valid medical excuse for their absences (93 LA 537, 92 LA 571, 92 LA 228, 91 LA 1174, 81 LA 943, 81 LA 330, 73 LA 414, 70 LA 1273, 70 LA 1046, 70 LA 935, 67 LA 638, 67 LA 97, 64 LA 625, 63 LA 982).

If a contract grants holiday pay without restriction, chances are that a laid-off employee is entitled to it—particularly if the layoff is brief. In deciding whether to award holiday pay to laid-off employees, an arbitrator may examine the specific language of the contract, the timing and length of the layoff period, or the employers' reasons for instituting the layoffs (96 LA 1218, 82 LA 1170, 71 LA 611).

## Work Requirements

*Incomplete day's work*—If employees must work both the day before and the day following a holiday in order to qualify for holiday pay, do they have to put in *full days?* What if employees are absent *part* of one of the qualifying days? It is generally recognized that the real purpose of such a provision is to prevent stretching of holidays. Going on this assumption, most arbitrators hold that employees who take time off for good reason on the day before or after the holiday have fulfilled their requirements under this kind of holiday clause.

● One arbitrator made the distinction between "stretching" a holiday and "arranging the necessary adjustments to make the holiday available." Thus, he said that an employee who left work a half hour early the day before a holiday so he could catch a train was eligible for holiday pay (*John Deere Tractor Co.*, 9 LA 21).

● Where an employee was 36 minutes late to work on the day before a holiday, he was held to be qualified for holiday pay because he had worked on the scheduled working day as required by the contract (*Lake City Malleable Inc.*, 25 LA 753).

● An employee who received permission from her foreman to visit her doctor during pre-holiday shift was entitled to holiday pay for Dec. 30 and 31, an arbitrator decided, because she returned to finish her shift as requested by the foreman (*ITT-Phillips Drill Division*, 69 LA 437).

● It has been held that partial absences are to be considered as depriving an employee of holiday eligibility under a before-and-after-work requirement. One arbitrator held that employees who received permission to leave early on the day before or after Christmas Day were not entitled to holiday pay under a strict interpretation of the requirement. He based his decision on the fact that the parties had discussed the clause at great length and agreed upon it in order to avoid disputes over excused absences

(*American Bemberg & North American Rayon Corp.*, 10 LA 384).

*Definition of 'working day'*—Is a "working day" the day that actually precedes or follows a holiday, regardless of whether an employee was scheduled to work on that day, or is it the first day preceding or following a holiday on which an employee is told to come in and work? An arbitrator would probably hold that "working day" was the first day on which management expected work from an employee.

● A contract obligated any employee "to work his full shift on both the working day before and the working day after the holiday."

A holiday fell on Thursday. An employee worked the preceding Wednesday, and was told not to work on the day following the holiday, Friday. She was scheduled to work on Monday, but did not report.

The employee contended that Friday should be considered the "working day after the holiday." Management argued that "working day" meant a day on which an employee was actually scheduled to work, and that Monday should be considered the "working day."

The arbitrator agreed with management. He held that ordinarily "working day" referred to a day on which an employee was expected to work. He noted also that minor variation from schedules were the rule. In other words, there was no evidence that the instructions to some employees not to work on the Friday following the Thursday holiday were connected with the occurrence of the holiday (*American Thread Co.*, 10 LA 250).

*Eligibility days not in holiday week*—Under a holiday clause requiring work on the day before and day after the holiday, do these eligibility days have to be in the same week as the holiday? In many instances arbitrators have held that they do not.

● An employer promised to pay holiday pay "provided such holiday falls or is celebrated within the regularly scheduled workweek, and provided further that such employee works the workday previous to and the workday following such holiday."

A holiday fell on a Thursday and the plant was closed for the rest of that week. An employee was denied pay for the holiday because he was absent the next Monday. An arbitration board majority upheld the employer's position that the days preceding and following a holiday on which work was required did not have to fall in the same workweek as the holiday. The opinion stated that it was "likely that the union will discover upon investigation, that in nearly all cases where a clause such as this is in a contract, it is applied so that the "workday" before or after the holiday may be in a workweek other than that in which the holiday occurs" (*Veeder-Root Inc.*, 11 LA 33; see also 12 LA 886, 41 LA 776).

*Saturday as 'work day'*—If Saturday is a scheduled work day, can employees who fail to report for overtime on Saturday be denied pay for a Monday holiday that follows? In answering this question, arbitrators look at the exact wording of the agreement.

• Under a contract that required employees to work the regularly scheduled work day before and after the holiday to be eligible for holiday pay, employees were held entitled to pay, for a Monday holiday, even though they failed to report for work scheduled for the preceding Saturday. The arbitrator found that the contract defined a regular week's work as consisting of 40 hours, Monday through Friday, inclusive. In view of this, he said, Saturday could not be considered a regularly scheduled work day (*Hinde & Dauch Paper Co.*, 22 LA 505).

• At another plant employees failing to report for Saturday work were held ineligible for holiday pay for the following Monday because the contract did not limit the hours employees could be required to work. The arbitrator decided that they had not met the contract's requirement of working on the last scheduled work day, even though it was overtime (*Great Lakes Spring Corp.*, 12 LA 779).

• In order to count Saturday as a scheduled work day, when it is overtime work that is involved, an arbitrator ruled that the employer must have the right to force such overtime work. In this case, where the contract spoke of normal Monday-through-Friday workweek and of "requests" to work on Saturday or Sunday, Saturday was not allowed to be counted as the last "scheduled" work day before a Monday holiday (*Amron Corp.*, 47 LA 582).

• Where an employer had the right to require Saturday overtime work, an arbitrator held that employees who failed to report for such work prior to a Monday holiday thereby failed to meet the requirement that they work the last scheduled work day prior to the holiday (*Sargent-Welch Scientific Co.*, 54 LA 923; see also 73 LA 777).

*Failure to work scheduled holiday*—Many contracts state that holiday pay is not required for employees who fail to report on holidays when work is scheduled. In spite of such apparently clear contract language, many problems have come up when employees have claimed their holiday pay, even though they did not work. In such cases, arbitrators give considerable weight to the method used in informing employees that work had been scheduled, as well as to past practice.

• In one instance an arbitrator ruled that it was enough for an employer to post notices a week beforehand that work was scheduled for the following Monday, a holiday. Because many employees on vacation called in to find out if work was scheduled for the holiday, the arbitrator decided that others on vacation had no valid claim to holiday pay on the ground that they had not received sufficient notice (*Bethlehem Steel Co.*, 22 LA 781).

• At another plant it was held that employees who failed to show up for scheduled work on Christmas day were properly denied holiday pay. The fact that the foremen asked them whether they planned to work on the holiday did not mean that they had a choice of working or not, the arbitrator said (*Bethlehem Steel Co.*, 25 LA 680).

• Workers who refused to report for holiday work, after an emergency call-in, lost their right to holiday pay, under a provision making ineligible those who were requested or scheduled to work and failed to do so. An arbitrator held that this did not require advance requests or scheduling for holiday work as contended by the union (*Firestone Tire & Rubber Co.*, 29 LA 469).

• Although one arbitrator recognized an employer's right to make changes in the work schedule, he ruled that one day's notice to report for work on a holiday was not enough. Thus, in spite of the contract provision denying holiday pay to those failing to report for work on a holiday when scheduled, the arbitrator concluded that the absent employees were entitled to holiday pay. (*Bethlehem Steel Co.*, 23 LA 271).

*Holiday pay after termination*— When terminated employees receive accumulated vacation pay, they also may be entitled to pay for holidays falling within the period covered by the vacation allowances, according to one arbitrator.

• Some employees who were terminated in May and June received from one to three weeks' accumulated vacation pay. The union contended that certain of them should have received additional pay for Memorial Day and the Fourth of July because these holidays fell during the weeks covered by their vacation pay. In rejecting this claim, the employer relied on two contract provisions—one stating that an employee had to work his scheduled work days before and after a holiday to qualify for pay and another saying that a laid-off employee would get holiday pay only if the layoff occurred in the holiday week.

An arbitrator found neither clause controlling. He reasoned that the purpose of the work requirements was to prevent holiday stretching; and that, although the layoffs did not take place during the holiday weeks, the employer by granting vacation pay deferred the effective dates of the layoffs beyond the holiday weeks. Hence he concluded that the applicable clause was one granting holiday pay in addition to vacation pay for a holiday falling during an employee's vacation (*Continental-Emsco Co.*, 31 LA 449).

**Effect of Shutdown**

*Permanent shutdown*—Are employees eligible for holidays that come after a plant closes down permanently? Although arbitrators have ruled both ways on the problem, their decisions seem to turn on whether individual employees are otherwise eligible for the holiday pay rather than the facts surrounding the shutdown itself.

• Where one plant shut down on New Year's Eve, an arbitrator held that employees were not eligible for pay for New Year's Day because they had not worked the following day as required by the contract (*Calif. Metal Trades Assn.*, 11 LA 788).

*Temporary shutdown*—Most arbitrators have ruled that employees fulfill their work requirements for pay for a holiday falling during a temporary shutdown if they work the last scheduled working day before it and the first scheduled working day after it. Such a ruling is usually based on the assumption that a plant's closing down is something that employees cannot control.

• In one case an arbitrator pointed out to the employer that the contract required work on the working days before and after a holiday rather than the day before and after the holiday. In light of the fact that the employees had worked December 30 and had been told not to report again until Jan. 5 the arbitrator held that these were the working days. So, he concluded, the employees were entitled to pay for New Year's Day (*Aerolite Electronic Hardware Corp.*, 10 LA 215).

• Employees who worked the day before the Christmas day holiday that fell on Thursday, and who did not work on the succeeding Friday because the employer temporarily had shut down operations were entitled to holiday pay for Christmas Day, an arbitrator decided, even though they failed to work the following Monday. The employees, the arbitrator stated, were qualified for the holiday pay because they worked the day before the Christmas holiday and were excused from working on the day after the holiday (*Reilly Tar and Chemical Corp.*, 66 LA 835; see also 75 LA 651).

● In another case, employees who did not work the last shift on the workday before the start of a two-week vacation shutdown were not entitled to holiday pay for the fourth of July holiday that fell during the shutdown period, an arbitrator held, because there was a past practice requiring employees, when a holiday falls during a shutdown, to work the day before and the day after the shutdown to be eligible for holiday pay (*Regal Ware Inc.*, 65 LA 795).

● It has been held that a month-long shutdown does deprive employees of holiday pay under a before-and-after work requirement, whereas a brief shutdown of only three days does not have this effect (*Vulcan Detinning Co.*, 4 LA 483).

● An arbitrator held employees were properly denied pay for a holiday falling during a shutdown where the contract specified that holidays must fall within a scheduled workweek. The arbitrator ruled that no scheduled workweek was in effect (*Sefton Fibre Can Co.*, 12 LA 101).

*Involuntary shutdown*—When an employer was shutdown because of a strike by another union, an arbitrator decided that the employees were not entitled to pay for the holiday that fell during the shutdown. Certain of the assumptions underlying a labor contract precluded the holiday-pay claim, he said, and primary among these was that the employer must be operating and able to provide employment opportunities. Because the employer had to suspend production involuntarily through no fault of its own, the arbitrator concluded that a liberal reading of the contract would raise an obligation never expected or intended by the parties (*Publishers' Assn. of New York City*, 40 LA 140).

## Effect of Layoff

*In lieu of eligibility requirements*—When a contract contains no specific eligibility requirements, are employees on layoff entitled to holiday pay? A common argument for awarding them pay is that companies might lay off their employees for the express purpose of avoiding holiday payments if laid-off employees were held ineligible. Some arbitrators have

held that those on just a temporary layoff do not lose their rights to holiday pay.

● One arbitrator ruled that the equities of a situation required that employees laid off because of a machine breakdown should be paid holiday pay because the breakdown was not their fault (*Thompson Mahogany Co.*, 5 LA 397).

● Another arbitrator found that, in a somewhat seasonal industry where layoffs were fairly regular, employees would suffer a serious inequity if they lost holiday pay just because of a layoff when they had worked throughout most of the contract year (*Otto Guggenheim & Co. Inc.*, 11 LA 1130; see also 10 LA 887).

● In keeping with the strict language of the contract, an arbitrator required that an employer abandon a past practice of 14 years. The only requirement for holiday pay was that the "employee actually works during the payroll week in which the holiday falls." A separate clause said that an employee would lose his standing as an "employee" if he was laid off for 12 consecutive months. When seven employees, who had been laid off for a little over nine months, were recalled the day after Labor Day, they qualified for holiday pay under the terms of the contract. The employer's practice of not granting holiday pay if the return followed the holiday was ruled improper (*Anaconda Aluminum Co.*, 48 LA 219).

● It has been held that if the layoff is bona fide, employees should be denied holiday pay. One arbitrator noted that, if holiday pay were granted, laid-off employees who had secured jobs somewhere else would get holiday pay from two companies (*Tenney Engineering Co.*, 10 LA 307).

*Before and after holiday work requirement*—Are laid-off employees considered as having met a requirement for working on the days preceding and following the holiday?

● One arbitrator ruled that the parties must have intended that employees on layoff should receive holiday pay even though they did not work on the days before and after the holiday. His reasoning was that there would have been no reason to write a contract clause requiring employees to have earned some wages within the 30 days before the holiday if the parties had meant to exclude laid-off employees from holiday-pay eligibility (*Thomas L. Leedom Co.*, 21 LA 740; see also 75 LA 729).

● Another arbitrator decided that employees who were laid off indefinitely between 1 and 3:30 p.m. on the day before a Thanksgiving holiday, which was their last scheduled workday prior to the holiday, and who otherwise met the employer's work requirements, were entitled to a full holiday's pay for the holiday. The arbitrator concluded, however, that the employees were not entitled to holiday pay for other holidays that fell during the layoff period that lasted from five to seven months (*Premiere Corp.*, 67 LA 376).

● It has also been held that laid-off employees are not exempt from work requirements.

One arbitrator reasoned that if he ruled otherwise, employees laid off for a whole year could claim pay for all six holidays provided by the contract. This, he said, would conflict with the fundamental purpose of the work requirement, that is, to cut down the monetary cost to the employer (*Chrome-Rite Co.*, 12 LA 691; see also 82 LA 1170, 72 LA 528, 71 LA 609).

*Employees on payroll*—If the holiday-pay clause of a contract applies only to those employees on the payroll, are laid-off employees considered on the payroll? Generally arbitrators hold that laid-off employees are not technically on the payroll, and thus are not entitled to the benefits of that status.

● In trying to define "on the payroll" one arbitrator found help in another section of a contract. The sick-leave clause specified that employees were on the active payroll if not laid off. So he reasoned that persons who were laid off were not on the payroll and, therefore, not entitled to holiday pay (*Armour & Co.*, 9 LA 338).

● Under another holiday clause with an on-the-payroll requirement an arbitrator ruled that laid-off employees did not go on the payroll until they went back to work (*The Flintkote Co.*, 26 LA 526).

*Recalled after holiday*—Are employees who are recalled from layoff after a holiday entitled to holiday pay? One arbitrator has ruled yes.

● Employees were recalled from layoff within two to three weeks after the Memorial Day holiday. The arbitrator ruled that the employees were entitled to pay for the holiday, because the contract entitled an employee who has been absent as a result of a short-term layoff to holiday pay if he has worked "within" 30 calendar days of the holiday (*Consolidated Aluminum Corp.*, 66 LA 938; see also 72 LA 840).

*Workers on disciplinary layoff*—Can employees who fail to meet the work requirements because of disciplinary layoff be denied holiday pay? In most cases arbitrators hold this practice to be justifiable.

● In one situation an arbitrator concluded that if the parties had meant to provide holiday-pay eligibility for employees on disciplinary layoff, the contract would have said so. He based his decision on the fact that other sections of the contract specifically mentioned "disciplinary layoff" as being covered (*McInerney Spring & Wire Co.*, 11 LA 1195; see also 11 LA 1181).

● At least one arbitrator has held that the employer was wrong in denying holiday pay to an employee who was on a two-day disciplinary layoff on the days immediately preceding and following the holiday. The arbitrator pointed out that the purpose of requiring an employee to work the days before and after a holiday is to discourage him from stretching the holiday on his own volition. But in this case the employee was not absent by his own choice. Because he had been ordered not to report for work, the arbitrator said he could not be held responsible for missing the days that the contract required for eligibility. Accordingly, the employer was ordered to pay him for the holiday (*Inland Steel Co.*, 20 LA 323).

### Effect of Strike

*Workday before or after holiday*— Even where employees failed to work the full workday before a holiday because of a breach-of-contract walkout, arbitrators have held the employees entitled to holiday pay, absent a showing that the strike was a result of a premeditated plan and that the part-day's work was intended only as token compliance with the holiday-pay eligibility requirements (20 LA 349, 16 LA 317).

• Other arbitrators have held that employees who, because of a work stoppage, do not work the complete day before or after a holiday do not qualify for holiday pay (93 LA 473, 85 LA 51, 62 LA 681, 68 LA 835, 35 LA 117, 11 LA 462, 40 LA 673).

*Absence of agreement*—Holiday pay normally does not accrue during a strike if there is no collective bargaining agreement in effect when the strike occurs. This principle has been applied to strikes that take place after the expiration of a contract, to lawful strikes under a wage re-opener, and to unauthorized strikes during the contract term (74 LA 1058, 37 LA 3, 43 LA 539, 36 LA 1276, 33 LA 681, 30 LA 671, 24 LA 561).

• As one arbitrator explained, "when an employee has chosen to detach himself temporarily from the contract effects by a strike or stoppage running through a holiday, he has surrendered the holiday benefit just as surely as he surrenders pay on any other day of such a stoppage. The surrender is certainly not lessened by the fact that the stoppage is an unauthorized one during the life of the agreement and barred by its terms" (*Hellenic Lines, Ltd.*, 38 LA 339).

• One arbitrator allowed holiday pay for New Year's Eve Day where a legal strike beginning on the day after a contract expired made it impossible to work the "next scheduled workday" (*A. O. Smith Corp.*, 51 LA 1309).

*Retroactive agreements*—A special problem arises when a strike-settlement agreement is made retroactive to the starting date of the strike. Does this mean that the strikers should be paid for holidays occurring during the strike?

• In one case, a claim for holiday pay was denied on the grounds that: (1) the new contract required work on scheduled work days before and after the holiday, (2) the plant was operating during the strike and work was available on the pre-

and post-holiday work days, and (3) the strikers had failed to meet the eligibility requirement by working on those days (*Alside Inc.*, 42 LA 75).

• Strikers were not entitled to holiday pay for the Labor Day holiday that fell during the strike period, an arbitrator ruled, even though the parties entered into a strike settlement agreement that retroactively reinstated expired contract provisions that were not modified in the new contract, including the holiday pay provision. Noting that the strike prevented the employees from complying with the employer's holiday work requirements, the arbitrator pointed out that the parties did not make a special provision for requiring payment of holiday pay for Labor Day (*Packaging Corp. of America*, 62 LA 1214).

*No work requirement*—If employees are out on strike at the time a holiday comes up, does that make them ineligible for holiday pay? Sometimes, if there was no work requirement for holiday-pay eligibility, it has been held that employees on strike were entitled to pay for holidays falling during the strike (*Royle & Pilkington Co. Inc.*, 18 LA 451).

*Refusal to cross picket lines*—Can employees who are absent because they refuse to cross picket lines be denied holiday pay on the ground that they do not meet work requirements? Generally arbitrators have held that holiday pay does not have to be paid in such cases even if the contract gives employees the right to respect picket lines.

• One arbitrator with this view said that it is one thing for an employer to agree that employees may respect picket lines, but it is something else again to approve their absence when they do (*Schlage Lock Co.*, 30 LA 105; see also 54 LA 754, 25 LA 687).

• An arbitrator ruled that an employer was not obligated to pay holiday pay or birthday pay to employees for July 4 holiday and birthdays of some of the employees that fell during the time when they were honoring picket lines of another union. In absence of a contract provision requiring such payments, the arbitrator concluded that the union should bear economic loses falling within the period of its economic and adversary struggle with the employer (*Pearl Brewing Co.*, 68 LA 221).

### Effect of Vacations

*When vacation includes holiday*— When a scheduled vacation period includes a holiday, are employees still entitled to pay for the holiday? Several arbitrators have held that eligible employees have the right to pay for a holiday even though it does fall within a vacation period.

● In one situation where a plant shutdown for vacations beginning July 3, an arbitrator ruled that the employees were justified in their claim for pay for the Fourth. The employer argued that, even though the contract said July 4 was a holiday, it should not have to give employees vacation pay and holiday pay for the same day. But the arbitrator said that, once the employees had qualified for paid vacation and paid holidays, the right to these earnings could not be cut off by the employer's timing of the vacation period (*Koler Cigar Co.*, 8 LA 143).

● In a similar instance an arbitrator held that employees should be paid for holidays falling within their vacations even if they chose the time of their vacations themselves. He said this was not shifting any loss to the employer, but only requiring it to pay the employee as much if he chose a vacation in which there is a holiday as he would have received if he chose one without a holiday (*Tioga Mills Inc.*, 10 LA 371).

● An employee was not entitled to pay for a holiday that fell during a scheduled vacation, an arbitrator decided, where the holiday also fell during a wage re-opener strike. The employee, the arbitrator held, was not excused from working on the last regularly scheduled workday before and the first workday after his vacation in order to be eligible for holiday pay (*Union Carbide Corp.*, 65 LA 189; see also 65 LA 795).

*Late return from vacation including holiday*—When an employee returned from vacation a day late, was he entitled to pay for a holiday that fell during the vacation period? One arbitrator held that he was, because eligibility tests for vacations and holidays were separate.

● The contract provided for an extra day's pay when a holiday fell during a vacation period, and also stated that employees must work the day before and after a holiday to be eligible for holiday pay. The employer argued that the employee did not meet the work test for holiday-pay eligibility because he did not show up the day after his vacation.

The employee did qualify, the arbitrator decided, because the holiday-during-vacation clause had to be entirely separate from the work-test clause. Otherwise, he reasoned, the contract could be interpreted to require employees to show up for work on the days "immediately" preceding and following a holiday, even though they were on vacation (*Streitmann Supreme Bakery of Cincinnati*, 41 LA 628).

### Effects of Absence

*Absence for illness*—Are employees who are out sick entitled to holiday pay? Arbitrators' reasoning leads to different conclusions on this question (93 LA 537, 92 LA 571, 92 LA 228, 91 LA 1174, 81 LA 943, 81 LA 330, 73 LA 777, 73 LA 414, 72 LA 607, 71 LA 1067).

● One contract stated that employees would not lose straight-time pay because of holidays. So an arbitrator denied pay for New Year's Day to an employee who was absent for illness from December 29 to January 5. He reasoned that the sick employee did not lose pay because of the holiday because he would not have worked if the day had not been a holiday (*General Mills Inc.*, 10 LA 53).

● An employer was not required to pay holiday pay to an employee who was sick and missed a workday following Thanksgiving holidays, an arbitrator ruled, where a doctor's statement confirming the employee's sickness was insufficient to constitute a grant of "sick leave" for purposes of establishing holiday pay eligibility (*Rheem Mfg. and Steelworkers*, 62 LA 837).

● An employee who failed to obtain a doctor's certificate certifying to his illness on the day after Christmas holiday was not entitled to holiday pay for the Christmas holiday, an arbitrator decided, despite the employee's contention that he was too sick to consult his physician (*Weil-McLain Co. Inc. and Sheet Metal Workers*, 64 LA 625).

• An employee who sustained an injury to his finger but who was certified as capable of returning to work on a workday that fell on a legal holiday was not entitled to holiday pay, an arbitrator held, where the contract limited holiday pay only to employees who worked the last full scheduled workday prior to and the first full scheduled workday after a holiday (*Belknap Inc.*, 69 LA 599).

• Where a contract provided for both paid sick leave and paid holidays, an arbitrator held that an employee who was receiving sick pay for Christmas and New Year's Day could not get holiday pay for those days, too. The arbitrator reasoned that if the parties had meant to duplicate sick pay and holiday pay for the same days, they would have clearly stated it in the agreement. He noted further that this had never been done in the past (*Standard Oil Co. (Indiana)*, 26 LA 206).

• An employee who was absent on his last scheduled workday prior to a holiday was entitled to holiday pay an arbitrator decided, despite his failure to obtain a physician's statement as required by his employer. The employee was unaware that when he became sick the day in question was his last scheduled work day prior to the holiday because the work schedule had not been posted, the arbitrator reasoned (*United States Steel Corp.*, 67 LA 97).

• An employee who claimed to be sick on the day after a holiday was entitled to pay for that holiday, an arbitrator ruled, notwithstanding the employer's contention that the employee failed to provide a legitimate doctor's excuse for his absence. Noting that the contract did not provide for substantiation of excuse for holiday pay in order to render a qualified employee eligible for such pay, the arbitrator concluded that the employee's post holiday sickness constituted a legitimate excuse, absent any challenge to the truthfulness of his claim of illness (*Hubbell Metals Inc.*, 67 LA 638).

• Where a contract clearly waived a day-before-and-after work requirement for holiday pay in the case of sickness, an arbitrator said, it meant that employees out sick were entitled to holiday pay, no matter when their illness began (*Bakers' Negotiating Committee*, 24 LA 694).

**Absence caused by on-the-job injury**—Are employees who are absence because of an on-the-job injury entitled to holiday pay? Some arbitrators have ruled yes.

• Employees were entitled to holiday pay for holidays falling while they were receiving workers' compensation as a result of on-the-job injuries, an arbitrator decided, notwithstanding the employer's contention that the employees were on "leave of absence" and, thus, disqualified from receiving the pay under the contract. Pointing out that the leave of absence provision in the contract related to unpaid leaves for reasons of "sickness, personal injuries or further educational study," the arbitrator observed that the fact holidays were paid days, as opposed to days off with pay, suggested that the holiday pay was part of the employee's regular wage (*Walworth County*, 71 LA 1118).

• Another arbitrator decided that in accordance with established past practice, as well as the contract, an employee who was ill and who suffered an occupational injury, certified by a doctor, was entitled to pay for only the first holiday occurring during the period in which more than one holiday occurred (*Chardon Rubber Co.*, 71 LA 1039).

**Absence for union business**—If employees do not meet holiday eligibility requirements because they are absent on union business, are they entitled to holiday pay? In one case an arbitrator answered "Yes" to this question. The holiday clause required employees to work on the day preceding and following a holiday in order to be eligible for holiday pay. The arbitrator based his decision on a contract provision stating that time lost in conducting union business would be counted in figuring service and attendance records (*International Harvester Co.*, 11 LA 1166).

***Involuntary absences***—Is an employee entitled to holiday pay if his failure to meet work requirements was caused by circumstances beyond his control? Some arbitrators have ruled in favor of the employees in such cases.

• This problem came up under one contract that required employees to work the scheduled days before and after a holiday to be eligible for holiday pay, except in the case of "justified absence." On the last scheduled workday before the Fourth of July, some employees could not get to work because of a bus strike.

Arguing that their absence was not justified, the employer denied them holiday pay. But an arbitrator held they were entitled to it. Noting that the purpose of a work requirement in a holiday clause is to prevent holiday stretching, he concluded that these employees were absent because of the bus strike and not because of a desire to lengthen their holiday (*Bemis Bros. Bag Co.*, 25 LA 429; see also 28 LA 390).

• An employee who was three minutes late in reporting for work after New Year's holiday because of an ice storm was entitled to holiday pay, an arbitrator ruled, despite a contract provision requiring the employee to work the last full scheduled work day prior to and after a holiday in order to be eligible for unworked holiday pay (*Vertex Systems Inc.*, 68 LA 1099).

• An employer properly refused to approve the absence of an employee on a workday after Thanksgiving holidays because of adverse weather conditions, an arbitrator decided. Therefore, the arbitrator concluded that the employee also was properly denied holiday pay (*Tennessee Dickel Distilling Co.*, 69 LA 189).

• An employee who did not report for work on the workday after New Year's Day holiday, despite the lifting of a road blockade that had been imposed several hours earlier in the day because of bad weather conditions, was not excused from submitting a reasonable excuse for his absence for purposes of establishing holiday pay eligibility, an arbitrator ruled (*Electrical Repair Service Co.*, 69 LA 604).

***Effect of disability or retirement***—Are employees who are out on a disability leave of absence or who retire from the employer on the day before a holiday entitled to holiday pay? Arbitrators have expressed varying views on this issue.

• One arbitrator ruled that an employee who went on disability retirement immediately after his disability leave of absence had expired was entitled to be paid for eight holidays occurring during his leave of absence. Despite the employer's contention that the employee had lost all of his holiday benefits because of his failure to return to work for one day after his extended absence, the arbitrator finds that management's interpretation of the contract's holiday provision did not bear a reasonable relationship to its purpose of preventing an employee from improperly extending his holiday absence. The alleged past practice of the employer of not paying holiday pay in similar situations was not binding, the arbitrator concluded, in view of the evidence that the employer followed this practice without the knowledge of the union (*Ideal Basic Industries Inc.*, 68 LA 928).

• Another arbitrator ruled that an employee whose last day of work was Dec. 30, 1975, and who was placed on retirement status on Jan. 1, 1976, was not entitled to holiday pay for New Year's Day holiday, notwithstanding the contention that because the employee did not work the regularly scheduled working day after New Year's Eve and New Year's Day holidays but nevertheless was given holiday pay for New Year's Eve holiday he should be paid for the New Year's Day holiday as well. Finding that the employer's decision to allow payment for the first holiday was in the nature of a gift for the employee who was about to retire, the arbitrator concluded the employee's entire standing changed on Jan. 1, when he no longer was considered an employee (*Westvaco*, 67 LA 128).

## Holidays Falling On Non-Work Days

***Saturday holidays***—Holiday clauses that simply designate certain days as paid holidays invite the question: When those listed holidays fall on Saturday what happens to employees' eligibility? Are they still entitled to pay for the holidays, or have they lost their rights?

In finding an answer to this as well as other eligibility problems, many arbitrators construe a provision for paid holidays as a negotiated wage increase. Pay for a certain number of holidays is often considered to be part of the employee's annual compensation. Thus, in the absence of clear contract language prohibiting it, it is frequently held that, no matter what day a holiday falls on, employees should be paid for it.

- In one case where the holiday clause was ambiguous, an arbitrator reasoned that if he denied employees pay for holidays falling on Saturday, he would be adding to a proviso to the contract that was not intended (*Carson Electric Co.*, 24 LA 667).

- Many arbitrators back up management's viewpoint that the purpose of a paid holiday clause is to protect employees from loss of pay caused by a holiday falling during the regular workweek. They reason, then, that if employees are not ordinarily scheduled to work on a day when a holiday occurs, they can not draw holiday pay under an unrestricted holiday clause. Thus it has been held that a Saturday holiday should not be paid for when a contract merely lists paid unworked holidays without going into the matter of the days the holidays fall on (*Standard Grocery Co.*, 7 LA 745).

***Saturday as scheduled work day***—If a contract limits holiday pay to those holidays that fall on a scheduled work day, and a holiday falls on Saturday, do employees rate the pay for it if they have been working overtime on Saturdays? In several instances arbitrators have denied pay for Saturday holidays under this kind of requirement.

- Under a contract granting pay for a holiday "falling on the employee's scheduled work day," a union demanded pay for New Year's Day, which fell on Saturday. Until November, the plant had been on continuous operations, with employees working a five-day week and sometimes overtime. From November on, however, business fell off, and employees worked no more than five days a week, Monday through Friday. The union contended that because management had scheduled work for some employees on some Saturdays during eleven-twelfths of the year, it should pay all employees for the Saturday New Year's holiday.

Ruling against the union, the arbitrator stressed the contractual requirement that the holiday must fall on "the employee's scheduled work day," and concluded that "New Year's Day not having been a scheduled work day for any of the employees, none of them under the provisions of the agreement are entitled to pay for that day" (*Minnesota Mining & Mfg. Co.*, 12 LA 165).

# Pay for Holiday Work

## OVERVIEW

Nearly all collective bargaining agreements that address the subject of holidays specify premium pay for holiday work. The premium pay may be expressed as holiday pay plus pay for hours worked, or simply as pay at a given rate for hours worked.

It is the latter type of clause that gives rise to most of the disputes over pay for holiday work. The question is whether employees are entitled to the premium rate only, or to the premium rate plus what they would have received had they not worked. The answer to this question must be based on a careful reading of the contract.

## KEY DECISIONS—

After reviewing prior rulings, one arbitrator held that a holiday provision that calls for straight-time pay for holidays and double-time for work on a holiday has been interpreted to call for triple-time only where:

- it is provided that the premium time for work on a holiday shall be given "over and above straight holiday pay" (26 LA 573);
- there has been an established practice of awarding holiday pay in addition to the premium pay provided for actual holiday work (16 LA 1951); or
- the provision for holiday pay fails to contain the limiting words "when not worked" (26 LA 491).

On the other hand, this arbitrator continued, where a contract is silent on the question of whether holiday pay as such should be awarded in addition to premium pay for working on a holiday, two reasons prevail for denying it.

- If triple pay is contemplated, it should be expressly provided for in the contract inasmuch as it is not usual in industry practice (22 LA 564.
- An award of holiday pay in addition to premium pay for the work performed on a holiday would permit two provisos of the contract to apply to the same hours (25 LA 432, 39 LA 1262).

From this review of prior awards, the arbitrator concluded that triple-time for holiday work was not required under the contract before him (*Southern Standard Bag Corp.*, 47 LA 27).

## SUMMARY OF CASES

### Failure To Meet Work Requirements

Even though employees at one plant failed to meet the work requirements for pay for an unworked holiday, an arbitrator ruled that they were entitled to premium pay for work on a holiday as provided by the contract.

- One provision of a contract said that an employee would receive pay for certain holidays not worked, provided the employee worked a full schedule on the days before and after the holiday. Another provision stated that an employee who was required to work on a holiday would be paid double-time for all hours worked. Two employees who did not work on the days preceding and following a holiday but who did work on the holiday were paid only straight time for their holiday work. The employer claimed that this was proper, because they had not met the requirements applying to unworked holidays.

The arbitrator disagreed. He said that the two provisions, although they appeared in the same section of the contract, were independent of each other and had different purposes; one was intended to penalize the employer for scheduling holiday work, the other to discourage the practice of stretching holidays. So, he concluded, an employee was entitled to double-time for holiday work even if he did not meet the eligibility requirements for pay for an unworked holiday (*Alpha Cellulose Corp.*, 27 LA 798).

• Employees were entitled to premium pay for working scheduled work on Thanksgiving Day holiday, an arbitrator ruled, under a contract provision entitling employees to eight hour's pay at two times the regular rate for required work on specified holidays. The employer had contended that the employees did not report for scheduled work on the day after the holiday and thus were not entitled to premium pay under a separate contract provision barring employees from receiving holiday pay unless they work the last scheduled work shift prior to and the next scheduled work shift after the holiday.

Rejecting the employer's argument, the arbitrator noted that the contract provisions were inconsistent and susceptible to two different constructions. Emphasizing that he did not accept the employer's construction that would cause a forfeiture of premium pay, the arbitrator said that although the parties may have intended that no employee was to receive holiday pay for days not worked unless he complied with the work requirement, employees were nevertheless entitled to premium pay for holidays actually worked regardless of attendance on day before or

day after holiday (*Rangaire Inc.*, 66 LA 775).

• Employees who worked their scheduled shift on the Thursday before Good Friday holiday and the holiday itself but who did not work their scheduled sixth day of work on Saturday did not meet the employer's post-holiday work requirement, an arbitrator decided, and thus were entitled to only time and one-half for their Friday work (*Tenco Tea Co.*, 68 LA 214).

## Work on Holiday That also Is Premium-Pay Day

When an employee works on a holiday, which also happens to be a premium pay day (such as the sixth or seventh day of work), complicated questions are likely to arise. The principle problem seems to be whether pyramiding (paying overtime rates on overtime rates) should be required. Arbitrators have held that employees are entitled to two overtime rates.

• Certain employees worked on a Saturday holiday, after having worked the regular workweek of Monday through Friday. They were paid time and one-half for the Saturday holiday worked, and claimed they should have received triple-time. They contended they were entitled to time and one-half for having worked more than 40 hours a week plus time and one-half for having worked on a holiday.

The contract provided that time and one-half would be paid for work after eight hours a day or 40 hours a week; no overtime would be paid on overtime; and when certain holidays, including the one involved here, were worked, "time and one-half" additional wages would be paid.

An arbitration board ruled that the provision prohibiting pyramiding of overtime was applicable only to daily and weekly overtime work, and that the word "additional," in the holiday pay clause meant "additional to such other pay as would be received on the day involved." Therefore, it was concluded that employees were entitled to triple-time—time and one-half for hours worked over 40 in the week and time and one-half for holiday work (*L. A. Jewish Community Council*, 11 LA 869).

● Another arbitrator decided that employees were entitled to contractual triple-time pay for work that they performed on a Friday holiday after they rejected the offer of the employer to trade the Friday holiday for Saturday and to waive triple-time pay for work on Friday, in favor of time and one-half pay for Friday as if it were Saturday work, in order to accommodate employer's production needs.

Pointing out that the contract provided that holidays that fall on Saturdays will be celebrated on preceding Friday and that the employer will pay triple-time pay for work performed on holidays, the arbitrator held that absent the employees' agreement to the proposal, they were contractually entitled to Friday holiday in celebration of New Year's Eve and to triple-time pay should they be required to work on Friday. However, employees who agreed to trade the Friday holiday for the Saturday holiday and to waive triple-time pay for work on Friday are estopped from claiming that they were paid improperly, the arbitrator concluded (*General Tire & Rubber Co.*, 71 LA 813).

● An arbitrator ruled that employees were entitled to be paid at two and one-half times their regular wage rate for working on their sixth consecutive working day, which fell on Memorial Day holiday. The employer's past practice, for at least five years, had been to pay employees who worked on holidays, which were their sixth day of a payroll week, two and one-half times their regular rate for that holiday (*Epicurean Inc.*, 85 LA 1109).

● Arbitrators have ruled against pyramiding of premium pay for weekly overtime on top of premium pay for a worked holiday.

A contract provided time and one-half pay for Saturday work, straight-time pay for certain unworked holidays, and double-time for work done on holidays. The parties also had agreed that a holiday falling on a Saturday would not be paid for if it were not worked. The union requested triple-time pay for any Saturday holiday on which work was performed. It argued that work on a Saturday holiday should be paid for at the premium rates for both the Saturday (an overtime day) and the holiday.

The arbitrator ruled that the parties had agreed on double-time as the appropriate premium for holiday work, but there was no necessity that this meant double the overtime rate when the periods coincided. The purposes of overtime and holiday pay are separate, he said, pointing out that for work on Saturday the parties agreed on a rate of time and one-half. "If the Saturday should coincide with a holiday the higher premium for holiday work will prevail." The arbitrator said he was not convinced that the premium should be pyramided, adding that it was "a reasonable provision that holiday work shall be paid for at double-time, but that this be uniformly applied as double the straight-time rate" (*Heating & Air Conditioning Contractors*, 11 LA 816; see also 74 LA 345).

## Daily Overtime on Holiday

What rate should be paid an employee for overtime hours on a holiday? Under a contract providing double-time for holiday work and time and a half for more than eight hours work in one day, one arbitrator allowed employees to collect pay at triple-time because the contract did not expressly prohibit pyramiding of premiums. On the basis of the same reasoning, the arbitrator also held that time and one-half the double-time rate was in order for work on a sixth day (after 40 hours' work) when the sixth day also was a holiday (*Phelps Dodge Refining Corp.*, 9 LA 474).

● Under a contract providing that all hours worked on a specified holiday shall be paid for at a rate of two times employee's regular hourly rate plus regular holiday pay, an arbitrator decided that an employer improperly denied employees triple-time rate for work performed on a Labor Day holiday (*Theodore Mayer & Brothers*, 62 LA 540).

● An arbitrator decided that the 40 hours beyond which overtime was payable to employees should include the hours that employees worked on a holiday and daily hours worked in excess of eight, even though the employer paid overtime rates for hours worked in excess of eight in any one day and already had paid premium rate for work performed on the holiday (*Northwest Protective Service Inc.*, 65 LA 930).

### Holiday Rate for Incentive Workers

Under a contract providing double-time for hours worked on a holiday, incentive employees were entitled to twice their full earnings, according to one arbitrator. The employer thought that it only had to pay employees their full straight-time earnings plus a premium of eight times the base rate. It argued that this had been the practice for eight years without protest from the union. But the arbitrator said that past practice is immaterial where it is clearly in conflict with the plain language of the contract. The agreement said that employees would "receive double-time for hours worked on any of the designated legal holidays." Clearly, the arbitrator ruled, this meant the incentive base rate plus incentive earnings plus shift premium, all multiplied by two (*Ford Motor Co.*, 27 LA 142).

### When Does Holiday Begin?

Premium pay was meant to apply to all time worked during the "calendar day" definition of Thanksgiving, according to one arbitrator.

• The night shift did not end until 1 a.m. Thanksgiving morning, but the employer refused to pay double time as the employees demanded. It argued that because the contract was silent as to whether holiday premium pay was based on the work day or calendar day, its past practice of paying straight time only when a regular shift overlapped a calendar holiday was controlling. According to the arbitrator, Thanksgiving Day is not a technical term with special meaning in labor-relations parlance; therefore, its normal meaning of midnight to midnight was binding, and the employees were entitled to double pay for the hour worked on the holiday. In addition, the "past practice" had not been used often enough to render it binding (*Grand Rapids Die Casting Co.*, 44 LA 954).

### Birthday/Holiday Pay

An employee was entitled to holiday pay for his birthday that fell on a Sunday, an arbitrator ruled, under a contract provision requiring the employer to recognize employee's birthday as holiday but "where individual's birthday falls on his regularly scheduled day off, he shall receive holiday pay for that day treating it as a birthday holiday." The decision was made notwithstanding the employer's contention that the employee was required to observe his birthday on following Monday pursuant to separate contract provision stating that any holiday falling on Sunday be celebrated on the following Monday. The arbitrator reasoned that the provision relating to birthday holidays is specific and thereby controlling, and that the specific provision equalizes long-run holiday allowances to employees (*American Smelting & Refining Co.*, 65 LA 1217).

• An employer was obligated to pay double-time pay to an employee for work that he was scheduled for on his birthday, which was paid for at double-time pay under the contract, an arbitrator ruled, notwithstanding the employer's contention that scheduling the employee on his birthday was an error. Because the contract clearly gives the employer the right to direct its working forces; having made the choice to schedule the employee on his birthday, the employer was bound by that choice, the arbitrator concluded (*Thomas Truck & Caster Co.*, 74 LA 1276).

• An employer did not have the right to discontinue a past practice of allowing employees to work on their birthday-holiday, an arbitrator ruled, because (1) the management rights provision of contract did not give the employer the right unilaterally to eliminate the practice, and (2) absent an effort by management during contract negotiations to get the union to agree to discontinuance of the practice, the union had the right to believe that the practice was part of the agreement covering holidays by custom and usage (*United Salt Corp.*, 72 LA 534).

### Gift Giving

In deciding whether management can unilaterally alter or discontinue a gift-giving policy, arbitrators usually consider whether the gifts constituted a past practice that had become a part of the collective bargaining relationship (69 LA 1250, 67 LA 979, 67 LA 769, 64 LA 571, 62 LA 879, 62 LA 209).

● One arbitrator held that an employer improperly discontinued a practice of giving employees gift certificates that were redeemable for $10 worth of food. Emphasizing that the certificates had gained the status of an employee benefit and a mutually recognized past practice, the arbitrator ruled that the employer was bound to continue the practice unless it could be altered or eliminated through negotiations with the union (*Advance Die Casting Co.*, 65 LA 810).

● An arbitrator decided that an employer properly discontinued its practice of giving Christmas turkeys to employees following a decrease in demand for the employer's products. Finding no express language in the contract that required the employer to distribute food on an annual basis, the arbitrator held that the turkeys were, at most, voluntary gifts. Reasoning that the employer's voluntary gift policy was predicated upon the attainment of favorable economic results, the arbitrator concluded that the turkey distribution could be discontinued as a result of an "adverse, unprofitable earnings period" (*Proform Inc.*, 67 LA 493).

# Part 9

# *Health and Welfare Benefits*

# Health & Welfare Benefits

## OVERVIEW

Disputes rarely arise between management and the union over the amount of benefits due employees under a health and welfare plan. Typically this information is spelled out in detail in the policies issued by the insurer and thus usually is out of the parties' hands. In some instances, however, where the collective bargaining agreement was more liberal than the insurance policy purchased by the employer, arbitrators have held that the bargaining agreement was controlling factor in resolving a complaint.

In the absence of specific contract language, the eligibility for coverage of employees who are absent from work because of layoff or for other reasons may be a source of disagreement. The employees' seniority status under the basic contract and the employer's past practice often are the determining factors in such cases.

## SUMMARY OF CASES

### Arbitrability of Insurance Disputes

Disputes under an insurance plan are generally not proper subjects for arbitration when the insurance is separate from the contract. Settlements of disputes of that nature are generally held to be topics for negotiation (*Mobil Oil Co.*, 43 LA 1287).

• Where the insurance plan has been mentioned in the collective agreement and figured in the parties' contract settlement, arbitration becomes the method for settlement of grievances on these issues (*Torrington Mfg. Co.*, 45 LA 1176).

• In another case, a contract stated that any difference arising between parties over working conditions or interpretations of contract that could not be adjusted amicably by parties had to be settled through arbitration. In a grievance where an employee sought insurance benefits after suffering a heart attack, an arbitrator determined that the case was arbitrable, despite the employer's contention that the dispute was between the employee and the insurance carrier. Doubts regarding the proper contractual interpretation should be resolved in favor of arbitrability, the arbitrator concluded (*Louisville Cooperage Co.*, 63 LA 165; 91 LA 62).

### Coverage/Eligibility

In determining which employees qualify for coverage under an employer's insurance plan, an arbitrator may focus on the parties' definition of who is a "regular" employee. In addition, an arbitrator may take into consideration any past custom or practice regarding employees' eligibility or specific contract language ( see *Rubber Workers Local 302*, 103 LA 667, in which an arbitrator held there was no authority to overturn an employer's denial of health insurance benefits where a contract's general exclusion provisions stated that the insurance company determined the necessary charges).

• According to one arbitrator, an employer's 20-year practice established a longer-than-normal waiting period for purposes of life insurance coverage. Although employees were considered "regular" for most purposes at the end of their probationary period, the arbitrator pointed out that it had been the custom to wait six months before issuing life insurance to them. Noting that the employees were aware of this practice, the arbitrator disallowed a claim for an employee who had died after working only four months (*Clinton Paper Co.*, 48 LA 702).

• In another case where an employer tried to treat employees who worked less than 30 hours a week as "not regular employees" for purposes of welfare-fund coverage, an arbitrator said that this was improper. Any employee whose hours systematically were scheduled in advance was a regular employee, the arbitrator concluded (*Veterans Linen Supply Co.*, 46 LA 741).

• A contract providing that welfare benefits were applicable only to regular and full-time employees did not preclude a sick employee's receiving benefits, an arbitrator decided, despite the employer's contention that the employee no longer was a regular employee when he was discharged for being physically unfit to perform his job. The contract, the arbitrator reasoned, was designed to exclude only part-time and temporary employees but did not exclude sick employees who might be able to return to work within a specified time (*Witco Chemical Co.*, 61 LA 1188).

• An employer was not required to place salaried employees in a common pool with hourly employees for the purpose of computing employee premiums for a long-term disability insurance plan, an arbitrator decided, even though placing employees in separate groups resulted in a premium increase for hourly employees and a decrease in benefits for salaried employees. Notwithstanding a contract provision that stated that unit employees will be "extended the same general benefits under the same terms and conditions as other employer hourly employees," the arbitrator concluded that conditions of employment, including insurance benefits, that the employer established for its nonunion salaried employees was not subject to union review (*Charter International Oil Co.*, 71 LA 1073).

• An arbitrator held that an employee working two part-time jobs that totaled 20 or more hours per week was not eligible for full-time health insurance benefits. Although the collective bargaining agreement defined "full time" as a position in which the employee worked 20 or more hours each week, eligibility for full-time benefits was contingent on the position held, not the actual number of hours worked, the arbitrator concluded (*Garaway Local School District*, 101 LA 181).

## Coverage of Dependents

Frequently, arbitrators are called on to resolve disputes that focus on whether an employee's dependents are entitled to benefits under an employer's insurance plan. In determining whether there are any restrictions or limitations on dependent coverage, an arbitrator may review the labor agreement, the language of the insurer's policy, the intentions of the parties, as well as any conventional and recognized practice of insurance companies that may have a bearing on the issue.

• In one case, employees' claims that were submitted for surgical fees for their dependents were subject to a "customary and reasonable" limitation under the major medical portion of an insurance agreement, an arbitrator decided. The union contended that it obtained an agreement from the employer that the disputed limitation had been eliminated from the plan. Arguing that this was not the parties' intention, the employer claimed that deleting the limitation applied to surgical charges only and not to the major medical portion of coverage.

In order to reach a decision, the arbitrator said it was necessary to rely on what would be considered as a generally understood and accepted practice. The arbitrator conferred with various insurance companies, insurance consultants, members of the medical profession, and executives of a county medical society. Finding that none of those experts indicated that they knew of any agreements that did not leave some limitation on surgical charges such as the "customary and reasonable" constraint, the arbitrator ruled that the limitation had not been eliminated under the major medical portion of the insurance agreement. Noting that the union itself realized that there must be some limitation, the arbitrator concluded that no employer can be expected to open itself up to uncontrolled medical charges (*CWC Textron*, 73 LA 15).

● A employer had a hospitalization plan for office employees with somewhat lesser benefits than the plan covering the bargaining unit. Company policy stated that employees who were also dependents of employees could not have double coverage. While one bargaining-unit employee's wife was employed in the office, she became pregnant, and quit her job five months later. When she had the baby, the employer paid her hospitalization benefits under the office plan. Her husband claimed the higher benefits for her as his dependent under the bargaining-unit plan, but the employer argued that because she was an employee at the time she became pregnant, she could not be insured as a dependent. Even if she could, it claimed, maternity coverage required a nine-month waiting period in either case, and it had not been that long since she quit and became covered as a dependent.

The arbitrator said the nine months should be figured starting with the date the husband's insurance became effective, not the date the dependent became covered. In addition, the arbitrator threw out the employer's argument that the woman was an employee when her pregnancy began. Her status as her husband's dependent when she went to the hospital was what counted, the arbitrator concluded (*Minnesota Mining & Mfg. Co.*, 32 LA 843).

● An employer did not violate its contractual obligation to provide major medical and life insurance benefits when its insurance carrier rejected an employee's application for dependent coverage for his wife under group health insurance on the ground that the spouse was not insurable based on her past medical record, an arbitrator ruled. Even if the carrier erred in its determination that the employee's wife was not insurable, the employer provided benefits through the carrier's plan, the arbitrator pointed out. Thus, the grievant's dispute was with the carrier and not the employer, the arbitrator concluded (*TSC Industries Inc.*, 71 LA 787).

## Coordination of Benefits

Insurance companies in their agreements with employers often insert a "co-ordination of benefits" clause that has the effect of prohibiting a family's recovery of double benefits in cases where the husband and wife work for separate employers who provided separate hospitalization coverage for each. Arbitrators are split over the effect of such clauses on the employer's obligations under the union contract (See, e.g., *Elgin School District U-46*, 104 LA 405, where an arbitrator held that an employer did not violate a contract requiring health insurance coverage on a "fully paid basis" when it failed to coordinate the benefits of spouses who chose the same health plan; see also 62 LA 493, 58 LA 984).

● One school of thought is that the possibility of double coverage is one of the benefits under the bargaining agreement and that it therefore may not be terminated unilaterally by the employer without the union's consent (54 LA 583, 52 LA 557).

● Other arbitrators take the position that the intent of the parties in negotiating for insurance benefits was not to permit an employee to make a profit out of the group insurance plan. They therefore find no objection to coordination of benefits (54 LA 335, 49 LA 833, 47 LA 1142).

## Coverage of Absent Employees

Generally, in determining whether an employee who has been absent from work because of layoff, sickness, or a leave of absence is entitled to health and welfare benefits, arbitrators must analyze and interpret the specific provision of the contract relating to those benefits. Where the contract's language is ambiguous, arbitrators must look to any established custom or past practice to interpret its application.

● One arbitrator ruled that an employee, who was recalled from a layoff but prevented from reporting back to work because of illness, was entitled to disability benefits because there was no past practice of denying sickness benefits in such cases. Although the employer conclusively proved that sickness benefits were never paid to laid-off employees who had not returned to the active payroll, the arbitrator concluded that the employer's denial of the benefits to a "recalled" employee who failed to report to work because of illness did not have the "support of an established and accepted practice" (*McCabe Powers Body Co.*, 64 LA 958).

• In another situation where a contract required the employer to pay 75 percent of the cost of hospitalization and surgical insurance for all employees, an arbitrator ruled that the employer had to keep up its share of the premiums for employees on indefinite layoff. He noted that the contract provided for the retention of seniority rights for two years after layoff. So these employees were still employees, and for this reason, the arbitrator held that the employer had to make insurance payments for the laid-off employees for at least two years (*National Lead Co.*, 30 LA 333).

• In a similar manner, one arbitrator held that management could not terminate the insurance coverage of an employee on a two-year disability leave. Noting that because the employee had retained her seniority and that her name was on the latest seniority roster, he decided that she was still an employee within the meaning of the contract (*Dayton Economy Drug Co.*, 40 LA 1182).

• Another arbitrator ordered an employer in a similar situation to keep up insurance payments for sick and injured employees for the duration of its contract. He based his decision on the employer's practice under the previous contributory plan, which was to go on paying its share of the premiums for employees on extended absence as long as they paid their share as well (*Dayton Steel Foundry Co.*, 28 LA 595).

• In some cases companies have not been required to make premium payments to health and welfare plans for absent employees. One arbitrator, for example, allowed an employer to continue to make payments into a group insurance fund only for persons on the payroll at the time the payments became due because it had done this for eight years without protest from the union (*Crown Upholstering Co.*, 20 LA 422; see also 94 LA 924, 94 LA 770).

• In cases where an employee is prevented by illness from being at work at the time life insurance benefits are negotiated and thereafter dies without returning to the job, arbitrators might examine various sources, other than the contract, to determine if the employees' beneficiaries are entitled to any compensation (64 LA 676, 53 LA 304).

• In deciding whether to deny payment to the beneficiaries of an employee who died while on sick leave, one arbitrator emphasized that the group policy issued by the insurance carrier to the employer, as well as the explanatory handbook prepared by the insurance employer for distribution to employees covered by the plan, had to be considered (60 LA 69, 39 LA 198).

## Coverage of Pregnant Employees

In determining an employer's obligations to pay health care benefits for pregnant employees or pregnant dependents, arbitrators generally examine and interpret the specific language of the insurance plan and the collective bargaining agreement.

• An employee who took maternity leave was not entitled to sick pay under a contract obligating an employer to provide sickness and accident benefits for employees who were absent due to "illness" or "accident," an arbitrator ruled. The employee did not suffer medical complications during the prenatal period and otherwise experienced a normal delivery, so she was not "ill" within the meaning of the contract, the arbitrator reasoned (*Miller Brewing Co.*, 64 LA 389).

• A single female employee who had a miscarriage was entitled to maternity benefits under a contract providing group insurance benefits to eligible employees including "usual reasonable customary-maternity benefit," an arbitrator held, notwithstanding the employer's contention that the employee was ineligible because that "usual reasonable customary" benefit applied only to employees who were under "family coverage" and not to the employee because she had "individual coverage." The arbitrator found that maternity benefits were available to single employees who had individual coverage in absence of clear contract language to the contrary (*Lear Siegler Inc.*, 63 LA 593; see also 95 LA 942).

## Coverage of Strikers

Are employees who are out on strike, or who have not been recalled after a strike, eligible for health and welfare benefits? There is no consensus on this issue, although a number of arbitrators do consider strikers eligible for such benefits.

• During contract negotiations, union workers went out on strike. As part of the settlement of the dispute, the employer agreed to reinstate all the strikers as they were needed. One of the strikers died before he was recalled for work, and the employer refused to pay death benefits under the life insurance policy in effect "for all employees covered by this agreement," because the employee had not been working at the time of his death. The arbitrator said the employer had to pay the benefits because it would have treated the employee as a continuing, rather than a new employee if he had returned to work before his death as he had planned to do (*Sidney Blumenthal & Co. Inc.*, 12 LA 715).

• When employees went on strike, the employer cancelled the hospitalization program without notifying the union or its members of his action. Management contended that the strike had in effect terminated the contract and that cancelling the insurance was a legitimate tactic. The arbitrator held that the union's exercise of its right to strike did not destroy the contract relationship, and the employer had no right to cancel the insurance, so it was held liable for the claims of two men who were hospitalized during the strike (*National Seating Co.*, 45 LA 476).

• In another case, cancellation of sickness and accident insurance during a strike was in keeping with the terms of the contract. Several employees suffered disabilities before the parties reached a settlement that again extended the coverage. These employees claimed benefits but were not awarded them by the arbitrator, who noted that to do so would be to

backdate the coverage to the period of the strike, which would be contrary to the terms of the contract (*E.J. Lavino & Co.*, 43 LA 213).

## Retroactive Coverage

Suppose some employees are out sick when a new health insurance plan goes into effect. Can they claim benefits under the plan? At least one arbitrator had decided that although persons who are out sick may be employees as far as other benefits are concerned, they are not covered employees for health insurance purposes until they return to work.

• Several employees who were out on sick leave when a health insurance plan went into effect put in claims for health benefits, saying that under NLRB rulings they were "employees," and that the plan covered "employees in the bargaining unit." The arbitrator rejected their claims on two counts. First, he noted that because the plan limited the coverage with respect to laid-off employees, it was logical to make a similar distinction for those on sick leave. Second, he pointed out that insurance is by its nature prospective and designed to protect employees against future contingencies. He ruled, therefore, that employees could not be covered until they returned to active status with the employer (*Schlitz Brewing Co.*, 23 LA 126).

## Discrepancy Between Contract & Insurance Policy

When an employer-union contract conflicts with the terms of the insurance policy covering the employees, which one takes precedence? Arbitrators generally have held that an employer must live up to the agreement made with the union. In the case of a discrepancy, therefore, the employer usually is held liable for benefits that the insurance carrier will not pay but that employees are entitled to under the union agreement.

• An employee was laid off because of illness and drew sick benefits for a period of 13 weeks. He did not return to work and died more than a year after his absence started. His family claimed benefits provided by the contract and the insurance policy at the time of the employee's sickness layoff even though the insurance policy for the employee had expired. The family, backed by the employee's union, maintained that he had been on a layoff status for the entire period of his illness and therefore had been covered by the union contract and its insurance clause for the same period. The employer insisted that the employee's layoff had ended when his 13 week's sick benefits ended and that liability under the insurance clause had stopped there.

An arbitration board, however, went along with the employee's family and the union and ruled that the employee was in the same position as a laid-off worker. Hence the employer had to pay the claim, even though the carrier was no longer liable. The board pointed out that the contract provided for seniority accumulation during a continuous layoff period of up to two years. Furthermore, they said that the contract provided insurance for "the employees and their dependents" but did not mention the status of employees on layoff or leave of absence. Given that there was no distinction in the contract between active and laid-off employees with respect to benefits, the board ruled that the employer should have kept up the insurance, and because it did not do this, must pay the insurance benefit (*Jenkins Brothers*, 22 LA 364).

● An employee at one employer lost four weeks' work because of illness. When she applied for the $10-a-week sick benefit specified by the union contract, the insurance carrier rejected her claim on the ground that she had been treated by a chiropractor rather than by a physician or osteopath as required by the insurance policy. An arbitrator ordered the employer to pay the sick benefits, adding that the employee clearly was entitled to them because the contract granted them after three months' service and did not call for a doctor's certificate or other proof of illness (*Crown Cotton Mills*, 32 LA 3).

### Who Pays for Insurance Rate Increase

If the insurance carrier raises its rates on a contributory health and welfare plan,

who is responsible for paying the increase—the employer or the employees? There is no problem, of course, if the agreement states that both the employer and the employees pay a specified percentage of the cost. Then the parties would share equally the burden of any increase.

● Where a contract said that employees would pay a certain dollars-and-cents amount, and the employer would pay the difference, one arbitrator required the employer to pay the increase. He ruled that by agreeing to pay the difference, the employer had assumed the risk of a possible change in rates (*Goodman Mfg. Co.*, 15 LA 489).

● In a case where the employer paid a flat dollar amount and employees picked up the balance plus any increase, one arbitrator held that management had to pick up any increase for retirees. The contract stated that the "above mentioned" plan applied to retired people but did not fix any limit on the employer's contribution for them. Because the contract required management to provide medical coverage for retirees, and in fact the employer already was paying more than the contract specified for their insurance, the arbitrator said management had to pick up the increases as well (*National Lead Co.*, 38 LA 772; see also 104 LA 18, 71 LA 699, 54 LA 472).

● Even though employees were supposed to pay the full cost of the premium for dependents, management could not pass on an increase to them, another arbitrator held. Dependents' coverage was a negotiated benefit offered to the employees at a monthly price of $1.95. In light of the fact that the contract bound the employer to maintain existing benefits "for the duration of the agreement," it had to pay the premium boost, the arbitrator concluded, emphasizing that any change in the amount of the employees' contribution would have to be negotiated (*Goshen Rubber Co.*, 38 LA 1231).

● An arbitrator held that retirees affected by an employer's letter announcing that it would cap payments for their health benefits were entitled to file a grievance over the matter. He based his decision on several factors, including the fact that the contract was silent on the issue of retiree grievances, giving them free rein in the matter; the agreement did not expressly bar retirees from filing a grievance over the change; and the arbitrator's view that the term "employees" in the contract should be interpreted as applying to retirees (*Commonwealth Telephone Co.*, 100 LA 611).

## Successor Employer

An arbitrator held a successor employer (a purchaser of a business' assets) was liable for health insurance contributions where the employer had signed a memorandum promising "to adopt all the terms" of its predecessor's collective bargaining agreement (*Teamsters Local 350*, 103 LA 705).

## Who Gets Insurance Dividends

If a negotiated insurance plan says that costs are to be split equally between the employer and its employees, dividends from the insurance employer should be divided 50-50, one arbitrator held. A union negotiated a package deal that included increased hospital and medical benefits. The cost of these benefits was to be shared equally by the employer and the employees. After the plan had been in effect for a while, the employer received some dividends from the insurance carrier. It pocketed half of these and applied the other half against future employee contributions. The union protested, arguing that the dividends represented deferred wages and therefore belonged entirely to the employees.

The arbitrator, however, said the employer acted properly. The insurance agreement, he pointed out, did not provide for a fixed contribution by the employer but stated that costs were to be shared equally. Insurance dividends are an element of these costs, so it was fitting to divide them equally, the arbitrator concluded (*Philip Carey Mfg. Co.*, 27 LA 651).

*Part 10*

# *Management Rights*

# Management Rights

## OVERVIEW

Many arbitrators recognize that, in the absence of a bargaining provision to the contrary, an employer retains all managerial rights not expressly forbidden by law. In many cases, arbitrators have ruled that a specific contractual clause, containing either an express or implied limitation, is necessary in order to restrict management rights.

In other cases, some arbitrators, at least with respect to certain issues, have taken the view that limitations upon management rights are not necessarily confined to those rights listed in a specific provision of the bargaining agreement. However, the restrictions may exist as "implied obligations" or "implied limitations" under a general provision of the contract, such as a recognition, seniority, or wage clause.

Additionally, arbitrators may in effect modify management rights by imposing a standard of reasonableness as an implied term of the contract. Moreover, many arbitrators are reluctant to uphold arbitrary or bad-faith managerial actions that adversely affect employees, even where the contract expressly permits management complete discretion in the disputed matter.

Management rights continue to be limited by federal legislation designed to protect employee rights. Recent examples include the Worker Adjustment Retraining and Notification Act (WARN), requiring employers to give their employees 60-days' advance notice of covered plant closings and mass layoffs; the Drug-Free Workplace Act, requiring covered employers to establish drug awareness programs; and the Employee Polygraph Protection Act limiting employers' use of polygraph examinations on applicants and employees.

## SUMMARY OF CASES

### Rights Retained When Not Limited by Contract

Most arbitrators agree that management retains all its rights that are not given up in the contract. This is so even if the agreement does not list all the rights that have been retained by management or has no management-rights clause at all.

● An employer had the right to suspend employees for infraction of plant rules, an arbitrator ruled, notwithstanding the union's contention that the contract permitted discharge for just cause but was silent on suspensions. Pointing out that the right to dismiss employees necessarily includes the right to impose lesser penalties, the arbitrator observed that the omission of a management-rights clause does not divest the employer of its inherent right to take disciplinary action less than dismissal for just cause.

Noting that the employer's failure to suspend employees for the last several years did not negate that right, the arbitrator concluded that a related contract provision recognizing the right of the employer to take "disciplinary action including discharge" was an express acknowledgment that management had the right to suspend employees (*Sequoia Rock Co.*, 76 LA 114; see also 96 LA 1033, 91 LA 1251, 74 LA 1139, 71 LA 632, 41 LA 506, 15 LA 274).

• The fact that an employer retains all rights not given up through specific contract provisions does not mean it has a free hand to take any action it wants in the name of management rights. It is well established that an employer's decisions made under a management-rights clause are subject to arbitration just like any other disputes over the interpretation or application of the agreement (*McInerey Spring & Wire Co.*, 9 LA 91).

• An employer was required to apply "cause" or "just cause" as the standard for determining the propriety of an employee's discharge, an arbitrator ruled, notwithstanding the employer's contention that the contract did not contain an express limitation of its right to discharge the employee, and therefore it retained discretion to terminate employees at will. Noting that the agreement did state that certain acts would not be cause for discipline, the arbitrator concluded that it was reasonable to infer that the parties contemplated that any disciplinary action would be taken only for cause (*R L C & Son Trucking Inc.*, 70 LA 600).

## Rights Surrendered by Negotiating

By asking the union's advice on a certain matter, management may lose its right to assert exclusive control over the subject, according to many arbitrators. In making awards, they attempt to find the intent of the parties at the time of the discussion. A employer may intend only to obtain the union's views on a subject, but if it has actually become a matter of collective bargaining and an agreement is made, arbitrators insist that the employer live up to such agreement.

• One employer association could not reduce the number of electricians on a ship to five after having agreed with the union that eight would be employed, even though there was no specific contract provision for this. The arbitrator said that an employer could not submit a managerial function to collective bargaining, reach an agreement on it, and then repudiate the agreement (*Pacific American Shipowners Assn.*, 10 LA 736).

• If an employer brings up a matter in negotiations and fails to reach agreement with the union on it, management may lose the right to take action on the matter, even though it would otherwise be able to do so under the management-rights clause.

During contract negotiations an employer demanded a clause making overtime work compulsory, but the union refused to agree to one. The employer signed the contract without it. Later, when some employees were suspended for refusing to work Saturdays, the employer claimed it had a right to require overtime work because the agreement was silent on the point. But the arbitrator decided that because the matter had been brought up in negotiations and no agreement was reached, the employer had lost its absolute right to require employees to work overtime (*Sylvania Electric Products Inc.*, 24 LA 199).

## Plant Transfer

*Relocation of operations*—What effect does a contract between an employer and a union have on management's right to move the entire plant or relocate some of the operations to locations outside the union's jurisdiction?

The U.S. Supreme Court has ruled that an employer that moves a plant to a new location may be required to arbitrate the question of employment rights at the new plant even though: (1) the new plant is a considerable distance away and (2) the contract has expired (*Carpenters v. Kimball Co.*, U.S., 1965, 57 LRRM 2628).

• In one case, an arbitrator said management had a right to shut down, buy out a competitor, and transfer operations during contract term. As to its duty to bargain, this meant consulting with the union on its decision to move, he held, not yielding to union opposition to the move. In this case, management refused to give employees any transfer rights, which the union contended violated seniority provisions. The arbitrator decided the employees had no seniority at the other plants, because these were under contracts with other locals (*Sivyer Steel Casting Co.*, 39 LA 449).

• An employer had the right to transfer its bar soap operation from its plant at which employees were represented by a union to its out-of-state plant at which employees were represented by another union, an arbitrator held, because the contract prohibited interference with the right of the employer to "permanently eliminate jobs" (*Lever Bros. Co.*, 65 LA 1299; see also 91 LA 849, 74 LA 407, 71 LA 873, 71 LA 120).

***Remedy for improper relocation—*** Depending on the circumstances and the wording of the contract, arbitrators have fashioned remedies for the employees affected by plant closing and relocation ranging from severance pay to an order directing the employer to re-establish the original plant.

An employer that relocates or closes a facility notwithstanding a collective bargaining agreement to the contrary may be required to reactivate the closed facility to allow bargaining unit employees to perform their former jobs for the life of the contract (*Sears Logistics Services*, 95 LA 229, clarified at 97 LA 421).

• A contract between a union and a clothing manufacturer specifically prohibited removal of the plant or the manufacture of garments in any other factory without the consent of the union. After a shutdown that the union was told was temporary, the manufacturer moved his operations to a new plant in another state. The move was accomplished at night and over weekends without the union's knowledge.

Finding that the move violated the contract, an arbitrator directed the manufacturer to discontinue operations in the new plant, re-establish the factory in the state from which he had moved, and pay the union damages of over $200,000 covering wage, vacation, and welfare-fund payments for 300 employees (*Jack Meilman*, 34 LA 771; see also 36 LA 1364).

• When one employer announced that it was going to move its finishing operations from Danbury, Conn., to Philadelphia, the union charged that this would be a lockout in violation of its contract.

An arbitrator found that the shift was being made for business reasons. In light of this, he said, only an express contract provision could stop the move, given that an employer's freedom to move is not limited by the mere existence of a contract. Nevertheless he ruled that management should have discussed the move in advance with the union. Moreover, he said, available jobs should have been offered to those employees willing to go to Philadelphia, and their moving expenses paid. Those who did not make the move, he decided, were entitled to severance pay plus a share of the pension fund.

The employer voluntarily offered to pay supplemental unemployment benefits totalling about $45,000 to employees staying in Connecticut, but the arbitrator figured this was not enough. He was not sure that he had authority to order payment of severance benefits; but to the extent that he did, he ordered the employer to set aside $100,000 for severance pay and moving expenses (*John B. Stetson Co.*, 28 LA 514).

• An employer was obligated to compensate employees for their loss of pay caused by the relocation of its distribution facility to its main plant in another locality, an arbitrator decided, because the management-rights clause did not entitle the employer to close the distribution facility for economic reasons (*Sealtest Dairy*, 65 LA 858).

• An employer that phased out its roller bearing operations at its plants in one area was obligated, according to contractual language, to give eligible senior employees hiring preference at its existing plant in another location to which production of some of its rolling bearing operation had been transferred, an arbitrator ruled (*Federal-Mogul Corp.*, 61 LA 745).

• A contract that recognizes a union as the bargaining representative of employees at a specific plant "and no other," and that gives the employer an exclusive right to decide where to locate its plant, leaves the employer free to move operations to a different plant without providing the union any information or the opportunity to bargain (*Zebco Corp.*, 104 LA 613).

***Failure to give contractually required notice—*** An arbitrator held an employer violated a collective bargaining agreement by giving a union the 60-day notice required under the WARN Act rather than the longer, 120-day notice specified in the agreement. The arbitrator found no "extraordinary" circumstances that would justify giving late notice. As a penalty, the arbitrator ordered the employer to make whole any terminated employee that suffered a loss because of the late notice. The arbitrator determined that employees should be awarded the difference between their actual income and the income they would have earned if they had still been employed during the extra 60-day period (*American National Can Co.*, 104 LA 191).

### Technological Change

*Introduction of new machines*—Employers generally claim the absolute right to install new and improved machinery. When it seems likely that it would result in rate changes or a cut in the workforce, the union may challenge management's right to make the change. Usually, however, arbitrators have held that a union cannot block technological improvement unless there are specific contract restrictions.

- Where one contract specifically allowed an employer to install new machines, an arbitrator ordered the employees to run them to their full capacity in good faith, even though it meant the piece rates would have to be lowered. The arbitrator stated that there was sound economic justification for upholding management's right to introduce technical improvements. To rule for the union, he said, would lead toward economic stagnation (*Associated Shoe Industries of Southeastern Mass. Inc.*, 10 LA 535; see also 84 LA 788, 83 LA 39).

*Transfer of work because of mechanization*—When work is mechanized, does management have the right to assign it to employees outside the bargaining unit? Awards suggest that it depends on how much change takes place in the way the work is done. If a union can show that the employees in the unit are capable of continuing the work after the new ma-

chines are installed, then its complain against transferring the work is likely to be upheld.

- Employees in the bottling department of a brewing employer had performed a manual testing operation on beer cans for seven or eight years; then the firm purchased a machine that could more efficiently prepare the cans for testing, thus sending the work to its machinists, who were in another bargaining unit.

The arbitrator found that installing the machine would not really change the nature of the testing operation but would simply allow it to be done faster. Accordingly, he concluded that the proposed transfer would violate two sections of the union contract—the recognition clause, which gave the union jurisdiction over the customary work of the bargaining unit; and the job security clause, which reserved jobs in the bottling department for employees on the seniority list there.

All the signs were that the bottlers would be able to operate the machine satisfactorily, the arbitrator noted. If they could not after a fair trial, he added, the employer could then give the work to the machinists (*Hamm Brewing Co.*, 28 LA 46).

- If an employer can show that the nature of the work has changed so that the employees who were assigned to it can no longer handle it efficiently, an arbitrator will no doubt uphold a transfer decision.

- Timekeepers claimed that their seniority rights were violated when the employer installed automatic data processing equipment that eliminated some of the duties formerly performed by them. In rejecting the time-keepers' claim, an arbitrator said that the employer had the right to mechanize its work procedures by utilizing data processing equipment. Moreover, he noted, the eliminated duties were not performed by any employees within or outside the bargaining unit, but by a machine (*Bethlehem Steel Co.*, 35 LA 72; see also *Van Norman Machine Co.*, 28 LA 791).

- A union's recognition clause did not guarantee that bargaining unit work would continue unchanged indefinitely, according to the arbitrator; hence he did not bar transfer of unit work to another department. When a publisher installed a computer in the subscription department, there was no longer any need for an addresso-graph operator. The arbitrator held that the recognition clause extended to departments, not to types of work. Thus the union could not claim jurisdiction over a new system introduced into another department (*McCall Corp.*, 44 LA 201).

• An employer had the right to assign technicians, instead of unit personnel, to develop a procedure for producing fuel rod simulators under a test program, an arbitrator decided, because the contract gave the employer the right to use management personnel for "experimental purposes." Rejecting the union's argument that because unit personnel used the same tools, instruments, and procedures used by the technicians, it followed that the work performed by the technicians was bargaining unit work, the arbitrator stressed that this contention overlooked the needs and purpose of the employer's experimental and research work. The assignment of such work was specifically granted to management under the contract and retained under the recognition clause, the arbitrator noted, concluding that to hold for the union would mean finding that management could not engage in essential developmental work (*Union Carbide Corp.*, 72 LA 1318; see also 93 LA 227, 91 LA 329, 85 LA 681, 84 LA 875, 83 LA 838, 82 LA 680, 72 LA 927).

## Assigning Work

*Right to control plant operations*—In general, arbitrators have recognized broad authority in management, absent clear limitations in a contract, to determine and control the methods of its operations (see, e.g., *Simpson Industries*, 104 LA 568; see also 95 LA 840, 93 LA 48, 92 LA 225, 88 LA 963, 88 LA 580, 88 LA 251, 87 LA 853, 85 LA 1079).

• An arbitrator ruled that a publisher had the right to use its presses to train management personnel, notwithstanding the union's contention that the

bargaining agreement established the union's jurisdiction over operation of the presses. The arbitrator pointed out that if the union desired to prevent the publisher from using the presses in this manner, it should have included specific language to that effect in the contract (*Sacramento Newspaper Publishers Assn.*, 62 LA 1112).

• Arbitrators have upheld management's right to schedule work hours and to require overtime (67 LA 257, 66 LA 1326, 66 LA 1338, 66 LA 577, 63 LA 1, 61 LA 16, 60 LA 905).

*Work not covered by job descriptions*—According to one arbitrator, management's freedom to assign work is not restricted by job descriptions unless the contract expressly says so. The purpose of job descriptions, he said, is to describe duties for classification purposes; they seldom list all job requirements. Unless the contract says otherwise, he added, management is free to change duties and assignments; employees must perform assigned tasks, saving their protests for the regular grievance channels (*Pittsburgh Steel Co.*, 34 LA 598; see also 53 LA 1130, 61 LA 808).

• When a new contract dropped the status quo provisions that had prevented unilateral changes in work assignments, management was no longer bound by a past practice of only assigning one job at a time to mold makers, according to another arbitrator. His ruling was that past practice under a prior contract is not binding unless the language giving rise to that practice is continued in the current contract. Therefore, he concluded, dual work assignments could be made unilaterally by management (*Overmyer Co.*, 43 LA 1006).

• Another arbitrator ruled that a publisher had the right to assign the work of filling, transporting, and cleaning new portable ink tank equipment to paperhandlers, instead of to pressmen. Because there was a lack of evidence clearly establishing that the work in question was within the traditional scope of pressmen's work, the arbitrator decided that the assignment constituted a reasonable management decision (*Detroit News*, 62 LA 313).

*Eliminating jobs*—Does a contract clause giving management the right to assign work forces permit the employer unilaterally to eliminate a job? A number of arbitrators have held that management can eliminate or combine jobs in the interest of efficiency or economy, so long as its action is not arbitrary and is not prohibited by the contract.

● An employer had the right to assign to "unrepresented" personnel duties that its receptionists had performed prior to the elimination of their jobs as a economy measure, an arbitrator ruled. Pointing out that the effect on the bargaining unit was minor, because the work had not been performed exclusively by unit employees, the arbitrator emphasized that the job elimination was for good business reasons. Noting that there was no contract language expressly prohibiting the employer from assigning work to non-unit employees when the assignment has been made in good faith and for good reasons, the arbitrator upheld management's right to transfer the work (*Lake City Elks Lodge*, 72 LA 643; see also 96 LA 844, 91 LA 329, 29 LA 324, 23 LA 561, 15 LA 783).

● A contract may have other clauses that restrict an employer's decision to do away with a job under the management-rights clause.

● Where a contract gave the employer the right to assign work forces, but also prohibited changes in job classifications except where a new job was created or changes made in the production process, one arbitrator would not permit the employer to wipe out a mouldman-leader's job that had not changed in content (*Bethlehem Steel Co.*, 17 LA 295).

*Eliminating classifications*—If there is no longer any work required in a job classification, can an employer do away with it? Awards apparently depend upon the wording in individual contracts.

● One arbitrator held that an employer was prohibited from dividing up the duties of the welder-inspector classification and abolishing it without getting the union's approval because its contract specifically said that job descriptions and classifications would remain unchanged

unless both parties agreed to change them (*Lone Star Steel Co.*, 26 LA 160).

● Even where there was no specific restriction but where the contract established rates of pay for several classifications, an arbitrator ruled that the employer could not unilaterally eliminate a classification. He said that the combining and elimination of classifications was a subject for negotiation between the parties (*Kansas Grain Co.*, 29 LA 242).

● Although a "bargaining unit work" clause did not freeze work, an employer was not allowed to abolish a unit job only to reassign its duties as a non-unit job. The employer contended that, because the jobs were clerical, they should not be considered part of the unit. However, the arbitrator found no evidence in the contract that the parties had intended to limit the bargaining unit to actual production work (*Gisholt Machine Co.*, 44 LA 840; see also 84 LA 788).

● Several arbitrators believe that in the absence of contract restrictions, management has the right to eliminate a classification by transferring its duties to others. One arbitrator decided that an employer did not violate the seniority provisions of the contract by laying off workers in one classification and assigning their duties to employees with less seniority. Seniority rights do not guarantee that a job will remain in existence or that its content will not be changed, he reasoned (*Axelson Mfg. Co.*, 30 LA 444; see also 90 LA 758, 90 LA 67, 89 LA 118, 71 LA 396, 54 LA 365).

*Combining jobs*—If the work on a certain job is reduced through technological changes, can the employees be required to take on duties belonging to another classification? In one case an arbitrator found nothing in the agreement to prevent combining jobs in this way. But, he warned, such combinations could not be used to fill vacancies.

● Because of technological changes, a time clerk and a die setter did not have enough work to occupy them full time. To keep them busy, the employer had them spend part of their time on work in other classifications. The union argued that this violated the seniority provisions of the contract; if more people were needed in these other classifications, it said, the regular procedure for filling vacancies should have been followed.

An arbitrator found nothing in the contract forbidding out-of-classification assignments. On the other hand, he said, the employer could not use this device to fill vacancies. To determine whether a vacancy existed, the arbitrator applied this rule: If either the time clerk or the die setter spent more than 50 percent of his time on work in some other classification, he filled a vacancy in that classification. Given that neither employee did so, the employer acted within its rights (*Fletcher-Enamel Co.*, 27 LA 466; see also, 53 LA 33).

• Another arbitrator found nothing wrong with the action of an employer who combined the duties of three jobs into one classification and offered to negotiate with the union over a wage rate for the new job. He said that the job-protection clause primarily was aimed at maintaining the pay scale, not at preventing all changes in classifications (*Sewanee Slica Co.*, 47 LA 282).

*Moving jobs between shifts*—Where there was no specific contract ban on it, at least one arbitrator ruled that an employer could move a vacant job from one shift to another in the interest of efficiency.

• When a day-shift cleaning job opened up at one employer, management posted it as a night-shift job. It figured the cleaning work could be done better when regular employees were out of the way. It assured the union that it was not going to transfer any of the day-shift cleaners but would simply move jobs to the night jobs to the night shift as vacancies occurred. The union nevertheless contended that the job should have been posted as a day-shift vacancy.

An arbitrator noted that the posting provision of the contract was of the ordinary type, requiring the posting of new jobs and vacancies. In his view, nothing in the clause limited the employer's choice of the shift to which a particular job was assigned. The union's claim that upholding the employer's action would pave the way for a wholesale transfer of jobs to the night shift did not impress the arbitrator; the existence of night-shift premiums was an effective deterrent, he remarked (*White Motor Co.*, 29 LA 153).

*Determining and filling job vacancies*—Arbitrators have upheld management's contractual right to determine whether a job vacancy exists and whether it should be filled.

• Under the management-rights clause of a contract, an employer had the right not to fill three computer jobs that it previously posted, an arbitrator decided, because contrary to the union's contention, the contract did not limit management's authority to determine whether job vacancies existed in the plant (*Computing & Software Inc.*, 61 LA 261).

• An employer had the right to temporarily fill a vacant production utility job during the period in which the job was being posted, an arbitrator ruled, because the contract gave management this right (*Right Away Food Corp.*, 60 LA 230; see also 94 LA 1183, 90 LA 577, 86 LA 1102, 86 LA 173, 84 LA 390, 84 LA 36, 83 LA 801, 83 LA 445, 82 LA 708).

• Where duties associated with the vacancy are reassigned and continue to be performed by employees in other jobs, arbitrators will examine whether the employer intentionally has avoided contractually required procedures for filling jobs (*Homestake Mining Co.*, 88 LA 614; see also 85 LA 449, 85 LA 290, 84 LA 390).

## Work By Supervisors

*Absence of contract ban on work by supervisors*—Does management have the right to assign production work to supervisors if the contract does not specifically say they cannot do the work usually performed by members of the bargaining unit? Under these circumstances arbitrators permit employers to assign production work to supervisors only so long as the rights of bargaining-unit employees are not violated.

• One arbitrator said that although an employer had the right to assign certain work to supervisors, it could not exercise this right if it would deprive employees in the unit of their right to work when sufficient work was available (*Bethlehem Steel Co.*, 14 LA 159; see also 39 LA 530).

• Under a contract where the job of gang-boss was made a part of the promotion sequence, an employer was not allowed to assign this job to supervisors outside the unit because it violated the seniority provisions (*West Virginia Pulp & Paper Co.*, 12 LA 1074).

• Another arbitrator held that an employer could not assign duties of shopping checker to a foreman without the union's consent because the transfer meant changing the job's content, which had been set by the agreement (*Kraft Foods Corp.*, 10 LA 254).

• One arbitrator said that under its contract management was allowed to transfer supervisors to bargaining-unit jobs during slack seasons. The contract said that the employer could retain as many as 30 employees regardless of their seniority if in the sole judgment of the employer, their special training, experience, or ability was needed. Although the union argued that this clause applied to technical employees only, the arbitrator said it extended to supervisors. In light of the fact that the employer was "sole judge" of who needed to be retained, it has the right to make 30 transfers of non-unit employees to bargaining-unit jobs, he decided. The only limit on management, he added, was that it could not act in bad faith in selecting the men for transfer or use the clause to subvert the union (*Jefferson City Cabinet Co.*, 35 LA 117).

**Work by supervisors during emergency**—Contract bans on supervisors' performance of bargaining-unit work often contain an exception permitting such work in an "emergency." Arbitrators generally take a narrow reading of such exceptions and require firm evidence of a true emergency.

• Sending a supervisor to an airport to pick up a cylinder was held not to be an "emergency" (*Masonite Corp.*, 53 LA 965). Nor were "emergencies" found in the use of supervisors to make withdrawals and requisitions for employees (*Masonite Corp.*, 53 LA 965), or in the performance by supervisors of Sunday washroom work caused by a temporary breakdown at another plant (*F.W. Means & Co.*, LA 54 874).

• An employer had the right to assign supervisors to replace a sprinkler valve that had blown off and caused water to spill into an oil room, an arbitrator decided. Despite the fact that the work customarily was done by pipefitters, the arbitrator upheld management's action because the work was of an emergency nature (*Diamond National Corp. and Paperworkers*, 61 LA 567).

• An arbitrator held a brewery did not violate a contract's provision barring supervisory personnel from performing unit work, when, during the course of repair of a malfunctioning crowning machine by a machinist who was not wearing a safety shield, a supervisor pushed away bottles on a conveyor that was moving toward the machine. The danger of an explosion arising from the flow of the bottles constituted an "emergency," the arbitrator reasoned (*Anheuser Busch Inc., Jacksonville Plant and Teamsters*, 62 LA 1130; see also 74 LA 1175, 71 LA 454).

**Application of 'de minimus' principle**—Arbitrators may decide to overlook a technical violation of a ban on supervisors performing bargaining unit work, where the violation was so minor as to warrant application of the "de minimis principle," which calls for ignoring inconsequential violations.

• No substantive violation was found in a supervisor's distribution of hand tools to pipefitters while the counterman was off duty (*Stauffer Chemical Co.*, 53 LA 706), or in a supervisor's dusting and sweeping an office where there was no indication that an employee was adversely affected (*Ideal Cement Co.*, 52 LA 9).

• A mine operator did not violate a contract when a foreman loaded roof bolting supplies found in a "unitrack" that he used to transport himself to a certain section of the mine, an arbitrator held. Even assuming that the operation of the unitrack with bolting supplies in it was "classified work," the operation, which lasted for 25 minutes, would be covered under the de minimis rule, the arbitrator concluded (*Consolidation Coal Co.*, 65 LA 892; see also 75 LA 569).

**Effect of other clauses**—Even under contracts that do not clearly forbid supervisors to do bargaining-unit work, some arbitrators have found the parties' intent in other clauses.

● In one such situation a working foreman was advanced to assistant superintendent but kept doing production work. The union complained that this violated a clause limiting the number of supervisors to three. But an arbitrator held that this must have been meant to limit only the number of working supervisors because an employer's right to employ any number of nonworking supervisors is not ordinarily restricted. The employer had not exceeded this limit, so the arbitrator ruled that the superintendent could continue doing production work (*Mt. Carmel Public Utility Co.*, 16 LA 59).

● Under another contract lacking a definite ban on production work by supervisors, an arbitrator found help from a clause stating that no employee would be temporarily transferred to a job in another department where the employee regularly handling the job was on layoff. This, the arbitrator said, prevented the employer from letting a foreman do a job ordinarily done by a bargaining-unit man who was laid off (*Sayles Biltmore Bleacheries Inc.*, 26 LA 585).

**Effect of past practice**—When faced with ambiguous contracts some arbitrators have answered questions of work by supervisors by looking at the employer's past practice.

● One arbitrator, noting that a contract definition of bargaining-unit work was ambiguous, focused on the way in which the definition had been applied. Over a period of three years, he noted, management had always withdrawn supervisors from assignments that the union claimed were bargaining-unit work. Because management itself had given this consistent interpretation to the contract, the arbitrator found it binding, despite the fact that the union had tried unsuccessfully to negotiate a specific ban

on supervisors' doing production work (*Los Angeles Drug Co.*, 29 LA 38; see also 88 LA 406, 84 LA 549, 83 LA 792, 82 LA 534, 75 LA 963, 74 LA 13, 73 LA 529).

● One arbitrator would not let an employer continue assigning supervisors to bargaining-unit work merely because it had done so for several years without the union's forcing arbitration of the issue (*Great Lakes Pipe Line Co.*, 27 LA 748; see also 75 LA 450).

**Monitoring of automated machinery**—Can management, after installing automatic equipment to operate its machines, assign supervisors to monitor the equipment and eliminate the job of machine operator? Even where the contract contained a prohibition on the performance by supervisors of "work normally performed" by bargaining-unit employees, an arbitrator ruled that this was permissible. The machine operator's duties had been taken over by mechanical devices rather than by supervision, he reasoned. Control-room monitoring, he stated, is closer to the normal duties of supervisors than to the work done by bargaining-unit employees.

At the same time, the arbitrator held that it would be improper for supervisors to operate the machines manually or to do physical work in cleaning, repairing, or adjusting them (*Goodyear Tire & Rubber Co.*, 35 LA 917).

**Work by supervisors to test standards**—Under a contract containing a general ban on the performance of production work by supervisors, one arbitrator ruled that management violated the agreement when it assigned supervisors to such work, outside regular hours, to prove that production standards were fair. However, in view of a clause stating that supervisors could do production work for the purpose of instructing employees, he said the assignment in question would have been proper if the employees who regularly performed the work had been called in to observe the demonstration (*National Lead Co., of Ohio*, 34 LA 235).

**Effect of strike**—A ban on assigning supervisors to bargaining-unit work does not apply during a strike, in the opinion of one arbitrator. Such a ban is designed to protect the job rights of union members on duty or available for work, he said. It has no application when the members refuse to work, he reasoned, because in such a case they are not displaced by supervisors (*Texas Gas Corp.*, 36 LA 1141; see also 75 LA 1302).

*Ban applied to other nonunit workers*—At least one arbitrator has decided that a contract clause forbidding supervisors to do bargaining unit work applied to other employees outside the unit as well.

• At one employer, requisitions for materials on night and weekend shifts were too infrequent to justify having a stock clerk on duty. Plant guards, who were not in the bargaining unit, handled the occasional requisitions on those shifts. The union protested. It would have been okay to have some other bargaining unit member take over stock-clerk duties, the union said, but it was wrong for plant guards to do the work.

The arbitrator agreed. Although having plant guards handle bargaining-unit work was not specifically forbidden by the contract, the arbitrator thought the effect of using them was the same as that of using supervisors; it deprived members of the bargaining unit of work that should have been theirs. Unit members have a vested right in bargaining-unit work, the arbitrator stated, and no employee outside the unit has the right to horn in on it (*Reynolds Metals Co.*, 26 LA 756).

## Production Standards

*Right to establish production standards*—If the contract does not provide yardsticks for measuring employee efficiency, can management adopt its own standards? Most arbitrators hold that an employer can, so long as whatever standards it sets are fair and reasonable (90 LA 570, 85 LA 254, 70 LA 1152, 65 LA 405, 65 LA 380, 65 LA 270, 64 LA 885, 60 LA 491, 33 LA 725).

• One employer gave an employee a warning stating that he was producing only 42 percent of the average of other employees doing comparable work. The union complained, pointing out that the contract made no reference to production

or efficiency standards. Neither side meant for such standards to be used in evaluating performance, it claimed. The employer, though, figured its action came within the scope of the management-rights clause, under which it retained the right to manage the plant, direct the work force, and suspend and discharge employees for just cause.

An arbitrator upheld the employer's position. The right to manage the plant and direct the work force would be almost meaningless, in his opinion, if the employer could not judge efficiency and require a reasonable level to be maintained. If some benchmark was to be used to measure performance, he added, management had to discipline all those individuals whose records compared least favorably with the standard. Failure to apply the standard in an evenhanded manner would violate the "just cause" requirement, he commented (*Menasco Mfg. Co.*, 30 LA 264).

• Another arbitrator said management could establish production standards where employees previously had set their own standards. Nothing indicated that the parties intended old practices to be continued indefinitely, he noted, and the union had been notified that the establishment was being contemplated. There was no evidence that the new standards were unreasonable, he said, and the employer's failure to exercise a right did not waive that right. Further, the contract allowed management to "establish production and work standards" and to eliminate practices that were inefficient or unreasonable (*Mead Corp.*, 41 LA 1038).

• An employer did not have the right to establish a productivity improvement program that imposed predetermined discipline on employees for failing to meet production standards, an arbitrator ruled. Rejecting the employer's contention that establishing the program was an exercise of its exclusive and unilateral right to manage the plant, the arbitrator decided that the arbitrary application of discipline changed the conditions of employment for the employees. Such a change requires mutual agreement by the parties, the arbitrator noted, pointing out that the evidence established that there were no negotiations or mutual agreement with respect to the program, or any implied waiver by the union of such negotiations. The employer would have been entitled to establish the program had it not included the disciplinary features, the arbitrator concluded (*Union Carbide Corp.*, 70 LA 201; see also 86 LA 6).

***Right to change size and composition of work crew***—If the contract mentions the number of employees to be used in the work crew on a particular job, can the employer adjust the size of the crew because of changes in the volume of business or other factors?

Under a contract that stated that "no less than three men shall be employed in a crew ..." an arbitrator ruled that, regardless of workload, the employer could not cut the size of the crew for the duration of the contract (*Weston Biscuit Co. Inc.*, 21 LA 653).

● In another case, where the contract banned reduction in existing crew size but permitted negotiations on size in certain situations, an arbitrator held that management could not negotiate for a smaller crew. Although the contract did not expressly confine negotiations to increasing, rather than decreasing crew sizes, the arbitrator thought it was the parties' intent to maintain the state minimum staff levels, at least for the contract term. Nothing barred them from resolving the issue when the new contract negotiations occurred, he added (*Sinclair Oil Corp.*, 41 LA 878).

● When a salt employer installed new conveyor equipment, it did not have the right to eliminate employees engaged in sacking the salt, an arbitrator decided. The contract's wage schedule specified that the crews consist of 11 employees, and, for this reason, the employer was not allowed to reduce the size of the sacking crews, despite the fact that only nine men were needed (*Barton Salt Co.*, 46 LA 503; see also 92 LA 453, 86 LA 357).

● Another arbitrator upheld an employer's action in reducing the size of a work crew after the work had been

mechanized and thus required fewer employees. The contract required a certain crew size "under present conditions." The "present conditions" mentioned in the contract no longer existed, the arbitrator said (*Theo. Hamm Brewing Co.*, 35 LA 243).

● In the absence of a contract requiring an employer to employ a specified number of electricians to operate mechanical devices used at its racing tracks, the employer had the right to employ two, instead of three electricians, to perform the work, an arbitrator decided (*West Flagler Assoc., LTD*, 61 LA 1253).

● An employer that purchased a folding carton plant of another employer properly required pressmen to operate the cutting press machine without help, an arbitrator ruled, because the employer made technological modifications on the equipment that rendered a reduction in crew size feasible (*Container Corp. of America*, 65 LA 517; see also 92 LA 553, 76 LA 1099, 76 LA 903, 74 LA 820, 71 LA 185).

## Miscellaneous Problems

***Right to promulgate reasonable plant rules***—It is well established that management has the right unilaterally to promulgate reasonable rules—not inconsistent with law or the collective bargaining agreement—and to enforce such rules through disciplinary action (96 LA 499, 95 LA 729, 92 LA 497, 92 LA 390, 92 LA 181, 92 LA 68, 91 LA 1251, 91 LA 969, 91 LA 375, 90 LA 729, 89 LA 1069, 89 LA 1065, 87 LA 529, 84 LA 688, 77 LA 705).

● In one case, the arbitrator emphasized that the employer clearly has the right, and in fact, the responsibility, to impose the ultimate penalty of discharge where plant rules definitely have been violated (*Walker Manufacturing Co.*, 60 LA 645).

● Although management generally has the right to promulgate reasonable plant rules, arbitrators may restrict that right where the rules are deemed unreasonable, vague, ineffective, or arbitrary (77 LA 807, 75 LA 975, 74 LA 770, 74 LA 252, 73 LA 443, 73 LA 684, 72 LA 588).

***Regulation of coffee breaks***—Can management, during the term of a contract, unilaterally establish definite rules regarding coffee breaks to replace a practice of allowing individual employees to select their own coffee-break times? According to one arbitrator, such an action is a legitimate exercise of management's rule-making powers.

• For years employees at one employer had been permitted to take breaks for coffee and other refreshments according to their individual wishes. In time this arrangement reached the point where it was seriously hindering production—an employee might take a break that would stop a production line and when he returned another might knock off, and so on down the line. To remedy this situation, the employer made a rule limiting breaks to set periods in the morning and afternoon. The union immediately protested that this amounted to a change in working conditions in violation of its contract.

An arbitrator pointed out that the firm's action did not end the practice of allowing breaks but actually gave it official recognition and status. This was not a change in working conditions, he concluded (*Dover Corp.*, 33 LA 860; see also 74 LA 312, 39 LA 1265).

• An employer could not unilaterally reduce the number of rest periods that had remained the same for five years. According to the arbitrator, such a seasoned practice took on the status of an obligation binding on both parties. It was a working condition set by past practice, and, as such, was not subject to unilateral action (*Formica Corp.*, 44 LA 467).

• An employer that had a past practice of giving three paid coffee breaks to its transfer drivers improperly discontinued the third break following the effective date of a new collective bargaining contract, an arbitrator decided, because the practice was of long standing and the parties specifically agreed during contract negotiations that the practice would continue under the new contract (*Pacific Clay Products*, 62 LA 706).

• An employer was not entitled to make a unilateral change in coffee breaks from the "honor system," under which employees could take breaks when they wished, an arbitrator held, because the

honor system was a practice of long standing and the change to a seven-minute break was an unreasonable alternative in view of management's failure to establish that the break period was of sufficient duration (*Ohmstede Machine Works Inc.*, 62 LA 45; see also 72 LA 470).

***Installation of time clocks***—Does management have the right to install the clocks without first getting the union's go-ahead? Time clocks are a condition of employment over which an employer is obligated to bargain, one arbitrator has said. But if the subject of installing them is raised in contract negotiations and the union registers no objection, management may be able to put in time clocks without discussing the matter further with the union.

• Shortly after signing a union contract, an employer started requiring office employees to punch time clocks. The union claimed this step violated a contract clause requiring the employer to negotiate with the union on conditions of employment. The employer maintained that it merely had exercised a management right. Even if the issue were bargainable, the employer argued, the union had waived its right to bargain about installation of time clocks by failing to negotiate on the point when management representatives brought it up in negotiations.

An arbitrator decided that the employer did have an obligation to bargain over the time clocks, but he agreed with management that the union had lost out by failing to pursue the matter in negotiations. The union might have ground for complaint, he added, if the time clocks were used in an unfair way (*Motor Wheel Corp.*, 26 LA 931).

• The exact procedures for clocking in and out were within the exclusive authority of management, an arbitrator decided. Even though manual time clocks had been used in the past, the arbitrator found nothing wrong with the employer's introduction of IBM units for clocking in and out. He said that the installation of new equipment was not a condition of employment, and therefore, not a subject for union involvement (*Babcock & Wilcox Co.*, 45 LA 897).

• An employer had the right to install a special time clock outside the restroom and to require employees to punch their time cards on entering and leaving, under guidelines that were instituted to prevent the abuse of emergency use of the restroom, an arbitrator ruled. Rejecting the contention that the use of the time clock by female employees was "humiliating and undignified," the arbitrator concluded that it was inconceivable that female employees under a female supervisor would experience any embarrassment among practically all female employees (*Cagle's Poultry and Egg Co.*, 73 LA 34).

• An employer did not have the right to institute a rule requiring employees to keep a time clock record of all their visits to the toilet in an effort to solve the problem of too much loss of work time loitering in the washrooms, an arbitrator decided. Even though the rule may have resulted in an increase in production, the arbitrator rejected its implementation, because it also resulted in a loss of dignity and embarrassment to employees. Although no one can blame the employer for wanting to curb wasteful practices of a small number of loiterers, other methods can be found to reduce the incidence of loitering without imposing onerous and humiliating timekeeping procedures on all employees, the arbitrator concluded (*Schmidt Cabinet Co. Inc.*, 75 LA 397).

***Change in pay periods***—Does management have the right to change the frequency of pay periods during the term of a contract without getting the union's consent? It probably does, arbitrators' rulings suggest, if the contract does not say when employees are to be paid.

• When an employer decided to pay employees on a bi-weekly basis instead of weekly, the union argued this was a change in past practice that violated its contract. The arbitrator disagreed, pointing out that the dispute was not even arbitrable because the contract said nothing about pay periods and specifically stated that only grievances arising out of the operation or interpretation of the agreement could be arbitrated.

Despite what the agreement said, the arbitrator noted that he might have ruled on the merits of the case if the parties had had an informal understanding about pay periods. The employer had had a weekly pay system for years, but the union never said anything about it, and such "mute acquiescence" did not establish a binding past practice, the arbitrator concluded (*Cone Mills Corp.*, 30 LA 100).

## Compulsory Retirement

────────────────────────── **OVERVIEW** ──────────────────────────

During the late 1940s and early 1950s there could not be any dispute as to the right of an employer to unilaterally set a mandatory retirement age in the absence of specific contractual restriction, according to one arbitrator. In the mid-1950s, however, a different theory began to emerge under which if the union did not acquiesce, but instead objected to the institution of a compulsory retirement plan, forcible retirement of an otherwise physically able employee would be held to violate the job security provision of the existing collective bargaining agreement (*Cummins Power Inc.*, 51 LA 909).

Since then there has been a split of authority on the employer's right to set a mandatory retirement age without negotiating with the union or in the absence of a specific contract restriction.

## KEY DECISIONS—

One arbitrator ruled that because retirement is such an important condition of employment, and a union has the right to bargain over employment conditions, it also has the right to bargain over retirement issues (*Consolidated Packaging Corp.*, 51 LA 47).

● Another arbitrator decided that discharge, as used in collective bargaining, is not synonymous with termination by retirement, and it is "a well-established principle in arbitration" that in the absence of any contract restriction, the employer has the unilateral right to establish and administer a compulsory retirement policy (*Brown Line Co.*, 50 LA 597).

● Still another arbitrator ruled that the forced retirement of a physically able and competent employee is a violation of the worker's security and seniority rights, especially where the retirement policy and plan was unilaterally announced and not spelled out in a jointly established agreement (*Armour Agricultural Chemical Co.*, 47 LA 513).

● In addition, the prohibitions against compulsory retirement incorporated in the 1978 amendments to the Age Discrimination in Employment Act, and in some state fair-employment-practice laws, have caused more split decisions in this area. The ADEA amendments removed the 70-year age limitation applicable to employees who are protected by the ADEA; therefore, with limited exceptions such as persons in a "bona fide executive or a high policy-making position," compulsory retirement of employees 65 or older is prohibited (87 LA 985, 87 LA 137, 74 LA 1121, 74 LA 278, 70 LA 245).

Several inferences can be gleaned from recent arbitration cases.

● Because no consistent pattern has emerged in arbitrators' rulings on whether an employer may require employees to retire at a fixed age, all the circumstances of the particular case must be examined, including what the collective bargaining agreement states about the issue, what the employer's past practice has been, what has happened in past negotiations, etc.

- Generally, a long-standing policy of retiring employees at a certain age may be continued by an employer, despite the existence of a bargaining agreement.

- If the union has had an opportunity to bargain on the subject of retirement and has failed to do so, the employer may be within its rights in putting a policy into effect during the contract term.

- It has usually, though not always, been held that a forced retirement does not violate a just-cause discharge provision.

- A compulsory retirement policy, to be valid and enforceable during the term of a contract, must have been announced in clear terms to employees and applied consistently.

─────────────── **SUMMARY OF CASES** ───────────────

### Long-Standing Policy

If the employer has had a compulsory retirement policy in effect for several years before it ever signs a contract with a union, does it retain the right to follow this policy after the contract goes into effect?

- An employer properly ordered an employee to retire when he reached his 65th birthday based on the company's retirement plan that it uniformly and consistently administered for almost seven years, an arbitrator decided. Although the contract on its face was silent on the subject of mandatory retirement, the arbitrator noted that the employer and the union had acknowledged, at a special meeting during contract negotiations, that pre-existing and uniformly applied mandatory retirement plans would continue. Although the employer's failure to communicate the mandatory retirement plan to employees was inexcusable, the arbitrator concluded that this failure by itself did not negate the plan's validity (*Illinois-California Express Inc.*, 63 LA 805).

- A school board that had a practice of retiring teachers at age 70 improperly established a new policy compelling them to retire at age 65, an arbitrator held. The contract barred the employer from changing past policy or practice in matters affecting employee wages, hours, or working conditions, without mutual agreement between the employer and the union. An employee's expectation as to

the duration of his employment permeates his job performance, his attitude toward his employer, and his job morale in a manner that makes the expectation an "employee working condition," the arbitrator concluded (*Jefferson County Bd. of Education*, 69 LA 890).

- Even though an employer's mandatory retirement policy predated the bargaining contract and was uniformly imposed on employees in other parts of the country, an arbitrator ruled that the employer improperly forced an employee to retire when the person reached the age of 65 because neither the union nor the employees knew that the policy existed (*Simpson Building Supply Co.*, 73 LA 59).

### Effect of Negotiations

According to many arbitrators, management's right to force employees to retire is strengthened if the union has had an opportunity to negotiate but failed to do so, or brings up the matter in negotiations but fails to get agreement and signs a contract that makes no mention of the policy.

- A pension plan providing for automatic retirement at age 65, adopted unilaterally, had been in effect for five years before the union brought a grievance over an employee's forced retirement. An arbitration board said the employer could continue to follow its established practice until such time as the policy was restricted through collective bargaining. Generally, the board concluded, employees are entitled only to the rights they have won in the contract. If the right to work beyond age 65 is not specified in the contract, the arbitrators said, the right does not exist (*Hercules Powder Co.*, 23 LA 214).

Arbitrators believe that if a union consistently objects to a compulsory retirement policy, or if the policy contravenes the contract, the employer may not be allowed to force employees to retire against their will.

● In one case, an arbitrator found that the union not only demanded bargaining when a compulsory retirement plan was set up—a request that was refused—but had protested every time the employer threatened to enforce it. The arbitrator noted that the agreement set forth circumstances under which seniority was lost but did not mention forced retirement. Thus, he ruled that the employer had introduced a new reason for loss of seniority without giving prior notice to the union and bargaining as required by law (*TransWorld Airlines Inc.*, 31 LA 45).

● An arbitrator ruled that an employer did not have the right to require two employees, aged 68 and 72, respectively, to accept compulsory retirement because they both were older than 65. Noting that in the past, the retirement of employees at age 65 had not been enforced, the arbitrator pointed out that a new pension plan, which the employer accepted during contract negotiations and that in effect became part of the collective bargaining agreement, did not require retirement at age 65. The arbitrator concluded that compulsory retirement clearly violated a contract provision prohibiting discrimination against employees on the basis of age (*Waterbury Hospital*, 62 LA 113).

● An employer improperly compelled employees to retire at age 65, an arbitrator decided, following management's failure to agree to a union proposal that the parties' new contract contain an express provision regarding mandatory retirement. Noting that mandatory retirement was proscribed by the contract's provision barring discrimina-

tion against employees "on account of age," the arbitrator rejected the employer's contention that the obvious intent of the provision referred to applicable statutory provisions, both federal and state, which did not protect employees who were 65 or older (*MaGee-Women's Hospital*, 62 LA 987).

● An employer violated the contract when it terminated employees when they reached age 65, an arbitrator ruled, because there was no compulsory retirement age in the contract's annuity plan. Emphasizing that the evidence did not establish that any employee previously had been involuntarily retired, the arbitrator concluded that requiring employees to accept mandatory retirement at age 65 was an attempt by management to impose a new condition of employment that was not negotiated by the parties (*Chicago Zoological Society*, 61 LA 387).

## Contract Specifying 'Normal Retirement Age'

Where either the contract or a pension plan agreed to by the union and the employer expressly provides for compulsory retirement, arbitrators find little difficulty in upholding the employer's right to compel an employee to retire. If, however, the contract is silent on the subject and there is no long-standing policy acquiesced to by the union, arbitrators generally hold that management does not have the right to compel an employee to retire. In such a case, language specifying a "normal retirement age" and the manner in which the parties have interpreted the language may be important.

● A contract stated that "age 65 is considered the normal retirement age." The employer retired an employee against his wishes when he reached 65, and the union filed a grievance. In upholding the employer's right to retire the employee, an arbitrator noted that "normal retirement date" was defined in an earlier pension agreement between the parties as the date beyond which an employee could not continue working unless specifically requested to do so by the employer. The only logical interpretation of that language, the arbitrator said, was that the parties intended to carry over the same concept of compulsory retirement that had existed under the pension plan (*National Airlines*, 35 LA 67).

• Under a pension plan that stated that an "employee may be permitted to remain" at work after the normal retirement age of 65 until he reached age 70 provided he was physically able to do the job and performed his duties satisfactorily, and permitted continued work after age 70 "only at the request of the employer," an arbitrator said management could not force retirement on a 65-year-old employee who met the plan's standards. The pension plan was not originally negotiated but was written by the employer, the arbitrator noted. Thus, if the employer had wanted to make the 65-to-70 privilege exclusively within its control, it could have stated so in concise language, just as it did in the provision for employees older than age 70, he reasoned. Because this was not done, the arbitrator concluded that the employee must be allowed to remain at work if he fulfilled the qualifications set out originally by the employer (*Central Soya Co.*, 41 LA 370).

## Discriminatory Retirement Policy

Some retirement plans allow employers to retire employees at different ages depending on the ability of the individual. Generally arbitrators have approved the use of such flexible retirement policies only as long as they are administered consistently and fairly.

• A policy that allowed older employees to continue working only as long as they continued in the same job was held to be discriminatory and a violation of the contract (*Barrett-Cravens Co.*, 12 LA 522).

• Another arbitrator ruled that there must be substantial proof that an employee's work was unsatisfactory before he could be forced to retire under a contract that gave the employer discretion in retiring employees 65 or older (*Ford Motor Co.*, 20 LA 13).

• An employer did not have the right to require three 65-year-old employees to retire, an arbitrator decided, where the

employees performed their duties satisfactorily, accepted required overtime, had exemplary attendance records, and did not have any disciplinary measures on their records. Noting that the document containing management's unilateral policy requiring compulsory overtime was not placed in the employee's work area, the arbitrator pointed out that the policy was not posted until after two of the employees had been notified that they had been retired. Emphasizing that the collective bargaining agreement denied the employer the right to unilaterally terminate employees because of old age, the arbitrator observed that the contract also incorporated an express declaration that prohibited discrimination because of age (*Air California*, 67 LA 1115).

• Where a retirement policy permitted employees who reached the age of 65 to keep working if their continued service was recommended by the department head, cleared by the employee health service, and approved by the administration, an arbitrator decided that an employer had the right to force retirement of a 69-year-old employee who was unable to adapt to certain operational changes that required expanded duties and responsibilities. Even though management's policy did not establish a fixed date of retirement and this fact created an impression of inconsistency, the arbitrator said that the employer's action was in effect a benefit to some employees who desired to work longer. The fact that the employee was not fully apprised of the mandatory retirement programs was insufficient to nullify his retirement, the arbitrator concluded (*City of Hope National Medical Center*, 67 LA 518).

## Physical Conditions Warrant Retirement

Arbitrators also have upheld management's decision to compel an employee to retire when the employee's physical condition warrants retirement (66 LA 1207, 66 LA 849).

• An employer properly refused to defer retirement of a 66-year-old employee who failed to pass a required physical examination because of a liver ailment and other physical problems, an arbitrator ruled. Emphasizing that the physical health of employees who are 65 years old or older is an important factor affecting job performance, the arbitrator concluded that there was no evidence of bias on the part of the employer's doctor who recommended the worker's retirement (*Kendall Co.*, 66 LA 1285).

## Psychological Test To Determine Fitness for Duty

An arbitrator held that an employer violated a collective bargaining agreement that permitted physical or psychological testing of employees to determine their fitness to return to work because the employer lacked just cause to believe a particular employee who was forced to be tested was "not fit for duty." The arbitrator determined that the employee, a police officer returning from disability leave for a shoulder injury, should not be subjected to psychological testing because he had not been disabled by any psychological or emotional problem (*City of Monmouth*, 105 LA 724).

## Subcontracting

────────────────────────── **OVERVIEW** ──────────────────────────

There has been a changing climate concerning the legality of subcontracting within the context of arbitration. Several decades ago, arbitrators looked with disfavor on subcontracting, but in recent years subcontracting has become the norm.

Unless a collective bargaining agreement contains language that specifically bars subcontracting, a union will have a difficult time blocking it. Labor organizations are less and less successful in convincing arbitrators that subcontracting is barred by implication, although there are instances in which unions have had success in inferring a ban on subcontracting from contract language.

## KEY DECISIONS—

An employer's right to subcontract, in the absence of specific contract restrictions, has been the subject of numerous grievances. Where the bargaining agreement is silent on subcontracting, one important factor considered by arbitrators is the effect of the subcontracting on the bargaining unit or the unit's employees. Also relevant is the employer's justification for the subcontracting, that is, what sort of business rationale it can provide to justify subcontracting (see, e.g., *James River Corp.*, 104 LA 475 *and Food and Commercial Workers Local 227*, 104 LA 1152; see also 92 LA 271, 91 LA 245, 88 LA 185, 82 LA 805).

In earlier cases pertaining to subcontracting issues, arbitrators generally held that management had the right, if exercised in good faith, to subcontract work to independent contractors. Later cases, however, have held that management's right to subcontract is not unrestricted but must be judged against the recognition, seniority, wage, and other such clauses of the bargaining agreement. Standards of reasonableness and good faith are applied in determining whether these clauses were violated.

• One arbitrator, for example, observed that management is prohibited from subcontracting unless it acts in good faith, unless it acts in conformity with past practices, unless it acts reasonably, unless the act deprives only a few employees of employment, unless the act was dictated by business requirements, if the act is barred by the contract clause in which the employer recognizes the union as the employees' representative, if the act is barred by seniority provisions, or if the act violates the spirit of the agreement (*American Sugar Refining Co.*, 37 LA 334).

Generally, arbitrators apply the following standards; typically more than one standard applies in each subcontracting case.

*Compelling Economic Reasons*—If the subcontracting was motivated by "compelling economic reasons" (e.g., costs, attempt to regain competitiveness, etc.), and assuming the subcontracting was done in good faith, and the bargaining agreement contained no specific restrictions on subcontracting, arbitrators usually will look favorably on the employer's actions (see, e.g., *Miller and Co.*, 102 LA 197; see also 100 LA 1208).

*Justification*—If the subcontracting was done for reasons such as economy, maintenance of secondary sources for production, plant security, etc., it is likely to meet with the arbitrator's approval (62 LA 421, 61 LA 530).

*Past Practice*—An employer's use of subcontractors in the past also weighs in its favor, especially if the union has not objected to the practice (see, e.g., *Merchandise Mart Properties*, 105 LA 704; *Consolidated Freightways*, 105 LA 1; and *Simonds Industries Inc.*, 104 LA 41).

*Effect on Union*—Arbitrators tend to look askance at subcontracting practices if the employer is using subcontracting as a method of discriminating against the union and substantially prejudicing the status and integrity of the bargaining unit (64 LA 602).

*Effect on Unit Employees*—Another way that employers cast doubt on the legitimacy of their choosing to subcontract is if members of the union are discriminated against, displaced, laid off, or deprived of jobs previously available to them, or stand to lose regular or overtime earnings because of the subcontracting (see, e.g., *Consolidated Freightways*, 105 LA 1 (low volume of outside work); *Mead Coated Board Inc.*, 105 LA 117 and *Hillsdale School District*, 104 LA 718 (job displacement); *United Central Telephone Co. of Texas*, 104 LA 246 (layoffs), but compare *Simonds Industries Inc.*, 104 LA 41 (layoffs); *Merchandise Mart Properties*, 105 LA 704 (size of bargaining unit); see also 100 LA 676, 100 LA 474, 100 LA 78).

On the other hand, if the subcontracting has little or no effect on the unit or its members, it is likely to be upheld by arbitrators (see, e.g., *Mead Coated Board Inc.*, 105 LA 117; see also 97 LA 64, 95 LA 1139, 95 LA 89, 93 LA 101).

*Type of Work Involved*—Other factors that arbitrators take into account is whether the work normally is performed by unit employees; frequently is the subject of subcontracting in the particular industry; is of a "marginal" or "incidental" nature; or is the type of work for which subcontracting is not limited under a collective bargaining agreement (see, e.g., *Lockheed Aeronautical Systems Co.*, 104 LA 803, in which an employer's ability to subcontract non-maintenance work was not limited under a bargaining agreement, and *Goodyear Tire & Rubber Co., Houston, TX*, 103 LA 1099; see also 100 LA 856, 97 LA 1216, 97 LA 782, 97 LA 650, 97 LA 614, 97 LA 214, 96 LA 816, 74 LA 1128, 71 LA 155, 62 LA 474).

*Availability of Sufficient, Qualified Manpower/Man Hours Within Bargaining Unit*—Arbitrators also evaluate whether the skills of the available bargaining unit members are sufficient for the task being subcontracted and whether the number of available employees is adequate for the task (see, e.g., *Oglebay Norton Taconite Co.*, 107 LA 1153; *Owens-Brockway Glass Container*, 106 LA 868; *Willamette Industries Inc.*, 106 LA 230; *United Technologies*, 105 LA 1214; *Republic Engineered Steels Inc.*, 104 LA 547; and *Beckett Paper Co.*, 104 LA 1107; see also 100 LA 387, 97 LA 614, 74 LA 616, 74 LA 269).

*Availability of Equipment/Facilities*—Another factor to be considered is whether, in the employer's own facility, there is sufficient and appropriate equipment to perform the tasks that would otherwise be subcontracted or whether the employer can easily and economically purchase such equipment (see, e.g., *United Technologies*, 105 LA 1214, *Mead Coated Board Inc.*, 105 LA 117, and *Beckett Paper Co.*, 104 LA 1107; see also 64 LA 1244, 63 LA 82, 62 LA 505).

*Regularity/Duration of Subcontracting*—Yet another factor arbitrators look at is whether the particular work is frequently or only intermittently subcontracted and whether the work is subcontracted for a temporary or limited period, or for a permanent or indefinite period of time.

*Unusual Circumstances Involved*—Arbitrators must also consider whether an emergency, "special" job, strike, or other unusual situation exists that necessitates bringing in subcontractors (see, e.g., *Pittsburg & Midway Coal Mining Co.*, 102 LA 631).

*History of Negotiations*—Another significant issues is whether management's right to subcontract has been the subject of contract negotiations (*Lockheed Aeronautical Systems Co.*, 104 LA 803).

*Management-Rights Clause*—Subcontracting may be proper if a contract's management-rights clause gives an employer the right to manage the workforce, especially where subcontracting is not expressly addressed in the contract or permits an employer to abolish/eliminate or reconfigure jobs and/or job specifications (see, e.g., *Simonds Industries Inc.*, 104 LA 41; *James River Corp.*, 104 LA 475; see also 101 LA 574).

*Quality of Work/Workmanship*—One arbitrator held that an employer did not violate a bargaining agreement when it contracted out certain work routinely performed by bargaining unit employees, in part because the unit employees' work was "dismally below expectation" (*Armco Steel Co.*, 102 LA 396).

## SUMMARY OF CASES

### Notification Requirement/ Duty to Bargain

A collective bargaining agreement may require management to notify the union of its intent to subcontract. In such cases, the notification requirement may be strictly construed because in effect it precludes the union from exercising its rights under a contract to discuss alternatives to subcontracting (see, e.g., *AK Steel Corp.*, 105 LA 869; 102 LA 396, 54 LA 1207, 53 LA 993, 46 LA 724).

• When a contract was silent on the issue of subcontracting, an arbitrator emphasized that prior notification generally should be given (*Pittsburgh Brewing Co.*, 53 LA 470).

• An arbitrator ruled that an employer's one-day notice to a union that it planned to subcontract bargaining-unit work violated a contract because it failed to give the union time to invoke the agreement's expedited procedure before a joint, labor-management contracting out committee and also because there was no emergency situation that made subcontracting a business necessity (*Armco Steel Co.*, 102 LA 396; see also *United Technologies*, 105 LA 1214).

• In another case, a hospital violated a contract allowing subcontracting of unit work only after 30-day advance notice to the union when it did not give the required notice before subcontracting work involving transcription of medical reports, an arbitrator ruled. In effect, the notice requirement restricted the employer's right to subcontract the work, the arbitrator reasoned. If the required 30-day notice was given, then the criteria and standards generally applicable to the various aspects of subcontracting became applicable to any work subcontracted by the employer, the arbitrator concluded

(*Kaiser Foundation Hospitals*, 61 LA 1008; see also 98 LA 13, 93 LA 666, 75 LA 485, 73 LA 1036).

• Another arbitrator decided that an employer properly contracted out construction and/or installation of manufacturing equipment, following the maintenance manager's meeting with union officers during which the manager gave the officers forms containing a brief description of the project, the contractor to whom the job would be awarded, and other details (*J.T. Baker Chemical Co.*, 76 LA 1147; see also 95 LA 668, 75 LA 810, 74 LA 1128).

• An arbitrator ruled that, even though a collective bargaining agreement requires a notice of intent to subcontract, the contractual notice requirement is not violated if the employer lacks the necessary equipment and qualified employees and if the subcontracting of work is not expected to become routine (*M.A. Hannah Co.*, 88 LA 185).

## Duty to Bargain

The current NLRB approach for determining whether an employer's decision to subcontract work is a mandatory subject of bargaining is reflected in *Otis Elevator Co.* (269 N.L.R.B. No. 162, 1984, 115 LRRM 1281), where the NLRB ruled that a duty to bargain arises when the decision turns on labor costs, rather than on a fundamental change in the direction or nature of the enterprise.

• An arbitrator ruled that a union has the right to bargain over the impact of subcontracting on the bargaining unit, even where it is clear that the employer has the right unilaterally to contract out the work in question (*Witco Chem. Co.*, 89 LA 349).

## Significance of 'Residual' Rights Clause

Generally, reliance on recognition, seniority, and other such clauses is not persuasive to arbitrators where there is a weak subcontracting clause in the agreement. In all probability, the arbitrator will allow the employer to use its "residual" rights to manage its workforce to determine whether to allow the subcontracting.

• In one case, an arbitrator indicated that the subcontracting clause required "good-faith" efforts by the employer not to subcontract work that was normally performed by regular employees. The arbitrator did not specifically repudiate the contract's recognition clause, but chose instead to treat the issue as if the contract were silent on the subcontracting question, thus basing his decision on the implications of the employer's right to determine how to manage its operations (*Sealtest Foods*, 48 LA 797).

## Subcontracting Where Work Is Customarily Performed by Unit Employees

Usually, arbitrators confronted by a clause that restricts management from subcontracting for work involving the production of parts and equipment normally made by unit employees will hold for the union if there is a significant detriment to the bargaining unit.

• An employer did not have the right to unilaterally contract out bargaining unit work during the time that maintenance mechanics were on layoff, an arbitrator ruled, even though the magnitude of the job, in addition to the rush nature of the work, justified contracting out a portion of the task. Pointing out that the subcontracting deprived unit employees of work they would customarily perform, the arbitrator emphasized that the injuries done to the workers and the potential damage to the union were paramount. Rejecting the employer's contention that contracting out the work was not an effort to undermine the union, the arbitrator concluded that the adverse effect that the subcontracting caused the unit was the same as if the employer had intended to undermine the union (*Consolidated Aluminum Co.*, 66 LA 1170; see also 97 LA 983).

• Another arbitrator ruled that an employer did not commit a subcontracting violation when it purchased stock parts from a supplier. Despite the fact that the contract prohibited subcontracting where employees were on layoff and the work subcontracted was work that they normally performed, the arbitrator reasoned that the purchases were not subcontracting because they were ready-made stock parts in a catalogue and thus no bargaining unit members were deprived of work (*Iowa Manufacturing Co.*, 68 LA 599).

## Subcontracting Where Employer Lacks Equipment and Facilities

An employer's right to subcontract out work may be restricted even when the employer lacks the equipment or facilities to do the job.

• An employer was obligated to pay lost overtime to employees for subcontracting unit work, an arbitrator ruled, despite the fact that the employer did not have the equipment the subcontractor used and the employees did not have training to operate the equipment. The contract prohibited the employer from subcontracting even if it had to rent part of the equipment and train the affected employees in the operation of such equipment, the arbitrator concluded (*Ashland Chemical Co.*, 64 LA 1244).

## Employer's Negligence As Cause of Need for Subcontracting

An arbitrator held that a hospital's subcontracting of a backlog of medical transcription work normally performed by bargaining unit employees violated a collective bargaining agreement that obligated the employer to make a good-faith effort the preserve bargaining-unit work. The arbitrator found that the transcription backlog had accumulated over an extended period of time, that unusual dictation requirements had not contributed to the backlog, and that the employer's ob-

ligation of good faith was hardly satisfied when it sought to justify the need for subcontracting on the basis of a situation that the hospital itself negligently had allowed to develop (*Fairmont General Hospital*, 105 LA 247).

## Subcontracting to Save Business

Subcontracting did not violate the contract when a technology company that was struggling to stop a financial "free fall" centralized operations and moved much of its basic work from small unionized sites to larger nonunion regional centers, an arbitrator found.

When the company in question lost nearly $345 million in net revenue in two years, it was compelled, management said, to lay off about 1,200 employees and close more than 50 warehouses. The union objected to the loss of warehouse jobs, arguing that the contract stipulated that subcontracting was permissible unless it was used as a union-busting tactic. Because more warehouse work was being done by nonunion subcontractors while union members were being laid off, the union called the strategy union-busting. It did not seek the reopening of facilities but asked the arbitrator to determine a remedy for laid-off members.

In denying the grievance, the arbitrator said the union's "theory of the case is premised upon an inherently illusory status quo ideal" of expanding work opportunities. The employer, however, was overwhelmed "in a collapsing sector of a recessionary economy" and business as usual would guarantee disaster, he said, in finding for the employer (*Nexitra*, 116 LA 1780).

# Part 11

# *Union Rights*

# Union Rights

## OVERVIEW

Although a union's prerogatives usually are specified in the collective bargaining agreement, problems involving the right of a union to conduct business, handle grievances, receive information, or visit an employer's premises to discuss employee complaints do arise in the arbitral setting.

More frequently, however, arbitrators must resolve labor-management disputes centering on the manner in which unions exercise their rights or on the reasonableness of limitations placed on such rights by an employer. Trouble also may occur with contract provisions pertaining to the use of union bulletin boards. Arbitrators usually have interpreted such provisions broadly, holding that any intended restrictions should be written expressly into the contract.

In this area perhaps more than any other, what the contract says is only part of the story. The union also has important grievance-handling and information rights under the National Labor Relations Act. According to one arbitrator, "the law of labor relations is relatively clear that an employer has no right to interfere with an employee's performance of his valid union activities and his obligations to his union, the same as the union and employee have no right to interfere with the employer's right to manage and operate the plant" (*Greif Bros. Corp.*, 67 LA 1001).

## SUMMARY OF CASES

### Union's Right to Information

Most arbitrators agree that the union should have any information necessary for the processing of grievances and for making sure that the contract is not being violated with respect to the employer's wage administration practices. As one arbitrator pointed out, "the object and purpose of arbitration is to arrive at a fair and just decision, and to this end parties should be assisted in obtaining competent and material evidence where such may reasonably be had" (*Chesapeake & Potomac Telephone Co. of West Va.*, 21 LA 367).

- One employer whose contract specified that it would furnish complete data and figures on the operation of its merit review system refused to disclose the names and department numbers of employees who had received increases. The arbitrator ruled that the agreement required the employer to give the union such information (*Sperry Gyroscope Co.*, 18 LA 916).

- Where a contract required the employer to furnish the union with detailed information pertaining to changes in work assignments, another arbitrator ruled that this meant it had to supply all the basic time-study data, not just summaries (*Celanese Corp. of America*, 27 LA 845).

- Still another contract did not explicitly state the employer's obligation to give the union specific information, but an arbitrator said the employer must give the union a list of pay rates so that it could bargain effectively on merit increases (*I. Lewis Cigar Mfg. Co.*, 12 LA 661).

- Given that a union was entitled to bargain over an employer's proposed amendments to the retirement plan, the employer had to give the union the text of all proposed and existing amendments and all actuarial data concerning all participants, an arbitrator ruled. The actuarial data was considered absolutely necessary to evaluate the presence or absence of benefits resulting from employees' contributions, the arbitrator concluded (*Anti-Defamation League B'Nai B'Rith*, 53 LA 1332).

● Another arbitrator decided that an employer who discharged an employee for exceeding his allotted amount of sick leave was obligated to give the union the names, addresses, initial employment dates, and seniority dates of other employees who had been allowed to return to work after being absent in excess of their authorized sick leave (*Mobil Oil Corp.*, 63 LA 263).

● Under a supplementary unemployment compensation benefit trust plan providing that the employer "will comply with reasonable requests by the union for other statistical information on the operation of the plan," an arbitrator held that the union was entitled to monthly lists of names of recipients and amounts paid. The employer's contention that the lists were not "statistical information" placed an unduly narrow restriction on the term, the arbitrator said (*Mack Trucks, Inc.*, 36 LA 1114).

● Under a contract that said nothing about seniority lists, one arbitrator agreed that the union had a right to seniority information only when it specifically asked for it (*Bethlehem Steel Co.*, 24 LA 699).

● Contract provisions making payroll data available on request did not require an employer to furnish such records for uncovering claims during a dispute over seniority in layoffs, an arbitrator held. The records were to be used only for testing the validity of specific claims, he said (*Santa Clara & Central Calif. Meat Processors' Assn.*, 36 LA 42; see also 77 LA 1008, 74 LA 96, 72 LA 57).

## Right to Represent Employees at Investigative Interviews (Weingarten Rights)

The U.S. Supreme Court's *Weingarten* decision (1975, 88 LRRM 2689) held that individual employees have the right under the NLRA to have a union representative present at any employer investigatory interview that the employee reasonably believes may result in disciplinary action (See, e.g., *Chevron Chemical Co.*, 60 LA 1066).

*Weingarten* and other union-representation cases have gained general acceptance among arbitrators, who have generally focused their decisions on the presence or absence of *Weingarten* principles (see, e.g., *S & J Ranch*, 103 LA 350; see also 98 LA 201, 97 LA 271, 96 LA 255, 95 LA 148, 93 LA 203, 92 LA 544).

[**Note:** The U.S. Supreme Court let stand an appeals court decision that extended *Weingarten* rights to nonunion workers (*Epilepsy Foundation of Northeast Ohio v. NLRB*, 2002, 168 LRRM 2673). Over time, arbitration cases can be expected to play "catch-up" with the courts' rulings.]

● Where an employee fails to request or waives union representation, arbitrators generally have found employers' denial of representation not to be a violation of either the bargaining agreement or *Weingarten* (86 LA 350, 83 LA 1248).

● In setting the limits to which *Weingarten* applies to employer investigations, some arbitrators have limited the right to union representation to investigatory interviews only. Consequently, there is arbitral authority to prevent union representation during employer searches for physical evidence in employee cars (84 LA 562), and in meetings informing employees to submit to drug screening during a physical examination (84 LA 1272).

● In another case, an arbitrator denied an employee union representation during a performance evaluation, holding that the union had no right to accompany an employee to a supervisor's evaluation before there was a grievance or a grievable event (84 LA 516; see also 97 LA 728, 97 LA 303).

● Arbitrators have held that where the purpose of a meeting was to administer discipline and not to conduct an investigatory interview, employer denial of union representation did not violate *Weingarten* (87 LA 572, 87 LA 568, 83 LA 1248; compare with 95 LA 82, 94 LA 1229).

● An arbitrator upheld the discipline of an employee, even though she was deprived of union representation during an investigatory interview, where she responded to a supervisor's initial, direct inquiry and failed immediately to request a union representative (*Grand Blanc Community Schools*, 97 LA 162).

● An arbitrator upheld a sexual-harassment discharge even though an employer improperly limited a union's role at a second investigatory interview because a union representative fully participated in the first interview, and any prejudice through procedural defect was overcome by clear and convincing evidence that the grievant engaged in the harassment of several employees (*Shell Pipe Line Corp.*, 97 LA 957; see also 97 LA 343, 96 LA 1020).

● On the other hand, an arbitrator held that an employee was improperly denied the right to union representation at an investigatory meeting about an incident for which he was later disciplined. Even though the employee did not ask that a union representative attend, several factors triggered *Weingarten*: the meeting clearly had the potential for discipline, the employer failed to inform the employee of the meeting's purpose or that it could lead to discipline, and the employee clearly could not have known or reasonably suspected the purpose of the meeting or the potential for discipline so that he could have asked a union representative to attend (*County of Cook*, 105 LA 974).

## Decertified Union's Right to Process Grievance

A decertified union still has the right to prosecute a grievance, one arbitrator held. Thus, where a union had processed a grievance but was decertified before the case reached arbitration, the arbitrator said it had a right to settle the dispute. A distinction exists between the collective bargaining function and the processing of a grievance, he noted. Though a decertified union may not bargain for the employees, he said, federal law does not bar it from representing them in arbitration (*Trumbull Asphalt Co.*, 38 LA 1093).

## Right to Post Union Notices

Usually a union is free to put up any notice dealing with union business, and the employer cannot withhold approval unless the material is slanderous or derogatory to the employer. Types of union notices against which companies have protested, but that arbitrators have found acceptable include the following:

● a notice urging members' support for striking members of another union (*Wisconsin Tissue Mills, Inc.*, 73 LA 271);

● a letter from a union international representative that attempted to avoid an imminent wildcat strike and assure members that the union would fight their grievances through legal means (*Freuhauf Corp.*, 54 LA 1096);

● a notice stating that the purpose of a forthcoming union meeting was to consider strike action against the employer (*Fairchild Engine & Airplane Corp.*, 16 LA 678);

● a seniority list drawn up by the union after the parties had failed to agree on such a list (*Lennox Furnace Co.*, 20 LA 788); and

● a notice urging union members to register for voting (*Warren City Mfg. Co.*, 7 LA 202).

● One arbitrator has held that a clause permitting the posting of union "announcements" could not be stretched to include organizational material (*General Electric Co.*, 31 LA 924).

● When the union posted a listing of nonmembers under the title "Scabs," it was acting improperly, according to an arbitrator. The lists smacked of coercion and created an atmosphere of intimidation, the arbitrator pointed out. The underlying purpose was to blacklist employees, an unlawful recruitment tactic and misuse of information, the arbitrator concluded (*Union Carbide Corp.*, 44 LA 554).

● The discharge of an employee for posting unauthorized inflammatory notices pertaining to the employer was upheld by an arbitrator, where the employee had been given repeated warnings concerning other notices he had posted and had been ordered not to post the notice that led to his discharge (*Beaver Precision Products Inc.*, 51 LA 853).

• Another arbitrator held that a union's posting of notices stating "Effects of Being Nonunion" and "Why Join the Union" violated a collective bargaining agreement clause prohibiting the posting of "notices containing solicitation," because the contract's ban included soliciting for union membership. The arbitrator also held that the union's posting of a letter to its membership on the status of grievances violated the contract's no-solicitation clause, where the tone of the letter set forth reasons to join the union and thus constituted solicitation for membership (*Leggett & Platt Inc.*, 104 LA 1048).

***Offensive or Controversial Notices—*** An arbitrator ruled that a union's posting of cartoons that depicted an employer kicking employees, employees being bound and gagged, management using whips on employees, and portrayals of the employer's open-door policy as the proverbial "spider and fly" relationship violated a collective bargaining agreement's ban on offensive or controversial union notices (*Leggett & Platt Inc.*, 104 LA 1048).

## Restrictions on Right to Represent Employees

Most contracts place restrictions on the union's methods of handling grievances by requiring, for example, that union representatives and employees obtain proper authorization from their superiors before they absent themselves from their work areas to discuss a grievance (67 LA 887, 67 LA 1123).

• In one case, an arbitrator held that an employer properly determined that a chief steward was on unauthorized leave instead of administrative leave when he left his workstation to give employees advice concerning various problems they were experiencing on the job. Although it had been the employer's custom to grant administrative leave to elected union officials for investigating grievances, the arbitrator ruled that the steward violated the contract by failing to identify either

the specific bargaining unit in which he planned to make the investigation or the particular supervisor who had been contacted (*National Institutes of Health*, 67 LA 788).

In addition to restricting the time and place in which union representatives are authorized to discuss grievances, contract provisions also may specify the union's role at each step of the grievance procedure.

• Where a contract provided that an employee filing a grievance could be represented at the first step of the grievance process "by an appropriate steward," an arbitrator ruled that an employee was not entitled to have the union's "business" representative represent him at the first-step meeting. Agreeing with the employer's contention that the presence of the union business agent, rather than a steward, at the first step created "an atmosphere of undue sophistication," the arbitrator decided that the parties had intended to try to settle disputes initially through the efforts of the lowest levels of employer and union representatives (*Navy Commissary Store Complex*, 62 LA 576).

## Right to Investigate Departments Not in Unit

Do union representatives have the right to investigate in departments not covered by the contract? One arbitrator ruled that an employer had no business refusing to allow a union representative to investigate a possible grievance involving a department specifically excluded from the bargaining unit when there was a charge that the department was doing bargaining unit work.

• By decision of the NLRB, engineering department employees were excluded from the bargaining unit of an employer. When the union got wind of a report that people in the department were doing bargaining unit work, the chief steward sought to enter the department to find out whether the report was true. The employer blocked his attempt, saying he should tell what he knew to the personnel manager. The latter would then investigate and report on his findings, the employer said. One reason given by the employer for its stand was that some of the work in the engineering department was classified, and the union representative did not have security clearance.

An arbitrator found no merit in the employer's contentions. The contracts, he pointed out, permitted the union to file grievances on its own motion; the union was not limited to processing grievances that came to it from employees. So if it got word that the contract was not being adhered to, it had a right to investigate without the personnel manager's intervention, regardless of the source of its information.

As for the employer's fears about security, the arbitrator saw no problem in the idea that the company could assign a "conductor" to accompany the union investigator and make sure no violation of security regulations occurred. The employer's action, the arbitrator concluded, amounted to a violation of the recognition clause of the contract (*Librascope Inc.*, 30 LA 358).

● Another arbitrator held that where a union cannot initiate grievances, it also could not go all over the plant looking for contract violations. A union suspected that unit work was being done in a department where none of the employees belonged to the unit. To investigate the situation, it requested access to the site but was turned down. Under the contract, management noted that union officers could leave their work for "the proper handling of grievances," but that did not mean the union could go where there were no unit members and look for trouble.

The arbitrator agreed that the union had the right to police the contract, but in his opinion the right was limited to cases of existing disputes. By the terms of the contract, only the employer and the employees could be parties to grievances. Because the union could not bring up grievances on its own, it could not roam the plant looking for them, the arbitrator concluded (*Bendix Aviation Corp.*, 39 LA 393).

## Right of Access to Plant

Many bargaining agreements provide for nonemployee union representatives to come into the plant to investigate grievances or for other purposes. Furthermore, some arbitrators suggest that such plant access is inherent in agreements whether explicitly guaranteed or not (36 LA 815, 32 LA 1004, 30 LA 358).

Although arbitrators have upheld union access to a workplace for grievance-related investigations, they often hold other nongrievance-related activities under greater scrutiny.

● An arbitrator held that an agreement, which required union representatives to make arrangements with an employer before entering the plant to "discuss matters of contract administration," did not allow solicitation of membership by a nonemployee union representative (*Montgomery Ward & Co.*, 85 LA 913).

● Where an employer repeatedly refused to give a union representative access to a plant to investigate violations of a union security clause and even had the union representative arrested for trespassing, an arbitrator ruled that the employer interfered with the union's contractual right to visit the premises. The arbitrator held the employer responsible for creating a confrontational situation where the circumstances called for "a spirit of cooperation and consideration" (*Piper's Restaurant*, 86 LA 809).

● An arbitrator found that, where an agreement permitted union safety officials access to an employer's premises, the employer's requirement that union officials sign a waiver releasing the employer from all liability was on its face unreasonable. Because the union officials were covered by employees' compensation and given that without the waiver, union officials would be given greater rights than employee members, the employer's requirement of waiver of liability for specific visits by union officials was reasonable (*Utah Power & Light*, 88 LA 310).

● Arbitrators also have held that when union representatives do not behave in a civilized manner while exercising visitation rights, they may be denied access to the plant (*Associated Hospitals of San Francisco*, 67 LA 323).

● A union representative visited the company president in his office to discuss an alleged contract violation by management. During a heated argument the representative suddenly got out of his chair, stepped behind the president's desk, and began to twist his arm and poke him in the chest. He then invited the president outside to settle the matter, after which the employer refused to allow the representative back into the plant. Although the contract said that the union agents would have access to the plant during working hours to take up complaints and determine whether the contract was being complied with, an arbitrator ruled that the denial of access was justified because of the representative's poor conduct (*Glendale Mfg. Co.*, 32 LA 223).

● A state's unilaterally imposed requirement that union representatives give one-week written notice before visiting an employer's work area violated a collective bargaining agreement that allowed union representatives to visit work areas if the visits did not disrupt work activities and required representatives to receive permission for such visits, and the contract mentioned neither written nor time notice requirements, an arbitrator held (*State of New Hampshire*, 108 LA 209).

● One arbitrator used the following guidelines in determining the propriety of a union representative's visit to the worksite.

1. Visitation rights must be exercised at reasonable times and in a reasonable manner.

2. The employer cannot legitimately interfere with the representative's business so long as the visitation rights are exercised reasonably.

3. In judging the reasonableness of a visitation's timing, not only the particular hours of visitation but also the number of visitations must be considered.

4. The employer cannot place a restriction on visitation rights that is contrary to contractual terms and past practice.

5. The employer may establish reasonable rules governing access to the premises as long as they do not unreasonably interfere with the legitimate purpose of

the visit (*Roy Demanes & Assoc. Inc.*, 60 LA 1039).

● An arbitrator ruled that an employer improperly denied a union's request for use of a former conference room for an after-hours meeting of a union's executive board. The denial, originally based on security, and later on the ground that employer facilities could be used only by employer bargaining-unit employees, was improper, the arbitrator said. The bargaining agreement provided that the employer grant meeting space to whatever subdivision of "the union" requests it "where feasible," regardless of whether the individuals are employees. In addition, the refusal was improper because the employer could have provided space without undue cost or inconvenience, the arbitrator said (*Ohio Dept. of Health*, 97 LA 310).

● In a case where management denied the chief steward access to the plant except during his own shift, an arbitrator held that the steward had the privilege of entering the plant at all reasonable times. If he were limited to his own shift, the arbitrator said, he would be no different from a departmental steward, and his plant-wide constituency would be ignored (*Buddy-L Corp.*, 41 LA 185).

### Right to File Grievance

The grievance-settlement machinery is one of the most vital elements in the union-management relationship. As such it has been the subject of numerous arbitral decisions.

● A union president had the right to present a grievance, even though the grievance-arbitration clause mentioned only disputes between "an employee and the employer" and the subject of the complaint did not affect the union head as an "employee." The protest was on behalf of a union member and was allowed because, according to the arbitrator, "it would be inappropriate to impose a legalistic restriction on the right of the parties to settle their disputes by use of the grievance machinery" (*Ohio Power Co.*, 45 LA 1039).

● An arbitrator decided that a union could file a grievance even if the employees involved wanted no part of it. If the union could not file on its own, there would be no procedure under which controversies as to interpretation or claims of violation could go to arbitration unless some employee actually affected brought up the matter (*Atlantic Seaboard Corp.*, 42 LA 865).

### Right to Repudiate Changes in Grievance Procedure

When an employer and a union orally agreed to certain changes in the grievance procedure, it made no difference that the membership did not formally approve the changes, an arbitrator ruled. An attempt was made to repudiate the changes when the union elected new officers; however, the arbitrator decided that if the union were free to invalidate agreements made by its previous officers, the employer would be able to invalidate all agreements by merely replacing its representatives (*Gertman Co.*, 45 LA 30).

### Right to Wear Union Insignia/Buttons

An employer will not have just cause under a collective bargaining agreement to prohibit employees from wearing union-sponsored insignia/buttons if the buttons are not provocative/threatening, the language used on the buttons is factually accurate, and/or the employer has permitted employees to wear similar items that were not detrimental to the employer, an arbitrator found, even though the items in this particular case were worn by employees who had contact with the public (*University of Iowa Hospitals and Clinics*, 112 LA 360).

# Part 12

# *Strikes and Lockouts*

# No-Strike Provisions

## OVERVIEW

Prohibitions against strike activity during the life of a collective bargaining agreement are included in nearly all labor-management agreements. Generally, arbitrators take the position that any union-inspired activity that interferes with production, whether or not called a strike, is in fact a strike (see, e.g., *Lucky Stores*, 100 LA 262, 98 LA 41, 97 LA 297, 71 LA 1151, 69 LA 1201, 69 LA 93, 67 LA 805, 67 LA 934).

In some instances, however, where, for example, production suddenly falls off or several employees call in sick simultaneously, the situation may not be quite so clear (see, e.g., *Plainville Concrete Services*, 104 LA 811).

## SUMMARY OF CASES

### Union Meetings on Company Time As Strike

Union meetings called during working hours usually result from some employer action that employees do not like, or are intended to allow employees to reach a decision on some matter that the union thinks requires fast action. Most arbitrators have held that such meetings amount to strikes.

● One arbitrator declared that a planned mass departure from the workplace that halts productive work and disrupts the employer's production schedule is a work stoppage and violates a contract's no-strike clause (*Nathan Mfg. Co.*, 7 LA 3).

● An arbitration board threw out one union's argument that a stoppage has to be for an indefinite period of time to be a strike. The board reasoned that a union meeting during working hours is a strike just as certainly as the employer's action would be a lockout if it stopped production to hold a directors' meeting (*Atlantic Foundry Co.*, 8 LA 807).

### Employee Gathering as Strike

Situations may arise where employees feel they have an urgent request or question that must be taken care of before they start working. They may then gather together and say they would not work until management listens to them. Most arbitrators take management's side in this situation and consider that when employees gather together informally instead of working they are in effect striking.

● Employees were engaged in an unlawful work stoppage, an arbitrator ruled, when, after meeting with their supervisor with respect to an incentive dispute, they refused to go back to work until after a private half-hour session with the union grievance chairman. Both supervisor and higher management officials who came into the meeting later made it clear to the employees that they were to return to work, the arbitrator noted. Group pressure of this type to resolve grievances is completely unsanctioned by the contract, the arbitrator emphasized, concluding that the agreement provided an orderly method for settling such disputes (*Kaiser Steel Corp.*, 51 LA 1041; see also *Republic Steel Corp.*, 6 LA 85).

● At least one arbitrator believes that a gathering of employees does not amount to a strike where they are not making any demands but rather are seeking information concerning a change in their working arrangements.

An employer decided to change the departmental organization of its crane operators. Under the old arrangement, crane operators were all together in one department and were assigned by supervision in that department to particular cranes in the various departments. Under the new plan, management intended to place the crane operators permanently in the various departments instead of assigning them each day to a department. At the beginning of their shift instead of their time cards crane operators found cards telling them to go to other locations to punch in. There was considerable confusion and the operators were about an hour late in starting work. Management maintained that the delay in starting constituted a strike violation of the contract.

The arbitrator held, however, that management itself caused the delay by its failure to tell the employees beforehand about their transfer. This was not a strike but rather a delay resulting from a failure of information, comparable to a delay resulting from a power failure, the arbitrator concluded (*Ford Motor Co.*, 10 LA 148).

### Simultaneous Absences as Strike

Unless a union can show evidence that simultaneous absences by employees are a coincidence and that each absent employee's excuse is legitimate, an arbitrator will probably consider this to be a strike.

● Shortly after a union meeting, a group of 20 employees in two departments failed to return to work. Each phoned the employer to report that he was sick. The employer charged that the mass absences were a strike in violation of the contract and discharged the employees. An arbitrator, asked to decide whether the absences were a strike, ruled that they were. Although testimony was presented to show that several of the employees actually were ill, the excuses of most were not backed up by evidence. It was this lack of proof that led the arbitrator to conclude that the mass absence was more than a coincidence and constituted a strike (*American Cyanamid Co.*, 15 LA 563; see also 87 LA 424, 54 LA 569).

● An arbitrator ruled an employer's drivers who called in sick on a Saturday that they were scheduled to work overtime violated a no-strike provision contained in a collective bargaining agreement. The arbitrator held the employer had established, albeit based on circumstantial evidence, that the employees' action most likely was concerted and prompted by nonunion drivers from another company facility who also were working that day. Furthermore, the arbitrator noted the employees presented no evidence they actually were sick (*Plainville Concrete Services*, 104 LA 811).

● A school board did not have the right to add one day to the school schedule to make up for a day it closed the school because one-half of the work force called in sick, an arbitrator decided, where the school waited for six weeks and made ratification of the contract contingent on the teachers' making up the lost workday. Finding that the purpose of the additional workday was to discipline employees for the alleged one-day work stoppage, the arbitrator ruled that the attempt was untimely and, therefore, not based upon just cause. Although management may view the decision as rewarding illegally striking employees, the arbitrator concluded it was too late to determine whether there was a concerted and unlawful work stoppage because the employer did not see fit to discipline culpable employees in a timely fashion (*White Cloud Public Schools*, 72 LA 179).

### Refusal to Work Because of Health & Safety Hazards

Employees who refuse to work under dangerous health or safety conditions may not be considered on strike by arbitrators.

● An employer was not justified in discharging employees who walked off their jobs following management's failure to install fire extinguishers that an OSHA inspector had ordered installed, an arbitrator ruled, notwithstanding the employer's contention that the employees should have filed a grievance, instead of engaging in a strike in violation of the contract. As a general rule, no employee is required to render services in a place that may be a hazard to his health and safety, the arbitrator emphasized, concluding that conditions existing at the plant were such that the health and safety of the employees were in jeopardy (*RI-JA Machining Co. Inc.*, 66 LA 474; see also 89 LA 1227).

● Another arbitrator did not feel that a good-faith belief that working conditions were a health hazard was enough reason to justify a walkout. According to his interpretation of the issue, it must be demonstrated that a hazard actually does exist. Thus, he denied the request for holiday pay or sick-leave passes for the employees who left work prior to quitting time because they felt the poor ventilation coupled with prevailing high temperatures presented a health hazard (*Wilcolator Co.*, 44 LA 847; see also 52 LA 259).

● Where it was found that employees had refused to work until management agreed never to operate under alleged dangerous conditions in the future, an arbitrator held that they were clearly engaging in an illegitimate strike. He said that this was more than just a mere refusal to incur an undue health hazard (*Ford Motor Co.*, 6 LA 799).

● Employees were not entitled to be paid for the time that they did not report for work because the employer would not provide a nurse in the First Aid room in its main building, an arbitrator ruled, because the employees' action constituted an unlawful strike under the no-strike clause of their contract. Although the employees were allowed to refuse work assignments on the ground that working conditions were unsafe, the arbitrator concluded that the absence of a nurse on duty did not constitute such a condition (*Quaker Oats Co.*, 69 LA 727).

**Slowdown as No-Strike Violation**

In some cases, a slowdown in production by employees may constitute an unlawful strike in violation of the contract. According to one arbitrator, any union action, including a pause at work, that interferes with the employees' duty to do their jobs amounts to a contract violation, particularly where there is a no-strike pledge covering any slowdown, work stoppage, strike, picketing, boycott, or

other job action (*Restaurant-Hotel Employer's Council of Southern California*, 24 LA 429; see also 55 LA 372, 50 LA 1157, 48 LA 1224, 41 LA 1253).

● Employees were held responsible for a work stoppage that resulted in a stay-in in violation of a contract, an arbitrator decided, notwithstanding the union's contention that it was management that decided to close the plant and shut down operations. Finding that the employer shut down the plant only after it had unsuccessfully tried to stop the stay-in through the use of plant guards and local policemen, the arbitrator upheld the employees' discharges because they had been apprised by both the union and the employer that the stay-in violated the contract (*Chrysler Corp.*, 63 LA 677).

Not every slowdown in the rate of production need constitute a strike.

● In deciding that the slowdown of several crews was not a "slowdown" in violation of the contract, an arbitrator noted that there was no labor dispute involved. In its normal usage a slowdown implies a dispute in which employees intend to get some advantage from their action. Although it was true that the crews were not producing as much as they had previously shown they could, they still were performing at a rate that was considered satisfactory for other employees. He concluded that the only fair way to judge effort and production was by the job, not by the individual (*Kelly-Springfield Tire Co.*, 42 LA 1162; see also 49 LA 1236, 41 LA 1339).

**Observance of Picket Line**

Where there is no contract provision permitting employees to refuse to cross a picket line, arbitrators generally agree that a no-strike clause is binding upon the employees concerned. Such employees, governed by a broad no-strike, no-work stoppage clause, must cross a peaceful picket line, or face disciplinary action or discharge by the employer, according to the arbitrators.

● An electrical union violated a contract provision barring authorization or sanction of "any" strike, an arbitrator ruled, when the union's president addressed a letter to a clerks union that was picketing the employer, stating that the electrical union members would "support" any sanctioned strike within the jurisdiction of the clerks union. Pointing out that during the course of the picketing, the electrical employees left the plant with their tools, did not report the following day, and returned to work only after the strike ended, the arbitrator said he could not accept the unified action of some 30 to 40 employees statewide as individual judgments, and thus must rule that it was taken in "concert." Noting that the contract contained a broad no-strike clause, the arbitrator concluded that the agreement did not allow the union either to render assistance or to engage in a sympathy strike (*American Totalisator Co.*, 74 LA 377).

● A carpenters' union violated a no-strike pledge when its members refused to cross a picket line set up by striking members of another union that had a contract with the employer, an arbitrator decided, notwithstanding the union's contention that the refusal to cross the picket line resulted from the personal conviction of each striking member. Pointing out that the union admitted to doing nothing to convince its members that they should honor the no-strike clause, the arbitrator emphasized that the union was responsible for the employees' action because it did not make a good-faith effort to get members to honor their contract. Absent a provision permitting employees to refuse to cross a picket line, the no-strike clause was binding upon the employees, the arbitrator concluded (*National Homes Mfg. Co.*, 72 LA 1127; see also 75 LA 36, 68 LA 401, 54 LA 140).

Where two or more unions bargained with an employer for different groups of employees, members of one union were entitled to honor the picket line of the other union, because the picket line was set up as the result of a genuine labor dispute, even though the contract had a no-strike clause.

● Clerical employees of a waterfront terminal employer went on strike to enforce their demands. Longshoremen employed by the employer refused to cross the picket line set up by the other union.

The employer claimed that their contract with the longshoremen required them to cross the picket line, because they had agreed to settle all disputes through final arbitration, without a strike or lockout. Asked to rule whether the longshoremen were required to cross the picket line, one arbitrator ruled that this was the type of legitimate picket line that union members could refuse to cross. The contract contained no promise from the union to pass through another union's picket line, he pointed out.

And in view of a union's basic teaching that it cannot be used to break the strike of another union, the employer should have known that the longshoremen would not cross such a line. The clerk's picket line was a legitimate one that grew out of a common and typical labor dispute and could be observed by employees belonging to another union or another unit of the same union (*Waterfront Employers' Association of the Pacific Coast*, 8 LA 273).

Where employees of neutral employers refused to cross picket lines set up by another union against another employer working at the same job site, an arbitrator held that the employees did not violate contractual no-strike provisions, in face of valid picket-line clauses.

● When unions representing employees of a general contractor and a mechanical contractor at a construction site honored the picket signs of another union that were directed at another electrical contractor on the same project, they did not violate the no-strike clauses in their contracts, an arbitrator decided. Even though the other union had restricted its picketing to a separate gate of the electrical contractor, the arbitrator found no violation, because the decision of the employees of the neutral general contractor and the mechanical contractor to consider the picketing as being at their own employers' gates was protected under the picket-line clauses of the unions' contracts. Finding that the striking union's picketing was protected primary activity, the arbitrator concluded that the picket-line clauses may be used to protect the individual decision of neutral employees to honor such activity (*Associated Gen-*

*eral Contractors of Minnesota*, 63 LA 32).

• An arbitrator ruled a picket line established by a union against an employer, whose plant it also was picketing, was not a "legitimate and bona fide picket line" that members of another union properly could honor under the employee's collective bargaining agreement. The arbitrator said that, because the picketing union did not represent a majority of the employer's workforce and had not filed a petition with the National Labor Relations Board to represent the employer's workers, the picketed employer was not a "direct employer" with which the union had a "bona fide" labor dispute "over wages, hours, or working conditions" (*Victory Marine & Alaska Cargo Transport*, 102 LA 421).

### Handling Struck Work

If there is a clear provision in a contract permitting employees to refuse to handle work going to or coming from a struck plant, then there may be no problem when they refuse to handle "struck work."

In the absence of a hot-goods clause, arbitrators have held that employees cannot refuse to handle struck work.

• Communications employees at a cable employer refused to forward messages through an employer that was on strike during a period when an emergency condition made it impossible to transmit the messages over their own employer's facilities. They were suspended for refusing to handle the so-called "hot traffic."

The arbitrator held that neither the contract nor past practice gave employees the right to refuse to handle the messages bound for a struck employer. He noted that the work in question was not part of the ordinary work flow, but was caused only by a cable break. Allowing employees to refuse to handle the work would amount to adding something to the contract that was not put there by the parties, according to the arbitrator. Finally, it was noted that the union should have followed the contractual grievance procedure rather than taking matters into its own hands. The suspensions were upheld (*Commercial Pacific Cable Co.*, 11 LA 219).

• An international and its local unions violated a no-strike clause when the international threatened to pull the union label on rotogravure work that a customer for a primary employer had placed with the secondary employer following another union's strike against the primary employer, an arbitrator decided.

Finding that the international improperly determined that the work was "struck work" under the contract, and then ordered the local to refuse to process any of the customer's requirements on the secondary employer's presses, the arbitrator ruled that the dispute should have been submitted to arbitration. Pointing out that the local was the agent of the international with respect to the union label, and that the use of the label was indispensable to the secondary employer's uninterrupted production, the arbitrator concluded that liability should be apportioned 99.8 percent upon the international and .2 percent upon the local (*Sterling Regal*, 69 LA 513).

### Union Liability for No-Strike Violation

A union may be liable when its members violate a no-strike clause, if there is evidence that the union, actively or passively, was involved in the unlawful action.

• A union was liable for damages that an employer sustained when a union steward encouraged picketing against the employer in protest against a subcontractor's employees' performing bargaining unit work, an arbitrator ruled, even though the steward's interpretation of the contract may have been knowingly wrong. Finding that the steward was acting within the scope of his authority when he rendered the interpretation, and the union was responsible for his actions as its agent, the arbitrator concluded that this responsibility continued until the union's business agent took action to overrule the incorrect interpretation, and carried out reasonable means for getting members back to work (*Rust Engineering Co.*, 77 LA 488).

• A union that represented mechanics and drivers under separate agreements was liable to an employer for damages for not directing employees to return to work after the mechanics refused to cross picket lines set up by the drivers when their contract expired, an arbitrator ruled. The no-strike clause and the provision expressing the union's commitment to see that its members obey all reasonable rules contemplated that the union would order its members to ignore picket lines and take all reasonable steps to end strikes, the arbitrator concluded (*Westinghouse Transport Leasing Corp.*, 69 LA 1210; see also 66 LA 388, 66 LA 82).

# Strike Penalties

——————————— **OVERVIEW** ———————————

Violation of a no-strike clause can lead to disciplinary action, up to and including discharge. In most cases, arbitrators uphold an employer's decision to penalize employees who engage in unlawful strike activity, unless the union can prove that the penalty the employer imposed was based on anti-union bias or discrimination.

Other factors that arbitrators consider in determining the propriety of strike penalties include the predominance of union members or leaders among those discharged and those offered reinstatement, the degree of union activity by the individual employee, and the position of the employer with regard to union membership.

Penalties against union officials who participate in or fail to try to prevent an unlawful strike frequently are harsher than those meted out against rank-and-file violators because union officials have a greater degree of responsibility than the average bargaining unit member.

——————————— **SUMMARY OF CASES** ———————————

### Discipline of Union Leaders

Union officials are supposed to set good examples for the rank and file to follow. Holding this view, most arbitrators have ruled that if union officers do not carry out their responsibility of seeing to it that employees live up to a contract's no-strike clause, they can be disciplined (69 LA 459).

● Indeed, many arbitrators have upheld the discharge of union leaders who incited, led, or refused to try to prevent an unlawful strike (88 LA 1230, 84 LA 1315, 69 LA 93).

The following cases are instances in which arbitrators have sustained disciplinary actions against union officers.

● Discharge was acceptable punishment for a union steward who violated a work rule and a settlement agreement by leading a work stoppage over an assignment that was allegedly contrary to past practice. The settlement agreement ordered his discharge if any further work stoppages occurred at his "direction or participation" (*San Francisco Newspaper Agency*, 87 LA 537).

● Discharge of a union steward for violating a no-strike clause by attempting to impede the work of probationary employees also was upheld by an arbitrator (*Vernitron Piezoelectric Div.*, 84 LA 1315).

● Discharge of a union president for failure to take affirmative action to prevent a wildcat strike and to put an end to it as soon as it occurred was upheld by an arbitrator (*Ford Motor Co.*, 41 LA 609).

● Discharge was appropriate for a shop steward who made no convincing effort either to prevent a walkout or to secure a return to work after it occurred, one arbitrator determined (*Gold Bond Stamp Co. of Georgia*, 49 LA 27).

● Discharge was upheld for union committeemen who probably were the instigators of a walkout but who, in any event, were derelict in their duty as union officers to try to get employees back to work (*Bell Bakeries*, 43 LA 608).

● Discharge of union officers for participating in an unauthorized work stoppage was found to be appropriate by an arbitrator who held that union officers cannot discharge their responsibility via a passive attitude that would allow them to merely be swept along by rank-and-file action (*Drake Mfg. Co.*, 41 LA 732).

● Suspensions were found to be appropriate for a union president and a recording secretary who recommended through their actions that unit employees not show up for scheduled inventory overtime that they previously had volunteered to perform (*Zellerbach Paper Co.*, 73 LA 1140).

On the other hand, arbitrators have rejected or reduced penalties imposed on union officials where:

● there were mitigating circumstances;

● the employer could not show that union leaders were more to blame than other strikers; and

● union officers fulfilled their responsibilities by urging employees not to strike, even though their efforts failed and the strike proceeded (65 LA 1245, 64 LA 1210).

The following cases are instances in which arbitrators have set aside or reduced strike penalties against union officials.

● A steward had his suspension set aside because the suspension had been based on uncorroborated statements that the steward had encouraged an employee to slow down her production rate and had threatened reprisals if she failed to do so. The evidence of bad conduct was insufficient to overcome the greater latitude accorded a steward in the performance of his or her office duties (*Associated Wholesale Grocers Inc.*, 89 LA 227).

● Disciplinary suspension, rather than discharge, was the appropriate penalty for a steward who urged a work slowdown in violation of a contract, but where there was no evidence of an actual slowdown (88 LA 1230).

● Similarly, disciplinary suspension, rather than discharge, was the appropriate penalty for a steward whose expression of dissatisfaction at the way the employer and the union committee had handled a grievance led to an unlawful work stoppage (*Quanex, Mac Steel Div.*, 73 LA 9).

● Participation by a union official in a wildcat strike was not grounds for discharge given that he later tried to halt the work stoppage. The employer failed to prove that the union official promoted the strike; however, his participation was sufficient for a one-year probation (*Cyclops Corp.*, 45 LA 560).

● When a union president failed to get the workers back on the job within five minutes, the employer placed him on 60-day suspension. The arbitrator set this aside because it was not clear whether the president caused the wildcat strike or was simply caught up in it (*Weatherhead Co.*, 43 LA 422).

### Discipline of Rank and File

As a general rule, arbitrators hold that an employer who is confronted with an unlawful wildcat strike is not required to deprive itself of the services of all employees participating in the strike. The employer may select those for punishment whom it deems deserve to be penalized, provided the employer's selection is not capricious.

● The employer has the right to assign varying penalties, up to and including discharge, on the basis of its evaluation of the degree of seriousness of the conduct of participants in an unlawful strike—again, subject to the general principle that the evaluation cannot be arbitrary or capricious. The employer also should exercise its right of discipline within a reasonable time limit (98 LA 41, 97 LA 297, 93 LA 1097, 90 LA 24, 89 LA 1296, 86 LA 622, 85 LA 1017).

● An arbitrator upheld the discharge of a number of employees for participating in a strike that violated a no-strike clause, given evidence that the strikers rejected pleadings of union and employer officials to cease and desist the job action. The arbitrator, however, reduced the discharge penalty to disciplinary suspension for an employee who appeared at the plant on two separate days during a strike to get an explanation of a restraining order he had received in the mail, and also for another employee who attempted to prevent the wildcat strike and who worked the first five days of the strike and missed the last three days because of threats against him and his wife (*Grumman Flexible*, 72 LA 326).

• An arbitrator ruled that an employer improperly placed a letter in an employee's file threatening discipline for alleged violation of a no-strike clause by his refusal to cross a sister local's picket line. The no-strike clause did not cover sympathy strikes, the arbitrator pointed out, adding that the established practice had been that bargaining-unit members would not cross legal picket lines and the employer would give them alternate work. The arbitrator also noted that no employee had ever received such a letter in the 16 years that the provision had been in effect (*GTE North Inc.*, 94 LA 1033).

• An employer had just cause to fire an employee whom it determined to have participated in a wildcat strike to a greater degree than other strikers, an arbitrator decided, rejecting the union's contention that the employer must establish the employee's participation by a preponderance of credible evidence. Management did not have to prove that the employee participated to a greater degree than other strikers before it can impose discipline, the arbitrator emphasized, concluding that the employer need only establish that it acted fairly and in good faith (*Price Bros. Co.*, 74 LA 748).

The employer must be able to show some basis for selecting individual strikers for discipline.

• One arbitrator set aside suspensions imposed on five employees accused of being the first to walk out of the plant during a wildcat strike; their identification was based on a supervisor's observing them from a window about 50 yards from the gate where the employees exited (*W. S. Hodge Foundry Inc.*, 55 LA 548).

• Another arbitrator held that a two-week suspension was too stiff a penalty for some wildcat strikers, even though they probably were guilty of inciting the strike. The arbitrator reasoned that the employees probably did not need much encouragement to strike anyhow and found no evidence that the strike would not have occurred even absent their actions (*International Minerals & Chemical Corp.*, 28 LA 121).

## Discipline of Strikers Heeding Back-to-Work Order

According to one arbitrator, employees who strike in violation of a contract can be disciplined even though they return to work at the union's request.

• In a contract the parties had agreed that the employer maintained the right to discipline employees for just and proper cause, the union would not engage in any unauthorized work stoppage, and the employer would not hold the union liable for damage resulting from an unauthorized work stoppage provided the union immediately instructed its members to return to work. The last clause further provided that the employer could take any disciplinary action it considered appropriate if employees ignored a back-to-work order. Employees who walked off the job on one occasion returned to work at the start of their next shift. When the employer slapped them with five-day disciplinary layoffs, the union filed a grievance. In its view, the contract permitted the employer to discipline strikers only if the union failed to tell them to go back to work and they continued their walkout. In this case, the union pointed out, it had issued the required instructions, and the men had in fact returned to work.

An arbitrator rejected the union's argument, asserting that the union's claim was that because the employer had the right under the contract to act in one set of circumstances, it necessarily had forfeited the right to act in other circumstances. Because the contract did not specifically cover the case at hand, the arbitrator decided it came under the provision affirming the employer's general right to impose discipline and determined that the suspensions should be upheld (*Bell Aircraft Corp.*, 30 LA 153).

## Damage Awards as Penalty

Arbitrators have assessed damages against unions that violate a no-strike pledge (77 LA 488, 75 LA 189).

• Although an arbitrator found that full compensatory damages were not required because of the limited nature of a union's violation and the employer's share of blame for the underlying dispute, he allowed damages for breach of the no-strike clause that included out-of-pocket expenses and lost profit on a specific transaction that the employer was unable to complete due to the violation, and a reasonable portion of overhead expenses and general loss of profits arising from the shutdown. The arbitrator refused, however, to allow recovery of attorneys' fees sustained in an effort to get an injunction to end the strike (*Mercer, Fraser Co.*, 54 LA 1125).

• As a remedy for a strike against a construction employer on a highway project, an arbitrator allowed damages including labor costs, rental value of its own equipment, rental value of rented equipment, and the prorated costs of traffic protection (*Foster Grading Co.*, 52 LA 197).

• An arbitration board decided it had power to award damages for a union's breach-of-contract strike, even though the contract made no mention of this remedy. The board would not, however, award damages for loss of good will because that was too speculative (*Oregonian Publishing Co.*, 33 LA 575).

### Arbitrators' Injunction versus Strikes

In some instances, and particularly where the parties have a permanent arbitrator, the employer may be able to get a back-to-work order from an arbitrator similar to a court injunction.

• After finding that the union's work stoppage violated the no-strike clause in its contract, an arbitrator ordered the employees to return to work and the union to secure compliance with the no-strike provisions. The order was issued on an ex parte basis in the absence of the union, because the union had received proper notice and an invitation to appear and had not objected to the employer's taking the dispute to arbitration on an ex parte basis (*Pacific Maritime Assn.*, 52 LA 1189).

### Cancellation of Seniority as Penalty

Even though employees who strike in violation of a contract can be disciplined,

at least one arbitrator thought that cancellation of seniority was an improper penalty for such conduct.

• When employees staged a wildcat strike, the employer notified all 2,500 strikers that they were suspended for five days and would be terminated if they failed to return to work by a certain deadline. It later informed the strikers that those who failed to report before the deadline would be taken back as new employees.

An arbitrator held that the employer had the right to fire the strike leaders but ordered it to reinstate the others with the seniority they had before the walkout. He did not think the employer really intended to discharge all the strikers; it had no reason to think it could find enough replacements. The contract mentioned suspension and discharge as disciplinary measures, the arbitrator noted, but said nothing about loss of seniority. Such a penalty was inappropriate, he said, because seniority is in the nature of a vested right and affects the relative standing of all employees. Upholding the penalty, he commented, would lead to continuing dissension between employees who stayed on the job or returned before the deadline and the "new hires." The award called for gradual reinstatement of the strikers, in order of their seniority, over a nine-month period (*Lone Star Steel Co.*, 30 LA 519; see also 64 LA 955, 63 LA 736).

### Docking for Lost Time During Stoppage

Awards suggest that arbitrators will allow an employer to dock the pay of employees for time lost during a work stoppage if certain conditions are met. These are that there is sure proof that *all* employees took part in the work stoppage and that there was work that could have been done during the stoppage when none of the employees were there to do it.

• A work stoppage occurred in one department of a company, and management docked every employee who participated for the time lost. The union contended that only those actually responsible for the stoppage should have had pay deductions and also asserted that because management could not determine exactly which employees caused the stoppage, the deducted pay should be restored to all employees.

The arbitrator held that if innocent employees had been forced to stop working because of others' activities, they should not have been penalized. Here, however, there was work that could have been done, so "it is quite manifest that each employee who stopped did so upon his own responsibility and should suffer any resultant consequences of such action." He concluded, therefore, that the pay deductions were warranted (*Fruehauf Trailer Co.*, 1 LA 155).

• On the other hand, when an arbitrator found it impossible on the basis of the evidence to conclude that all the employees in one shop participated in a stoppage, he decided that none of them could be docked (*S. Co. Inc.*, 10 LA 924).

• Although production had been halted by a strike, an employer broadcast over the radio the message that it would be operating. As a result, some employees showed up for work but were later told to go home. Others never showed up because they had been told not to do so by their supervisors. The arbitrator held that both of these groups of employees were entitled to pay even though the contract specified that no one would be paid for time lost to strikes. He reasoned that their lost time was primarily attributable to the employer's instructions, not the job action (*U.S. Steel Corp.*, 45 LA 509).

## Partial Strikes

According to one arbitrator, employees can be penalized for engaging in an intermittent work stoppage lasting for part or all of a shift even though the contract does not contain a no-strike clause.

• When an employer refused to arbitrate grievances over the pay of skilled trades—as it had a right to do under its contract—the union proceeded to hold meetings that lasted two hours on each of three shifts. The third time this happened, the employer warned that further meetings would lead to disciplinary action. The next day, another series of meetings was held, and the participants were

each given a one-day suspension. Claiming that the discipline was a contract violation, the skilled tradesmen staged a one-day strike, and management told the union that one-day suspensions would again be imposed unless the union promised there would not be any repeat performances. The union did not give any such assurance, and the employer followed through with the suspensions.

An arbitrator upheld the employer's actions. Although the contract gave employees the right to engage in a "whole strike," that was not the same as a "partial strike," he said. An employee must either work or strike, and the worker cannot set his or her own working conditions, the arbitrator held. The union's attitude suggested that more stoppages might occur, and under these circumstances, the arbitrator decided the penalties were justified (*General Electric Co.*, 31 LA 28; see also 39 LA 629).

## Discipline for Slowdown

Arbitrators are likely to hold that discharge is too severe a penalty for employees who take part in a slowdown.

• In one case a group of employees was fired because they had collectively decided not to increase their output when production standards were raised as a result of job changes. An arbitrator reduced their penalty to a month's layoff in view of their long seniority and the fact that they did not actually decrease their output (*Armour & Co.*, 8 LA 1).

• Even though another arbitrator was convinced that an employee had deliberately engaged in a slowdown, he changed the penalty meted out from discharge to a four-week layoff because of the employee's long record of satisfactory performance (*Reed Roller Bit Co.*, 29 LA 604).

• An employer was not justified in discharging a member of a union shop committee for telling employees to slow down production, an arbitrator decided, notwithstanding the employer's contention that the employee violated a contractual provision barring the union from causing or sanctioning work stoppages, strikes, or slowdowns. Emphasizing that the employer failed to apply progressive discipline, the arbitrator concluded that the employee was not adequately warned about his discharge (*Stevens Air Systems*, 64 LA 425).

## Discipline of 'Silent Partners' in a Slowdown

If a slowdown occurs on an incentive operation, can employees be disciplined who are down the line from the bottleneck and therefore do not have primary responsibility for the drop in production? If such employees do not call management's attention to the fact that they are not getting as much material to process, they must be regarded as "silent partners" in the slowdown, one arbitrator determined, and they should be regarded as being just as much at fault as those who take the initiative in restricting production (*John Deere Harvester Works*, 27 LA 744).

● Disciplinary suspensions were in order for shop committeemen who took part in a slowdown, thus giving it their silent, if not active approval, one arbitrator ruled. He agreed with the employer that although the committeemen did not initiate the slowdown, they did avoid their responsibility under the contract's no-strike pledge in not trying to stop it. The employer tried to identify the leaders but could not, he noted. The next best approach, the arbitrator reasoned, was to make an example of those who had shirked their responsibility to lead (*Philco Corp.*, 38 LA 889).

## Pay Cut for Slowdown

● One arbitrator decided that if incentive employees engage in a slowdown, they could be denied pay guarantees under an incentive plan and be paid only for actual output (*American Steel & Wire Co.*, 6 LA 392).

● Another arbitrator said that cutting pay below guaranteed levels was a contract violation and therefore an improper penalty for a slowdown (*Jacobs Mfg. Co.*, 29 LA 512).

## Discipline for Strike Misconduct

Employees can be disciplined for misconduct during strike activities. Violence is the principal charge leveled against strikers for which management feels it may issue discharge or suspension slips.

● Arbitrators generally will consider the evidence in each case closely. If the accusation is of the more serious type (such as attacking a supervisor) and the evidence supports the charge, the discipline may be allowed to stand (69 LA 351, 68 LA 706, 66 LA 1020).

● Where the charge of strike misconduct is not substantiated by the evidence, the arbitrator likely will disallow the disciplinary action taken (77 LA 483, 75 LA 929, 74 LA 726).

In considering cases involving dismissals for misconduct on a picket line and during a strike, respectively, arbitrators have developed general criteria.

● How satisfactory is the evidence?

● What is the extent of each person's participation? In any mob situation the degree of involvement of the individual in any action taken is important.

● What was the nature of the violence? This has both quantitative and qualitative aspects. Participation in several incidents is more serious than in only one. Some actions are more reprehensible than others. Shouting insults and shoving are of a different order from striking a person.

● Was the violence provoked? To the extent the violence is retaliatory and defensive it is less culpable than if undertaken as an act of aggression.

● Was the violence premeditated or undertaken on the spur of the moment? Premeditated violence is the more inexcusable.

● What will be the impact of the punishment? Discharge is more of a penalty for an old man than a young one; for a long service employee than a short service employee.

● Was the disciplinary action discriminatory? An employer is under some obligation to treat persons similarly situated in a comparable, although not necessarily identical, manner. Violence can hardly be said to be the real basis for discharge if other unjustifiable factors enter in.

● What is the general context of the situation (*Cudahy Packing Co.*, 11 LA 1138)?

- Was the alleged misconduct of the aggrieved proved to the complete satisfaction of the arbitrator?
- If the misconduct is proved satisfactorily, was it of such a nature as to warrant discharge?
- If the misconduct is proved, was it the result of certain provocation that mitigates the guilt of the aggrieved?
- Is there evidence that discrimination was a factor in the discharge?
- Was the misconduct of such a nature as to affect employer-employee relationship or was it more appropriately the concern of civil authorities (*Swift & Co.*, 12 LA 108)?

## Amnesty Pledges

The following cases illustrate how arbitrators view management's offer of amnesty to striking employees.

- When several employees engaged in a wildcat strike, the superintendent promised amnesty to those who began work "without further delay." Of those on strike, 17 did not return until an hour later. They were given one-day suspensions, which they claimed was a violation of the amnesty pledge. The arbitrator disagreed, saying that the pledge was not a continuing offer to be accepted whenever the employees felt like returning (*Bethlehem Steel Corp.*, 47 LA 524).

- Although an employer's amnesty pledge following a wildcat strike barred discipline for "passive nonviolent participation," it did not bar the discharge of two men who tried to promote a secondary boycott. According to the arbitrator, the evidence established that they were guilty of concerted misconduct above and beyond actions protected by the amnesty agreement (*Falls Stamping & Welding Co.*, 48 LA 107).

- An employer's blanket offer of reinstatement "without recrimination" after an unlawful strike extended to all employees, including the steward who instigated the strike. The arbitrator, however, directed the employer to deny back pay as a penalty for her part in the unlawful strike (*Strombeck Manufacturing Co.*, 45 LA 37).

# Part 13

# Union Security

# Union Security

_____ OVERVIEW _____

A significant percentage of collective bargaining agreements contain union-security provisions that require employees to become union members and maintain their membership in good standing as a condition of continued employment.

A union may be entitled to demand the discharge of an employee who fails to join the union and pay dues, but the National Labor Relations Act sharply limits the conditions under which a union may take this action. Even though an arbitrator may uphold the discharge of an employee for failing to maintain union membership, the National Labor Relations Board may order the employee reinstated with back pay if it finds the employee's protected rights under the NLRA have been violated.

Under union-shop agreements, the obligation of employees to join the union is clear. However, the lesser forms of union security, such as modified-union-shop and maintenance-of-membership, often give rise to special problems—which employees must join, what constitutes union membership, when employees may resign from the union, etc.

_____ SUMMARY OF CASES _____

### Types of Union-Security Agreements

There are several types of union-security clauses. Following are the principal ones:

• *Closed-Shop Agreement*—Closed-shop agreements, which require union membership as a condition of employment, are unlawful under the NLRA.

• *Union-Shop Agreement*—Union-shop agreements require nonunion new hires to become members of a union within a prescribed period after initial employment, and for nonunion employees to become members within a prescribed period after the union-shop contract becomes effective. Under the NLRA, the union-shop contract may not require the employer to hire only union members.

• *Modified-Union-Shop*—Modified union-shop contracts limit membership obligations to new hires, while permitting currently employed employees to continue their nonunion status.

• *Agency-Shop Agreement*—Agency-shop agreements also condition employment on the payment of regular union dues and initiation fees, but, unlike a union shop, it does not require actual union membership. Employees who choose to remain nonunion must pay the labor organization a union-service fee, which usually is equivalent to union dues and initiation fees, because the union must act as a bargaining representative for all employees within a bargaining unit. (94 LA 1272, 93 LA 732, 90 LA 973, 89 LA 1181)

Agency-shop provisions are limited by state right-to-work laws (currently in 21 states), which regulate union-security agreements more rigorously than federal law, and by religious objections. Also, nonmembers, under *Communications Workers v. Beck* (U.S., 1988, 128 LRRM 2729), may object to a union's use of agency fees for nonrepresentational activities—i.e., not related to collective bargaining, contract administration, or grievance adjustment. Further, nonmembers are protected by First-Amendment free-speech provisions (*Chicago Teachers Union, AFT, Local 1 v. Hudson*, U.S., 1986, 121 LRRM 2793; see *City of Bucyrus*, 100 LA 427, where an arbitrator held a public-sector employer's failure to deduct employees' fair-share fees was arbitrable where contract violations were alleged).

• *Maintenance-of-Membership Contracts* —Require employees who are union members on the effective date of the agreement to retain that membership for the duration of the agreement.

• *Hiring Arrangements*—Require the use of union hiring halls as employment agencies. A union may charge non-members a fee to help pay the expenses of a hiring hall, but the fee cannot be equal to the dues paid by union members.

## Union Membership

*Application for membership*—Can an employee be considered a union member if he has never signed an application card? Often when a union and an employer sign a contract with a maintenance-of-membership, union shop, or other union security provision, the problem comes up of determining which employees were union members at the time the contract was signed.

One arbitrator has laid down the following standards for determining what constitutes union membership:

• The individual must have signed an official application card showing his intention of joining the union and his desire to have the union act as his representative for collective bargaining.

• The employee must have paid his first month's union dues.

• The union must have issued him an official receipt for the first month's dues payment.

• The union must have furnished him with an official membership card showing that the employee has been accepted for membership.

Only if all these conditions are fulfilled according to the arbitrator, can an employee be considered as having joined the union. At the same time, payment of an initiation fee is not necessarily a condition of union membership; the arbitrator observed that unions frequently waive payment of an initiation fee, particularly during an organizing drive (*Bendix Aviation Corp., Pacific Division*, 15 LRRM 2650).

*Employees behind in dues when contract is signed*—Granted that an employee was a union member at one time, the question frequently arises whether he or she was still a member of the union at the time a maintenance-of-membership contract went into effect. If not, the employee is not bound to keep up his or her membership in the union unless subsequently the employee voluntarily rejoins the union.

Most arbitrators who have ruled on this question have based their decisions on the provisions of the constitution or by-laws of the union holding the contract. Ordinarily, the union constitution will provide for automatic suspension of members behind in their dues a certain number of months.

When the record of an employee's dues payments shows that he was so far behind at the time the contract went into effect that he was under automatic suspension from the union, the arbitrator will usually hold that he is not bound by the maintenance-of-membership requirement (*Bendix Aviation Corp., Pacific Division*, 15 LRRM 2650).

*Members in arrears carried in good standing*—Can a union by its action in carrying a delinquent member as a "member in good standing," bar escape of the member from the union at a time when such escape is possible?

This situation usually arises when a membership-maintenance clause is enforceable only against "members in good standing" at a certain date. Arbitrators have actually held that the employees must be "members in good standing" and not merely carried as such by the union (*Electrical Workers*, 4 LA 443).

• One arbitrator stated that a union could waive the delinquency of its members when no third party interests were affected. It is proper, he said, for a union to continue to carry members even if they are in arrears in their dues because of illness or financial difficulties, if the members do not object. But when he found that carrying a delinquent member as one in good standing meant depriving him of his right to withdraw from the union under the escape clause, he ruled that the employee did not have to be discharged for not maintaining membership (*Monsanto Chemical Co.*, 12 LA 1175).

***Failure to pay dues after signing membership application***—Are employees "in good standing" with the union if they have signed a membership application card, but have not remitted dues since signing of the application?

This situation is frequently presented when unions are successful in organizational drives and obtain many membership applications. Some months later when the unions are successful in securing a contract, they find that many of the employees who have signed the applications have failed to keep up their dues.

• An employee who signed an application form to become a union member at the request of a friend and in the belief that its only purpose was to get the union certified was improperly discharged for failing to pay union dues, an arbitrator ruled. Finding that the employee demanded that his application card be returned to him and that he did not intend to belong to the union in advance of the effective date of the contract, the arbitrator concluded that the employee was induced to sign the card under mistake of fact (*Rexnord Inc.*, 77 LA 1166).

***Employer's obligation to discharge for delinquency***—An employer may be obligated to accede to a union's demand to discharge an employee who is delinquent in paying dues, according to arbitrators.

• An arbitrator ordered an employer that refused to discharge employees to whom it had served timely notice of nonpayment of union dues or agency fees to discharge all such employees who, within 10 days from date of award, fail to resolve their financial problems with their union. The union's failure to inform the employees of their agency-fee option could not be used as a defense against the grievance, the arbitrator said, because unfairlabor-practice claims are not cognizable in arbitration (*Great Western Carpet Cushion Co.*, 95 LA 1057; see also 95 LA 1175).

• An employer was obligated to terminate employees after the union notified management that the employees, who were expelled from the union for nonpayment of dues, had not tendered the required dues, an arbitrator ruled. Pointing out that the demand that the employees be discharged for not paying dues was in full compliance with the Labor-Management Reporting and Disclosure (Landrum-Griffin) Act (LMRDA), the arbitrator concluded that the union was not treating the employees arbitrarily or unfairly by requiring them to pay an initiation fee in order to be reinstated (*Times Journal Publishing Co.*, 72 LA 971).

• An arbitrator ruled that an employer was obligated, under a union-security agreement, to accede to the demand of unions to terminate employees who refused to pay union dues and fees of varying amounts charged by the jointly certified unions, despite the contention that the charging of different fees and dues by three unions, that must be operated as a "single union," was not compatible with the concept of joint representative in a single unit (*Frazer & Johnston Co.*, 66 LA 251; see also 77 LA 424, 76 LA 71, 68 LA 261, 42 LA 989).

***Employer Failure To Compensate Union for Lost Dues***—Where a collective bargaining agreement expressly exempted an employer from any liability resulting from its violations of the contract's union-security clause, an arbitrator held the employer was not required to compensate a union for lost dues after the employer violated the agreement by failing to discharge employees who did not pay their union dues (*Yukon Manufacturing Inc.*, 105 LA 339).

• An arbitrator ruled that a union did not have the right to seek the termination of a newly promoted supervisor because of his failure to pay union dues during a 60-day period in which he continued to accumulate seniority and could decide to return to a bargaining unit. The supervisor was not a member of the bargaining unit during the 60-day period and has no responsibility to remain a union member in good standing, the arbitrator held (*Electric Energy Inc.*, 92 LA 351).

***Dual union membership***—Can a union withhold membership from employees who belong to a rival union, even though lack of membership is cause for dismissal under a union-shop agreement? One arbitrator said no.

● Three employees were not members of the union that held bargaining rights at the employer where they worked. They arranged with a competing union, of which they were members, to pay their dues to the incumbent. The latter union denied them membership until they disaffiliated with its rival and signed a checkoff agreement with it. The men refused, and the union demanded their discharge under the union-security clause because they would not sign the checkoff form and were tardy in paying their dues.

There is no prohibition against an employee's belonging to two or more unions, the arbitrator noted. Although the dues were delinquent, he found that they were paid before the deadline. Because their dues were in order, the arbitrator ruled that the employees were entitled to membership in the incumbent union and the employer had no reason to dismiss them (*Hawaiian Brewing Corp.*, 35 LA 420).

*Refusal to join union because of religious belief*—Can employees be fired for refusing to join a union and to pay dues on the ground that it is against their religion? One arbitrator has held yes.

● Under a contract requiring an employer on written request of the union to discharge employees who fail to become members of the union in good financial standing, an arbitrator ruled that an employer was obligated to discharge an employee who refused to pay the required dues because it was against her religion to join associations such as unions. Despite the contention that requiring the employee to pay dues when her religion forbids her to join unions violated her constitutional guarantee of freedom of religion, the arbitrator found no provision in the contract that exempted bargaining unit employees from the obligation to pay dues. Emphasizing that the requirement to pay dues applied to all unit members, and therefore was not discriminatory, the arbitrator concluded that the dues amount required was not onerous (*Benson Shoe Co.*, 62 LA 1020).

*Part-time employees*—Can a union require part-time employees to pay union dues and fees under a contract that requires full-time employees to join the organization? One arbitrator has ruled no.

● Under a contract that recognized the union as exclusive bargaining representative of "full-time" employees and that permitted part-time employees to be used to augment regular staff on an on-call basis, an arbitrator decided that a union was not entitled to require a part-time employee, who was performing fill-in duties, to pay union dues and fees. Finding that the part-time employee was not subject to the terms and conditions of the contract, particularly the contract's agency-shop provisions, the arbitrator ruled that the employee was not included in the bargaining unit, because he received no benefits under the contract (*Saginaw County Juvenile Home*, 67 LA 446).

## Escape Periods

*Premature resignation letters*—Employees who submit their letters of resignation from union membership prior to the escape period nevertheless may be held to have effectively resigned, particularly where the letters were sent close to the escape period.

● A maintenance-of-membership agreement provided a 15-day escape period immediately following the anniversary date of the agreement. This was variously interpreted as meaning a 15-day period beginning Nov. 7 or Nov. 8. Prior to this first anniversary date, 19 employees submitted letters of resignation in the period Oct. 17 through Nov. 5. On Nov. 22, the union informed these employees that their attempted resignations were not effective, because the 15-day escape period ran from Nov. 7 through Nov. 22.

Holding the resignations effective, an arbitrator noted that the employees obviously intended their resignations to become effective on the first possible date. He added that the union was guilty of bad faith in waiting until the last day of the escape period to inform the employees that their resignation letters were invalid (*Carson Mfg. Co.*, 52 LA 1057).

● Under a contract providing that any employee may withdraw from the union during the seven days prior to April 1 of each year, an arbitrator decided that an employee gave timely notice of resignation from the union where he spoke to union officials about resigning and handed a letter to the payroll department requesting his withdrawal from the union "as of April, 1972." Notwithstanding the union's contention that the letter was untimely, in that it carried a date that was before the beginning of the escape period, the arbitrator concluded that, the crucial date in the letter was the effective date of the withdrawal (*Continental Oil*, 61 LA 610).

*Absence of escape clause*—In the absence of an escape clause in renewed maintenance-of-membership agreements, can an employee resign from the union on the date an old contract expires and a new one becomes effective?

Most arbitrators hold that the union-security relationship between parties to the contract is a continuing one that may be interrupted only by formal action of the parties and not by an individual who has benefited by the contract. If the parties do not provide an "escape" period, then none can be implied.

● One arbitrator with this view said that when the parties to a labor contract resort to every known technique to continue their relationship, that continuing character should be recognized and given effect in proceedings such as arbitration. In this case, he said, because it was a collective agreement, no single employee had any power to create an escape period not provided for by the contract (*Monsanto Chemical Co.*, 12 LA 1175).

*Effect of renewed contract on escape period*—In the absence of specific reference to it, is the escape period in an old contract carried forward to the new contract by the terms of a renewal agreement?

Renewal agreements usually provide that all the provisions of the old contract shall be carried forward in the new contract except those specifically modified by the renewal agreement. An arbitrator has held that it is not necessary to provide specifically for the renewal of the escape period as it is renewed with all other provisions (*Fulton Sylphon Co.*, 7 LA 286).

## Resignation From Union

*Meaning of resignation*—Under a contract providing for maintenance of membership for union members until they properly resign, what is the meaning of "properly resign" when it is not defined in the contract? In this situation arbitrators often will look at the union's constitution for the proper procedure for resigning from the union.

● Where one union's constitution provided for a 10-day period for resignations, an arbitrator ruled employees who had not resigned within this period were still members and thus subject to the maintenance-of-membership clause of a collective bargaining agreement (*Bridgeport Rolling Mills Co.*, 18 LA 233; see also 66 LA 875).

● Where a union's constitution does not provide for resignation but the labor contract it signs with a firm does have an escape clause, arbitrators are likely to hold that members can withdraw during the escape period. The agreement a union makes with an employer comes first, they say, regardless of what its constitution provides (*Shell Oil Co.*, 14 LA 153; see also 70 LA 230, 61 LA 610).

*Verbal resignation*—Can a union member resign from the union just by giving word-of-mouth notice to his department steward? In addition to a strict scrutiny of the constitution and by-laws of the union, the arbitrators look to past practice and custom before making their determination

● An employee, during a 15-day escape period, verbally informed the chief union steward of his desire to resign from the union. He then refused to pay any further dues. The union requested his discharge for violation of the membership-maintenance clause of the contract. The arbitrator found that under the constitution and by-laws of the union, it was clear that the steward was a designated contact person between the union and its members. Therefore, the employee had a right to tender his resignation to the departmental steward. The arbitrator further found that neither the constitution and by-laws nor custom and usage in the union required that a resignation be submitted in writing (*Onsrud Machine Works*, 9 LA 375).

● Another arbitrator has held that "proof of knowledge held by responsible union officers, no matter how received, that a member wishes to drop out of the union" determines whether or not the employee has resigned. He also held that the union's efforts to get the employee to sign a union membership card upon his rehire as a new employee constituted proof of the employee's claim that he had resigned from the union when he left the employer (*Chicago Metal Mfg. Co.*, 9 LA 429).

## Transfer Into Bargaining Unit

*Status of transferred workers under modified union shop*—Under a modified union shop, employees who are not members of the union when the contract goes into effect are not required to join, but new employees, hired after the effective date of the contract, must become union members after a specified period of time. Under this arrangement, are old employees transferred into the bargaining unit required to join?

● Some arbitrators have ruled that employees transferred into the bargaining unit must be treated like new hires and required to join the union (*Chrysler Corp.*, 18 LA 664; see also 35 LA 274, 19 LA 85).

● Another arbitrator held that an employer was justified in refusing to discharge a salaried employee for refusing to join the union on her return to the bargaining unit, because she could not be considered as a "new hire" under the modified union-shop agreement. The employee had been with the employer for nearly 28 years and had not been a union member before she was transferred to the salaried supervisory job (*Lord Mfg. Co.*, 55 LA 1005).

*Extension of modified union shop contract to new unit*—If a master contract containing a modified union shop is extended to cover a new unit, are all employees in the new unit required to join the union on the theory that they were hired after the effective date of the master contract? In this situation, one arbitrator has held, the union-security provision cannot be considered retroactive.

● The union-security clause in the master agreement between an employer and a union became effective April 19, 1951. It provided that employees who were not union members on the effective date did not have to join, but that all employees hired after that date had to become members within 30 days. On Nov. 13, 1952, a new unit was brought under the master agreement and the union claimed that all of the employees in it had to join because they were hired after April 19, 1951. The arbitrator disagreed. For purposes of the new unit, he said, the agreement became effective on Nov. 13, 1952. Hence, employees in the unit at that time who were not union members were not required to join, the arbitrator concluded (*Chrysler Corp.*, 21 LA 45).

# Part 14

# Dues Checkoff

# Dues Checkoff

## OVERVIEW

Checkoff is the means of dues collection under union-security agreements. By law, dues checkoff must be authorized voluntarily by each employee, and authorizations cannot be irrevocable for more than one year or the duration of the contract, whichever is the shorter period.

Within this legal framework, various problems may arise. For example, resolving the disposition of an employee's checkoff authorization when an employee is discharged or transferred out of the bargaining unit and resolving whether an employer may check off higher amounts when a union representing its employees raises its members' dues obligations.

## SUMMARY OF CASES

### Effect of Discharge

When an employee signs a checkoff authorization that is automatically renewed each year if he fails to revoke it, does the authorization remain effective if his employment is terminated, and then he later returns to work for the employer as a new employee? Or will a new authorization be necessary?

● One arbitrator ruled that an employee's discharge ended his checkoff authorization, even though the contract did not specifically cover the matter. Any other conclusion, he commented, would lead to the "preposterous" result of having a checkoff authorization hanging in a state of suspended animation for a period of several years if a discharged employee did not think to revoke it (*Link Belt Co.*, 16 LA 242).

● An arbitrator held that an employer properly refused to honor an old dues checkoff authorization that had been signed by two employees before they were fired and subsequently re-employed (*Samsonite Corp.*, 53 LA 1125).

### Effect of Promotion

The status of a checkoff authorization by an employee promoted out of the unit may be unlike that of a discharged employee.

● One arbitrator decided that, instead of being cancelled, the authoriza-tion merely remained in a suspended state. He noted that the authorization cards contained the phrase "future employment" and ruled that this applied to *any* future employment in the unit. To support his decision, the arbitrator reminded the employer that it had a policy of automatically renewing authorizations for other employees who left the unit because of layoff or who returned to the unit within the life of a single contract (*Temco Aircraft Corp.*, 23 LA 93).

● Five employees who were promoted to supervisors were obligated to pay their union dues until they completed one year of work outside the bargaining unit, or until they sent written notice revoking their dues checkoff authorization, an arbitrator decided, in a case where the contract stated that any employee who transferred from the unit after January 1 of a year had to pay union dues during that first year in exchange for the right to accrue seniority.

Notwithstanding the employer's contention that the supervisors were no longer members of the union and had the option of paying dues or of forfeiting their accumulated seniority, the arbitrator concluded that the obligation to pay dues was mandatory in face of the supervisors' existing and valid dues checkoff authoriza-tion (*Minnesota Mining & Mfg. Co.*, 62 LA 1013).

• An employer that stopped checking off union dues for union members on their promotion to supervisory positions was justified in not resuming checkoff on the supervisors' return to the unit due to a reduction in workforce, an arbitrator ruled, despite the union's contention that the supervisors had not revoked their dues authorization cards. Finding that the supervisors ceased being "employees" within the meaning of the contract upon their promotions, the arbitrator concluded that the employees had returned to the unit as new employees who might or might not elect to execute new dues deduction authorization forms (*Armstrong Cork Co.*, 65 LA 907; see also 65 LA 1035).

### Dues Revocation

Arbitrators have held that employers may be obligated to continue to deduct union dues from an employee's wages where the employee's revocation of checkoff authorization was ineffective.

• An employer was required to deduct union dues from the wages of an employee who gave notice to the employer that he was withdrawing from union membership, an arbitrator decided, where the checkoff agreement was renewed automatically, unless "specific" notice of revocation was communicated. According to the arbitrator, the employee's communication to both the employer and the union was to the effect that he was withdrawing his union membership, not that he was revoking his dues authorization.

Distinguishing withdrawal of membership from revocation of authorization, the arbitrator pointed out that an employee could for personal or other reasons wish to terminate his union membership but still wish to contribute to the cost of contract administration and thereby, be able to claim assistance from the union, in the event of difficulties with the employer. Consequently, it did not automatically follow that communication of an intent to withdraw from the union necessarily implied an intent to no longer pay dues to support the administration of the contract, the arbitrator added.

Emphasizing that cancellation or revocation of the wage authorization required a notice sufficient to apprise the parties "unequivocally" of that purpose, the arbitrator concluded that at best the employee's notice indicated that he may have, or probably intended, to revoke or cancel his dues checkoff (*Asarco, Inc.*, 71 LA 730; see also 72 LA 937, 71 LA 228, 70 LA 58, 41 LA 1073, 36 LA 933).

• A struck employer violated a contract's maintenance-of-membership clause, an arbitrator ruled, when it failed to deduct union dues from wages of employees who sought either to revoke their dues checkoff authorizations or to resign from the union after the old contract had expired. Notwithstanding the employer's contentions that because there was no collective bargaining contract containing a union-security clause in effect during the period the employees were free to resign from the union and were not obligated to pay dues to the union after resigning, the arbiter held that the dues checkoff authorizations remained in effect despite the contract hiatus.

The employees failed to revoke their authorizations in a timely fashion because they acted after the contract had expired and when the escape periods of their anniversary dates either had passed or were too distant, the arbitrator reasoned. Even assuming that the employees had resigned effectively, the resignations were not revocations, the arbitrator concluded, adding that even if they were, they should have been lodged in a timely fashion in accordance with the irrevocability provisions of the authorizations (*Washington Post Co.*, 66 LA 553; see also 90 LA 946, 88 LA 497, 66 LA 875, 55 LA 770).

• An arbitrator ruled that an employer violated the recognition clause of a collective bargaining agreement when it unilaterally ceased deducting union dues from the paychecks of eight employees who had sent the employer written notice that they resigned their union membership, which the employer interpreted as lawful revocation of its authority to deduct the employees' dues. The arbitrator held that the relevant contract provisions did not extend to circumstances where the employer unilaterally changes working conditions without advance notice to the union (*City of Kent*, 103 LA 1049).

### Effect of Decertification

Arbitrators have ruled that after a union has been decertified, the employer need not continue paying checked-off contributions to it until the collective bargaining agreement expires.

● One union claimed that the decertification cancelled only those provisions concerning recognition and representation, while the rest of the contract remained in effect until the normal expiration date. The arbitrator disagreed, noting that the contract was a bilateral agreement, and when the union no longer was able to comply with its contractual obligations as the employees' representative, the employer no longer was bound by the contract (*Ferris Sales & Service*, 36 LA 848).

● A similar decision was reached when a union that lost a deauthorization election claimed that the voiding of the union-security provision did not affect the separate checkoff clause. The arbitrator based his decision on contract law and said that the commitment to pay dues was made in the light of an assumed right of the union to compel membership. Because that assumption turned out to be erroneous, the checkoff authorizations became voidable at the option of the employees (*North Hills Electronics*, 46 LA 789).

### Dues Increase versus Assessment

Suppose a union has a checkoff arrangement calling for the deduction of union dues but not assessments, and then it imposes a levy in addition to regular dues for an indefinite period of time. Can the employer refuse to check off the additional amount on the ground that it is an assessment? According to one arbitrator, an employer could not refuse to do this.

First, the arbitrator found that the dues hike was voted by the membership in the form of an amendment to the bylaws, in accordance with the union constitution. Assessments, on the other hand, could be levied by the local executive board without a vote of the membership. Second, the additional money was to be used to carry on the regular business of the local, whose treasury had been depleted by a number of strikes, but it was not earmarked specifically as a strike fund, nor was the levy for any set length of time. Finally, the arbitrator noted that when the union had put similar (but smaller) dues increases into effect in the past, the employer had not refused to check off the additional amounts. So it could not refuse to do so in the present situation, the arbitrator concluded (*Bates Mfg. Co.*, 24 LA 643; see also 41 LA 65).

● An employer's refusal to deduct two hours' pay that a union had certified as monthly dues and fair share assessments for members in the unit was improper, an arbitrator decided, because the union's discretion to decide the amount of dues and assessments that effect each employee in the "same form, manner, and degree" satisfied the contract's uniformity requirement (*Rock County*, 64 LA 887).

### Increase in Fees Subject to Checkoff

If fees are subject to checkoff, can a union increase the amount of the initiation fee, once the checkoff agreement has gone into effect? Unless the contract puts a definite limit on the amount of fees to be checked off, the employer can do nothing to stop the union from raising it, according to one arbitrator.

● When a union upped its initiation fee from $5 to $25, the employer protested that the fee was "unreasonable and excessive." When it agreed to the union shop and checkoff provisions in the contract, the employer argued, it did so with the understanding that the initiation fee was $5, not expecting such a significant increase to $25. Requiring new employees to pay this amount, it said, might hinder its recruiting efforts. The arbitrator, however, found nothing in the contract to prevent the union from raising the fee; neither the agreement nor the checkoff form, he noted, said what the fee should be. Noting that the National Labor Relations Board had already ruled that the increased fee was not "excessive or discriminatory," the arbitrator concluded that the employer had no voice in setting the amount of the fee, and that the union was under no obligation not to change it (*Engineering & Research Corp.*, 23 LA 410).

## Failure To Enforce Checkoff Provision

An arbitrator ruled that because of an employer's failure to enforce a collective bargaining agreement provision requiring employees to join the union as a condition of employment , it must pay as damages to the incumbent union. The amount had to equal the aggregate regular dues that would have been collected from the employee for a period beginning 30 days after the date of hire and extending to the date the particular employee left the bargaining unit. The arbitrator cautioned he had no arbitral authority to order a nonunion employee to pay dues retroactively (*Servco Automatic Machine Products*, 100 LA 882).

# Part 15

# *Wages and Hours*

## Incentive Pay Plans

─────────────────────── **OVERVIEW** ───────────────────────

The Department of Labor's Bureau of Labor Statistics has defined incentive pay or wage plans as "a method by which employees receive extra pay for extra production." BLS elaborates that in established incentive pay plans, consideration must be given to the base rate for a job; the amount of work required to earn the base rate; and the relationship between extra work above the base and extra pay for extra performance. Further, BLS divides incentive pay plans into "piecework" plans or a form of a "standard-hour" plan.

Most collective bargaining agreements that address incentive operations do not elaborate on the details of such systems. Almost all contract clauses dealing with incentive pay place some limitation on the employer's right to revise standards (86 LA 6, 85 LA 1183, 82 LA 1145, 82 LA 738, 62 LA 756, 61 LA 132, 61 LA 171).

Generally, arbitrators have interpreted such provisions to mean that employees' earnings opportunities must be protected when standards are revised (*Elkhart Brass Mfg. Co.*, 67 LA 184), and that where a change in the workload is negligible, the employer is not required to negotiate a change in the incentive rates (*Jack T. Baillie Co.*, 84 LA 285).

## KEY DECISIONS—

Following are basic guidelines for establishing incentive pay rates:

- "The essential standard should be that the employees affected should have free access to the relevant information so that any injustices in the final result may be corrected through the regular grievance procedure."

- "Employees should be informed of the results of time studies; of the basis for any employer estimates of efficiency of the employees that are timed; and employer allowances for such factors as fatigue and personal needs."

- "Pieceworkers affected by any new rate are entitled to a clear and prompt statement of exactly what the new rate is."

- "An elementary standard of piecework administration requires that a piece rate, once established, should not be changed unless the relevant conditions of work are subsequently changed or unless an error or oversight was made on establishing the original rate" (*International Harvester Inc.*, 1 LA 512).

## SUMMARY OF CASES

### Time Limit on Revision of Incentive Rate

Most contracts dealing with incentive systems provide that management (sometimes with the advice or consent of the union) can revise existing incentive standards or rates, or set up new rates, when there are changes in the content of the job involved. If there is no time limit on the period during which the rate can be changed, is management free to set a new rate at any time after there have been changes in the job?

According to most arbitrators, management has an obligation to revise incentive standards or rates within a "reasonable" time after changes are made in job content.

• One arbitrator, decided that two years was far more than a reasonable time limit for changing an incentive rate (*International Harvester Co.*, 14 LA 1010; see also 34 LA 497).

• Overnight notification of a speedup in the rate of output of a potato-chip bagging machine did not meet the contract's requirements of "reasonable prior notice," according to an arbitrator. A change in rates could occur only if the union were notified sufficiently in advance to permit meaningful discussion, the arbitrator concluded (*Daniel W. Mikesell Inc.*, 47 LA 986).

• A delay of 13 months after changes were made before establishing a new rate for the job was okayed in another instance, because the arbitrator found that this period of time was necessary to allow a complete restudy of the operation (*Mosaic Tile Co.*, 16 LA 922).

### Basis for Rate Changes

Where the workload of incentive employees changes, arbitrators in reviewing the incentive rates may apply the standard of maintenance of prior earnings on the theory that incentive employees should be able to earn as much under the new standard as under the old (28 LA 259, 26 LA 812, 17 LA 472).

• The maintenance of prior earnings standard may not. however, be applied where the contract expressly recognizes that the employer, at its discretion, may find it necessary or desirable from time to time to establish new incentive rates or adjust existing incentive rates because of certain conditions (*Timken Co.*, 85 LA 377; see also 90 LA 1279).

• A more nebulous standard requires the maintenance of the same ratio of earnings to effort expended. Use of this standard means that employees receive increased earnings for that part of the increased production that is due to their effort, and management receives the benefit for that part of the production increase that is due to technological improvement (28 LA 129, 22 LA 450, 10 LA 20).

• In one case a union objected to an increase in the number of units required and a decrease in the percentage standards on the ground that employees could not earn as much as under the old rates. But an arbitrator found that the new method of calculation would permit employees to earn as much as before (*Timken Roller Bearing Co.*, 28 LA 259).

• Where another arbitrator found that greater productivity was the result of machine and engineering changes, he allowed the employer to revise the incentive rates. He noted that the stated aim of the incentive agreement was to give employees more money for extra effort above normal. If the rates had remained the same, he reasoned, earnings would have gone up in direct ratio to the increased productivity, even without any extra effort from the employees. He concluded that the rate change did not violate the contract's ban on revisions that lessen the earnings potential of employees (*Libbey-Owens-Ford Glass Fibres Co.*, 31 LA 662; see also 65 LA 643).

• An arbitrator held an employer's change of an incentive pay plan violated a collective bargaining agreement, which allowed the employer to change the incentive plan only to correct "errors in application of rates of pay." Despite the employer's contention that its employees manipulated figures under the plan to keep the rate high, the arbitrator pointed out that the time of certain employees, whose work was counted as the basis for incentive for their department, worked on other jobs was not counted and the employer had acquiesced in its 10-to-20-year practice of allowing employees to perform other work. The employer had complained about incentive rates in the past, the arbitrator said, but had backed down when employees explained that, under the team concept, other employees helped them on incentive work, which in turn freed them up to do other jobs (*Wheeling Pittsburgh Steel Corp.* 105 LA 298).

## Reduction of Rates

Reduction of incentive rates has been allowed where the introduction of new machinery has resulted in increased production without requiring an increase in effort (63 LA 384, 11 LA 432, 3 LA 677).

• An arbitrator ruled that an employer did not violate a contract when it reduced the incentive time standard for cut, splice, and wind-up elements on a cutting machine because an upgrading of the machine to provide automatic feed without excessive jam-ups justified a review of the operation, and the change in the standard was commensurate with the degree of change in job content (*Armstrong Tire Co.*, 95 LA 1050).

• Reduction of incentive rates has been ordered where employees controlled production on new machines at a very low level (10 LA 534).

## Changing Job Standards During Strike

An employer violated its contract by revising incentive standards during a strike following the expiration of the previous contract and then putting them into effect after the strike had ended and the new agreement had been signed, an arbitrator ruled.

• The strike-settling contract, like the pre-strike agreement, said there were to be no changes in incentive standards unless changes were made in the methods of operation. While the stoppage was in progress the firm kept production going after a fashion, but all employees were paid on an hourly basis. Meanwhile, the employer's job standards people were told to do some tinkering with certain standards that were considered loose. The tighter standards were made effective when incentive work was resumed a week after the new contract had been signed. The union was told nothing of all this; it became aware of the situation only when employees began complaining about the speed-up.

The arbitrator conceded that the employer could do as it pleased while the union was on strike. But if it meant to make new standards effective during the term of the new agreement, he said, it had to inform the union of its intention during the negotiations over the new contract, so that the parties could negotiate on the basis of full information. By failing to do this, the arbitrator concluded, the firm violated the agreement (*M.H. Rhodes Inc.*, 25 LA 243).

## Allowances

Following is a general statement of a standard for allowances to be paid pieceworkers and examples of its application:

"In all cases where allowances are deemed necessary, the pieceworker should be paid his occupational earned rate or his average piecework earning rate, depending on the degree of effort expected and the responsibility placed upon him under the particular conditions that gave rise to the grievance.

"By way of example, it seems obvious to us that, where an employee encounters hard stock, faulty material, or is given erroneous instructions, and is required to continue with the job after calling the situation to the attention of his supervisor, he has every reason to expect to be guaranteed his average piecework earning rate.

"Similarly, where, because of his special skill and aptitude, he is called upon to leave his regular job to perform experimental or other work not a regular part of his assigned duties and that he performs for the convenience of management, he should also receive his average piecework earning rate.

"However, it seems equally obvious that, where a temporary breakdown occurs and he is called upon to perform some other work to occupy his time, which work does not call for anything more than day-rate effort or efficiency, industrial practice generally does not call for the payment of the average piecework earning rate" (*International Harvester Inc.*, 1 LA 512).

## Machine Breakdown

At what rate should incentive employees be paid for periods during which their machines are down for repairs? One arbitrator, ruling on the equities of the situation, agreed with a union that incentive employees should be paid average hourly earnings rather than base rates during periods of machine breakdown (*Pantasote Co.*, 3 LA 545).

● Another arbitrator ruled the other way in interpreting a contract that stated that waiting time caused by machine breakdowns would be paid at the "regular earning rate." The arbitrator said that the employer need pay only on the basis of the hourly rate and not on the basis of average earnings, as the union contended (*Kensington Steel Co.*, 13 LA 545).

● A machine operator who worked on an incentive basis and whose machine broke down was entitled to refuse assigned work on a new machine that had the potential of diluting his earnings, an arbitrator ruled. The contract, the arbitrator noted, provided that if an employee reported for work, and his work was not available, the employer would assign him any available work, and that if any work was refused, the employee would be paid only for elapsed time registered on his time card.

Rejecting the employer's contention that the employee only had the right to refuse work at the start of his shift, the arbitrator concluded that there was no doubt as to the meaning of the contract giving the employee the right to refuse assigned work (*Mueller Company*, 76 LA 965).

## Temporary Rate for Materials Shortage

Under a contract calling for payment of a specified hourly rate when a shortage of materials "substantially" reduces an employee's output, how far must the employee's production drop before he is entitled to receive that rate?

● A union argued that such a provision meant that an employee should get the specified hourly rate whenever a materials shortage caused his production to drop below the point in the incentive range that is on a level with the hourly rate. But an arbitrator ruled that the hourly rate should be paid only when his production drops below the incentive base rate (*Maytag Co.*, 20 LA 43).

## Spoiled Work

If a crew of employees working under a group incentive system has to stop work while one or two members of the crew rework parts that they spoiled, should all the members of the group be paid hourly rates or average earnings?

● In one arbitrator's opinion, the rest of the crew should not be penalized for work spoiled by one or two members of the group. The employees responsible for the spoiled work should be paid their hourly rate, the arbitrator said, but the others should get average earnings for the time they waited while the parts were being reworked (*International Harvester Co.*, 23 LA 184).

● One arbitrator ruled that under a group incentive plan management was justified in apportioning among all employees in its production line the cost of reprocessing work damaged by two men. The union protested that penalizing all the employees for the mistakes of two was unjust. The arbitrator, however, held that the earnings deduction was not really a penalty, but the result of an accurate count of acceptable products. Had the men at fault been made to correct the error, they would have earned less than base wages, a contract violation. Furthermore, he said, the assembly line would have been stopped and the other employees paid only base wages. He pointed out that by continuing to operate, the line made up the reprocessing cost and still earned incentive pay (*Westclox*, 34 LA 777).

## Denial of Incentive Pay for Quality of Work

An arbitrator held an employer properly denied incentive pay to a department's employees where the quality of their product runs was unacceptable and ultimately cost the employer money. The arbitrator found the employer was not liable under the parties' collective bargaining agreement to pay an incentive rate to employees when their work performance was unacceptable and substandard (but where no disciplinary action is necessary). The arbitrator added that incentive pay is payable when an employee would have earned payment but for some action of the employer (*Lawrence Paper Co.*, 100 LA 384).

## Built-In Delay Allowances

If allowances for delays are built into the rates under an incentive plan, should employees still be paid their hourly rates for down time? Awards differ on this problem depending upon the circumstances in each case.

● In one instance where a crew of incentive employees were held up for an hour and a half because their supervisor had not got certain equipment ready for them to use, an arbitrator ruled that they were entitled to straight-time pay for the down time. He agreed with the union that such long periods of lost time that were the fault of management were not the kind of delays allowed for in the incentive rates (*Bethlehem Steel Co.*, 29 LA 360).

● Another arbitrator turned down a union's claim that incentive employees deserved standard hourly rates for a delay that began in the preceding shift and continued into theirs. The union argued that the incentive plan was not in effect until a crew actually started work. But the arbitrator disagreed, saying that, in the absence of contract language to the contrary, an incentive plan with built-in delay allowances must be considered as covering all delays no matter when they start (*Kaiser Steel Corp.*, 31 LA 447).

## Hourly Workers Assigned to Piecework

If some employees fill in as utility men on piecework operations in addition to their regular jobs at hourly rates, should they be paid their hourly rate or at piece rates for their piecework assignments?

● The common complaint of employees who are assigned piecework on a casual or part-time basis is that they are unfamiliar with the work or the machines and, as a result, may not be able to make as much as they would on their regular jobs at their hourly rate. Taking this fact into consideration, one arbitrator ruled that employees in a "hybrid classification" who do piecework in addition to their hourly-paid work must be paid at least the rate of their hourly scale. He noted that, under the contract, regular pieceworkers customarily were paid at a straight hourly rate or at their piece rate, whichever was greater. In the absence of contract provisions covering hourly employees assigned to piecework, the arbitrator reasoned, casual pieceworkers should receive the same treatment. The arbitrator further pointed out that standard practice elsewhere called for hourly rates in such a situation (*John Deere & Co.*, 21 LA 449).

● An arbitrator decided that electricians who were not on an incentive wage rate, but who were assigned to work with electricians who were on incentive, were not entitled to be paid incentive pay, in the absence of a past practice by which employees who are not on incentive pay are paid such rate when working with incentive pay employees. Despite the union's request for the arbitrator to study "very carefully" the entire contract provisions, that included a joint-incentive committee, continuation of wage rates, or new wage rates for new jobs, the arbitrator concluded there was nothing in the agreement that supported the union's position (*Jessop Steel Co.*, 76 LA 641).

## Education Incentive Pay Plan

An arbitrator held an employer's denial of contractually provided education incentive pay was proper where an employee already had received tuition reimbursement for the same claimed courses. The arbitrator reasoned the employer's tuition reimbursement program was a noncontractual item and was a separate and distinct program from the employer's education incentive pay policy, which was a contractual item. Further, the arbitrator distinguished the two programs by saying the educational incentive pay was designed to reimburse an employee a fixed amount for a designated time block of pre-approved training, whereas the tuition reimbursement program was set up to reimburse an employee for college or trade school courses (*City of Miamisburg, Ohio*, 104 LA 228).

---

# Job Evaluation

## OVERVIEW

In the absence of an express contractual provision, it is generally recognized that management has the right to establish new jobs or job classifications and change existing jobs and classifications without first bargaining with the union (93 LA 623, 91 LA 1003).

However, where an agreement contains rigid job classifications, an employer may not be permitted unilaterally to establish new classifications (84 LA 989). Arbitrators have often rejected the contention that job classifications in an agreement automatically preclude elimination or modification of jobs or classifications (91 LA 329).

Even where management has the right to alter its classification system, the union normally may question changes through the grievance procedure.

## KEY DECISIONS—

Arbitrators generally agree that an employer has the right to eliminate jobs— and allocate any remaining jobs—(93 LA 227, 86 LA 880, 84 LA 788, 83 LA 792, 82 LA 534, 82 LA 225, 46 LA 43, 30 LA 444, 25 LA 188, 16 LA 955)—or classifications (91 LA 329, 84 LA 875) when justified by improved technology or production efficiencies, and if not expressly prohibited by an agreement. Further, arbitrators have held that an employer may combine jobs or job classifications in determining methods of operation (85 LA 1026, 83 LA 214, 30 LA 81, 19 LA 797).

Unless restricted under a bargaining agreement, changes in methods of operation (see, e.g., 39 LA 939, 46 LA 43, 17 LA 268, 6 LA 681) or changes in a product (46 LA 43) have been held to be within the prerogatives of management (19 LA 797, 30 LA 81).

On the other hand, an employer's act of recognizing a union has been held to carry with it the obligation to refrain from making major changes in employment conditions and circumstances without consulting with the union (25 LA 611). Such obligation may be found to exist under the National Labor Relations Act, as well as under the contract (71 LA 244).

## SUMMARY OF CASES

### Management's Right to Change Job Descriptions & Classifications

Does an employer have to get the union's permission to change the makeup of a job or classification before putting the change into effect?

Even though job classifications, job descriptions, and job evaluation procedures have been agreed on in the past and have become part of the contractual relationship with the union, the employer may still have the right to introduce new jobs or take apart existing jobs. As long as the employer pays the established rates and accepts union complaints through the grievance procedure, jobs can be put into effect, described, and evaluated by the employer, according to most arbitrators.

• An employer had the right to establish new job classifications and rates for positions, following the advent of a new production process that demanded new skills, an arbitrator ruled. Because the contract expressly gave management the power to add to negotiated classifications and rates, the arbitrator concluded that the employer's action was taken pursuant to its authority to establish new classifications, which it exercised properly according to the evidence (*T.N.S. Inc.*, 76 LA 278; see also 76 LA 1220).

• Another arbitrator decided that an employer's contract did not obligate it to freeze job titles and duties pending the union's consent to a change. Such a requirement, he said, would place the employer in an intolerable position (*Dow Chemical Co.*, 22 LA 336; see also 31 LA 744, 14 LA 510).

• Arbitrators, however, also agree that even where the contract specifically gives management the right to establish new or revised job descriptions, the union still retains the right to challenge management's evaluation through the grievance and arbitration machinery (*Emhart Mfg. Co.*, 23 LA 61; see also 23 LA 206).

Many arbitrators, however, believe that management does not have the right to change the job classifications that are agreed to in a contract without the union's consent.

• An employer violated a contract obligating it to notify the union of proposed changes affecting rates of pay, hours of work, and other conditions of employment, an arbitrator decided, when it unilaterally created a new work group during a reorganization of its operations (*United Telephone Co. of the Carolinas*, 71 LA 244).

• Another arbitrator ruled that an employer could not make a major transfer of job duties from one category to another without the union's consent because it would upset the bargain the parties made when they incorporated the rates and classifications into the contract (*James Vernor Co.*, 26 LA 415; see also 24 LA 713).

• An employer did not have the right, under the management-rights clause of the contract, unilaterally to subdivide a job classification into three classifications. Although the change was made in good faith to eliminate a production bottleneck, management was restricted in its freedom to make such changes by other sections of the contract, according to the arbitrator. Contrary past practices could not justify the action, because the specific contract language governed the situation (*Barcalo Mfg. Co.*, 31 LA 269).

## Changes in Job Duties Warranting Wage Adjustment

A change in an employee's job duties may or may not warrant (in the opinion of an arbitrator) a wage adjustment under a particular collective bargaining agreement, depending on how substantial the changes are.

Some examples include the following.

• The installation of a computer that enabled truck operators to input certain information, eliminating the need for some shipping clerks, was found not to entitle the operators to the shipping clerks' higher pay, where the operators did not perform all the functions of the clerks' jobs (*Union Camp Corp.*, 110 LA 820).

• An arbitrator found that a 30 percent increase in output was attributable to improvements in new equipment and did not justify a wage adjustment for machine operators because the essential nature of their jobs did not change (*Menasha Corp.*, 108 LA 308).

• In another case, a perceived inequity between the pay rate for workers in one department and that of workers who had less responsibility in other departments was deemed sufficient to justify an arbitrator's order of a wage increase in the lower paid department in lieu of negotiations on the issue (*International Paper Co.*, 106 LA 645).

• An arbitrator denied a grievance over an employer's refusal to grant a request for an upward adjustment in the contractual wage rate of a salt mining company's bulk loaders after the installation of a new computer system changed their job requirements. He determined that the changes in the employees' job duties were not "substantial" enough to warrant a wage increase (*Morton Salt*, 112 LA 110).

## Changes Warranting Job Reclassification

Some contracts require reclassification of jobs in which there have been substantial changes since they were classified and the rates set. Arbitrators must often determine whether changes in job content are substantial enough to warrant a reclassification (95 LA 1081, 95 LA 412, 69 LA 198, 54 LA 918, 22 LA 721, 20 LA 463, 11 LA 490).

● An arbitrator decided that an employer improperly reclassified students in its training program as "trainees," rather than as "helper apprentices" belonging to the bargaining unit, after a change in the work duties of the employees. The students' training for production jobs in the shipyard was sufficient to make them "production" employees under the contract, the arbitrator reasoned, concluding that the fact that none of the employees' training actually was used in the shipyard did not preclude their classification as "production" employees (*Ingalls Shipbuilding Division*, 69 LA 294).

● An employer had the right to require molding operators to train new employees on pick off or hydraulic presses, an arbitrator ruled, rejecting a union's contention that the action constituted a "significant change in job content" requiring a new evaluation for the molding operators. Pointing out that the parties agreed that the molding operators were responsible for training other operators on small presses before the job evaluations became part of the collective bargaining agreement, the arbitrator noted that if there were any changes, they were not either as large as, or expansive as, claimed by the union. The complete record failed to show that there had been a significant change in job content of the operators, the arbitrator concluded (*Powder Metal Products Inc.*, 77 LA 499).

## Reclassification After Technological Changes

Where an employer introduced a new machine substantially different from machines in an existing wage rate classifications, it was required to negotiate with the union over rates to be paid the operators of the new machine, and not merely insert the job in an existing classification, an arbitrator decided (*Lockheed-Georgia Co.*, 48 LA 518).

● In another case, however, a publisher-employer had the right to change job classifications following conversion from a hot metal process to a cold metal process that resulted in a substantial change in equipment and procedures of its composing room, an arbitrator ruled, because management had the right to make changes in job duties, to create new job classifications, to eliminate jobs, and to combine jobs by unilateral action, absent a provision in the contract imposing a limitation on such action (*Leavenworth Times*, 71 LA 396; see also 93 LA 227, 91 LA 329).

## Factors in Establishing New Rates

When a new job is set up that does not fit into the existing classification scheme, various factors should be taken into account in establishing the rate for the job.

● According to one arbitrator, the following factors should be considered in setting up the rate range for a new job: (1) nature of the duties and responsibilities of the job as compared to other jobs at the plant; (2) existing wage rate structure; and (3) existing method of in-grade rate progression (*Dumont Electric Corp.*, 13 LA 763; see also, 62 LA 511, 62 LA 574).

● Another arbitrator determined the job rate for a new classification in light of the employer's past practice, prevailing practice in comparable plants, and the effect on intra-plant wage relationships (*Wetter Numbering Machine Co.*, 13 LA 177).

● When two jobs are combined into one, the new job should be evaluated as though it were a completely new job and the rate set accordingly, another arbitrator ruled (*Republic Steel Corp.*, 20 LA 370).

## Upgrading Under Classification System

Generally, the test that arbitrators use for determining if an employee is entitled to be upgraded to the next higher classification is whether the employee is actually performing or is capable of performing the higher classification (67 LA 1094, 67 LA 23).

- Employees classified as specialists third class claimed they should be reclassified to specialists first class because they were qualified to do higher-rated work and they were performing the same job duties as employees with the first-class rating. The arbitrator turned down their arguments because he found that their job duties had not changed since they got their third-class ratings; there was no practice of upgrading employees merely on the basis of added skill without the addition of more difficult job duties; and the only reason they were performing the same job duties as employees with a first-class rating was that more difficult work, which would have been assigned to the first-class specialists, was not available at the time (*Bethlehem Steel Co.*, 19 LA 521).

- An arbitrator held that an employer was not obligated to classify "production layout artists" as "creative artists," even if they had the ability to do the work of the higher classification, because they were not required actually to do this work. An employer is not required to pay for talent he does not use, the arbitrator held (*Gill Studies Inc.*, 52 LA 506; see also 75 LA 531).

- An employee who held the job of loader crater B for about two months properly was denied upward reclassification to the position of loader crater A held by another employee on leave of absence, an arbitrator decided, because the employer had reason to believe that the employee was not capable of performing a significant portion of the loader crater A job duties (*FMC Corp.*, 61 LA 1240; see also 69 LA 1239, 63 LA 907).

- A federal government employee who held a GS-13 classification when detailed to perform duties of a higher-rated job of GS-14 was entitled to be promoted to the higher-rated job, an arbitrator ruled, where the employee continued to perform the higher-rated job duties for a period of two years (*Economic Opportu-*

*nity, Office of and Government Employees*, 64 LA 164; see also 75 LA 1298).

## Downgrading Under Classification System

Arbitrators are likely to approve management's action in downgrading an employee if there is a clear showing that the employee is performing lower-rated duties.

- A federal agency employer did not improperly reclassify an employee when it changed his job description from "supervisory occupational analyst" to "occupational analyst" during the course of a job survey in the division, an arbitrator held. He pointed out that under civil service rules, employees who held management titles had to supervise at least three professionals, a requirement that the employee did not meet (*U.S. Department of Labor*, 64 LA 357).

- One employer moved an employee to the next higher classification as part of a negotiated plan to eliminate wage inequities. Six years later it discovered that the employee had been performing the duties of his old classification all along, so he was downgraded to his original classification. The union argued that once the employee's classification had been agreed on jointly, it could not be changed. The arbitrator decided, however, that the job descriptions were clear enough to show that the employee's duties fitted his old classification and ruled that the employer was free to reclassify him (*Erie Forge & Steel Corp.*, 22 LA 551).

- An employer arbitrarily downgraded three employees on the basis of gradual changes in their duties, an arbitrator ruled. This action would have been okay under the contract, the arbitrator said, except that the employer left six or seven other employees doing similar work in the higher classification (*John Deere Harvester Works*, 20 LA 665).

## Where Job Overlaps Two Classifications

If the contract states that employees performing the duties of two classifications should be paid the rate of the higher classification, they must be paid the higher rate even if they spend only a small part of their time on the higher-rated job duties or do not have the skills originally required for the higher job, an arbitrator ruled (*Hotpoint Co.*, 23 LA 562).

In situations where this point was not covered in the contract, however, arbitrators have relied on various factors in determining which job rate should apply.

● One arbitrator said employees should get the lower rate because they performed only a few of the duties of the higher job, even though these duties made their jobs as a whole more difficult than those of other employees in the lower classification (*Douglas Aircraft Co. Inc.*, 18 LA 387).

● Another arbitrator decided that the proper rate for an employee performing the duties of two jobs was not the one for the job at which he spent most of his time, but the rate for the job for which he had been trained and was responsible—the higher of the two (*Soule Steel Co.*, 21 LA 88).

● Still another arbitrator ruled that employees were not entitled to the pay for a higher classification than their own just because they were voluntarily performing some of the duties of the higher-rated job (*Phelps Dodge Copper Products Corp.*, 25 LA 64).

## Elimination of Classifications

When it comes to eliminating existing job classifications, management may have less freedom than it does in setting up new or revised classifications. arbitrators sometimes have ruled that where job classifications are included in the contract, the employer has no right to abolish any of them without the union's consent as long as the job functions of the classification continue to exist (*Flintkote Co.*, 41 LA 120).

● In another case, however, following what he saw as a modern trend among arbitrators to give management more leeway in changing and abolishing jobs, one arbitrator upheld management's right to abolish job classifications and assign the work to higher-rated jobs. The fact that the classifications were listed in the con-

tract did not mean they were frozen, he said; they were not contracted for, but were bases for rates of pay. Hence, the employer could not have given the duties to lower-rated employees (*Georgia-Pacific Corp.*, 40 LA 769).

● Another arbitrator decided that where a larger part of a job's duties had been eliminated, management could abolish the job, even though the contract required it to maintain local working conditions (*Pittsburgh Steel Co.*, 40 LA 70).

● Job elimination has also been upheld where duties were reduced or eliminated by extensive changes or automation (*Pittsburgh Steel Co.*, 40 LA 67; see also 40 LA 65).

● If all the duties of a job classification are eliminated by technological or other changes, what the employer can do, one arbitrator suggested, is merely refrain from assigning any employees to that classification. Although it cannot formally abolish the classification without union consent, there's nothing to require the employer to keep on assigning employees to the job. This action would have the effect of leaving the classification in a dormant state, he pointed out, which might be useful if the job duties of the classification were ever resumed (*Lone Star Steel Co.*, 23 LA 164).

## Eliminating Red-Circle Rates

Most arbitrators agree than an employer cannot get rid of red-circle rates by withholding negotiated general increases. The time and place to do this, they say, is at the bargaining table.

● Where one employer tried to withhold an increase 10 months after discovering that some employees were being overpaid, an arbitrator said that it had waited too long to correct the error (*Celluplastic Corp.*, 28 LA 659; see also 72 LA 1178, 27 LA 858).

● In another case, an employer properly discontinued paying the red-circle rate to an employee after the signing of a new contract that did not carry over the old contract's clause recognizing the existence of red-circle rates, an arbitrator ruled, despite the employee's contention that his red-circle rate was provided for in a separate contract that negotiators had no authority to alter (*Everlock Charlotte Inc.*, 62 LA 1018).

• Under a contract granting wage increases according to the employees' classifications, former painters who had been reclassified as laborers and permitted to keep their higher painters' wage scales as "red-circle" rates within the laborers classification were not entitled to increases negotiated for the painters' classification. The former painters were classified as laborers when the contact was executed and, therefore, were entitled only to increases applicable to laborers (*Bethlehem Steel Co.*, 31 LA 104; see also 72 LA 87).

## Effect of Transfer & Promotion on Red-Circle Rate

Where a red-circle rate exists for employees on a particular job, it is not likely that the employees can carry the top-plus rate with them in the event they are transferred, even if they stay within the same classification.

• One arbitrator ruled that a red-circle rate applied only to the job involved and was not the property of the employee to take with him wherever he went. This same arbitrator held that an employee who is promoted from a red-circle rate and later demoted back to the same classification has no right to the red-circle padding after demotion. In other words, the promotion has the effect of cancelling the extra red-circle amount (*International Harvester Co.*, 22 LA 674; see also 53 LA 694).

• Another arbitrator, however, ruled that incentive employees were entitled to retain their red-circle rates following their transfer from nickel-line to zinc-line jobs as the result of senior employees bumping into their old jobs (*H.P. Snyder Mfg. Co.*, 64 LA 801).

• An arbitrator held that an employer that had agreed to a 15-cent red-circle add-on for certain employees improperly discontinued an employee's red-circle rate when he elected to bump to a lower-rated job. The red-circle advantage had been significantly restricted through grievance settlements and contract negotiations, the arbitrator pointed out, but a bumping provision remained silent as to red-circle rates. Further, there was no indication that the union had agreed to give up the red-circle add-on in connection with bumping rights, the arbitrator found (*Schauer Manufacturing Corp.*, 94 LA 1116).

# Overtime Work & Pay

## OVERVIEW

Grievances concerning overtime work generally fall into one of three categories: challenges of the employer's right to require employees to put in overtime; complaints that overtime work has not been distributed properly; and complaints that work has not been paid for at the proper rate.

Although there have been rulings both ways, arbitrators have held more often than not that management can require employees to work overtime if the contract does not expressly limit the length of the workday or workweek. Such demands, however, must be exercised reasonably.

In general, the Fair Labor Standards Act requires employers to pay employees overtime compensation "at a rate of not less than one and one-half times" the employee's regular rate. It does not, however, prohibit an employer's paying an overtime rate of more than 150 percent of an employee's regular rate.

## SUMMARY OF CASES

### Overtime Pay Requirements

For the most part, an employee's right to have his or her overtime pay computed in accordance with methods approved by the FLSA and its implementing regulations is a right that cannot be waived and that the employee cannot be prevented from asserting.

Nonetheless, an arbitrator ruled that the FLSA was irrelevant where a contract expressly states the method for computing overtime, and an advisory opinion on law had not been requested (see, e.g., *Potlatch Corp.*, 95 LA 737).

### Management Right to Require Overtime

Many cases have reached arbitration over the issue of whether management has the right to compel an employee to work overtime or discipline one who refuses such duty. If the issue is not expressly settled in the collective bargaining agreement, arbitrators have generally ruled that management does have that right.

- Arbitrators may rule that management acted unreasonably in compelling employees to work overtime where the employer has not considered the legiti-

mate excuses of employees who refuse to work, does not attempt to find substitute employees who are willing and able to perform the work, or gives insufficient notice that overtime work is required (76 LA 205, 75 LA 849, 74 LA 1020, 74 LA 967).

- One arbitrator stated that the burden is not on the employer to find a contractual provision expressly authorizing it to require overtime work. On the contrary, the arbitrator found, the burden rests with the union to point out the contractual prohibition against such mandatory assignment (*Seilon Inc.*, 51 LA 261).

- Another arbitrator stated that the "vast majority of arbitral awards" support the position that "overtime is compulsory in the absence of a specific prohibition in the collective bargaining agreement" (*Douglas Aircraft Co.*, 55 LA 1155).

- Other arbitral methods of confirming management's overtime powers involve finding implied support of the right in existing contractual provisions, such as clauses recognizing management's authority to control or direct the workforce or setting pay rates for hours worked beyond a certain number in a week (55 LA 31, 52 LA 493).

• Furthermore, it has been found that specification in the contract of a "normal" workday or "normal" workweek implies that there will occasionally be "abnormal" workdays or workweeks. Such provisions may serve to affirm management's right to require overtime (*Jones & Laughlin Steel Corp.*, 29 LA 708).

• In a case where the contract stipulated that changes in the work schedule must be mutually agreeable to both the employer and the union, the union held that an employee should not have been disciplined for refusing to work overtime because such overtime constituted a change in the work schedule. The arbitrator found, however, that the overtime was for a limited, specified duration and hence, not a change that would require union approval. Therefore, management was permitted to require an unwilling employee to work overtime (*McConway & Torley Corp.*, 55 LA 31).

• In another instance, an arbitrator ruled that a statement in the contract that it was the policy of the employer (as opposed to a requirement for the employer) to assign overtime to employees willing to accept it did not deny management its right to compel an employee to work overtime—provided management had exhausted all possibilities of locating willing employees (*General Telephone Co.*, 53 LA 246).

• A provision of an agreement giving the employer sole discretion in scheduling production has been determined to be legitimate basis for management to require overtime. Past practice—even of many years' duration—of relying exclusively on volunteers to work overtime did not constitute a waiver of this right (*Colt Firearms Div.*, 52 LA 493).

• An employer that previously assigned overtime to its employees on a voluntary basis was justified in making assignments mandatory, an arbitrator decided, because there was nothing in the contract that specifically limited the right of employer to require overtime. Emphasizing that it is a settled rule that employers retain all power to manage the plant, make rules, and set working hours, the arbitrator concluded that the employer's reasonable assignment of overtime did not violate the contract (*Powermatic/Houdaille Inc.*, 63 LA 1).

• An employer that failed to pay overtime to employees who worked more than 80 hours in a two-week period did not violate its contract. Police officers in a New Jersey township had a 28-day work schedule in which they worked 14 days. When the department went through changes in patrol squad assignments, four officers worked more than 80 hours during the two-week pay period. The officers were paid annually in 26 biweekly pay periods. Because the contract defined overtime as any time spent working either before or after the workday, the four employees were not paid overtime.

The union filed a grievance, arguing that in the past, officers were paid overtime when they worked more than 80 hours in a two-week period. The union said this problem could have been avoided by changing squads at the beginning of pay periods, rather than in the middle, but the employer maintained that overtime was only owed when officers worked more than 160 hours in the 28-day schedule. According to the contract, the officers were not entitled to overtime, the arbitrator determined, in rejecting the grievance. "The contract does not state that employees are entitled to receive overtime simply because they work more than 80 hours during a pay period," he said, adding that the officers did not work more than 160 hours during the 28-day period (*Washington Township*, 115 LA 1206).

## Equal Distribution of Overtime

Contracts frequently provide for the equal sharing of overtime, with equalization generally limited to employees in the same job classification, from the same department, or on the same shift. Ordinarily, when two or more employees have accumulated the same amount of overtime, the one with the greatest seniority is given the option of the overtime assignment.

• In a case where the contract called for equalization of overtime with consideration given to seniority, management scheduled a specific overtime assignment for all first-shift employees and promised to even up the overtime of second-shift employees within the allotted time period for equalization. When management subsequently failed to do so, second-shift employees with greater seniority than some of the first-shift workers filed a grievance, which later came to arbitration. The arbitrator upheld the grievance, stating that under the contract it was required to cross shift lines if necessary to equalize overtime with consideration to seniority (*Eaton, Yale & Town Inc.*, 54 LA 1121; see also 75 LA 608, 75 LA 275, 75 LA 99, 74 LA 699).

• In another ruling, the arbitrator found that failure of an employee to show up for prior overtime assignments does not justify passing over that employee for a new overtime assignment when the contract specifies that extra-hours work is to be distributed equally (*Grief Bros. Corp.*, 55 LA 384).

• Under a contract providing that overtime in each department would be divided equally among employees to the extent that it was practical to do so, an employer improperly awarded overtime during a holiday weekend shutdown to one member of a labor pool, an arbitrator ruled, instead of to another member who had fewer overtime hours (*Logan-Long Co.*, 61 LA 963).

• An employer violated a contract provision requiring equalization of overtime, an arbitrator decided, when stockroom clerks who belonged to finished goods department that had only day shift were allowed to work overtime, instead of night-shift stockroom clerks who belonged to parts-in-process department that had both day and night shifts (*Akron Brass Co.*, 67 LA 267).

• An employer who failed to contact vacationing employees to determine their availability for scheduled overtime on the date they would have returned to work violated a contract requiring equalization of overtime, an arbitrator held, notwithstanding the employer's contention that the employees were not eligible for overtime because they failed to sign the over-

time sheet (*General Mills Chemicals Inc.*, 66 LA 1012; see also 73 LA 1087, 76 LA 1159).

### 'Equalization' Period

Recognizing that it is not always possible to equalize overtime exactly, many contracts specify a permissible spread in the number of overtime hours worked by different employees.

• One such contract had a provision stating that the company would distribute overtime work as equally as possible within a 36-hour limitation and that the employee who had the fewest hours of department overtime would be scheduled first.

An arbitrator interpreted these two provisions to mean that the employer should assign scheduled overtime to the employee who had the least amount of departmental overtime credit, but could properly give overtime to an employee whose overtime credit does not exceed that of another employee by 36 hours. He further ruled that when an employee is properly assigned extra-hours work, but his or her overtime credit increases between the assignment and performance of that overtime, management need not reschedule that overtime for another employee (*National Lead Co.*, 53 LA 687).

In the absence of a contractual time limit, what is a reasonable length of time in which to equalize overtime assignments?

• One employee complained that an employer violated a clause requiring equal distribution of overtime by failing to give him any overtime work during a two-month period when other employees worked as much as 24 hours overtime. In the following two months, his overtime was brought up to that of the other employees. The union claimed he was entitled to pay for overtime missed during the first two months. The arbitrator, however, ruled that four months was a reasonable period in which to equalize overtime because the contract did not set any time limit (*North American Aviation Inc.*, 17 LA 320).

### Avoiding Double-Time Pay

Arbitrators have consistently ruled that management may not assign overtime in such a manner as to avoid paying double-time when such an assignment violates the scheduling of overtime stipulated in the collective bargaining agreement.

• A contract called for equal distribution of overtime, and provided for double-time pay for hours worked in excess of 12 in any one day. The employer scheduled a group of employees for overtime and then dismissed them after they had worked a total of 12 hours during the day. Another group of employees, who had accumulated more overtime but were not eligible for double-time pay, were assigned to complete the overtime work. The arbitrator ruled that the employer was not entitled to avoid paying double-time by assigning overtime to employees with more accumulated extra-hours work, even though the contract failed to specify within what time period overtime had to be equalized (*Continental Can Co.*, 52 LA 118).

• In two similar situations, the contracts provided for double-time pay for the seventh consecutive day worked and equalization of overtime. Failure to assign extra-hours work to employees with the least amount of accumulated overtime in order to avoid paying double-time constituted a violation of the contract, it was held in both cases (*American Enka Corp.*, 52 LA 882; *U.S. Borax & Chemical Corp.*, 54 LA 387).

### Transferred Employees

In two cases, arbitrators found that when overtime is to be shared equally throughout a department or work group, employees temporarily transferred to another area are entitled to overtime assignments scheduled in their regular group. As one arbitrator pointed out, to rule otherwise would mean that management could avoid giving overtime to a particular individual merely by temporarily transferring him prior to assigning overtime (*Massey-Ferguson Inc.*, 53 LA 616; see also 54 LA 252).

### Qualifications to Perform Overtime Tasks

Certain overtime tasks may require more skill and time than others. This may result in a lack of uniformity in the distribution of overtime, because of some employees' inability to perform frequent-overtime tasks.

Arbitrators have reached differing conclusions regarding management's discretion in assigning overtime when a certain group of employees is able to perform the overtime task but is not the most proficient group for the task.

• In one instance, the contract called for equal distribution of overtime departmentally; however, it had been the employer's practice to assign maintenance overtime on the basis of special proficiencies of the maintenance employees. The arbitrator ruled that this practice violated the contract, except in cases where the employee having the least overtime was totally unqualified to perform the overtime task (*National Lead Co.*, 53 LA 687).

• It was the policy of another employer not to require female employees to lift more than 50 pounds. Yet, it was frequently necessary for women on the staff to do so during regular hours. When an overtime assignment occurred that necessitated lifting more than 50 pounds, the female employees (who were in line for overtime) were bypassed, and they filed a grievance. The arbitrator ruled that the employer had violated the contract because the women had shown during regular hours that they could do the work (*Standard Brands Inc.*, 54 LA 732; see also 75 LA 275).

• Another arbitrator held that it was legitimate to assign overtime for purposes of taking inventory on the basis of ability, despite a contractual provision for overtime assignments to be made on a seniority basis. The arbitrator reasoned that special skills are needed for taking inventory, and inventory is totally unrelated to production activities (*Myers Drum Co.*, 55 LA 1048).

### Overtime by Job Classification

A contract called for overtime work to be performed by the classification of employees who normally performed that type of work. Given such a provision, an arbitrator ruled that it was a violation of the contract for overtime to be assigned to another classification of employees even though the job was to be performed in their work area and they had on occasion performed that particular task (*American Shipbuilding Co.*, 54 LA 1216; see also 74 LA 699).

## Overtime by Seniority

Arbitrators also have upheld contracts that provide for overtime to be distributed on the basis of seniority.

• One such contract contained a clause stating that overtime would be allocated according to departmental seniority unless production would be substantially impaired by strict adherence to such a rule. In one instance under this agreement, management made no attempt to contact the senior employee in the affected department but gave an overtime job to an employee from another department who was on hand performing other overtime activities. The arbitrator held that management had violated the contract (*Harris Brothers Co.*, 53 LA 293).

• An electrician who was fifth in seniority standing in his department was entitled to eight hours of overtime pay because he was bypassed for the overtime in favor of another electrician who was sixteenth in seniority standing, an arbitrator held, notwithstanding the employer's contention that the employee's grievance was invalid because the four other more senior employees did not elect to file grievances (*Celotex Corp.*, 63 LA 521).

• Nonetheless, where a contract specified that overtime must be distributed according to seniority, an arbitrator ruled that an employer did not violate the contract when it offered overtime to a junior employee after finding that the senior employee who might have been offered the overtime had already left the plant (*Kellogg Co.*, 62 LA 1217; see also 77 LA 217).

• An employer was under no obligation to assign overtime work on the basis of seniority, an arbitrator decided, where the collective bargaining agreement did not specifically state that seniority rights applied to overtime distribution. The

union objected to an employer's practice of assigning overtime in a random manner and demanded that senior employees be paid for extra-hours work given to junior workers. The contract said nothing about overtime distribution, but it did contain a clause stating that seniority rights for employees would prevail. The union contended this meant that seniority would apply in all situations except as specifically limited by the agreement. The employer, on the other hand, argued that the clause meant seniority rights would operate only in the manner spelled out in detail in other parts of the contract. The arbitrator agreed with the employer that without a provision making seniority applicable to overtime work, the union did not have cause for complaint (*Crowe-Guide Cements Co.*, 30 LA 177).

## Probationary and Temporary Employees

When the contract fails to specify whether probationary employees are to be given overtime, the facts in the individual case may determine the arbitrator's ruling.

• A collective bargaining agreement stipulated that overtime was to be distributed equally among employees in a department. When necessary to get additional help from outside the department, overtime was to be given to the senior employee with the least overtime. The contract defined probationary employees as employees. In a grievance arising under this agreement, the arbitrator ruled that the employer acted properly when it assigned a probationary employee in the department to overtime work rather than going outside the department (*Hess & Eisenhardt Co.*, 53 LA 95).

• Under a contract provision stating that an employer was not required to offer overtime to employees who were not qualified to perform work, an employer had the right to assign overtime involving filling of a large order in warehouse department to experienced temporary employees, an arbitrator ruled, instead of to two office employers. Noting that the employer was not obligated to train office employees before using outside help, the arbitrator concluded that the employer had the right to assign the overtime to the temporary employees absent a clear showing of discriminatory or arbitrary treatment of the office employees (*Nissan Motor Corp.*, 66 LA 132; see also 77 LA 393, 72 LA 996).

• On the other hand, an employer improperly assigned overtime on its Valentine's Day candy line only to temporary employees instead of to regular employees in the unit, even though the entire line was staffed by temporary employees, an arbitrator ruled, because there existed a past practice under which regular employees were given the first consideration for available overtime whenever there was a mixture of regular and temporary employees on a particular line (*Zachery Confections Inc.*, 77 LA 464).

### Notification of Available Overtime Work

To what extent is management obligated to attempt to reach an employee at home whose turn it is to work overtime?

• A contract called for equalization of overtime. The employer called the employee who had the least overtime to come in from home for an overtime assignment, but the employee failed to answer the phone. The assignment was properly given to someone else.

Twenty minutes later, however, another overtime assignment became available. The employer assumed that the previously called employee with the least overtime was still unavailable and failed to try to contact him for the new assignment. The arbitrator ruled that the employer should not have assumed that the employee had not returned home during the 20-minute interval and therefore, it violated the contract by failing to call him a second time (*Goodyear Aerospace Corp.*, 52 LA 1098; see also 76 LA 1159, 76 LA 1024, 74 LA 110).

• In another case, the contract provided for overtime to be given to the most senior employee classified to do the work. Overtime was necessary for Labor Day, and it was scheduled late in the afternoon of the last working day before the holiday. The most senior employee had been on his honeymoon and was not due back until after Labor Day. The foreman made no attempt to contact the senior employee and instead assigned the overtime to someone else.

The employer argued that it would be unreasonable to have to try to contact the senior employee throughout the holiday weekend. Furthermore, if he were unavailable, it would be very difficult to get a substitute at the last minute. The arbitrator upheld the employer's contention and agreed that the overtime was properly assigned to someone else (*Carey Salt Co.*, 51 LA 1170).

### Responsibility for Error in Assigning Overtime

Arbitrators generally hold that any mistakes an employer makes when assigning overtime, even if they are perfectly honest and understandable errors, are management's responsibility.

• Because of a computer error, overtime was improperly assigned to an employee. The arbitrator concluded that the aggrieved employee must be compensated—despite the fact that he should have been aware of the error and should have called it to management's attention before the scheduled overtime was performed (*Goodyear Aerospace Corp.*, 54 LA 579).

### Remedy for Overtime Missed

The usual remedy awarded when management makes an erroneous overtime assignment is make-up overtime or payment of money the employee would have earned had the overtime been properly assigned. Arbitrators are frequently called upon to determine which of the two remedies is appropriate.

• Under a contract providing for equal distribution of overtime within the appropriate overtime group in a classification, the employer improperly gave an overtime assignment to an employee from a different classification. The arbitrator ruled for a monetary award—rather than make-up overtime—for the employee who should have been given the assignment. The arbitrator explained that to give the grievant make up overtime would adversely affect the contractual overtime rights of the other employees in his classification (*Trane Co.*, 52 LA 1144).

• In another instance, an employee was mistakenly bypassed for an overtime assignment under a contract stipulating equal distribution of overtime. The assignment was given to another employee in the same overtime group. The contract failed to specify any remedy for improper overtime assignments, so the arbitrator imposed an award of makeup overtime for the grievant. He felt that the remedy was appropriate because the bypass occurred within the same overtime equalization roster and no inequities would result from make-up overtime. Furthermore, the bypass was unintentional, and the employee would suffer no loss of earnings as long as he received the make-up assignment within a reasonable period (*Kaiser Aluminum & Chemical Corp.*, 54 LA 613).

• An employer that committed an honest mistake in its bypass of an employee to perform emergency overtime work was directed to (1) provide make-up overtime of eight hours for employees at a time convenient for them and at a time when they otherwise would not be working; (2) ensure the overtime given did not take away from the employee's other overtime opportunities; and (3) provide eight hours of overtime pay to employees without requiring them to work any make-up overtime if they ceased to be an employee or were unable to work the make-up overtime within a reasonable period of time (*Kimberly-Clark Corp.*, 61 LA 1094; see also 76 LA 10).

When the award granted is monetary, arbitrators generally will award pay for missed overtime at the overtime rate rather than at straight time.

• A series of grievances came before an arbitrator in which he found that certain employees had been denied their proper opportunity for overtime work. The union argued that the employees should be paid the appropriate premium rates for the hours of work they were denied. The employer, however, maintained that they should be paid straight-time rates, saying that the contract specified straight-time as the appropriate rate of pay for any hours not worked. The employer also pointed out that it had been established practice at the plant to pay only straight-time in such cases.

Despite the employer's past practice, the arbitrator ruled for the union. He said that the most important consideration was that the employees would have been paid at overtime rates had they worked the hours in question (*John Deere Ottumwa Works*, 20 LA 737).

## Definition of 'Day' for Overtime Purposes

Where overtime pay is required for all work beyond a designated number of hours a day, the manner in which a day is measured becomes crucial.

Some companies use a calendar day, others a 24-hour period following a specified time, and still others recognize the 24-hour period following the start of the particular employee's regular shift.

• In one case, several employees who normally worked from 3 p.m. to 11 p.m. were ordered to work from 7 p.m. to 7 a.m. on Monday and Tuesday, resuming their normal work schedule on Wednesday. The contract defined the workday for purposes of computing overtime as "24 consecutive hours commencing with the starting time on an employee's regularly assigned shift."

The union contended that the employees were entitled to overtime pay for the hours worked between 3 p.m. and 7 p.m. on Wednesday. The union argued that the 24-hour period began for these employees at 7 p.m.; hence, 3 p.m. to 7 p.m. Wednesday was the same workday that began Tuesday at 7 p.m. The employer countered that the workday began at 3 p.m., the starting time of these employees' regularly assigned shift; and all work performed on Wednesday was to be paid at the straight-time rate. The arbitrator ruled for the employer (*Chicago Pneumatic Tool Co.*, 42 LA 1240).

• In another case, a problem arose with the initiation of Daylight Saving Time. The contract required overtime pay for all time worked in excess of eight hours in any one day and defined a day as "24 hours beginning at the time an employee starts work on his regular or assigned schedule." The arbitrator held that the employees who worked the 7 p.m. to 3 p.m. shift and the 3 p.m. to 11 p.m. shift on the Saturday before Daylight Saving Time went into effect were entitled to overtime pay for the first hour worked on those same shifts the following Sunday. He commented that the contract was very specific in defining a day as 24 hours long, and only 23 hours had elapsed between the start of the Saturday shifts and the start of the Sunday shifts (*Neches Butane Products*, 49 LA 1195).

### Overtime on Holidays

● Under a contract that failed to specify the manner of computing compensation for hours worked in excess of eight on premium-pay days such as holidays, an arbitrator found that employees are entitled to one and one-half times the applicable premium hourly rate for such hours. The contract called for time-and-one-half pay for overtime work and triple-time pay for holiday work. The arbitrator upheld the union contention that the triple-time holiday pay was the proper base rate to be used for computing overtime on a holiday; hence, overtime on a holiday was to be compensated at four and one-half times the straight-time rate (*Fry's Food Stores*, 44 LA 431).

● In another case, however, an employer properly paid the time-and-one-half rate rather than double-time pay to employees who were scheduled to work on a contractual holiday, on a Tuesday, an arbitrator decided, notwithstanding the union's contention that the payment of time and one-half was not in keeping with the intent of the contract. The employer, the arbitrator reasoned, was entitled to compute the employees' pay by not considering the exception to the contract's no-pyramiding clause, which applied only to work performed on Sunday (*Inland Container Corp.*, 63 LA 1294).

### Holiday As Time Worked for Overtime Purposes

When contracts are silent on the subject of whether or not an unworked holiday is to be counted as hours worked for purposes of calculating weekly overtime, arbitrators have ruled either way, based on each case's particulars.

● One employer's contract stated that time-and-one-half wages would be paid for all work beyond 40 hours in a week and specified a Monday-through-Friday workweek. When employees worked a Saturday during a week that included an unworked holiday, the union and the employer disagreed over whether the employees were entitled to overtime pay for the Saturday work. The employer claimed that because the contract did not specifically say so, holidays need not be counted as time worked.

The arbitrator ruled that holidays should be counted as time worked; otherwise, employees would lose pay (the overtime premium) for the sixth day worked because of a holiday. Concluding that the parties meant for employees to enjoy holidays without losing any money, the arbitrator said the employer must count holidays as time worked (*Martin Aircraft Tool Co.*, 25 LA 181; see also *Fairbanks North Star Borough*, 103 LA 614, in which an arbitrator held an employer wrongly denied shift workers overtime pay for Saturday holiday work).

● Another arbitrator declared that if the contract is silent on the matter, management need not count an unworked holiday as time worked in figuring when overtime pay starts. The contract stipulated time-and-one-half pay for work after 40 hours a week. It stated that "hours lost by employees from their regular scheduled shift at the request of the employer shall count as time worked for the purpose of computing weekly overtime."

In one week, employees put in a total of 40 hours of actual work, apart from time off on a holiday. The union insisted that the time off on the holiday should be counted as time worked—for a total of 48 hours' work in the week, eight of them compensated at the overtime premium.

The arbitrator decided that it was not time lost at the request of the employer. He considered the unworked holiday comparable to an unworked Sunday, which should not be viewed as time worked for overtime purposes (*Goodyear Clearwater Mills*, 6 LA 117).

## Pyramiding of Daily and Weekly Overtime Pay

Collective bargaining agreements generally provide for overtime or premium pay for work in excess of some specified number of hours per day or in excess of some specified number of hours in a week. It is common for these agreements to also contain a clause prohibiting pyramiding of overtime premiums—hours of daily overtime worked and compensated for cannot be counted again as time worked toward weekly overtime. Problems can arise, however, in determining whether certain hours worked are in fact overtime hours and consequently cannot be counted toward weekly overtime.

● In one such case, an employee worked 12 hours on his birthday. The contract recognized employees' birthdays as holidays, and provided for time-and-one-half pay for work done on a holiday. The contract also prohibited pyramiding of overtime premiums. The employee was paid time-and-one-half holiday pay for the first eight hours worked on his birthday and time-and-one-half overtime pay for the remaining four hours. The union contended that the first eight hours he worked should be counted in computing the weekly overtime because these hours were compensated as holiday work, not overtime work. The arbitrator agreed, rejecting the employer's argument that such action would amount to pyramiding (*Hooker Chemical Corp.*, 50 LA 1091).

● In another case, an employee had received time-and-one-half pay for the hours she worked on her scheduled day off. The arbitrator ruled she was also entitled to receive overtime pay for the hours worked in excess of 40 during the week, despite the fact that the contract prohibited payment of both daily and weekly overtime for the same hours. The premium pay that the employee received for her off-day work is analogous to "penalty pay" for Sunday and holiday work, the arbitrator said, rather than to daily overtime (*Safeway Stores Inc.*, 45 LA 244).

● An employee who worked from 3:00 a.m. through 3:00 p.m. on Monday was entitled to (1) double time pay for working from 3:00 a.m. to 7:00 a.m. Monday, which was considered part of Sunday under the contract; (2) regular pay for working from 7:00 a.m. to 11:00 a.m.; and (3) time-and-one-half pay for working from 11:00 a.m. to 3:00 p.m., an arbitrator ruled, despite the employer's claim that the payment constituted pyramiding. The arbitrator noted that pyramiding meant "piling on" by paying two different rates for the same hours of work (*King-Seely Thermos Co.*, 61 LA 544).

## Compensatory Time in Lieu of Overtime Pay — Public Employees

● State and local government employers can require their workers to take time off to reduce their accrued compensatory time, which was allocated in lieu of overtime pay under the Fair Labor Standards Act, the U.S. Supreme Court ruled.

Congress amended the FLSA in 1966 to extend its coverage to state and local government employers and amended it again in 1985 to allow these employers to use "comp" time instead of cash overtime. The FLSA caps the number of comp time hours government employees can accrue before the employer must switch to overtime pay. Employers can reduce or eliminate the amount of accrued comp time by making cash payments instead of allowing employees to take time off from work.

In this case, county deputy sheriffs agreed to accept comp time in lieu of overtime pay. The sheriff's department became concerned about its obligations to pay overtime to employees who reached the cap on accrued comp time and to make cash payments to employees who left work with substantial accumulations of comp time when it required its deputies to use up their accumulated comp time. The deputy sheriffs argued that the law implicitly prohibits the practice unless there is a prior agreement authorizing it.

A federal district court ruled in favor of the deputy sheriffs, saying the employees had the right to decide when they would use accrued comp time. The U.S. Court of

Appeals for the Fifth Circuit reversed. On appeal, the Supreme Court agreed with the appeals court, holding that nothing in the FLSA or Department of Labor rules says the sheriff's department cannot require deputy sheriffs to use their comp time rather than let it accumulate. According to the court's decision, however, federal law does not prohibit state or local government employees with collective bargaining rights from negotiating agreements allowing them to use accrued comp time when they please (*Christensen v. Harris County*, U.S., No. 98-1167, 5/1/00).

[**Note:** The decision does not apply to the private sector, where employers generally are required by the FLSA to compensate their employees in cash for overtime work. ]

## Refusal to Work Mandatory Overtime As Voluntary Quit

An arbitrator held that a refusal to work mandatory overtime by an employee who claimed he was sick constituted a "voluntary quit." The employee in question had been reminded less than a month before the incident that precipitated his termination that, under company policy, a refusal to work mandatory overtime was a voluntary quit, the arbitrator noted. In addition, the employee had claimed illness when he had been required to work overtime in the past, he had not gone to a medical examination his employer had arranged, and he had been advised one month before his discharge that he should claim illness before, not after, he was asked to work overtime (*Land-O-Sun Dairies Inc.*, 105 LA 740).

# Premium Pay for Weekend Work

## OVERVIEW

Arbitration awards involving premium pay for weekend work provide few general guidelines for application to everyday problems.

Settlement of disputes over premium pay generally depends on a close reading of complex contract language and its application in the context of the particular bargaining situation (97 LA 45, 94 LA 271, 94 LA 52, 92 LA 23, 91 LA 1043, 90 LA 225, 74 LA 1195, 65 LA 975, 65 LA 636, 62 LA 1008).

## SUMMARY OF CASES

### Sunday Premium

Frequently, contracts call for premium pay for work performed on Sundays. For purposes of such provisions, many contracts limit Sunday worktime eligible for premium pay to work begun after some specified hour on Sunday in order to avoid premium payments for work that is part of a Saturday night shift. Without such a limitation, arbitrators will generally hold employers liable for premium pay for all work performed on "Sunday" as defined by the calendar day.

● One contract defined the "workday" as beginning at 7 a.m. and provided for double-time pay "for all hours worked on Sunday." Third-shift employees regularly scheduled to work from 11 p.m. Saturday until 7 a.m. Sunday claimed that they were entitled to double-time for all work performed after midnight Saturday night until the end of their shift. The employer denied their contention, insisting that the Saturday workday began at 7 a.m. and continued for 24 hours until 7 a.m. Sunday. Hence, all work performed by the third shift employees fell on Saturday, the employer claimed.

The arbitrator, however, found that the contract made no such definition of Sunday. Absent any contractual provision specifically defining the day for overtime or premium pay purposes in some other manner, a day is generally held to mean the calendar day, the arbitrator explained. He concluded that in this contract "Sunday" meant from midnight Saturday to midnight Sunday and, therefore, awarded third shift employees double-time pay for all work performed after midnight Saturday (*Trent Engineering Co.*, 55 LA 1232).

● Employees who worked on Sunday from 7 a.m. through 2:15 p.m. were entitled to eight hours' pay at double-time rate rather than the seven hours' pay they received, an arbitrator decided. Despite the contract's ambiguity, the arbitrator held that the union's interpretation that an employee who works more than four hours in a workday is entitled to eight hours' pay was confirmed by past practice (*Construction Industry Committee*, 69 LA 14; see also 86 LA 827, 77 LA 1030, 74 LA 1214, 66 LA 1096).

● An arbitrator ruled that a public-sector employer violated a collective bargaining agreement when it eliminated Sunday premium pay under the claimed authority of the Prevailing Rate Systems Act, which generally provides that nonsupervisory operation and maintenance employees in the federal workforce should be paid comparable wages for similar positions in the private sector, even though the agreement stated that premium pay can be changed if required by law, and the agency that promulgated the wage rates for the particular government agency under the PRSA found that comparable rates did not constitute "law" and that additional monies paid for premium work were negotiable items (*U.S. Army Corps of Engineers*, 104 LA 469).

• Engineers were not entitled to double-time pay for work performed on Sundays after the employer began opening its stores to the public as a regular business day because the Sunday Blue Laws were struck down as unconstitutional, an arbitrator ruled, notwithstanding the union's contention that the contract stating that "employees who work on Sunday shall receive double the straight-time hourly rate for hours worked" meant what it said (*Alexander's Personnel Providers Inc.*, 68 LA 249).

• Under a contract stating that "double-time shall be paid for all work performed on Sunday, excepting shift that overlaps into Sunday," an arbitrator ruled that a publisher was not obligated to pay double-time pay to an employee who worked a portion of a Sunday on a new shift that started at 10 p.m. Sunday and ended at 6 a.m. on Monday (*Baltimore News American*, 68 LA 1054; see also 90 LA 663, 74 LA 1042).

• A company violated its collective bargaining agreement by imposing a three-day, 12-hour shift schedule on some of its employees, an arbitrator decided.

A manufacturer assigned three shifts to workers, including a three-day, 12-hour shift for which employees were given 40 hours of pay. Other schedules specified in the contract provided premium pay for weekend work, but the new schedule made no mention of that. The employer said it had the right to "schedule at its whim," but the union contended that the employer had violated the contract's provisions on shift work and premium pay because the new schedule was imposed without any negotiations. Calling the scheduling unreasonable, the arbitrator stated that any new type of work schedule should still permit premium pay to conform to the contract. He ordered the employer to drop its three-day, 12-hour workweek until a new plan could be negotiated with the union and said the company must compensate any employees who worked Saturdays or Sundays for any premium pay they had been denied (*South Charleston Stamping and Mfg.*, 115 LA 710).

## Seventh-Day Premium

Rather than specify Sunday as a premium day, some contracts generalize and call for premiums on the seventh day worked. Similar problems can arise in determining when the "seventh day" actually begins.

• An employee at one employer regularly worked Monday through Friday, beginning at 7:30 a.m. After working his regular week, he was called in at 11:00 p.m. Saturday, and worked until 8:36 a.m. Sunday, with an hour break for a meal.

The contract provided for time-and-one-half for the sixth day worked and double-time for work on the seventh day. The workday was defined as eight hours. The employer consequently paid the employee time-and-one-half for the sixth day and double-time for only a few minutes on Sunday morning, claiming that the seventh day did not begin until eight hours had been worked on the sixth day.

The arbitrator ruled, however, that the seventh day began at 7:30 Sunday morning because the employee's regular starting time was 7:30 a.m. He ordered that the employee be paid at double-time rates for all work done after 7:30 a.m. Sunday (*City of Lansing*, 53 LA 855; see also 87 LA 1269, 83 LA 480).

• Under a contract provision requiring payment of double-time rate to all employees for all work performed on Sunday when it is the sixth or seventh day worked in the workweek, an arbitrator ruled that an employer was not required to pay employees at double-time rate for work performed before the start of the workweek commencing at 7:00 a.m. Monday, even though the workday was considered a 24-hour period extending from 7:00 a.m. to 7:00 a.m. The pre-shift hours, being continuous with Monday, could not be considered an extension of Sunday, the arbitrator held, since there was no reason to conclude that "Sunday" as used in the contract meant anything other than the normal calendar day. Moreover, past practice supported the employer's contention that employees performing the pre-shift work in question were paid time-and-one-half, rather than the double-time rate, the arbitrator concluded (*Certain-Teed Products Corp.*, 61 LA 689; see also 86 LA 992, 76 LA 1037).

## Pyramiding Premiums

A contract called for time-and-one-half pay for an employee working his first scheduled day off or the sixth day in the workweek, and double-time for working his second scheduled day off or the seventh day in the workweek. The contract also contained the following clause: "The Company shall not be required to pay overtime twice for the same overtime hours worked."

An employee was scheduled to have Tuesday and Wednesday off. However, he was called in to work Wednesday, his second scheduled day off. He also worked Monday and Thursday through Sunday of that week. He was paid time-and-one-half for Wednesday and straight-time the remainder of the week.

The union claimed the employee was entitled to time-and-one-half for Sunday because it was the sixth day worked in the week. The employer argued that such payment would be pyramiding, which was prohibited in the contract clause quoted above, as the employee already received a premium for the Wednesday worked and that time could not be counted again.

The arbitrator rejected the employer's argument, however. He pointed out that there were two different days involved, and these were not, therefore, "the same overtime hours." He explained that the clause did *not* state that overtime hours worked and compensated for under one provision could not be counted as hours worked for overtime purposes under any other provision. But rather, he said, the clause was intended to prevent paying a double premium in such situations as an employee working the sixth day in the workweek, that same day also happening to be his first scheduled day off (*Dow Chemical Co.*, 49 LA 480; see also 97 LA 45, 91 LA 1043, 87 LA 130).

● An employer properly paid the straight-time rate, rather than overtime, to employees for work performed on Friday in a workweek consisting of Sunday, Monday, Tuesday, Wednesday, Thursday,

and Friday, an arbitrator ruled. Contending that the contract provided for overtime for all work over 40 hours in a payroll week and on a Sunday to Friday schedule, the union argued that overtime should be paid for Friday work because Friday was an overtime day, while Sunday was a premium pay day.

Rejecting the union's contention, however, the arbitrator pointed out that if premium pay and overtime pay are the same, as he viewed it, payment for Friday work in a Sunday to Friday schedule would be pyramiding overtime, which was prohibited by the contract. The denial of the employee's grievance was consistent with the generally accepted concept in today's industrial world providing one overtime day in a six-day workweek, the arbitrator concluded (*Utah International Inc.*, 75 LA 212; see also 94 LA 271, 94 LA 52, 92 LA 23, 90 LA 225).

## Unworked Days Affecting Premiums

Holidays and other time not worked but paid for may or may not influence the rate of pay on what are normally premium days. Specific contract language is crucial (68 LA 1006, 63 LA 1294, 62 LA 1008).

● A contract called for time-and-one-half for all work performed on Saturday. Another provision of the contract provided for "bereavement pay"—pay for up to three days of missed work when an employee attended the funeral of an immediate family member. The contract stipulated that the employee was to be paid bereavement pay for the time he "would have had the opportunity to work" at his "standard hourly wage rate."

An employee under this contract was scheduled to work on Saturday. However, due to a death in his family, he was excused from work that day. The employer subsequently paid him eight hours' bereavement pay at the straight-time rate.

The employer contended that the "standard hourly wage rate" meant the "straight-time" rate. The union argued that the employee was entitled to eight hours' pay at time and one half, the "standard hourly wage rate" for Saturday. The arbitrator agreed with the union's view and awarded for the grievant (*Marlin-Rockwell Co.*, 54 LA 99).

• A contract provided that all work performed on the seventh consecutive day of the employee's workweek was to be paid at double-time. The contract further stipulated that employees were not to lose pay for worktime lost while serving on jury duty.

An employee was absent from work Monday and Wednesday one week while serving on jury duty, for which he was paid by the employer for eight hours each day. He worked Tuesday, Thursday, Friday, Saturday, and Sunday of that week. The employer paid the employee at the straight-time rate for Sunday.

The union argued that time spent on jury duty and compensated for by the employer was to be counted as time worked. Thus Sunday was the seventh consecutive day worked in that employee's workweek, and should have been paid at double-time, the union insisted. But the arbitrator found no provision in the contract stating that time spent on jury duty, and compensated for by the employer, was to be counted as time worked. Concluding the employee had been properly paid, the arbitrator said that, absent any such provision, he could not sustain the grievance (*Cabot Corp.*, 52 LA 575).

• Another arbitrator also concluded that without specific contractual provision to that effect, pay for jury duty was not to be counted as hours worked when computing overtime (*Coleman Company Inc.*, 52 LA 357).

# Premium Pay for Shift Work

## OVERVIEW

Contract clauses that provide for payment of a wage differential to employees who work on afternoon or night shifts ordinarily do not give rise to many disputes. Almost all employers that require night work pay a shift bonus. The rate of payment usually is specified in the collective bargaining agreement, and employees assigned to the particular shift automatically are compensated at those premium rates.

Occasionally, however, there may be questions related to the payment of shift differentials to night watchmen and similar groups, or to employees who divide their time between shifts. By law, and in the opinion of most arbitrators, shift differentials must be included in figuring an employee's overtime rate.

## SUMMARY OF CASES

### When Regular Work Schedule Extends into Another Shift

If portions of employees' regular work schedule fall into two different shifts, are they entitled to a shift premium for any of the hours? One arbitrator held they were not.

• Workers who normally worked the evening shift (3 p.m. to 11 p.m.) received a 15-cent premium shift differential. When management unilaterally changed the schedule for this shift to 11 a.m. to 7 p.m., the employees claimed they were entitled to shift differential for the hours of 3 p.m. to 7 p.m. The arbitrator rejected their contention, stating that the shift differential was only applicable to the eight-hour evening shift and not to a few hours worked during that time span (*Diamond Shamrock Corp.*, 55 LA 827; see also 73 LA 677).

• An employer that changed the starting time of the period worked by orderlies from a 6:30 a.m. to 3 p.m. shift to a 7:30 p.m. to 4 a.m. shift on certain workdays was required to pay the employees contractual premium pay for the split shift, an arbitrator decided, because the employees were now required to work portions of two shifts (*Miami Inspiration Hospital*, 68 LA 898).

• An employee whose shift began on Friday and extended into Saturday was entitled to straight-time pay for work hours that extended into Saturday, and an employee whose shift began on Saturday and extended into Sunday was entitled to time-and-one-half the rate for the hours worked on Sunday, an arbitrator ruled, under a contract that stated that time-and-one-half the employee's regular hourly wage would be paid for all work done on Saturday and double the employee's hourly rate would be paid for all work performed on Sunday.

In adopting the words "all work performed on Saturday," the parties meant "Saturday" to consist of shifts beginning on Saturday, and in using the words "all work performed on Sunday," they meant to cover the shifts that began on Sunday, the arbitrator emphasized, concluding that this interpretation was supported by the parties' past practice (*Vlasic Foods Inc.*, 74 LA 1214).

If an employer agrees to pay employees the premium rate required for a shift in which the majority of their working hours fall, what rate should be paid an employee who works exactly half his time on the day shift and half on the second shift? In one such situation, the arbitrator rejected the employee's claim for a shift premium.

• The employee worked regularly from 12:30 p.m. to 9 p.m., with a half-hour for lunch between 4:30 p.m. and 5 p.m. The regular second shift hours began at 4:30 p.m.; therefore, excluding his lunch period, this employee worked exactly half his hours on the day shift and half his hours on the next shift. The arbitrator pointed out that because the lunch period could not be counted as hours worked, the employee could not show that a majority of his work time was put in on the second shift and denied his claim for the second-shift premium (*Canfield Oil Co.*, 7 LA 322).

### Night Premium for Nonproduction Workers

Rulings have gone both ways on whether nonproduction employees on premium-pay shifts are entitled to shift differentials. Arbitrators frequently base their decisions on the employer's past practice or specific language in the contract.

● Under a contract that provided a shift differential for night work, an arbitrator ruled that the employer violated the contract by denying the shift differential to janitors who worked on the night shift. Although janitors had not received the differential prior to the current contract and the subject was not mentioned during negotiations, the contract language neglected to specifically exclude janitors from receiving the premium (*Journal-Tribune Publishing Co.*, 51 LA 606; see also 98 LA 312, 95 LA 479, 89 LA 581, 83 LA 17, 81 LA 1118, 81 LA 903, 77 LA 1220, 73 LA 1305).

● It was held in another case that night shift premiums did not apply to watchmen, even though the contract did not specifically exclude them. In this instance, the award was based on a past practice of several years of not paying such employees the premium (*John Lucas & Co.*, 19 LA 344).

● In another case, an employer was again not required to pay shift premiums to cleaning staff for night work because they had not received such pay in the six years that they had been covered by the contract. This past practice overrode the fact that the contract made no exceptions to the payment of premium pay for those

hours, according to the arbitrator (*Morgan Engineering Co.*, 33 LA 46).

● A housekeeper was not entitled to premium pay for working a four-hour afternoon schedule from 12:30 p.m. to 4:30 p.m., an arbitrator decided, notwithstanding the union's contention that the contract provision requiring payment of seven-cents-an-hour night premium for all regularly scheduled "night employees'" obligated the employer to give premium pay to the employee because "night employees," and "second shift employees" working the 11:00 a.m. to 7:00 p.m. shift were one in the same. Finding that the term "shift employees" referred only to employees working for eight hours' duration, the arbitrator held that that interpretation was in keeping with the commonly accepted definition of "shift" (*Huron Valley Public Schools*, 63 LA 49; see also 97 LA 447, 74 LA 884).

### Inclusion of Shift Premium in Calculating Overtime Pay

If an employee is entitled to a shift premium, his or her overtime pay must be based on the regular rate plus the shift premium, according to the wage and hour laws and previous arbitral rulings.

● An employer agreed in its union contract that a bonus of five cents an hour would be paid to workers laboring on the second and third shifts. When an employee on a late shift performed overtime work, the employer contended that he was entitled only to one-and-one-half times the day rate, while the union argued that he was entitled to one-and-one-half times the day rate plus five cents.

The arbitrator, in upholding the union view, pointed out that the differential for late-shift work becomes an integral part of the employee's wage. Therefore, he ruled that an employee who worked overtime was entitled to receive compensation for those hours at the rate of one-and-one-half times his full hourly wage, including the shift premium (*Public Service Electric & Gas Co.*, 2 LA 2).

### Overtime Extending into a Premium-Pay Shift

Arbitrators generally rule that an employee working a day shift who occasionally is assigned overtime that extends into a premium-pay shift is not entitled to have the shift differential included in overtime pay. If, however, the overtime occurs on a regular basis or the contract language suggests that the differential is to be paid, the arbitrator may award the shift premium.

● One arbitrator found that employees on the first shift were not entitled to a shift differential for the hour worked after the shift's normal quitting time. He ruled that the shift differential was intended only as additional compensation for second-shift employees who had to give up their "socializing time." Occasional overtime work performed by the first shift did not alter their status as first-shift employees, and the contract specified that the second shift, not the first, was to receive the differential, the arbitrator concluded (*Idal Corrugated Box Co.*, 46 LA 129).

● In another instance, a case came to arbitration over an employer's practice of paying employees who worked overtime on their day off on the basis of the shift differential applicable to the shift actually worked rather than on the basis of the shift to which they were regularly assigned. Employees who regularly worked a premium-pay shift were called in on their day off to work the day shift. The employer did not include their usual shift differential when computing the overtime pay for the day shift worked.

The arbitrator upheld this procedure because the practice had been in effect for several years, and the union had never challenged it before (*Bonanza Air Lines Inc.*, 44 LA 698).

● Under a different contract providing a shift differential for second-shift work, another arbitrator held that an employee who regularly worked a ten-hour day was entitled to the shift differential for the two hours worked daily on the second shift, in addition to the overtime premium for those two hours. The arbitrator explained that payment of overtime alone is sufficient for first-shift employees who only occasionally work overtime into the second shift. The additional shift differential must, however, be paid to employees who work overtime into the second shift on a regularly scheduled basis, he added (*Brighton Electric Steel Casting*, 47 LA 518).

● Where a contract called for shift bonuses for second and third shifts for "all work on these shifts," the employer had to include bonuses in the base rate for purposes of computing overtime worked on those shifts by employees who were regularly assigned to the preceding shifts (*Stauffer Chemical Co.*, 35 LA 529).

# Reporting & Call-In Pay

## OVERVIEW

Generally, a contract clause that requires an employer to provide reporting pay does not also apply to pay for call-ins for emergency work. Usually a distinction is made between the two.

Where an employer is relieved of its reporting-pay obligation when it tells an employee not to report, a properly addressed telegram is usually considered the appropriate form of notice even if the employee ultimately does not receive it. If, however, the contract specifies that the employee must "receive" the notice, then, in fact, the employer does not fulfill its notice obligation merely by trying to contact the person but must actually succeed.

Even if work is unavailable through no fault of the employer's, an employer nevertheless must notify employees not to report if this is feasible. A failure to give such notice may make the employer liable for reporting pay.

## SUMMARY OF CASES

### Overtime or Call-In Pay

Problems may arise over whether specific time worked outside the normal work schedule is to be compensated as overtime or as "call-in" time.

● One arbitrator made the following distinction between overtime and a call-in. Overtime is time worked in a continuous stream with the regular work schedule—whether it precedes or follows that shift. Call-in pay, however, is intended to compensate an employee for making a special trip to work, so it is necessary for the employee to be released to leave the workplace immediately after completing an assignment in order for that assignment to qualify as a call-in (*Owens-Illinois Inc.*, 55 LA 1121; see also 73 LA 478, 69 LA 908).

● An arbitrator held that an employee (who normally did not work on Saturdays and Sundays) who was called on Saturday to work at a garlic mill on Sunday, and returned to the mill on Monday was entitled to contractual double-time call-in pay for Sunday, because the employee was not given the required notice before the end of his last regular shift (*Basic Vegetable Products Inc.*, 90 LA 666; see also 92 LA 766, 92 LA 361, 88 LA 1307, 85 LA 500, 83 LA 491, 82 LA 1104, 82 LA 48).

### Reporting or Call-In Pay

A collective bargaining agreement contained a provision guaranteeing employees a minimum of four hours' work or four hours' pay if called in at some time other than their regular shift or as a continuous extension thereof. The contract further provided for a minimum of four hours' work or pay to any employee reporting for work at the start of his normal shift—with certain exceptions, such as when no work was available because of a power failure.

The second shift employees were instructed on Friday afternoon to report for work the following afternoon. Saturday was not a normal workday, but Saturday overtime occurred frequently. A power failure occurred Saturday morning, and when employees reported for work as instructed, the employer told them to go home.

The employees filed a grievance claiming four hours' call-in pay. The employer contended that the situation came under the provisions governing reporting pay, and it was therefore not liable for payment to employees because of the power failure exception. The arbitrator upheld the employer's view, stating that the reporting-pay provisions applied because of the established practice of an extended workweek schedule (*General Dynamics Corp.*, 54 LA 405; see also 84 LA 675).

## Exceptions to Reporting-Pay Requirements

Reporting pay provisions generally list certain situations in which the employer is not required to make reporting payments to employees. These exceptions may be when work is unavailable for reasons beyond the employer's control or where the employer has given employees prior notice not to report. Arbitrators are frequently called on to determine if a given situation is truly beyond the employer's control or if the employer has given employees proper notice not to report.

Some of these situations are discussed below.

*Civil disturbances*—A contract guaranteed four hours' reporting or call-in pay, except where employees were denied work for reasons beyond the employer's control. During a period of civil disturbances, the employer canceled a regular evening shift because of a curfew imposed by the governor. Management made reasonable attempts to notify employees through radio announcements, although such notification was not required under the terms of the contract. When the employees demanded reporting pay, management balked, and the arbitrator upheld the employer's stance, holding that the situation was "a classical illustration of 'other causes beyond the control of the company'" (*Koppers Co. Inc.*, 54 LA 408).

• Civil disorders in another city prompted a citywide curfew starting at 3 p.m. Several second-shift employees reported for work at 3 p.m., but were sent home. They subsequently claimed four hours' pay under a reporting-pay clause requiring such pay for employees sent home for lack of work. The arbitrator interpreted "lack of work" to mean absence of the need for the product with adjust-

ments in the work schedule to reduce output. Because that situation did not exist, the arbitrator rejected the employees' claim (*Lockheed-Georgia*, 51 LA 720).

*Bomb threats*—An employer received a bomb threat, and because two previous threats had proved to be hoaxes, management assumed this too was a hoax. The employer gave employees the option of going home and being paid only for the time actually spent on plant premises or staying and working the entire shift and getting full pay for the time worked. The employer said it would not give four hours' reporting pay to employees who elected to go home, under a contractual provision that exempted the employer from such reporting pay if there were an explosion.

The union later claimed the workers were owed reporting pay, arguing that no explosion actually occurred. The arbitrator denied their grievance, however, pointing out that if an actual explosion would exempt the employer from reporting pay, the same should hold true for the mere threat of an explosion. Otherwise, "any mischief maker could drive the corporation out of business with threats of one sort and another" (*General Cable Corp.*, 54 LA 696; see also 73 LA 1252, 62 LA 463).

• An employer was obligated to give reporting pay to employees who claimed loss of wages during two separate bomb scares, an arbitrator decided. The contract's provision exempted the employer from providing reporting pay if inability to provide work was caused by "labor disputes, riots, fire, flood, tornado, lightening, power failure, or act of God." The provision was not, however, applicable, the arbitrator held, because the actual reason was not among those specified in the contract (*Miller Printing Machinery Co.*, 64 LA 141; see also 73 LA 280, 72 LA 1232, 69 LA 511).

*Equipment failure/power outages*— To determine whether employees must be paid for reporting to work during equipment failures and power outages, arbitrators will look very closely to determine if the incidents were within the employer's control.

• A contract provided for reporting pay for employees who report for work but find none available, except "if the plant delay results from causes beyond the control of the employer." A flue collapsed at the plant, necessitating the shutdown of a furnace used in production operations. The union argued that because the flue had not been inspected for three years and proper inspection could have prevented the collapse, the situation was legitimately within the employer's control. The arbitrator agreed and awarded the employees reporting pay (*Bunker Hill Co.*, 51 LA 873).

• Under another contract requiring reporting pay unless the lack of work was caused by a major power interruption or equipment breakdown over which the employer had no control, the arbitrator awarded reporting pay when a leak in a boiler made work unavailable. The leak occurred following a shutdown and repairs on the boiler, and such leaks were common after boiler shutdowns. Although the leak was beyond the control of the employer, the arbitrator said that the employer should have foreseen the possibility of the leak and made every effort to discover it in time to notify employees not to report to work (*Rubatex Corp.*, 52 LA 1270; see also 74 LA 1037, 74 LA 513, 54 LA 1218).

• Another arbitrator ruled that employees who were sent home after a power failure in the main electric feeder line were not entitled to four hours' reporting pay under a contract providing for such payment except where the employer "is not able to operate the plant because of reasons beyond its control." The union contended that because the burn-out that precipitated the power failure occurred within the plant, its occurrence was management's responsibility and therefore was within its control. The arbitrator accepted the argument that the main feeder line was management's responsibility, but because the power failure could not have been anticipated, it was beyond the employer's control (*Erie Artisan Corp.*, 51 LA 850).

• A power failure precipitated by a malfunction in new equipment was judged to be beyond an employer's control, an arbitrator determined, exempting the employer from providing four hours' reporting pay to employees (*E.W. Bliss Co.*, 55 LA 522; see also 73 LA 1117).

• Another arbitrator held that an employer violated a collective bargaining agreement by failing to provide reporting pay even though production was halted by a power outage that was beyond the employer's control. The employer's obligation to the employees was triggered at the point when they reported to work, not when the power outage occurred, the arbitrator said, ordering the employer to pay employees whom it had sent home for two hours' work, as guaranteed by the contract's reporting-pay provision (*AKRO Corp.*, 102 LA 191).

**Lack of heat**—When employees reported to work Monday morning, an employer's plant was without heat because an oil tank had run dry over the weekend. The employer had been aware of the oil shortage on Friday, but managers felt there would be enough to last until Monday. An unexpected, though not uncommon, drop in temperature caused the oil to run out earlier than anticipated. Employees refused to work without adequate heat. A short time after the shift began, however, the company president told employees that the oil shipment was on its way, there would soon be heat, and to either get to work or leave. They all went home, and the employer did not pay the employees at all that day.

The union demanded four hours' reporting pay or at least compensation for the time spent at the plant that morning. The arbitrator awarded payment for time spent in the plant, because the situation was within management's control, but denied four hours' reporting pay because of mitigating factors in the employer's favor (*Dietz Machine Works Inc.*, 52 LA 1023).

**Health hazards**—While first-shift employees were at work, a mechanical detector sounded an alarm indicating the presence of unsafe levels of carbon monoxide in the workplace. The employees evacuated the area, but 20 minutes later the employer announced that the alarm was a result of a malfunction in the detector, and instructed employees to return to work. Seventeen of them refused to do so, believing conditions were genuinely unsafe, but they requested other work for the hour remaining in their shift. The employer said it could not make substitute work available on such short notice.

The 17 employees subsequently filed a grievance requesting the pay they had been denied for the last hour of their shift. Their claim was based on a contract provision stating that employees who report for their normal shift without prior notification not to report will be given eight hours of work. The arbitrator found that the employees were justified in refusing to return to work under the circumstances. He further found that the contract failed to limit the employer's liability to pay the employees in this situation, and thus awarded each of the 17 workers one hour's pay (*Miller Printing Machinery Co.*, 54 LA 69).

● In another case, when several employees were suddenly taken ill at work, the employer tried to ascertain the cause, but was unable to do so. On the advice of the state health department, the employer closed the plant two hours after the start of the workday and paid the employees for the two hours worked. An arbitrator denied a grievance for four hours' reporting pay, explaining that the employer had made every effort to locate and control the cause. Given that its efforts failed, the situation was obviously beyond the employer's control, and it was therefore not liable for reporting pay under the provisions of the contract (*Lasko Metal Products Inc.*, 51 LA 1119).

*Inclement weather*—In two cases, employers decided to close down production because they felt that there would be substantial absenteeism as a result of a snowstorm, making operations inefficient. In both instances, the arbitrators awarded reporting pay to those employees who did show up for work. The decision to shut down because of anticipated absenteeism was within the managements' control, they held (*Westinghouse Electric Corp.*, 51 LA 298; *Muskegon Piston Ring Co.*, 55 LA 685; see also 73 LA 627).

● An employer was not obligated to offer reporting pay to employees who were prevented from working by closing of the plant caused by freezing rain and icy roads, an arbitrator ruled, because such conditions are an "Act of God" exempting the employer from reporting-pay liability. The fact that the employees travelled on the icy roads without difficulty on their way to the plant and had not seen any accidents was not controlling, the arbitrator held (*Bangor Products Corp.*, 63 LA 213; see also 74 LA 191, 73 LA 962, 72 LA 845, 71 LA 1015, 71 LA 716).

*Daylight saving time*—Under a contract guaranteeing a full day's pay if employees work more than half the shift except when they are sent home early for reasons beyond management's control, the employees demanded a full eight hours' pay even though they only worked seven hours on the evening that daylight saving time went into effect. Management claimed it was not liable to pay for the last, unworked hour because the institution of daylight saving time was beyond its control. The arbitrator upheld the union's position, saying management could have scheduled the employees for eight hours, even though it would have created confusion at the start of the next shift; the situation, therefore, was not beyond management's control (*Magma Copper Co.*, 51 LA 9).

*Proper notification*—The facts of the individual situation may dictate whether management's attempts to notify employees not to report to work were sufficient to exempt the employer from reporting pay liability (67 LA 1029, 67 LA 792).

● Massive riots broke out in the city where a plant was located, and out of concern for its employees' safety, company management announced on the radio that its second shift was canceled.

The contract provided for four hours' reporting pay when employees were sent home for lack of work unless they were notified the night before not to show up. Several second shift employees who did not hear the radio announcement reported for work. Along with employees sent home early from the first shift, they asked for four hours' reporting pay. The arbitrator denied their request on the grounds that attempts to notify second-shift employees were reasonable under the extreme circumstances, and there was no "lack of work." Furthermore, the arbitrator held, the employer should not have any present or future deterrent placed in its way when confronted with a decision whether to shut down for the safety of its employees (*Electronic Communications Inc.*, 51 LA 692).

• In a different case, a severe snow-storm caused management to close a plant. Announcements of the closing were broadcast on four major radio stations, but 112 employees did not hear the announcements and reported for work as usual. They were sent home.

Under a contract provision allowing for at least four hours' straight-time pay to be given any employee who reports for his regular shift without having been instructed to the contrary, the 112 employees claimed four hours' reporting pay. The arbitrator awarded them the pay because, despite the employer's efforts to notify all employees, these 112 had not received instructions to remain at home (*Niagara Machine & Tool Works*, 55 LA 396).

• Employees who were not given advance notification that a plant would close because of heavy snowfall were entitled to reporting pay, an arbitrator decided, because the snowfall did not make it impossible to carry on operation of the plant. Finding that there were already four or five employees at the plant when the employer decided to close and that 13 of the regular workforce lived within a mile of the facility, the arbitrator ordered the employer to compensate the employees for a full shift at the applicable rate of pay (*Hamilton Press Inc.*, 65 LA 274; see also 71 LA 1106, 71 LA 551, 70 LA 150).

• An arbitrator ordered an employer to pay its night-shift employees four hours' reporting pay for showing up at the start of the day shift in which they were scheduled to be laid off, despite their employer's claim that the employees were not scheduled to work and that the employer had given the workers' union two days' notice of its intent to lay off the workers. The arbitrator held that the employees had reported to work as ordered by their employer, the facility was operative and work was available, the notice of the layoff intent did not constitute adequate notice under the parties' collective bargaining agreement, and the employees were not given notice until after reporting (*Fritz Co.*, 101 LA 507).

**Disciplinary action**—Arbitrators have ruled that an employee is not entitled to reporting pay if he is sent home early for disciplinary reasons, or if he is disciplined, but reports for work anyway (64 LA 609, 63 LA 483).

• A little more than an hour after starting work, two employees were sent home for threatening a supervisor, a violation of an employer rule. The two employees maintained that they were entitled to four hours' reporting pay under the provisions of the contract. The arbitrator disagreed. Although the contract was not particularly clear on this issue, he felt certain that it was not the intention of the parties in negotiating the agreement to protect or reward employees in such a situation (*Unarco Industries Inc.*, 55 LA 421).

• In another case, an employee who had a poor attendance record failed to show up for work one day and did not call in his absence. When he reported to work the next day, his foreman stopped him immediately after the employee punched in and asked him why he had been absent. He said he was sick. The foreman did not believe him and suspended him for three days, sending the employee home right away.

The employee filed a grievance requesting four hours' reporting pay for the day he was sent home (but not challenging the suspension). The arbitrator denied the grievance explaining that the foreman could not know of the suspension prior to the employee's reporting to work because he did not know if the employee's absence was legitimate. Consequently, he could not have given the employee prior notification not to report. Furthermore, the conditions precipitating the foreman's sending the employee home were beyond management's control (*Barber-Greene Co.*, 53 LA 1244).

• Employees were entitled to pay for work time that they lost on the day after they had been absent when the employer refused to allow them to work because of their failure to comply with a modified attendance rule. The modified rule required absent employees to notify the employer of their absence at least one half-hour before the start of their shift, or within two hours after the start of the shift if the absence was caused by an emergency. Although the arbitrator found that the employer had administered the modified rule in a fair manner, he concluded that the employer's implementation of the rule without giving the union an opportunity to negotiate on the subject was sufficient reason to allow the pay (*National Can Corp.*, 63 LA 766).

• An employer was obligated to pay call-out pay to employees for the time that they were required to spend at an employer disciplinary investigation during their off-duty hours, an arbitrator ruled, despite the employer's contention that the phrase "called back to work" applied only to cases when employees were brought back to perform production activities. If there is to be an exception to the call-out provision for disciplinary meetings, it should be stated in the labor agreement, the arbitrator concluded (*Mobil Oil Corp.*, 76 LA 3).

*Application of premium rates*—Under a contract providing that double-time rates apply for all work in excess of 12 hours in one day, and further providing for a minimum of four hours' pay at time and one-half for call-in, an employee who had already worked 12 hours was called in for another hour and one-half. The employer paid him double-time for the one and one-half hours actually worked, but only time and one-half hours for the remaining two and one-half hours of the four-hour call-in guarantee.

The grievant maintained that he was entitled to double-time pay for the entire four-hour period, but the arbitrator held that there was no expressed or implied requirements in the contract that an employee is entitled to the high premium rates for the entire four hours of call-in pay unless he actually works the entire period (*General Portland Cement Co.*, 53 LA 653).

# Hours Schedules

## OVERVIEW

Arbitrators generally agree that an employer may set or change working hours if the change is not arbitrary, capricious, or discriminatory, and is not restricted by the collective bargaining agreement. An employer is more likely to be given the prerogative to schedule work hours than to be able to change established schedules. Some—though very few—collective bargaining agreements permit a change in schedules only by mutual labor-management agreement, or require the employer either to discuss with or to notify a union of schedule changes.

## SUMMARY OF CASES

### Scheduling Shifts

As long as the contract does not limit an employer's right to schedule shifts, most arbitrators hold that the union's consent is not required to change the schedule (98 LA 1099, 92 LA 418, 92 LA 48, 90 LA 922, 90 LA 559, 88 LA 969).

Even where a contract expressly prohibits an employer from making schedule changes without the union's consent, some arbitrators have upheld management's unilaterally doing so.

• An employer did not violate a contract provision barring a change of present tours of duty without consulting with the union when it changed the tour of duty for file clerks in its radiology service so as to require them to work weekends and holidays, an arbitrator ruled. Noting that the employer met its obligation to notify the union about the proposed change and agreed to negotiate over the impact of the change, the arbitrator pointed out that meetings with union representatives failed to produce agreement on the matter. The employer, the arbitrator concluded, was not required to wait until the union agreed to the change before implementing it (*Veterans Administration Medical Center*, 72 LA 374).

• Under a contract obligating an employer to notify a union of any change in the start of a shift, an employer had the right, without notice to the union, to re-quire a new employee to commence work no later than the normal shift time, an arbitrator decided, because the employee in effect was not working the shift but was working a period of time on his first day of work with the employer (*Carnation Co.*, 73 LA 827).

• Arbitrators have ruled that an employer may alter employees' work schedules if it has a legitimate business reason (74 LA 1254, 73 LA 621, 73 LA 418).

• An employer did not have the right to unilaterally assign a trash truck loader to the 6:30 a.m. to 2:30 p.m. work shift in an effort to facilitate earlier trash pickup, where the contract set the regular starting time for the second shift as 7 a.m. to 8 a.m., an arbitrator ruled, because the management-rights clause could not be construed to deprive the union of the right it clearly had under the contract's hours-of-work clause (*Cyprus Wire & Cable Co.*, 71 LA 925).

• An employer did not have the right to assign mine inspectors to a "mantrip-to-mantrip" work schedule that required inspectors to go inside the mine in the morning with the mine crew, to stay with the mine crew, and to come back out with the crew at the end of the shift, without notifying the union as required by the contract whenever changes were made in policies, practices, or working conditions, an arbitrator decided. Notwithstanding the employer's contention that it had an inherent right to direct its workforce, the arbitrator concluded that the change in the schedule was not merely direction of work, but involved revision of an established working condition (*Mine Health and Safety Administration*, 75 LA 369; see also 95 LA 221, 91 LA 1121, 87 LA 9, 85 LA 1144).

### Contracts Specifying 'Normal Week'

Arbitrators have differed on whether a specified "normal week" bars management from changing shift schedules.

• In one case, an arbitrator approved an employer's setting up a seven-day, continuous-shift operation, even though the contract specified an eight-hour day, five-day week, Monday through Friday. Absent language to the contrary, he held that the "normal week" clause should not be interpreted to bar continuous operations; otherwise management would be prevented from introducing new products that necessitate such methods (*Stanley Works*, 39 LA 374; see also 95 LA 210, 88 LA 129, 86 LA 992).

• Another arbitrator ruled that such a contract clause clearly required a fixed workweek, so management had no right to schedule continuous operations (*Traylor Engineering & Mfg. Div.*, 36 LA 687).

### Hours Schedules for Weekend Work

Arbitrators have decided that an employer does not have to pay any attention to the Monday-through-Friday shift hours in assigning overtime work on a weekend.

• One employer called in a first-shift worker to handle a rush job on Sunday. Because of production difficulties, the worker did not clock out until nearly midnight. The union complained that the "first-shift man" should not have been allowed to work the second-shift hours. Rejecting the union's argument, the arbitrator said it would lead to undesirable rigidity in scheduling overtime if the employer had to follow the standard shift hours for weekend work. Such an interpretation would defeat the purpose of overtime work, which is to get the job done quickly, the arbitrator said (*Menasco Mfg. Co.*, 26 LA 312).

• An employer was not obligated to pay overtime to employees for work performed on Saturday after changing the workweek schedule from Monday through Friday to Tuesday through Saturday because of an economic recession, an arbitrator decided. Notwithstanding the union's contention that five-day schedules have always run from Monday through Friday and that Saturday was considered a day off that was paid at premium pay if worked, the arbitrator held that the employer did not violate a contractual provision that stated that "40 hours per workweek shall constitute a normal week's work." The arbitrator noted further that there was no provision in the contract limiting the "normal workweek" to Monday through Friday (*Stephan Chemical Co.*, 65 LA 630; see also 89 LA 364, 86 LA 992, 77 LA 23, 76 LA 154).

### Changing the Workweek

Whether or not the employer can change the workweek schedule without getting union approval depends on the wording of the contract.

• One arbitrator found that a clause setting a regular workweek from Monday through Friday limited the employer's right to change its work schedule from Monday through Friday and alternate Saturdays to Tuesday through Saturday and alternate Mondays. Although a different production schedule was needed, the arbitrator said, the employer had to reach agreement with the union first (*Seamless Rubber Co.*, 26 LA 758).

• Where a contract established Monday through Friday as the basic workweek wherever "possible," an employer did not have the right to institute unilaterally a workweek of Tuesday through Saturday, an arbitrator held (*Norfolk Naval Shipyard*, 54 LA 588; see also 92 LA 430, 89 LA 1313, 73 LA 810, 72 LA 411).

• The fact that a contract said the parties "may negotiate" necessary schedules differing from the standard Monday through Friday workweek did not mean the union's consent was required before changes could be made, another arbitrator ruled (*Menasco Mfg. Co.*, 30 LA 465).

• Where the management-rights clause of an agreement gave the employer the right to schedule work, and where 40 percent of the workforce had been on a seven-day workweek for a number of years, the employer was allowed to put the rest of the employees on the same schedule. The arbitrator held that the employer did not have to get the union's approval to do this (*Celanese Corp. of America*, 30 LA 797; see also 87 LA 1290).

## Change in Schedule to Avoid Premium Pay

Even though an employer may have the right under its contract to change work schedules, it may be violating the agreement if it makes such changes merely to avoid providing premium pay.

• A contract gave an employer the right to revise operations in any way within its discretion. Using this right, the employer changed a Monday-to-Friday schedule to a Tuesday-to-Saturday one for one week in which Monday was a holiday. In this way, employees had to work on Saturday at straight time, instead of at the time-and-one-half rate that would have been in effect had the Monday-to-Friday workweek not been changed. The union protested and the arbitrator found in its favor, noting that it was clear that the employer had the right to change schedules, but that "it is also clear that it was not the intent of the parties that the employer should be allowed to abuse this right by changing shifts in order to avoid the payment of legitimate overtime" (*Kennecott Copper Corp., Nevada Mines Div.*, 6 LA 820; see also 65 LA 1133, 35 LA 893, 30 LA 465).

## Change in Schedule to Avoid Contract Benefits

After negotiating a contract granting benefits to part-time employees working 25 hours or more a week, can management limit the working hours of those employees to less than 25 per week? Given that the practice of assigning part-time workers to 25 hours or more a week had been in effect for some time, an arbitrator ruled against the reduction. Man-agement pointed out that the contract did not guarantee 25 hours to part-time workers or prohibit reducing the hours of work of such employees. However, the arbitrator decided that the contract was negotiated on the assumption that the past practice would continue, so the employer was bound by that to continue scheduling hours as before (*Kroger Co.*, 36 LA 129).

## Shutdown Before, During, or After Holiday

If an employer thinks that very little work would be done on the day before or after a holiday, can it shut down over the union's objection? One arbitrator held that a contract permitting shutdowns for lack of work or "other legitimate reasons" allowed an employer to do this.

• One employer scheduled no work on Christmas and New Year's Eves because it was afraid employees would start their holiday celebrations on the employer's time. The union demanded pay for the time lost, relying on a clause stating that the employer would maintain an eight-hour day and a 40-hour week. An arbitrator pointed out that the contract itself said that the hours-of-work clause was not to be construed as a guarantee of any fixed amount of work. Moreover, he said, the agreement had features, such as a reporting-pay clause, that were inconsistent with the idea of a work guarantee. Noting that there was no showing of bad faith on the part of the employer, the arbitrator decided the shutdown did not violate the contract (*Pittsburgh Screw & Bolt Co.*, 29 LA 615; see also 85 LA 398, 83 LA 314, 64 LA 287, 62 LA 1191, 29 LA 795).

• An arbitrator held that an employer violated contractual seniority, workweek, and maintenance-of-standards provisions of a contract by instituting continuous layoff plans under which certain employees were laid off for four Fridays and recalled on the following Mondays. The result, the arbitrator found, was a systematic, perpetual reduction of the workweek from 40 to 32 hours for a portion of the workforce (*Ace Hardware Corp.*, 88 LA 594).

## Scheduling Lunch Periods & Rest Periods

If a contract provides lunch and rest periods but does not say when they are to be taken, does the union have a say in when they should be scheduled? In one case where the contract did not schedule the lunch periods, an arbitrator upheld the union's objection to the employer's changing them.

• The practice at one employer had been for employees to eat in four half-hour shifts from 11 a.m. to 1 p.m. Then management decided that five lunch periods would work out better than four, so it changed the lunch schedule to run from 10:45 to 1:15 p.m. When the union claimed this was an unreasonable break with past practice, the employer pointed out that the contract, although it provided a half-hour lunch period, said nothing about when it should be taken. The arbitrator, however, agreed with the union. The obligation to provide a lunch period implied scheduling at a reasonable time, and by custom this meant near the middle of the work shift. In this case, the arbitrator decided, past practice had been so consistent that 11 a.m. and 1 p.m. must be regarded as the outside limits for lunch periods (*Bakelite Co.*, 29 LA 555).

• An arbitrator upheld management's right to stagger rest periods after instituting a continuous operation. Under the contract, times for rest periods were determined by foremen, stewards, and workers in each department. This right, the arbitrator said, was dependent on the shifts and hours set by the employer. When management decided to go on continuous operations, it necessarily followed that rest periods had to be staggered; hence the workers had no cause to complain, he said (*Philco Corp.*, 40 LA 490; see also 88 LA 599, 75 LA 16, 62 LA 374).

• Where a collective bargaining agreement expressly stated an employer must provide a 15-minute afternoon break sometime after lunch, an arbitrator held that an employer wrongly rescheduled the afternoon break for the last 15 minutes of the workday, even though nothing in the agreement restricted the employer from rescheduling employee rest periods beyond the fact that breaks could not be connected to lunch. Under the agreement, "rest period" was defined as a "short interruption during the work period," the arbitrator said, and a rest period at the end of the day does not constitute an interruption between periods of work. The arbitrator concluded the employer had the right under the contract to reschedule breaks, but simply not at the end of the workday (*Air System Components*, 104 LA 477).

## Working During Paid Lunch Period

If a contract provides for a paid lunch period, can employees be required to work during that time? If some employees are not required to look after any job duties during their meal time, but others are, an arbitrator is likely to rule that this is an unfair practice.

• A contract provided for a 20-minute lunch period as part of the normal workday paid for by the employer. Employees were relieved from all duties during this paid meal period, except for boiler firemen, who were asked to keep watch over their boilers while they ate. The union asked that relief men be furnished the boiler firemen so that they could eat without disturbance. The employer claimed that there was ample time for them to eat and still keep an eye on the boilers.

The arbitrator ruled that the firemen were entitled to relief. Because no exception was made for these employees in the contract, and because they did not receive any extra payment for the additional time spent on the job during their eating time, the arbitrator reasoned that they had to be treated like other employees (*Ford Roofing Products Co.*, 5 LA 182).

• An employer violated a contract provision requiring lunch periods to be arranged by mutual agreement between the parties, an arbitrator decided, when it compelled employees to operate their looms during scheduled lunch periods. Notwithstanding the employer's contention that continuous operation of the looms was dictated by the need to maintain its competitive position in the marketplace, the arbitrator ruled that the clear provision of the contract must be enforced in the absence of a subsequent agreement modifying its terms (*Atlanta Wire Works Inc.*, 62 LA 945; see also 71 LA 1128).

• An arbitrator held that an employer was not required to pay employees for their lunch period when they were asked to perform minor tasks of short duration during their lunch period. The contract called for the employer to pay for the lunch break if a worker "works straight through without stopping to eat" and called for "up to thirty minutes" for meals that suggested to the arbitrator that uninterrupted meal periods were not intended (*Chevron Oil Co.*, 52 LA 928).

## Coffee Break as Rest Period

Should a coffee break be viewed in the same light as ordinary rest periods? Several arbitrators ruled that there is no basis for distinguishing between coffee breaks and ordinary rest periods. Therefore, under a contract specifying that the employer would continue its past practices with respect to rest periods, it did not have the right to eliminate the practice of allowing certain employees to take a 10-minute coffee break in the morning in addition to their regular two 15-minute rest periods during the day (*International Harvester Co.*, 21 LA 194; see also 76 LA 1203, 73 LA 34).

## Paid Wash-Up Time

Where a contract is silent on the subject, can management discontinue paid wash-up periods on its own? In one case, an arbitrator ruled that it could not, pointing out that for many years, workers had been allowed to clean up during working hours. Arbitrators usually find unwritten practices involving specific benefits for workers to be binding for the duration of the contract, the arbitrator concluded, saying the employer could not discontinue the practice unilaterally (*Harnischfeger Corp.*, 40 LA 1329).

• Another arbitrator held that an employer could reduce, unilaterally, two 15-minute wash-up periods per day to two five-minute periods (*Ruralist Press Inc.*, 51 LA 549; see also 68 LA 94, 62 LA 179, 61 LA 891).

## Payment for Unrecorded Work

An employee was not entitled to pay for "off-the-clock" work that he could not prove he had performed, an arbitrator ruled. He made no claim to the pay until after he resigned from the supermarket at which he was employed, the arbitrator noted, concluding that there was no "clear and convincing evidence" that the work actually was performed (*Wrigley Stores*, 43 LA 225).

# Wage Guarantees & SUB Plans

## OVERVIEW

Guaranteed pay provisions and supplementary unemployment compensation benefits trusts or "SUBs" are likely to be fertile sources of grievances. One reason for this is that an employer usually tries to interpret such guarantees as narrowly as possible because it receives no work in return for payments made in fulfillment of a guarantee (95 LA 1187).

Generally, arbitrators have not interpreted a statement of normal working hours as constituting a guarantee of work or pay. Similarly, a listing of weekly salaries for employees probably does not mean the employer cannot pay pro-rata salaries when a reduced workweek is in effect.

## SUMMARY OF CASES

### Regular Workweek Not Guarantee

If a contract establishes a regular workweek of a certain number of hours, is this a wage or work guarantee? Most arbitrators agree that such a contract does *not* guarantee wages or work.

● A union, arguing for such a guarantee, relied on two provisions of a labor contract. One provided that the regular workday should be eight hours and the regular workweek 44 hours in six days, Monday through Saturday. The other required the employer to maintain standards at least at the levels prevailing when the contract was signed. Putting these two clauses together, the union claimed the employer violated the contract when it decided to eliminate Saturday work.

The arbitrator approved the employer's action because there was no discussion in negotiations of whether the employer was guaranteeing 44 hours' work; if there had been any such intention, it would have been stated in explicit contract language; the workweek clause was intended merely to set forth hours of work for purposes of computing overtime; and a clause providing four hours' reporting pay implied that there were occasions when a full schedule of work would not be available. This was inconsistent with the concept of a guarantee, the arbitrator concluded (*Consumers Service Co.*, 29 LA 447; see also 97 LA 39, 95 LA 482, 83 LA 314, 81 LA 14, 10 LA 312).

● An employer was not obligated to pay a full day's pay to employees for each day on which management decided to close the plant and send employees home during a power failure, an arbitrator ruled, because neither the contract nor past practice provided a guarantee of hours of work. Emphasizing that the contract provision establishing an eight-hour workday and five-day workweek was construed to provide only usual or "standard" workday or workweek, and the word "standard" was not synonymous with "minimum," "maximum," or a "guarantee," the arbitrator concluded that the emergency nature of the event causing the plant closure freed the employer of an obligation to make the payments (*Caribe Circuit Breaker Co.*, 63 LA 261).

● An arbitrator decided that an employer had the right to shut down its plant on the Monday preceding Christmas Eve and the Christmas holidays after the union rejected an offer to work the preceding Saturday at straight-time rate, because the separate contract provision stating that "five days, Monday through Friday, shall constitute a week's work" did not imply a guarantee of 40 hours as a standard workweek (*T M Fab Inc.*, 64 LA 287).

• An arbitrator held that employees were not required to do outside work to make up for hours lost when their employer failed to assign them 40 hours of work per week, as guaranteed in the contract (*Market Wholesale Grocery*, 86 LA 147; see also 97 LA 724, 91 LA 1118, 82 LA 1026).

## Statement of Weekly Salary

The fact that a contract lists weekly salaries for clerical employees does not mean the employer cannot pay them pro rata salaries if a reduced workweek is in effect, an arbitrator ruled.

• Protesting a cut in salaries of clerical employees in a steel mill during a period when the workweek was 32 hours instead of 40 hours, a union pointed to a wage table in the contract listing the "guaranteed salary" of various clerical grades. The union said the employer had to pay the "guaranteed salary" whether the workweek was one day or five. The arbitrator, however, thought the union was confusing a guaranteed rate with guaranteed earnings. The "guaranteed salary" is a promise that a salaried employee will be paid at a certain rate, the arbitrator said, and the contract also made it clear that the rates shown were based on a 40-hour week. The employer could cut these rates according to the actual workweek, he said, because the contract did not specifically say it could not (*Bethlehem Steel Co.*, 26 LA 784).

## When Employees Refuse Assigned Work

Can employees be deprived of a weekly guarantee of work or wages if they refuse to do available work that is different from their usual job? Most arbitrators have upheld employers' right to transfer employees to jobs where they are needed in order to make use of them for the guaranteed time.

• Even where a contract did not specifically deny the guarantee to employees refusing transfer to available work, an arbitrator ruled that the guarantee did not apply when employees refused such work. He reasoned that it was clear that the employer's guarantee of hours involved a corresponding responsibility on the part of employees to perform the work offered (*Kroger Co.*, 5 LA 154).

• Where a prior arbitration award (42 LA 228) interpreted a supplemental unemployment benefit plan's provisions relating to "lack of work" in terms of plant practice of allowing employees for whom there was no work to decline alternate work, senior employees who declined alternate work when there was not enough alternate work for all of the employees were awarded benefits by an arbitrator. Junior employees were also entitled to short-week benefits where the employer failed to exercise his power to "compel acceptance of another job offer," that is, notify an employee of alternate work, order him to accept it, and advise him that refusal to accept such work would result in the loss of benefits (*Pittsburgh Steel Co.*, 46 LA 774).

## Effect of Strike on Guarantee

If one group of employees has a guarantee of hours or wages in its contract and cannot work because of a strike by another group, is it entitled to the guarantee? Much depends on the wording of the guarantee provision.

• One arbitrator ruled that a clause like this did not require a bakery to pay drivers their weekly wages during a time they could not work when the bakers were on strike. The arbitrator said that the pay guarantee applied only when the drivers could do work (*Junge Bread Co.*, 1 LA 569; see also 74 LA 987, 53 LA 550).

• Even where a contract contains a specific guarantee of work, one arbitrator held, the guarantee is suspended when employees cannot work because of a walkout by members of the same union under a different contract. He reasoned that all union members must accept responsibility for the actions of any portion of the membership (*Kroger Co.*, 5 LA 154).

• In one case an arbitrator ordered an employer to pay the guarantee where the contract clearly guaranteed 40 hours of work in a week, employees had already worked the first day of the week, and they had no work for three days during the week because members of another union were on strike (*Wheatality Baking Corp.*, 11 LA 526; see also 74 LA 867).

## Effect of Strike on SUB Eligibility

The extent of an employee's involvement in a strike situation may have some influence on whether he is eligible for supplemental unemployment compensation benefits trust payments.

• Workers who were suspended for engaging in a wildcat strike were not entitled to supplemental unemployment benefits, even though they received state unemployment compensation benefits, one arbitrator ruled. The union argued that, under the SUB agreement, an employee was entitled to benefits, even though laid off by reason of a strike, if he was awarded unemployment compensation benefits for the same week of layoff. The arbitrator reasoned that the employees were not laid off because of a work stoppage, but for disciplinary action connected with a work stoppage. The contract language clearly treated layoffs for disciplinary reasons differently from those resulting from strikes, he added (*Lehigh Portland Cement Co.*, 37 LA 996).

• Another arbitrator decided that employees on layoff who were eligible for SUB before a strike did not become ineligible when the stoppage began. Following the expiration of the SUB agreement and the beginning of a strike, the employer stopped paying SUB to employees who prior to the strike had been laid off from the bargaining units that went on strike. It continued the plan in effect for certain employees outside these units. Under the SUB plan's termination provision, the union argued, as long as the plan continued to exist, it had to apply to employees "to whom it had been made applicable."

The arbitrator agreed. Although the employer was free to terminate the entire plan when the agreement expired, it could not terminate coverage in these units only. Because none of the employees had originally been laid off because of the strike, he reasoned, the continuance of their layoff could not have been a consequence of the strike. The benefit eligibil-

ity rule could not be applied as an additional "strike situation" eligibility rule, he concluded (*Allegheny Ludlum Steel Corp.*, 37 LA 689).

## Guarantee Applied to Partial Workweek After Strike

If employees are called back to work after a strike in the middle of the workweek, are they entitled to a full week's pay under a weekly work guarantee? According to one arbitrator the answer is yes. Otherwise an employer could get around the contract simply by withholding work on the first day of a regularly scheduled workweek, the arbitrator concluded (*Wilson & Co. Inc.*, 5 LA 454).

• Another arbitrator ruled that employees were not entitled to short-week benefits under a SUB plan that contained a strike disqualification clause for full weekly benefits. The arbitrator held that if unemployment resulting from strike disqualified the employees from benefits while "wholly unemployed," it surely disqualified them from benefits while "partially unemployed" (*E. J. Lavino & Co.*, 43 LA 213).

• Employees were not entitled to short-week benefits under a SUB plan for having worked less than their 32 hours scheduled during a week of contract negotiations, an arbitrator ruled, where the employer slowed and later shut down the plant. Although the union contended that the reason the employees did not work was the lack of available work, the arbitrator held that the evidence established that the shutdown, in addition to lost time resulting from preparations upon agreement on the contract, was reasonably related to the union's threat to strike unless an agreement on the new contract was reached (*Bethlehem Steel Corp.*, 62 LA 54).

## Effect of Layoff on Guarantee

Does an employee lose a weekly hours guarantee if he is laid off before the end of a workweek?

• One arbitrator decided that unless the contract says otherwise, an employee coming under the guarantee probably does not lose the amount guaranteed if removed from the payroll by the employer during a workweek. Once the employee starts to work he is entitled to a full week's pay, the arbitrator concluded (*Keeshin Motor Express Co. Inc.*, 2 LA 57).

• Employees who were laid off as a result of a permanent plant shutdown were entitled to supplemental unemployment benefits, an arbitrator ruled, despite the employer's contention that the employees were terminated upon receiving severance pay (*Ajax Forging and Casting Co.*, 64 LA 1309).

• Another arbitrator made a distinction between employees who were laid off temporarily and those who were permanently terminated. The arbitrator held that a weekly guarantee provision did apply to employees who were laid off during the week with the expectation that they would return when more work was available but did not apply to those whose employment was ended permanently before the end of the workweek (*Walsh, Perini, Groves, & Slattery Cos.*, 21 LA 117).

### Effect of Lockout on Guarantee

If an employer locks out employees during an impasse in negotiations for a new contract, are the employees entitled to a full week's pay under the guarantee provision of the expired contract?

• Where the expired contract guaranteed employees 40 straight-time hours of work or a full equivalent of pay for a regular workweek, the arbitrator decided that employees who worked the first part of the workweek in which the expiration date of the old contract fell were entitled to be paid for the remainder of the workweek when the employer locked the employees out because negotiations reached an impasse. Finding that the guarantee of a week's work or equivalent pay was triggered by employees' being "put to work" the first part "of the regular workweek," the arbitrator held that the right of the employer to lock out employees did not necessarily excuse it from obligations that attach to other contractual provisions (*Edward Don & Co.*, 65 LA 1307).

### Exclusions From Guarantee

Most wage guarantees contain language relieving the employer of the obli-

gation to pay the guarantee if work is lost because of specific circumstances. This exclusion might be stated generally in terms of conditions "beyond the employer's control," in which case disputes are almost certain to arise concerning whether in a given situation the loss of work was "beyond the employer's control." In other cases, the exclusion might list specific circumstances under which the guarantee would not be applicable. In such cases, arbitrators tend to restrict the exclusion narrowly to the listed situations.

• An exemption from a weekly wage guarantee for time lost because of causes beyond employer control did not apply where a meat packing employer laid off the workforce because of disruptive absenteeism. The contract specified exemptions for layoffs due to "flood, fire, power failure, breakdown of plant equipment, or other causes beyond reasonable control of employer." According to the arbitrator, the employer was freed from the guarantee only where a layoff was due to "physical" causes such as those listed. The layoff for absenteeism did not fall in this category, so the employer was not relieved of his obligation under the guarantee (*Ohio Natural Casing & Supply Co.*, 43 LA 888; see also 71 LA 817, 71 LA 283, 68 LA 986, 63 LA 257).

### Effect of Snowstorm on Guarantee

When a severe snowstorm prevented a large part of the workforce from reporting to work, an arbitrator ruled that the employees were entitled to an automatic short-week benefit as provided in the contract. The arbitrator held that in the past the employer had declared employees on layoff in similar situations and should have done so in this instance. He went on to state that the mere fact of a snowstorm did not entitle employees to SUB payments; each storm would have to be appraised on its own "with the test of reasonableness being the decisive criterion" (*Kelsey-Hayes Co.*, 49 LA 666).

• Where the contract exempted the employer from SUB liability for time not worked due to an "act of God," employees were not entitled to benefits when a severe snowstorm caused a high degree of absenteeism and forced the suspension of production, resulting in several employees being sent home. As the absenteeism resulted from an "act of God" the employees were not considered on layoff for purposes of SUB payments (*International Harvester Co.*, 49 LA 892; see also 74 LA 55, 53 LA 9).

## Effect of Holiday on Guarantee

Should a holiday be considered a scheduled workday for determining wages under a clause guaranteeing 40 hours' pay for those reporting a certain number of days per week?

● A contract guaranteed 40 hours' pay to each person who reported for work, on request, either five or six days in any week, depending on the department's schedule. Several employees reported for four scheduled workdays one week, but each worked less than 32 hours. They were paid for their time on the job plus one unworked holiday. The employer maintained that an unworked holiday could not be considered a fifth day of work for purposes of the pay guarantee.

The intent of the parties in establishing the 40-hour pay guarantee was to stabilize wages, the arbitrator decided. To accomplish this, the employer was to schedule production so employees would qualify for the guarantee, the arbitrator said. Therefore, he ruled that the occurrence of a holiday did not remove the obligation to do so. The workers could count the holiday as a day on which they reported for work, he concluded (*Colonial Baking Co.*, 35 LA 686).

● Under an SUB plan providing benefits in an amount equal to 65 percent of after-tax pay when added to state benefit and other "wages" or remuneration, an arbitrator ruled that employees laid off for a holiday week were entitled to benefits, even though state benefits plus holiday pay paid by the employer came to more than 65 percent of normal take-home pay. The state unemployment compensation agency defined "wages" for a holiday week as not including holiday pay, and the parties had agreed to apply the agency's definitions. The arbitrator concluded that the employer's contribution did not count, reducing the pay below the 65 percent level (*Pittsburgh Steel Co.*, 42 LA 228).

● Another arbitrator stated that the closing of a plant on Fridays, following Thursday holidays, did not constitute a layoff under the meaning of the SUB plan, and that the employees were not entitled to benefits (*Western Tool Inc.*, 42 LA 1064).

## Overtime Included in Guarantee

When the contract does not specify whether or not a weekly wage guarantee includes overtime pay, should overtime pay be added to employees' regular earnings before applying the minimum guarantee?

● At least one arbitrator ruled that overtime pay should be added to employees' regular wages in calculating gross weekly earnings to which the wage guarantee applies. Given that the contract clause did not specify whether or not the guarantee included overtime, the arbitrator's decision was based on the fact that the overtime rate was computed from the daily base rate rather than from the weekly guaranteed rate. If the parties had intended to exclude overtime, the arbitrator said, they would have figured the overtime rate on the basis of the weekly guarantee (*Boller Beverage Co.*, 19 LA 860).

## Eligibility for SUB While Receiving Social Security

If a supplemental unemployment benefits plan disqualifies employees who receive a retirement pension financed wholly or partially by the employer, is an employee who is drawing federal Social Security benefits entitled to payments under the plan?

● Interpreting the basic steel SUB plan, one arbitrator ruled that an individual cannot be considered to be disqualified just because he receives old-age insurance benefits. Even if Social Security were considered a pension, he added, it could not be said to be financed either partially or wholly by the employer because it is financed by federal taxes

(*Various Steel Companies*, 32 LA 529; see 88 LA 232, 82 LA 1261).

## Disability Retirement

Where a contract provided for an income extension arrangement for use in the event of layoff, a grievant who retired on a disability pension because of a permanent physical disability was not entitled to benefits under the plan. Although income extension aid may be a form of severance pay for employees who are separated through no fault of their own, it is not available to all separated employees, the arbitrator noted, but only to those laid off for lack of work or plant closing (*General Electric Co.*, 49 LA 62).